FINDING ROSE

FINDING ROSE

The Search for My Grandmother

Andrew A. Dahl

Finding Rose: The Search for My Grandmother

Heritage Narrative Press

ISBN: 979-8-9917562-2-8

Copyright ©: 2024 by Andrew A. Dahl

FINDING ROSE

Dedication

This book is dedicated to my wife Ziva and my children, Lara and Evan, who have been steadfast in their support of my writing efforts over the past six years. They have patiently endured listening to my numerous anecdotes regarding newly found facts about my family. Their continued encouragement allowed me to see this work to its completion. My family has painstakingly assisted me with the enormous task of editing this book.

I am grateful to Jutta Faehndrich, Ph.D., of Leipzig, Germany, not only for her vital skill in deciphering and translating old German handwriting, but also for making critical suggestions based on her experience in historical research and genealogy.

I feel both humbled and honored in being able to be the spokesperson for my grandmother Rose and the many other family members who did not survive to tell their own stories.

Table of Contents

PREFACE

I never met my grandmother Rose even though I am her only grandchild. Undoubtedly, she hoped and prayed that each of her three children would provide many grandchildren for her to love. The last letter my parents received from her, reaching us in Shanghai through the International Red Cross, was written in March 1942, having passed through multiple censors in Nazi Germany and Japanese-occupied China. That communication verified that she knew I had been born 6 months earlier and, in the letter, limited to 25 words, she asks about my welfare. My mother, her daughter, often showed me that letter when I became old enough to understand and she would point out that the stains on the yellowed paper were likely the results of tears having fallen from Rose's eyes as she penned those words.

In some respects, she seems almost as real as my other grandmother, my father's mother Sara, whom I loved and who often cared for me in Shanghai. My mother's mother was always spoken about in hushed tones, never by name, often out of range of my hearing, permeated with feelings of hopelessness, helplessness, guilt, and heartache. When my mother went to her room and cried, I was told she had a headache. I assume this was to spare me anxiety and the contagion of sorrow. Any good parent would have done the same. Today, as lucid nightmares of real and imagined dangers often disrupt the sleep of my safe and secure world, I can only envision the recurring horrors that invaded and occupied my mother's mind during those wartime days, and worse, the endless nights.

My mother and her immediate family attempted to ensure my grandmother's safety during the mid-1930s. After 1938, they went to extraordinary means to preserve her life and, after 1942, continued to hope that she, through some miracle, had remained alive. Even following the liberation of the large concentration camps, they continued their efforts to locate my grandmother. They never could find her. It is now my turn. Although my writing cannot reverse what happened more than eighty years ago, this book is my personal attempt to find Rose's spirit and understand her life.

Finding my grandmother would not have been possible without the contents of my mother Gerda's "suitcase of sadness" carefully carried and stored by her for fifty years and then by me, following her death more than thirty years ago. We never looked through this suitcase together for more than a few minutes - much longer would have been too painful. It is full of official documents, newspaper clippings and personal information about my family. Within that blue and white suitcase, held together by disintegrating rubber bands, were letters containing tiny German script crowding every square inch of the thin crinkled paper. It took much emotional effort on my part to gently handle them individually and attempt to translate the letters' words. I procrastinated until my eightieth year and finally realized it was now or never. Günter, the brother who came to America, had his own storehouse of grief, although it was less well organized than his sister's and came to me in bits and pieces in large envelopes or small packages after his death in Baltimore in 1999. They were sent to me by Faith, the woman with whom he shared his home and his life after he became a widower. Although on occasion I broached the subject with my uncle Günter, at first directly and later only circumspectly, he would tell me good-naturedly that he did not wish to speak about his childhood, the War years, or the search for my grandmother. The many letters and other memorabilia retained by Helmut, Rose's middle child, who had escaped to Palestine, came to me by a more circuitous route.

I have tried to fill the gaps in Rose's story with my recollections of stories told, acquired knowledge of 19th and 20th century history, along with the vast resources available in libraries and online, as well as written and spoken first-person accounts of those who experienced similar events of the period.

INTRODUCTION

The railroad platform was a great deal smaller than the one Rose recollected, where Albert had said his last goodbye to their son. Given the events of the past 24 hours, she was not surprised that she had initially failed to notice any distinguishing signage mounted on the slab where she now stood. She now realized that there had been none to see. The empty track looked different and any painted yellow markings on the concrete, which ordinarily might have identified the specific location, were obscured by the masses of people around her. It was definitely cold, March often is in Aachen, Germany, although the last light snowflakes had fallen more than two weeks earlier. She held Else's gloved right hand, ostensibly to prevent their separation, but also to comfort each other as they embarked on their forced journey into the unknown. She wondered how far away from the actual track she had stood, five years earlier, then in a blustery heavy summer rain, holding her umbrella in the wind as she waved goodbye to her youngest child leaving by himself at barely age 17 on a train bound to Antwerp to board a ship for America. She missed him greatly, as she did her daughter in Shanghai and her other son in Palestine, the middle child of three. Although the majority of those nervously waiting on the platform were elderly, there were some people of her children's age waiting for the train's arrival. Rose was glad that her family would not have to suffer through this with her and her sister.

Her legs were tired from standing, and her right shoulder ached from alternating between carrying and dragging the small suitcase, although it was lighter now than it had been the previous day before she repacked. She was a bit hungry, having skipped breakfast, and thought out loud that they should wait to have their *gebäck* until they were onboard the train, but her sister could not hear Rose's soft voice, drowned out by the cacophony of sounds of children asking questions of their parents, former neighbors anxiously questioning each other, and, of course, the yelling of the brown-shirted men clasping guns, some holding leashed barking German Shepherd dogs, trying to maintain a sense of order. The train to Koblenz was to leave at 2:46 and German trains always leave on time.

They had been waiting there for hours, having been aroused before dawn in preparation for the pickup by the Gestapo. They and the others had been driven to the Aachen *Hauptbahnof* in a windowless van. She and her sister had hardly slept the previous night, their natural anxiety having been made worse by the after-dinner arguments by those leaving the house as to whether they were destined to go to Trawniki or Izbica. These places were foreign to her, although she had learned the names of the major Polish cities in her secondary school in Bücken. "Prepare for deportation to the East" was what they had all been told a few days earlier.

She thought of her husband Albert, now gone for almost four years, and what she had experienced since then. *Gottseidank* that Grete Berger had been able to persuade the Nazis that their mother Fanni would not survive the journey and that the two sisters had been able to leave her comfortable in their shared room at the *Aachen Judische Altenheim*. Rose hoped that Fanni thought that her daughters would return in a brief period of time. It was a recurring wish, and she attempted to clear her mind of any doubts by paying attention to her surroundings.

Rose could hear the increasing sound of the train approaching the station and she and Else were jostled back and forth by the crowds surrounding them as the multitude gathered their belongings, the remnants of everything that had been important in their lives. It was March 21, 1942.

CHAPTER 1: Beginnings Liepmann

My mother and father always told me to "clean my plate," whether hungry or not and irrespective of whether the fare was to my liking. Of course, this was during the Second World War, when Shanghai was occupied by the Japanese and food stuffs were scarce, including ordinary staples such as rice, sugar, and flour. I never had fresh milk until after the War and tasted my first chocolate in 1945, a few weeks following the Japanese surrender after the Enola Gay accomplished its designated task. My hand was held high waving an American flag while my mother and I watched a parade of marching U.S. troops in Shanghai a few weeks later. There were huge crowds, primarily Chinese, whose Shanghai municipality had been occupied by the Japanese since their military victory in 1937, but also including Europeans, whose French Concession and International Settlement had endured Japanese occupation since a few days after Pearl Harbor. A uniformed marching American G.I. saw me standing in the front row just inside the curb on the Bund and walked over to me and took something out of the right pocket of his green jacket and held it out on his open palm towards me. My mother whispered, "take it" and "say thank you" and this small object was now in my right hand. I had no idea what this strangely shaped object, glowing in the sunlight, signified. My mother took it from me and removed the bright silver wrapper and told me to open my mouth. I can still recollect that distinctive initial texture followed immediately by the suffusion of prolonged sweetness of the slowly melting chocolate Hershey's kiss.

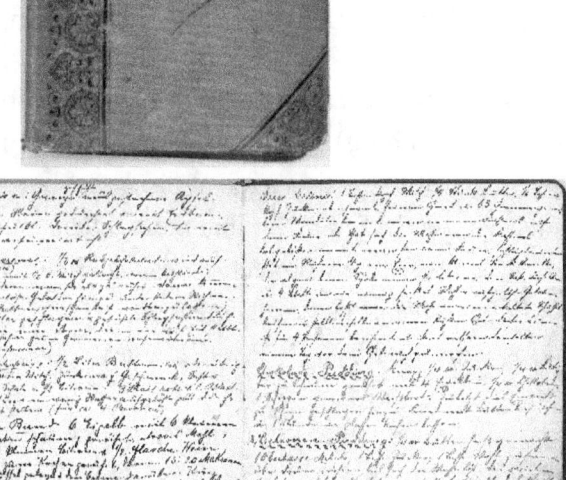

Rose Liepmann/Oppenheim Recipe Book with page of luscious desserts, written in Kurrent script,   c. 1912

My mother Gerda was a skilled cook, having learned the art in the kitchen of her mother, Rose Oppenheim. Rose's husband owned one of the two general stores in the village of Velmede, located on the banks of the Ruhr River in the *Hochsauerland* district of *Nordrhein-Westphalia* (North Rhineland-Westphalia), Germany. The store primarily sold dry goods, fabric, and apparel, but also purchased produce for resale, brought to the store daily by local farmers. In addition, horse-drawn wagons passed through Velmede, selling vegetables, meats, and dairy products to the local population. As the principal food purveyor in the area, my grandfather Albert knew everyone in town and had excellent relationships with the local farmers and vendors, providing Rose with the opportunity to obtain fresh chicken, beef, veal, and lamb for her recipes, together with a treasure trove of seasonal vegetables. Although they did not keep a kosher household, they abstained from eating pork in their home, as did my parents.

My grandmother Rose Liepmann married my grandfather Albert Oppenheim on July 1, 1909, when she was 23 years old. The Liepmanns and the Oppenheims, two Jewish families who had lived in Germany for hundreds of years, had now come together. Over centuries, these two families, my ancestors, had survived repeated murderous pogroms, expulsions, burning and looting of their homes, together with exclusionary laws and exorbitant taxation, all directed at them because of their religion. Yet they considered themselves proud Germans. Germany was their homeland and had been their relatives' *Heimstatt* seemingly forever.

Rose's family originally came from Hannover, where there is documentation of Jews residing in the *Alstadt* (old city) dating back to 1292. The *Stadtrecht* (municipal law) of 1303 contained a clause, revoked later, to the effect that no one was to molest the Jews "by word or deed." This resulted in significant growth in the Jewish community. By 1340 even kosher ritual slaughter was permitted in the city. As often the case for the Jews of Europe, the relatively "good" times rarely lasted, promptly replaced by new oppressions. During the 14th century "Black Death," Jews were accused of causing the bubonic plague pandemic in Hannover and were banished from the city. A handful of families illegally returned during the 15th century but were forced to wear a distinguishing badge on their clothing, yellow rings on the breast of men's overcoats, and two bluish stripes on the women's upper garments. By the beginning of the 16th century there were eight Jewish families in Hannover. They employed a rabbi and maintained a synagogue, where they were frequently forced to listen to the preaching of Martin Luther's evangelical disciple, Urbanus Rhegius, known as the "Bishop of Lower Saxony," who attempted to convert them to Christianity.

The region around Hannover was then ruled by *Herzogtum Braunschweig und Lüneburg* (dukes of Brunswick and Lüneburg) within the Holy Roman Empire. Between 1553 and 1601, these dukes issued six additional orders of expulsion against the Jews, but Hannover's municipal behavior at that time resembled the "sanctuary cities" of today in that these edicts were ignored by the city council, who felt that the Jewish population was under their protection, especially since the Hannoverian Jews were uniquely subject to the payment of *Opfer-pfennige* (taxes, interest, and rents) to the city for this special status. However, all business relationships with Jews by non-Jews were forbidden by the city council.

After 1584, when Duke Julius of Brunswick took possession of the area including Hannover, Jews were again officially permitted to reside there. This did not obviate the hostility of the populace towards Jews, often incited by Hannover's clergy.

During this period and later, Hannover's city council would frequently grant "letters of protection" to Jews. Issuance of such a document required a lump sum payment or an annual fee to the city, or both.

The Duchy of Hannover was formed out of the former territories of Brunswick and Lüneburg in the 17th century. In 1613, the Hannover synagogue was torn down under the order of the ruling royal family. It was rebuilt on the same site ninety years later.

The dukes continued to establish their rights of taxation and guardianship over the Jews, expressed in the *Judenordnung* of 1723, in force until 1842, including severe restrictions of the number of Jews allowed to live in Hannover.

During the Seven Years' War (1756–1763) between England and France but also involving territorial disputes between Prussia and Austria, the Jews of Hannover were assigned the obligation of providing 2,000 bed linens and 1,000 shirts for the soldiers. This was in addition to the duty of paying a per-head war tax plus 10 percent of all personal property, consistent with the requirement of Jews elsewhere in Germany.

For many generations, Jews moved in and out of Hannover, often not on their own volition, beholden to the cyclothymia of hatred generated by the various rulers and populations of the region.

Every year, at Shavuoth, the holiday commemorating the giving of the Ten Commandments to the Jewish people at Mount Sinai, they would, in their synagogue or home, recite the Haftorah portion from Ezekiel 11:17. "Therefore say: 'This is what the Sovereign LORD says: I will gather you from the nations and bring you back from the countries where you have been scattered, and I will give you back the land of Israel again.'" Furthermore, although every year's Passover Seder would end with the phrase "next year in Jerusalem," there was rarely significant discussion regarding the possibility of a Jewish nation being established in the area from which my far-removed forebears had been expelled by the Roman Empire almost 2,000 years earlier. Most German Jews did not vocalize that they were living within a diaspora—their goal was to have families, ensure their sustenance, education and safety and achieve more freedom from generation to generation within their German homeland.

At some time in the 18th or early 19th centuries, my grandmother's ancestors conducted their own mini-exodus from the affliction of their time, moving their families away from the city of Hannover to the more rural areas of *Nordrhein-Westphalia.*

One branch, the Liepmanns, went 80 kilometers northwest to Bücken, a town in *Niedersachsen* (Lower Saxony) in *Grafschaft Hoya* (county of Hoya), still located within the Hannover territory, then ruled jointly by local royalty and, following the political merger with George I of England in the early 18th century, by the British House of Hannover. This mutual control of the region persisted for 120 years, broken only by 10 years of the Napoleonic wars. In 1814, the Congress of Vienna established Hannover as an independent Kingdom, although it continued to be co-ruled by King George III of England. When Queen Victoria succeeded to the British throne in 1837, the 123-year union of Great Britain and Hannover ended, since it had been decreed that only male rulers of Britain could share in such power. In 1866 the Kingdom of Hannover was annexed by Prussia and, five years later, became part of the German Empire, which existed until the end of World War I.

Bücken had its first Jewish settlers in 1715, a married couple whom I cannot identify as relatives because the husband's name, Isaack, lacked a surname, customary for that period in Jewish history. Jews were considered servants of the *Kaiser* (King), Frederick William at that time, and therefore were not allowed to own property. Jewish families in Bücken were provided with living quarters to rent and were required to pay money to the municipality for "protection." Isaack and his wife's rented abode was promptly broken into by two intoxicated townsmen, who smashed all the windows and pelted the Jews with stones. Another two Jewish families numbering an additional eight people moved there in 1758. By 1828, there were six Jewish families in Bücken, which then had a population of seven hundred people. The records of the town reveal that Jews made their living as tanners, merchants, or butchers. Some continued to receive renewals of their *Schutzbriefe* (Letters of Protection) while other families had theirs revoked and accordingly suffered the loss of their rental home or expulsion from the city.

There had been a synagogue in the nearby town of Schweigen since at least 1828. On November 24, 1843, by an order signed by the local Royal ruler, the members of that synagogue were allowed to merge with a new synagogue in Bücken, established by 38-year-old Abraham Liepmann, (1805-1897), Rose's paternal grandfather and my second great-grandfather. Abraham had married Rosalie (known as "Rosette" or *Rahel* within the religious setting) Alexander, four years his junior, also a resident of Bücken, and they had three children. Abraham had originally been a livestock dealer and later in life became a successful fabric merchant. Jews were able to own property beginning in the early 19th century and Abraham Liepmann purchased a spacious house directly across the street from Bücken's *Stiftskirche*, the Romanesque 12th century, twin-turreted Protestant-Lutheran collegiate church of St. Materniani and St. Nicola, popularly known as *"Bücker Dom,"* on *Brückstrasse*. On the first floor, with a separate entrance, was a large room serving as a synagogue for the men together with an adjacent side room for the women to pray.

The Liepmann home in Bücken where Rose was born and grew up, with the Bücker Dom in the background.

By 1852, there were 46 congregants from Bücken renting space in my ancestors' home for both a prayer sanctuary and a religious school, which, by 1854, was teaching twelve children. My family lived upstairs. The congregation had no burial ground of its own; the deceased were interred in the cemetery in neighboring Hoyerhagen. In the early 1860s, several Jewish families left Bücken resulting in the synagogue facing challenging financial times, forcing it to merge with the more sizeable Jewish congregation in the adjacent larger community of Hoya. The Liepmann house in Bücken became a private home once more.

My 2nd great grandparents, Abraham Liepmann (1805-1897) and his wife Rosalie Alexander (1809-1881), c. 1855

Abraham and Rosalie had an older daughter and two sons including Moses Liepmann, Rose's father, my great-grandfather, who was born in that house in 1850 and attended the synagogue and religious school in his home.

Abraham Liepmann (1805-1897), my second great-grandfather, c. 1865

Abraham Liepmann (1805-1897), my second great-grandfather, c. 1892

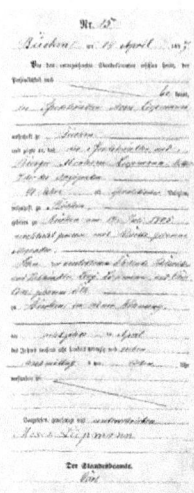

Abraham Liepmann, death certificate, 1897

The other branch of Rose's family, the Vorreuters, had similarly left the city of Hannover in the last half of the 18th century to move to Enger, a small town in the Herford district in *Nordrhein-Westphalia*, west of Hannover. My second great-grandfather, Gottschalk "Samuel" Vorreuter was born there in 1805 and in 1838, married a local teenager, Henrietta Ganz, almost twenty years his junior. They had a son, Gottfried, known as "Solly," a year following the wedding and then had two daughters much later in the marriage, including my great-grandmother Fanni, born in 1855. Fanni Vorreuter was to become Rose's mother.

Confirmation book of my great-grandmother,
Rose's mother, Fanni Vorreuter, c. 1868

In 1869, Prussian King Wilhelm I promulgated the North German Confederation Constitution, which officially gave Jews civil and political rights in 22 German states. In 1871 the now unified German Empire granted all German-Jews emancipation. This led to many changes in both Jewish and non-Jewish society. Some Jews continued to fully identify religiously with their families' Judaism, others sought to remain Jewish but behave more like their Christian peers and the remainder, realizing that this "emancipation" still precluded Jews from achieving high-profile social positions, converted to Christianity.

Fanni (Vorreuter) Liepmann (1855 -1942) my maternal great-grandmother, c. 1877

In 1880, Moses Liepmann married Fanni Vorreuter. They settled in Bücken, where Moses had joined the family textile business. They had five children, Gustav Liepmann, born in 1881, followed by Max, two years later, and Rose in 1885. Rose's sister, Elsbeth, known as Else, arrived two years later. Else, who never married, was to be Rose's playmate and lifelong companion. They were rarely separated in their life journeys from Bücken to Izbica. Paul, the baby in the family, was born in 1894.

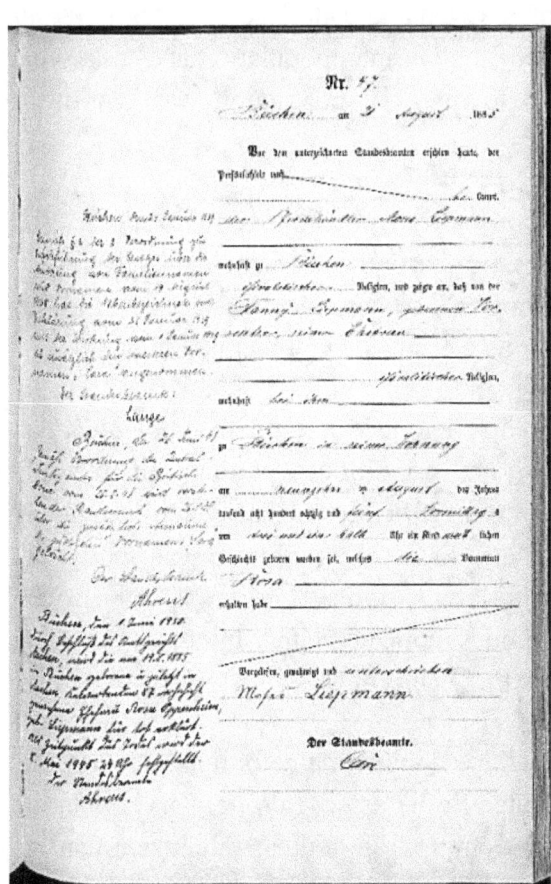

Birth certificate of my grandmother, named Rosa (but always called "Rose"): Dated 8/21/1885, the certificate states that a child of female sex was born to the "horse-dealer" Moses Liepmann, of "Israelitischer" religion and his wife, Fanny Liepmann, born Vorreuter, also, of "Israelitischer" religion, in Bücken in their residence on 8/19/1885 at 3:30 in the morning. The document is signed by Moses Liepmann. On the left side of the certificate are three later handwritten entries made by German officials in 1939, 1948, and 1950. There is similar documentation on the birth certificate of Rose's younger sister, Else. I will discuss these entries later in this book.

Rose with her maternal grandfather,
Abraham Liepmann, 1886

The five Liepmann children including Rose grew up in the large house on *Brückstrasse*, which, even though it had housed both the synagogue and the Jewish school twenty years earlier, was indistinguishable from the other adjacent half-timbered buildings. The children went to local schools and spent their free time both indoors and out. The girls enjoyed playing with their dolls and amusing themselves with make-believe, while the boys played soccer, rode their bicycles and, in the summer, swam and paddled canoes in the *Weser River*, which ran through town. Jews made up under one percent of the German population and, to a great extent, were assimilated, especially in the smaller villages and towns. The population was two-thirds Protestant, both Reformed and Lutheran, and one-third Catholic.

Most Jews were middle-class, working in or owning small businesses or employed as tailors, civil servants, doctors, lawyers, journalists, bank clerks, factory workers, professors, and teachers. Rose's family engaged in both secular and religious community affairs, and although they saw themselves as a religious group who lived in Germany, they preferred to think of themselves as Germans who practiced Judaism.

The Liepmanns maintained a discernible identity and culture. They belonged to the Hoya *Gemeinde*, an organization informally centralizing local Jewish activities. Rose and her siblings participated in youth groups and singing companies. After World War I, such *Gemeinden* were officially empowered by the newly created Weimar Republic to consolidate local Jewish communal and ritual affairs, hire rabbis, build and maintain synagogues, and, in larger cities, run a variety of institutions, among them newspapers, social associations, libraries, health facilities, and charity funds. Tax revenues, collected either by the government on behalf of the Jews or by the Jewish community itself, supported these activities.

Rose's family, both on the Liepmann and the Vorreuter sides, had lived in Germany for hundreds of years and did not identify with the Jewish families who had recently migrated from Eastern Europe. This population had left Poland and portions of the Austria-Hungarian and Russian Empires, all hotbeds of antisemitism, to come to Germany for a better, more secure life for their families. These new arrivals were unable to obtain citizenship despite the nascent German Empire having embraced culturally liberal policies. They lived in distinct traditional immigrant communities, primarily speaking Yiddish, a language used among Central and

Eastern European Jews, rather than German. Their clothing was distinctive of Eastern European Orthodox Judaism, and they were far more observant of Jewish religious law and, in contrast with the largely middle-class German Jews, often eked out humble existences as industrial workers, artisans, or peddlers.

There were approximately ten Jewish families living in Bücken in the last quarter of the 19th century, with a few more living in Hoya, the district capital. None of these were Eastern Ashkenazi Jews with origins in the Slavic nations, who tended to settle in major German cities. In Berlin, which had been the capital of Prussia and maintained that role within the German Empire, there was a strong tradition of Teutonic nativistic behavior. This Prussian reactionary mentality found a convincing anti-Jewish argument in the "*Masseneinwanderung*," the alleged mass immigration of unwanted East European Jews (*Ostjuden*) into Berlin. The 1883 pogroms in Russia caused tens of thousands of Jews to come to German cities, leading to a resurgence there of antisemitic propaganda, eventually leading to the expulsion of many of these Russian Jews back to Poland and Russia in the east and to France, England, and the United States in the west.

The Liepmann family, both subconsciously and deliberately, hoped to offset similar hostile responses by embracing the modernity of the Enlightenment. They stopped well short of conversion to Christianity but opted for a form of Judaism which did not include traditional rituals and religious practices such as rigorous observance of the Sabbath, strict dietary laws, and the injunction to cover their heads. They clearly distinguished between Jewish ceremonial law and Jewish moral law, and primarily adopted the latter in their attempt to assimilate.

Rose and her family were indistinguishable in dress, appearance, and outward religious signs from their Christian neighbors. Although they may have embraced ambivalent attitudes regarding the newly arrived Eastern Ashkenazi Jews, they would have been appalled by the repellent imagery employed by members of the highest governmental circles against these very poor and frightened refugees.

The word *Yekke* or *Jecke* refers to a Jew of German-speaking origin, whether still in Germany or elsewhere in the world. It is a colloquial term, which depending on context and the specific person using it, may convey esteem or may be utilized in a derogatory sense. There are a number of theories regarding the etymology of the word. The best known is that it originates from the cultural differences in dress that developed between the more westernized German Jews who wore shorter "jackets" ("yekke," cf. German *Jacke* with an initial y-sound instead of the English j-sound) distinguishing themselves actually and symbolically from Eastern European Jews, who typically garbed themselves in traditional longer coats as their outer clothing.

Another notion regarding the origin of Yekke is that it stems from the Western European pronunciation of the name "Jacob," the Jewish biblical patriarch who "wrestled with God" as "Yekkeor" or in the diminutive "Yekkel," differing from the Eastern European pronunciation of "Yankef" or "Yankev" as the name for Jacob.

Rose's father, Moses Liepmann, was often away on business, leaving her mother, Fanni, to not only care for the household and the children, but also to tend to the needs of her father-in-law, Abraham Liepmann, who had become a widower in 1881 and now lived with them. Fanni was also the arbiter of the common disputes that occur among siblings close to each other in age.

Westphalia was a center of the German textile business, and Moses Liepmann travelled by train to the nearby larger towns of Hannover and Bremen for the day and to the cities of Hamburg and Münster overnight or longer. He bought and sold contracts for wool, linen and occasionally silk materials or took possession of actual fabrics from manufacturers and delivered them to the tailors or factories that would produce finished goods of clothing, upholstery, bedsheets, and carpets. His return to Bücken was highly anticipated by the children when they were young because their father would always arrive bearing five small gifts, either candy or small toys.

L-R: Fanni (Vorreuter) Liepmann (1855 - 1942), my maternal great-grandmother, and her sister Hermine "Eva" Vorreuter (1858-1943), c. 1895. Fanni was to become a widow two years later.

In 1897, when Rose was only 11, her father Moses died after a brief illness, four months after the death of her paternal grandfather, Abraham Liepmann, at the age of 91. The responsibilities for the family fell solely upon Fanni, who would remain a widow for 46 years. My grandmother's brothers Gustav and Max were 15 and 13 and stopped their education to find work to support the family. Rose initially continued in school while, as the elder daughter of the family, sharing the responsibility of caring for a large home and for her 3-year-old brother, Paul.

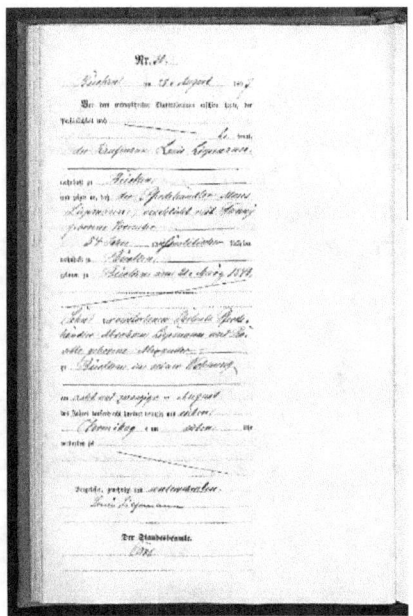

Death certificate of Moses Liepmann, Rose's father, 1897

Fragment of Gedenkblatt an den Sterbetag, memorial for the death (Yahrzeit) of Moses Liepmann, my maternal great-grandfather (1850-1897)

Although in 1763 Frederick the Great of Prussia had mandated regular school attendance for all children from the ages of 5 through 13, most girls lacked educational opportunity much beyond that age. The most intelligent boys might continue schooling in the *gymnasium*, a secondary school with rigorous academics, classical languages, modern languages, and mathematics and science, in preparation for university admission. Girls were not allowed admission into a *gymnasium* until 1908.

The education of women in the 4th quarter of the 19th century was considered unimportant within the highly patriarchal German society. Male children had always been considered superior and women could not inherit any land from their father's estate. Kaiser Wilhelm II, the German Emperor and King of Prussia, known as William by his maternal grandmother, Queen Victoria of England, defined the role of women as "*Kirche, Küche, Kinder*" (church, kitchen, children.) Governmental policies made it difficult, if not impossible for German women to attend universities, which required passage of the *Abitur,* the German "leaving certificate," equivalent to today's A levels or International Baccalaureate Diploma. Secondary schools were separated by sex and there were no girls' schools offering the *Abitur*. German universities only began to officially admit women in 1909.

Although more formal education for middle and upper-class girls was the norm in Germany's cities, it ended at the onset of menarche, when a girl was 14 or 15. After this, her education might continue at home with tutors or occasional lectures.

So it was with Rose, who, not by choice, left school in 1901 to help at home and work as a salesperson in a number of shops in Bücken. She spent her teenage years in a small town without much opportunity for expanding her world. She learned to cook, sew, and manage a household, the skills that would make her a wonderful wife and mother.

Realschule (10th Grade) class of Rose Liepmann (third row, third from left), age 16, 1901. Note that there were only male teachers.

Rose Liepmann, 1902, age 17

Rose Liepmann, on left, 1906, with local friend.

She met her future husband and my grandfather, Albert Oppenheim, in 1908 through a family connection. Albert lived in Velmede, about 2 hours southwest of Bücken by train. His family had originally been from Frankfurt, where Jews had lived for more than 800 years.

My grandmother Rose, 1906

My Grandmother Rose, 1908

Chapter 2: Beginnings Oppenheim

The Jewish population of Frankfurt, Germany dates back at least to the middle of the 12th century when they established a "Jewish Quarter" adjacent to the present-day Frankfurt cathedral. This small community, including my Oppenheim ancestors, initially prospered after being given imperial protection by the Holy Roman Emperor Frederick II (1194-1250). Jewish people realized a degree of security with the emperor, who claimed the right of possession and protection of all his Empire's Jews. A synagogue was constructed in Frankfurt, and although their housing was within the Quarter, people could freely walk in or out of that area. Frederick's granting the Jews an official charter could not, however, prevent what was to be the first of many violent attacks on my family because of their religion. The first Frankfurt "pogrom," occurring in 1241, was sparked by the refusal of a Jew to convert to Christianity. More than 150 of the Jewish Quarter's 200 residents were killed and the remainder quickly abandoned their homes, fleeing into the surrounding countryside. The emperor expressed extreme concern, not so much at the loss of life but more with the decline in tax revenue from the wealthy Jewish community. He now ordered strict penalties to be levied against anyone who would attack the Frankfurt Jews. Some of those who had survived did return to the same area, rebuilt the synagogue, and the community once again grew in number, although selectively forced to submit to crippling taxes to pay for protection against any physical persecution.

Less than 100 years later, in 1349, Frankfurt's Jewish population was also blamed for the Black Plague and, throughout Europe, Jews were killed and their homes were burned. A few years later, when a fire occurred in the Cathedral, a not-infrequent occurrence in that age of wooden buildings, a rumor spread that it had been set by Jewish Quarter residents. The community was completely massacred, and many Jews chose to burn down their own houses while still inside rather than face death from the angry mob. Jews "poisoning the well" was yet another variation of the Hellenistic pre-Christian blood libel that still exists even today-- that Jews kidnap and slaughter non-Jewish children before Passover to use their blood for baking *matzoh*.

In 1462, the Frankfurt City Council ordered the resettlement of their remaining Jews within a specially constructed alley, *Judengasse*, built on a former moat, only 5 yards wide, surrounded by high thick walls and located along a 400-meter stretch of the city's eastern walls. For the next 350 years, as many as 2,200 Jews resided there, crammed into 160 tiny houses. The three gates, *Judenbrückchen,* to the area were closed and locked at night, on Sundays, and during Christian holidays. Residents were only permitted to rent their homes, with ownership remaining in the hands of the city. Jews could leave their narrow alley through the guarded gates only on workdays and were now required to wear distinctive clothing (usually a yellow ring on their outer garment) and were prohibited from visiting public baths.

Compulsory segregation of Jews was common in medieval Europe, with segregation of Jews having been mandated in Prague in 1262. This Frankfurt *Judengasse* was the first legally constructed ghetto space in the Holy Roman Empire. Although the term "ghetto" (derived from the Italian word *gettare*, meaning casting of metal) was not used until 1516 in Venice, when authorities required the 900 Jewish Venetians to move to the island of Cannaregio, the concept of an enclosed place where European Jews were relegated to live was applicable to the area in Frankfurt where my Oppenheim ancestors were confined. In 1555, Pope Paul IV issued a proclamation requiring the Jews of Rome to live in separate quarters in a crowded and unsanitary area that regularly was flooded by the Tiber River, together with also severely restricting their rights, including what businesses in which they were permitted to engage. The purpose of this edict was to encourage conversion to Catholicism, an act that would serve as a ticket out of the ghetto.

In the mid-20th century, the word "ghetto" eventually was reappropriated to refer to poor, urban, primarily African American neighborhoods in the United States, but two generations later, the phrase was deemed offensive and is now often euphemized by the term "inner city."

The *Judengasse* in Frankfurt was home to Germany's largest Jewish community, becoming one of the most important centers of Jewish life in late medieval and early modern central Europe. It was there that my eighth great-grandfather, Menachem Levi, was born in about 1510.

In the Biblical period, animal names were commonly used as human names. For example, the name Rachel is derived from the Hebrew word for "ewe" and the name Jonah springs from the Hebrew for "dove." This practice was discontinued 2,000 years ago but was restarted in the 14th century by Ashkenazi Jews who, lacking surnames at that time, distinguished individual families by adding ornamental German or Yiddish vocabulary words denoting wildlife to a person's Hebrew name. Thus, my early 16th century ancestor was known as Menachem Levi *Zum Hirschen*, the latter from the German word meaning "deer" or "stag," perhaps because of the association of the deer with Naphtali, who was blessed by his father Jacob as "a hind let loose." (Genesis 49:21)

By 1580, when Menachem's grandson, Lazarus, was born, the family name had been changed from Levi to HaLevi (The Levite in Hebrew, signifying a Jewish male descended patrilineally from the tribe of Levi). Because the area of the ghetto remained confined, Jews subdivided their houses and built extra stories to accommodate the exponential population growth. At some time in the late 16th century, the family home was now designated as the "*Haus Zum Goldener Hirschen*," a gilded image of a stag having been painted on the house to distinguish it as belonging to my family. Today, more than 400 years later, there are scores of hotels, guesthouses, and bed and breakfast establishments named *Goldener Hirsch* scattered throughout Germany and Austria.

When my sixth great-grandfather Lazarus Halevi was 34, the entire Jewish ghetto in Frankfurt was looted in what is known as the *Fettmilch* Uprising. This was a violent political protest by Frankfurt's merchant class, who rebelled against the control of the municipal council by a few patricians. As usual, the Jews, lacking any representation in the government, were targeted as having colluded with the city fathers. In August 1614, armed citizens led by Vincenz Fettmilch, a gingerbread baker, entered the *Judengasse*, Frankfurt's "Jewish Lane," and drove the almost 1,400 residents, including my HaLevi family, from the area, before ravaging the quarter and plundering its movable property.

In 1611, Matthias had become Holy Roman Emperor and after his army had defeated that of his brother, Emperor Rudolf II, conjunctly held the title of King of Germany. Matthias, as other Emperors before and after him, felt that he was the successor of the first century CE Roman emperor Titus, who claimed to have acquired the Jews as his private property after he burned Jerusalem and took the Jews to Rome as slaves. The German emperors apparently claimed this right of possession more for the purpose of taxing the Jews than of protecting them. Emperor Matthias acted to quell the rebellion but by that time the Jews were fearful of return and had resettled in the nearby towns of Hanau, Hoechst, and Offenbach.

Eighteen months after the *Fettmilch* rebellion, in February 1616, the Emperor formally announced that the Jews could come back to the *Judengasse,* and he rebuilt their homes and institutions. At the same time, their request to be compensated for lost or damaged property was refused. The quarter's synagogue was repaired and reconsecrated, and above the gates to the Judengasse a stone imperial eagle was mounted, accompanied by an inscription reading "Protected by the Roman Imperial Majesty and the Holy Empire." On February 28, 1616, Vincenz Fettmilch, together with six of his fellow rebels, was executed for his crimes.

My ancestors again were able to live in the *Judengasse* and occupy the rebuilt "Haus zum Goldener Hirschen." They declared their return a "little Purim," reminiscent of the Biblical rescue of the Israelites in diasporic Persia 2,000 years earlier, when Esther and her extended family, the descendants of King Saul, were spared by King Ahasuerus and the Jews avowed executioner, Haman, was hanged.

Lazarus' son, my fifth great-grandfather, Joseph HaLevi, was born in 1616 in Frankfurt's ghetto, shortly after his parents returned there from "exile." His mother, my sixth great-grandmother, was likely carrying him in her womb when they returned to the *Judengasse*.

The Halevi family continued to live in Frankfurt's ghetto for the next hundred years. Some of my relatives were musicians and supported themselves through their performing for and teaching music to fellow Jews. In 1711, the ghetto burned to the ground after an accidental fire spread out of control, but the homes and businesses were quickly rebuilt, and my ancestors rushed back to their walled-in existence.

In that same year, my fourth great-grandfather, Abraham (Levi) Lazarus HaLevi was born, received musical tutelage by members of my family and, while still a young man, moved 100 kilometers north to become Court violinist to Count Ludwig Ferdinand of Sayn-Wittgenstein at his 13th century castle in Berleburg. The Berleburg Castle is one of the few noble residences in Germany inhabited by the same family for the past 750 years.

Abraham (1711-1790) had four sons, the oldest being Moses Abraham Levi Oppenheim (1748-1808), my third great-grandfather. At age 20, Moses left home to live in the town of Attendorf, 60 kilometers to the west, first to apprentice for and then to work with the merchant Aaron Lazarus (Ursell). In 1780, he again moved, this time to the neighboring village of Neuenkleusheim, a tiny iron mining and agricultural community. According to *"Die Geschichte der Juden in Neuenkleusheim,* a book written by Claus Heinemann, a German pediatrician and a Christian fourth cousin (once removed) of mine, Moses became the first Jewish resident in the community and was the first Jew to serve on a jury within the rural district of Olpe in the *Sauerland* region. Moses, then still a young man, made his home into the village's synagogue. His brother, Nathan Abraham Levi Oppenheim (1760-1810) was a teacher of Jewish studies and joined him in Neuenkleusheim, residing three houses away from his brother Moses.

1836 Contract between Clara Leiffman Oppenheim (1759-1837), the widow of Moses Abraham Levi (Oppenheim) (1748-1808), my third great-grandfather and her son, Jacob "Bachor" Oppenheim (1797-1891), my second great-grandfather, regarding the transfer of assets from mother to son.

In 1787, Emperor Joseph II of Austria established a law mandating that all Jews in Austria and Germany adopt last names. Names derived from the Hebrew were no longer permitted and had to be legally changed to "Germanized" names. Thus, Abraham's four sons took on the "Oppenheim" surname, one of the 156 choices considered acceptable by the authorities. All other names were forbidden, and their use, or the maintenance of the customary Hebrew surnames, was punishable by severe fines.

The introduction of permanent last names into European Jewish life came with the decision of European governments to make their Jewish populations, previously granted a large measure of communal autonomy, fully subject to the same state regulations and bureaucratic record-keeping as all others. During this Enlightenment period, citizenship was finally granted to Jews in Austria and Germany, something that they had never possessed before. In theory, Jews had achieved a situation approaching equal rights, but in practice the story was vastly different. Jews were accepted into society as long as they were not too Jewish. Many Jews saw conversion as the best way to advancement in enlightened Europe. A classic example was Benjamin Disraeli, born Jewish, who was twice the Prime Minister of England during the reign of Queen Victoria and was only able to achieve that position because his family converted to the Church of England.

For most German Jews, after centuries of physical and economic marginalization, the concept of belonging to a nation as a citizen was intoxicating. Many desired nothing more than to prove their loyalty to their host country and the best way to do this was to join the army, which for centuries had been closed to Jews. In Prussia, and later in Germany, disproportionately large numbers of Jews volunteered for military service. Jews in early 19th century Germany were able to modify their religious beliefs to effectively participate in most aspects of public life, becoming artists, intellectuals, professionals and holding civil office in increasing numbers. This general acceptance, however, rarely led to their residential integration and they continued to be excluded from certain professions and social groups.

Being a Jew in early 19th century Europe conveyed a set of realities which confounded many individuals, leading some to assimilate intellectually and physically with the Christian majority and others to leave Judaism entirely behind through conversion to Christianity, allowing accelerated assimilation into society in both their public and private lives.

Early 19th century German nationalism increasingly demanded total loyalty from its citizens, and any suggestions that a group might consider themselves a nation rather than only a religious group was met with scorn. In 1783, the German Jewish intellectual, Moses Mendelssohn, advised "Adopt the mores and constitution of the country in which you find yourself…but be steadfast in upholding the religion of your fathers too. Bear both burdens as well as you can." The emergence and growth of the Jewish Reform religious movement in Germany in the 1840s was fueled by that sect's official rejection of the Jews as a nation and surrendering the Messianic idea of the return to Israel, the concept that had sustained some oppressed Jews throughout the Diaspora in the Mediterranean basin and Europe.

Prior to the 1790s, Jewish conversion to Christianity in Germany was rare, although pastors, as well as the nobility, welcomed such events and often encouraged them by handing out lavish gifts and money to the new addition to the Christian faith. Some of these converts were encouraged to travel, and sometimes forcibly sent, to distant towns to remove them from the "bad" influence of their Jewish former family and friends.

The contemporary attitude toward conversion could be best summed up by the German Jewish writer Heinrich (whose original name was Chayim) Heine, who was baptized as a Lutheran in 1825. "From the nature of my thinking you can deduce that baptism is a matter of indifference to me, that I do not regard it as important even symbolically... The Baptism certificate is the ticket of admission to European culture."

After centuries of continual persecution, and having been shut out from German cultural life, most German Jews struggled to assimilate while holding on to Jewish religion at the same time, but others felt that assimilation into German-Christian culture was the highest prize to pursue, and that differences between both religions could easily be reconciled. In Germany, there were thousands of converts between the 1790s and 1850s, some of them famous poets, musicians, and socialites. The majority of converts were rather well-educated, middle-class Jews. During the reign of Prussian King Frederick William III, about 2,200 Jews were baptized between 1822 and 1840, most of these being residents of the larger cities.

This search for societal inclusion and integration through voluntary conversion to Christianity affected the Oppenheim family. My 4th great- uncle Nathan Oppenheim's oldest son, Abraham, was born on June 11, 1803, in Neuenkleusheim and, at age 26, "had a vision of the baby Jesus" and was baptized, changing his name to Franzizcus Oppenheim. He became a cattle dealer and butcher and moved his family to the neighboring town of Kirchhunden in the district of Olpe. All of his descendants are Christians, some of whom emigrated to the United States in the 19th century.

Moses' only son, Jacob "Bachor" Oppenheim, my second great-grandfather, was born in 1797 and, as his grandfather had been, was a talented violinist. Rather than pursuing this skill as a career choice, he chose instead to become a merchant in Neuenkleusheim and lived with his parents in the synagogue. While on a business trip to *Nordrhein-Westphalia*, he stopped in the tiny village of Velmede and fell in love with a young woman, Jette Strauss. They married in 1838, and they returned to live with his parents and had a family.

After Moses died, Jacob sold the home in Neuenkleusheim in 1858 and moved to Velmede, the village of his parents-in-law, with his wife, three sons and a daughter.

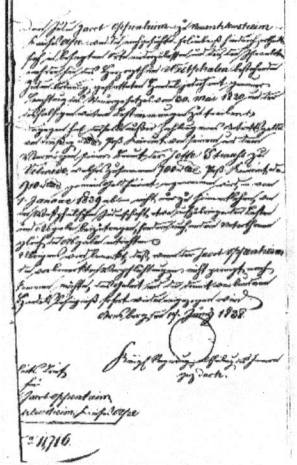

Marriage certificate of my 2nd great grandparents, Jacob "Bachor" Oppenheim (1798-1891) of Neuenkleusheim and Jette Straus (1814-1878) of Velmede, 1838.

Jacob Oppenheim frequently travelled to neighboring villages either by foot or by horse to sell or trade food and soft good items. His business visits to Berlar, five kilometers south of Velmede across a few rolling hills, are recalled in a memoir entitled *"Baßmes" Hof. Sauerländisches Dorfleben im 19. Jahrhundert. (Bassmes Yard, Sauerland Village Life in the 19th Century)*. It was written by Wilhelm Kathol (*Baßmes Willem*) in 1938, when Kathol was 84 years old and, reminiscing about his youth in the mid-19th century, put his thoughts to pen and paper. According to Kathol, Jacob Oppenheim ("Oppenhäim") frequently visited Kathol's village of Berlar to trade. Jacob was "an older, clever and intelligent man who could also play chess and probably no longer had to make a lot of money by trading goods." In Kathol's words, "The Jew from Velmede Oppenheim was about 70 years old, had white frizzy hair on his head. He carried a heavy pack on a stick, thrown over the shoulder and dangling on his back with him. So did his sons Pheylipp, Moses and Isaack, who wanted to trade with the lead and zinc miners in the mountain settlement of Alexander." (Of these three "sons," only Moses was the progeny of Jacob. Other relatives, employed servants or students/apprentices were often also referred to as "sons." Pheylipp and Isaac were certainly such).

Kathol continues in his memoir regarding the events of around 1865, "He (Jacob Oppenheim) enjoyed playing chess with my eldest brother Franz during the lunch break when they stayed with us on the farm in Berlar. The old Oppenheim always thought for a long time. Sometimes he put a chess piece on another square but didn't release his fingers and pulled the piece back after half an hour. At 2 P.M., my brother Franz had to return to work in the fields. Often Mr. Oppenheim remained seated in front of the chessboard until Franz came back in the evening. Then the chess game continued. When it was time for dinner, the chessboard was carefully put away. Mr. Oppenheim picked up his pack and, in the darkness of night, spent a good hour walking back from Berlar via Halbeswig to Velmede."

"On the next day or so, he would again come with his backpack and the game would be played on, just like yesterday, until late in the evening. That went on for five to six days until it was really called 'done' and the game was over. I do not know who won. All I know is there were a lot of chess games played out by the two over the years."

There is another Kathol anecdote circa 1870 regarding my second great-grandfather: "One day Mr. Oppenheim came into our house without his backpack. 'Oh, Mr. Oppenheim, where is your pack?' 'Oh, I was just in the Koers' house, I most certainly left it there. Run over there and get it for me!' Quickly I returned with the pack. Mr. Oppenheim was pleased and said: 'Wilhelm, as a reward for that I will give you a beautiful colorful vest with blue buttons made of crystal, which I'll bring you tomorrow.' But many days passed, he had always forgotten it. Every time Mr. Oppenheim came to our house, I asked for the promised vest with the blue buttons. In the end, he probably got weary of the endless questioning. One day, Mr. Oppenheim pulled a piece of red cloth from his breast pocket, appearing to be a very large handkerchief with green flowers together with a small container holding six etched glass blue buttons, and handed it to me. Now I was very pleased, and everything was good again. The handkerchief and the buttons were placed into Mother's special drawer. I was able to look at everything there from time to time. But a vest was never made from this. After a little more than a year, the colorful cloth became a curtain in front of the folding window between the living room and the kitchen. I took the nice buttons one day and put them in my pants pocket and lost them while I was playing. But I got a lot of spanking from my mother when the true story came out."

Jacob's first son and heir, Moses Oppenheim, named after his paternal grandfather, was born in 1839 in Neuenkleusheim. He was educated in the intricacies of the contemporary merchant trade by his father and, according to an entry in the handwritten January 1861 diary of the linen weaver, Bernard Mengeringhausen, of Niederslohe, a town 50 kilometers southwest of Velmede, my great-grandfather Moses sold Mengeringhausen's wife "coffee, tobacco, oil, laundry starch and pocket handkerchiefs." Their sizes were described in "Ellen," a now archaic German measure of length which traditionally was the distance between the elbow and fingertip, usually about two feet, although this number historically ranged from 16 to 31 inches. A few years later Moses Oppenheim received a calf in trade from the Mengeringhausens in exchange for "tallow, cotton cloth, and various other fabrics" for the manufacture of a coat and a pair of trousers in addition to a few *groschen,* a coin of the period made of .900 silver, equivalent to ten *Pfennig* (1/10 of a Mark) after the unification of Germany in 1871.

According to my translation of the Kathol memoir, The Oppenheim merchants "were well-respected, real businesspeople, otherwise they would not have found buyers in the whole area."

Velmede, Hochsauerland, c. 1880

Wishing to have a retail location for his business, my great-grandfather Moses Oppenheim opened a general store in Velmede in 1868 just prior to getting married to Lina "Caroline" Amant.

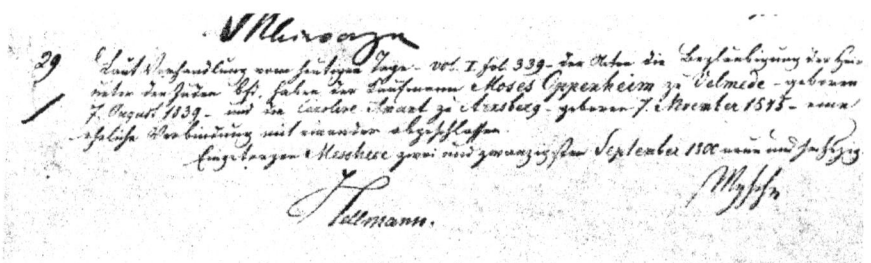

Marriage Certificate of my great grandparents, Moses Oppenheim (1839-1913) of Velmede to Caroline Amant (1845-1900) of Arnsberg, 1869, in Meschede, Westphalia.

The Oppenheim family was registered in Westphalia as landowners in 1871. On May 21, 1872, Moses purchased a seven-pound shoulder of bacon from the linen weaver Mengeringhausen for three *thaler*, a large silver coin weighing about one ounce and minted in the Holy Roman Empire and later in the Austro-Hungarian Empire. The English form of *thaler*, "dollar," survives as the name of a number of modern currencies. Although the Oppenheim family did not maintain a kosher household, they did not cook pork in the home. The large slab of bacon was likely destined to be divided for sale at the store.

Lina (Caroline) Amant and Moses Oppenheim, my great-grandparents, c. 1887

Lina (Caroline) Amant and Moses Oppenheim, my great-grandparents, c. 1892

Moses Oppenheim and Caroline Amant had seven children between 1873 and 1885, four boys and three girls, with my grandfather Albert born in 1875.

Moses Oppenheim with six of his seven children, 1904: Top row l-r: Luis born in 1884, Max, born in 1873. Albert, my grandfather, born in 1875, and Eduard, born in 1879. Bottom row l-r: Henriette, born in 1877, Moses (1839-1913), and Minna, born in 1885. A seventh child, Johanna, born prematurely in 1876 with severe developmental disabilities is not pictured.

The general store in Velmede became the family business, named eponymously *M. Oppenheim*. Moses' oldest son Max was sent to the United States in 1895 after a brush with the law, and his second son, Albert, my grandfather, began to work in the business part-time while in secondary school, and following graduation from *gymnasium*, worked there full-time, both in purchasing and sales.

My grandfather Albert joined the German army and served for two years from 1897 through 1899 in the Hessian division of the Infantry, stationed in *Cassel* (now Kassel). Germany was then at peace and the leading land power in Europe. The unification of Germany in 1871, following the French defeat in the Franco-Prussian war and the French ceding of Alsace and parts of Lorraine to Germany per the Treaty of Frankfurt, was facilitated by the Prussian statesman Otto, Prince of Bismarck (1815-1898), later known popularly as the Iron Chancellor. This resulted in a surge in nationalism among the Germans, including its Jewish citizens, who felt special obligation for military service to the nation that was at the forefront of the world in providing Jews emancipation and equal opportunity.

Discharge certificate of Albert Oppenheim from German Army, 1899.

Jewish emancipation had a darker side, however, often leading to a new and sometimes more virulent form of antisemitism, a term that was first coined in 1879 in Wilhelm Marr's pamphlet, *The Victory of Judaism over Germanism,* which sought to single out Jews as inferior because of their racial impurity, rather than their failure to adhere to Christianity. Marr also opined that Jews were conspiring to run the state and should be excluded from citizenship. Although the publication quickly became a best-seller, my family did not feel threatened as Jews during that time.

France, on the other hand, was in the midst of a period of antisemitism, as evidenced by the Dreyfus affair and its aftermath from 1894-1898. Alfred Dreyfus, a French army officer from a prosperous Jewish family, while an artillery captain for the General Staff of France, was suspected of providing military information to the German government. Dreyfus was found guilty of treason in a secret military court-martial, during which he was denied the right to examine the evidence against him. The French Army stripped him of his rank in a humiliating ceremony and shipped him off to Devil's Island, a penal colony located off South America's coast in French Guiana. The initial conviction was annulled by the French Supreme Court after a thorough investigation. In 1899, Dreyfus returned to France for a retrial but was found guilty again. The renowned French author Emile Zola risked his own career in January 1898 when he decided to stand up for the Jewish officer, writing an open letter, *J'Accuse*, to the President of France, Félix Faure, accusing the French government of antisemitism and falsely convicting Alfred Dreyfus. Ultimately Dreyfus was pardoned in 1906.

At the same time in Czarist Russia, Czar Alexander III (1881-1894), emulating his grandfather's anti-Jewish policies of 70 years earlier, was implementing laws designed to harm Russian Jews' economic, social, and political status. Alexander's secret police published a forged collection of documents known as *The Protocols of the Elders of Zion,* extensively detailing a secret plot by rabbis to take over the world. The text was widely translated and became a powerful propaganda weapon for antisemitic elements worldwide, including the United States, where the auto magnate Henry Ford was among those openly sponsoring its circulation. The Russian imperial police applied antisemitic discriminatory laws in a strict fashion, while the Russian media engaged in unrestrained anti-Jewish propaganda. In 1891, all Jews were systematically expelled from Moscow and violent pogroms plus repressive legislation resulted in the mass emigration of 2.5 million Russian Jews to western Europe and America during the years 1881-1914, one of the largest group migrations in recorded history.

Albert Oppenheim, my maternal grandfather, c. 1901

In 1900, Velmede was a village of approximately 1,500 residents, located within the municipality of Bestwig, a rural area in the *Hochsauerland* district, in *Nordrhein-Westphalia*, Germany. Velmede is on the south bank of the Ruhr River with the nearest train station being in Bestwig, a larger village two kilometers away. *M. Oppenheim*, located on the main street, *Provinzialstraße (*now named *Bundesstraße),* was one of two general stores in Velmede, the other one being owned by the Bachmanns, the only other Jewish family in town.

During the first decade of the 20th century, my grandfather Albert gradually assumed management of the business from his father Moses, who was aging and spending more time at the nearby family home on *Baumhofstraße*. It took only a few minutes for Moses to come into the store, which he did at least once a day, to make sure that his son was doing a good job, the employees were working hard, and all was in order.

A picnic in the Ostenberg hills, c. 1904: Albert Oppenheim, 2nd from left; Henriette Oppenheim, 5th from left; Minna Oppenheim, 6th from left, Johanna Oppenheim, 7th from left; others unknown.

According to the 1997 publication, "*Judisches Leben im Synagogenbezirk Meschede (Jewish Life in the Synagogue District of Meschede),* edited by Wilfried Oertel, "under his (Albert Oppenheim's) management, the company (*M. Oppenheim*) developed to provide great satisfaction to its customers. There was a rich offering of the finest textiles, fabrics, bed linen and everything you need to sew yourself." Further quoting Oertel, "Mrs. Mathilde Schiene, née Humpert, bought her wedding dress there. Mrs. Grete Schlicker, née Hermes, also bought almost all of her trousseau from *M. Oppenheim* and was very satisfied with it."

At the beginning of the 20th century in the rural *Sauerland*, it was customary for children to continue to live in their parents' home unless the boys went off to pursue a trade in other communities, while the girls married and moved in with their new husband's family. The Velmede Oppenheim family home was large and accustomed to multi-generational occupancy. Max, my oldest Oppenheim great-uncle, had emigrated to Philadelphia in 1895 at the age of 22 and, a few years later, moved to New York and became a textile salesman. Eduard, Moses' third son, three years younger than my grandfather Albert, also left Velmede during the first decade of the century, moving to Querfurt, a small town near the city of Halle in the German state of Saxony-Anhalt which in 1949, during the Cold War, became part of East Germany. He also entered the textile business. Luis left Velmede in 1902 to go to Philadelphia to work in the woven goods business with his older brother Max. Older sister Henrietta, born in 1877, known as "Hennie," married Adolf Vorreuter and moved to Natzungen, a village 90 kilometers to the east in the Detmold region of *Nordrhein-Westfalen*, where he had a business. Albert's younger sister, Minna, born in 1885, had married Albert Baum, a businessman from Mengede, near Dortmund, and had moved there in 1907. The large Velmede house was ready for some new occupants.

Chapter 3: An Ordinary Life 1909-1914

Rose Liepmann and Albert Oppenheim, 1908, the year before they married.

Rose Liepmann and Albert Oppenheim were married in Hannover, Germany, on July 1, 1909. He was 34 years old; she was 10 years younger. That difference in age between groom and bride was common at the beginning of the 20th century. As has happened from time immemorial, she met her future husband and my grandfather in 1908 through a family connection. Albert's sister Henrietta had married a man who was the nephew of Rose's mother, and they had been introduced at that wedding a year earlier.

The Oppenheim-Liepmann wedding was a large affair, attended by friends and family not only from Westphalia and other portions of Germany, but also from outside of the country with Albert's brothers Max and Luis coming from New York and some cousins travelling from German Southwest *Afrika*.

*Rose and Albert, 1909, the
year they wed.*

The Oppenheim home in Velmede was large and somewhat empty, occupied only by Moses, Albert's widower father, and the newly married couple. Within the next few months, they were joined by Rose's widowed mother Fanni and Rose's sister, Else, who had sold the Bücken house and moved 200 kilometers southwest to Velmede. Else was Rose's best friend and confidante throughout their childhood and they had shared the giggles, tears, and innocent secrets of being teenage girls together. Else would never marry and these three strong women were to live under the same roof for more than the next thirty years, until that fateful day in 1942 when the daughters had to leave their mother forever in Aachen.

*Oppenheim family home, Velmede, Sauerland,
Nordrhein-Westphalia, Germany, c. 1900*

Home births continued to be the norm of the times. My mother Gerda (Gerta) was born in 1910, followed by her brother Helmuth (Helmut) two years later. To say that they garnered most of the attention of their grandmother, aunt and mother would be a vast understatement. They were nurtured, protected, and well fed. Being among the first of the new generation of Oppenheims and Liepmanns, the babies received frequent visits on weekends and holidays from proud uncles and aunts, including Minna (Oppenheim) Baum from Meschede, Hennie (Oppenheim) Vorreuter with her baby, Walter, from Natzungen, Max Liepmann and his wife Paula from Bücken and young bachelor Paul, still in his hometown of Bücken.

My mother, Gerda Oppenheim, c. 1913

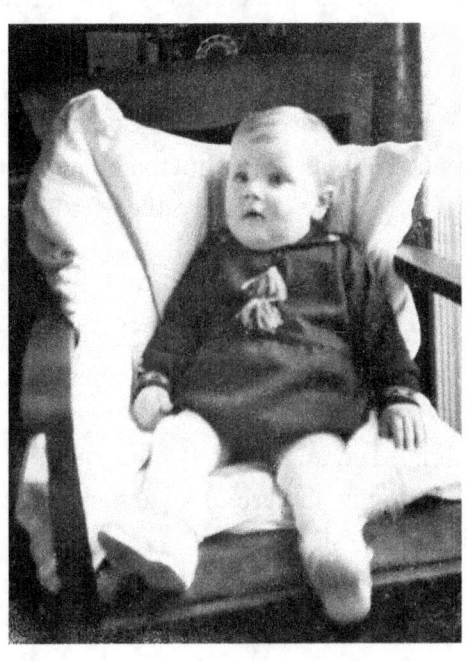

My uncle, Helmut Oppenheim, c. 1913

Whenever families gather, they frequently reminisce regarding happy days gone by and share memories about those departed. They also are eager to enthusiastically speak about new information about those relatives not present for reasons of geography: Max Oppenheim, Albert's eldest brother, was apparently less than eager to replicate his father Moses' small-town life. As a child growing up, sitting at similar family gatherings, Max had frequently heard the success story of a branch of the family: Joseph Schnellenburg, born in Germany in 1802, became a clothing merchant, and left Padberg, *Hochsauerland, Nordrhein-Westfalen,* Germany, with his wife and young children to go to the United States in the late 1840s and found his own promised land in Philadelphia. After changing his last name to Snellenburg, Joseph began a clothing manufacturing establishment and then opened a retail shop on a triangular piece of property he purchased on South Street, part of Philadelphia's largely Jewish garment district. One of his sons, Nathan, opened another clothing store in 1869, named *N. Snellenburg & Co.*, aiming its marketing at a middle-class population, using the slogan "The Thrifty Store for Thrifty People." The company sold directly from the workroom to the wearer, allowing clothing to be competitively sold for lower prices.

Incidentally, Joseph's son, Isaac, born in Pennsylvania in 1847, was a Union soldier who lied about his young age in order to volunteer for service in the American Civil War. He was killed in the battle of Richmond in 1862 and buried on the battlefield.

Nathan Snellenburg, born in 1844, married Minna Amant in Philadelphia in 1871 through a rather circuitous route. While a young woman in Germany, a good friend of Minna's had been bartered in marriage to a "one-armed Albuquerque businessman." Whether the limb had been lost in the American Civil War or perhaps in a less heroic fashion such as a barroom fight, is unknown. Albuquerque was then truly the Western frontier, located in the New Mexican Territories, captured by the United States in 1846 during the Mexican-American War. The young German woman refused to make the arduous trans-Atlantic and transcontinental voyage to her betrothed unless her best friend Minna, the younger of the two daughters of my second great-grandfather, Abraham Amant (1810-1853), accompanied her. Minna agreed and the two women, each less than twenty years old, left Bremen, Germany in late 1863 to take the voyage across the Atlantic to New York. From there, they travelled by train to the most western train stop, Marion, Ohio, where they arranged for transportation by stagecoach to Albuquerque. The population of Albuquerque in those days was less than 1,500, its buildings were mud huts, and the economy was supported by a US Army Depot located there, that military presence there to reduce the incidence of deadly raids by members of the Apache Nation. A year earlier, in 1862, there had actually been a brief occupation of the town by a group of Texan Confederate soldiers as part of an unsuccessful plan by Confederate political and military leaders to conquer California using Civil War Texas troops. After Union troops soundly defeated them at the battle of Glorieta Pass, the Texas contingent retreated from Albuquerque to return home.

According to family legend, Minna and the bride-to-be were novices to the adventures of outdoor life and travelled slowly on various wagon trains across the USA under significant hardship, eating buffalo meat when available and sleeping in taverns of "doubtful" reputation, finally arriving in Albuquerque just after the end of the Civil War. That town's single unpaved street, replete with thriving taverns and houses of ill repute, was still pockmarked from artillery fire by the Union Army. The railroad did not reach Albuquerque until 1880.

My second great-grandparents, receiving letters from their daughter Minna describing the dangers she faced daily and, fearing the worst, communicated with the Snellenburgs in Philadelphia, who arranged for Minna to be brought east, where she was introduced to Nathan, her future husband. Minna's older sister, Lina "Caroline" Amant, had married my great-grandfather, Moses Oppenheim, Albert's father, a few years earlier, in 1865.

N. Snellenburg & Co. became Philadelphia's leading clothier for generations, moving to a more fashionable downtown location on Market and 12th Streets in 1889, ultimately closing in 1962. At its height, the family-run company employed more than 3,000 people, and included a manufacturing operation on North Third Street, which for a period of time was the largest clothing manufacturer in the world.

Thus, Max Oppenheim, with dreams of his own financial success, left Germany to initiate a fresh start for himself in the United States, arriving in New York City on October 16, 1896, at age 23. He worked in the garment industry, first in New York, and then moved to Philadelphia in 1902 and, three years later, settled into an apartment at 230 Market Street in Newark, New Jersey. He returned to Germany for 3 months in the summer of 1908 to regale any and all receptive listeners about his adventures in the New World. Max had become a naturalized US Citizen on November 5, 1904, but only became a true "American" when, in 1911, he married Boston-born and bred Sophie Edith Brande, the oldest daughter of Bernhardt Brande, who had emigrated from Germany in the early 1870s and promptly changed his first name to Bennett.

Luis Oppenheim, Max and Albert's younger brother, greatly preferred the experiences described in Max's letters to the more familiar routine of Albert and their father Moses. In 1902, Luis, age 21, crossed the Atlantic to be with his older brother and enter the fabric and garment industry in New York City. Changing his name to Louis Joseph Oppenheim, he ended his bachelorhood after meeting Max's wife's sister, Pauline Brande, whom he married in 1916. The twists and turns of life sometimes produce unusual outcomes; two brothers marry two sisters and prosper in a new environment.

The Velmede family gatherings to observe and praise the developmental milestones of new babies inevitably turned to tales, first transmitted by mail, and then perpetuated orally, of the members of the family who had moved to the Southern hemisphere.

Beginning in the 1870s, Britain, France, Germany, Belgium, Italy, Portugal, and Spain competed for European pre-eminence through acquiring territories around the world, including Africa. By the beginning of the 20th century, European powers had colonized much of that continent.

Germany was late to enter this economic scramble for assured sources of raw materials, guaranteed markets, and profitable investment outlets. European nations acquired colonies to relocate their "surplus population," a consequence of industrialization, including unemployment, poverty, homelessness, and social displacement from rural areas.

To level the playing field and allow ease of German entry, Otto Von Bismarck, the mastermind of the unification of Germany in 1871 and its first Chancellor, convened a diplomatic summit of European powers in late 1884 at the Berlin West African conference (the Berlin Conference). The meeting, devoid of any representatives from Africa, produced a treaty known as the Berlin Act, with provisions to peacefully guide the conduct of the European imperialist competition in Africa.

In that year, 1884, the German flag was raised on the coast of Southwest Africa in an area which is now Namibia and a Dutch-speaking German provincial judge, Heinrich Ernst Göring, was appointed commissioner of the area. (His son Hermann Göring was a key member of Hitler's inner circle until the end of WWII, followed by his conviction as a war criminal at the Nuremberg war trials.)

In the following year, 1885, a group of bankers, industrialists and politicians formed the German Colonial Society for Southwest Africa and was given full rights to exploit mineral deposits in German SW *Afrika*, including gold, platinum, copper, and diamonds. In 1886, a dual legal system was passed, with one set of laws for Europeans and different statutes for the indigenous population.

Local opposition to mining created difficulties for the Germans, despite the signing of various treaties with the native inhabitants and, in 1894, a contingent of German troops was sent in to quell a rebellion by the local population that had killed 150 German settlers in more remote farmlands.

It was in 1895 that 23-year-old Max Vorreuter, Fanni Liepmann's nephew (and Grandmother Rose's first cousin) took his wife and baby to German SW *Afrika*. By the year 1902, there were approximately 2,500 Germans living in a large area, 1.5 times the size of the European German Empire.

Max settled in the new German village of Swakopmund on the deep blue sea of the Atlantic, surrounded on three sides by the towering golden dunes of the Namib Desert. Since the German military was positioned in the interior of the vast region, where the mines were located and farmland was fertile, it is likely that he was in SW *Afrika* to seek his destiny in the mineral industry as a middleman, not to serve with the troops, farm the land or work in the mines. When he returned to Germany briefly in 1906 for a visit, he regaled his family with stories of the fortunes that could be made on the *Afrikan* frontier.

Max and his wife, Johanne (née Wieneke), had three more children together while there but the family returned to Germany in 1915 when, during World War I, German South West *Afrika* was invaded by the South African and British forces of the Western Allies. After the end of the War, the administration of the area was taken over by the Union of South Africa, then part of the British Empire and administered as South West Africa under a League of Nations mandate.

The day-to-day ordinary activities of earning a living, consuming food and drink, sleeping, cooking, cleaning, commerce, love, and friendship, are punctuated by the special occasions of births, deaths. engagements and weddings, bar mitzvahs (and, today, bat-mitzvahs), funerals and relocations. What one remembers most vividly may be a special occasion or a nondescript encounter lasting a few moments, which when it occurs, may seem unimportant. We have surprisingly little control of what becomes deeply imbedded into our brains. We anticipate events and they occur when they happen and not one minute sooner. Waiting for them often becomes a fruitless occupation.

So it was with Rose's life in Velmede during those years. She attended to the needs of her mother, husband and children, and until 1912, to her widowed father-in-law, shopped, cooked, and maintained a clean home where family and friends could gather. The house was heated with coal and cooking was done over a coal stove. The Oppenheim home was one of the first in the village to have internal plumbing although any hot water needed required heating the water on the stove. They had the luxury of a new water-closet, a radical departure from the chamber pots and outdoor toilets with which they had grown up.

Although Thomas Edison had unveiled his light bulb to the public in New York in 1882 and the technology crossed to Berlin in that same year, electricity did not arrive in the homes of Velmede until the late 1920s. The three principal thoroughfares of Velmede were illuminated in the evenings by gas streetlamps. My grandfather, Albert Oppenheim, always dressed in a starched shirt, necktie, and jacket, kept the *M. Oppenheim* store open until shortly before dark every day and returned to his adjacent home which by then had been illuminated by candles and oil lamps. Given the presence of open flames and considerable wooden potential tinder, it is hardly surprising that a well-functioning local fire department was a practical necessity. Albert was very involved as a volunteer for that busy service in Velmede, as had his father, Moses, before him.

According to the unpublished manuscript by Wilfried Oertel, *Judisches Leben im Synagogenbezirk Meschede*, in a section authored by Rita Romer, the mayor of Velmede convened a meeting about "the establishment of a voluntary fire brigade" in 1899. A total of 63 people reported and registered with their signatures. Among them were Moses and Albert Oppenheim. As Romer writes, "It was a matter of course for the businessman Albert Oppenheim to volunteer as a fire fighter in charitable service for the citizens of Velmede." On March 16, 1902, the volunteers were divided into four sections, namely the hydrant and hose department, the security group, a regulatory team, and the rescue department. Albert Oppenheim was elected to the regulatory department. "At the 25th anniversary of the volunteer fire brigade in 1924, Albert Oppenheim, a businessman, was also particularly honored for his work for the volunteer fire brigade over the previous 25 years."

Weeks and months went by uneventfully with efforts devoted to the growing of a local business and the rearing of young children. Else, Rose's sister, was physically strong and energetic and, wishing to earn her keep, worked long hours at *M. Oppenheim* as both a buyer and salesperson, travelling the *Sauerland* by horse and carriage to buy materials and make deliveries. After she returned home and the dinner table had been cleared and the dishes put away, she always had lengthy conversations with her sister Rose, while Albert smoked his pipe doing the day's business accounting or reading a book.

The sisters spoke about the mundane affairs of the day—who had come into the store and the gossip they had overheard, who was getting engaged or getting into trouble, and about the effects of the weather on the neighboring farms. Although Tesla had demonstrated wireless communication in 1893 in St. Louis, Missouri, radios would not be part of everyday life until the 1920s and the Oppenheims first listened to the radio at home in 1927. The sisters read every newspaper available and frequently spoke to each other regarding the rapidly changing state of the world.

Velmede was located in the southeastern portion of the Prussian province of Westphalia in a region called the *Sauerland*, a hilly, heavily forested, sparsely populated rural area. The nearest larger towns were Meschede, 16 kilometers to the west, and Arnsberg, 40 kilometers to the west. The nearest city was Dortmund, 60 kilometers to the west, still in Westphalia but no longer a part of the *Sauerland*, with a population of approximately 100,000 people at the turn of the 20th century.

Germany had no national newspapers at that time. Towards the end of the 19th century, the word *Generalanzeiger* became the term for mass newspapers that described themselves as politically and denominationally independent. The "preference of the message over the commentary" as well as the "emphasis on entertainment and instruction over opinion-forming" corresponded to the attempt to win over broad sections of the population as readers. Velmede was within the circulation zone of the *Generalanzeiger* of Dortmund, founded in 1890 as the *Dortmunder Nachrichten* (Dortmund News) with the slogan, "an independent organ for everyone." Its editor, Karl "Karlchen" Richter and its publisher Friedrich Wilhelm Ruhfus were considered left-liberal in their politics.

Germany in 1900 had a population of 60 million people, of whom 1% were Jewish, numbering approximately 600,000. A wide variety of Jewish newspapers and periodicals were available in Germany at that time.

These included the *Israelitisches Familienblatt* (Israelite Family Paper), a weekly newspaper, founded in 1898 and published in Hamburg, directed at Jewish readers of all religious alignments. This was the only newspaper dealing with primarily Jewish issues in Germany which was run by a private business not aligned to a Jewish organization of any kind. It was politically rather conservative and avoided the current controversies regarding assimilation and Zionism. The *Familienblatt* provided broad-scale information and news about life in the Jewish communities, Jewish celebrities, Jews around the world, Judaism in general, Jewish traditions and history, and recipes for kosher cooking. Its circulation included about one quarter of all the Jewish families in Germany.

The organization *Zionistische Vereinigung für Deutschland* (Zionist Federation of Germany) founded in 1897 in Berlin, began to publish *The Jüdische Rundschau (*Jewish Newsmagazine*)*, another popular weekly publication, in Berlin in 1902. This periodical emphasized the new political movement begun by Theodore Herzl to establish an independent Jewish state. Herzl, born in 1860, was a successful Viennese journalist and playwright who published his Zionist manifesto *Der Judenstaat* (The Jewish State*)* in 1896 and convened the first Zionist Congress in the following year in Basel, Switzerland.

The *Allgemeine Zeitung des Judentums* (AZJ, General Journal of Judaism) was one of the first modern and certainly the most important of German Jewish periodicals of the 19th century. The AZJ was published biweekly in Leipzig and later in Berlin between 1837 and 1922. The publication understood itself as the main organ of the Jewish emancipation movement in the 19th century. It advocated moderate religious reform and closer relations with non-Jews. After the foundation of the German Reich in 1871, when full legal rights had been achieved on paper, the fight against antisemitism became the main focus of the AZJ.

The *Centralverein Deutscher Staatsbürger Jüdischen Glaubens* (Central Association of German Citizens of Jewish Faith) was founded by German-Jewish intellectuals in 1893 in Berlin, with the aims of unifying German citizens of Jewish faith, fighting for the Jews' rights as citizens and to combat rising antisemitism. Commitment to the German nation was an important part of their agenda and the members saw themselves primarily as German citizens with their own religion. This newspaper repudiated political Zionism. In 1895, this group began publishing a monthly newspaper entitled *Im Deutschen Reich* (in the German Empire) as its official organ. In 1922, this publication merged with the AZJ and was replaced by the weekly *Central Verein Zeitung* (Central Association Newspaper).

The Oppenheim family received the general newspaper daily and assiduously read one or more of the Jewish newspapers. They were concerned about economic stability and felt assimilated into the community, interacting on a friendly basis with their neighbors many times a day. Although the largely Catholic population knew that the Oppenheims were Jewish, this difference did not create strife and was only readily noticed on Sundays when my family's neighbors attended church services and wore their best clothing, those often having been purchased at *M. Oppenheim.* Although they were familiar with Herzl's young movement and discussed among themselves its pros and cons, the Oppenheims/Liepmanns neither embraced nor rejected Zionism since they felt it would not directly concern them.

In the early years of the second decade of the 20th century, Rose and Else often discussed until late in the evening what they had recently heard or read regarding the politics of Europe and, if the conversation grew louder or more animated, were often joined by Albert. The topics usually inevitably included various signs of the upcoming war.

Germany, aware that Great Britain was developing the world's largest Navy and Russia was enlisting large volumes of troops, was rapidly building its military. Germany's perennial enemy, France, had been badly defeated in the Franco-Prussian War of 1870-1871 and had paid Germany huge war reparations and ceded the provinces of Alsace and Lorraine to Germany.

Otto Von Bismarck, who almost singlehandedly had unified most Germans into the German Empire in 1871 (leaving the Austrians and Swiss-Germans outside the Empire), then becoming its chancellor, was the main practitioner of *Realpolitik* (politics as the art of the possible). Bismarck took full charge of German foreign policy from 1870 until his dismissal in 1890. It was through the *Dreikaiserbund* (League of the Three Emperors (Germany, Austria-Hungary, and Russia)), established in 1873, that Bismarck intended to prevent the ever-present tensions in the Balkans from getting out of hand – although he rightly knew that Russia and

Austria were competitors for German influence in the Balkans. In 1878, he convened and brokered the "Congress of Berlin" to de-escalate the dispute between Austria and Russia over the newly independent Bulgaria. He thereby succeeded in averting a Balkan-driven European War by 36 years, but not by one year longer.

In 1888, 29-year-old Wilhelm became Kaiser Wilhelm II, Germany's new ruler. He was the grandson of Queen Victoria of England and, although the military and imperial competition between the two nations had diminished somewhat based on this family tie, after Victoria's death in 1904 Germany again began an ambitious warship building program to challenge Britain's superiority on the seas.

In 1882, Germany had secretly entered into a Triple Alliance with Italy and Austria-Hungary. For Italy, the agreement promised to provide military support against France in case Italy was attacked without provocation. However, Italy reached an understanding with France in 1902 by signing another secret pact, stating that each of the countries would remain neutral in case of a war. When this agreement with France became public, Italy's position in the Triple Alliance was questioned. France and Britain were understandably concerned about the Triple Alliance, and France felt especially threatened by the German Navy. Thus in 1904, England and France signed an *Entente Cordiale*, a friendly understanding to encourage cooperation against a German threat. Russia joined the alliance three years later in 1907 to form the Triple Entente. The primary difference between the Triple Alliance and the Triple Entente was that the latter did not promise military support if war broke out but merely pledged moral support for each other. The Russian government also made a promise to help Serbia in case of attack by any members of the Triple Alliance.

The "Iron Chancellor," Otto Von Bismarck, had strong negative views of the Balkan people and had little sympathy for what he considered their troublesome aspirations of independence. Although Bismarck believed in fighting wars that were in the national interest of his country, he was particularly against starting wars in the Balkans due to the region's ethnic and religious complexity and its troubled political past. Bismarck arranged for a secret "Reinsurance treaty" between Germany and Russia in 1887.

In 1888, Bismarck is quoted as saying "One day the great European War will come out of some damned foolish thing in the Balkans."

The young Kaiser Wilhelm II frequently clashed with the aging Chancellor Bismarck. The Kaiser believed in the divine right of the monarch and wanted a rapid expansion of Germany's colonial and naval power in order to gain a "place in the sun." In 1890, Bismarck resigned because of his belief in the politics of negotiation and unwillingness to submit to what he felt were the warmongering dictates of Wilhelm II. Bismarck, a confirmed anti-socialist, had always been fearful of a French-Russian alliance but Wilhelm II and many of his advisers believed that ideological differences and lack of common interest would keep Republican France and Czarist Russia apart.

In 1891, France and Russia began to have friendly contacts and in 1894 the two nations developed a secret treaty called the Dual Alliance. In that same year, with Bismarck out of the picture, Germany and Russia failed to renew their former treaty of friendship and Germany became more fearful of the growing leftist discontent in Russia and its military conscription efforts. In 1908, the Austro-Hungarian Empire annexed the Balkan Provinces of Bosnia and Herzegovina, and diplomats travelled back and forth among nations to try to avert a war. Russia now was the main obstacle to the expansion of the German and Austro-Hungarian empires, with Serbia the only regional Russian ally.

This dizzying combination of shifting mutual defense alliances, imperialistic competition of the European powers for economic control in Africa and Asia, the buildup of the military and its growing influence within political systems, and the growing nationalism of the Balkan nations all contributed to the build-up to World War I. The two Balkan Wars of 1912 and 1913 were preludes to the coming Great War. The weakened Ottoman Empire, Serbia, Bulgaria, Greece, Montenegro, Romania, Macedonia, and Bosnia fought with each other on a rotating basis, with invasions followed by retreats, forming and breaking alliances with brief armistices and diplomatic breakthroughs promptly followed by failures.

The tipping point of all this European strife, the immediate cause of World War I, was the assassination of Archduke Franz Ferdinand of Austria-Hungary, the nephew of Emperor Franz Joseph I of Austria, and the heir presumptive to the Austro-Hungarian throne. In June 1914, a Serbian-nationalist, Gavrilo Princip, enraged by Austria-Hungary's control of Bosnia and Herzegovina, believing strongly that these areas should be part of Serbia, assassinated Franz Ferdinand and his wife while they were in Sarajevo, Bosnia, a part of Austria-Hungary.

Thus began the expansion of the war to include all those involved in the various mutual defense alliances. On July 28, 1914, Austria-Hungary declared war on Serbia. In response, Russia formally ordered mobilization in the four military districts facing Galicia, its common front with the Austro-Hungarian Empire. That night, Austrian artillery divisions initiated a brief, ineffectual bombardment of Belgrade across the Danube River. On August 1, after its demands for Russia to halt mobilization were met with defiance, Germany declared war on Russia. Russia's ally, France, ordered its own general mobilization that same day. A secret treaty was concluded between the Ottoman Empire and the German Empire on August 2, 1914. The Ottomans entered the war on the side of Germany and Austria-Hungary (the "Central Powers") one day after the German Empire declared war on Russia. On August 3, France and Germany declared war on each other. The German army invaded neutral Belgium on August 4 enroute to attacking France, prompting Britain to declare war on Germany. President Woodrow Wilson declared that the United States would remain neutral in the conflict.

The First World War and its aftermath would have a profound effect on my grandmother Rose's life.

Chapter 4: World War I

For my grandmother and her family in the first part of the second decade of the 20th century, the threat of Germany going to war was far less troublesome than the fear of being ruled by their Russian neighbors. German Jews had the most political, educational, and economic freedom that they had ever enjoyed and, especially in the large cities, Jewish social status continued to improve. The new, open, cosmopolitan atmosphere had its impact on religion as well, with many urban German Jews, deeming traditional Jewish observance as overly restrictive and irrelevant to modern life, joining the Jewish Reform movement. Even the historically Orthodox congregations began to combine their strict traditionalism with the pursuits of worldly affairs.

The Jews of Germany contrasted their status as citizens in full with the situation of their brethren in neighboring Russia. Of the approximately 11 million Jews living in the world of 1900, almost 4 million resided in Russia. They had been confined by the various Russian Czars to live in an area called the Pale of Settlement, a political entity formed in 1791 by Catherine the Great. This consisted of the easternmost twenty percent of the territory of European Russia, extending eastwards from the border with the German Empire to include what is now Lithuania, Belarus, and Moldova together with much of Ukraine and Poland and relatively small parts of Latvia and the western Russian Federation. Even some cities within the Pale (derived from the Latin word *palus*, a stake, to mean the area enclosed by a fence or boundary) excluded Jews from residency. Life in the Pale was economically bleak, especially when contrasted with the German-Jewish situation. Czar Alexander II, the monarch of Russia from 1855 to 1881, was interested in expanding the opportunities of rich and educated Russian Jews, but following his assassination in 1881, anti-Jewish sentiment skyrocketed. Partially fueled by rumors that he had been killed by Jews, new laws were passed that granted Russian peasants within the Pale the right to expel Jews from their towns. In addition, the new Czar, Alexander III, was known for his fierce hatred of the Jews.

Rose and her family knew all of this on an intellectual basis, but what truly stoked their concern and fears regarding Russia was the use of a new medium, photography, within the Jewish publications that they read, to vividly display the destruction and plundering of Jewish property and physical attacks on and murder of Jews with impunity and without fear of consequences, resembling those scenes that the Liepmann and Oppenheim ancestors had personally experienced and witnessed for centuries in Hannover and Frankfurt. My grandmother Rose had heard the stories and thought all this was far in the past but reading eyewitness accounts of the victims and seeing the published photographs of the Russian pogroms in Kishinev (1903) and Kiev (1905), telegraphed from the scene, drove home in graphic detail the terrible brutality of the Russians and ignited a visceral terror and trepidation about all things Russian. In the three years between 1903 and 1906, about 660 pogroms were recorded in the Pale, all carried out with the Russian government's complicity, many typified by extreme savagery and mutilations of the wounded, taking the lives of as many as 250,000 Russian-Jewish men, women and children.

This violence across the Pale prompted a huge wave of Jewish migration westward that the Russian government did not oppose and even encouraged. In the first ten years of the 20th century, one of every seven Jews in Russia left the country to escape the carnage and widespread intolerance they were experiencing. For their own safety, they abandoned their *shtetls* to emigrate to the Americas or to Europe, including Austria and Germany, where they primarily settled in tenement buildings in the big cities with their families, finding subsistence and employment as tailors, artisans, peddlers and factory workers, while continuing to dress in a traditional manner and speaking Yiddish or Russian in the streets and in their homes.

None of these Eastern European Jews had any reason to find their way to Velmede. Rose and her family had seen a few of the recent immigrants when they visited Dortmund, Frankfurt or Hannover and, although they were well aware of the dire circumstances which prompted their having departed the Pale, could not personally identify with the different appearances that they presented, the women with their long dark dresses and head coverings and the full-bearded men with their long black coats, black pants, white shirts and fur hats. Yes, they were religious brethren, but they were not family.

As the war clouds loomed ever closer, my grandmother could not envision the changes that would occur in her life within the next few years.

Ivan Stanislavovich Bliokh was a Polish Jew who converted to Calvinism in the 1850s and to Catholicism in the 1860s when he married into a prominent banking family in Warsaw. He made a fortune in the railway boom of the 1860s, funding the construction of successful rail-lines in southwest Russia.

Bliokh was an avid reader and keen observer and spent more than twenty years investigating military history, geography, and finance. He assembled an interdisciplinary group of specialists to write a huge book on the technical economics and politics of modern industrial war. Bliokh's five-volume book entitled *"The Future of War in its Technical, Economic and Political Relations"* was published in St. Petersburg in 1898. Although he was an optimist and a pacifist, he predicted a general European war which the capacities of modern economies would transform into a protracted and bloody conflict, leading to social crisis and revolution. Defense would dominate the offense, making impossible a single, decisive battle. Maneuvering would give way to firepower and positional warfare. Indecision, when coupled with the capacity of modern economies to generate war materials of destruction for the front, would result in a war of yet unseen devastation.

In his book, Ivan Bliokh explicitly stated that the future war would be a battle of motors, rather than heroes. Engineers and managers, rather than commanding officers, would play the major role. The realities of the future conflict would be shaped by rapid-fire rifles, machine guns, massive use of artillery, and extensive use of minefields. War would no longer be associated with heroic engagement of with armies marching down the roads and confronting each other but would rather develop into a bloody slaughter. Major battles would be fought on fronts thousands of kilometers long, where each advance of a few kilometers would be paid for by tens of thousands of lives.

Bliokh, writing 16 years before the beginning of the Great War, was truly prescient: He predicted automatic rifles made of aluminum, machine guns, bullet-proof armored gun carriages, barbed wire obstacles, trenches and controlled mine fields, armor shields, individual armor, aerial combat and bombardment, and unrestricted naval warfare, all resulting in terrible attack casualties, including entire units being annihilated in minutes by modern rifles, shrapnel, and machine-gun fire from camouflaged shelters. Fighting for a piece of terrain would last for many days. There would be high mortality rates resulting from shell bullets and the lack of medical personnel and doctors. Training of conscripts would be substandard and commanding officers would be inadequate. The outcome of the war would be decided not so much by actions on the frontlines as by the economic potential of the belligerent countries, the strength of their political regimes and, in particular, the state of industrial production, the stable performance of agriculture, and the uninterrupted operation of railroad communications. The terrible conditions of war and its horrible human toll would cause widespread distress among both soldiers and civilians. The final blows would be the depletion of resources of all belligerent sides, the inability to pay reparations and finally revolution.

Bliokh wrote: "In the future war everyone will be dug in the trenches. It will be great trench warfare. It will inevitably involve almost the entire continent, will last many years, and will cause casualties in terms of millions of lives to be lost and result in unprecedented economic disasters. The war will deprive millions of people of their daily bread, while prices will rise exorbitantly. The troops, irritated by the terrible losses and hardships, and going wild in the midst of unseen heretofore bloodshed, on their return home will find poverty — then a pernicious temptation may appear: to overthrow the existing system."

"The war for Russia, regardless of its outcome, would be no less disastrous than for her enemies." Specifically, Bliokh predicted, "Due to the relative backwardness of the Russian military and civil industries, the instability of agricultural performance and its dependence on weather conditions, and taking into consideration the lack of railway transportation, the future war will affect Russia more painfully than other parties to the conflict. Because of the war, the prospects for famine, public unrest, and the revolution will eventually increase enormously."

During the majority of the First World War, German Jews and gentiles stood proudly together in defense of their country. Jews welcomed the war as a fight for justice, freedom and, most important of all, German culture. For many German Jews, the war harbored the hope of being treated equally to non-Jewish Germans on a social basis for the first time. Many Jews also held strong patriotic feelings for Germany and the belief that the war in the East against the Russian Empire would bring the liberation of their fellow Eastern European Jews from pogroms and persecution. At the start of the war, 12,000 German Jews immediately volunteered for the German Army. Of the 100,000 Jews who served with the German military, 70,000 fought at the front line, 12,000 were killed in action, and 3,000 were promoted to officer ranks. However, they could only become officers of the reserve, not the regular army. The Iron Cross was awarded to 18,000 German Jews during the war.

My family was no exception. Every Liepmann or Oppenheim able male in Germany volunteered or was enlisted into the German Army, with most serving on the front lines. Within two months of the beginning of the War, Gustav Liepmann, Fanni's oldest son and Rose's brother, had sent a picture postcard from the Meuse (*Maas*) river in Belgium, which the German army had quickly crossed on their first offensive.

Back of postcard from Gustav Liepmann, October 28, 1914, in Belgium, "Watch on the Meuse," sent to his family in Bücken, lower Saxony

Gustav Liepmann, on far left, October 28, 1914, in Belgium, with sign saying, "Watch on the Meuse," front of postcard.

The Meuse *(Maas)*, one of Europe's major rivers, arising in France and flowing north almost a thousand kilometers through that country, Belgium, and the Netherlands to drain into the North Sea, throughout history has been the natural line of resistance against an enemy advancing from east to west over the Belgian highlands. Some of the banks of the Meuse are fairly flat, others are cliffs nearly 300 feet high bordering the river's channel. The entire Meuse valley was in the front line of World War I, culminating in the 300-day-long battle of Verdun in France, where hundreds of thousands of young men died. The last major clash of the War, the Argonne Forest (France) offensive of 1918, was also fought on the banks of the Meuse River, involving 1.2 million American soldiers, the majority of the American Expeditionary Force (AEF).

It is certain that Rose's brother, my great-uncle Gustav Liepmann, traversed the Meuse many times in the Great War, either on foot, by boat or by bridge since his assignment was to defend the river in Belgium against an Allied offensive. He was with the Second German Army under the command of General Karl von Bülow, which crossed the Meuse in Belgium east of Namur and west of Andenne within the first few days of World War I. That Army then turned south and met unexpected resistance from both the Belgians and the Fifth French Army under General Joseph Jacques Césaire Joffre, just to the west of Namur, again on the banks of the *Maas*. The German Army won that battle of Namur on August 22, 1914, and on the following day was able to advance into France. The Germans pursued the retreating Allied Armies for 200 kilometers over the following two weeks, finally being halted at the river Marne, just outside Paris.

On September 9, after four days of intense fighting, the German armies found themselves unable to maintain their position on the Marne and were driven back 75 kilometers to the river Aisne. Here both Armies entrenched themselves in the "Western Front" that formed, and they would remain centered near this position in continuous conflict for the rest of the war. Germany's master plan for the conduct of the war, named the Schlieffen Plan, according to which Germany would have quickly attacked and defeated France before Russia could mobilize and attack Germany, had failed.

Great-uncle Gustav was sent back to the village of Sclaigneux, Belgium, from where he had sent the postcard of October 28, 1914. He remained stationed there for many months, well to the east of the Western Front.

Gustav Liepmann, Rose's brother, 1915-1916, Belgium

I do not know how many of the numerous rivers in Belgium and France my mother's other direct ancestors crossed in uniform during the years 1914 to 1918. I know that Max Liepmann and Paul Liepmann, Rose's two other brothers, served Germany with distinction in the Great War, with Paul becoming an officer. Likewise, Albert Oppenheim, Rose's husband and my maternal grandfather, and Eduard Oppenheim, my great-uncle, both left their wives and two young children to enlist in the German Armed Forces.

Max Liepmann, Paul Liepmann and Albert Oppenheim, 1917

Four of the five members of the Liepmann and Oppenheim family in the German Army received the Iron Cross, a medal given to members of the German military for demonstrating bravery on the battlefield.

Albert Oppenheim (center) in a bunker, 1916

Albert Oppenheim, Paul Liepmann and Max Liepmann, 1916.

Iron Cross awarded to my father, Max Dahl, M.D., who served in the German artillery at age 17. He was to become Rose's son-in-law.

Albert and Rose with Helmut, 1915, on a respite from the Great War. The man on the left is unknown.

The United States declared war on Germany and officially entered World War I on April 6, 1917. Six weeks later, Congress passed the Selective Service Act, authorizing President Wilson to increase the size of the military. As a result, every male living within the United States between the ages of eighteen and forty-five was required to register for the draft in three separate enrollments. The first registration was for men aged 21 to 31, the second for those who had turned 21 since the previous registration, and the third, on September 12, 1918, added both men aged thirty-one to forty-five and all those between age 18 and 21. My great uncles Max and Louis Oppenheim, now citizens of the USA, registered for the draft in New York City on September 12, 1918, as directed, with Max appearing at the draft board at Broadway and 89th Street and Louis registering at the office at Columbia University at 116th Street on the West Side of New York City.

United States Draft registration documents of Max and Luis Oppenheim, 1918

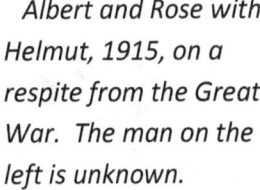

U.S. troops did not actively participate in the effort in Europe until May 28, 1918, at which time 650,000 American servicemen had arrived in France. By September 12, 1918, the end of the War was in sight and one month later, the German government was requesting armistice discussions with President Wilson. Rose's brothers-in law, Max and Luis Oppenheim were never called for active duty. They would never have to return to Germany to fight against their brothers Albert and Eduard.

Gerda Oppenheim, my mother, 1916

In late 1915, Albert returned from the War for a brief visit with Rose, Gerda, and Helmut in Velmede. It was time for a family photograph and for Albert to tell Rose about the day-to-day life in the Army, with days of boredom interspersed with days of anxiety. Albert did not enjoy sleeping in army tents on the cold ground nor did he fancy the rations that he subsisted on. It was wonderful to get a few days of Rose's home cooked food and see how the children had grown. In the evenings, Albert talked to Rose and Else about the supremacy of the German Airforce, the success of the German submarines (U-Boats) and the use of poison gas by the British in the Third battle of Artois on the Western Front. They realized that with the failure of the Germans to overrun France within the conflict's first few weeks, this would be a lengthy war to be fought on two fronts. In Russia, on the Eastern Front, the hardship of the War led to the Russian people revolting, the forced abdication of Czar Nicholas II, and the establishment of a provisional government. They continued to wage war until the collapse of the Russian army and the Bolshevik Revolution. The new Bolshevik government requested an armistice from Germany and quickly signed the Treaty of Brest-Litovsk, removing them from the war and granting Germany huge territorial concessions and promises of reparation. Even after this, with German morale briefly improved, Albert would return home for short visits every few months and, having observed the reality rather than merely reading the German press accounts of the War, told Rose that Germany would soon lose the war and that they should both hope that life would return to the way it had been prior to 1914.

Albert, Helmut, Rose and my mother, Gerda, 1915

During the War, life in Velmede went on with most able-bodied males involved directly in the war effort and far away from home. The store, *M. Oppenheim*, was operated by Else and some female employees, while Rose was participating to a greater extent than usual with its business aspects. Most repairs on the home and shop would have to wait until workmen returned from the Front. The men who came home to Velmede before the end of the War were those who had been permanently crippled. Any wounded soldiers who partially recovered were sent back to the trenches.

Max Vorreuter, Rose's first cousin, visited Velmede with his family after coming back to Germany from Southwest *Afrika* after the German defeat there by the British and South African troops in 1915. He was thankful that at age 43, he was too old to be conscripted into the armed services. His younger brothers Emil and Felix were not so fortunate. They enlisted in the German army and served on the Eastern front and, like 500,000 other German soldiers, were taken prisoner by the Russians. Although the war with the Russians was won by the Germans in 1917, there was little, if any, repatriation of the prisoners by either the interim or Bolshevik governments. Felix Vorreuter and Emil Vorreuter, both Rose's first cousins, died in the Russian prisoner of war camps on January 25, 1918, and March 24, 1918, respectively, likely from a combination of malnutrition and infectious disease, long after Russia was no longer an active combatant.

The British naval blockade severely restricted food supplies in the large German cities, causing malnutrition and civilian susceptibility to disease in urban areas. Velmede was essentially a farming community and, fortunately for my family, did not suffer food shortages, bread rationing or the despair that this brought elsewhere. Hungry people in the cities were being fed by thousands of newly opened soup kitchens and they complained that the farmers were keeping the food for themselves, which was indeed the case in the rural areas such as Velmede. Even the army had to cut the rations for soldiers. The morale of both civilians and soldiers continued to sink. Coal was in short supply due both to the blockade and the drafting of German mine workers into the military, making the winters even colder.

The people of Velmede never saw an enemy soldier. Unlike in World War II, there would not be a single Allied combatant on German soil until after the end of the War. There would be no foreign armies devastating the German landscape. There would be no civilian casualties from the use of weapons. However, the enthusiasm for war among the German people rapidly faded in 1918 and a grimmer attitude began to prevail amongst the general population as the supply of manpower and essential supplies dwindled, the casualty reports increased, and the force of American ground troops and artillery began to be felt on the Western Front. The Germans were suffering twice as many casualties as they inflicted, and the new German troops sent into battle were under-aged youth or embittered middle-aged family men in poor condition. The German people became more despondent and with no victory in sight, just wanted the War to end. On October 4, 1918, German Chancellor Max von Baden, newly appointed by Kaiser Wilhelm II just three days earlier, sent a telegraph message to President Woodrow Wilson requesting an armistice between Germany and the Allied powers, based on the terms President Wilson had laid out in his famous Fourteen Points address in January 1918. After a month of indecision and squabbling among various factions within the German military and the fractured German government, World War I came to an end on November 11, 1918. The Kaiser and all the royal families had abdicated, and the German Empire had been replaced by the Weimar Republic.

As Germans recognized that the War was not going well for them, the Dolchstoßlegende (the stab-in-the-back myth), an antisemitic conspiracy theory, became widely believed and promulgated in right-wing circles in Germany. This belief was that the German Army did not lose the First World War on the battlefield but was instead betrayed by the civilians on the home front, an unpatriotic populace, Socialists, Bolsheviks, and especially the Jews, who were said to foment labor unrest and strikes. It was hardly surprising that the majority of the German public was perplexed at the request for an armistice, since the censored German press had only been reporting Central Power victories and Allied defeats.

When Adolf Hitler and the Nazi Party came to power in 1933, they made the Jewish people an essential part of the traitorous group which had "stabbed the nation in the back," leading to the German defeat. To many Germans, the expression "stab in the back" was reminiscent of Siegfried, the hero of Richard Wagner's 1876 opera Götterdämmerung, being murdered by the villain Hagen by a spear in his back. The vast majority of Germans would eventually come to believe this conspiracy theory, which effortlessly eradicated any guilt in beginning and losing the War, replacing it with anger at their weakness in losing the War. Hitler was to heavily capitalize on this sense of communal shame, using the idea of Jewish betrayal during and after the war to bring the Nazi Party to power, a party that saw Jews as not merely traitors, but a poisonous group of *untermenschen* (subhumans).

A 1919 Austrian postcard with a caricatured Jew stabbing a German soldier in the back with a dagger

The *Dolchstoßlegende* actually began well before the end of World War I. Although in August 1914, eighty-one German rabbis volunteered to serve as *Feldrabbiner* (Field Rabbis), something that had not existed before in the German Empire, rumors began to spread that the Jews were not sufficiently supporting the War effort and were, instead, personally profiting from the engagement. In October 1916, the army ordered a *Judenzählung* (Jewish census) of the troops, with the intent to show that Jews were under-represented in the fighting forces and that they were over-represented in non-fighting positions. To their surprise, this tally showed just the opposite, that Jews were over-represented both in the army as a whole and in fighting positions at the front. The Imperial German Army promptly suppressed the results of the census.

The commander of the German Army, Field Marshal Paul von Hindenburg and his Chief of Staff, Erich Ludendorff, were to a great extent responsible for the creation and popularization of the myth that the army was not defeated on the battlefield, but rather was betrayed on the German home front. After the end of the War, in the autumn of 1919, Ludendorff was having dinner with the head of the British Military Mission in Berlin, British Major General Neill Malcolm. Malcolm asked Ludendorff what his opinion was regarding why Germany lost the war. After Ludendorff replied with a list of reasons including that the home front failed the army, Malcolm is said to have asked him, "Do you mean, General, that you were stabbed in the back?" Ludendorff rose to the bait and pounced on Malcolm's phrase. "Stabbed in the back?" he echoed, "Yes, that's it, exactly, we were stabbed in the back."

Later that year, Ludendorff and Hindenburg appeared before the *Untersuchungsausschuß für Schuldfragen* ("Committee of Inquiry into Guilt") of the Weimar Republic's National Legislature, which was investigating issues regarding World War I. Hindenburg refused to answer any questions, but instead read a statement that had been written by Ludendorff, a statement that ended with Hindenburg declaring that: "As an English general has very truly said, the German Army was 'stabbed in the back'." This testimony of Hindenburg contributed heavily to the widespread acceptance of the *Dolchstoßlegende* in post-World War I Germany.

When I came to the United States from Shanghai in 1949 as the only child of stateless refugees, my natural inclination was to become an American patriot, which I continue to be to this day. For many years of my life, I felt some shame that members of my family, including my father, had at one time been enemies of the United States, my newly adopted home, during World War I. I had considerable anxiety in trying to reconcile the fact that my father, my grandfather, and numerous great-uncles had been part of a fighting force whose actions prompted American entry into the World War in 1917 and that my family may have been responsible for injuries or deaths to citizens of my new home.

The Nobel-Prize winning writer, Thomas Mann, whose non-Jewish family had lived in Germany for many generations, was eager to defend his nation throughout the First World War and was a supporter of the Weimar Republic but became rabidly anti-Hitler even before 1933. In his "*Reflections of a Nonpolitical Man*," published in 1918, he writes about his bitter arguments with his brother, Heinrich, also a novelist, who, as a "social justice warrior" before his time, viewed the Great War as a battle between French civilization and German barbarism. Thomas was not a rabid nationalist but was extremely skeptical of the ideas of his brother, for whom French bombs were logical and peaceful, while German ones were a result of mere viciousness. Thomas could not understand how Heinrich, an ardent supporter of the universal rights of man, could, at the same time, accept France's alliance with the arch-reactionary Russian czarist government.

I have now come to realize that the world of 1914 was a quite different place than it would be in 1933. This was especially true for the Jews of Germany and, to a lesser extent, for the Jews of the United States. The traditional Jewish values of freedom, both religious and political, equality under the law, access to education, family ideals and upward mobility were arguably more attainable in pre-WW1 Germany then they had ever been anywhere in the world in the prior 2,000 years. In the United States at that time, Jews had significant limitation of employment opportunities, were excluded from living in certain areas, were unable to join certain social clubs and could not bring their families to vacation at many resorts. There were quotas on enrollments at certain American colleges and universities and access to becoming faculty at these institutions was restricted. Many prestigious New York and Boston law firms denied employment to Jews and hospitals throughout the United States refused to allow Jewish physicians privileges to admit their patients.

According to Jerome Karabel's 2005 sociological treatise, "The Chosen, The Hidden History of Admission and Exclusion at Harvard, Yale, and Princeton," at the beginning of the 20th century preparatory schools such as Groton, St Paul's and Choate and universities such as Princeton, Yale and Harvard were interested in having students (and professors), who were socially polished, charismatic, athletic, brave, born leaders, rather than those who were academically superior, serious scholars or openly ambitious. In 1904, the Yale yearbook boasted of having "more gentlemen and fewer scholars than any other class in the memory of man." Although a limited number of Jews were accepted to these institutions based on their truly exceptional intellectual merit, in the first thirty years of the 20th century no single Jew of the 1,200 who attended Yale was elected to a "senior society." This attitude was pervasive in other American academic and non-academic institutions. In 1914, the Protestant Establishment clearly still dominated American business and society. They or their ancestors had worked hard to possess privileges, and they were eager to protect them as their most valuable possessions.

The Jewish newspapers in 1915 Germany were consumed by reporting on the lynching of Leo Frank in Marietta, Georgia. My family found it horrifying that the centuries' old blood libel could manifest itself in a presumably civilized nation such as the United States. A Jewish-American in Atlanta, Leo Frank, was accused and convicted of the rape and murder of Mary Phagan, a 13-year-old Christian girl, despite only fabricated circumstantial evidence. 31-year-old Frank was found guilty of murder and sentenced to death by hanging, a verdict met with cheers and celebration from the crowd. Following the Governor of Georgia's changing the punishment from death to life imprisonment, a mob stormed the prison where Frank was held, seized him, and hung him from a tree. America might be a land of opportunity for some, but it was also home to the Ku Klux Klan, who disseminated the view that Jews, among others, were subverting American values and ideals. It was also the place where many recent Jewish immigrants, primarily from Russia, suffered economic hardships, laboring in sweatshops alongside their children for seemingly endless hours, and living in crowded vermin-infested apartments without sanitary facilities within the slums of the large cities.

My family, like other German Jews were patriotic nationalists, perhaps not as passionately so as *Volk* Germans, but nevertheless supportive of the war effort. Theodore Herzl, President of the Zionist Congress, felt that he had made progress in convincing Kaiser Wilhelm II of the necessity for a Jewish State in Palestine, an area controlled by the Ottoman Empire since 1516. In 1898, Herzl, seeking support for his concept of a

Jewish homeland including Jerusalem, the capital of ancient Israel, secretly left Vienna to join the Kaiser on a trip to Palestine and they met publicly there on two occasions. He was hoping to convince the Kaiser to influence the Turkish Sultan to seriously consider the proposals of the Zionists. By the time of the outbreak of war in 1914, the offices of the Zionist Organization had been located in Berlin and the Zionist policy had become to maintain strict neutrality in the event of war and "to demonstrate complete loyalty to Turkey," the German ally controlling Palestine.

In 1915, David Ben Gurion, who was to be Israel's first prime minister and Yitzhak Ben-Tzvi, the future President of Israel, both volunteered for the Turkish Army to fight against the Allies. Despite their actively calling on Jews to become Ottoman citizens and attempting to assemble a militia in Jerusalem to fight on the Ottoman/German side in the First World War, they were rejected for military service and exiled from Palestine to Egypt. They moved to the United States and met with members of the *Poale Zion* (the socialist Jewish Labour Movement) to encourage them to fight on the Ottoman side. In that same year, many German-Jewish philosophers, politicians, and academics travelled to the United States to encourage American Jews to try to persuade the still-neutral American government to enter the war on Germany's side.

In the United States at that time, most Russian and German Jews supported the Germans. With Czarist Russia on the side of the Allies, the advancing Germans were regarded as liberators by the Jews. The non-Jewish German-American community and the largely anti-British Irish Americans had similar sentiments.

German-Jewish politicians and intellectuals praised the German entry into the war. Jewish member of the *Reichstag* (Parliament) Ludwig Haas commented that Russia, when it entered the war, had committed "the greatest crime in world history." Russia was the oppressor of the Jews; therefore, it was Germany's enemy and worthy of their fighting a holy war to deter them. It is likely that Rose read the issue of the Zionist *Jüdische Rundschau* when it proclaimed that Germany was fighting "to free Russia and the world from unprecedented tyranny." German Jews were prominent supporters of their army's efforts to colonize the East. The territory won from Russia, they argued, properly belonged to Germany. Since the *Ostjuden* (Eastern European Jews) spoke Yiddish, a dialect of German, they were Germany's racial compatriots. Although there was frequently cultural friction between the German and the Eastern European Jews, the latter mostly welcomed the Germans who were attempting to deliver them from Russian rule.

In October 1914, the German-Jewish playwright Ludwig Fulda wrote, "We shall fight this war to the very end as a cultured people to whom the legacy of Goethe, Beethoven and Kant is as sacred as hearth and home." German Jews were integrated into their country's forces, and anti-Jewish insults in the military were rare. The Bavarian Army Regiment, which counted the young Adolf Hitler as one of its enlistees, had fifty-nine German Jews. There was a vastly different situation in the Russian Army, where the Jews were suspected of collaboration with the enemy, and 600,000 of them were banished from the front by the czarist army, a policy very compatible with the Czarist government's pogroms, restrictive decrees, administrative pressure and frank encouragement of the emigration of 2,000,000 Jews from Russia in the thirty years prior to World War I. The majority of the Jews in the world of 1914 prayed for the victory of Germany and the Central Powers against Russia and its allies, Britain and France.

*Gerda and Helmut Oppenheim,
Velmede, 1919*

CHAPTER 5: A Time of Normalcy: 1919-1930

The future 29th President of the United States, Warren Gamaliel Harding, during the 1920 Presidential campaign, successfully employed a recurring phrase: "America's present need is not heroics, but healing; not nostrums, but normalcy; not revolution, but restoration." Although the word "normalcy" was not one that Harding invented, his repeated use of it in his speeches during the weeks leading up to his election made it more widely used by the English-speaking world than its common synonym "normality." Harding was nominated by the Republican party, albeit on the tenth ballot, after an all-night debate in a "smoke-filled room." The actual origin of that term stems from that June 1920 location in a room at the Blackstone Hotel in Chicago where Harding's nomination was decided upon in a private meeting by a handful of cigar-smoking power-brokers. The Republican National Committee's decision to support Harding, even though the junior senator from Ohio was a relatively minor candidate who had nothing controversial to espouse, was based on their understanding of what the American male (and female for the first time given the recent passage of the 19th Amendment) voters wanted: Peace, economic prosperity, family life, nothing stressful, in other words, Harding's normalcy.

Normalität is the German word for either "normalcy" or "normality." My grandmother Rose wanted nothing more than emotional relief from the stresses of the War years. My grandfather, Albert, her husband, was home from the conflict physically uninjured and seemingly prepared to resume the management of *M. Oppenheim* and do whatever necessary to grow the business. He had gotten older during his time away, certainly understandable in light of the horrors he had seen and the terrors he had felt. He was perhaps a little quieter than he had been and definitely seemed to toss and turn in his sleep more than she could remember.

In the early morning hours of May 4, 1920, there was a great deal of excitement at the Oppenheim home in Velmede. Gerda and Helmut, now 10 and 8 years old, were told not to go to school and the store was closed. In the early afternoon, Albert came down the stairs and excitedly told his children *"Sie haben einen brüderchen."* (You have a little brother). My mother told me this story many times and, frankly, I am not certain whether grandfather Albert used the word *brüderlein* or *brüderchen*. In any event, the meaning was the same. A baby in the house was the first step towards *normalität*.

For Rose and Albert, the arrival of their son, Günter, was a true blessing. A third-born child usually enters a household with parents already possessing years of experience in raising children, parents who are more relaxed about a fever, rash, or emotional outburst. Gerda and Helmut were old enough not to feel the usual jealousy or resentment when a baby is born and wanted to be involved in entertaining and educating their younger brother. Third children separated by five or more years from their older siblings in age are often calmer, more easy-going children, and their sunny disposition is amply rewarded by their older siblings and parents, either consciously or subliminally.

I have often been perplexed by the observation that children who are products of the same biological parents and similar upbringing possess marked differences in character and social development. Parent-child and peer relationships are critical determinants of social skills and personality in childhood. Birth order and external forces can certainly influence the ultimate nature and behavior of an individual. If one had asked my grandmother in the late 1920s to describe each of her children through the use of unique adjectives, she likely would have said the following: "Gerda is intelligent, quick to learn, stable, serious, logical, orderly, conscientious, dependable, realistic, trustworthy, hard-working, thoughtful, reliable, responsible, stable, and kind to her family and friends; Helmut is introverted, curious, a detached intellectual, dogmatic, opinionated, idealistic, bookwormish, withdrawn, intensely creative, logical, blunt, inflexible, private, stubborn, quixotic, dreamer, at times unreasonable and willing to take risks; Günter is extroverted, predictable, calm, positive, spontaneous, adaptable, secure, reliably loquacious, fun loving, jovial, distractable, friendly, adaptable, confident, industrious, athletic and lovable." Three children exhibiting a wide range of personalities despite similar biological disposition and experience. Traits observable in childhood are strong predictors of adult behavior and were I to describe my mother and uncles as I knew them, I would use similar descriptors.

After the armistice of November 11, 1918, Kaiser Wilhelm II abdicated and went into exile in the Netherlands. The Weimar Republic was established, but not without significant infighting among various factions. The new government reluctantly accepted the terms of the 1919 Treaty of Versailles, including loss of significant territory and population to France, Belgium, Denmark, Poland, Czechoslovakia, and Lithuania. All of its colonies outside Europe were taken away. There was a cancellation of the territorial losses and payments due Germany from Russia under the Treaty of Brest-Litovsk, severe reduction in the size of the German military, acceptance of a "war guilt" clause and payment of massive reparations to the Allied powers, payable in gold, Allied currency, agricultural goods, intellectual property, or commodities including coal and steel. There also existed a huge amount of domestic debt liability for funding of the War and previously promised pension payments to German soldiers, now out of work. Since tax revenues were insufficient to finance these outlays, the *Reichsbank* started running their monetary printing presses. Although Germany was not permitted to pay the Allies directly with German Marks, the German treasury could produce more Deutschmarks and convert them into Allied currency. As the government began printing more money to pay both its foreign and domestic debts, it created astronomical "hyperinflation," the worst ever seen in the history of civilization. The buying power of German money simply disintegrated. The value of one German Mark decreased by a factor of twenty versus the United States Dollar between 1914 and 1921 and would be further drastically reduced in value by the end of 1923, when hyperinflation reached its peak. At that time one US dollar was worth 4.2 trillion (4,200,000,000,000) Marks. On paydays, employees brought suitcases and backpacks to work to collect their wages, and then dashed off to purchase goods at the nearest shop before the exchange rate again changed. People suffered from food shortages and froze in their unheated homes. Political extremism was on the rise.

1923: German hyperinflation at the grocery store with payments by huge stacks of money.

1923 German money: a 100 billion Mark bill, commonly used when shopping for groceries.

On November 15, 1923, decisive steps were taken to end the nightmare of hyperinflation in the Weimar Republic: The *Reichsbank*, the German central bank, stopped monetizing government debt and established a new currency, the *Rentenmark*, which was backed by mortgages on agricultural and industrial land. The value of the *Rentenmark* was fixed at the old Marks exchange rate of 4.2 *Rentenmark* for one US dollar. Although this stabilized the future German economy, the old German *Papiermark* was now worthless, and the German people had lost all their hard-earned savings. Together with this, the German unemployment rate reached 19.1 percent in October, 23.4 percent in November, and 28.2 percent in December 1923. Hyperinflation had impoverished the great majority of the German population, especially the middle class.

The rural location of Velmede, more than 500 kilometers from Berlin and 600 kilometers from Munich, gave my family there a buffer against the economic and political unrest occurring in Germany during the early 1920s. Goods were not in short supply. There was simply no stable currency with which to buy them. People stopped dealing in cash and started bartering instead. Although any bank savings that my family had accumulated was now worthless, the large amount of dry goods inventory that had built up at *M. Oppenheim* during the War and added to by Albert after he returned from the War, purchased with Marks that had not, as of yet, seen major inflation, was invaluable as a trading vehicle. One could always buy food, coal, or a train ticket with a bolt of cloth or pay a store employee or a worker at home with a few pairs of socks or a pair of trousers, regardless of what the Mark was worth at that minute. If customers of *M. Oppenheim* insisted on using a wheelbarrow of money for payment for goods at the store, Albert would quickly send someone to a supplier or a factory with the money in a different wheelbarrow to purchase more goods that day, before the cash had a chance to be devalued yet again.

After the November 1923 peak of Germany's postwar economic and political chaos, the country made a remarkable recovery over the next six years, fostered by the actions of the German Central Bank, the end of the Allied occupation of the industrial Ruhr Valley, the USA agreeing to lend Germany money in the new mood of international cooperation and the Allies granting German government a more realistic payment schedule for war reparations.

Velmede was a wonderful place for Rose's children to grow up. It was small enough so that one could easily walk from one end to the other. Everyone knew each other, making it safe for youngsters to be out playing in the street or at a friend's house until evening. The surrounding hills provided opportunities for hiking and in the winter, for cross-country skiing and sledding. The Ruhr River, flowing through town, besides providing drinking water, was a perfect location to canoe, row, sail, or swim in the summer.

Days turned to weeks, then months and years for my Velmede family, as they do for all of us. Albert enjoyed reading a good book and spending time with his family, occasionally going out in the evening to play chess or skat (a 3-handed trick-taking card game that originated in Germany in the early 19th century, combining elements of bridge, hearts, euchre, pinochle, and poker) with friends. Rose was content with caring for the home and children and making sure her husband was comfortable in all respects. Else worked long hours at *M. Oppenheim* and, once Gerda and Helmut began to commute to school, often was at the train station in Bestwig to accompany the children home after their ride home if they were returning late in the day or the rain was heavy. Fanni, who was to turn 75 in the year 1930, mostly stayed at the house but was always eager to greet the children and inquire about their school day. She stayed well informed and often had pithy things to say about local and national politics.

Helmut, Günter and Gerda, 1922

Albert (R.) playing chess at a professional exchange meeting, 1924

Norderney is one of the Frisian islands off the North Sea coast of Germany. Reachable only by ferry, it has been a popular resort since the end of the 18th century. The Oppenheim family frequently travelled there for summer vacation.

56

*Albert and Else (2ⁿᵈ row) in
Norderney on holiday, 1925*

*Norderney, c. 1927. Else
Liepmann, third from left.*

*Gerda Oppenheim (R) on vacation at
Tegernsee lake resort with friend, upper
Bavaria, 8/5/1929. She was 19.*

*Norderney, c. 1929. Albert Oppenheim
in hat, dark jacket and tie, fourth row, left*

Norderney, c. 1930. Rose and Albert 2nd row, third and fourth from left.

My family were members of the Synagogue in Meschede, a 10-minute train ride from Bestwig, which was less than two kilometers distant from the Oppenheim home in Velmede. The Meschede Synagogue was built in 1879 and destroyed in 1938 during *Kristallnacht*. The ideology of that congregation was what I would term modern German Orthodox, where attendees wore normal dress clothing, rather than all in austere black, and men's hats were either street hats or yarmulkes rather than the fur hats favored by the Eastern European Jews. Women did not wear wigs, men sat downstairs while women at prayer were upstairs and women did not actively participate in any activity in front of the Ark of the Torah (pulpit). Although the Jewish Reform movement originated in Germany in the middle of the 19th century and was designed to bring Judaism into line with the ideas of the western European enlightenment, this branch of Judaism had not yet penetrated the more rural areas of Germany, such as the *Sauerland*.

Rose and Albert did not maintain a kosher household, although they did not bring pork or shellfish into the home. This departure from the dietary restrictions of Judaism was the source of some consternation on the part of Fanni, especially in the first few years she lived in Velmede. She had, after all, married Moses Liepmann, the son of the founder of Bücken's synagogue almost 100 years earlier and her own Vorreuter family in Enger had observed Jewish dietary law.

The Meschede Synagogue, c. 1890. Note the pentagram stars in the windows and clerestory, rather than the six-pointed stars of David.

Rose, Albert, Else, Fanni and the children always attended the synagogue for High Holy Day services (Rosh Hashanah and Yom Kippur), fasted on the day of atonement and went to Meschede to say *Yahrzeit* (the prayer on the anniversary of a death of a close relative). Although *M. Oppenheim* was open on Saturdays and closed on Sundays to conform to the habits of the primarily Lutheran and Catholic customers of the store and residents of the area, the family would sometimes attend the weekly Shabbat morning service in Meschede. If Albert participated, the store would be managed by one of the employees for the three hours that he would be absent in the morning. Trains ran five or six times an hour in each direction and in the spring and fall the walk to the Bestwig train station was very pleasant and punctuated by conversation among the members of my family. Pesach (Passover) eve was always celebrated with a bountiful Seder. All the beautiful silver dishes and serving platters were taken from the highest cupboards and were carefully removed from their blue felt protective coverings and shined with silver polish. A special set of German porcelain, either Villeroy and Bosch, passed down through the Oppenheim family, or Meissen, courtesy of the Liepmann ancestors, was carefully hand washed, but only by Else or Rose, since they did not fully trust the help to take enough time to not a break a plate or cup handle. Rose and Albert had recently purchased an additional china service of the newly popularized Rosenthal brand of dishes, but tended to use the other older, more historical, sets at special occasions. The Seder was officiated by Albert, and he sang the traditional melodies used by his father, Moses, and countless generations before him, perhaps slightly altered by Liepmann interpretations of similar prayers. The Seder was attended by friends and family, often coming from miles away and the Oppenheims would occasionally also invite some Christian friends from Velmede, so that they too could share in the commemoration of the festival of freedom, the recounting of the Jews' deliverance from the tyranny of Egypt. In certain years, the Oppenheims would travel to Dortmund or Hamm to be included in a Seder at a relative's home. The minor holidays of Chanukkah and Purim were always observed at home, with gift-giving to the children and recounting of the exploits of the Maccabees and Esther and Mordecai.

Christmas and Easter were annual solemn events in Velmede and there would, of course, be a decorated Christmas tree on the *Provinzialstraße* and in many families' homes. The neighbors recognized that the Oppenheims respected these occasions, closing the store on the Christian holidays, but also realized that these commemorations had no religious meaning for their Jewish friends and acquaintances.

Rita Romer writes, "The Jewish children had grown up among all the others. You played with them, you quarreled and made up again. At Easter there was a way for the neighborhood children to get a taste of Jewish matzo bread. In the Jewish homes (at Christmas), there was also a tree in their houses and there, too, the children received small gifts that day."

According to Wilhelm Kathol's (*Baßmes Willem*) 1938 memoir entitled *Baßmes' Hof. Sauerländisches Dorfleben im 19. Jahrhundert*, "The Jewish families took part in the village festivals. For example, on April 25, 1926, at the general assembly of the St. Andreas Protective Society, Lazarus Senger and Albert Oppenheim were elected, to check the bills and the ledger. Again in 1927, the two were supposed to check the books prior to the upcoming general assembly. When there were parades passing their homes, they put out flags decorated with their jewelry like all other residents. Their children looked for flowers outdoors in the meadows and made carpets made of flowers for the corridors."

There was only one school in Velmede. It was a public *Hauptschule*, teaching reading, writing, and arithmetic and preparing children for trades and blue-collar work. After the third grade, classes were segregated by sex, and education usually ended when children were eighteen, although many, especially the girls, were taken out of school earlier to work on farms, as housekeepers or as apprentices to tradespeople.

Kathol writes, "The (Jewish) children also attended the local village school. The only thing they did not usually take part in was religious instruction. But when the Old Testament was dealt with, they were there and contributed to the teaching with their knowledge."

Albert and Rose felt that Gerda was too intelligent to continue in the local *Hauptschule* and made the decision that she would receive a better education at the Catholic School in Arnsberg, which educated girls in a *gymnasium*, an academic high school.

Gerda Oppenheim, 1921, age 11

Gerda began attending the *Mariengymnasium* in Arnsberg when she was 12 years old. Since classes began at 7:45 in the morning, she would get up early in the morning and walk or ride her bicycle to the train station in Bestwig. It was still dark at that time in the winter months. Trains ran every ten minutes and the train ride to Arnsberg took 40 minutes and the school was another 5 to 10 minutes from the station on foot.

The Mariengymnasium in Arnsberg was founded by the Order of the Poor School Sisters of Notre Dame in 1889 for the express purpose of allowing girls to also have access to a decent education. The school had about 250 students, half of whom were boarders and the others being day students, as was my mother, Gerda.

In the mid-1920s, the Sisters recognized the need for women to also have access to professions that required university studies. Curricular and examination changes were made. Following this, Mariengymnasium had the right "to hold the matriculation examination" for Universities (*Abitur* examinations).

The initial purpose of the school, as expressed in 1890, was "Fortification and Christian religious education and endowment with the knowledge and skills for the full and joyful fulfillment of the duties of later life, with special attention to handicrafts and the learning of the household."

There was, of course, a dress code for the girls, who always wore skirts and were never allowed to wear trousers. In addition, they were not permitted to wear short-sleeved tops even in the warmest weather. In physical education classes, everyone wore dark blue gym pants with a skirt over them. The skirt could be removed from over the trousers only when participating in gymnastics.

By the time my mother arrived and classes started in the morning, the boarding students had already attended morning prayer and eaten breakfast.

My mother was the only Jewish girl in her class. Her teachers were religious Sisters of the Order and her relationship with them was good, but they always had clear rules for all students. As part of her education, she attended church services daily together with the other girls and had minimal instruction in catechism. There were occasionally social events with other schools.

From 7:45 a.m. to about 12:30 p.m., the lessons took place in the classrooms of the school. At 1:00 p.m., lunch was eaten in the dining room with twenty students sitting at each large, long table, joined by one or two Sisters. Each girl had her specific place with its own napkin drawer. After a prayer, the boarding students were served lunch, while the day students, including Gerda, brought their own food. From 2:00 p.m. to 6:00 p.m., with a brief coffee break at 3:45 p.m., there was mandatory study time, with the imposition of absolute silence so that the girls could concentrate on their tasks. The Sister supervising this time was fair but observant, intolerant of even the slightest bit of nonsense. The class of young women graduating from *Mariengymnasium* in 1928 was the first to sit for the *Abitur* examination. My mother was included in that group passing the examination and qualifying her for admission to university.

School pageant with a boys' school, 1928. Gerda Oppenheim, seventh from the right in back row.

Young women leaving home to study at co-educational institutions of higher learning was a relatively new concept in rural Germany in the late 1920s and Albert and Rose, after much discussion, with Gerda included, decided that it would be best for her to go to a women's finishing school for six weeks. There, in a large mansion in Switzerland, my mother learned proper manners and etiquette that would serve her well as a future wife. There were lectures on topics as varied as how to manage a budget for the home, staff management of servants in the home, menu preparation and being a polite hostess including issues of international protocols when entertaining guests from varying backgrounds. Every day there were practical sessions of floral arrangement for the home and for the dining table, cooking, setting a beautifully decorated dinner table with the proper placement of napkins and eating utensils, decision-making regarding seating arrangements, home management, and menu preparation.

With today's updated roles of men and women in society, it's difficult to imagine the role of a finishing school within the education of a woman to prepare her for family life. My mother certainly had been taught how to behave properly at home. The finishing school's traditional mission would polish those social skills so that she could be an asset to her future husband when he brought clients or friends to their home. Although this appears very stilted and extraneous today, there is even an etiquette to eating cheese: Hard cheeses are eaten with a knife and fork, never put on bread, but soft cheeses can be spread on a small piece of bread that one daintily, without fanfare, breaks off from a slice located on the bread plate. The exception is mozzarella which is a soft cheese which one eats with a knife and fork.

At finishing school, my mother was also taught the art of making polite conversation with guests in the living room and at the dining table, with an emphasis on staying away from the taboo subjects of religion, politics, sex, and finance. All matters regarding money were best left to the male members of the party, who would retire to the library after dinner to discuss these matters over cognac and a cigar without the women being present.

Helmut Oppenheim, c. 1922

Helmut attended the Velmede *Hauptschule* and after the sixth grade was sent to the non-religious rectory school of the City of Meschede, which was a less than 15-minute train ride from Bestwig/Velmede. In 1928, while Helmut was a student in his junior year there, the city of Meschede contracted with the monks of the Königsmünster Benedictine Abbey, a monastery of the Benedictine Congregation of St. Ottiliene, to run that school and announced that the school from that time onward would be a strict religious institution. Helmut was adamant regarding his unwillingness to continue his education at a Catholic institution and spent his final year of high school year at a non-sectarian *gymnasium* in Neheim, a part of Arnsberg, the town where his sister had attended school in the *Mariengymnasium* two years earlier.

Helmut, kneeling in first row, fourth from right, *1923*

In 1928, at age 18, Helmut left home to become an apprentice at the *Sternheim & Emanuel* department store in Hannover, a company that his father Albert had dealt with professionally for many years. The merchants Louis Sternheim and Max Emanuel had founded the store in 1886, initially as a textile and manufactured goods store located in rented rooms. A few years later they bought the building and replaced it with a new building in 1896. They created, "a department store worth seeing for the time" at *Osterstrasse* 99 in Hannover. By the time Helmut arrived they had expanded to a large department store with more than 300 employees, selling articles for daily needs, women's, men's and children's clothing, linen and fabrics of all kinds, haberdashery, cleaning supplies and handicrafts, curtains, furniture, carpets and beds in all price ranges, just as *M. Oppenheim* did on a much smaller scale. Thousands of customers visited *Sternheim and Emanuel* every day. Helmut rotated through the various departments in sales and customer service and worked in the office in purchasing, accounting, and business management.

In 1929, during the global economic crisis, an antisemitic leaflet circulated in Hannover that stated that *Sternheim and Emanuel*, among other Jewish businesses, were "robbery institutes, which systematically plundered the working Germans."

Helmut wrote home about this in a rather jocular manner, but he was already recognizing the rising popularity of Adolf Hitler's *Nationalsozialistische Deutsche Arbeiterpartei*, (NSDAP, or National Socialist German Workers' Party), the successor to the pan-German nationalist and antisemitic German Workers' Party (DAP), founded in early 1919 as a response to Germany's defeat in World War I. The Weimar Republic was a parliamentary democracy with a large number and variety of political parties. The most popular political party during the 1920s was the left of center Social Democratic Party of Germany (SDP). The SDP was repeatedly forced to ally itself with more conservative parties to form coalition governments. With the decade of the twenties experiencing a rapid decline in the popularity of SDP coalition partners such as the center-left German Democratic Party (DDP) and the Centre Party, representing Roman Catholics concentrated in southern and western Germany, the SDP was unable to win a parliamentary majority. Each coalition government was a little more unstable than the prior one and majorities could not be maintained for significant periods of time, with calls for new elections being frequent. In this setting, there was a void on the far left which was filled by the German Communist Party (KPD).

The 1930 German general election occurred while Helmut was serving his retail apprenticeship in Hannover. That election drew a record 82% voter turnout. The SDP remained the strongest party and won 143 of 577 total parliamentary seats, a loss of ten seats from the election two years earlier. Hitler's NSDAP became the second-largest party and gained 107 seats, a massive increase from the 12 seats they had won in 1928. The only other major party to significantly increase its seats was the KPD winning 77 seats, 23 more than in the last election. The more than thirty other political parties shared the remainder of the votes.

The outward idealism of the KPD (communists) was appealing to young German students who saw their country's entry into World War I as an expression of fascism, rather than one of nationalism. The Communist Party of Germany in 1930 regarded the SDP as their main adversary and thought of them and the other centrist parties as "social fascists." Helmut, at age 18, living away from his family for the first time, was not immune to the Leninist and Stalinist concepts of redistribution of wealth and removal of power from the well-entrenched. He frequented the coffee houses and bars of Hannover, a city of 400,000 people at that time, many of them young intellectuals, artists and Bohemians looking for an end of the ruling elite and the ascent of the common worker perhaps, if necessary, by revolutionary means. Helmut participated in lengthy discussions about political philosophy, often until almost dawn, and by late 1930, had become an active and vocal member of the KPD.

In 1931 Helmut returned to Velmede to work for *M. Oppenheim*, with the understanding that he would take over the business once Albert retired. That was not to be.

Günter, *"der Kleine"* was called "the little one" not because he was the baby of the family. He was born prematurely and was a small sickly baby. He nursed sparsely and infrequently, and grandmother Fanni was up two or three times every night for the first six months of his life to offer him a bottle and insisted on Günter at least partaking some of it until she returned briefly to her bed until the next feeding. Following this he thrived, becoming bigger and stronger with each passing month. There was no question that he was the favorite of Fanni, Else and Albert, although Rose was equally devoted to all her children.

Günter, sitting in chair on left, 2nd grade 1928

Günter attended the Velmede *Hauptschule*, coeducational for the first three years and then in a boys-only class. He was popular and athletic and occasionally got into a row with some of the local lads.

In 1929, the Oppenheims were among the first residents of Velmede to purchase an automobile. Albert and Rose did not wish to learn how to drive and designated Gerda to take driving lessons and become the family "chauffeur." My mother was the first woman in Velmede to obtain a drivers' license and could often be seen in her car in Meschede and Arnsberg running errands or visiting friends.

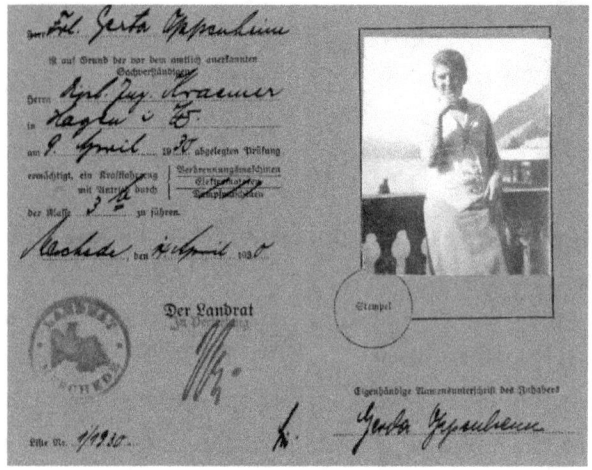

*Gerda Oppenheim,
driver license, 1930*

Gerda Oppenheim, driving in Meschede, 1930

Günter, age 10, with Eugenie Fröndhoff, a longtime employee of M. Oppenheim, in her family garden in Bestwig, 1930.

Günter, 1929

Günter, Gerda and Helmut, 1928

*Oppenheim Home and Store,
Velmede, Sauerland, Nordheim-
Westphalia Germany, c. 1928*

Gerda Oppenheim, 1929

*Günter (top row) and friends in front of
M. Oppenheim store window, c. 1929*

*Albert, Rose, Fanni, and Else in
garden of Velmede home, 1930*

*Rose and Günter, 1930 vacation,
Hohegeiß, Harz mountains, Lower Saxony*

Chapter 6: 1931-1932

Late in the evening on December 31, 1930, Rose, Albert, Else and Fanni toasted the arrival of 1931. Although the worldwide depression, triggered by the New York stock market crash of October 1929, had caused Germany to see investment by foreign money withdrawn, businesses crashing, wages dropping and unemployment soaring, Velmede, because of its sparse population and agriculturally based economy, was, to the greatest extent, spared, as it also had been during the hyperinflation of the early twenties.

Albert was 55 years old and had recently been diagnosed with diabetes. Although the Nobel Prize in Physiology and Medicine had been awarded to Drs. Banting and Macleod for the isolation of insulin in 1923, its utilization by the general population only became widespread in the late 1940s, when insulin syringes became available. Its use in Germany in the 1930s was confined to clinics and hospitals, so Albert's treatment was essentially dietary, including carbohydrate limiting and portion control. He was easily fatigued and was looking forward to his son Helmut returning from Hannover later that year to take over many of the business responsibilities at the store.

My grandfather Albert Oppenheim, c. 1930

Rose was 45 and kept herself busy with her home, family and various functions in town. Gerda was now almost 21 and had a number of male suitors, including Edgar Bachman from Velmede, the son of the other Jewish family in town. It was common to send a chaperone whenever a young woman went out on a "date" with a gentleman and Günter was usually the one to tag along to make sure everything was kept scandal-free. Gerda understood the necessity of this is but was still extremely annoyed when she was seen with Günter,

Günter, Rose, and Albert on vacation in Hohelete, a mountain resort in Bavaria, June 1930

ten years younger than she was, and was told on two separate occasions, "You have a very good-looking son."

Else was 43 and essentially was the manager of *M. Oppenheim*, able to handle all routine and unique problems that arose on a daily basis and only asking for Albert's help when customers insisted on speaking to a man regarding an issue. Although she was a spinster, she was pleased to have her beloved family to come home to every evening.

Fanni was 75 and felt fortunate to have her family around her. She took especial pride, of course, in everything Günter did, and also spent considerable time with her newest grandchild, Ruth, who was born in 1929 to Paul, Fanni's youngest son, and his wife Agnes. Paul Liepmann was also in the textile business, and he lived with his family in the small city of Horn, 70 kilometers from Velmede. On January 1, 1932, her oldest son, Max Liepmann, Rose's brother, died unexpectedly at his home in Hannover. He left a wife, Paula, née Hornthal and two children, Margot and Erich Liepmann.

Else Oppenheim, my great-aunt, c. 1930

My great grandmother Fanni with newest of six grandchildren, Ruth Liepmann, 1931

At the end of 1930, Helmut was 18 and would be completing his training in textiles and retail in Hannover in about six months and then planned to join the *M. Oppenheim* business, which he did in the middle of 1931. By the time he returned to Velmede, he had become a full-fledged member of the German communist party. During the summer of 1932, he felt somewhat socially and intellectually constrained by the provincial nature of life in rural Velmede, where the streets and shops closed down at 8 p.m. He missed sitting in cafes into the late night with friends and arguing the politics of Germany. Being woken up by his mother at 6 a.m. to work at *M. Oppenheim* or to catch a train for a business trip was not to his liking. In September of 1932, Helmut went on an extended camping trip by bicycle throughout the Italian mountain region with a friend. There he had an opportunity to collect his thoughts and reflect on the importance of life's choices. When he returned to Velmede he told Rose and Albert that he was going to move to a larger city, leave the employment at *M. Oppenheim* and get a job in the fabric industry on his own. Although his parents were disappointed, they respected that decision and were pleased that he would not be far away. He promised to visit them frequently in Velmede. Throughout all of Helmut's life, he was destined to move from job to job, never really putting down roots and often living hand to mouth.

My uncle, Helmut Oppenheim, 1929

Helmut cycling in the mountains of Italy, 1932

Helmut's youth hostel card, 1932

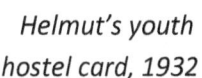

Else, Rose and Albert on vacation in Bad Ems, 1932

Gerda Oppenheim, 1930, Velmede

Günter was 10 years old and growing up fast, had many friends, and was an excellent soccer player. He was a fast learner in school and was looking forward to being sent away to a *gymnasium* once he completed eighth grade at the local *Hauptschule*.

Günter (center) and local buddies, 1930

My uncle Günter, 1931

Gerda, on vacation in France, 1932

Gerda was twenty and very independent, working at *M. Oppenheim*, driving a car, cross-country skiing or hiking with acquaintances on weekends and taking overnight trips to the beach in Norderney with Helmut and vacationing with various girlfriends in Bavaria and France.

Gerda, on vacation in Bavaria, 1931. She was 21 years old.

My mother, Gerda Oppenheim, far right, skiing, 1931

Gerda met her future husband in June of 1932, and they became engaged in October of that year. Max Dahl was ten years older and was a physician with a successful general medical practice in Lüdenscheid, a small city also in the *Sauerland* region of *Nordrhein-Westphalia*, Germany, located about 120 kilometers west of Velmede. He was the oldest child of Nathan Dahl, a teacher of Jewish Studies and leader of prayer in a synagogue, and Sara née Goldberg, who had been a student of Nathan's in one of his classes and was also ten years her husband's junior. Max was born in West Prussia in the German town of Schwetz, located where the Weichsel River empties into the Baltic Sea. Just after his graduation with highest honors from *gymnasium* in mid-1918, he enlisted in the German Army, where he briefly served in the artillery and was awarded the Iron Cross for bravery in battle. He then enrolled at Berlin University for one year followed by the study of medicine at the University of Giessen, near Frankfurt, one of the oldest and finest medical schools in Europe, founded in 1607.

The region of West Prussia where my father was born was ceded to Poland by the Treaty of Versailles in 1919 and my father, having left home to pursue his studies, never returned to Schwetz after the transfer of the area from Germany. However, despite never having set foot in Poland, he was considered to be of Polish nationality under international law. Because of post-War political uprisings in the area between the Germans and Poles, his parents moved west, first to Oberlahnstein in the German Rhineland and then, in 1922, to Hamm in Westphalia.

Max Dahl, 1920, wearing KC (Kartell-Current) fraternity sash

Max Dahl's medical school graduation certificate, 1924

Rose and Albert felt that Max was the ideal fiancée for Gerda. He had an excellent classical education, good moral values, knew eight languages, was a decorated War veteran, had a noble profession, and was economically well established, He was an active member of Kartell-Convent (KC), the pre-eminent Jewish fraternity, founded in 1896, whose purpose was a lifelong "fight against antisemitism in the German student body and the education of its members to [be] self-confident Jews who … are ready and able at any time to stand up for the political and social equality of the Jews." Members of that association were bound to the understanding "that the German Jews form a part of the people indissolubly linked to the German fatherland by history, culture and legal community."

Gerda Oppenheim
Dr. med. Max Dahl

danken herzlich für die ihnen
anläßlich ihrer Verlobung er-
wiesene Aufmerksamkeit

Velmede / Lüdenscheid, im November 1932

Printed thank you card for
engagement congratulations
and gifts, November 1932

Gerda Oppenheim and Max Dahl, M.D., the
engaged couple, 1932

1932 ended on a happy, hopeful note for Rose. Although Helmut no longer lived at home, she often was surrounded by her children, was in the midst of planning a wedding and Albert's business was thriving. Günter, "der Kleine" would have his Bar Mitzvah in the Spring. Although she would attempt to remain optimistic throughout the rest of her life, 1933 would be the first of many years of upheaval and pain.

My grandmother Rose, 1932

Chapter 7: 1933

Gerda was married in Essen, Germany, a large city in *Nordrhein-Westphalia* on Sunday, February 12, 1933, at the Glückauf-Loge (Good Luck Lodge) immediately followed by a seated reception. Hundreds of people attended including Liepmann relatives from Enger and Bücken, Oppenheim relatives from Arnsberg, Dortmund, Hacken, Mengede, and, of course, Velmede, Vorreuter relatives from Natzungen and Herford, the Dahls and Goldbergs from Hamm and Datteln, Gerda's friends from school and her many travel companions, Max's friends, K.C. brothers and colleagues from medical school and Lüdenscheid, and Rose and Albert's close friends, including the Bachmanns, the other Jewish family in Velmede and their Christian neighbors, the Nieders, Müterigs, Bamfastes and Bückers.

Wedding reception seating card for Frau Erna Oppenheim second wife of Eduard Oppenheim. His first wife Meta Brandenstein had died at age 43 leaving him with three children.

The groom, Max Dahl, M.D.

The bride, Gerda Oppenheim, 1933

The wedding reception was followed that evening by a *Glückauf* dinner buffet in the main hall of the Dortmunder Union, the largest brewery in Germany, known for its pale lager beer (pilsener), less than a twenty-minute train ride east of Essen. The *Speisenfolge*, literally "order of courses" or menu included many delicacies, each served with choice German wines.

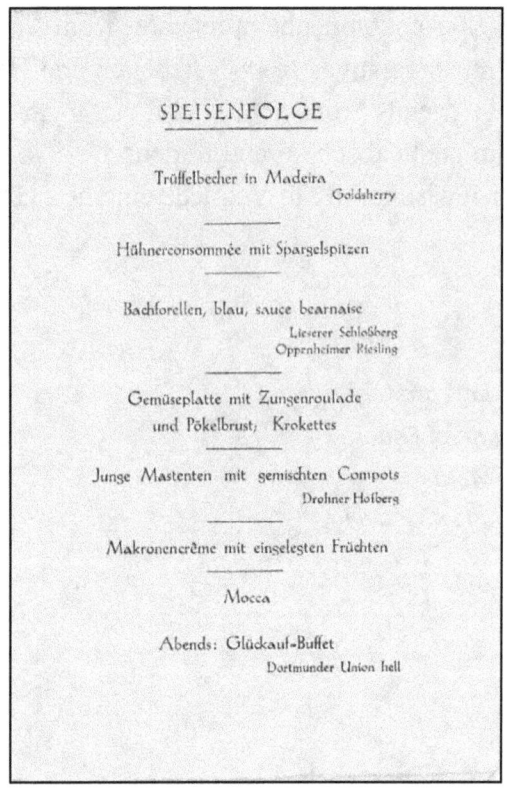

Minced truffles in Madeira, accompanied by golden sherry

Chicken consommé with asparagus tips

Poached book trout with Béarnaise sauce, accompanied by a Lieserer Schlossberg Oppenheimer Riesling

Vegetable plate with galantine of tongue, brined beef and potato croquette

Young duckling with mixed fruit, accompanied by a Drohner Hofberg (regional Riesling)

Macaroon Crème Brulé with pickled fruit

Mocha (a coffee with chocolate flavoring)

Hundreds of congratulatory telegrams and wedding cards arrived for the newly married couple.

From the moment the engagement was announced, my grandmother Rose devoted herself to making her daughter's wedding perfect. Just as mothers do today, she wanted the wedding to be a magical moment in Gerda's life, an event about which her guests would talk for years to come. With her usual efficiency she, with my mother's input, managed the guest list, the venues, the seating arrangements, determined the color schemes and dress for the wedding party, arranged for a rabbi to officiate and kept track of all progress using only a pen, a notebook, and her keen mind.

The young couple wished to honeymoon in Italy but since it was rather cold there in February, they postponed their trip until the weather moderated. After the wedding, they lived in my father's apartment in Lüdenscheid, where my father resumed his medical practice while Rose's daughter, my future mother, began to establish her own household and promptly became the well-liked wife of a prominent professional. Rose and Albert looked forward to their frequent weekend visits to see the family.

Letter addressed merely to "wife of "Dr. Max Dahl Lüdenscheid," 1933. Everyone knew the Doctor.

Despite the beauty and peacefulness of the wedding, Rose, her family, the wedding party, and the other guests must have had grave underlying concerns regarding President Hindenburg's appointment of Adolf Hitler as Chancellor of Germany only two weeks earlier.

In 1933, there was a profound sense of hopelessness among the German people, still reeling from the worldwide economic depression that began in 1929. The German government was subjected to increasing attack from both the left and right of the political spectrum. Paul von Hindenburg, a World War I hero and President of The Weimar Republic, was becoming older and politically weaker. In the 1930 general elections, the Nazis (NSDAP, National Socialist German Workers' Party) under Adolf Hitler had gained over 100 seats in the *Reichstag* (parliament) and smaller increases were achieved by the Communists.

In the spring of 1932, Hitler ran against incumbent Hindenburg for President, with the Nazi Party making an impressive showing and receiving 30% of the vote. Hindenburg led all the candidates with 49% of the vote, just under the majority needed to win. In a run-off election a few weeks later, Hitler gained over two million votes more votes to achieve 36% of the total votes. Hindenburg gained only one million votes over the prior election but did reach 53% of the total electorate, sufficient to be elected to another term as the German President. Although Hitler had lost the election, his personality, policies, and party were rapidly gaining support.

On June 16, 1932, Germany received a reprieve from the overwhelming financial burden of post-World War I reparations payments when the United Kingdom and France agreed to suspend disbursements imposed on Germany by the Treaty of Versailles. Despite this, the *Reichstag* was unable to achieve consensus on most issues and was again dissolved that month. In the absence of any legislative branch of government, the country was briefly solely ruled by President Hindenburg together with his reactionary chancellor, Franz von Papen.

In the July 1932 *Reichstag* election, Hitler and the Nazi party gained an additional 123 seats, making them the most powerful party in the *Reichstag*. Together with its coalition partner, the German National People's Party (DNVP), it had gained a *Reichstag* majority, the first time since 1930 that a governing coalition had held a parliamentary majority. Functionally, however, because of divisions within the DNVP itself, this would not result in any meaningful legislation coming from the *Reichstag*. At the election of 1932, the Nazis and the Communist Party, both declared enemies of the parliamentary system, together held an absolute majority of the seats. At the time of the swearing in of the new Parliament, the speaker of the Parliament, Hermann Göring, one of the leaders of the NSDAP, recognized a Communist deputy who wished to dissolve Parliament, and the Communists and the Nazis combined to vote out the new legislature before it had ever conducted any business.

In the next Federal parliamentary election on November 6, 1932, the Nazi vote decreased from the prior 37% to 33% while the Communist and the National Conservative seats in the *Reichstag* increased. This election was to be the last free election in Germany for the next 17 years.

With Parliament continuing to fail to attain a majority vote on any constructive legislation, Kurt von Schleicher, minister of defense in the chancellorship of Von Papen, persuaded Hindenburg to appoint him as Chancellor in December of 1932. Schleicher attempted to reduce Hitler's influence within the *Reichstag* by putting together an anti-Hitler coalition but was unable to do so. Although both he and Hindenburg intensely disliked Hitler, their fear of a successful far-left alliance between the Communists and the socialist Social Democratic Party of Germany (SDP) was even greater. On January 30, 1933, at the urging of Von Papen and a handful of German industrialists, Hindenburg appointed Adolf Hitler as his Chancellor, providing him with the opportunity to form an effective government. Hindenburg, Von Papen, and Schleicher were comforted by their knowledge that Hitler's powers as Chancellor theoretically were limited by the Constitution and Parliament.

Two weeks prior to the wedding of Rose's daughter, the downfall of the German republic had officially begun.

Hitler immediately called for new elections and appointed fellow-fascist and Nazi Hermann Göring to be his Minister of the Interior of Prussia, giving Göring control of the largest police force in Germany. Göring, in his *Schießerlass* (shooting decree) of February 17, allowed the Prussian police unrestrained use of firearms in operations against political opponents. This encouragement of the use of force and removal of all restraints on police actions rapidly spread to the rest of Germany.

Under Hitler and Göring's direction, Nazi *Sturmabteilung* (stormtroopers, SA, colloquially called "brownshirts"), the NSAPD paramilitary wing, began a campaign of violence and terror against trade union and Communist party offices and attacked the homes of prominent left-wing individuals. Campaign meetings of the Social Democrats (SPD) were broken up and their newspapers were banned. Centre Party meetings and speakers were also disrupted. Only the Nazis and DNVP were allowed to campaign unmolested. Josef Goebbels was appointed Minister of Information and Propaganda.

My parents were visiting Rose and Albert for the weekend in Velmede when, on the morning of February 27th, 1933, Albert knocked on their bedroom door and came into the room saying *"Haben sie gehort? Der Reichstag Brennt!* (Have you heard? The Parliament Building is burning!)" This fire destroyed the *Reichstag* building and Hitler immediately blamed the catastrophe on the Communists, although it is the consensus of most historians that the act was perpetrated by the Nazis themselves.

Article 48 of the constitution of the Weimar Republic allowed the President to take emergency measures without the prior consent of the *Reichstag* "If public security and order are seriously disturbed or endangered" within the German Reich. Hitler persuaded President Hindenburg to pass the *Reichstag* Fire Decree as an emergency action, effective immediately, February 28, 1933, suspending most Constitutional civil liberties, including *habeas corpus*, property rights, freedom of speech and the press, the right to public assembly, and the right of free association. It allowed the Reich central government to assume powers normally reserved for the federal states and established harsh penalties for offenses previously considered minor. It mandated the death penalty for arson to public buildings, allowed for the arrest of thousands of Communists, consolidating the position of the Nazis. The decree was unaccompanied by any written guidelines, giving the Nazis free reign in its interpretation.

Hitler did not formally ban the Communist Party at that time, fearing an uprising if he did so and also expecting that the KPD's presence on the ballot would take votes away from the SPD. In the election of March 5, 1933, the Communists managed to win 81 Parliamentary seats. These new legislators were quickly thrown into jail by the Nazis before they could assume their place in the *Reichstag*, now convening at Berlin's Kroll Opera House. The courts and prosecutors, hostile to the KPD for many years, readily agreed with the premise that since the *Reichstag* fire was a Communist plot, KPD membership was an act of treason. For all intents and purposes, the KPD was therefore banned as of the day after the election. Many of the SDP (*Sozialdemokratische Partei Deutschlands*, Social Democrats) legislators fled Germany, also fearing imprisonment or worse.

The election allowed Hitler, with the support of the conservative *Deutschnationale Volkspartei*, (DNVP, German National People's Party) to control the majority of seats in Parliament. He then persuaded the Centre Party to vote with him to attain the supermajority to pass the *Ermächtigungsgesetz,* officially titled *Gesetz zur Behebung der Not von Volk und Reich* ("Enabling Act" or Law to Remedy the Distress of People and Reich). This law gave the German Cabinet under the control of the Chancellor the powers to make and enforce laws without the involvement of the *Reichstag* or consult with Weimar President Paul von Hindenburg. More importantly, any law agreed to by the Chancellor could override individual rights and any checks and balances within the Weimar Constitution. The bill was passed on March 23 with 444 votes for and 94 against, turning Germany into a legal dictatorship with Hitler at the helm. Once this Enabling Law was in place, the Nazis could bypass the *Reichstag* and rule by decree – seemingly creating laws that stabilized Germany and got rid of its "internal enemies." In reality, the laws that the Nazis put forward secured their political future as the sole ruling party in Germany.

Thomas Mann, writing in his diary on March 27, 1933, called the Nazi victory "a revolution of an unprecedented kind: without ideas, against ideas, against everything that is good, noble, and decent, against freedom, truth, and justice. Nothing comparable has ever happened in the whole history of mankind." Hitler had nullified the concepts of decency and truth, those tenets which are essential to the sanctity of the private individual and human existence.

The Nazis immediately used the Enabling Law to remove all civil rights. The Nazis could now imprison their political opposition for an indefinite period for any, or even no, reason. They justified this measure as implementing necessary security measures, rather than revealing their true motive – to remove opposition.

The Nazis also took several more steps to reduce their political opposition "legally." On May 2, 1933, trade unions were banned. Just two months later, on July 14, 1933, the Nazis used the Enabling Act to ban all political parties except the Nazi Party. To ensure that they could not be openly opposed in the press, on

October 4, 1933, it was declared that all newspaper and magazine editors must be Aryan. Censorship was heightened, and any person publishing actively anti-Nazi material was threatened or imprisoned. Within the next two years, more than 1,600 newspapers were closed.

These acts removed people's ability to oppose the Nazi Party in any form. However, it did so under the guise of legality, and "protecting" the German people and their democracy.

Within four months, the other political parties had been stripped of all power either by outright banning or Nazi terror, and Germany had become formally a one-party state with the *Reichstag* merely a rubberstamp legislature comprising only Nazis and pro-Nazi guests. Although three more elections were held during the Nazi era, voters were presented with a single list of Nazis and guest candidates, and voting was not secret.

My parents left on their honeymoon shortly after the election and just prior to the passage of the "Enabling Act," the law investing Chancellor Hitler with full legislative authority. That same month, 50 concentration camps were opened in Germany, set up by local authorities on an ad-hoc basis to handle the masses of people arrested as alleged political opponents of the regime. Hitler and his Nazi party mounted their assault on the labor unions, the Labor Party, and the Social Democratic Party. Hitler had become absolute master of Germany.

On Saturday, April 1, 1933, following instructions by party officials, a 24-hour organized boycott of German-Jewish shops and businesses by the Nazis began (*Judenboykott*). On that day, Germans were not supposed to shop at stores and businesses that the Nazis identified as Jewish. They were also expected to not visit the offices of Jewish doctors and lawyers.

This would be the first of many similar initiatives to force the permanent closure of Jewish businesses. The restrictions specifically stated that the boycott "is directed exclusively against the German Jews." Protection from this edict was granted to "all foreigners without regard to their religion, origin, or race." The homes and offices of all Jewish professionals (doctors, lawyers, teachers, professors, dentists, etc) were marked with special signs saying, "Don't Buy from Jews" and "The Jews Are Our Misfortune." Some non-Jewish business owners posted signs identifying their establishments as "German-Christian," meaning not Jewish.

SA (*Sturm Abteilung*) storm troopers or Hitler Youth were strategically stationed to discourage frequenting these offices. Throughout the country, many professionals were arrested at their places of employment for disobeying the boycott. In some towns, the SA marched through streets singing anti-Jewish slogans and party songs.

Six days later, on April 7, 1933, the Law for the Re-establishment of the Civil Service or "Aryan Law" expelled all non-Aryans (defined initially on April 11, 1933, as anyone with one Jewish parent or two Jewish grandparents) from the civil service. For the first month, exceptions were made for those working since before August 1914, German veterans of World War I, and those who had lost a father or son fighting for Germany or her allies in The Great War. That same law also barred the admission of lawyers of non-Aryan descent to the Bar and denied non-Aryan existing members of the Bar the right to practice law. Jewish judges were no longer permitted to work at all. This prohibition was quickly extended to include Jewish assessors and commercial accountants and Jews were also banned from serving on juries, the very right that my third great-grandfather, Moses Abraham Levi Oppenheim, had been granted in Olpe more than 150 years earlier.

These decrees in the first week of April 1933 set the stage for a stream of antisemitic legislation with increasing restrictions and regulations regarding racial identification. On April 22, 1933, Jews were prohibited from serving as doctors in State-run insurance institutions. Reimbursement by the National Health Service on behalf of any patient consulting with "non-Aryan" physicians was thereby denied, thus excluding Jewish doctors from the medical system and, by extension, from German society.

During the last week of April 1933 my parents, Dr. Max and Gerda Oppenheim Dahl, came back to Germany from their six-week Italian honeymoon well rested, prepared for my mother to settle into family life in Lüdenscheid and my father to resume his office and hospital medical practice. The new politics of Germany would prevent that from occurring. Since my father had been receiving payment for patient care from the central German government social insurance program, he was considered a civil servant according to the "Aryan Law" and, because he was Jewish, his expulsion from the civil service was automatic. His successful medical practice was essentially terminated overnight.

When Rose and Albert greeted the young couple in late April, the conversation quickly turned from glowing descriptions of Rome's grandeur, Venetian canals, and Florentine museums to the markedly changed political situation. Gerda's livelihood depended on her new husband's ability to practice medicine. Although Albert argued that his son-in law would be left alone because of his German military service, Max knew that any initial exemption from the Law would only be for one month, which would end after the first week in May. Rose could not believe that this state of affairs could occur in her Germany, but Max informed her that implementation and enforcement of the Law was ongoing in the large cities of Berlin and Munich and, according to his Jewish colleagues in Lüdenscheid, had already begun there.

The comfortable domain of the 500,000 German Jews had been turned topsy-turvy. My father insisted that he and Rose's daughter, just turned 23 that month, needed to leave Germany so that he could practice medicine and support her. Over the course of two days, he told Rose and Albert the facts they did not want to hear. The world was still in the throes of an economic depression with unemployment rampant in most civilized nations. Relatives in the United States were writing with tales of economic woe, urging those without guaranteed employment not to emigrate to there. The United States had the strictest of immigration policies and required the onerous task of obtaining visas, which could take months or even years to obtain. In order to practice medicine in the United States, Max would be required to take examinations which were infrequently given and purposefully made difficult for foreign physicians to pass. He could be forced to take additional training to attain admitting privileges at most American hospitals, many of which were not eager to have foreign or Jewish physicians as staff members. The countries of Western Europe also would not accept him as a practicing physician without him surmounting various hurdles. Italy was romantic and charming, and Max could speak Italian reasonably well, but Il Duce, Benito Mussolini, had gradually dismantled all democratic institutions since declaring himself dictator eight years earlier. Although there were no racial laws there yet, it was a fascist government very similar to the one Hitler now controlled in Germany, hardly a place to start a new life. Spain had an unstable government and was in the early throes of a civil war. The long enmity between France and Germany made it improbable that Max could be successful in that nation since he would be considered a German doctor. With Hitler having come to power, German-trained physicians were similarly unlikely to be popular in Great Britain, England, Australia, New Zealand, and South Africa.

Max had done his homework well and presented the argument that he and Gerda go to Shanghai, China, for the period of time necessary for Germans to come to their senses, rid themselves of Hitler, and repeal the new laws. Shanghai was an open city, where no visa or other documentation was required to gain entry. One could emigrate there without a police certificate, affidavit of health, or proof of financial independence. There were no quotas on immigrants. However, there would also be no food, shelter, or social services available to anyone who could not pay for them. Max had lived frugally as a bachelor and had accumulated sufficient money to initiate a new beginning. Shanghai already contained a thriving international community of British, French, Russians and Americans who had arrived during the prior sixty years. Western-trained physicians were in high demand by both Europeans and the wealthier Chinese. The Shanghai Jewish community dated back to the 1840s when a few Sephardic Jews came from places like Baghdad, Cairo, Bombay and Singapore. Sephardic Jewish families with the names of Sassoon, Kadoorie and Hardoon had built hugely successful business empires and many of the city's famous landmarks. Early in the 20th century a new influx of Ashkenazi Jews emigrated from Russia, first fleeing pogroms and then the Communist Revolution. Most of them earned modest livings as small business owners. Germany was no longer a land of opportunity for my parents, and China offered the young couple a new prospect. Going to Shanghai, the "Paris of the Orient," to weather the political storm was an idea both exotic and exciting, although family on both sides would be sorely missed.

Rose, Albert, Fanni, Helmut, and Else
in Velmede, 1933, a week prior to
Günter's Bar Mitzvah

Rose protested that Shanghai was the end of the world, and all communication would be by mail, letters that would only be read as much as a month after being written, assuming that they were not lost in transit. True, but Max and Gerda assured her that it would only be for a brief period of time until the political climate in Germany reverted back to normalcy.

My mother did not want to leave Germany before her brother Günter's *Bar Mitzvah*, which was to take place in mid-May 1933. Helmut came to Velmede to be with the family a week before the event. Three days before the Bar Mitzvah, there was a knock on the door of the Oppenheim home in Velmede and some members of the SA (Nazi storm troopers) came into the house and arrested Helmut for being a member of the Communist Party and plotting to overthrow the new Nazi government. Months before, he had been out at a café, and he had been overheard arguing politics by a Nazi informer. This resulted in the Nazis constantly spying on all his movements and activities. A few days before that knock on the door, the SA had discovered that Helmut had personally delivered a communist flag to St. Andreasberg, a mining village in the Harz mountains near Braunlage, Lower Saxony, where the Oppenheim family occasionally had gone on weekend summer vacations. Helmut was immediately taken to the holding area of the Bestwig jail, adjacent to Velmede, charged as a traitor and placed in that prison. He was to be transferred to Arnsberg, a larger neighboring community, for proper interrogation by the SS in three days, the day of Günter's *Bar Mitzvah*.

Albert was at the shop when the storm troopers came to the house to confront Helmut. Friends came to *M. Oppenheim* and informed Albert of his son's arrest. He ran down the street to their home because he wanted to see Helmut before he was taken away, thinking that Helmut would be given time to change clothes or gather his possessions. According to the unpublished manuscript edited by Wilfried Oertel, *Judisches Leben im Synagogenbezirk Meschede*, (Jewish Life in the Meschede Synagogue District), Albert saw the police car speeding away with Helmut inside. He then rushed back to the store and "threw himself over the counter and screamed… 'You just took him with you, without a way of saying goodbye. Now it's all over.' Then he cried in complete dismay. All the employees were deeply saddened and shaken, but also sad with the loving parents."

My grandfather Albert was a respected member of the community and knew all the local policemen in Velmede and Bestwig, many of whom had shopped at *M. Oppenheim* for two generations. These officials had not yet become Nazi Party enthusiasts. On the following day, Albert Oppenheim went to the Bestwig jail where Helmut had spent the night and was able to pay a large fine to the local police in order to have his son released. The police warned them that the Brown Shirts would soon return, and that Helmut needed to quickly disappear from sight. Heeding the advice, Helmut left Velmede that day to lose himself in the German population elsewhere. In order to protect his family, he told no one where he was going. Oertel writes, "After he was released again, he had to constantly flee from the HJ (*Hitlerjugend*-Hitler Youth) and the SA. He was chased and hunted by them like a bird... Once… Helmut had been travelling by train and, like all passengers, went through the station barrier in order to be able to surrender his ticket. Then he was kicked from behind… He was shouted at: '*You Jews* are *lying, are you still here?*' He was scared and felt threatened again. A horde of SA men followed him as he began to run. They hunted him every time they met him."

The Bar Mitzvah was a bittersweet occasion for the Oppenheim family, with Günter's sister and brother-in-law about to leave for China and Günter's brother having just made a forced hasty departure. Nevertheless, Günter came of age, reciting the same portion *(Parshah)* of the Torah (Leviticus: 21:1, Emor) that his great-nephew, my son Evan Dahl, would recite 58 years later in Poughkeepsie, New York.

In August 1933, Max and Gerda Dahl left their families, friends, and native country to travel to the very foreign land of China. They put their furniture into storage and emptied both the medical office and rented apartment in Lüdenscheid. My parent's adventure in Shanghai, which was to be only a brief interlude until

Germany came to its senses, lasted sixteen years. Had my parents not made this decision, it is doubtful that you would be reading these words today.

The young Dahls left with their clothing, some personal possessions and Max's medical office equipment packed into two steamer trunks. They took the train to Genoa, Italy, where they boarded a ship which took them to Shanghai in four weeks, going around the toe of Italy's boot, across the Mediterranean, through the Suez Canal into the Red Sea, then stopping in Goa, Colombo, Singapore, Jakarta, and Hong Kong, before entering the East China Sea and sailing up the Wang Po River to the large port of Shanghai.

Max Dahl, Singapore, Sept 26, 1933, on a stopover on his and Gerda's voyage from Germany to China, photograph sent in a letter to Rose and Albert

Rose received letters, often including photographs, from her daughter mailed from every city visited by the ship. In Trieste, the young Dahls met a cousin of Gerda's, Gisela Heinemann Lenneburg, and her husband, who owned a department store in Olpe, Westphalia, where their common great-grandfather, Jacob Bachor Oppenheim, had lived. Gerda tried to convince them to also move to Shanghai but the Lennebergs said they had far too many business commitments to do so. In a condolence letter written to me shortly after Gerda's death in 1990, Gisela related that "she was sorry they went back home." Ultimately, Gisela and her husband were able to immigrate to the United States in 1939, but only after, earlier that year. they were among the 937 Jewish passengers on the *MS St. Louis*, which departed from Hamburg, Germany, ostensibly bound for Havana, Cuba. The Cuban government refused entry to the passengers, and the liner then travelled to Florida, where the United States also rejected them. The ship returned to Germany and many of the passengers on this "voyage of the damned" ultimately were deported and murdered in Nazi concentration camps.

My parents were among the first of the German refugees to emigrate to Shanghai. By November 1933, twenty-six German-Jewish families had arrived in Shanghai. By the spring of 1934, there were eighty refugee physicians, surgeons, and dentists in China. By the end of 1934, several thousand well-educated Jews of Germany and Austria had fled their countries of birth to go to China, many of them attorneys, academics, professors, businessmen and artists. As their departure from Germany was for the most part relatively unhurried and physically not difficult, most brought significant assets with them. Many were able to start businesses immediately. Some dealt with small existing enterprises. Others practiced their previous professions, became schoolteachers or became artists and musicians. New import and export businesses thrived.

Gerda Oppenheim Dahl and Max Dahl,
China 1933

In weekly letters from Gerda in Shanghai to Rose and Albert in Velmede, my mother wrote of her new experiences in Shanghai. She and her husband had settled into a boarding house in the French Concession, where, in 1849, the Chinese governor of Shanghai had granted the French Consul to Shanghai certain territory for a French settlement. Most of the other German Jewish immigrants lived in this portion of Shanghai, which had become the intellectual and artistic heart of Shanghai with high-end residential developments, retail shops, cabarets, and concert halls, all built with European money in the first third of the 20th century. Her husband, Max, my mother wrote, was in the process of establishing a medical practice on Kiukiang Road (now Jiujiang Lu) near the Bund and hoped to care for both international and Chinese patients.

In a letter to friends, written after arriving in Shanghai, my mother wrote,

"After we have landed here safely and have settled down a bit, I am slowly starting to deal with my long-failing correspondence.

It is impossible to describe to you the vast extent of what we have experienced and seen. First of all, a little bit about the travel on large trains, then about the voyage across the seas.

Venice, the city of gondolas and canals, the magnificent buildings and sweet songs; - Brindisi with almost tropical vegetation under a burning sun; - Port Said, the gateway to the Orient, Africa's alluring torch, at night with intrusive deceitful traffickers and handlers, deeply veiled women; - The Suez Canal on the banks of which African vistas spread out on one side and Asiatic deserts on the other, where alongside modern railways that connect Cairo with Jerusalem, picturesque camel caravans travel majestically indistinguishable from 1000 years ago; - the Red Sea with oppressive, indescribable heat and humidity that together does not allow even a drop of sweat to evaporate; - then another 8-day journey in the Arabian Sea interrupted by my sea sickness: - Bombay! the city of palaces and huts, the most wonderful facilities and the most appalling filth, the city of the "Tower of Silence" in which the corpses of the "Parsi" people are laid down for the vultures to eat; - Colombo on Ceylon, situated in a lovely location, well put together women, screeching monkeys in the directly adjacent jungle: a "paradise at the seashore"; then Singapore, already quite Chinese due to the migration necessitated by the incredible birth rate of the yellow race; the city of pineapples (2 pieces for 20 cents); - and then Shanghai: all these impressions are so overwhelming that they cannot be digested quickly.

Once we had been here for a month, we became truly Chinese. Now we hardly notice the many beggars, the many women with infinitely small, twisted feet, we hardly smell the stench of the food stalls that can be found on every street corner, and we are also used to the noise that the traffic of the world's largest city traffic brings with it. Shanghai is a cosmopolitan city in every respect, large shops in which you can buy everything imaginable, wide paved streets, cars, buses, large, elegant hotels, cinemas, cabarets, cafes, etc. In addition, the convenience of the rickshaws rarely is bested by the greater speed of automobiles. Police officers regulate the massive amount of traffic in an exemplary manner.

Of course, there is the image of China, as we know it from having read books, but living right in the middle of it, all descriptions are dull compared to the realities: Poverty with all its attendant symptoms: filth, disease, prostitution, and crime are evident here like nowhere else. In contrast to all that, there again are the Europeans in their elegant cars, dressed in splendid clothes, who make all Chinese be their servants.

We first looked for an apartment in a boarding house and then went about the task of setting up the medical practice. My husband immediately had patients on the first day. We hope to be able to complete this successfully here, even if the competition is very tough, especially in Shanghai. There is no other homeopathic physician here or, as a matter of fact, in all of China, and that provides us much encouragement!"

For my grandmother Rose, 1933 had begun optimistically with her daughter about to enter a good marriage and "der Kleine" to be called to the Torah for his *bar mitzvah*. Yes, these events did both occur, but Hitler coming to power had an even greater impact beyond forcing her daughter and son-in-law to settle thousands of miles away and her older son, Helmut, to be evading arrest, hiding deep in the bowels of an unknown German city.

In July 1933, legislation (*Gesetz über den Widerruf von Einbürgerungen und die Aberkennung der deutschen Staatsangehörigkeit,* Law for the Repeal of Naturalization and Recognition of German Citizenship) was passed stripping naturalized, as opposed to native-born, German Jews of their citizenship, creating a legal basis for immigrants from Eastern Europe to be deported. The issue here for Rose was that this law could cause her new son-in-law to lose his German citizenship since he had been born in West Prussia (easternmost part of Upper Silesia), which after World War I was granted to Poland in the Treaty of Versailles. Although my father had always considered himself a German and fought and received the Iron Cross in World War I, this legislation might, in fact, lead to his deportation from Germany as "a Jew from Poland," were he ever to return from China.

86

Johanna Oppenheim, Albert's younger sister by a year, was born with severe developmental disabilities including deafness and mutism and had been enrolled in a nearby residential care facility since when she was a girl. There, she was well cared for and was visited frequently by Rose and Albert. In July 1933, the *Gesetz zur Verhütung erbkranken Nachwuchses (*Law for the Prevention of Hereditary Diseased Offspring) was passed, calling for the compulsory sterilization of people with a range of hereditary, physical, and mental illnesses. The existence of this new statute gave Rose and Albert much concern regarding Johanna's future safety.

Before the end of 1933, Hitler and his henchmen were able to establish additional laws and decrees further reducing the civil rights of all Germans with many more restrictions on German Jews. These included the Law against the founding of new political parties, the exclusion of Jews from employment in the cultural sector by denying them membership in the newly founded Chambers of Literature, Press, Broadcasting, Theater, Film, Music, and Fine Arts, the *Reichserbhofgesetz* (Hereditary Farm Law), stipulating that *Erbhöfe* (hereditary farms) could only be inherited by German farmers able to document that they had no Jewish or "colored" ancestors back to January 1, 1800 and the Law against Dangerous Habitual Criminals, which allowed the courts to order indefinite imprisonment of "habitual criminals" if they deemed the person dangerous to society and additionally provided for the castration of male sex offenders.

Chapter 8: 1934

The political climate in Germany further deteriorated for the Jews in 1934. Government-planned boycotts of Jewish businesses in the larger cities continued intermittently, often accompanied by violence. Jews in those cities were intimidated by the increasingly visible presence of the SA (*Sturmabteilung*), Hitler's paramilitary force, also known as the Brownshirts or the Stormtroopers, a group dating back to 1921 that now numbered more than 2 million men, many of them disgruntled former German soldiers, a force now much larger than the size of the entire German Army. Even more threatening was the newly expanded SS (*Schutzstaffel*), which had begun in 1925 as a group of personal bodyguards for Adolf Hitler. The SS came under the control of Heinrich Himmler in 1929 and was an exclusive group, with Himmler answering only to Hitler himself.

In 1933, up to 200,000 people were seized and imprisoned by the SA and the SS. Prisons soon became stretched for space and the Nazis were forced to improvise, using any land they could get their hands on to create temporary "camps." In March of 1933, Himmler had announced the opening of the first Nazi concentration camp, in the town of Dachau, Germany, within a broken-down munitions factory. The camp initially housed political prisoners who opposed the Nazi regime. Although inmates here were tortured and abused under extremely unsanitary conditions, it was paradise when compared to the Nazi concentration camps of the near future in places yet to be heard about such as Auschwitz/Birkenau, Sobibor, Belzec or Treblinka.

SS Members considered themselves the self-selected elite of all the world's society. They were required to profess undying fidelity to Hitler and unquestioningly acknowledge him as their one and only prophet. Their motto was "Loyalty is my honor."

The SS was recognizable by their black uniforms, whose collar had two staggered S's, which looked like lightning bolts. Other recognizable insignias included death's head badges and silver daggers. By 1934, the SS had more than 50,000 members and would grow to a quarter of a million men by 1939. An SS member was either a part of the *Allgemeine-SS*, in charge of the various police forces, such as the *Sicherheitspolizei* (Sipo), *Kriminalpolizei* (Kripo), and *Gestapo*, or the even-more elite *Waffen-SS*, further divided into three groups, the *Leibstandarte* (Hitler's bodyguards), *Totenkopfverbände* (administrators at concentration and death camps), or *Verfügungstruppen (*combat support forces*)*. The *SS-Sicherheitsdienst* also oversaw the intelligence department, known as the SD.

Many of those individuals that were harassed by the SA and the SS or imprisoned in camps were terrified to speak out about their ordeal, fearing that they would be further abused or re-imprisoned and that other members of their immediate families would meet similar fates.

The SS and the SA did not always agree on political matters. In late June 1934, the SS purged the leadership of the SA in the *Nacht der Langen Messer* (the Night of the Long Knives), murdering 150 SA members including the *Sturmabteilung's,* head, Ernst Röhm, allegedly for having plotted an overthrow of Hitler by the German military. Following this purge, Hitler demanded that any media coverage of that night present it as a preventative measure against a revolutionary, violent, and uncontrollable force, rather than a series of political murders.

On August 2, 1934, the aged, feeble, and powerless German President Paul von Hindenburg died at the age of 87. Hitler, supported by the German armed forces, quickly added the Presidency of Germany to his position as Chancellor. Only three weeks later, he abolished his new role as President and declared himself "Führer of the German Reich and People" while retaining his position as Chancellor. In this expanded capacity, Hitler now became the absolute dictator of Germany, without any legal or constitutional limits to the extent of his power or authority.

Hitler stated that he would occupy this new role but requested agreement from voters. On August 19, 1934, the German people were asked to vote on whether they approved of the merging of the two offices of Chancellor and President and Hitler's new role as Führer. 96% of registered voters turned out to vote on the referendum question which asked,

> "The office of the President of the Reich is unified with the office of the Chancellor. Consequently, all former powers of the President of the Reich are demised to the Führer and Chancellor of the Reich Adolf Hitler. He himself nominates his substitute.
>
> Do you, German man and German woman, approve of this regulation provided by this Law?"

90% of the voters voted "yes," intimidated by the public, rather than secret, voting in many districts, having storm troopers stationed at polling stations and forcing clubs and societies to march to polling stations attended by Nazi storm troopers and then casting their ballots in full view of their escorts. In some places, polling booths were removed or banners reading "only traitors enter here" hung over the entrances to secret voting booths to discourage this type of voting. In some areas, the number of votes recorded cast was greater than the number of people able to vote. Nevertheless, the British historian, Sir Ian Kershaw, considered a leading expert on the social history of that period in Germany, has written that even after accounting for the manipulation of the voting process, the results "reflected the fact that Hitler had the backing, much of it fervently enthusiastic, of the great majority of the German people" at the time.

I do not know whether Rose, Albert, Fanni and Else participated in that election. Had they been able to do so secretly, I am certain that they would have cast a "no" vote. They considered Hitler to be a rapidly increasing danger, and they were beginning to doubt that he would shortly disappear from public life and power. This was the last national vote in which Jews and other minorities were allowed to cast ballots before they were stripped of citizenship the following year by the enactment of the Nuremberg Laws.

In 1934, yet another Hitlerian edict commenced, removing Jews from receiving medical care under the Germany National Insurance system. This had a direct financial effect on the Oppenheim family, since they, especially Fanni and Albert, were having more medical problems as they grew older and sought health care more frequently.

In Velmede, *M. Oppenheim* remained reasonably busy, continuing to be their favored place to shop by many of the families who had frequented it for generations. After all, the only other place to shop was at *Bachmann's*, which also had Jewish ownership. The SA or SS was rarely seen in this rural village unless they were searching for Helmut or other "opponents of the state."

Letters from Gerda in Shanghai arrived at least weekly. Some were brief and others were detailed but almost all urged Rose and the family to leave Germany and come to Shanghai until Hitler became history. Rose read this advice but decided that Grandma Fanni's physical condition would not allow her to tolerate such an arduous journey.

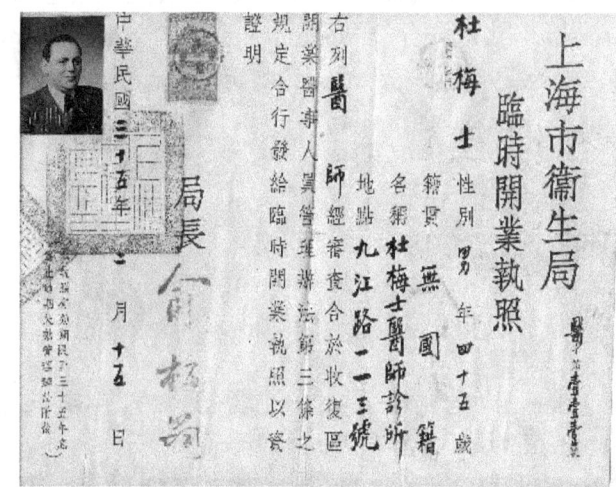

Chinese Medical License,
Max Dahl, MD, 1934

Gerda wrote a friend in Germany:

We already have many pleasant friends, we are often invited to their homes, and we go out a lot. In the meantime, we are hard at work studying English ad have classes every day and soon will have completed learning the language. If there is something that I need to purchase to buy and I don't know how to do so economically, all my new acquaintances are willing to show me where to go.

My husband received his official Chinese Medical License and has also found pleasant doctor colleagues and other gentlemen to befriend, whose families have invited us into their homes. So, in many ways we don't miss anything. I am sorry that we could not bring along our beautiful apartment. The boarding house life cannot be compared with the atmosphere of a home.

If everything works out, I will soon, meaning in 1 ½ years, be able to go to Germany again, and I'm already looking forward to seeing all of you then.

Write to me soon. I will always answer you promptly and will further describe many things in detail that I have only hinted at today. You can see so much in a city where people from 40 nations live side by side.

Many warm greetings for you, your mother, and all good friends,

In love, your G e r d a

In Germany identity cards were required to be carried at all times by everyone, including children.

1934 identity card, Günter

,

Summers in Shanghai were long, hot, and humid. Odors of rotting food and sweating bodies permeated the streets. There was no air conditioning and the ceiling fans in my parents' boarding house did little to ease the stickiness. The wealthier Chinese and some Europeans would escape to the inland mountains for relief from the heat during the summer. In the late spring of 1934, after the opening of my father's medical office, my parents made the decision to leave Shanghai for two months during the summer.

LuShan (Kuling in English) is an area that has long been known in China for its great beauty. Poets and painters have immortalized it, although it is recent history that has again popularized the region. Before the middle of the 19th century, Buddhist and Daoist temples, Confucian academies, and sightseeing pavilions were the main types of buildings on Mount LuShan. After China's defeat in the Opium Wars (1840-42), priests and businessmen from British, Russia, France, Germany, Italy, together with some important governors in China, began to rush into *LuShan* to construct their summer residences. Villas in European and American styles appeared one by one in the valley or by streams and brooks. On Mount LuShan (mount Lu), Kuling Town was built amid peaks and clouds at an altitude of about 3,500 feet. It had permanent residents numbering around 20,000, and 30,000 to 40,000 additional wealthy visitors rushed in during the hot summer months. There were more than 1,000 villas of various styles - American, English, French, German, Russian, Finnish, Dutch, Austrian and Italian. Because of its mild summers, this mountain town of *LuShan* was often referred to as "Nature's Air Cooler."

My parents had come from Germany with some money and were at that time unencumbered by financial pressure or major responsibility. My father, recognizing that there was an opportunity to combine a respite from Shanghai's heat with a medical practice opportunity to treat the summer crowd and then possibly continue their care after they returned to Shanghai, sent my mother by herself to Kuling in late May of 1934 to rent an office for my father and an apartment for the two of them for the coming summer.

After returning from her scouting expedition, Gerda Oppenheim Dahl, then barely 24 years old, wrote Rose, Albert, and the rest of the family in Velmede:

"I took a 12-hour night train from Shanghai to JiuJing, the capital of Jiangxi Province, and then found a bus which would drive for an hour to bring me to the base of Mount LuShan in two hours. After getting off the bus and collecting my small suitcase and parasol, I was immediately surrounding by scantily dressed men who were shouting at me in a mixture of Chinese and Pidgin-English, trying to persuade me to choose their sedan-chair to carry me up to the top of the mountain. They presumably thought that I, a reasonably dressed European woman, was rich and would have no problem paying the price they were asking. The only way up the mountain was to be carried or to walk and, as I surveyed the rocky steps going up seemingly endlessly, I realized that I could not navigate that path with my luggage and high heels. I had to be carried and, having learned from friends and experience that price is always to be bargained when dealing with the Chinese, I knew enough to bargain with various pairs of eager bearers seeking my business until I reached what I felt was a reasonable price for the trip to Kuling, at the top of Mount LuShan.

I climbed into the chair, which was padded with some dusty pillows. The chair had a canvas roof of sorts and was attached both in front and in back to two bamboo poles. A bearer in the front and one in back took each of the poles and lifted my seat up to approximately their waists and began to quickly carry me up the mountain on that narrow path. There were similar chairs carrying other train passengers both in front of me and behind me and the Chinese bearers chatted shrilly among themselves almost continuously. The route had been actually carved out of the rocky side of the mountain and undulated with high perpendicular cliffs on the left side and steep banks leading to deep valleys on the right. The path was shrouded in a deep fog with visibility sometimes being only a few yards.

As we went higher and higher, the bearers occasionally would stop to catch their breath and one or the other, or often both, would say to me "cumshaw." This is a pidgin English word from the Chinese word *gamsia*, which is an expression of thanks. I had learned in Shanghai that in colonial China, "cumshaw" was a request for a tip or a gratuity. Realizing tht it would be a simple matter for my bearers to tilt my chair to the right and almost effortlessly send me into the rocks below, I quickly answered, 'good cumshaw' and 'much cumshaw' every time they made the request. Since I am writing you this letter, I obviously made it to the top, although my heart was beating rapidly. I tipped the bearers, stayed in that beautiful place for three days, made the necessary arrangements for Max's office and a nice apartment for the two of us, and was emotionally prepared for the chair ride back down. The descent is even more dangerous than the ascent, especially so until one has reached the foot of the cliff."

Bearers and their passengers on the rocky
trail up to KuLing Town, Mount LuShan, c. 1934

In July 1934, my parents made the same journey together, the climb up the mountain now requiring two sets of bearers to carry my parents, plus additional coolies to carry their luggage up the mountain. That summer in Kuling, my father was professionally busy caring for the Europeans and Chinese officials, and my mother hired a cook and spent her days hiking in the mountains with new friends.

Gerda and Max,
Kuling, China, 1934

They made that identical trip again in 1936 and for the third and last time during the summer of 1937. In 1934, Soong Mei-ling, then first Lady of the Republic of China, was given a villa in Kuling. She and her husband Chiang Kai-shek both loved the villa very much, naming it *Mei Lu Villa* to symbolize the beauty of Mount Lu. President Chiang Kai-shek chose Mount Lu as the summer headquarters for his nationalist Kuomintang government. By 1937, Max was a well-known physician in Kuling and could count many high-ranking officials of Generalissimo Chiang Kai-shek's government among his patients. General George Marshall (of the Marshall plan) was to take the same sedan chair ride six times up and down in 1946, when the United States was attempting to prevent a Chinese Civil War and negotiate a settlement between the Nationalist Chiang Kai-shek, situated on top in Kuling Town, and the Communist Mao Tse-Tung, living at the foot of Mount LuShan.

Max Dahl in a rickshaw,
Kuling, China, 1934

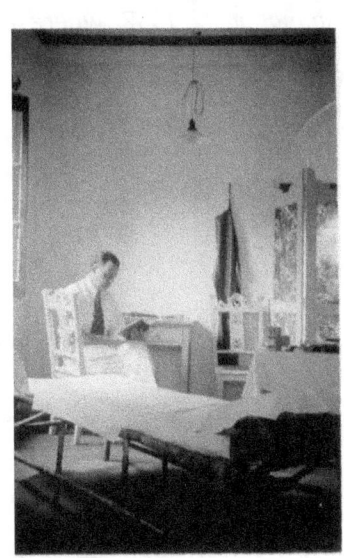

Dr. Max Dahl in his
office, Kuling, China, 1934

Gerda Oppenheim Dahl,
hiking in the LuShan
mountains, 1934

Gerda wrote her family in Velmede later in 1934 that they had been able to afford and find a comfortable 7th floor large one bedroom apartment on Rue Cardinal Mercier (now *Miaming* Road) in the French Concession and had joined the *Cercle Francais Sportif* (French Club), where they played bridge, tennis and badminton, and had made many friends among the other refugees who sought freedom from oppression and a new life in China during that period of time. My parents would come to recognize that, at least in Shanghai, labor was cheap, taxes were low, and foreigners enjoyed special privileges.

Gerda and Max's apartment house in Shanghai, c. 1937, where I lived for seven years on the 7th floor.

The one relevant and serious issue with Hitlerian ideology that Rose was experiencing on a daily basis in 1934 was related to Günter, now 14 and attending the public school with the same local boys with whom he had grown up. He told his mother that he was noticing a change in the attitude of some of his teachers and marked deterioration in the relationships with his friends. Everyone at school knew that he was the only Jewish boy in his class, since he had never before been forced to hide that fact.

His teachers were now emphasizing the rise of Hitler and glorifying the Nazi ascendancy to power. Günter was being asked to draw swastikas in his written exercise books and was being taught that World War I and the reparations that Germany had been forced to pay were "Jewish problems," and shortly everything would begin to improve under Hitler's leadership. He, together with the other students, had been required to write a poem of praise on the occasion of Hitler's birthday, April 20th.

Many of his friends had joined the Hitler Youth, a Nazi group designed to indoctrinate impressionable children with Hitler's ideology. In January 1933, there were 50,000 members of the Hitler Youth. By the end of the year, there were more than 2 million and by 1939, over 90 percent of German children were part of the Hitler Youth organization. This organization especially appealed to teen-age boys due to its impressive uniforms, frequent marching parades, emphasis on athletic prowess, multi-day adventures in Germany's forests, and emphasis on mutual brotherhood. Similar to the Boy Scouts, which like all other competing youth groups, Germany banned in 1936, there were hiking and camping trips, summer camps, and campfires where pledges were made and stories told. These boys were trained in survival skills and often were taught to use knives and other weapons. Over time, some members of Hitler Youth developed an almost religious devotion to the Führer, often to the point of becoming informants to the SA or SS about any "devious activities" on the part of their neighbors or even their own parents. Ultimately the children who had been saturated in Nazi ideology for years made obedient, fanatical soldiers in the Nazi *Wehrmacht* (Army).

In this three-dimensional theater of history, Günter was forced to frequently hear his classmates sing the Horst Wessel song, named after a SA storm trooper who was murdered in 1930 at age 23 and became a martyr in the party's struggle with their Communist opponents. A poem Wessel had written was put to music and became the marching song of the SA and later the official song of the Nazi Party and unofficial national anthem of Germany.

Hold high the banner! Close the hard ranks serried!
SA marches on with sturdy stride.
Comrades, by Red Front and Reaction killed, are buried,
But march with us in image at our side.

Gangway! Gangway! Now for the Brown battalions!
For Storm Troopers clear road o'er land!
The Swastika gives hope to our entranced millions,
The day for freedom and for bread's at hand.

The trumpet blows its shrill and final blast!
Prepared for war and battle here we stand.
Soon Hitler's banners will wave unchecked at last,
The end of German slav'ry in our land.

Rose and Albert had been planning to have Günter commute to a secondary school in a nearby larger town, just as they had done with his sister Gerda and brother Helmut. However, his experiences made them feel that he would be happier and safer staying closer to home and enrolling in Velmede high school until the time when he could be sent for training in the art and science of retailing.

Rose and Albert, 1934

Chapter 9: 1935

By the spring of 1935, the Nazification of Günter's school in Velmede had become intolerable. He was being abused mentally and emotionally and was getting into physical altercations almost daily. Rose and Albert's plan of sending Günter for a training program to a retail establishment was accelerated. They needed to find a city or large town where their 15-year-old son would have a safe place to live and be well fed and taken care of when not at his apprenticeship.

Gerda's in-laws, Sara and Nathan Dahl, my paternal grandparents, had moved to Hamm, Germany, a small city 70 kilometers northwest of Velmede, in 1922. Nathan was employed by the local Jewish community as a teacher. Their daughter, Ilse, born in 1908, still lived with them in 1935. Rose's husband, my maternal grandfather Albert, had over many years developed a business and personal relationship with the Alsberg family, builders and operators of textile shops, specialized fabric department stores and general department stores in a number of German cities. He was able to procure an apprenticeship for his son with the *Alsberg* department store in Hamm. This was located on *Bahnhofstrasse* near the Dahl home. There Günter would be taught all aspects of merchandising and retailing over two or three years. Although he would receive no salary, it was a marvelous career opportunity.

Sara and Nathan Dahl,
my paternal
grandparents,
Hamm, Germany, 1935

In June of 1935, "der Kleine" left Velmede to live with the senior Dahls in Hamm and begin his training in the retail industry. In addition to his work, Günter was able to participate in sports and social activities within the Hamm Jewish community, including enrolling in the local and regional Jewish sports competition through the Maccabee Club. As a Jewish boy, he had been excluded from organized sports in Velmede since 1933.

Now Rose, Albert, Else and Fanni no longer had any children living with them in the big house in Velmede. They were pleased with their decision regarding Günter but missed the presence of the young people in their family.

Januar	Februar	März
April	Mai	Juni
Juli	August	September
Oktober	November	Dezember

Name:
Adresse:
Verein:
Ort:
Abteilung:

Maccabee enrollment Günter, 1935 in Hamm

On September 15, 1935, the German *Reichstag*, at a special meeting during the annual Nuremberg Rally of the Nazi Party, passed the first two of what would be many *Nürnberger Gesetze* (Nuremberg Laws). The first, the Law for the Protection of German Blood and German Honour, prohibited marriages and extramarital intercourse between Jews and Germans, and forbade the employment of German females under 45 in Jewish households. The second of the Nuremberg Laws, the Reich Citizenship Law, declared that only those of German or related blood were eligible to be Reich citizens; the remainder were classed as state subjects, without citizenship rights. The language of the Citizenship Law included that a person must prove "by his conduct that he is willing and fit to faithfully serve the German people and Reich." This law was effectively a means of stripping Jews and other "undesirables" of their legal rights and, of equal importance, of their citizenship, marking a major step in clarifying racial policy and removing Jewish influences from all aspects of German society.

The Nazis enacted the Nuremberg Laws because they wanted to put their ideology regarding race into law. They believed that the world is divided into distinct races that are not equally strong and valuable. The Nazis considered Germans to be members of the supposedly superior "Aryan" race. They saw the so-called Aryan German race as the strongest, and most valuable race of all. According to the Nazis, Jews were not Aryans but, rather belonged to a markedly inferior separate race, rather than merely a separate religion. The presence of Jews in Germany threatened the German people and, in order to protect and strengthen Germany, Jews must be clearly identified and separated from other Germans.

For my grandmother Rose, this was more than just a vague law to define, control, and dehumanize Jews and eventually to expel them from "Aryan" society. She was troubled and apprehensive about the personal safety of her daughter, Gerda, who was then visiting the family in Velmede after having been in China for two years.

In the late spring of 1935, my parents in Shanghai were acutely aware of the deterioration of the political situation in Germany not only through newspapers, radio, and letters from friends and family in Germany, but also from frequent disturbing conversations with similarly afflicted Jews in Shanghai. Rose, in letters to her daughter and son-in-law, continued to insist that her 80-year-old mother, Fanni, my great-grandmother, would not be able to tolerate the major physical and emotional upheaval that a lengthy and strenuous journey to leave Germany for China entailed. Gerda and Max had grave concerns about all four of their parents and agonized daily about their responsibilities for them as the oldest children in their respective families.

My mother, Gerda Oppenheim Dahl, realized that their sojourn in China would not be as limited as she had imagined two years before. She was only 25 and was homesick, missed her parents and decided that she wanted to see her family again. My father, now lacking a German passport due to his birthplace in what was now Poland and also trying to build his medical practice, decided against going with her to visit his own parents in Hamm.

In the summer of 1935, my mother Gerda made the long trip back to Germany. This time it would be overland rather than by sea as it had been in 1933. She traveled on various trains for two full weeks, first north to Harbin and then transferring to the Trans-Siberian Railroad. This would take her westward through Mongolia and all of the remainder of Asia into European Russia. From there she journeyed through Austria, Switzerland and into Germany. She was reunited with her parents, maternal grandmother and her younger brother, Günter, all of whom she had not seen for two years.

She spent the next two months visiting her large family of many aunts, uncles, and cousins, socializing with school friends, and writing letters to her husband, my father, in Shanghai. She expended considerable time sorting through the furniture and other possessions that they had left behind in storage in 1933, selling some items and arranging for the rest to be shipped to China.

Albert Oppenheim, 1935

Gerda on her visit to Germany to be with her parents, 1935

Albert and Rose with Gerda on her summer, 1935, visit to Germany from China

My maternal uncle Helmut had been able to surreptitiously come to Velmede on a few occasions in late 1934 and early 1935 to briefly visit with his parents, *tante* Else and *großmutter* Fanni. Every time he returned to Velmede he would do so with considerable trepidation, for he was well known by everyone in the village, having grown up and gone to school there. His father Albert was no longer certain of the degree of influence that he had on the local police officials. Helmut, who was being pursued by Hitler's confederates as an enemy of the Reich, was unaware which of his school friends or their families were people who would not divulge his presence to Nazi officials or which had become so indoctrinated in Nazi ideology that they were eager to report him immediately to the SS, were they to see him in the streets of Velmede. After all, he remained a wanted criminal, a "communist." Occasionally he would meet Rose in the evening in Dortmund, Meschede, or Hannover, where local Nazi officials were not actively searching him out. He was supporting himself with various odd jobs but had continued to participate in anti-Nazi organizations and so far, had remained below the Nazi's radar screen where he resided and had avoided being jailed again. His plan was to leave Germany within the next year. He never came to Velmede and did not see his sister during the two months that my mother was visiting in Germany in 1935.

Gerda also frequently drove to Hamm to spend time with Günter and her in-laws, Sara and Nathan Dahl.

Ilse Dahl, Gerda, Sara and Nathan Dahl, Hamm, summer, 1935

Helmut and Rose, meeting in Hannover, 1935

In late August 1935, a close friend of the Oppenheim family, whose relatives had also emigrated to China, approached my mother in Germany and asked her to transport a significant amount of money to his family when she returned to China. There was no way to transfer funds from Germany to China other than hand-carrying cash or gold, both of which were forbidden by the Nazis. German *Marks* could buy a great deal in Shanghai. Although it was illegal to take more than 100 *Marks* out of the country, this law was frequently being broken by Germans. My mother, still a German citizen at that time, agreed and was given the cash in a plain white envelope.

The Reich Citizenship Law was passed while Gerda was still in Germany and the lengthy bureaucratic task of stripping German citizenship from "non-Aryans" began slowly. However, Albert learned that her name had been placed on a list of people whose citizenship had been specifically revoked, likely because of her having left Germany two years earlier. By the stroke of a pen, my mother had lost, as my father had a year before, her German citizenship and now had no civil rights and was stateless. Although she still had a current German passport in her possession, it had been officially invalidated. She needed to get back to China to be with her husband. She also had the envelope of money and was no longer a protected citizen.

For my mother, a promise had been made and she had been brought up understanding that it needed to be kept. My mother knew that once the train crossed over the German border into Switzerland, she would have reached safety and would not be subject to arrest for smuggling money out of Germany. The border passage into Germany a few months earlier had been smooth. The train had not even stopped, and she hoped this crossing would be as uneventful. As the train approached the Swiss border without any indication of a halt, she felt her anxiety lifting. Once she crossed the Rhine River, the natural boundary between Germany and Switzerland, all would be well. A few minutes prior to crossing into Switzerland, however, there was an announcement that the train would stop for about an hour, passports would be checked, and luggage would be inspected. The train pulled into *Büsingen am Hochrhein*, the border station, and my mother saw groups of both SS (*Schutzstaffel*), the paramilitary arm of the Nazis, and German soldiers getting into the front cars of the train. Fearing that all was lost, she took the envelope out of her purse and tucked it under her seat cushion and quietly left her compartment to go back to the dining car at the very rear of the train, where she sat and ordered a cup of black coffee. She waited there with trembling hands as, through the window, she observed the soldiers leading some other passengers from the train. The SS never reached the dining car within the designated time and my mother returned to her seat after the train entered Switzerland, finding the envelope with the money exactly where she had left it. The train journey back to China, although certainly exhausting, was otherwise thankfully unexciting. Although China would never truly be "home," Germany had forever lost that appellation for Gerda.

She would never see her parents again.

Rose in her garden, Velmede, 1935

Chapter 10: 1936

By the end of 1935, Helmut's energy was sapped from attempting to stay one step ahead of the Nazi authorities continuing to search for him. No matter where he was, he became uneasy every time anyone, for whatever reason, approached him. He could not work because of fear that any potential employer could be a Nazi informant. A friend who had emigrated to Palestine in 1934 encouraged him to come there, since work was readily available, Jews were welcome and living costs were relatively inexpensive. Helmut, now 23 years old, made the lifesaving decision to go to Palestine. However, he wished to see his parents again prior to his departure.

Helmut neared Rose and Albert's home in the afternoon on some familiar paths in the woods after walking to Velmede from the train station in Bestwig, less than two kilometers away. He noticed some uniformed Nazis strolling in the street near the house and was apprehensive about coming close to his parents' home. According to *Judisches Leben im Synagogenbezirk Meschede,* he returned into the woods, heard someone running after him and ran to a house at the other end of Velmede, where both the Hermes and Schlicker families lived. They had been old friends of the Oppenheims, and Helmut felt they could be trusted not to give him up to the Nazis. Mrs. Schlicker opened the door and found Helmut, "snorting violently… behind the door and wrestling for air. He said, 'They're behind me again!' He came into the house and now felt safe and was able to regain his breath and his composure."

It was late afternoon when he sought shelter at the Hermes/Schlicker home. Helmut said, "They've been chasing me all over the village!" The older Mr. Hermes left the house and started pacing up and down Velmede's *Provinzialstraße (*named *Bundesstraße* following WW II). He knew that Albert Oppenheim was in the regular habit of getting some exercise walking in the fresh air. By 1936, the Nazis had already forbidden anyone from speaking to the Jews in Velmede on the street. Hermes continued to pace along the street, always looking in front, behind and to either side. He finally saw Albert coming towards him on the main street. As the two men crossed each other's path, Mr. Hermes hissed between his teeth, "Helmut is with us, don't worry. Leave the door open at the back, he will come through the gardens in the dark." The message at first was rather unclear and it took a number of brief furtive encounters in the middle of Velmede's main street before Albert subtly nodded his approval.

Rita Romer writes in *Judisches Leben im Synagogenbezirk Meschede* that, "at that time, *'Oberm Kirchhof'* (the upper churchyard) did not yet have any development." There were only leased gardens between *Provinzialstraße and Baumhofstraße.* The gardens were unfenced so that Helmut was able to slip into the house from the rear in the middle of the night.

Helmut stayed hidden in the Oppenheim home for several days and spoke to Rose and Albert regarding his final decision to go to Palestine. He now needed to escape unseen from Velmede with only a few of his belongings and get to the international port of Trieste on the Mediterranean Sea, where he would take a ship to Tel-Aviv. The former free city of Trieste was located on the Italian-Yugoslavian border and had been annexed by Italy as a prize for its late entry into World War I on the side of the Allied Powers. Whether he would reach Trieste by going east through Germany and Austria or south through Switzerland and Italy remained to be seen.

The Oppenheim family decided that he would first need to get to Frankfurt, approximately 150 kilometers away and located in the State of Hesse, just southeast of *Nordrhein-Westphalia*. In that larger city, Helmut could remain anonymous for a period of time before leaving. Frankfurt had frequent trains leaving in all directions, giving him the opportunity to determine his further route to Trieste at the last minute.

Tante (aunt) Else was by now an excellent automobile driver and delivered goods ordered from *M. Oppenheim* to the surrounding areas three or four days every week. The sight of Else driving with empty boxes in the back seat was a familiar one for all the residents of the Velmede-Bestwig area. One evening, after completing her deliveries, she parked the car at the back of the house and left the empty boxes in the back seat of the automobile. Before dawn on the following day, Helmut left his parents, entered the car, and crawled into the back seat under the pile of boxes with his one suitcase. As soon as the sun rose, Else left the house in her usual manner, got into the front seat of her car, and drove Helmut to Frankfurt.

From Frankfurt, Helmut was able to escape by train and bus to Trieste, Italy, where he boarded the Steamship *Tel Aviv*, which took him to Palestine. The SS *Tel Aviv* had been a United States ocean liner named the SS *Martha Washington* and, during World War I, an American Navy and Army troop ship by the same name. The liner was sold to the Italian Cosulich Line in 1922 and operated out of Trieste, renamed the SS *Tel Aviv* in 1932. Helmut's ship was scrapped a year after his Mediterranean Sea voyage.

The Steamship Tel-Aviv, on which Helmut left Europe after escaping from Germany in 1936.

Once in Palestine, Helmut settled in a *moshav* (a Zionist agricultural co-operative where all residents work and receive compensation in the form of housing and food*)* called Magdiel north of Petah Tikvah and northeast of Tel Aviv. Magdiel had been founded in 1924 by a group of twelve Ashkenazi families who purchased the land from local Arabs, facilitated by the Palestine Land Development Company.

Rose immediately wrote to Gerda in Shanghai regarding Helmut's abrupt departure. On February 18, 1936, Gerda wrote to Helmut, addressing the envelope to a Liepmann cousin who lived in Tel-Aviv. These are passages from that letter, translated from the German, with selections from other translated letters to follow. I have italicized my personal explanations or additions to the various letters.

Shanghai, February 18, 1936

From: Gerda

Dear Helmut,

So that it doesn't take a long time until you get news from us, I don't want to wait for your first letter, but rather write to you now. I am hopeful that this letter will reach you via the detour of Hans Spanier and find you in the best of health. You can't imagine how excited we are about receiving your first letter from there. There is so much to ask you; I am hoping that you write us with all the details. Did you have a nice trip? Are you seasick in spite of Vasano *(A popular medication of the 1930s, related to scopolamine, intended for the prevention and treatment of seasickness)*? And what about all the other things there? I assume that you accepted the first position that Heinz *(Heinz Oppenheim, Eduard Oppenheim's son, a contemporary first cousin of Helmut's. who had emigrated to Palestine a year earlier)* had set up for you, that is, that is being employed by a former lawyer Cohn from Berlin. How difficult it must be for you in the beginning, lacking the English and Hebrew language skills! - So just work hard to learn the languages, you will probably have nothing else to do. How is the climate there at this time of the year? Hopefully you will not feel lonely, you will have your work to do during the day, and there are enough relatives and acquaintances there. *(In their letters, members off my family frequently use the German word "hoffentlich," which I have translated to the English word "hopefully." Prior to the 1960s, the English adverb "hopefully" could only be used to mean "in a hopeful manner". It was frequently misused as an adverbial disjunct to mean "it is hoped," which has become more acceptable in modern English. In German, "hoffentlich" has always meant "it is hoped" or "I hope that…").*

The commune of Petah-Tikvah *(Founded in 1878, Petah Tikvah means "opening of hope")* to which you can go, I gather from mother's last letter, is probably very close to Tel-Aviv, and there are so many acquaintances there that you will certainly not be homesick.

I wish you all the best today from the bottom of my heart, I just hope that you will feel good there and that you will again be a joyful satisfied person. When I was in Germany this last summer, you never visited me at all. Well, I can understand that you are unhappy with the atmosphere at home. I myself became so nervous and fearful but why do I need to tell you this? We should not mince any words in our letters. I think you should tell us in detail about the conditions in Velmede. What especially interests me is why you could not appear at the house *(their parents' home in Velmede)* anymore. Who wanted to harm you? How did you behave with Paul Muetterig *(a school classmate of Helmut's from Velmede)*? Did you say goodbye there? Also, please, write me with careful detail. Mother is not allowed to ever write the way she would like, and we, who live so far from the conflict, are interested in everything.

You must have been so happy when you crossed the German border. I found that as soon as I arrived in Basel a heavy weight was lifted from my heart. But it was not until I arrived in Italy that I felt very safe. One always thinks that Switzerland is far too close to our sad fatherland and that the Gestapo can always bring us back from there, even if you have done nothing.

Did you go through Switzerland or via Munich to get to Trieste? I can imagine how astonished you were at the sight of the Alps! It has been exactly three years since I saw Switzerland for the first time, and in the meantime I've been there three more times. I hope that it was not terribly difficult for mother and father to say goodbye. You know, Helmut, that the saddest thing for me about the situation is that our parents will soon be all alone because Günter cannot remain in Germany. That is very clear to me. I only wish that things for you go well so that you can arrange for father and mother to come to you there.

Helmut--always write home diligently; that's really the only thing with which we can delight our loved ones. And be careful in the letters, please do not make any political comments, so many letters are opened and such things would not be useful. You of course know that. One has to be careful with complaining even outside Germany. I don't know what the situation is in Palestine where one is predominantly among Jews, but here in China one cannot express one's true opinions openly, as long as you have loved ones in Germany, because there are informers everywhere. I am a little bit envious of you: I believe that in two years you will be a Palestinian citizen, right? Or an English subject, while we remain only "Germans."

There is not much to tell about us. The medical practice is not especially busy, in the autumn it was much better, but that is not uncommon here—one just has to wait until it improves. Here it is often very cold, perhaps you would like to send us a little of the warmth of where you are. It is my understanding that it is not too hot this time of year where you are.

I am going to wait with the next letter until I have received your correct address directly from you or from Velmede. The letters will probably take about four weeks to reach you, since they have to go by sea.

Finally, all heartfelt greetings and again I wish you all the best. Give Heinz my regards.

Your Gerda

From Max, my father and Rose's son-in law:

Dear Helmut, I send you good wishes. I am thankful that you have found your personal freedom and that all is well. Let's hear from you soon. Max.

Steven John Carell, (1962-), an American actor and comedian, has written "Sending a handwritten letter is becoming such an anomaly. It's disappearing. My mom is the only one who still writes me letters. And there's something visceral about opening a letter – I see her on the page. I see her in her handwriting." My mother's letter above expresses so well her lifelong controlled emotions of both optimism and pessimism during very trying times. Without mentioning the Gestapo itself, Gerda communicates her concerns about local German informers and the inability to express oneself openly in public because of the fear of harm to family members in Germany, any of whom could undergo investigation by the police, unrestrained by any legal limits. Arbitrary searches, public denunciation and brutal interrogations often were the result of tips from the public. A neighbor, acquaintance, colleague, friend, perhaps even a family member, local police forces, and Nazi organizations could inform the Gestapo that a person or a family member abroad was behaving illegally or suspiciously, creating a potential crime or threat. In Nazi Germany, these types of tips were referred to as denunciations. They were often motivated by ideology, politics, or personal gain. The consequences for those people who were denounced could be severe. In the end, Gestapo agents held in their hands the fate of the people they arrested, often without cause. The Gestapo did not need a warrant to read a suspect's mail, enter a home, or listen to telephone conversations.

Gestapo agents had the power to determine the total future direction of a human being's life. Individual agents could choose to be lenient or ruthless. They could let people go, dismiss cases, merely issue warnings and fines, or detain someone in prison indefinitely or condemn someone to a concentration camp. The only monitoring of these decisions came from within the Gestapo itself.

On February 28, 1936, the family in Velmede sent a letter to Helmut in Magdiel, the *moshav* where they thought he was living. Apparently, Helmut's suitcase did not arrive in Tel-Aviv with him and the ship.

Helmut's grandmother Fanni "Oma" wrote,

> How happy we were today when your long-awaited letter finally arrived. But we also regretted that you didn't get your suitcase with the ship. Your father called Cologne today about it. I am hoping that you will have the suitcase by now. I'm so excited, dear Helmut, to hear more details about your arrival there. It is good that you were spared the seasickness... This week we are waiting in vain for news from Aunt Paula *(Paula Liepmann, wife of Fanni's son, Max Liepmann)*. Last week dear Erich *(Liepmann, Fanni's grandson, age 12)* went to a Jewish sanatorium to recuperate for 6 weeks, in Dürheim in the Black Forest. I hope that the dear boy will come back healthy from there. Erich has been sick for 4 weeks with no appetite.

Rose continues in this same letter of February 28, 1936:

> Dear Helmut,
>
> After dinner I want to add a few lines to Oma's. I hope you are healthy and happy like us, thank God... When will you finally get your luggage? Write us about it! We are of course very curious to learn more about the first days in Erez from you. *(Erez was the term used by my family for the biblical land of Israel. The Hebrew word Erez or the more commonly used Eretz means "land," and refers to the "promised land," given by God to the Jewish people, the descendants of biblical Abraham, after their exodus from Egypt. From the second Temple period (515 B.C.E. until 70 C.E) onward Erez (or Eretz) Israel became the current appellation of that land. It was the official Hebrew designation of the area governed by British mandate after World War I until 1948.)* ... You are fine, thank God. I sent your letter today to Günter, who, by the way, came Saturday evening and stayed until Sunday. We went on a nice car tour with him. ...The business is very quiet. ... Dear Helmut, did you take the sweatpants that belonged to Erich? We can't find them anywhere. Now I should send you greetings from Vater *(father Albert)* and Tante Else. Please write to us again as soon as possible and stay healthy.

> Love, your mother

The letters from Gerda in Shanghai to Helmut in Palestine continue during 1936. Pages in those letters provide an insight into the historical events of the time and my mother's thoughts regarding them.

> Shanghai, April 30, 1936

> Dear Helmut,

> Your detailed letter of March 20th made us incredibly happy for more than a week. I would have already written again earlier if there had been a fast ship available. These lines that I am writing today should go off tomorrow with the "Potsdam." *(The SS Potsdam was an ocean liner of the North*

German Lloyd company, one of three sister ships operating the service between Bremen and the Far East.) It is now time to think about your birthday. I congratulate you from the bottom of my heart and wish you all the best for the future. Hopefully, you continue to feel as well there as you wrote in your last letter! Thank you very much for your congratulations on my birthday. I received a lot of mail from home for that day, and that is always the best. Trude Goldschmidt *(my mother Gerda's lifelong girlfriend, who had emigrated to England)* even told me to send her warmest greetings to you from her; those have travelled a long way, haven't they?

Enclosed you will find half an English pound as a birthday present for you, for which you will certainly have use. *(At that time, this was a significant amount of money.)*

In the past few weeks there has not been any good news in the newspapers about Palestine. Hopefully, you in Magdiel have noticed nothing of the unrest that is occurring. *(Violence erupted in Palestine in April 1936 after Arab leaders overcame their personal rivalries and, under the leadership of the Mufti of Jerusalem, Haj Amin al-Husseini, began the terrorism of "The Arab Revolt." On April 15, 1936, an Arab attack on a Jewish bus near Nablus killed three Jews)* . But these incidents are very sad for us Jews; It makes us notice again that Eretz is not yet a country that belongs to us.

We are of course extremely interested in what you write about your daily activity. Hopefully, you can take it easy with your physical labor when it gets ridiculously hot! I like to believe that you are enjoying the oranges and grapefruit there, but in the long run you will certainly get tired of that kind of work. It is wonderful that you are earning what you need to live. Are you living in a kibbutz, I didn't really get the hang of it in your letter? Write a little more about your personal life. I don't mean to say that the descriptions about the country etc. are not interesting but we would like to know everything. Have you found nice acquaintances? Am I correct in thinking that it's extremely easy to make friends there? Is Magdiel in a beautiful setting? We envy you for swimming in the sea, or is it not possible to do that in Magdiel itself? But at least you are not so far away from Tel Aviv, so that on days off you can go to the beach there. Or is that awfully expensive to do?

How are you doing with your summer clothing? You need light fabrics clothes now, maybe shorts, like those worn here in midsummer. Do you have enough money to buy that, or should we send you something? Do not get upset, just get in touch with us, we'd be happy to send you something. In the last letter, we enclosed a few dollars—did you get that?

We receive regular weekly letters from home. Our mother always writes in great detail about everything that occurs in Velmede. Well, you probably know that Guenter recently sent me a nice summer dress from his own money that he has saved-- I was really touched, I tell you. I sent him a silk shirt for his birthday, I hope it will fit him.

Otherwise, I think nothing has changed in relation to the misfortune at home. The latest is now the law relating to Jewish pharmacies that are now compelled to sell their business and are subject to compulsory leasing. It's almost synonymous with expropriation. I don't think it's too pessimistic to assume that this will also happen with Jewish homeowners and all Jewish businesses over time. Business is now being done that way. The villains in Germany proceed very systematically, everyone is affected in turn.

The other day it didn't look so rosy for Germany in politics, that was when the Rhineland was militarized again, the whole world was extremely upset, it almost looked like war, but unfortunately the moods changed very quickly, everything calmed down again, and today it even appears that England is giving Germany a loan. That is just the worst-- that everything goes well for the dogs, even though they are throwing throw sand into the eyes of the people.

How did it go with your passport, by the way? It may have significance for Guenter, but I cannot figure out anything more precise.

We're doing fine. The medical practice was very bad for a few months, so we had to dip into our savings, something that we hadn't done for a whole year. Now it's gotten better again, and when that happens, we're in a good mood - I'll send you a few pictures soon from us too. We have recently started playing tennis so we can have a little exercise in summer. The tennis court we play on is diagonally across from our apartment, so it's convenient. We always want to play early in the morning because later on it becomes too hot. So far, however, you can't complain about the heat here. Summer is coming later this year than usual.

How is your knowledge of the Hebrew language doing? I believe it is rather difficult to learn this language, but it is absolutely necessary. Is it not? And now I want to end for today, I have to still write to Hamm *(to her parents-in-law)* and Velmede *(to her parents)*. Write us again soon and we sent you our heartfelt greetings and kisses.   From your Gerda.

Shanghai, June 2, 1936

My dear Helmut,

3 days ago, I was overjoyed with your letter of April 21st. Despite that it came via airmail, it was on the road for an exceptionally long time. I have already written you that airmail letters take the same time as ordinary letters. The best example is that an ordinary card from Uncle Eduard from Tel-Aviv dated April 20th came at the same time as your air mailed letter. So, in the future I plan to only send ordinary letters. I just must become accustomed to the fact that mail from here to there and vice versa takes at least 4 weeks. But despite this, I still cannot explain to myself that at the end of April, when I heard about Velmede, a letter from me to you from the end of March, I believe of the 26th, in which I put money for you, had not yet arrived there. Incidentally, I had sent it to Heinz in Tel-Aviv because I didn't know your address at the time. In the meantime, I have written to you again, another letter with enclosed money, which should have arrived there for your birthday. I sent that to you care of the postmaster in Magdiel. So, this is the fourth letter that I am writing to you, and as soon as I have confirmation of your receiving the money, I will send you something again.

I have been earning a little money myself for some time. I get some writing assignments from a medical company here making 25 dollars a month and recently I've been giving German lessons to an American woman, for which I also get $ 20 a month. So that gives me some freedom to go out. I wish we could share a little of the good life we lead here with you. God, boy, Palestine would not work out for me. But I hope that it will not be necessary for you to do this terribly hard work in Magdiel for too long either. You're not used to such manual toil.

I was delighted to hear that you might be able to get to work at the clothing factory of the Bicks. Uncle Eduard even wrote from Abbazia *(a seaside resort on the Adriatic, which was then part of Italy and now is Opatija in Western Croatia and, prior to World War I, was a portion of the Austro-Hungarian Empire)*, as if this position were as good as certain for you, I really will not believe that until I hear it directly from Velmede or from you.

The current newspaper reports about Eretz are terrible *(The Arab Revolt)*. Hopefully, you won't notice any of this in Magdiel! It is too sad that something like this had to happen, this is again fodder for the Nazis. In addition, one can again see that even Palestine will not now be a home for us. But we hope that everything will turn out for the better there, because we don't know what else there will be.

Yesterday I had a long letter from Velmede. I got a couple of photographs sent. I like our Guenter best with Ruthchen, really David and Goliath. Surely you got the pictures too. The "little one" seems to have grown again, hard to believe, since he was such a weak little baby that he would almost have starved if Oma hadn't come, right? No, I think you're right Palestine is not the right thing for him, but he can visit you in a few years.

We are planning on our next vacation to go home, God knows when that will be, to go through Palestine. So, you can see that you have all kinds of prospective visitors. I wish I could say that about us too. Mother also sent me an excerpt from Oskar Hoenigsberg's (*Oskar was a good friend of Helmut's in Germany who had gone to Palestine a year earlier*) letter, precisely at the point where he describes his visit to you in Magdiel. Describe for us what you actually have to do in the process of planting. There is not always fruit to pick. In general, you haven't answered so many different questions from me. How about the money that you were able to take with you? When will you get that? - Have you got your passport in order by now?

I believe that nothing has changed in Velmede since you left. The terrible problems continue to be never ending. Business is bad, of course. I just hope it continues to feed our parents. Of course, I am very worried about what will become of Guenter. But for the time being he is still with *Alsbergs* –he just should learn a great deal about business and competent salespeople are needed all over the world. It would be best, however, if something had changed in German politics by the time he had finished his training, but I don't believe that the hatred there has subsided. Today Hitler is generally considered to be the greatest man who made his fatherland strong, and when the countries abroad give in and come close to his demands, then he has won the game. I even believe that it won't take that long until Germany has colonies again. The Jewish question is as good as forgotten by all the others, whom it does not appear to concern.

I recently had a long letter from Egon. (*Egon Baum, Minna Oppenheim Baum's son, who had left Germany to work at the Snellenburg department store in Philadelphia in December of 1933 and was apparently doing very well*). He seems to have become a real Yankee; he writes in such typical American English that you almost have to laugh. The boy was lucky, a little proper protection, and one is almost a made man.

It must certainly be very hot there, it was still tolerable here until now, but soon the great heat will also set in here, which is said to be worse than the temperature in Eretz because of the terrible humidity. But what so many other people can endure will also be bearable for us, especially when you need to work as little as I do. Do you always wear a hat, Helmut? You know that you shouldn't expose yourself to the sun with your bare head. (*In these letters, Gerda often assumes the role of older sister, responsible for the health, comfort, and behavior of her younger brother*).

Did you also do anything special during Pentecost? (*Pentecost, also called Whitsun is a Christian holiday taking place on the 50th day (the seventh Sunday) after Easter Sunday. The Monday after Pentecost was a legal holiday in Germany and my family often used the term to describe the long weekend.)* We were out in the fresh air a lot on both days, and we even took a day trip on the first holiday, going on a ship for 1 ½ hours and picnicking on the banks of the Yangtze River. I tell you; we came back home sunburned in the evening. We have recently been playing tennis every morning so that we can exercise a little and enjoy that a great deal. I do not have too much new to tell you—one has one's friends with whom to get together, you go to the cinema, eat well and cheaply, and that is the pleasant life in Shanghai.

We recently enjoyed a good concert, the cellist Feuermann (*Emanuel Feuermann (1902-1942), a Polish Jew, was one of the great cellists of the 20th century*) was here, and I have to say, it was a real pleasure to hear him play, then we went to the English theater on the evening before Pentecost, which we really liked, although the actors were all amateurs. The medical practice is moderate to the greater extent—it was in May, and we do not know yet what it will be in June. The worst thing here is that you don't know what the next month will bring. Such irregular times were never known in Germany.

So, dearest Helmut, I don't know anything more to report for today. Hopefully, I'll get good news from you again soon. As soon as I have the first confirmation of the money, I'll send you something again.

Greetings and kisses for today   From Your Gerda

Shanghai, June 24, 1936

Dear Helmut,

I don't know much to tell you today, first of all there is no letter from you to answer, and then I wrote a long letter to you on June 2nd. Has it arrived? It seems to be a very peculiar thing that all my letters to you seem to be lost. Didn't the one on your birthday arrive with some money in it? A few days ago, exactly on June 18, we sent you $ 20 by postal order, which will be paid to you there in the Palestinian currency. No, they can't be lost. However, Mother wrote in her last letter that all the money sent from Bestwig did not arrive there. That is peculiar! I hope you can get it all at one time—that will make you a rich man.

Hopefully, you have work again by now! I heard from Velmede that there was currently little work in Magdiel. I can well imagine that the current conditions will cause a lot of unemployed people there. It is terrible that no peace and order can be restored at all. Do you notice this occurring in Magdiel?

How is the climate there now? We are at the beginning of the summer, we have already had a couple of very hot, humid days, and at the moment it is very pleasant again.   But as I said before, we are only in June. Fortunately, we are in good health, the medical practice could be better, but we do not wish to complain.

I'm in somewhat of a rush. We are about to get a visit from the Berges, the artist couple from Hamburg, who are doing very badly here. The two of them come to us for dinner every Wednesday. (*My parents on a regular basis invited less fortunate Jewish immigrants who had come to Shanghai from Germany to join them at their evening meal*). So today I just want to add warm greetings and kisses for you and end, as soon as I have another message from you, you will also get an answer.   Sincerely, your Gerda

Shanghai, August 17, 1936

Dear Helmut,

It has been a few weeks since your letter dated June 17th came into our possession, but the heat here has made me too lazy to write until this time. I have to answer your letter with a longer one because I waited.

We were pleased to see from your letter that you are fine. In the meantime, of course, we heard every week from Velmede about your well-being. In your letter there wasn't much else in it either. Perhaps you will write us a little more detailed, yes?- The fact that you notice little or nothing at all of the unrest in Magdiel calms us down a little. Otherwise, the situation in Eretz still appears just as worrisome as it did at the beginning of the dispute. Or are the reports very exaggerated in the newspapers?

You must see how advantageous it is to speak Hebrew and we both don't understand why you don't want to learn the language. If you intend to become at home in a country, you have to try to master your language as a basic condition, and you are not more stupid than everyone else who is learning it. So, sit yourself down with the Hebrew dictionary and the grammar book. It is better to get this done sooner rather than later.

How is it with your work? Do you have some every day? And do you get along with your money? Our last money sent to you by Postal order was posted as being in your possession.

By the way, you've never written anything about the £ 1,000 you were allowed to take with you. When can you access some of that? Did you also take some of our money from Arnsberg? I have already asked you that before, but you have forgotten to answer me. (*Throughout the correspondence from Gerda in Shanghai to her brother Helmut in Palestine, there was a consistent sense of frustration regarding her brother's failing to send her details regarding his life and not answering repeated questions.*)

Strange that they didn't renew your passport. It almost looks like deprivation of citizenship. If I were you, I would try to get my passport again, because I still prefer a German Pass to a stateless one 1000-fold. How long will it still be until you become a Palestinian citizen? Have you already accomplished the necessary formalities? Or will that occur automatically? Just inquire about everything, because it is so important to have the correct document and you probably don't know whether you have the correct passport.

How is summer getting on for you? Was it really hot in July (and August? I still have pleasant memories regarding your area from August last year when I came back here. It was terribly hot then. But we cannot complain; although this Shanghai summer is not without heat, everyone says that this year, it is not so bad. We have had a particularly good time since July 1. We have become members of the French club, which is located only 2 minutes away from our apartment. And there we can use a wonderful swimming pool, and also play on the magnificent tennis courts. And whether you believe me or not, I've learned to swim in the last few weeks, although you and Guenter have said I would never learn how to do that. Or was it just Guenter alone, who said that?

By the way, I recently heard that the Alsbergs in Hamm also want to sell their business too. Hopefully, it won't happen that rapidly. I hope that Guenter's apprenticeship will be finished before that happens. Once that occurs, we will probably still will not know what shall happen to him. I would really love the Snellenburgs *(of Philadelphia, USA)* to take him into their business like they did with Egon. And I believe that they will do that too if father repeatedly begs them to do that.

I am hoping that the messy situation in Germany will not be even more confused after the Olympics! You hear so much about it.

In Velmede, they again have no cleaning lady in addition to no boy helper. I think all the time about the fact that mother and aunt Else now have far too much work to do all the time. Max is just coming home right now and brought a long letter from our Oma. One is amazed at how beautifully and in wonderful detail the old woman can still write. From that letter, it seems that now they are getting a boy again at home. Hopefully, that will work out well!

Edgar (Edgar Bachmann, the son of the other Jewish family in Velmede, of about the same age as Gerda) will be leaving soon too; I think in September! When you think about everything like that, it is so sad for all the parents who stay behind alone in Germany. And it used to be so nice at home! How beautiful Germany was is often only noticed later. You will already have arrived at that realization. But what good is it at all to think of earlier times; In Germany, it won't be any different anytime soon, and as it stands now for us, we have lost nothing by not being there now.

Do you ever see Heinz *(Oppenheim)*, dear Helmut? - The day before yesterday was our father's birthday and the day after tomorrow is mother's birthday. On such days I always feel a little homesick. But you have to be sensible!

Well, now I don't have anything more to tell you today. We look forward to hearing from you again soon with good news! Be warmly greeted and kissed.

From your Gerda

Shanghai, October 4, 1936

Dear Helmut,

The most wonderful thank yous for your 2 letters of August 6th and 20th. In the last one you wished us a Happy New Year *(the Jewish New Year, Rosh Hashanah, occurring in the early autumn)*; the letter arrived punctually two days before. We were pleased to have the satisfactory news from you. It seems as if you now feel more comfortable in Eretz than in the beginning. I only wish that you would find lighter work to do there. The fact that you are earning money and can save what you had sent from home high on a shelf is really wonderful. But I can imagine how frugal you must be to get this done. But be sure to eat your fill! It's a shame that food supplies there, I mostly mean meat, is not as cheap as it is here. Now it will probably only take a short time until the oranges will be ripe. Yes, you will fill yourself with those.

The news from home, thank God, is quite good. I mean that the loved ones are at least healthy. I do not yet know what the consequences of this new attack on the Jews on the occasion of the party congress will be. Hopefully, it won't get any worse than it already is. I only wish that Aunt Minna is successful when she talks to Stanley about Guenter. You also know for sure that Uncle Max

(Oppenheim, located in New York and hardly as successful in business as the Snellenburgs) is not in the position to take over the guarantees of custody for him. You just keep learning English; you wrote that you read English books, you never know how you might need something like that again. There is a definite possibility that you will go to America later. *(Although Helmut had many opportunities to come to the USA in the mid-1930s and after World War II, he never wished to make the journey.)*

The situation in Palestine is extremely critical. You now have the English military there in major abundance. I hope that this move will deter the Arabs from their constant attacks. But that just seems not to be the case. It is great that you do not feel this in Magdiel at all. *(My mother certainly had all the latest news and her pessimism regarding the British was prescient.)*

Do you have some opportunity to read some good books? We recently had a few here which would also have interested you. One such book is called "The Yellow Spot" and was published by the Bishop of Canterbury. It consists purely of factual reports, photographs, and newspaper clippings regarding the antisemitic agitation in Germany today, a book that should mainly be given to non-Jews and non-Germans to read. Then a few days ago I read a book by Arnold Zweig: "The Reckoning of German Jewry," also particularly good. Recently there is a German monthly magazine published in Moscow, entitled "The Word," a publication reminiscent of the earlier Weltbuhne magazine resembling a diary, whose collaborators are the two Manns, Doeblin, both Zweigs and Bert Brecht and a whole host of other well-known German writers who no longer have a say at home. After we had seen a sample issue of "The Word," we have ordered a half-year subscription. Perhaps you can also have it lent to you. People there who may have more money perhaps have access to this publication. But please do not write anything about such matters when you correspond with home. *(Gerda is correctly worried about German censors reading mail sent from outside Germany to the Oppenheims in Velmede and placing them in danger).*

There is little else to tell you about us. Summer survived well and now we have the most beautiful and healthiest autumn weather that one can imagine. What is the weather there now? Enclosed are some prepaid envelopes that we received from Holland a few days ago. I'll send you several of them next time. And now that's it for today. Look forward to receiving good news again from you soon.

All the best, Your Gerda

Shanghai, November 30, 1936

Dear Helmut,

For the sake of experimentation, I will send this letter via Siberia. I can imagine that if mail goes directly from Moscow to Constantinople, or whatever the port south of Russia is called, this letter will then be with you in less than three weeks. And I really want this letter to get there quickly.

Specifically, two days ago I sent you a package of magazines on the Conte Rosso. *(The Steamship Conte Rosso was a large Italian ocean liner, the first one built after World War I and the largest to date. In the 1930's it sailed the Trieste-Bombay-Shanghai route, including traversing the Suez Canal, where mail bound for Palestine would be unloaded. Many Austrian and German refugees sailed on this ship from Europe to reach Shanghai).* I believe I had mentioned in my previous letter that we have subscribed to the Moscow magazine, "The Word, " and I gave you five of them, because I'm sure you would be interested in them. But last week for certain reasons, which I will explain to you, I did not get the chance to write a letter to you, and I wanted to tell you so urgently that you should not mention this magazine in a letter to home. You must know that there are Germans staying here in Shanghai, and you never know whether it will not harm us if the authorities find out that we are distributing such an anti-Nazi magazine. So please don't mention any of this. Caution is always good.

And now on to something else! Hopefully, you are as well as we are! To my delight, I always hear good things about you from Velmede every week! I hope that I soon will receive direct correspondence from you. Well, next week is Max's birthday, maybe a letter will come from you. Do you always have work? And how much do you earn in general? Can you get along on that well? Well, if you are now getting the £ 56 paid out, you're almost a rich man. *(Helmut had some money transferred to him from his parents and was supposed to be getting a portion of that every month).*

I'm so happy that our Guenter will be going to America next year. I always say that the Snellenburg connection is worth more than even if our family at home had won the big lottery. Don't you think so too? I was also really worried about what to do if the American plan failed. I hope father will find a good apprenticeship for him for another year, so that he will be a little more knowledgeable when he arrives in Philadelphia. It is tragic that we will then all live so far apart, but I hope all of this is just a transition; maybe you will go to America later, and who knows whether we'll stay here forever. Of course, for the time being we're not thinking of any changes. You have to be happy that one is here. Enclosed are a few new photos of us that we took last week when we went on a Sunday morning walk.

Since last week it has gotten very cold, the heat is in full retreat. What is the weather there?

A few days ago, we experienced something incredibly sad, that's why I didn't get back to my letter writing. You probably also knew Fraulein Eichengruen. She was with us last year in Velmede. Think about it, she died suddenly last week, she poisoned herself with veronal. *(Veronal is a powerful barbiturate which was available in Shanghai and was used as a sleeping pill. By taking a mere handful of these, one would sleep forever).* Isn't that terrible? I got really upset when you know someone as well as I knew her. Such an end is certainly not understandable. There was no really good reason for her act. She has probably never really felt good here in Shanghai, often had arguments with her brother, but that is still no reason to take her own life.

And now, dear Helmut. I don't know anything more to say for today. Surprise us again soon with some good news from you.

Hearty greetings and kisses,   Your Gerda

Helmut, Magdiel, Palestine, late 1936

Life in a kibbutz or *moshav* in Jewish Palestine in 1936 was challenging for all inhabitants. There was the constant threat of violence by surrounding Arabs, in addition to the hard physical labor and the social aspects of living in a commune. The population of each was multi-generational, including both residents who had lived there for many years and recently born babies, cared for in a 24-hour nursery while their parents worked in the fields or in light manufacturing. All men were expected to know how to use a gun and be proficient in hand-to-hand combat in case of attack. Helmut found the physical work extremely difficult. He had never been an athlete and was most content reading a good book or arguing about political philosophy well into the early hours of the morning. Although many dwellers in Magdiel shared Helmut's idealistic vision of socialism, he had to go to bed each evening shortly after dinner, so that he could arise before sunrise on the following day to work in the orchards.

Rose and Else frequently would take the train from Bestwig to Hamm to visit with Günter on the weekends when he did not work. They continued their friendship with the senior Dahls as they compared the news that they had received from their children in Shanghai. Paul, the youngest of the Liepmann family, lived in Horn, one hour east of Hamm and the two sisters would often combine their visits to *"der kleine"* to see Paul, his wife Agnes, and their child Ruth, who was growing up quickly.

In 1936, Albert noticed a marked decrease in sales at *M. Oppenheim* due to the increasing popular compliance with boycotting of Jewish retail businesses, which had begun three years earlier. Although there were no picketers in Velmede holding signs saying, "Don't Buy from Jews" and "The Jews Are Our Misfortune," the nationwide campaign against the Jews of Germany which would culminate in the Holocaust was having effects in even the more rural areas of Germany. The passage of the Nuremberg Laws in 1935 contributed to the evolution of the aryanization of German society and business.

The changes happened gradually in Velmede, rather than in staccato fashion. They affected personal status, the interaction of Jews with general society, and their economic situation. The restrictions affected individuals and the Jewish community as a whole. Jews were not only limited by the flurry of laws and decrees, but Rose and Albert felt deeply humiliated by them.

Else, Rose, Ruth Liepmann (age 7), Günter, May 1936, Horn, Germany

Under article 3 of the Nuremberg Law for the Protection of German Blood and German Honour, Jews were prohibited from "employing in their households' female citizens of German or related blood who are under 45 years old." This was prompted by "understanding that purity of German blood is the essential condition for the continued existence of the German people and inspired by the inflexible determination to ensure the existence of the German nation for all time." Rose had, of course, terminated employment of female household help a year earlier but Albert was determined to keep Eugenie Fröndhoff, who had worked at *M. Oppenheim* for 7 years, as an employee. According to Rita Romer, writing in *Judisches Leben im Synagogenbezirk Meschede,* Eugenie, who lived with her parents in Bestwig, had completed three years of unsalaried training as a saleswoman at *M. Oppenheim* after completing secondary school. She loved the work environment, was paid for overtime, and became a dedicated employee, thought of as family by Rose, and treated with dignity and respect by Albert, who often gave her new clothing as a gift for her devotion to the business. For lunch she always went home by bicycle to have the principal meal of the day with her family in Bestwig. Albert would often give her fruit or pastries to take home to share with her parents. "In her first year as a trained saleswoman, she received twenty marks as a monthly wage. This then increased over the years to 1938 to 60 marks. Her parents were extremely proud of her professional progress. However, her two brothers, who worked for the Civil Service and were threatened with dismissal if family members continued to be associated with *M. Oppenheim*, "begged her to stop working for the Jewish merchant." The Fröndhoff family continued to purchase items from *M. Oppenheim*, but fearing reprisals, would have Albert deliver them to their home, which he would do furtively after dark, driving "via the so-called 'Black Way' behind the railway embankment."

Over many years and two generations, it had become customary for the Oppenheim store (and also the Bachmann shop) to donate christening gowns and wedding dresses to the poorer families of Velmede so that they could truly enjoy these important milestones. In addition, the less fortunate households in the village would often find a package of fruit or other food on their doorstep on holidays or during difficult financial times, left there by the employees of *M. Oppenheim*.

However, continuous propaganda and the madness of crowds create short memories. Kathol writes, "Ms. Grete Schlicker found it abhorrent that the poorer Velmeders, of all people - previously grateful for a pair of trousers or another item of clothing given by the Oppenheims at cheaper prices - were now their worst enemies. Many poor children had been dressed for communion or marriage for free by the Oppenheims... For some poor families in Velmede on Christmas Eve, there was a parcel delivered from the Oppenheims, the only present they were to receive that year. Now, when they (the Oppenheims) were stunned and involuntarily abandoning their business and trying to bring their bare lives to safety, evil tongues would say about them: 'Now they have run away, have taken their gold, money and jewelry well hidden in car tires with them.'"

Some of the multi-generational families of Velmede continued to frequent *M. Oppenheim*. Gerda Susewind told the story, "Despite the ban, my mother and grandma continued to shop at the Oppenheims and Bachmanns... This was made public in various publications, including the '*Stürme*r'. The very next day, indignant relatives from Hagen and Berlin contacted them and insulted them as crazy just because they were loyal to their honest, Jewish merchant. Nazis and neighbors denounced every buyer." Some Velmeders complained about this public denunciation. Romer has written, "They wanted to continue shopping in the local shops undisturbed. There weren't any others. They simply felt restricted in their personal freedom. In the end, they bowed to the edict out of fear for their own safety. But who seriously considered the situation of the Jews? How did they feel? So restricted, excluded and disadvantaged in many ways. They have been deprived of their existence."

Rita Romer, in *Judisches Leben im Synagogenbezirk Meschede,* writes about the gradual but inexorable change in the enforcement of the Nazi racial edicts. There was a public notice board located in Velmede's town square, where local Nazi officials would place the names of residents who disobeyed the laws. Mathilde Humpert, the teenage daughter of longstanding customers of *M. Oppenheim,* had bought her wedding dress at the store a few years earlier and had been very satisfied with the quality and service. Her school classmate, "Mrs. Grete Schlicker, née Hermes, also bought almost all of her trousseau from *M. Oppenheim* and was very satisfied with it. At some point she was approached by someone: 'You, have you already seen, you are on the bulletin board'. When she, now curious, looked it up, the number 10 - among many other names, actually read: 'Miss Grete Hermes is a customer and bought from the Jew Oppenheim'."

Many of the old customers of the two Jewish shops in Velmede learned that they had been secretly photographed entering the stores. Within a few weeks the photo and the name of the resident would be made public in the local edition of the *"Stürmer,"* the Nazi newspaper. Their names were also displayed on the local bulletin board and often resulted in these *M. Oppenheim* customers being reprimanded by some of their neighbors. Despite knowing this, some faithful customers, either out of their need for an accessible, reasonably priced product or wanting to loyally support their long-time Jewish shopkeepers, continued to go to Velmede to shop at *M. Oppenheim,* but only in the evening after dark. As Rita Romer writes "They remained loyal to their courteous trader almost to the very end. They regretted the sad development but could not change it." Eventually, even they stopped shopping at *M. Oppenheim*.

Beginning in 1936, Albert would often return to the store on a Monday morning to find that the shop windows had been broken by bricks or large stones during Sunday night. For the first 3 or 4 episodes of vandalism, insurance paid for the damage but then the insurance company withdrew their coverage, and the local glazier would demand payment in advance for repairing the glass. This occurred as frequently as every other week.

The parades by Nazi officials and by the Hitler Youth had become more common in Velmede and also had developed into more threatening events. Rose was relieved that Günter was no longer in the public school and being subjected to this on a daily basis, although she did not know about the tone in Hamm, where he had been sent for his retailing apprenticeship. Willi Liese, of Ostwig, a village 6 kilometers from Velmede, told of his recollections of a specific Hitler Youth parade which interacted with Rose's mother, my great-grandmother, Fanni: "I had great respect for old lady Oppenheim or mother-in-law Lippmann (sic)." As a boy, he had marched with the Hitler Youth with childlike enthusiasm. He liked the uniform and the frequent adventure games. The brisk marching with the pennants in front of the group appealed to him as well and was fun. However, they had also been instructed to shout out vicious insulting songs as they marched by the homes of the Jews. They did the same in front of the Oppenheim house. "The old lady (Fanni) stood in front of the house with her parasol and watched the goings-on. When the troop with the pennant was exactly across from her and she had to listen to the mocking songs, she spat really powerfully in front of them. All the boys were stunned at this courageous opposition. They waited for an immediate punishment of the woman for insulting the members of their squad. After all, they were the organization in which Jewish hatred was espoused daily. Fortunately, the young Hitler Youth leaders ignored the woman's transgression and everyone breathed a sigh of relief."

All of these factors led Rose and Albert to the conclusion that there was no future opportunity for them in Velmede and there was no reason for them to continue to call it their home. Gerda was in Shanghai, Helmut was in Palestine and would not be joining the business, if there was any business remaining, and they would likely send Günter to the United States the following year. Their beautiful memories of Velmede as a wonderful place to work, live and raise families had been shattered. They began to write to friends living in Aachen, Germany, near the Belgian border, and others in Hannover, where Rose's family was originally from, to gather some information as to whether life in either of these locations was relatively unencumbered by daily exposure to antisemitism.

In late 1936, Rose and Albert began to make frequent visits to Hannover and Aachen to search for a new home.

Günter, 1936

*Albert, Else, Fanni
and Rose, in back of
house, Velmede. 1936*

Chapter 11: 1937

Early in 1937, Günter completed his apprenticeship at *Alsberg's* and obtained his first paying job at the Blum Textile Department store in Essen, a 40-minute train ride from Hamm. He was able to continue living at the senior Dahl home and save some money for whatever lay ahead.

In the spring of 1937, the dire political situation for Rose and my family continued to worsen. 150,000 of the more than half million Jews of Germany had already left the country, the majority emigrating to neighboring European countries such as France, Belgium, the Netherlands, Denmark, Czechoslovakia, and Switzerland. Most of these refugees were later caught by the Nazis after their conquest of western Europe in May 1940. By 1937, a minority had been able to relocate into more distant, but ultimately much safer, countries such as England, Australia, South Africa, and the United States, all of which had increasing reluctance to accept additional Jewish refugees and, consequently, were placing various additional obstacles to the already difficult process of gaining entry visas.

The German Jews desirous of leaving their native land during this period were still able to take the majority of their personal possessions with them. Palestine and Shanghai remained destinations with relatively easy access. However economic opportunities and entry-level housing in these locations were becoming relatively less available because of competition among the newly arrived people.

In late February and early March of 1937, the *Kripo*, an acronym for *Kriminalpolize,* the Criminal Police, the detective police force of Nazi Germany, rounded up approximately 2,000 convicted offenders and imprisoned them in specifically designated locations. This was the first mass roundup of persons not deemed to be political opponents for incarceration in concentration camps. As Rose read this in the newspaper, she experienced a sense of relief that Helmut was not one of those placed into such a camp.

Albert, Rose, Fanni and Else, the garden in back of the house, Velmede, spring 1937.

That feeling, however, was tempered by her knowledge that Helmut was in another dangerous part of the world. He was still working and living in Magdiel, located in an area inhabited by both Arabs and Jews. The entire area of the British Mandate in Palestine was in the midst of the Arab revolt, an uprising against the British administration there, demanding Arab independence and the end of the policy of allowing Jewish immigration and land purchase. This had begun the prior year and there was frequent violence and terrorism in the area, to the point that in September 1937, the British were forced to declare martial law within the Palestinian mandate.

Gerda wrote to Helmut in the spring of 1937 commenting on this and other matters.

Shanghai, March 25, 1937

Dear Helmut,

We haven't heard from each other for so long that I think it will be high time that one or the other of us breaks the silence. I am not certain who is to blame for this long standstill in our correspondence, but I do believe it is you, Helmut. It is a good thing that I regularly hear from Velmede that you are indeed fine. You have, as mother writes, a great deal of hard work which you now have to do, after you have had better things for a while, but have also not earned that much. New unrest is reported in the newspapers. Hopefully, it won't be as bad as last year.

We're fine. We are healthy, the practice is so-so, and if we about break even every month, then we don't want to complain. If we could of course save something, it would be even better, but if not, we just have to wait a little longer. We certainly won't get rich anymore. I always say, of course I am joking, that, when my brother finally is in America, I mean Guenter, and has earned millions there, then it will be good for all of us too. Guenter is already reorganizing the whole store in Blum; I am racking my brains about how they ever got along before without him. Yes, dear Helmut, and what kind of thing was that weak little boy…if our Oma hadn't come, and so forth.

I am always very happy with Guenter's long letters, he writes about every 3 weeks, probably more often to you. You will see, with his happy temperament he will go far in life, he will certainly one day be a very capable businessman. The Velmeders write, thank God, that they are not dissatisfied either. If our father is even thinking of buying a new car, then the business at the store cannot be so terribly bad either. I'm so happy that we ourselves don't have to worry about it.

Mr. Bachmann was denied his traveling trade license through some chicanery. This has major consequences, especially nowadays. I was very afraid that our father would also have his license renewal refused, but why it was given to him and not to Mr. B. is not yet clear to me. *(The Bachmanns were the other Jewish family in Velmede and derived their income from a business similar to that of the Oppenheims.)*

I do not think the political climate in Germany has changed in any respect. In every letter from home, you hear about other people who have emigrated to America or Africa. Only the old people stay at home.

What do you always do, I mean in your free time? Do you ever get together with Heinz and Werner? You certainly are aware that Werner's father was locked up for so long.

Tomorrow is the first Seder evening, we will have a lot of visitors, because Max can give a Seder very nicely. Do you get any Matzah balls and Lockschen *(Jewish egg noodles, a traditional dish for Passover)* to eat? How about your plans to accept a volunteer position to learn how to learn to breed poultry or grow vegetables? Try to find something like that! It's better. It is always better if one really becomes educated in something.

Let us hear from you soon. Hearty greetings and kisses. Your Gerda

Rose's concern for the safety of her children also extended to the Far East, where, in 1937, The Second Battle of Shanghai was raging, fought between the Imperial Japanese Army and the Chinese Nationalist Republican Army. At the end of the three-month battle, which included artillery barrages and bombing strikes by the Japanese in downtown Shanghai, the city fell, and Japan gained control over Shanghai.

While the weekly letters from Gerda and the infrequent letters from Helmut that Rose read and reread failed to mention their being in the midst of armed conflict, she could not avoid being drawn to news reports emanating from China and Palestine both in the press and on the radio. Although it would be more than difficult to send Günter, now seventeen, away to yet another foreign land, she realized that he would have an opportunity for a place in the sun in the peaceful United States.

It had been almost one hundred years since Joseph Schnellenburg left Germany and started a textile business in Philadelphia. His son Nathan had married Albert's maternal aunt in 1871 and would become the founder of *N. Snellenburg & Company*, commonly known as *Snellenburg's*, one of the major department stores in Philadelphia, with more than 1,000 employees in 1937. His youngest son, Stanley, born in 1892 and Albert's first cousin, now managed the store's operations.

Egon Baum, the child of Albert's sister Minna, went to the United States from Germany at age twenty on the *SS Bremen* in December of 1933, having been promised a job by Stanley. Now, four years later, Egon was writing his mother, still in Germany, that he was "well on his way to becoming a wealthy man."

Günter, Hamm, 1937

Stanley Snellenburg, age 20, Philadelphia, 1912

Minna had become a widow in 1925 and frequently visited Velmede to spend time with Rose and Albert. Her stories about Egon's success resonated with my grandparents. Various Snellenburg cousins from the United States had returned to Germany over the years and, whenever Rose and Albert welcomed them into their home or met with them in Dortmund or Düsseldorf, my grandparents were always impressed with the quality of their clothing and accoutrements. Although they realized that Philadelphia was not a mythical shining city on a hill whose streets were paved with gold, they were eager for their son to have a measure of security and a promise for a good life in the United States. They successfully initiated correspondence with Cousin Stanley and were able to secure an assurance that a job would be waiting for Günter if he indeed would leave Germany and come to Philadelphia.

Snellenburg's, 12th and Market Street, Philadelphia, c 1930, an immense, Renaissance-style retail emporium.

On March 5, 1937, Stanley Snellenburg sent a notarized affidavit from Philadelphia on behalf of Günter to the American consulate in Germany as part of an application for a visa to enter the United States. In this "guarantee," Stanley attested to being an American citizen, being in the "department store business," listed three life insurance policies and a savings bank account that he owned, attached a Dun and Bradstreet grading report on *Snellenburg's,* and further stated that "I do hereby promise, agree and guarantee, that I will properly receive and take care of … Günter…and that I will at no time allow (him)…to become (a) public charge upon any community or municipality." Stanley had been frequently assured in letters from his first cousins Albert and Rose that Günter was indeed industrious and dependable. Stanley was certain that Günter would be frugal and willing to work hard for a fair salary at *Snellenburg's.*

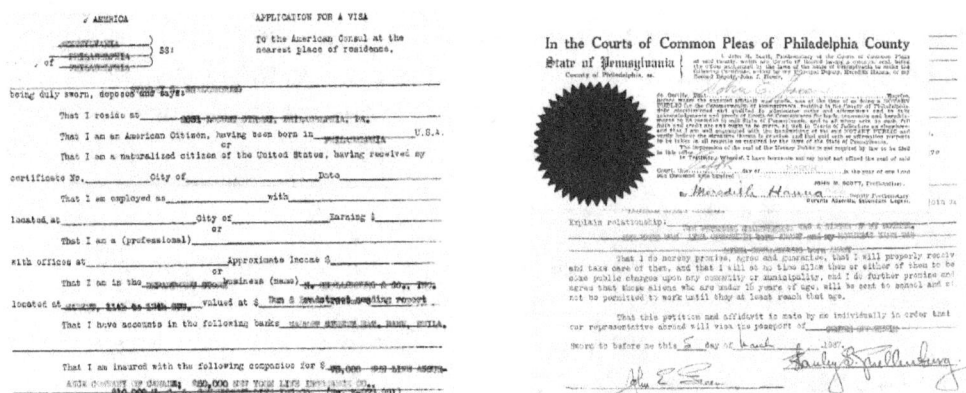

Notarized "Guarantee" documents submitted by Stanley Snellenburg for the successful U.S. visa application for Günter Oppenheim, 1937. Despite numerous requests, Stanley never provided "guarantees" for any of my remaining family until it was too late.

Gerda and Max, day trip on the Yangtze River, China, April 1937.

A letter from Gerda in Shanghai to Helmut in Palestine mixes the mundane with the serious.

Shanghai, April 22, 1937

Dear Helmut,

First of all, I would like to thank you from the bottom of my heart for your good wishes for my birthday, which arrived punctually on the day before April 6th. With the same post, I am sending you a silk shirt as a sample of no value, one similar to one you had already received from us. I hope that you do not need to pay any duty for it. *(Articles shipped often required duty, a sum of money to be paid to the government, by the recipient upon receipt. The amount was dependent upon the value, which in the case of used clothing, could be designated as worthless)*. You can say that the shirt had been previously worn. I also enclose an issue from "The Word." It is the last one we received; we no longer have the subscription.

We were very happy with the pages you sent us. But we hadn't heard from you for a terribly long time. As I already wrote to you, I think your last letter came in November, and the next one only again for my birthday. but I have the feeling that some of your postings to us must have gotten lost. *(It is wishful thinking on the part of Gerda to think that so many letters had been "lost." It is far more likely that Helmut failed to write)*.

I happily hear from home that you still like it so much in Magdiel. Among the people I have spoken to, you seem to really be one of the few who love Palestine. And that's simply good news. I hope you always have work! I really envy you for your plan to go to France in the summer. That will make father and mother and Guenter joy.

I last had news from Velmede 8 days ago. Lately so much has happened in the family, good and sad, that I can't digest everything. There is Bachmann's sell-out *(of their competing store in Velmede)* and their intention to leave. I think so often about whether it would not also be best if father would rent our business, but one never knows how everything will turn out. I am hopeful that our

Guenter will get his visa for America without further difficulties! Max sometimes jokes that if only one will not find him too weak during the medical examination!

And now I want to end for today. Let us hear from you again soon! Be warmly greeted and kissed,

From your Gerda

Rose and Albert went to Hamm to tell Günter that he would be going to America towards the end of August 1937. The thought of this was exciting but tempered by some apprehension about the various events that lay ahead, both anticipated and unexpected. He had just turned 17 and was mature beyond his years. After two years of hard work during his apprenticeship in Hamm and his job at *Blum* in Essen, Günter needed some rest and recreation. He and his brother Helmut, who had not seen each other in two years, made plans to meet and travel together for the month of July. Long-distance telephone calls at that time were only for the super-rich. That left messages sent through friends who were travelling between Palestine and Germany, telegrams, and old-fashioned letter writing, which is what they did. Helmut, rightly concerned about the Nazi censors reading letters coming from and going to Germany, had previously devised some subtle encryption language to communicate with Günter if an occasion arose to require it. Although Helmut certainly knew that expert cryptographers could quickly crack any homemade code, he felt that the SS had not yet associated him with the city of Aachen where his parents were spending some time searching for a new home, since he had never been in that location. Helmut used the word "Aachen" in his letters to Günter instead of the word "Velmede," so that if letters might be read by anyone who sought Helmut's arrest, they would search for him in Aachen, where he spent no time. He wished that a planned visit to Velmede to briefly see his family and connect there with Günter would not be subjected to intensive scrutiny.

With all arrangements in place, Helmut, in the summer of 1937, took the bus from Magdiel to Egypt's Port Fuad, which lies on the eastern bank of the Suez Canal and took the free ferry across the canal to the cosmopolitan city of Port Said. Helmut, who had always been an avid booklover, recalled reading the words of Rudyard Kipling "If you truly wish to find someone you have known and who travels, there are two points on the globe you have but to sit and wait, sooner or later your man will come there: the docks of London and Port Said." From that Mediterranean port city at the northern terminus of the Suez Canal, he boarded a ship bound for Genoa, Italy. He hitched a ride to the Genoa *Brignole* railroad station and then quickly left that busy terminus and traveled by train to Velmede, changing trains in Milan and Frankfurt.

He arrived under the cover of darkness in Velmede, where Günter was waiting for him, and was reunited with his parents, his grandmother Fanni and his aunt Else. He would never see his parents again.

Günter, Fanni, Else, Rose and Helmut, Velmede, July 1937. Fanni is no longer able to stand unassisted.

The two brothers left by train with their backpacks and headed to Italy. They had a marvelous time touring the country using rented bicycles. They slept under the stars and visited Venice, Padua, Trieste, and the Lake region in Lombardy. They swam, saw the sights, partied, and chased girls. Their meals were often *pane* from the local bakery and inexpensive local *formaggio* from a neighborhood *drogheria*. Every few days they would treat themselves to 200 grams of *prosciutto crudo*. At the end of the vacation, Helmut put Günter on the train heading north towards Velmede and he journeyed south to Genoa to board a ship returning to Palestine. Neither realized that they would not see each other again for 25 years.

Helmut in Venice, 1937

Helmut and Günter, Bellagio on Lake Como, July 1937

Lago di Garda

In preparation for his emigration to America, Rose and Albert booked passage for Günter on the *Steamship Pennland* leaving Antwerp, Belgium, on August 21, 1937, scheduled to arrive in New York City on August 31, 1937. That ship was a transatlantic ocean liner built in Ireland in 1920, and operated by Red Star Line, whose ships all had names ending in "-land." It had been originally outfitted with berths for 2,100 passengers: 600 cabin class and 1,500 third class. In 1935, the SS *Pennland* was refitted as a one-class ship with accommodations for approximately 500 tourist class passengers.

My grandparents wanted to accompany their son to Antwerp to escort him onto the ship, but Günter insisted that they only go with him to Aachen from where he would, by himself, take the train to Antwerp, changing in Brussels. It would be foolish and unnecessary, he said, for his parents to go the long distance to Antwerp and then immediately turn around and return to Velmede.

Just after dawn on the morning of August 21, 1937, Aunt Else drove Rose, Albert, and Günter to the Bestwig train station, where the three boarded the train to Aachen. They were putting Günter on the 11:30 a.m. train from Aachen to go to Antwerp, a trip of three hours including the train transfer in *Bruxelles*. He would have more than adequate time to board the ship, leaving at 6 p.m. that evening from the port. After they changed trains in Dortmund, the train car filled with people and their conversation became subdued. They had become accustomed to avoiding any meaningful discussions when they were in the presence of strangers. Anyone could be an informer. The *Gestapo Geheime Staatspolizei,* (the direct English translation is "Secret State Police") had over 150,000 informants throughout the country who would report any anti-Nazi sentiment to the Gestapo. Although those around them in the train seemed very pleasant, they had heard many stories about longtime "friends" informing on their Jewish neighbors.

It had been raining when they first stepped into their car in Velmede. As their train approached the *Bahnhof* in Aachen, the rain had intensified, and it had also become rather windy. Trying to think about anything but the imminent parting with her son, Rose's mind kept returning to her satisfaction that she had the presence, upset as she was, to have brought both umbrellas from their location in the hall closet.

Aachen's first railroad station was built in 1841 outside the city walls. It was relocated to the junction where *Romerstraße* becomes *Laagerhausstraße* in 1905, on *Bahnhofplatz*, half a mile south of the center of the medieval town. Rose had been there many times in the last few years while looking for a new home or visiting friends, but this occasion felt extremely different.

The Aachen railroad station is spacious with numerous trains every day, leaving there to go to all the major cities of Germany. Trains leave for Hamburg and go on to Berlin, Düsseldorf, or Munich via Cologne, and to Bremen, changing in Dortmund. As it is located proximate to the borders of Holland, Belgium and Luxembourg, trains leave multiple times a day bound for Bruges, Luxembourg via Liège-Guillemins and Amsterdam, via Heerlen. One can get to Paris directly or by changing trains in *Bruxelles*.

It was a Saturday, but the station was no less busy than during the week. In May 1933, in one of its first official acts, the NSDAP had banned labor private unions in Germany, and Hitler established the *Deutsche Arbeitsfront* (the DAF or German Labour Front). The DAF became, in essence, a government-run union, with membership dues payable weekly directly to the Reich by all workers. Currently, any person employed by large businesses or factories was working at least 10 hours per day, six days a week, and both the station and the trains were filled with people coming or going to work.

Rose did not notice the crowds in the main hall of the *Bahnhof*. She was concentrating her vision and her mind on Albert walking ahead with his arm around their son. Her husband, who was slim when they married 28 years earlier, had put on some weight during their years in Velmede but, for the past two years, had become thinner and at times appeared elderly and somewhat frail to Rose. Yet from the rear, watching both men pacing ahead in their suits, topcoats, and hats, it was difficult to detect an age difference between the smaller and the larger man. Günter was certainly a handsome figure with his well-knotted tie. He had been required to be well dressed every day during his apprenticeship and retail job, very different from the 15-year-old boy dressed in shorts that she had sent to Hamm two years earlier.

Her mind continued to be hyperactive with recurring thoughts regarding the decisions made and she had difficulty keeping her personal pledge to refrain from revisiting those choices. Especially at this last hour, it was impossible to not ask herself, "Did we really need to do something so drastic? How can we send him so far away? Should we have kept him in school? Will he be all right? What if he is homesick? When will we see him again?" Rose tried to calm down by saying to herself, "He will thrive, everyone will like him; He is strong and independent; We brought him up well; We are still his parents." This emotional turmoil of excitement, pride, regret, sorrow, and anxiety had been plaguing her for months and could have continued endlessly, but they were now at the doors of the passenger train car. The last thought Rose had, just before the beginning of the final goodbye hug, was that she knew that uncertainty dominated her future, a feeling like distant rain, something that might be overwhelming and cold and perhaps dark.

Rose and Albert, Velmede, 1937

Günter got onto the train carrying his suitcase. He sat down at a nearby window and waved goodbye to his parents as the train slowly left the station. His parents tried not to cry and he, with great difficulty, attempted the same. He had 168 American dollars divided among his various pockets, dollars he had received in exchange at a bank for the *Deutschmarks* he had saved over the past year together with money given to him by Rose, Albert, Else and Fanni, who all wished him good fortune. He would never see any of them again.

The SS Pennland left Antwerp on time and took ten days to reach New York, stopping for passengers in Le Havre, Southampton, and Halifax.

Red Star Line poster showing SS.
Pennland arriving in New York, c 1935.

When Günter arrived in his shared stateroom, he found a letter at his bedside written by Helmut from Magdiel, Palestine, August 14, 1937. It said, in part,

Dear Günter!

You will be very pleasantly surprised when the steward puts this letter on your bed... So now the time has really come. Germany lies behind you, a new life beckons. Boy, my best wishes are with you. You certainly have a lot to do to digest the many impressions of the last few days. Can you find your way around the ship yet? It never happened so quickly for me! Now you can get pretty seasick! Hopefully not! The things you have seen in the last few months and what you will see in the next few weeks!

I'm happy that we spent the 14 days together *(in Italy on vacation in July).* What do you think the official in full regalia in the mayor's office who said he had been personally instructed by Mussolini is doing right now? How about Marie and Cristina and the little Signorina. When am I going to get the pictures that you took of those girls?

Yesterday I received a postcard from the you and Eduard *(Oppenheim)* and his family in Eisenach which reminded me of the pork knuckle with sauerkraut that we ate there 4 years ago at 25 ° in the shade. I can still feel the heaviness in my stomach today. Here, *(in Palestine)* it is pitch dark in our room after 7 o'clock and 30 ° in our room without the slightest draft, which means that sweat is running down my back and chest. While you were there, you could have said hello to the veterinarian's daughter.

Now let yourself be lazy again and eat yourself up to the maximum on the ship! You won't have it that good again soon.

The first Rosh-ha-shanah over there should be spent well and at the next one you shall be satisfied with the course of the first year. Now our parents are all alone! But all you can do is write regularly. I pick up Gerta's packages from an address in Tel Aviv.

I am curious as to whether or not this letter reaches you. And now once again have a good trip, a pleasant welcome and good luck.

Helmut

Günter, just arrived in USA, 1937. He had turned 17 only 3 months earlier.

Exactly one week after arriving in New York, Günter started work at *Snellenburg's* in Philadelphia. In the meantime, he had found shared accommodations in a rooming house at 2223 North Park Avenue in North Philadelphia, a working-class neighborhood where he was to remain for a few years. This was a bus ride with a transfer from his place of employment.

Snellenburg's trucks, Philadelphia, 1937.

Günter, Philadelphia, 1937

Although he was hard at work, Günter still found time to be on the beach in Atlantic City before the winter cold set in.

Günter, Atlantic City, 1937

Rose and Albert continued to make day trips to various German mid-sized cities to find a new place to live while Else remained in Velmede to care for her mother and manage *M. Oppenheim.* They finally decided to buy a small home for the four of them in Aachen, near the border of Germany with Belgium, notwithstanding that Fanni had frequently expressed her wish to move to Hannover, a city with which she was extremely familiar.

Although Albert was still able to show a small profit in the majority of months by decreasing his staff, buying well and drawing down his large inventory of goods, the continued "Aryanization" of German businesses continued to gain steam. A*risierung*, the transfer of Jewish-owned businesses to German ownership throughout Germany was still "voluntary," but forced confiscation would become Nazi policy in 1938. Albert had personally seen advertisements that denounced Germans who bought products from Jews and uniformed guards posted outside Jewish businesses to harass customers, and he understood that all public institutions were forbidden to patronize *M. Oppenheim* and other Jewish businesses. He knew some Jewish business owners in larger cities who had been jailed until they agreed to give up their ownership. Both in Hamm and in Horn, the Nazis had confiscated businesses owned by personal friends and business acquaintances.

Prior to the Nazis coming to power in 1933, Jews owned 100,000 businesses in Germany, including stores, factories, publishing houses, newspapers, and private professional practices. This included 50,000 Jewish-owned stores that existed in 1933. By the beginning of 1938, only 9,000 remained.

Rose and Albert, having faced ever increasing economic and social discrimination for four years, sadly came to the realization that they needed to sever all relationships with Velmede. Albert, an excellent businessman all his life, recognized that it was the proper financial decision to sell *M. Oppenheim* at a radically reduced price from its actual value, since it would be either worthless or expropriated soon. In addition, they would make some repairs to their adjacent home and attempt to get some additional money through its sale.

In December 1937, the family in Germany wrote to Günter in Philadelphia. These are excerpts:

Velmede, December 14th, 1937

From Fanni:

My dear Günter,

Yesterday we enjoyed your letter and are pleased that you, dear Günter, are well and satisfied. Certainly, you have a lot of work now, just before Christmas. There is a lot to do here in business, especially in the evening, as the public now knows that the business will soon pass into other hands on January 1st. Then we also have to set up our kitchen and living room upstairs by summer. All extra furniture here, beds, etc. have already been sold. …We also had a letter from Gerda today and from Helmut yesterday. Both write satisfied thank God. …Uncle Paul will probably help us here with business after Christmas when the handover is going to happen... Right now, there has been a lot of snow here for days. My dear Günter, that's it for today. With best regards,

From Rose:

My dear Günter,

Now it's time to add a few lines to Oma's, because the letter has been lying around for a few days because I really didn't have the time. First of all, many thanks for your dear letter, which, as always, pleased us very much. Thank God we are alive and well, there is a lot to do in the business, many customers come to us from Bachmann's. The goods in our store have become very depleted from customer sales. Yesterday we had a large amount of cash receipts; today's was very little. Father went to Remblinghausen today to settle some accounts. Before I forget, dear Günter, it's Uncle Paul's birthday on January 5th, please congratulate him. The other day he gave me various reply coupons for you and is always so nice. You haven't written to Horn from there either, so please don't forget! We have had workers in our house since yesterday: the plumber Schmier and the electrician Hegener. They installed the kitchen sink on the top floor and Bamfaste is supposed to wallpaper afterwards. The wires for the light have been laid in the walls. There was a terrible mess as the tiles above the water pipe in our kitchen were removed to make the drain for the top floor. We're lucky to have help in the house again. We made a good swap in hiring the new boy. He is called Paul David, is 33 years old, very smart, knows everything, was a matzoh baker at *Marens* in Burgsteinfurt for four years and a worker at the power station in Coesfeld. It's good that we got rid of the "grandpa!" *(The Oppenheim's helper for odd jobs around the house had been an elderly man who no longer was physically able to do work efficiently).*

Thank God we had good news from Gerda and Max, the theater of war is now further away. *(Shanghai was no longer in the zone of active combat.)* Gerda had the second letter from you and was very happy with it, sends you her best regards. Helmut recently wrote all the best. Yesterday Mrs. H. Mieder *(a Velmede neighbor)* brought a sausage each for Helmut and you. Tomorrow I'll mail the one for you, I sent his to Helmut today. He wrote us that apart from the sausage we send him every week he doesn't have money to eat a lot of meat. Here are the photos, dear Günter! Glue them all into your album. It was really nice of your buying agent at Snellenburg's to give you a train ticket to New York for your visit. Is she a Jew? Do you have a lot of Jewish staff at all? Hopefully there won't be a strike with you! In any case, you know who to side with. Please give Stanley my best regards. Did you receive the money we sent you in October and December? Well goodbye dear boy, be hugged.

From Albert:

Dear Günter! For yourself, dear boy, I add many greetings. We are always very happy with your good and detailed news, which you should continue to send us regularly every week.

Yesterday our successor sent around the first notes announcing the takeover at the beginning of January. In terms of business, we have been busy for months, as in the best of times. Our warehouse has shrunk a lot so that, in my opinion, there is not much merchandise left over in excess of the amount to be paid immediately. *(A contract had been signed for the store to be sold for a certain amount with additional monies to be paid for remaining merchandise.)*

Your loving father

Chapter 12: 1938

On January 15, 1938, at 9 a.m., *M. Oppenheim*, the Oppenheim family business for seventy years at 79 *Provinzialstraße*, was reopened under the name of *Padberg and Müller*. Flyers announcing this were posted on bulletin boards in Velmede, Bestwig and surrounding towns and advertisements of the new ownership were placed in newspapers. These read,

> "We are communicating with the honorable residents of Velmede and the surrounding area that we have taken over the shop M. Oppenheim. The store is now installed with modern fixtures, and we have the best quality and largest selection of merchandise priced for value. We would be pleased if you would stop by. According to the economic report of the NSDAP (Nazi Party) of December 13, 1937, our enterprise has now been judged to be pure Aryan.
>
> Everyone therefore can come in and shop there."

The aryanization of the shop was complete. Although the transfer of ownership and payment was to have occurred on January 1, some last-minute issues resulted in my grandparents being forced to receive a promissory note rather than the cash which they had been guaranteed for the inventory in the store and warehouse. The business and real estate was sold to Padberg and Müller for a few *Pfennigs* on the *Deutschmark*, without a down payment and to be paid in installments. Rose and Albert had no legal recourse, and a similar "fire sale" situation would occur when they "sold" their home six months later.

The Germans euphemistically referred to this and similar transactions as "transfers" or "relinquishment" of property ownership. Whatever the term used, at best this was a confiscation, forced sale, a sale under threat or duress or unlawful dispossession. At worst it was equivalent to looting or theft.

A letter to Günter written on January 5, 1938, and marked as received by him on January 12, 1938, describes some of these happenings:

January 5, 1938, written on *M. Oppenheim* stationery,

From Rose:

> My dear Günter,
>
> I hope that you, dear boy, are healthy and happy like us, thank God. Only grandma and aunt Else caught a cold, which will hopefully be better soon. Incidentally, today father, who now always takes care of the mail, sent off a nice sausage for you, one for Helmut and some money for you. The handover of the warehouse brought a lot of work and excitement, because many things that were under the counters were no longer worth much. We were lucky that Mr. *Salm (an uncle by marriage of Gerda's)* helped us. He knows the hype, and without him we would not have been through. Dear Günter, Mr. Padberg… gave us bills of exchange for the rest, which we didn't spend and which we redeem every month three days before the due date. Of course, they also pay the interest for it. Mr. Salm advised us to do it that way. They changed a lot in the store…In the shop window there is a large sign that they will open on January 5th and, according to the confirmation of the NSDAP Gauleitung *(local Nazi leadership),* are recognized as a purely Aryan company. I wish them all the best. Hopefully they will have a great business here! Well, dear Günter, thank you very much for your December 23 letter which pleased us very much. At the same time one of Helmut's arrived, Gerda had written shortly before after a three-week break. The letter was on the way for 4 weeks and, thank God, contained good things about the practice.
>
> By the way, Bachmann's *(the other Jewish family in Velmede)* here recently had terrible excitement again at night. Strangers who have not been found until now (as always!) shot many shots with rifles through the shutters of the living room into the walls and also into the hallway. Many window panes were destroyed in the process. It's just awful! What do they have against the Bachmann's?
>
> Dear Günter, we are very pleased that you have started to save. Now stick with it! One thing leads to another. Did you ask Stanley if you could go into sales? It would be very nice if he allowed it and then you earn better. There is heavy snow here and it is very cold, minus 20° C yesterday. Can you ski there too? I close for today with best regards from Grandma and Aunt Else. Good night, it's midnight and I'm tired. In constant love, your mother.

From Albert:

> My dear boy!
>
> Although mother told you everything that was particularly worth knowing, I still want to add a few lines to tell you a lot about our changed situation in life. So since January 3rd we have finally withdrawn from business life and I have to admit the first few days of our private life are very comfortable, especially after a stressful and sometimes exciting week taking over the storage. Though we have to do with decent Seges (*Western Yiddish for non-Jews)* in every respect and with

absolutely no Nazis...there was nevertheless discord due to the enormous sales of the last few months, in which, understandably, all au-courant items, especially the hard-to-find white goods, of which we had no more, sold out. The leftovers led to serious differences of opinion with regard to setting the price, which, however, thanks to Mr. Salm's skills, were righted again to mutual satisfaction. I can say that even before, after all the raisins had been picked out of the warehouse, I was secretly afraid of the take-over, but everything went to our satisfaction. The accounting was also carried out without any discrepancies on both sides. I will still have plenty to do for the next few months. I will visit customers every month for payments, from which I expect more success than waiting for deposits.

Dear Günter, we are always very happy about your letters-- we are thereafter continually in a good mood. Gerda and Max have also calmed down and the practice is still good. How the situation in Shanghai will develop is still unclear. In any case, their continued stay there is guaranteed. Well, goodbye, boy. Your loving father hugs you and kisses you in spirit.

A letter to Gerda and her husband Max in Shanghai from Albert written a few days later describes the sale of the business further:

Letter to Gerda in Shanghai from the Velmede family, on M. Oppenheim Stationery, with notes by Rose, Fanni and Else at the outer borders of the typed letter, January 11, 1938.

January 11, 1938,

From Albert to Gerda and Max in Shanghai:

My dear children!

Although our dear mother has already told you everything that is particularly worth knowing, this time I will not fail to tell you a little more about our changed situation in life, which, my loved ones, I assume, will also be of particular interest to you. So first of all I would like to tell you that we are happy to have the handover behind us and that we are sitting comfortably and dignified up here. Yes, dear ones, it was a huge job, not to mention the uncomfortable move and the storage of the many chunks. Nevertheless, everything went to the satisfaction of both parties, I mean the handover of the warehouse, whereby not least Mr. Salm, as a specialist, did his part, and we were really happy to have had it here.

Even if we have really decent leaseholders who have the best reputation in the business world and absolutely no Nazis, there were often excited scenes when taking in the goods in view of the various leftovers that naturally accumulated over the years and of which I was always had a certain fear. According to the contract, the goods had to be accepted at the invoice price and completely *uncourant* items by agreement. I added the last passage because I thought it appropriate at the last crucial stage in November, because our warehouse had been thinning colossally after the enormous sales and almost all of the raisins *(choice items)* had been taken out. What was not yet completed by then was completed in December. Herr Padberg, an extremely driven and efficient merchant, almost passed out when, shortly before the takeover, he saw our cleared warehouse, in which not a meter of white goods could be found, for example, the most sought-after articles today, and he was forced to make new purchases for considerable sums, which in themselves are difficult to get hold of, which he did not consider necessary at his first inspection in August.

Everything was done very well, even though we often had to make extensive concessions for some items with regard to the price. *(When corresponding with the children, realizing that letters, especially those going abroad were being opened by censors and understanding that the Nazis were eager to enact excise taxes on Jewish transactions, Rose and Albert employed a simple pre-arranged number code when writing sums of Reichsmarks).* We ourselves estimated our remaining warehouse at about *ON mille,* but with the items previously chosen by Uncle Paul including shop fittings it resulted in *PK* which after calculating according to the agreement on December 30 was taken care of promptly. Today we are so happy that we did not sell the business as the tenants wanted to do back then, as early as the first or second of November, but took advantage of the Christmas business, which I had never known in terms of sales. I just want to give you a few numbers here. Since September, roughly since we became aware of our business closure, we had accredited an approximate cash receipt of approx. *ER* and approx. *OK* to *OP mille* to only flawless customers, including approx. *OE mille* cash and approx. *5 N mille* in December alone. Isn't that nice and reminds you of the best years and especially because the sales are still made with good earnings without a discount! I would like to mention here something that also weighs in, that since September I had only bought the bare essentials and since then the new items have hardly made-up *N mille.*

At the moment I am in the process of writing invoices, and collecting the accounts receivable, which I estimate to be over *PN mille*, which will have to continue at high pressure. I will continue to visit customers as before for the next months but expect it to take at least 2 years and also have to reckon with losses.

So, we hope to be able to live a carefree and humble life in peace. - As for the choice? Where will we go? We will think about it calmly and look around.

Helmut, from whom we just had a satisfied letter, will also receive his transfer shortly. Günther always writes very happily and is in good hands there.

These are excerpts from a letter written to Günter a few days later:

January 13, 1938, Velmede-Ruhr,

From Rose:

My dear Günter,

While grandma and father have their afternoon nap upstairs in our cozy living room, I want to chat with you and first of all thank you very much for your detailed letter yesterday, which, as always, pleased us very much. So please write to us every week and a lot, dear boy! We are interested in everything, and we are all always very happy when your news is good. I also wish you a healthy and happy 1938. If only we all stay healthy, we will thank God and be happy to be satisfied. Hopefully you are as well as we are, thank God! Today we had a letter from Gerda dated December 21st, she received mail from you with congratulations on Max's birthday. The practice was quiet around that time, as it is every year. Hopefully it will get better soon. Both Gerda and Max would like to take time off for a fortnight, but Max says it wouldn't work because of the practice. Helmut also wrote recently. He is still waiting for the money to be transferred from Germany by Hawara *(The Haavara Agreement, translated "transfer agreement" was a pact between Nazi Germany and Zionist German Jews signed on August 25, 1933. The agreement was finalized after three months of talks by the Zionist Federation of Germany, the Anglo-Palestine Bank and the economic authorities of Nazi Germany. It was a major factor in making possible the migration of approximately 60,000 German Jews to Palestine in 1933–1939. The agreement enabled Jews fleeing persecution under the new Nazi regime to transfer some portion of their assets to British Mandatory Palestine. Emigrants sold their assets in Germany to pay for essential goods, manufactured in Germany, to be shipped to Mandatory Palestine).* His friends think that Helmut's number will soon be called and then Helmut will get the money paid out in cash, whereas now it is only to be paid half in cash and half in Palestine securities that can only be sold at a great loss. I want the matter to be settled first! We miss you very much, dear Günter! I am very happy that everyone is so nice to you, dear Günter, just always be humble and courteous and make every effort to make progress, because who knows whether we can end our life here in Deutschland.

We are in the process of selling our furniture here before moving away. You can't keep all of the old things because such a large apartment would cost too much in the city. Grandma thinks you could take everything with you! That is not possible!

Fritz and Minna's husband in Lathen lost their trade license. What can they do but to emigrate? Father and I recently visited the Bachmann's in the evening and were able to see the bullets struck in the walls for ourselves. The bullets went through the closed wooden shutters! The shooting lasted for hours at night! If only they could find out the perpetrators!

A few days ago, OK went off. (a coded reference to money being sent abroad)

Did you recently ask Stanley to place you in sales? Or are you not speaking fluently enough yet? Well enough for today, dear Günter. Father wants the table! All loved ones here send you their best regards. Stay healthy, be hugged and greeted a thousand times by your loving

Mother

The notarized record of the purchase of *M. Oppenheim* by "Josef Padberg, businessman in Schmallenberg, Meschede district" from "Albert Oppenheim, merchant in Velmede earlier, now in Aachen" states that the purchase price was "17,000 Reichsmarks" and also notes that the land value alone, without the business and the goods, according to earlier assessment records, was "18,100 *Reichsmarks.*" The document also states that "It is noted that the seller is Jewish."

By an ordinance of January 23, 1938. the Velmede-Bestwig volunteer fire brigade was forcibly transferred to the police force. It was expressly emphasized that Jews are not allowed to belong to the volunteer fire brigade. From now on, only "national comrades" were allowed to take the oath on the Führer when they were accepted into the fire-fighting police. Jews were no longer considered Germans. My grandfather Albert, who had served as a volunteer for the brigade for so many years, as had his father Moses before him, must have been sorely disappointed at this development, but made no mention of it in any correspondence, perhaps fearing that Nazi censors would find such a sentiment worthy of arrest or worse.

In the late spring of 1938, Rose and Albert packed their personal belongings and, together with Rose's sister Else and mother Fanni, made the permanent move to Aachen, near the German border with Belgium. Else, always the optimist, was looking forward to the change and the sisters were anticipating daily walks in the gardens of the *Aachener Stadtpark* on *Monheimsalle*, within a short distance of the small house at 39 *Normannenstraße*, in the northeast portion of the city. Fanni, now approaching her 83rd birthday, rarely left the house in Velmede because of difficulty walking, and likely would also not do so in Aachen.

These are portions of letters written by my family in Velmede during the early spring of 1938:

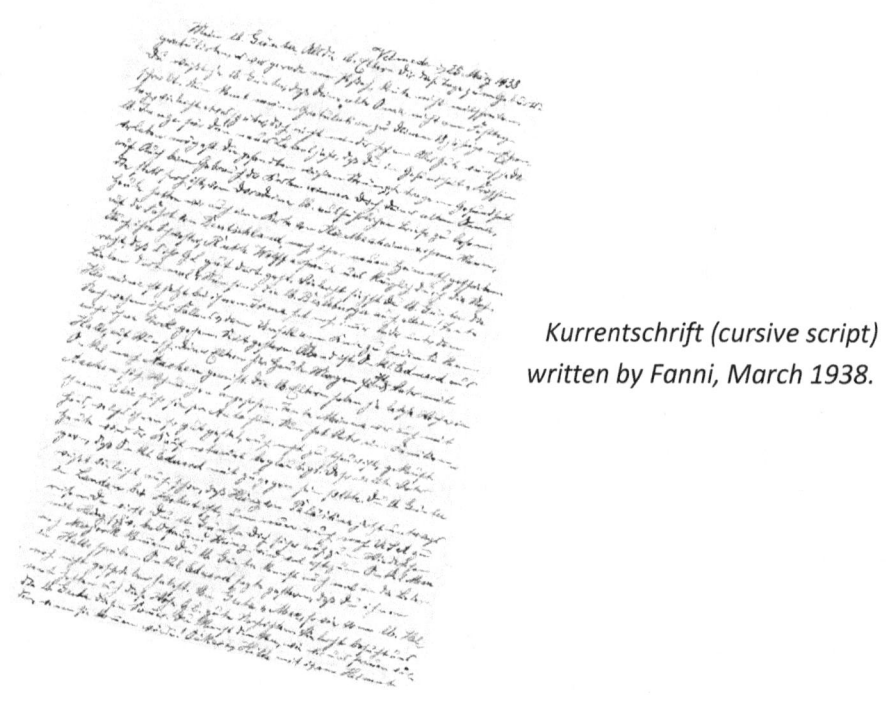

Kurrentschrift (cursive script) written by Fanni, March 1938.

Velmede, March 25, 1938

From Fanni:

> My dear Günter,
>
> Your dear parents congratulated you on your birthday on Passover so I couldn't take part, since you know dear Günter that your old grandma doesn't write on a holiday. (It *was customary for more orthodox Jews to not "work" on Shabbats and Holidays. "Work" included tasks like writing.*) Now comes my congratulations on your 18-year-old special day, maybe a little later, but no less warmly. I wish you all the best, dear boy, for your new year of life, which you shall experience in health and

happiness. The forwarded white stockings do wear in health. When you use the brushes, remember your old grandma, who is always happy to read your lovely, detailed letters. ...

Uncle Eduard (*Oppenheim*) from Halle has been here since yesterday evening, at the request of your parents. This morning father traveled to Aachen with the uncle. The dear parents took a look at apartments in Aachen last week... Else drove them there by car.

You dear Günter may already know that Heinz from Palestine is now on the way to London with Herbert *(Uncle Eduard Oppenheim's two sons, who had originally fled to Palestine and London)*, in order to travel to the USA. You dear Günter will be happy to see Heinz again soon, God willing? Heinz will probably first come to Uncle Max's *(Oppenheim)* in New York. Dear Günter, can you write again to the loved ones in Halle. Uncle Eduard said yesterday that you haven't written to them yet. Thank God, we had good news from Gerda and Max as well as from dear Helmut this week. Maybe dear Gerda is visiting us this summer. You can think how happy we would be if she came...

Now for today warm greetings from your loving grandma.

[P.S.:] Lotte Wolf from Dortmund is also going to America in 14 days. Karla Bachmann is here now and will also be going to the USA. Greetings and kisses again. Yours. Granny

From Rose:

My dear Günter,

First of all, I would like to ask you not to speak to anyone about Heinz's coming! Uncle Eduard begged us very much! I don't know why. So Silentium! Heinz will be leaving London on the Steamship Germany on May 6th. I'm curious to see if Uncle Eduard manages to get a passport for himself and Erna. He would so much like to see Heinz in London again, but has no passport.

We sent you a pair of brown shoes through Mannheimers. Get in touch with Ruth so that you can get them. Then please write us soon whether they fit well, because then we also want to buy you the pair of white ones. Aunt Else and I are about to go to the train station to pick up father, who is coming back from Aachen, where he went this morning with Uncle Eduard. Tomorrow I want to tell you about the result of this trip. I hope you are learning English well. With 1000 heartfelt greetings and love Your mother

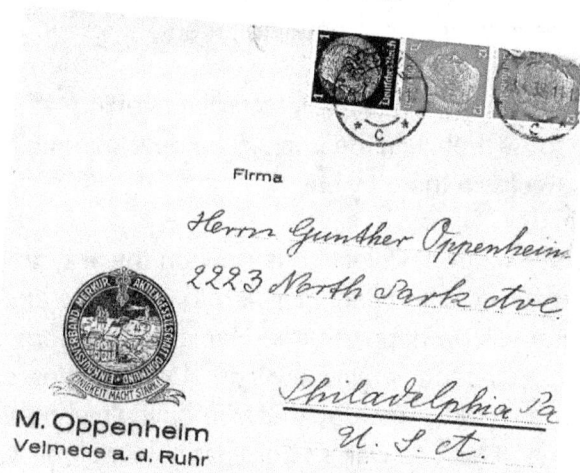

April 22, 1938, M. Oppenheim envelope

Velmede, April 22, 1938

From Rose:

My dear Günther,

Father had read your detailed dear letter dated April 12th out loud to us when he brought it home from the post office today. We are always immensely delighted us when the mail reports good things from you! I have just reread it in peace and quiet.

I hope these lines will find you as well as they leave us thank God. I haven't written to you myself for a long time because father and I were away, as Aunt Else wrote you, about an apartment. Now we have been to Aachen for the second time in this matter, this time by car, where we like it much better than in Cologne... Finding a suitable apartment is a tough job! There is something wrong with each and every one. We have various things on hand. When it all comes together, we will write it you. In case nothing should work out, father and I want to look around in Düsseldorf again. Many apartments rent out only to Aryans! Aachen has a beautiful landscape and that's why we like it so much there. There are wonderful residential streets and delightful houses. We hope that we get something suitable there.

Dear Günther, dear boy, first of all I want to wish you all the best for your birthday and the year to come! Stay healthy and good and keep making us happy as before. Above all else, make sure that you get ahead, dear Günther, and for this, in my opinion, it is extremely important that you speak fluent English very soon. I advise you, dear boy, to go to night school! I think that's much more important to you than a sports club at the moment! So go ahead, take my advice and study English hard. Do what Stanley advises you to do!

Ursel and Ernst *(children of Jewish friends)* have grown up... Their father paid a lot of *Reichsfluchtsteuer (The Nazi Reich Flight Tax "refugee tax "to strip emigrating Jews of their last funds)* tax on emigration from the Reich! We heard *O K K mille (number coding system used by my family who realized all letters would be read by the Nazis)* ... Lotte Wolf emigrates at the beginning of May. She is marrying a former engineer who now owns a grocery store in Newark... The Bachmanns are almost always in Eslohe. Anneliese is unfortunately ill with bronchitis and is in the

140

Meschede hospital, little Marianne is also there with pneumonia but is getting better. It's sad what B's go through. Carla has now left, her papers are already *(with the US consulate)* in Stuttgart, she will then emigrate soon.....

How did you like the matzo, dear Günter? We ate all sorts of varieties this year..., we were in Plettenberg with Adolf Sternberg for one day... Adolf is still very busy in his factory: a miracle from God.....

Had good news from Helmut today, who will now finally receive the transfer *(of money through Haavara)*. We also recently heard good news from Gerda, thank God. We haven't seen Ilse's *(Dahl)* fiancé yet, but we only hear good things about him. Now I want to give the other loved ones a little more space and therefore close with best regards for you, dear boy, and a birthday kiss from your very loving mother. How do you like the stationery?

a

Example of Rose's more modern handwriting above and Albert's florid Kurrent writing below.

From Albert:

My dear Günter!

This is the first time that you, dear boy, are celebrating your birthday far from home, to which I congratulate you all the more warmly and wish you all the best. Above all, stay healthy and continue to strive, as before, to secure the favor and benevolence of everyone who knows you. You dear boy are among our children relatively best off, because you are among many acquaintances and dear relatives, where you have now found a second home and, God willing, also will find a secure future.

Just like mother, I am of the opinion that you need something to improve your language skills, because this is, as one has heard over and over, the basic condition for rapid advancement. You say that you have already made good progress with the language in private life, but better is better!

Above all, surround yourself with good people, especially with Stanley, and seek and follow their advice, because they will certainly know it well and you are in safe waters! How happy we are about your detailed letters and the good news from Gerda and Helmut, I can hardly describe to you. We are always in such good spirits then.

In the meantime we are seriously seeking for an apartment. Aachen will probably be our future domicile, which makes us especially ... pleased.

Farewell my dear boy and take care. As always, continue to delight us with your weekly letters. Greetings from your father

Rose, 1938,
on a train

The Japanese novelist and essayist, Haruki Murakami(1949-), has written, "How wonderful it is to be able to write someone a letter! To feel like conveying your thoughts to a person, to sit at your desk and pick up a pen, to put your thoughts into words like this is truly marvelous."

Velmede-Ruhr, April 26th, 1938

From Rose to Günter:

My dear boy,

Yesterday evening father and uncle Eduard came back from Aachen, where the purchase was made official by a notary..., So, dear Günter, the house is very charming: a small flower garden in front, a larger one in the back (maybe as big as one of our beds in the garden). Very beautiful rose bushes, espalier fruits, a peach tree, plum tree and flower beds. Downstairs in the house are two living rooms (one with a large terrace facing the garden) and the kitchen. The bedrooms are on the first floor (one of which has a balcony overlooking the garden and an entrance to the lovely bathroom with a built-in bath). On the second floor there is a very large attic (guest bedroom). Everywhere running water, heating, hot water. The house was built in 1932 and is in very good shape. The owner is leaving Aachen, so he's selling. So, dear Günter, we are all very happy to have found something like this. The house is lovely, on a pretty street, a little out of town (but not far). Now God grant that we can all stay healthy and live in our house in peace and quiet for a few years. Uncle Eduard drove on that night because he still has a lot to do before going to see Herbert and Heinz. Hopefully he'll get the passport.

So, dear Günter, be very astonished when you see Heinz! Uncle Eduard said we shouldn't write it to you! ... Heinz didn't need any guarantees *(monetary guarantees that the US government required as part of the process of obtaining a visa to immigrate to the USA)* because he had money himself. I just wished, dear boy, that our Helmut could later go to the USA and you would be together! Maybe our Gerda will come to visit this summer! But it is not yet certain. That would be wonderful and a great joy for all of us! Well goodbye, my dear boy! Stay healthy, write to your loving mother again soon.

From Albert:

Dear Günter! We are happy to have acquired this lovely little house that mother has described to you with all the baffles and conveniences. We are our own masters in it and do not have to ask anyone else. The price turned out to be about 90,000 Marks and everything is already taken care of!

Greetings and kiss!

Father

Rose, front door of Aachen house, 1938

On April 26, 1938, a few weeks after the *Anschluss*, Nazi Germany's annexation of Austria, achieved with little to no opposition from the local population or any other foreign powers, Hermann Göring, Hitler's deputy for the "four-year" economic plan, issued the "Order for the Disclosure of Jewish Assets," requiring Jews to report all property with value in excess of 5,000 *Reichsmarks*.

Nothing was immune from this mandated decree, which included bank accounts, real estate, fine art, life insurance, and stocks and bonds. By July 31 of that year, German finance officials had collected paperwork from its Jewish citizens worth some 7 billion *Reichsmarks. T*his registration would shortly result in the systematic plunder of Jewish possessions, one that would allow the kleptocracy to keep German citizens well fed and continuing to support the Nazi regime. As the German historian Götz Aly has written in *Hitler's Beneficiaries*, "Aryanization was essentially a gigantic…trafficking operation in stolen goods... The Nazi leadership transformed the majority of Germans (into)… well fed parasites."

Adolf Eichmann established a similar system in August 1938, in Vienna, under the auspices of the *Zentralstelle für jüdische Auswanderung* (Central Office for Jewish Emigration). He described it as an "automatic factory" or "conveyer belt... You put a Jew and his property on one end and the Jew emerged with a passport and no property on the other end."

On July 11, 1938, the German Reich Ministry of the Interior, Wilhelm Frick, officially banned Jews from attending health spas. Immediately following this, the local administration of the island of Norderney formally barred Jews from coming there to vacation. They issued a special postage stamp with the inscription "Nordseebad Is Free from Jews" and requested that the inhabitants of the island affix the stamps whenever writing to friends or for business. The stamp was also sent to Jewish newspapers all over Germany with the request that they warn their readers not to come to Nordseebad, because they will be immediately deported.

Shortly after this, many German newspapers, primarily in the states of North Rhine -Westphalia, Lower Saxony and Bremen, published an article entitled *Einst und Jetzt* (Once and Now) contrasting the "old, Jew-filled" Norderney on the top of the article with the "current" German North Sea beach resort on the bottom of the page.

My grandmother Rose, who had, for many years, visited the resort with her family on vacation, was surprised when she opened the Aachen newspaper and read:

Einst und Jetzt (Then and Now)

"In the beautiful German North Sea is the island of Norderney. Not long ago it was the playground of the Jews. That clean and fertile land was despoiled by the dirty-born and foul-living Jews, who at every opportunity molested German maidens. The Jewish presence has been banned through the forethought of the German National Socialists movement. German men and women are now free to walk and laugh on the beach, as people who are good should be able to do, having enjoyment while they make the world a better place to live in."

Rose was even more startled when she recognized her daughter Gerda, my mother in the top row on the far left in the top picture and her son, Helmut, my uncle, in that same photograph in the bottom row on the far left, described as Jews who formerly defiled Norderney.

This 1938 newspaper article is typical of the contemporary ideology that regarded Jews as "parasitic vermin." Hitler believed that a person was defined by his race and traits of that race could never be overcome and would be passed from generation to generation. He claimed that "superior" races had not just the right but also the obligation to subdue and even exterminate "inferior" ones. The Nazis defined Jews as a "race," with Jewish religion being irrelevant to an unchanging biologically determined heritage which attempted to expand its influence at the expense of other races.

In order to fastidiously implement the Nazi policy of using legal measures to expel the Jews from society and remove their rights and property, in addition to abusing, terrorizing and later murdering millions of innocent civilians, with the ultimate goal that Germany and the world be *Judenfrei* (free of Jews), the proper identification of the less than one percent of the German population who were Jewish was necessary.

This process of establishing "racial purity" by the Nazis involved two steps, defining who was Jewish and subsequently legally marking those were identified as such. Immediately following the Nuremberg Laws in 1935, the Nazis issued the official definition of a Jew. According to German law, anyone with two or more Jewish grandparents was a Jew, as was anyone married to a Jewish person or who had one Jewish parent. The NDSP also defined people with only one Jewish grandparent as being a *mischlinge* (having mixed race). Descendants of families that had converted from Judaism could also, under certain circumstances, be considered *mischlinge* and certainly, if they looked like Jews, or "behaved" or "felt" like Jews, would be treated as Jews and, by 1941, could be deported or murdered as Jews.

In order to prevent Jews from attempting to escape their identity, the NSDAP, on January 5, 1938, passed the "Law on the Alteration of Family and Personal Name," which forbade Jews from changing their names. On April 22, the "Decree against the Camouflage of Jewish Firms" prohibited changing the names of any Jewish-owned businesses. On August 17, Hitler issued an "Executive Order on the Law on the Alteration of Family and Personal Names," requiring all Jews bearing first names of "non-Jewish" origin to adopt an additional official name, specifically designated as "Israel" for men and "Sara" for women. Jewish individuals had to report their new names to government offices and use both their given and added first names for business transactions. In addition, new Jewish parents were required to select a name for their newborn child from a government-approved list. All German Jews were obliged to carry identity cards that indicated their heritage.

In keeping with this directive, Rose now was forced to use the name "Sara" on the return address on all letters sent by her, including those mailed to her children in the USA, Palestine, and Shanghai.

The Nazi bureaucrats went to great lengths to enforce the name alteration of all Jews. The official birth certificate on file for Rose (and also for Else and Fanni) were altered in the German municipal records reflecting that imposed name change.

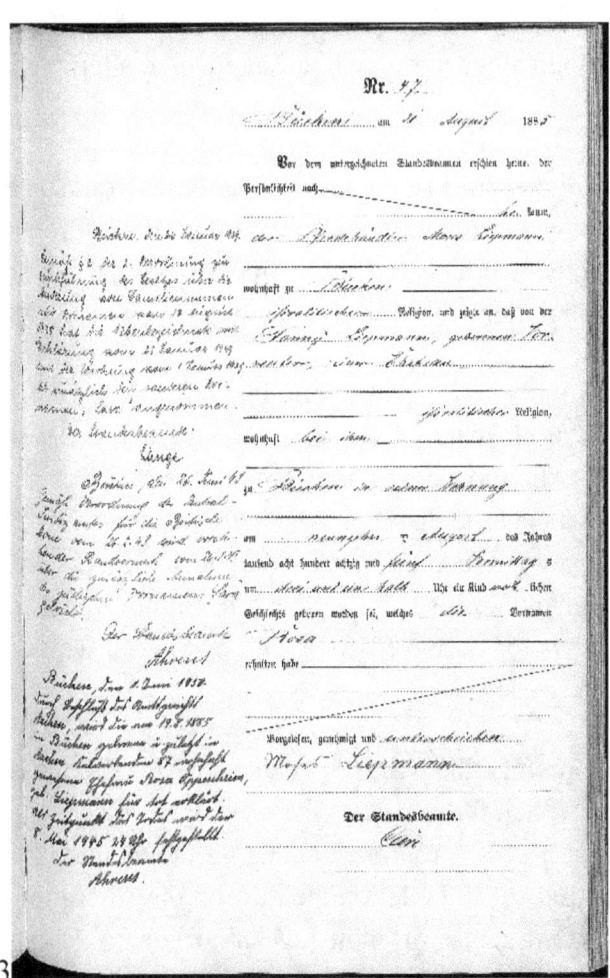

This is the original official birth certificate of my grandmother, Rosa (Rose) born in Bücken in 1885, on the right side of the document. On the left side, there are three later entries. The first, officially written by "Lange" in 1939 changed her name to "Sara," in keeping with the "Executive Order on the Law on the Alteration of Family and Personal Names." There are additional post WWII entries written by "Ahrens," a local bureaucrat, in 1948 and 1950, after World War II.

The 1948 entry officially removes her new name "Sara," restoring her name to Rose and the 1950 entry finally declares that she had died on May 8, 1945, five years earlier. That is the date of the German surrender in WW II and has absolutely no relationship with Rose's actual date of death.

Else's birth certificate was similarly altered.

There is never any mention, in the many letters Rose wrote to her children, of the unprecedented political events occurring around her. It is obvious that she knew all correspondence was being censored by the Nazis and punishment for any suggestion of dissent would be swift and severe. The forced resignations of the high-ranking military leaders Werner von Fritsch and Werner von Blomberg, who had expressed concerns regarding Hitler's movement towards war, allowing Hitler to personally take over the entire Germany military, were certainly well reported in the German press of the time. Undoubtedly, Rose, Albert and Else had private conversations about this and the other happenings of the times.

Following the success of the *Anschluss,* his unopposed "invasion" of Austria, Hitler's next target was Czechoslovakia, especially its northern part, called the *Sudetenland,* which had a population that was predominantly "ethnically" German. In the summer of 1938 Hitler, aware that the Allies were desperate to avoid war, demanded the annexation of the *Sudetenland* into Germany. On September 29, British, Italian, French and German leaders met in Munich to discuss the issue and, in less than two days, agreed, without the involvement or acquiescence by the democratic government of Czechoslovakia or its people, to concede the *Sudetenland* region to Germany in exchange for a pledge of peace. Hitler's Munich Pact would make the later invasion of the remainder of Czechoslovakia considerably easier.

My paternal grandfather Nathan Dahl, Bad Withungen July 1938, prior to emigrating to Shanghai with his wife Sara in 1939 to be with his son and daughter-in- law.

Rose and Albert 39 Normannestrasse, Aachen, 1938

On October 5, 1938, the Reich Ministry of the Interior invalidated all German passports held by Jews. My family was required to surrender their old passports, and these were returned to them as valid again only after the red letter "J," for *Jude* (Jew), designating Jewish ownership, had been stamped on them.

Rose and Albert's *Machatonim* (A Yiddish and Hebrew word for the parents of the person your child has married), Nathan and Sara Dahl, were fortunate to emigrate to Shanghai from Germany in early 1939 to join their son Max and daughter-in-law, Gerda. My grandfather Nathan's passport had the red "J," but his name had not yet been changed from "Nathan" to "Israel." There was a 6-month period between the announcement of the "Executive Order on the Law on the Alteration of Family and Personal Names," and its rigid implementation. He was leaving Germany within that window. One month later he would have been required to change his name to "Israel." It is ironic that his wife, my other grandmother, who was making the identical journey to "The Paris of the Orient," has a similar passport, stamped with a red "J," but her birth name already was "Sara" so no name change would have been proscribed had she still been in Germany a month later.

On November 7, 1938, a 17-year-old Polish Jew, Herschel Grynszpan, distraught about his parents' expulsion from Germany by the Nazis, went to the German embassy in Paris and shot the diplomatic official assigned to assist him, Ernst vom Rath. Rath died two days later from his wounds. At a coincidental meeting of Nazi Party leadership that day in Munich, propaganda minister Joseph Goebbels stated that "World Jewry" had conspired to commit the assassination. He announced that "the Führer has decided that ... demonstrations should not be prepared or organized by the (Nazi) Party, but insofar as they erupt spontaneously, they are not to be hampered."

The savagery against the Jewish population of Germany and Austria that erupted during the night of November 9-10 came to be called *Kristallnacht* (The Night of Broken Glass/Crystal) because of the shards of shattered glass that littered the streets of countless German communities after the vandalism and destruction of Jewish-owned businesses, synagogues, and homes. The perpetrators set fire to hundreds of synagogues, looted thousands of Jewish businesses and physically attacked and killed Jews throughout Germany and Austria.

Just after midnight, Reinhard Heydrich, head of the Security Police *(Sicherheitspolizei)* sent urgent telegrams to *Sturmabteilung* (SA) leaders containing specific directives regarding the riots. The Storm Troopers (SA) and Hitler Youth Members wore civilian clothes during the violence to support the fiction that the plundering, looting, and violent disturbances were expressions of "outraged public reaction."

Heydrich's orders instructed police officials to arrest as many Jews, preferably young, healthy men, as local jails could hold. During *Kristallnacht,* 30,000 Jewish males were rounded up, forced to march through the cities while German civilians lined the streets to watch. They were taken to local prisons, and many were transferred to concentration camps in Dachau, Buchenwald and Sachsenhausen. This was the first time Nazi officials made massive arrests of Jews specifically because they were Jews, without any further cause for arrest.

The Aachen Synagogue prior to Kristallnacht

Among the hundreds of synagogues that burned through the night, often in full view of the public and local firefighters who stood by to watch, was the Aachen synagogue near my grandparents' new home. Rose, Else and Albert had sometimes walked from *Normannenstrasse,* crossing the *Aachen Stadtpark,* to attend Saturday morning services and admire both the Moorish-inspired architecture dating back to 1862 and the magnificent ark at the synagogue on *Promenaden-Platz.* The Torah scrolls which had been housed within that ornate cabinet now were no more, either desecrated and thrown into the street or smoldering in the wreckage. The huge bronze candlesticks, hung on seemingly endless poles, had disappeared, likely taken by authorities to be transformed into armament for a future war.

Aachen synagogue, November 11, 1938, after its destruction.

Rose and Albert's synagogue in Meschede, which had been my family's place of worship since it was constructed in 1879, was desecrated, but not destroyed by arson because it was surrounded by non-Jewish-owned homes. According to Wilfried Oertel in *Judisches Leben im Synagogenbezirk Meschede*, "destructive SA men broke into the synagogue, smashed the stained-glass windows, smashed the Torah scrolls, shredded the prayer scarves and threw them and the prayer books…into the neighbouring moat." Another squad returned "to do more thorough work. An SA man took the stone tablets with the Ten Commandments from the roof gable and smashed them with a heavy sledgehammer." A few days later, the synagogue's board was coerced into selling the building to the city of Meschede for merely 1,000 *Reichsmarks*.

The *Alte Synagoge* in nearby Dortmund, one of the largest Jewish houses of worship in Germany, where Rose and Albert had witnessed many bar mitzvahs, weddings and funerals of family members and friends, was among the majority of Germany's more than 2,000 synagogues which were destroyed on *Kristallnacht*. Little of the sanctuary or its contents remained after the fire burned and then smoldered for the entire night. The Jewish cemetery was desecrated, as it was in many other German communities.

Rose, Else, Fanni and Albert were aware of fires and shouting in their Aachen neighborhood during that night but fortunately were not personally subjected to property destruction or physical violence on *Kristallnacht*.

This was not the case, however, with their *Machatonim* in Hamm. Construction of the synagogue in Hamm had been completed in 1868. Approval for building the sanctuary included a provision that a teacher should live on the property housing the synagogue. On *Kristallnacht* that educator was my grandfather Nathan, who had come to Hamm with his wife Sara in 1922 to be the teacher of Jewish studies. They resided in the building's upstairs apartment at 5 *Martin Luther Strasse*. The Jewish community school was on the ground level and the synagogue was in the back yard of the school, accessible from the street through a narrow driveway.

A reporter from the *Westphalian Gazette* newspaper reported that he was walking towards the Hamm train station at dusk when he observed a few Schutzstaffel (*SS*) men who were busy in the alley leading to the synagogue. When he asked what they were doing, they replied that they "wanted to set fire to the synagogue." The reporter pointed out they would also set fire to the surrounding buildings. The SS troops then limited themselves to destroying the interior of the synagogue and breaking the stained-glass windows. They smashed the 120 seats and desks for the men and the 60 galleries for the women and then the *Bimah* (podium or lectern) and the *Torahad* (the cabinet holding the holy scrolls) were completely destroyed using sledgehammers and axes. The *Tallith* (prayer shawls) and the velvet Torah cloaks, embroidered with lions and the Star of David, together with the prayer books, were thrown into a heap in the courtyard. With the SS members holding the reins, horse-drawn carts were driven over the piled up holy objects before they were set ablaze.

Later that night, uniformed men broke down my Dahl grandparents' wooden door, rushed into their apartment, smashed the windowpanes, hacked their furniture into pieces with hatchets and pickaxes and threw glass, radios, china, clocks, chairs, lamps, and paintings out of the windows into *Martin Luther Strasse* below. The looting of the neighboring Jewish houses dragged on for the entire night. My grandparents, huddled in their bedroom, were physically unharmed, while their friends, the Heymann family, husband and wife, living a few blocks away at 4 *Schützenstrasse*, were killed.

On the morning after *Kristallnacht*, my grandmother Sara went downstairs into the street to see what items she could salvage to bring back to their apartment. There she found their silver *kiddush* cup, dented but intact, which we use today as Elijah's cup at our annual Passover family Seder.

A few days later, a teacher from the local school brought his class to the nearby Jewish-owned house at 40 *Hesslerstrasse*, which had also been looted and then destroyed. He explained to his students, as they wandered through the wreckage, that this was how *Verräter des Volkes,* "enemies of the people," were treated.

A month later, because the synagogue was in such disrepair due to *Kristallnacht*, the city of Hamm demolished the synagogue and, to add insult to injury, charged the Jewish community for the costs.

In the aftermath of *Kristallnacht*, German leaders like Hermann Göring made an immediate pronouncement that "the Jews," themselves, were to blame for the damage caused and violence of *Kristallnacht* and imposed a *Suhneleistung* ("atonement payment"), also known as the Jewish Capital Levy ("JUVA"), a fine of one billion Reichsmark on the German Jewish community. The Reich government confiscated all insurance payouts to Jews whose businesses and homes were looted or destroyed, leaving their Jewish owners personally responsible for the cost of all repairs.

Three days after *Kristallnacht*, the "Decree on the Exclusion of Jews from German Economic Life" closed all Jewish-owned businesses. Rose realized that it had been good that they had acquiesced to the sale of *M. Oppenheim* one year earlier. She also felt more justification in having sent Günter to America at such a young age when, on November 15, all Jewish children were expelled from German schools.

Reinhard Heydrich and Heinrich Himmler were the principal architects of the Holocaust. They both believed that merely destroying overt, "visible" opponents of the Reich including "World Jewry," was insufficient to guarantee the security and survival of the German race. Finding and destroying "camouflaged" enemies possessing international ties, who sought from within to destroy the "natural" bond between the Nazi leadership and the German people, was also necessary. In 1936, Heydrich had explained that Germans must come to realize that the "effective struggle against the enemy must derive from recognition of the fact that all visible, apparent enemies are but the tip of the iceberg of eternal, unchanging dangerous spiritual forces." As part of his attack against "the enemy," he was instrumental in the implementation of the first roundup of 30,000 individuals after *Kristallnacht*, simply because they were Jewish. This "deportation" to internal (within Germany) "concentration camps" was done with the hope that the incarcerated victims would accelerate their decision and those of their families and neighbors to emigrate, making leaving of all assets behind less significant than the Jews' fear for their lives.

On December 25, 1938, the family wrote to Günter. In order to provide a reader with the true flavor of this letter, I have printed it in its entirety so that the reader can appreciate the contrast between the mundane (what Albert ate prior to going to the Castle Hotel) and the vital passages regarding life and the future.

Velmede to Günter

From: Grandma Fanni

My dear Günter.

I have just replied to dear Helmut to the letter we received yesterday. Dear Gerda and Max had also pleased us yesterday with a letter. All loved ones are now doubly worried if they are without news from here for a longer period. Unfortunately, it is also a [very] sad time here! Can't say a lot of good things from here. It is also not good that Aunt Minna cannot be in M. now. Aunt Sophie there in M. [we] also very much pity. How is Aunt Sophie doing there in New York? Is she well again? Uncle Paul, as well as Uncle Eduard in Halle and Walther in Natzungen are back home. In Horn they even sold the shop, house, and garden during Paul's absence! - We do not yet know where uncle will emigrate with Aunt Agnes and Ruth. It's too sad these times now! - Aunt Lieschen Sternberg and her 17-year-old daughter, Anneliese, will move here next Saturday. In Plettenberg they also sold their business and house. From Cologne, Aunt Paula, Uncle Robert, and Erich are in Hannover for Christmas with their mother, Aunt Marie Hornthal, where Werner from Berlin will also be. Erich pleased us yesterday with a very good picture of himself. Unfortunately, all loved ones have to leave here! You dear Günter will certainly meet Aunt Minna and Egon's sister more often. Please give my best regards to the loved ones. It has been very cold here for a week and a lot of snow has fallen. Even the radiator is frozen up in the attic. Is it that cold there too? Tomorrow, Günter, a sausage is being sent off from here for you. Enjoy it very much. Your old grandma, who loves you, greets you warmly.

From Rose:

My dear Günter,

Your lines from December 6th made us very happy on the 21st with the attached wage calculation. I wish you, dear boy, that there will soon be a 0 behind the total, I mean that you will increase your salary. Hopefully you are doing very well in terms of health and in every other respect. Thank God we are also doing well.

It's bitterly cold here and most beautiful in the cozy, warm room. Father got together with Uncle Eduard and what can be done for Aunt M. *(Minna Baum, née Oppenheim, Albert's sister who had left Germany for the USA without selling her house and possessions in Mengede)* will be done. Has Ensinghoff already written to you about the sale? Was the Christmas business good for you and did you also get a present? Our father has just gone to the Castle Hotel after we enjoyed our coffee with fine apple pie and rice pancakes (special pastries here!ⁱ). Maybe he'll find a group of Skat *(a card game that was a precursor of bridge)* players there. For a long time, he didn't feel like doing that!

How was it at the school prom? Did you like it with the young girl's parents?

Yesterday we had news from Gerda and Max. They seem to be very worried about us, which I am very sorry about. The loved ones now see a lot of misery and hear a lot! A young man named Stern from Meinerzhagen came to them without a penny, having been unable to get a work permit in Germany and left Germany to go to Shanghai.

Paula *(Paula Liepmann, widow of Rose's brother Max Liepmann, who had remarried Robert Brunell. Paula had two children, Margot and Erich)* and her husband as well as Erich have affidavits for the USA, are just waiting to have to go to Stuttgart *(where there was an American consulate).* They are counting on June / July. Erich will soon be going to Holland to stay with one of his mother's cousins. From there his parents take him with them. Margot is doing well, she is living with a rich family in New Orleans, who treat her as their own child. She also managed to get these rich people to give affidavits for their parents and Erich, which nobody should know! Everyone in Cologne believes that Robert's brother, who is a doctor in New York, had done it. But he couldn't do it yet!

We heard from Frieda in Hamburg that her son Fritz and his wife are going to Bombay *(British India)*, where Fritz signed a three-year contract with a company. Anna and her family will emigrate to the USA in the summer, and then Frieda wants to move to Hamm. Unfortunately, her brother Alex is doing so badly financially that he has to lay cables and his wife has to work as a servant. Hilde, her daughter, and her husband in Dortmund have acquaintances from Bücken in the USA, whom they reached out to, who immediately replied very nicely. They wanted to help them and get everything necessary done to get them to the US. Then Alex and wife with Edith are supposed to go at the same time. But if only England and America opened the gates! The misery is too great. Everyone regrets, but no one helps!

Dear Günter, how wonderful it would be if, if it were sorely needed, we could all find a home in the empty house that dear Aunt Minna and Uncle Nathan once lived in, these good people *(Minna Amant, the sister of Albert's mother-in law had married Nathan Snellenburg in Philadelphia and they owned a large unoccupied house there)*. It is already a great comfort for us just to know: where should we go in an emergency? Max and Gerda are now taking in their parents and probably first

Ilse and husband too. Max wrote so nicely yesterday, but we can't all go there! *(Shanghai)* Thank God and right on cue, we still like it so much here in our house that we prefer to stay here for as long as possible. We consume what we have, live on the substance. Until then you will hopefully earn better, dear Günther, and Max and Gerda will definitely do what they can to help us. Just make sure that you get affidavits for us in the course of time, dear boy, no matter from whom. We have absolutely no desire to go to Erez!

How are Erich Berg's parents doing? Buy simple stationery, dear Günter, even if your name is not on it and be very economical! Do you want to go to the expensive club? Better save the money for necessary things! Now Helmut should also hear from me. Therefore, for today I warmly greet and kiss you, your always loving mother. PS Don't you even have a good picture of yourself to send us?

From Else:

Dear Günter,

It's Christmas Day and a heavenly peace! No one to be seen far and wide. Father has just come back from a little stroll.

Man thinks and God steers. Things often turn out differently than you think they should.

Yours, Else

In 1938, in the United States, petitions were circulated by the Jewish Peoples' Committee of New York and sent to the President and to Congress, urging the passage of House Joint Resolution 637, providing for the admission of refugees into the United States, specifically raising the quota for immigrant Jews from Germany. These petitions included signers' names and addresses and were maintained by the Visa Division. Unfortunately, due to general anti-immigration sentiment in Congress as well as antisemitism on the part of some in Congress, the resolution was not approved, and no extra visas were issued.

Chapter 13: 1939

By the beginning of 1939, German Jews had been eliminated from the German economy, their capital had been seized, although some continued to work for Aryan companies. On January 1, 1939, at the recently established Buchenwald concentration camp in eastern Germany, Deputy Commandant Arthur Rödl ordered several thousand inmates to assemble for inspection shortly before midnight. He selected five men and had them whipped to a classical music melody played by the inmate orchestra. The whipping continued for the entire night.

The events which occurred on *Kristallnacht* represented a major turning point in the antisemitic policy of the *Nationalsozialistische Deutsche Arbeiterpartei* (Nazi Party, NSDAP). The indifference with which most German civilians responded to the violence of November 9-10, 1938, signaled to the Nazi regime that the German public was willing to tolerate even more extreme measures. In 1939, anti-Jewish policy became concentrated more and more concretely into the hands of the *Schutzstaffel* (SS) under the direction of Heinrich Himmler. In addition, on January 24, 1939, Herman Göring, Hitler's right-hand man, ordered the *Sicherheitsdienst* (SD. Security Police) chief Reinhard Heydrich to organize and coordinate a "total solution" to the "Jewish question."

On the day after New Year's, the family in Aachen wrote to Günter (at times spelled Günther), living at 3118 North 15th Street, a men's rooming and boarding house in Philadelphia. I am including this letter, with every square millimeter of the onion skin pages covered in script, in its entirety, to give the reader a sense of the balance of its contents. Else, Rose and Albert write of the ordinary goings on in life, the sending of sausages and socks, birthdays and anniversaries, the love and concern that they have for Günter, together with the wishes and advice to bring him much success. However, all of these common matters, familiar to anyone who puts pen to paper to communicate with a child in a faraway land, are dwarfed by the recurring theme of how Rose, her husband, her sister and her mother could possibly extricate themselves from an untenable situation in Germany and all be together again in a secure place. There is ceaseless talk of waiting lists, visas, guarantees, all obstacles to be surmounted to reach a safe haven in the United States. In order to reassure Gunter and also themselves, the Aachen family gives example after example of those who have had or are having some success overcoming these impediments to wellbeing and life itself.

January 2, 1939, Aachen to Günter

From Else:

Dear Günther,

I want to open the dance today and thank you very much for your last lines from December 17th, received on December 31st. I can tell you that you really comforted us with it. You would have made a good preacher or lawyer! God grant that better times will come for all of us. It would be too nice if we could experience them together!

Father has applied for a waiting number for everyone in Stuttgart. By the time it's our turn, this system might not even exist anymore. Everyone is pushing for emigration and how difficult it is! Good for those who are abroad and have that behind them.

You can imagine how glad we are that Paul and Uncle Eduard and Walter came back! Last week they had a lot of work with the inventory. But at least they were allowed to sell until the end. That was by no means the case everywhere. Oskar requested them for emigration to Erez. We hope to see Uncle Paul with us soon. One has a lot to discuss. The family members from Cologne will visit us on Sunday, they were with Aunt Marie in Hannover for Christmas.

These days the Sterns from Plettenburg moved here and stayed with us the night before the furniture arrived. They got the guarantee for USA from people they hardly know. Anneliese, the 17-year-old daughter hopes to leave with the aid organization even before.

Do you know, dear Günther, that the family from Halle will get the guarantee from Stanley? They'll go to England first; and wait there for their turn. Did the Arnsberg Sterns also get the guarantee from Stanley? Uncle and Aunt Dahl *(my paternal grandparents)* have passage for the end of March from Genoa, and Radts *(my father's sister and her husband and mother-in-law)*, for the end of February to Singapore. Fritz Goldschmidt *(great grandson of Abraham Liepmann, Rose's paternal grandfather)* and his wife emigrated to Bombay at the end of December; when the Heilbrunns *(Anna Goldschmidt Heilbrunn and her husband Frederick)* go to the USA, Aunt Frieda *(Frieda Liepmann Goldschmidt, paternal granddaughter of Abraham Liepmann)* will move to Hannover, what should she do alone in Hamburg? How is your friend Bill, are his parents emigrating too? Inquiries about Shanghai arrive here every day. Everyone who wants to leave quickly and does not know where to is going to the Far East!

Herbert Sternberg from Plettenberg. who already has a guarantee for the USA with his sister, but for whom it takes too long, wants to go to Shanghai first. He is an engineer and very ambitious. He was also out of town, just as his father who turned 70 recently, who, however, soon came home for health reasons 2x. *(This sentence contains cryptic meanings: "out of town" means arrested or put into prison or deported. "For health reasons" could signify a release from prison. "2x" means a similar thing happened to both.)*

Grandma asks whether the sausage she sent you arrived? Max and Gerda were so happy with your birthday letter as they write. How is old Mr. Stern doing? Are they all over there now? Greetings to them if you should ever see them. How happy they will be that they are all back together again. It is gratifying that your business has recently picked up. Here it was real Christmas weather, snow and cold as it should be. Good thing the cold didn't last long. Greetings to Aunt Minna in particular.

Write again soon, dear Günter; if you only knew how longingly one waits from one letter to the next! Good news from you is really the one thing that can please us. Stay healthy and be warmly greeted by your aunt Else, who loves you.

From Rose:

My dear Günter,

I want to chat with you tonight in the hope that you are healthy and well like us and that you are doing well in every respect. We are always delighted to hear that from your letters, dear boy, and I thank our Lord God every day that you are all three outside the country. God grant that we will be given the chance to spend our last years near you, dear Günter.

I cannot tell you how much your last letter delighted us and comforted us, dear boy! You can talk better than a pastor from the pulpit. At the same time a letter from Aunt Minna arrived, which I replied to immediately. It will also be a great comfort to her that Uncle Eduard is back and taking care of her matters. Father got in touch with him immediately and will eventually go to Mengede with him when the time comes. Aunt Minna thinks that, because Egon will become a citizen, she could be requested to come to the USA by him before long after she comes back. If so, in her place I would leave and liquidate everything here. As I said, that's my personal opinion. Most people advise against it.

Yesterday two gentlemen from here called us to inquire about Shanghai, where they want to emigrate to with eight people. How many have already asked us in writing! All countries have closed their gates and the miserable do not know where to go in their distress. Yet, as Gerda writes again and again, there is almost no opportunity for merchants to earn a living in China. Now, even after a lot of effort, the Dahl family from Hamm finally got passage from Genoa on March 29th and Ilse with her husband in mid-February. They want to go to Singapore. Gerda wrote that they wanted to set up their large, closed veranda as a bedroom for the parents with a large couch, which can indeed be done. During the day, the beds can disappear and then it's a living room. The loved ones in Shanghai were so happy with your letter, dear Günter!

We hope that Uncle Paul will visit us soon. If only he had an existence in Erez. Oskar will furnish the guarantee for him. That may be difficult enough for him, because he hasn't been there long and doesn't understand anything about agriculture.

Dear Günter, who would give us the affidavits in an emergency? It would be a great relief for us if we then won't have to worry! Now stay healthy and write to us again soon, dear boy. With heartfelt greetings in constant love, your mother.

From Albert:

My dear Günter,

The letter should not leave without adding a few lines for you, my dear boy. I was extremely pleased about your last caring letter to us, and it had a calming effect on us all. I am especially happy that the dear cousins are so very nice and see the plight of the Jews. Who will furnish the guarantee for us then? Did you get in touch again about this? We just had a letter from Gerda, who also said that there would be no staying here for us in the long run. She and Max as well are writing repeatedly that in an emergency we should come to them, since no visa is necessary for going there. But frankly we don't feel like going there as well, since Max's parents and possibly also Ilse and her husband are already going there. We get inquiries every day from strangers really about the possibility of emigrating to China, for example this morning the Habsberg's relatives from Essen and Herbert Sternberg from Plettenberg who is going to Shanghai as an engineer have contacted us.

Goodbye, write again soon, dear boy, then your father, who loves you, will always be very happy.

Hitler's goal of making Germany racially pure and *Judenfrei* (free of Jews) was pursued from 1933 to 1939 by making existence for the Jews in Germany so miserable or impossible that they would decide to leave the country and move elsewhere. The primary means of achieving this was both making them the pariahs of their communities and creating economic havoc with their lives. On January 24, 1939, Nazi

Generalfeldmarschall Hermann Göring ordered Reinhard Heydrich to establish a Jewish Emigration Office, and informed him to speed up the emigration of Jews. Heydrich appointed Gestapo chief Heinrich Müller to head this endeavor.

After *Kristallnacht*, the Nazis commenced open seizure of Jewish property. A major form of this confiscation was the imposition of the *Reichsfluchtsteur* (escape tax), to be paid by Jews on leaving Germany ironically even when they were deported to concentration camps outside Germany. The amount of the tax initially was 25% of registered assets. As a result of this tax together with various other levies, those Jews fortunate enough to emigrate were able to carry only a small portion of their financial resources with them. Whether Jewish citizens remained in Germany and Austria or left, they were doomed to lose much, if not all, of their property. Just under half of those assets went directly to the German state. For Jews remaining in Germany after 1938, whatever assets that they still possessed were registered and kept in blocked accounts in specified financial institutions, from which only a modest amount could be withdrawn for their living expenses. Five percent of the income in the German Reich's national budget for 1938-1939 was derived from the wealth confiscated from Jewish families. Other Jewish belongings in the form of houses, businesses and goods were sold to non-Jewish Germans for vastly less than their real value.

The *Suhneleistung* (punitive or atonement Tax) even affected German Jews living abroad. The *Deutsche Steuer-Zeitung* (German Tax Journal) reported: "The tax offices are thereby being sent into the front line in the struggle against the Jews." Anyone living abroad who had registered their property in Germany in the hope of saving part of it, as it was impossible to transfer more than a tiny fraction abroad by legal means, was thus affected. German authorities subsequently used these records to confiscate their remaining property through the mechanism of denaturalization.

At the beginning of 1939, primarily due to emigration, there were less than 800 Jews remaining in Aachen, slightly more than half of what there had been prior to 1933. Rose, Albert, Else and Fanni were among those, essentially reduced to receiving sustenance derived from the Oppenheims' own confiscated assets and provided to them on a monthly basis at the whims of the Nazi government bureaucracy. My family had no other means to support themselves but continued to be optimistic despite having lost all connections to their previous lives.

The rational fear of more *Kristallnachts* to come served as a spur to further emigration of Jews from Germany in the months to come. The "voluntary" decision to leave Germany was at its worst far better than the alternative of what was to come—the policy of forced emigration including deportation of the Jewish population "to the East," and ultimately the planning for and execution of the eradication of all of European Jewry. On the sixth anniversary of his appointment as chancellor, January 30, 1939, Adolf Hitler spoke to the *Reichstag* and indicated what those intentions were: "If international finance Jewry in and outside Europe should succeed in plunging the nations once more into a world war, the result will be ... the annihilation of the Jewish race in Europe." Ridiculing the Western Allies' lack of humanitarian action in regard to the Jews, he notes that "it is a shameful spectacle to see how the whole democratic world is oozing sympathy for the poor, tormented Jewish people, but remains hard-hearted and obdurate when it comes to helping them which is surely, in view of its attitude, an obvious duty."

All of the Nazi efforts including anti-Jewish boycotts, enacted anti-Jewish legislation, confiscation and taxation of property and the threat of physical harm and death markedly enhanced the desire for German Jews to leave their ancestral home. Many families, such as mine, had already seen their younger members depart for foreign soil such as China, Palestine, the United States, Latin America, and other countries in Western Europe. However, in order to leave a nation, one needs to find a country willing to allow one's entry, the formal acquiescence of the state one is emigrating to with the issuance of a visa and, equally critically, a means to travel there.

As 1939 evolved, these hurdles to emigration from Germany are constantly reflected in the correspondence from my family in Aachen to their children scattered to the far reaches of the world. For Nathan and Sara Dahl, the Oppenheim's *machatonim*, the choice to leave for China to join their son and daughter-in law in Shanghai had been made in 1938 and that election became more resolute by their personal involvement in *Kristallnacht*. Thankfully, after multiple temporary setbacks and hurdles to overcome, they left the European continent from the port of Naples on February 27, 1939, bound for Shanghai. No visa was necessary to enter Shanghai, where Gerda and Max Dahl would be waiting to assist the senior Dahls by whatever means was necessary.

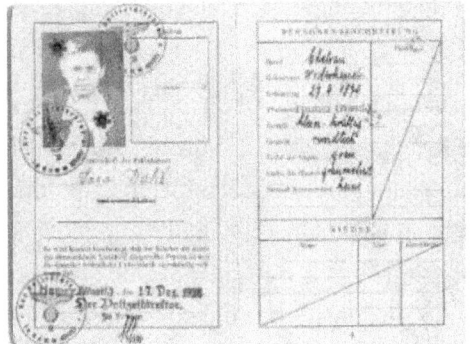
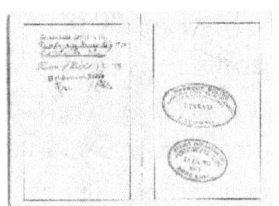
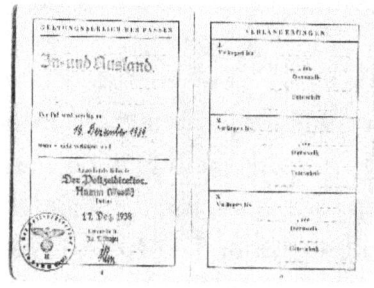

Travel documents for Sara Dahl, 1939

In mid-July 1938, representatives of 32 nations met at Évian-les-Bains, France, to specifically address the plight of German and Austrian Jewish refugees wishing to escape persecution by Nazi Germany and lacking a destination to which to flee. Rose and her family desperately listened to the radio and read the newspapers daily waiting in suspense for what occurred at Évian. President Franklin Roosevelt had initiated this meeting in part to divert attention and blame from specific American policy that severely limited the quota of Jewish refugees admitted to the United States.

Roosevelt appointed Myron Taylor as the US representative to the Évian Conference. Elected as chairman, Taylor sought to persuade the member states to accept Jewish refugees. During the nine-day meeting, delegate after delegate expressed sympathy for the Jews seeking to flee Nazi persecution, but all, with the exception of the Dominican Republic, refused to admit more refugees. The conference was a toothless charade. In 1979, the then US Vice President Walter Mondale described an alternative outcome, "At stake at Évian were both human lives – and the decency and self-respect of the civilized world. If each nation at Évian had agreed on that day to take in 17,000 Jews at once, every Jew in the Reich could have been saved."

Immediately after the Évian conference, the German Reich stated how "astounding" it was that foreign countries criticized Germany for their treatment of the Jews, but none of them wanted to open the doors to them when "the opportunity (was) offered." Hitler himself remarked "I can only hope and expect that the other world, which has such deep sympathy for these (Jews), will at least be generous enough to convert this sympathy into practical aid. We, on our part, are ready to put all these criminals at the disposal of these countries, for all I care, even on luxury ships."

In early 1939, the Wagner-Rogers refugee aid bill was introduced in both houses of the United States Congress, calling for the admission to the United States of 20,000 German refugee children under the age of 14, in addition to the immigration normally permitted. The bill was defeated in the committees of both chambers and never reached the floor for discussion. Had this legislation passed, it is highly likely that Rose's niece, Ruth Liepmann, then 10 years old, would have been sent to the United States by her parents, sparing her from her murder in Auschwitz four years later and providing my grandchildren with numerous Liepmann cousins.

During and shortly after World War I, legislation in the United States severely limited the number of immigrants who could enter the country each year. The Johnson-Reed Immigration Act of 1924 set national origin quotas, or limits, on the number of immigrants from particular countries allowed into the USA annually. The law provided that immigration visas would be provided annually to two percent of the total number of people of each nationality in the United States as of the 1890 national census, making the total number of yearly visas approximately 150,000. Potential immigrants had to apply for one of the slots designated for their country of birth, which, for German-born individuals, was 25,957 per year. After Germany's annexation of Austria in March of 1938, Austria's quota was combined with Germany's, making the annual total 27,370. These low numbers remained constant until after World War II.

The quota was the maximum number of people who could immigrate, not a target that State Department officials, many of whom were antisemitic, tried to reach. Unused quota slots did not carry over into the next year.

In 1933, the year Hitler became Chancellor of Germany, the US State Department granted only 1,241 visas to German-born citizens. More than 26,000 precious visas went unissued although there were more than 80,000 Germans on a waiting list, amounting to three years of the visa quota. From 1934 to 1937, an average of 7,053 Germans, more than 95% Jewish, received US visas annually, while a yearly average of approximately 19,000 went unissued, although there was an average of 88,000 Germans, with 99% being Jewish, on the waiting list at any given time. In 1938, more than 25% of US visas were unissued despite the waiting list growing to over 139,000 and antisemitic persecution rapidly increasing. In 1939, for the only time during the Nazi era, the State Department issued the maximum number of visas, yet nearly ten times that number remained on the waiting list. By the middle of 1939, 309,782 German-born individuals, more than 95% of them Jewish, remained on the waiting list for German-quota visas. This was almost 200,000 more than had been on that list only one year earlier. In July 1939, the US State Department would have had to issue the maximum number of visas allowable each year for more than 11 years to admit all the refugees on Germany's waiting list, a registry that would only become greater over the next two years.

In the 1936 US Presidential election, Franklin Roosevelt was re-elected with 61% of the popular vote. The Democrats gained twelve seats in the House of Representatives, furthering their supermajority over the Republicans in both the House and Senate. Roosevelt and Congress both had the power, but not the will, to alter the visa situation, both by increasing the quota and, even more importantly, insuring that people on the waiting list had easier access to visas that were left unfilled each year. Had they done so, the more than 300,000 German Jews who had applied for a visa and were unsuccessful, including my family, would have had their lives saved.

Rose, Albert, Else, and Fanni registered with the US consulate in Stuttgart, and were assigned quota numbers 46807, 46808, 46809 and 46810, extremely far down on the waiting list for American visas. They were required, while waiting for "their numbers" to be called, to gather all the necessary documents needed to obtain a visa, including identity paperwork, police certificates, exit and transit permissions, and a financial affidavit, commonly termed a "guarantee," which was achieved by obtaining financial sponsors in the United States, either relatives or friends who were US citizens, who would ensure that the alien coming to America would not place any financial demands on the United States.

Such a "guarantee" was typically a notarized document, signed by the American citizen "sponsoring" the applicant and attached to the visa application. This sworn statement typically would list the name and address of the sponsor, where he resided and, if he was a naturalized, rather than a native-born citizen, providing the certificate number and place of naturalization. An employment history of the guarantor was required together with his current salary, bank balances and life insurance policies in force.

An additional document, certified by a local Court of Common Pleas, was often attached to the guarantee to garner the attention of the small number of US immigration officials processing hundreds of thousands of "guarantee" forms. Such an affidavit named the relationship of the guarantor to the alien and furthermore stated that the undersigned "hereby promises, agrees, and guarantees, that I will properly receive and take care of them, and that I will at no time allow them to become public charges on any community or municipality, and I do further promise and agree that those aliens who are under 16 years of age, will be sent to school and will not be permitted to work until they at least reach that age."

Rose and the rest of my family also needed to have a valid ship's ticket before the actual receipt of a US visa. At the beginning of World War II in 1939, Germany had nearly 50 functioning U-boats (submarines) and ten more would be operational by the end of the year. The valid fear that U-Boats would target trans-Atlantic ships caused many passenger-ship lines to severely curtail or cease their Atlantic crossings. This made it much more difficult and costlier for refugees to find berths to the United States or Latin America.

Following *Kristallnacht*, the Nazis shut down the large number of Jewish newspapers available in Germany and, in their place, ordered the creation of one new Jewish newspaper, *"Das Jüdische Nachrichtenblatt,"* which was heavily censored. This publication published discussions and news items about the Jewish community, but only those found "acceptable" by the Nazi authorities. Many of the articles and advertisements concerned issues around Jewish emigration from Germany, which Hitler and his henchmen were still encouraging as a potential solution to the "Jewish problem." With China remaining one of the few places which a refugee could access without a visa, the demand for ship passages to Shanghai soared without supply increasing. Every issue of the *Nachrichtenblatt* had numerous advertisements by people seeking berths for ships going to the Far East, often offering huge amounts to secure such "tickets." In February 1939, the weekly letters to Günter in Philadelphia from Rose, Albert, Else and Fanni in Aachen continued and are excerpted here:

A typical page of personal requests for ship tickets out of Germany, many to Shanghai, in the classified section of the newspaper "Das Jüdische Nachrichtenblatt," 1939.

February 16, 1939, Aachen to Günter

From Rose:

My dear Gunther,

Kurt and Ilse *(Radt, sister and brother-in-law of Max Dahl, Gerda's husband)* have already been gone for 14 days and will hopefully get work in Singapore. so that they can stay where it is much better than in Shanghai... We had letters from them *(Max and Gerda)* yesterday. They are very agitated about the great misery of the refugees who arrive there in large numbers every day with no money. There is terrible misery and most of them have no income. But they don't know where else to go in their need. Very often Max and Gerda have poor Jews for dinner... You really have great musical enjoyment there. Unfortunately, we have to do without that here and we'd be so happy to hear a good opera! The radio still brings us music up to now...

Frieda from Hamburg wrote that her son Fritz and wife had a fabulous reception when they arrived in Bombay. It was more than they could ever have imagined. Fritz has a three-year contract. I hope they will stay healthy despite the nasty climate. Henny Bruck's eldest son from Berlin went to Siam three weeks ago, where he doesn't know anyone. Aunt Paula's husband, like so many others, no longer has a job and is sitting at home. They are waiting to be called up by US immigration, but that can take until late as they have high numbers.

We still have years of time with our high number, that is if we have that much time left, which few still believe. Aunt Paula sent us the attached leaflet. You can see from this, dear boy, that if you earn 25 Dollars a week and have the first papers, which is already the case with you, you can request visas for father and me as well as grandma, and we would be given preference. In an emergency you would have to try that, but only then, because where should Aunt Else go? I hope that we can all stay together.

Uncle Paul in Horn received a long letter from Oskar's parents in Israel, they urgently advised him not to come to Erez without affidavits for the USA, because they certainly could not stay there. Oskar and his family already have affidavits. and in time will move on to the USA. In Erez, people who cannot cultivate the land can only get ahead in rare cases. They consume what they have and would then be poor as a beggar. It is too sad! What shall Paul and the loved ones from Horn do? People are more likely to find work in the USA than in Erez. Uncle Paul can't farm! He is also trying to get guarantees so that he can get there from Erez. Helmut's plan to lease with his friend Pinto and run a large-scale chicken farm didn't work out because Pinto didn't feel like it, which Helmut regrets very much..... Stay healthy and be hugged by your always loving mother.

and from Albert:

    & father

From Else:

    Dear Günter,

        Grandma and I also greet you warmly and hope you are healthy. It's nice that children can request their parents' immigration in addition to the quota! But apropos of "aunts" there is nothing! I have been ordered to go to the police station tomorrow to receive my Jewish identity card. By the way, it has now turned out that Grandma's name is "Eva" just like Auntie Hermie.! (*Fanni's sister Hermine's nickname was "Eva." Fanni's identity card apparently called her "Eva" also*) We already had a good laugh about it!!

        Aunt Else

February 24, 1939, Aachen to Günter

From Rose:

    ...Erna from Natzungen and her fiancé also surprised us, he and Erna are a good match. If only they were out of the country with Walter (*Erna Vorreuter's brother*) already! Now Cuba is their hope where they have an acquaintance. I hope it works!

Ilse and her husband will have landed in Singapore by now. If only they can stay there and find work so they don't have to go to Shanghai! There must be terrible misery among the emigrants, as Gerda writes. They do not know how to accommodate them, and there is no longer any money. More and more people arrive, and the need is growing ever greater. Gerda and Max are at the end of their rope from all this sadness. They can only just invite people to dinner more often. ...

Trude Goldschmidt and Anneliese Bachmann want to accept positions in households in England and wait there until they are called up for the USA. In the meantime, Uncle Paul has also visited us. They haven't gotten any further with Erez, they are waiting, but they are also trying to get affidavits for the USA because everyone says Erez would be nothing in the long run, only for people who can farm.

Yesterday, Aunt Paula wrote to us that the information we recently sent you was incorrect. You can only vouch for us if you are a citizen! They are very much waiting for the call from Stuttgart, but it may be autumn by then.

How was your lecture received in evening-school, dear Günther? Speaking English won't be difficult for you, right?

I am surprised that Stanley doesn't even answer us a few lines to our letter on his birthday in response to father's request about the affidavits. I can read English, so he can write in English.....

Stay healthy, dear Gunther and be warmly greeted and hugged by your loving mother.

From Albert:

      & father

On February 21, 1939, yet another antisemitic law was enacted by the Nazis. The "Decree concerning the Surrender of Precious Metals and Stones in Jewish Ownership" required all Jews to turn in their gold, silver, diamonds, other precious stones, and jewelry of value to the Reich without compensation. I am certain that some German Jews complied with this request at least in part and other chose to hide away these items in "secret" places, bury them under cover of night in their back yards or send them in some camouflaged manner to relatives outside of Germany. All of these now illegal actions, if discovered, had the risk of severe punishment by officials.

Germany invaded the Czechoslovakian provinces of Bohemia and Moravia on March 15, 1939, thereby breaking the Munich pact signed less than half a year earlier.

In March 1939, the Aachen family wrote to Helmut in Palestine.

March 5, 1939, Aachen to Helmut

From Fanni:

      My dear Helmut

Happy to hear from your last letter about your well-being. God willing, these lines also reach you with the best of health, as they leave us. Since yesterday evening, dear Paul has been with us again for a day. Father actually wanted to be with Uncle Eduard in Mengede today, where they want to take care of Aunt Minna's affairs there..... The weather here these days is like spring. Today is Purim. Do you notice something of it there, Helmut?

The children from Eslohe left with a Kindertransport. Anneliese is supposed to take a job.

We had a letter from Günter this week too, thank God he is writing very satisfied. Tomorrow for you dear Helmut and also for Günter, a sausage is being sent off from here. Enjoy it very much. Since I also want to write to Günter, I will close with the warmest greetings and am your old grandmother with true love.

From Uncle Paul:

Dear Helmut!   Hopefully things will work out with our certificate, otherwise things will look bad for us! We didn't get any further with our things here either, but it will probably come soon. I will write you in more detail later. For today, greetings and kisses your Uncle Paul

From Rose:

My dear Helmut,

I have just written Günther, whose reports, thank God, are always good... A letter from Gerda and Max also arrived today. They are now having their veranda ready as a bedroom and living room for the parents (*Nathan and Sara Dahl*). ... With your detailed letter of February 18, we were very happy on the 28th, we had already worried about your long silence, dear Helmut. Hopefully, carrying heavy loads will not have any harmful consequences for you! ... Before you buy a car, dear Helmut, take someone with you who understands something about it so that you don't get cheated on. ... As for the transfer, father wrote to Paltren again and asked if it was still possible. In Horn as well as in Natzungen the goods are still exactly there as in January. Through Trude we heard that the children from Eslohe came to Brussels on a transport. She herself wants to go to England and take a job in a household there. She now lives with her parents in Cologne... We are in good health, thank God, our father is still on a diet, he just has a bit of a cold. He currently plays skat in the Castle hotel. ... If only Erna, Walter and Leo could get away! Herbert Sternberg from Plettenberg is not going to Shanghai now, he has two years of free sustenance with a company in London thanks to his excellent certificates. Well, dear Helmut, please us again soon with news and stay healthy. Grandma sent a sausage today. With heartfelt greetings in love, your mother!

On March 8, 1939, Sara Dahl wrote to my Aachen family to tell them that she and Nathan were coming to Aachen to visit. From there, the senior Dahls would begin their journey to Shanghai to join Gerda and Max. From the tone of the letter it is obvious that there were certain things Sara could not write about because of the Nazis opening all correspondence.

March 8, 1939, Hamm to Aachen

From: Sara Dahl:

My dear ones!

We will leave for Dortmund in the course of the afternoon, God willing, and will be at your place Friday afternoon God willing at ¼ to 4 o'clock.

We look forward to seeing you all again. We received the letter from the dear children *(Gerda and Max),* and we were very happy with it. When we are with them, we will be able to tell them many things or tell them what they thought were mistakes we made. One cannot arrange everything as one would like. Everything else verbally.

Best regards   Yours, Sara.

Throughout the many letters written by my grandmother Rose and family to Gerda, Helmut and Günter, frequent reference is made to the members of the Bachmann ("B.") family, the only other Jewish family in Velmede besides the Oppenheims. Just as Albert had assumed responsibility for the retail family business, *M. Oppenheim*, from his father, Albert's contemporary Max Bachmann had inherited the Bachmann general store from his father, Eliezer (Lese) Bachmann. Max Bachmann married Klara Wolf, originally from Bielefeld, and they had four children, Anneliese, born in 1906, Edgar, born in 1910, Carla, born in 1918, and Hilde, born in 1922. Edgar was a classmate of my mother Gerda in elementary school and was one of her unsuccessful suitors.

Paul Schumacher, a Velmede neighbor said, long after the end of World War II, "From 1936 to 1939, windows of the Jewish shops of Bachmann and Oppenheim were smashed in almost every second Sunday." Maria Bathen, née Schnettler, who grew up in Velmede, told a story when she was 94 years old: "On the day of the Reich's *Kristallnacht*, the Bachmann's shop windows were smashed, the duvets slashed and shaken out of the windows onto the street. In addition, pieces of meat were thrown around and many eggs were thrown. A destroyed plaster mannequin was also lying in the street."

The forced sale of the Bachmann business in Velmede occurred a few months prior to that of *M. Oppenheim*. The family then moved to Koln (Cologne), from where their children found their way to England and ultimately to the United States, settling, for the most part in Ohio. Their parents, Max and Klara, after being forced to deposit all of their assets into "The Reich Association of Jews" to purchase living accommodations at a *Reichsaltersheim* (old age home) in "the spa town of Theresienstadt," Czechoslovakia, were transported there by cattle wagons with other Jews from Cologne and then both died of "natural" causes, such as starvation, infectious diseases and suicide, before they could be moved to other Nazi extermination camps such as Auschwitz.

In March, the family in Aachen sent letters to Gerda and Max in Shanghai.

March 9, 1939, Aachen to Shanghai

From Fanni:

My dear two,

Even though we have not yet received an answer from you to our last letter, I see myself prompted again today to chat with you dear ones in writing. Because your birthday, my dear Gerta, reminds me to do so. So first of all I congratulate you heartily and wish you all the best for your new year, both of you, dear ones. Stay healthy and content, that's the main thing in this difficult time. Well, God willing it won't take much longer and you'll have the dear parents from Hamm there! You dear Gerda will surely have a particularly nice support in the household from the dear mother. The good woman has always been so efficient and hardworking so far ... If we only knew where Paul *(Fanni's son)* could start a new existence! It's all so difficult now. On Sunday father will go to Mengede here, where Uncle Eduard and Aunt Erna will be... Aunt Henny and Erna wrote to us from Natzungen this week that they also longed for the time when Walter and the bride and groom will know where they can go. Aunt Paula from Cologne writes today that Werner Hornthal and Marga now have an entry permit for Rio and will leave via Hamburg in April. Aunt Hermine, who is still in Soest together with Käthe, will also emigrate to the USA with Löwenbachs. Ruthchen from Horn now goes to Mr. Bernstein's class in Soest every week and then to Aunt Käthe. Aunt Agnes and Uncle Paul, as well as Grete and Fritz, also have weekly English lessons in Horn, the latter two have the guarantee for the USA.

Aunt Else or mother just have to find something practical in town for you, dear Gerda, for your birthday.

Now, dear ones, I wish you a pleasant birthday party and, with warm greetings, I am your old grandmother with true love.

The above section of this letter to Shanghai was written by Rose's mother, my great-grandmother Fanni, just shy of her 85th birthday. Her general optimism and faith in God shine through all the world events surrounding her, perhaps obscuring the fear of the unknown that could lie before her and her family.

It is indeed a tragedy that most of these real people Fanni writes about, all close relatives, scattered throughout Westphalia, were, in March of 1939, looking forward to some form of delivery from their current existence. They would only come together geographically three years later in the Nazi death camps of the east:

"Paul" Liepmann, Fanni's youngest son, was arrested and detained at Sachsenhausen concentration camp on December 16, 1938. He was released from there and deported from Dortmund, Germany, to Theresienstadt on July 29, 1942. He survived there for more than two years before being sent to his death at Auschwitz on September 28, 1944.

Paul's wife Agnes Sternberg ("Aunt Agnes") was deported from Dortmund to Theresienstadt, Czechoslovakia, on July 29, 1942, and died there on May 5, 1943.

Paul and Agnes' only child, their daughter Ruth "Ruthchen," Fanni's youngest granddaughter, was deported to Theresienstadt from Dortmund with her parents on July 29, 1942. She was there when her mother Agnes died and remained there after her father Paul was taken to Auschwitz. On October 6, 1944, she was murdered at Auschwitz concentration camp. It was four months after her 15th birthday.

"Uncle Eduard" Oppenheim, Albert's brother, was deported to Auschwitz in 1942. His wife Erna Baum Oppenheim, "Aunt Erna," was deported to the death camp in Sobibor, Poland, in 1942.

"Aunt Henny," Albert's sister Henrietta Oppenheim Vorreuter, was deported to Auschwitz in 1942.

"Erna," Erna Vorreuter, Aunt Henny's daughter, was deported to Lodz, Poland, in 1942 and then to the Chelmno killing center. She was the bride of "the bride and groom" in Fanni's letter. The "groom," Louis Levy, likely met a similar fate.

"Aunt Hermine," Hermine (Eva) Vorreuter Aronstein, Fanni's sister, was deported to Theresienstadt, Czechoslovakia, where she died in 1943.

"Aunt Käthe," Hermine's daughter, Käthe Aronstein Schild, never "emigrated to the USA." She was murdered in Sobibor in 1942. Her sister, Gertrud Aronstein, was deported to the Minsk Ghetto in Belorussia by the Nazis.

"Grete" Sternberg Frank, Agnes Sternberg's sister, and her husband Fritz Frank, who were having English lessons to prepare them for going to the United States, were deported to the east in 1943. Johanna (Spanier) Sternberg, the mother of "Grete" and "Aunt Agnes," died in Theresienstadt in 1943.

Having "the guarantee for the USA" as Grete and Fritz had secured, according to Fanni's letter of March 9, 1939, was meaningless. In order to gain entry to the United States, one needed immigration papers, specifically a visa. Although these "guarantees" were highly sought after and prized when obtained, in no way would they usually lead to the visa that was necessary to enter the USA. For Grete and Fritz and so many others who "have the guarantees," they were illusory and a diversion, albeit likely an optimistic one.

March 9, 1939, Aachen to Shanghai

From Albert:

> My dear ones!
>
> Today it is a bit of a special occasion especially my dear Gerda, to add a few lines for you, namely to think of you on your birthday. I warmly congratulate you, dear child, and wish you all the best, especially health and happiness for the future. If you my dear ones are also deeply affected by the many emigrants and their stories, which one can understand, you still have to hold your head up and be glad to be there.
>
> With love, your father

From Else:

Dear ones,

I hope you are healthy and in good spirits! It is time to go to bed, but first I want to wish you, dear Gerta, a very happy birthday. A few pieces of needlecraft that I am sending to you these days, I think, will bring you a little joy and if you use them, think of me. Yesterday Gertrude Levy from Hannover wrote that she and Ms. Stern were so happy about your hospitality towards Mr. *Stern (in Shanghai)*! Was he with you again? ... If only we could talk to each other! Who knows, things often turn out differently than you think! We are always happy when good news comes from you and the boys *(Helmut and Günter)*! And once again, all the best!

Your Aunt Else, who loves you.

From Rose:

My dear children,

For the rest of the day I want to chat with you and first of all tell you that, thank God, we are all doing well, which I hope will also be the case with you when these lines arrive. ...After we had several beautiful spring days, it has become unfriendly and cold again. Last night we even had a strong thunderstorm with snow flurries. The snow disappeared today... Tomorrow afternoon, the dear parents *(Sara and Nathan Dahl)* will come to us from Dortmund. We look forward to welcoming them here. I'm really curious what they will tell us, also about Ms. Radt *(Max's sister's mother-in law)*. I don't think they intend to let Kurt's mother live with you, so wait and see, dear children! It would be really lucky if Ilse and her husband find work in Singapore and can stay there. I always think that the mother will stay with them there too. So wait and see, dear children!

We received your dear letter of February 15th here on March 6th and, as always, were delighted with it. The fact that a letter from us takes 1 whole month to get to you, thank God, doesn't happen very often and I don't understand it. Tomorrow morning, Father and I have to pick up our *Kennkarten (identification cards, required of all Jews)* here at the police headquarters. Each cost 3 Mark! Aunt Else and Grandma already have them. Because Grandma cannot walk, an officer came to us and took her fingerprints here. Do you have to have these too, dear children?

Dear Gerda, we have the *(U.S. Immigration)* numbers 46808, 09 and 10. You are quite right, dear child, that will definitely take more than five years. As soon as he is naturalized, our Günter can not only request us outside of the quota, but also our grandma. We want to hope that we can stay here for that long! But it is a great comfort for us, dear children, that in an emergency we will find a refuge with you! The influx to there does not stop, on the contrary, it is still increasing, a sign of the great plight of the people, who surely know that they will not find work there. Uncle Paul was here when your last letter arrived. He also took the inserted letter for your dear parents*(Sara and Nathan Dahl)* with him as far as Hamm ... Do you already know that Helmut now and then accompanies a truck as a second driver. He often only has to sit for hours, but then again, while loading, has to carry heavy things. Hopefully he can tolerate it and advance with it! Günther has different plans every evening, and his letters are always cheerful. He and his friend Bill are often invited to the latter's very nice and wealthy relatives...

You received a nice present from Max for your wedding anniversary, dear Gerda! Your birthday is already around the corner. On this, dear child, I congratulate you wholeheartedly and wish you that you stay healthy, satisfied, and happy and that we can always enjoy good news. How much one would like to talk and see each other again! We want to hope that this wish will also come true! These days something is shipped off for you from grandma, I think stockings, dear Gerda, they always come in handy, and a bridge blanket from me... Well goodbye, dear ones, stay healthy and please write again as soon as possible. With heartfelt greetings and a birthday kiss in constant love

Your mother

The American actress, Diane Lane (1965-) has written "I love handwritten letters. The way the words get jumbled up when the writer's excited. The way the words get neat when the writer is trying not to make a mistake. I love the rebelliousness of snail mail, and I love anything that can arrive with a postage stamp. There's something about that person's breath and hands on the letter. I love handwritten letters."

The above letter was the last time Albert was able to correspond with any of his children. On March 20, 1939, he became severely ill and was taken to the hospital, as described by Rose in a card to Helmut dated the next day, written in handwriting that appears understandably shakier than usual:

Aachen, March 21, 1939

My dear Helmut,

Unfortunately, I am writing to you today from the hospital where yesterday we suddenly had to take our dear father, who is seriously ill. He came back from Mengede, where he had met with Uncle Eduard about Aunt Minna's financial affairs, with a swollen cheek and very sick. The dentist diagnosed an inflammation of the jaw and pulled 2 teeth, but it only got worse, so that yesterday we had to have it cut out from the outside on the right cheek immediately. Father is very weak and unfortunately can hardly swallow, so he gets injections with glucose and insulin, because that's the dangerous thing, he is diabetic. I am so miserable, dear Helmut, and I can't believe that our dear, good father is suddenly so seriously ill. God grant that he will get better and stay with us. Thank you very much for your letter yesterday! I can no longer write today, dear Helmut.

In constant love, your very worried and sad mother

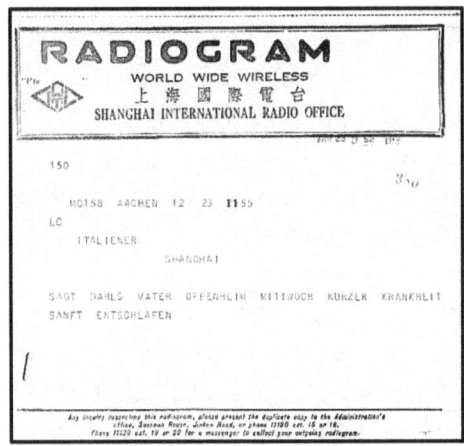

Telegram sent from Aachen to Gerda and Max Dahl in Shanghai, March 23, 1939: "Father Oppenheim Wednesday, short illness gently went to sleep."

March 21, 1939, Aachen to Shanghai

From: Fanni:

My dear Gerda and dear Max. You have probably received our last letter, dear Gerda, for your birthday. Now, unfortunately, I have to worry you again today.

Continued today March 27th: In any case, you beloved Gerda and Max already know that the beloved good father has meanwhile been released from all earthly suffering and has been resting in peace for days. Yes, who could even have guessed that the end would be so near! When I started writing this letter, a letter had just arrived that prevented me from continuing to write. Your dear parents from Hamm arrived here in the afternoon... Father came back from Halle four days later on Wednesday. Since then he has been examined by the doctor and the next day a second doctor, a dentist, was called in. Both Jewish doctors advised immediate transfer to Marien Hospital, where unfortunately he passed away there on the second day. Mother was always with him, besides a nurse. Yesterday, dear Max, your dear mother *(Sara Dahl)* surprised us. She had heard the death notice only shortly before she got here and wanted to come visit before she left for you *(to travel to Shanghai)*. Hopefully, when this letter arrives, the dear parents will have arrived safely with you, dear Gerda and Max. How have the loved ones, also Ilse and Kurt, survived the trip? After all such sad experiences, before their departure from Hamm, they had unfortunately already had to go through so much! Yes my dear ones it's too bad! We are just glad that we could still have our dear Paul here in these so sad times. Who is so loyal to us, and who is also at your mother's side with words and deeds. Today Paul has to go home again, unfortunately the loved ones there have so many worries right now! Aunt Paula from Cologne, as well as Mr. Bachmann and Trude Goldschmidt were here for the funeral. Uncle Adolf Sternberg from Plettenberg. From Horn Gustav Spanier. Aunt Henny from Natzungen left here yesterday. Walter, as well as Leo, Erna's fiancé, the latter, like Anneliese Sternberg, was so diligent in looking after all the guests. My niece from Düsseldorf, Wanda Aronstein, and Erich Wolff from Perleberg were here. From dear Helmut and Günter we already had telegrams from Erez and USA, also from Stanley. Aunt Erna and Uncle Eduard traveled back to Halle yesterday morning. God willing we will soon receive good news from you both as well as from the good arrival of your dear parents there. Paul has to leave for Horn soon. He's still in town with mother. That's it for today.

Dear ones, in true love I greet you warmly your old grandmother, grieving with you.

From Rose:

My dear children,

I find it so difficult to write, and yet I want to get myself up and send you a few words. I still can't believe that our good father has left us forever. Everything is like a bad dream and yet it is bitter truth. With us everything is now desolate and empty, everywhere we miss the dear one who has passed away. It is a great consolation to me that our dear father passed on so calmly and gently without a fight. It was just before 2 a.m. in the night from Tuesday to Wednesday. I sat by his bedside until his last breath with a nurse who was there at night. It looked exactly as if our good father was slumbering. In the morning he had once again spoken to me, later he almost always slept. The bad thing was that he couldn't swallow anymore. The three doctors at Marien Hospital tried very hard, but all the injections no longer helped. We never want to forget our dear and good father! Your good mother *(Sara Dahl)* was with us for a few hours yesterday, which made me very happy. Today on the 27th they left Hamm. She can tell you all the details.

How are you, dear Gerda and Max? Hopefully you are healthy. Could Ilse and Kurt not land in Singapore after all and are they there now? Did Ilse get sick on the way? Now I have to close for today and I hope to hear good things from you soon. We get a lot of letters of condolence.

Your very sad mother hugs you in constant love

From: Else

My Dear Two,

What unsettling, bad days we have behind us! Your dear good father, our faithful caring advisor has passed away! We just can't believe it! It is almost as if life no longer has a purpose for us. Who would have thought that the end would come so quickly. And yet we have to take courage and not lose our nerve, even if it is often too difficult! "Cheer up," beloved mother, grandma and aunt Else were telegraphed by the two boys, as if by appointment, and we want to heed that! Today, 8 days ago on March 21st, Uncle Paul and I were in the hospital in the afternoon and your dear father slept and slumbered all day. Mother, who devotedly cared for him, and did not leave his bedside, had gone there early in the morning, and stayed with him until the end. Little did we know that the end was so near, otherwise Uncle Paul would have stayed there. It was lucky that when we called on Sunday he came immediately and stood by us loyally. There was so much to do. All relatives who escorted Father send you warm condolences and greetings. It was a simple, impressive celebration in the cemetery. Mother and I were there, the other women stayed with Grandma at home. The Sternbergs (Dienchen and Anneliese), Aunt Henny, Aunt Erna, Aunt Paula, Aunt Wanda. Our little house has probably never had so many visitors. Everyone was absolutely thrilled with how beautiful it was here. Arnold Liepmann from Essen was also here. How happy the dear blessed father always was when he could show guests the house from top to bottom. Neither the attic nor the cellar was forgotten! The only thing that can comfort us and you is that he was spared a <u>long</u> sickbed and that he had such a gentle death as he deserved it! May the earth be light to him! He has no more worries. I silently squeeze your hands, and I am with you in spirit.

Yesterday Mr. Meier was with us to give condolences. He wants to emigrate to Shanghai with eight people; that is enough! He doesn't know any other way out. He asked us to ask you whether it would be profitable to make vinegar, oil, orangeade, and soup seasoning there; with which he could subsist well here. What do these articles cost there?

Today, thank God, we had good news from both boys... Dr. Schuster, father's attending physician, sends greetings to Dr Meyerbach *(A physician who had also emigrated to Shanghai).*

With love, your aunt Else.

Condolence card Fanni to Helmut, March 29, 1939:   "Warm Sympathy"

From: Grandma Fanni:

My dear Helmut,

Because I fear the letter will become too heavy, I have to express my condolences to you, dear boy, on the sadly sudden death of the beloved blessed father on this card. Yes, dear Helmut, I still cannot grasp that the dear departed is no longer with us! Unfortunately, I am spared nothing. I must see everyone die who was so close to me. Must survive all. In these sad times, our dear Paul is still so loyal at our side. He too has so much worry and grief himself, especially because his wife Aunt Agnes cannot get rid of her annoying cough. I also have to write to Günter and Aunt Minna and Uncle Max in New York.

Therefore, dear Helmut, for today only heartfelt greetings

from your grandmother who is grieving with you

Albert was buried in the *Jüdischer Friedhof Lütticher Straße* (the Jewish cemetery in Aachen on Liège Street), established in 1822, adjacent to the site of the ancient *Jakobstor* (Jacob's city wall tower and gate), later renamed the "Liège Gate" during the brief Napoleonic Empire's occupation of Aachen.

Anatole Paul Broyard (1920-1990), an American literary critic, wrote "In an age like ours, which is not given to letter-writing, we forget what an important part it used to play in people's lives."

March 28, 1939, Aachen to Helmut in Palestine

From Else:

My dear Helmut,

We have just written to Gerta, now you shall hear from us too. This morning we enjoyed your letter of March 18th, and a cheerful letter from Günter arrived at the same time. Little did we know then that the death of your dear and good father would bring us such great sadness. We can't believe

173

that he has passed away forever, the faithful advisor to all of us. It all came too suddenly. On Sunday he went to Dortmund with Dahls *(Sara and Nathan)*, where he stayed until Wednesday. Then he laid down and did not get up again. Mother told you that we had to take him to the hospital on March 21st, and on the 22nd he passed on peacefully. Mother did not leave his sickbed and cared for him self-sacrificingly. For days he consumed nothing but liquids; and was always thirsty. Uncle Paul came to us upon our phone call on Sunday and stood by us faithfully. On Monday he and mother took dear father to the Marien Hospital, where three doctors took care of him. On Tuesday, Uncle Paul and I went to see him, but he slumbered all day and at 2 1/2 o'clock at night he passed away peacefully. On Friday Mother and I escorted him to his final resting place. The funeral service in the hall and at the grave was simple and moving. The teacher spoke well. Many dear relatives were here to pay their last respects to the blessed father... The ladies all stayed at home with Grandma, who lost her best friend! How well she got on with father, they always had the same opinion and father always agreed with her... Now you have to always say Kaddish *(the Jewish prayer for the departed, recited on the anniversary of their death)* Helmut, for dear, blessed father. We have a little light burning for him day and night. May the earth be light to him! We also sent announcements to the old neighbors in Velmede. We have received a huge number of condolence letters also for you, since most of them do not know your address. Ms. Bachmann and Anneliese also wrote. Bachmann's house was bought by her across the street neighbor Strute. Next week it's already Passover. We are expecting Uncle Paul and if possible, Aunt Agnes will come along too. Ruthchen may go to school here, then we won't be so alone.

now dear Helmut, I must say goodbye and send my love.

From Rose:

My dear Helmut,

Even if it is very difficult for me to write, I will still pull myself together and add a few lines to Aunt Else's detailed report for you. By the coming night a week has now passed since our dear, unforgettable father closed his eyes in eternal slumber. I often cannot believe it, and yet it is the sad truth. It is a great consolation for me that our dear father had such a beautiful death; without a fight he fell asleep peacefully. I sat at his bedside with a nurse who was there at night. Father spoke to me early in the morning and said when I came: "It's good that you are here. But now we want to go home again!" Then I gave him something to drink, he was always very thirsty and he fell asleep again. The bad thing was that he didn't eat anything. All the injections were of no use. The diabetes was the worst part of it! In any case, you received my card from the hospital by airmail, dear Helmut. You and Günter sent dispatches at the same time, both with the same words: Cheer up! Stanley also sent a dispatch. Lots of letters arrived. The relatives all ask about you and express their condolences to you children. We haven't heard from Gerda and Max yet. Hopefully they are healthy.

Stockings, dear Helmut, Grandma will be very happy to knit for you. You can get many from our dear, blessed Father. Should the sweater be in blue again? ....

Have you found a place in Tel Aviv where you feel comfortable, dear Helmut? Hopefully you will find a job that suits you and that feeds you. Enclosed Günter's last letter that you can keep... Well, dear Helmut, please write again as soon as possible and often say kaddish for our unforgettable dear father. May he rest in peace!

Your very sad mother hugs you with heartfelt greetings.

The Marien Hospital in Aachen, where Albert died, was founded in 1853 by the Franciscan Sisters of the Poor. It was a full-service Catholic hospital with about 120 beds, which, in 1939, had neither given up its political independence nor succumbed to Nazi eugenics and exclusion of Jews from society. The 1934 law for the prevention of hereditary offspring was never implemented at this hospital. There is nothing to suggest that Albert, as a German Jew, received anything but good care.

The former health department of the city of Aachen was located at *Bahnhof Platz*. In the wake of the National Socialist racial madness from 1934 onwards, that department persuaded compliant local physicians to label several hundred women, men and children as "inferior" and forcibly sterilize them in seven Aachen hospitals or from 1941 to 1945 either to commit "euthanasia" to "prevent hereditary offspring" or to send them to various institutions where they were murdered in other fashions.

1939 letter from Fanni to Helmut, written in Kurrentschrift (cursive script), an old form of German handwriting based on late medieval cursive writing.

1939 envelopes addressed to Helmut

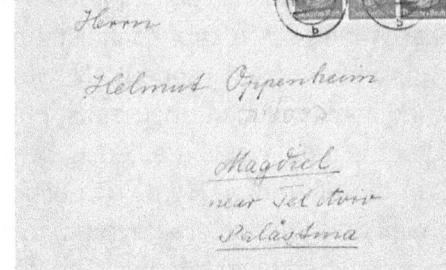

March 31, 1939, Aachen to Helmut

From: Grandma Fanni on *M. Oppenheim* stationery:

My dear Helmut,

Just now, your dear letter is a consolation to us, especially to your dear mother, in this sad time. At the same time, dear Günter's lines were so warmly welcomed. Yes, you dear children

175

unfortunately all too early, had to lose your best, loyal father! We must all seek to submit to the inevitable. There is still no news from dear Gerda. .... Erna's fiancé from Cologne was also here with Walter and Aunt Henny from Natzungen. If only the loved ones can finally move on with their emigration! We heard with delight, especially Mother, that you'll say Kaddish, Helmut. Günter will probably do it too. Uncle Paul is also very worried. At Easter he will probably come here with Aunt Agnes. We will send you stockings dear Helmut, which I have just knitted for dear blessed father, along with others soon.

In true love, Helmut, your grandma greets you.

Aachen, April 3rd, 1939

From Rose: .

My dear Helmut,

Only today can I add a few lines for you to Grandma's because I couldn't get myself up to write... Thank you very much, dear Helmut, for your comforting words on the 25th, which arrived here at the same time as a lovely letter from Günter on the 31st. Yes, dear children, you are right, all crying and wailing is of no use, our unforgettable good father has left us never to return. As hard as it is, we want to be brave and keep our heads up. But we all want to keep Father's memory in our hearts and never forget him! You children were his greatest joy and when mail arrived from you his face beamed. Lately he has been crying sometimes while reading your letters, so I read them out loud and said to him: "We want to thank God that all three are gone!" Yes, dear Helmut, our father always only looked after us; he thought of himself last. I and we miss him everywhere. Often I think it is a terrible dream and I will hear his step like before! Life lies before me dark without light! May God help us to face this stroke of fate steadfastly and may he save us all from further suffering! Have we already written to you, dear Helmut, that our father came home from the trip to Mengede with a swollen cheek and immediately lay down because he was not feeling well? The doctor came, brought a dentist with him, but who did not want to pull the tooth out of the swollen cheek and prescribed chamomile compresses, which I then kept administering. Father slept a lot, could only consume liquid food, and could not open his mouth properly. Now a lump formed on the outside of the right cheek, and as father's condition worsened, the dentist pulled his molar. Thank God our good father was no longer in pain. After the tooth was extracted in the morning, we took him to the Marien Hospital in Burtscheid (Aachen) in the afternoon. He didn't notice anything because he was always sleeping. There they cut the cheek and the doctors gave us hope. Dear Helmut, if it hadn't been for the sugar our good father would have lived still today. The sugar was the dangerous thing. He got insulin shots and others for the heart.

The doctors tried very hard, often came during the day, but everything was in vain. Our good father did not eat any more, and he slumbered quietly and peacefully into a better afterlife. This is a consolation for me, my dear boy, that I saw our dear, unforgettable father fall asleep without any struggle, Such a beautiful death is not bestowed on many people! I sat at his bedside with a nurse until the end. It was around 1 3/4 in the night from Tuesday to Wednesday when our beloved father fell asleep forever. Our father never complained beforehand, he ran like a rabbit, did most of the shopping for us and liked to go to (play) Skat often. But the excitement of the last time was also poison for him, and unfortunately nobody was spared that. Whenever he went away, he came back halfway sick, especially from what he heard of suffering and grief on the way. It would have been best not to go to Mengede! But who knows everything beforehand? It is not easy to sort out Aunt

Minna's business. That surely upset him too! At the funeral at the school, the rabbi described father as beautifully as he was. He said that his eyes shone when mail came from you children from China, Palestine, and America. We have a small electric light on in the room for father and it is a great joy for me that you, dear Helmut, say Kaddish as often as you can. Günter will probably not miss it either.

I'm worried because we haven't heard from over there after we sent a dispatch to China! Maybe Max didn't tell Gerda. Their nerves also seem at an end, as they often wrote. ... It must be terrible in Shanghai for the many immigrants, and it won't be long before Max's parents arrive. ... May God direct everything for the good! Tomorrow you will get two pairs of stockings. Do you prefer gray or black, dear Helmut? We have so many from our dear father. Can't you make use of nightgowns? It's Yontef, so enough for today. How much our father loved Passover and Mazze! Farewell, my dear boy, stay healthy and be hugged and warmly greeted by your so sad   Mother

From Fanni:

My dear Helmut.

Hopefully you have the festive season well behind you. I was pleased to see from your letter that you, like dear Günther, did not fail to say Kaddish for your dear, blessed father. How sad I certainly feel! The dear departed is well! - He has no more worries and sorrow! Did you, dear Helmut, tell Kerren that the dear blessed father unfortunately died here? ... Greetings from your old grandmother who is grieving with you.

Rose placed a notice of Albert's death in the Jewish newspaper, *"Das Jüdische Nachrichtenblatt."* It is translated "After a short severe illness my most beloved husband, our most caring and unparalleled father, father-in -law, brother, brother-in-law and uncle, Mr. Albert Israel Oppenheim, of Velmede, went to sleep on the 22nd of March in his 64th year. In deep sorrow, in the name of all those he left behind. Rose Sara Oppenheim, born Liepmann. 39 Normannenstrasse, Aachen. Shanghai, Magdiel, Philadelphia."

Death notice placed by Rose in the Jewish newspaper, "Das Jüdische Nachrichtenblatt," April 1939.

Albert's middle name was not "Israel" nor was Rose's middle name "Sara." The use of these names in the published death announcement was in accordance with the Nazi mandate as of January 1, 1939, that "If a Jew bears a name differing from those which can be given to Jews, he must adopt an additional first name, namely Israel in the case of a male and Sara in the case of a female."

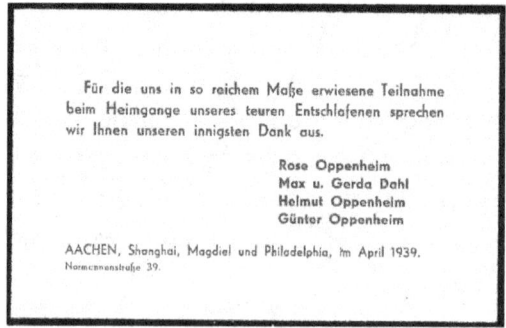

The correspondence from Aachen to Helmut continues:

April 14, 1939

From Fanni:

My dear Helmut,

... I just want to start answering your letter of the 8th that we received this morning. ... Did you receive the stockings and sausage? Your letter of today pleased us, because we saw your well-being from it. We are also healthy so far. Unfortunately, it is often so infinitely difficult to get used to the sad reality of having to do without the beloved blessed Father forever! But what good is all brooding and the dear departed is better off than us bereaved! Who can be resentful of God's acts? One has to endure with devotion what God has given us...

This week we also had the first letter from dear Gerda after the dear blessed father's death. Unfortunately, she also wrote so sadly and could not yet get used to the sad reality.

The loved ones from Hamm *(Sara and Nathan Dahl)* sent us a card en route from Italy this week. Ilse and Kurt are already in Shanghai, as Gerda wrote to us earlier. Hopefully they'll find employment. .... Thank God our Paul is coming next week and will bring Ruth, who is supposed to go to school here. ... The future of our Paul also worries us immensely... In the garden here the plum and cherry trees are in bloom. How much did father love the garden and the house...

Lilly Vorreuter is also in Essen, with her uncle who is supposed to be doing very well in financial terms... Günther wrote today that he also had a letter from Heinz, who is still getting on well in the aviation profession... We also had a letter yesterday from Ms. Hücker from Velmede, who ... writes, among other things, that Padberg and Müller are not that popular in Velmede, that customers don't like to come to them as much as they used to be at "Oppenheims!" As *Kaffers (the German pejorative for thick-headed people—this is as close as my grandmother came to using obscenities)* they are, did not even send condolences to the announcement of the passing of the dear blessed father! – On Sunday I also have Yorzeit of the dear blessed cousin and two days later also of the death of our dear blessed mother, which have been resting for 41 years. They died in the same year as my dear blessed husband, your grandfather. Dear Helmut. Uncle Paul was only 5 years old at the time. How much grief and misery we have seen since then! - But enough for today, dear Helmut. It will soon be Sabbath; I also want to write to dear Günther beforehand. Warm regards, dear boy, in true love, your old grandma

From Else:

Dear Helmut,

I hope you have long since received the due post from here and you don't worry unnecessarily about us... You will surely understand that we often have to muster all courage and all strength to find our way around. May God help us all and keep suffering and hardship away from us in the future. We have to accept what he inflicts upon us to bear. It all came too suddenly. One didn't even have to think about it until suddenly everything was over. I don't think your dear blessed father was expecting such a quick end. He hardly complained and is now better off than any of us. We want to give him the rest that we can only envy him for.

Eight days ago today, mother and I went to the cemetery; and decorated the grave with fir trees and blooming flowers. That will probably always be our destination for walks in the future. Above the portal is written in large letters: Here be peace, grant it to the weary one. The rabbi talked about it splendidly on Yom Kippur in the synagogue. We were also there at Passover for the service... Now, dear Helmut, until the next letter. With love,

Aunt Else

In May of 1939, any thought Rose had of joining Helmut in Palestine vanished, when the British government, in the "MacDonald White Paper," rejected the establishment of an independent Jewish state in the Middle East and severely restricted both future Jewish immigration to Palestine and future purchase of land by Jews in Palestine. British Prime Minister Neville Chamberlain supported this as part of his attempt to curry favor with the Arabs of the region and bring them into any coming war on the side of Britain. Chamberlain's appeasement efforts failed to persuade the Arabs, just as it had with the Germans at the Munich Conference. Although many Algerian Arabs fought with the French Army, tens of thousands of Arab Muslims fought for the Nazis in World War II. Hitler had a plan to extend the Holocaust to the Middle East and forged an alliance with Arab nationalists.

In September 1939, a few days after the beginning of World War II, David Ben-Gurion expressed the complexity of Zionist policy to Britain in his famous statement: "We must help the British army as if there were no White Paper, and we must fight the White Paper as if there were no war." After the White Paper, "illegal" immigration from Germany to Palestine was pursued by German Jews, with 27,000 taking this route before the end of 1940.

On May 13, 1939, the German liner *St. Louis* sailed from Hamburg, Germany, to Havana, Cuba. The 937 passengers were almost all Jewish emigrants, all holding landing certificates and transit visas issued by the Cuban Director-General of Immigration. The majority of the Jewish passengers had applied for US visas and had planned to stay in Cuba only until they could enter the United States. Even before the ship sailed from Hamburg, right-wing Cuban newspapers deplored its impending arrival and demanded that the Cuban government cease admitting Jewish refugees. Just one week before the ship sailed from Germany, Cuban

President Federico Laredo Bru issued a decree that invalidated all recently issued landing certificates. The Cuban government refused to allow the refugees to disembark from the ship. On June 2, Bru ordered the ship out of Cuban waters and the *St. Louis* sailed slowly toward Florida. It came close enough for passengers to see the lights of Miami, but the ship was denied entry into the harbor. Some passengers on the *St. Louis* cabled President Franklin D. Roosevelt asking for refuge. Roosevelt never responded. The State Department and the White House had decided not to take extraordinary measures to permit the refugees to enter the United States. A State Department telegram sent to a passenger stated that the passengers must "await their turns on the waiting list and qualify for and obtain immigration visas before they may be admissible into the United States." The *St. Louis* then returned to Europe and some of the passengers were finally permitted to land in western European countries rather than return to Nazi Germany. However, 254 *St. Louis* passengers were killed in the Holocaust. One of the survivors said, "You know, we always cling to the hope something is going to happen. They're not going to let us rot on the ocean. I mean, something had to happen to us. Of course, the fear was that we would go back to Germany."

Rose, Else and Fanni in Aachen say goodbye to Erich and Paula Liepmann, who are on their way to the United States, June 3, 1939. The person on lower right is Marie Hornthal, Paula's mother.

My father, Max Dahl, in Shanghai, 1939

Anton Bamfaste was the longstanding postmaster in Velmede and knew Rose and Albert and their family well. The following two translated letters from Rose to *Herr* (Mr.) Bamfaste are representative of her communication with non-family members.

June 14, 1939, letter from Rose to Anton Bamfaste in Velmede

June 14th, 1939

Dear Mr. Bamfaste,

I have always wanted to write you a few words of thanks for your words of comfort on the passing of my dear and unforgettable husband, whom a cruel fate tore from me too early. It is doubly hard for me and all of us because our children are far away, and yet I thank our Lord God every day that all three of them are gone and that we have always been delighted with good news so far. Thank God Gerda's husband has a good practice, and two months ago the in-laws from Hamm moved to them. The old people like it very much with the children, who ask us in every letter to come to them all. But we want to stay here as long as possible. It's so cozy in our house! The roses bloom in the garden and the fruit trees are full of fruit. Our old mother, who unfortunately can hardly walk, sits a lot on the large terrace and thinks about the good times past. Unfortunately, she has to experience a lot of sadness! How much my dear Albert liked it here. He was not allowed to enjoy the quiet here for long. But now, dear Mr. Bamfaste, how are you, your dear wife and three children? Hopefully they are all healthy. What is Tony doing? Does Meinolf still go to school and does Alfons work in your business? I think of all of you a lot! What else is new there? Thank goodness our two boys are doing fine too. Helmut is a chauffeur on a truck and gets to know the whole country in the process. It's hard work, but he likes it. Our Günther is our sunshine. His letters always delight the whole house. But he's also well and everyone likes him. If we stay healthy, we hope to join him in the future. Is Bachmann's house still empty? How is our old neighbor, Mr. Anton Mieder and the old Mrs. Meier and Mrs. Baker Burmann? Many greetings for the three of them and also for the dear accountant Schmier. Is the sick child still alive?... If someone from your family comes to Aachen, you are cordially invited. We live in a green area, just as quietly as in the country and yet close to the city. Well goodbye, very warm greetings from my mother and sister and especially from yours

Mrs. Albert Oppenheim   Greetings for your dear family.

July 7, 1939

Dear Mr. Bamfaste,

By answering your detailed letter quickly, I would like to show you how happy we were all about it... I was happy to hear from your report that you and your loved ones are doing as you wish. Thank God we too are healthy and, to our great joy, we receive good news from our children. So yesterday we had a long letter from Gerda and husband who, thank God, are very satisfied with the practice and have been taking in their parents for a few months now. The old people also like it a lot with the children, they just have to get used to doing nothing. In Shanghai there are still many refugees from here and from Austria who do not know where to go. They are terribly to be regretted, as the available funds are only sufficient for scant provisions.

I read the news from Velmede with great interest! Nieder Anton was certainly a jolly shooting champion. He must have been more pleased with the new honor than his father. I'm sorry that Frau Vogel had to die so young! How are things at Huber? Your Meinolf certainly looks dashing in his uniform! I think it's a good job that he wants to take up.

As for the matter of the promissory note, dear Mr. Bamfaste, I have to tell you that I have no doubt that your brother-in-law is right. I just cannot understand how my dear blessed husband could forget that he had given the note in payment. I know he was looking for the note and thought he had misplaced it. Would you please tell this to Mr Dröge and tell him at the same time that he may excuse me for having reminded him. But I couldn't have known it.

A few days ago, I visited my dear husband's grave, where the flowers bloom so beautifully. There is peace and quiet there, and all who sleep in eternal rest are to be envied. They have no more sorrow or worries and they are comfortable. I would be really happy if you or someone from your family came to visit us. Then we could chat about old times! Thank God we still like it here very much. We haven't longed to go back for one moment. Now farewell to you all and to you and your dear relatives the best greetings from my old mother, my sister and yours

Rose Oppenheim

In the letter above, Rose refers to the failure of the purchasers of *M. Oppenheim* to pay the promissory note that they had signed. Rose had been told by Mr. Padberg that it had been paid in full prior to my grandfather Albert's death. However, the payment was never recorded in Albert's notes and Albert had never told her about receipt of the money. Given my grandfather's attention to record keeping and the close relationship between Albert and Rose, I find that highly unlikely. It appears that even the pittance that was promised for the store was never paid.

In August, the family wrote to Helmut in Palestine. All these and future letters had to pass through the hands of both German and British censors, the latter located in Palestine, both of whom opened the letters and, after perusing their content, could continue them on their way or send them to another department, in the case of Germany to deal with punishment of the authors, and in Palestine, investigate the recipient of the letter.

August 20, 1939

From Fanni:

My dear Helmut.

Your last letter for mother's birthday arrived punctually and together with Gerda's and Günter's letters delighted us through reports of your well-being The heat here this summer is very easy to bear here and here in the garden, on the terrace it's always airy and not too hot. ...Uncle Paul was recently in Berlin and Bielefeld. But all to no avail. Hans Mosberg from Bielefeld is also in England

and wants to wait there until he can enter the USA. ... How happy Margot will be, who longingly awaits the time until her loved ones come! (*This refers to Paula Liepmann leaving for the USA with her son Erich, where his sister Margot had been for a few years.*)

Dear Erich also visited Aunt Frieda Goldschmidt in Hannover when he was with his grandmother Aunt Marie Hornthal. The latter wrote yesterday that she was so happy with Erich. I am also so sad that the dear boy will have to leave soon. So they leave one after the other! -... Now, dear Helmut, that's it for today. Your old grandma greets you deeply in true love.

From Rose:

My dear Helmut,

Grandma has already reported everything new from the family, so first of all I want to thank you warmly for your birthday wishes and for the coffee that Aunt Else fetched from customs today. It cost 75 pfennigs. Dear Helmut, you shouldn't send anymore. You'd better save the money you have to earn so arduously! .... What kind of work do you have with the car now? Did you find a nice apartment and have you furnished your room comfortably? ... Have you now answered Gerta and Günter's letters? I'm curious to see if the little one *(Günter)* went on vacation and where he went... ... Everyone who wants to work gets a job here, and everyone is treated well. *(This appears to be a reference to the Nazis imposing forced labor on the Jews, with Rose trying to pass this through the censors.)* Schuster Gerdes wrote on the order for payment that he wanted to pay in four installments of ten marks each month. Hopefully he will keep his word. Dreiers are really bad, despite their promise to send 10 marks in July and then every month they haven't sent a penny. I now have to apply for foreclosure. Treseken still owes the interest from last year and does not pay off the mortgage. I have to send the bailiff to her, although I hate to do it. They're Gäscht *(a Yiddish derogatory term for beggars—Rose is hoping that the censors will not know this word, since she is describing multiple non-Jewish people who still owe considerable money to M. Oppenheim).* In response to the payment orders, the following paid *(their debts to M. Oppenheim)*: Gödden (Muses) Nuttlar, widow Bernhard, Hücker and Hückelheim (Frau von der Hardt) Friedrich Gerdes from Ev. and Artur Büttner. The matter against Padberg and Müller will be dealt with in writing. I am very afraid that I will lose and have to pay a lot of costs on top of that. If only I had done nothing in this matter? But you can't put up with everything. Well, dear Helmut, I want to tell you that I am very happy when you light the lights for our dear blessed father and say Kaddish. I went to the cemetery with Aunt Else on Father's birthday. Now stay healthy, dear boy, and write to us again very soon.

With constant love, your mother

From Else:

Dear Helmut, we have just enjoyed our evening meal of "thick milk" *(a German form of yoghurt)*. Now I want to chat a little with you... This morning, I had to go to the dentist, also had other things to do, so I went to the customs office and picked up the delicious coffee from you. That's a long way from us! Next to the main station and I arrived there just before closing time, one o'clock; it was pouring down with rain and since the driving conditions here are miserable, we have to walk almost 20 minutes before we reach the tram stop, I said to myself: If you have now received the things, you'll be reckless and buy yourself a car! But first it comes differently, second then you think. For Günter's birthday present I was supposed to shell out so much that I gave it up. I had brought 20

Marks and it was still not enough! We were so sorry for the "little one" he wanted to make us happy and certainly did not suspect that it would cost us so much. A dress, he wrote cost only 1 dollar 39..., He should never send anything like that again. They are artificial silk dresses, light for the summer. So I went home on the tram, quite saddened. Aunt Minna always darns Günter's socks so nicely. He usually sends her about 20 pairs! I wonder if he's on vacation... Last year we went by car to see everything and then father and grandma were there too. One can't even begin to think. When grandma is alone at home, her time gets long and you don't have peace either. When we take her out in the wheelchair, we stay close by in the park. It's uphill almost everywhere here, and you can't get anywhere with the heavy chair. It's so nice on the terrace and there is fresh air there, too. Grandma is all tanned. But she also likes to see something different. It's a pity that you both, Günther or you can't take her to the park! Father did not let go at the time, grandma had to go with him to the top of the Lousberg, and he helped.   Cordially your aunt Else

In Lewis Carroll's 1871 book, *Through the Looking Glass*, the twins Tweedledum and Tweedledee recite a poem entitled "The Walrus and the Carpenter." One stanza of this reads

> The time has come,' the Walrus said,
>   To talk of many things:
> Of shoes — and ships — and sealing-wax —
>   Of cabbages — and kings —
> And why the sea is boiling hot —
>   And whether pigs have wings.'

As the beginning of World War II approaches, the letters from Rose, Else and Fanni written lovingly and carefully by hand to Gerda, Helmut and Günter continue to contain both the mundane "cabbages" and sausages together with the existential "kings" and survival. From this point forward, I have severely edited the many letters to concentrate on the phrases that are consistent with the issues that are foremost in the minds and hearts of both the authors and the recipients of these letters. In each letter, Rose articulates gratitude for having received correspondence from her children and expresses the joy of reading each word. Else and Fanni often echo her sentiments.

August 30, 1939, Aachen to Helmut

From Fanni:

> My dear Helmut,
>
> Yesterday I wanted to write a reply to your last letter...- It's too sad if war breaks out! Günter and the loved ones from Shanghai write contentedly too, thank God... We are unfortunately still very worried about our loved ones in Horn! If only they knew where to go with their old in-laws and Aunt Emilie!... And Uncle Paul! – has no prospect of getting away with his family either... Wish you, dear boy, good holidays and with heartfelt greetings, I am your old grandmother with true love.

From Else:

> Dear Helmut, ... You probably listen a lot to the news on the radio right now, just like us! God grant that the impending danger of war will pass again, it would be inconceivable! ... Earlier, mother cleaned the paths in the garden, now it's so beautiful to look at. I'm so sorry that you can't even come and see it. The fruit trees all have particularly beautiful varieties! The peaches, plums, apples, and

pears! It is a splendor! It is a pity that our dear blessed father did not see it, and yet he is better off than we are.

From Rose:

My dear Helmut,

... Hopefully by the time these lines arrive you will be as healthy as we were and completely rid of the annoying rash on your back... Uncle Paul is very keen on going to Australia and has requested the papers for it. The stay in England would take a long time and would cost far too much because Uncle Paul has such a high waiting number. For Australia you also need showcase money. If only the war won't break out! That is our greatest concern! Grandma made the enclosed handkerchief with loop hole embroidery for you, dear Helmut! Don't lose it!...

I am very sorry that the shirt was stolen! It was from our dear father. ... Well, dear Helmut, we are already at the turn of the year. The last one brought us endless suffering through the loss of our dear father, whose grave I visited yesterday. I brought him beautiful roses from our little garden. He does not need to take part in all the hardship that the future brings and is to be envied... Stay healthy and may your hard work be rewarded by success and may you advance in life.......Write to your loving mother again soon.

Following the annexation of Czechoslovakia, Poland was already partially surrounded by German controlled territories in mid-1939. As such, it was in a geographically weak situation.

In response to Hitler's occupation of Czechoslovakia in March 1939, the British pledged military support to Poland in the case of an attack from Nazi Germany. The French supported this agreement. This became known as the Polish Guarantee. Hitler responded by renouncing the German-Polish Non-Aggression Pact and the Anglo-German Naval Agreement.

During the night of August 23-24, 1939, Hitler and Stalin signed the German-Soviet Nonaggression Pact, known as the Molotov-Ribbentrop Treaty. Their nations agreed that they would not attack each other and secretly divided the countries that lay between them. Hitler had long planned an invasion of Poland, to which Great Britain and France had guaranteed military support if it were attacked by Germany. The pact with Stalin meant that Hitler would not face a war on two fronts once he invaded Poland and would have Soviet assistance in conquering and dividing the nation itself. Poland was surrounded. Hitler thought it was unlikely that Britain and France would respond militarily to an invasion of Poland, but even if they did respond, Hitler's pact with the Soviet Union would allow the German Army to retaliate.

On September 1, 1939, Hitler invaded Poland from the west. On September 3, 1939, having received no reply to their demands sent to the Nazis and unwilling to accept further German expansion, Britain and France, together with India, Australia and New Zealand declared war on Germany. The British government cancelled all visas previously granted to "enemy nationals." One effect of this was that German Jews could no longer immigrate to safety in England.

The Second World War had begun.

On September 17, Soviet troops invaded Poland from the east. Under attack from both sides, Poland fell quickly. On September 28, Germany and the Soviet Union signed a secret amendment to the Pact, geographically dividing their occupation of Poland. One of the covert articles attached stated that neither party to the treaty would allow on its territory any "Polish agitation" directed at the other party.

Poland surrendered on September 28, 1939, and the country, with its population of 3.3 million Jews, was partitioned between Germany and the Soviet Union. Within the next weeks, *SS* chief Heinrich Himmler and *SS* Security Service chief Reinhard Heydrich cleared all Jews from Western Poland so that the region could be prepared for resettlement by ethnic Germans. In November 1939, all Polish Jews were ordered to wear white armbands with a blue Star of David whenever appearing in public. Destruction of all Polish synagogues began.

The expulsion of the Jews of Germany to Poland commenced shortly. On November 29, 1939, *SS* chief Himmler ordered the death penalty for German Jews who refused to report for deportation. It was to be almost two and a half years before Rose and Else received the deportation order that would ensure their deaths.

The British foreign office warned central European governments that if they shipped their Jews to Palestine, the British would "expect the governments to take the immigrants back."

In the United States, a 1939 Gallup poll reported that 83 percent of Americans opposed the admission of a larger number of Jewish refugees. Based on instructions coming from the State Department, a United States consular official in Stuttgart, Germany, told numerous German Jews who had American sponsors and were waiting for a visa that all U.S. immigration quotas were filled and that they should reapply for admission to the United States in three years.

Hitler's goal of a *Volksgemeinschaft,* a new German society which rejected old religions, ideologies, and class divisions, and instead created a unified German character based around ideas of race, struggle, and state leadership, was progressing according to plan. The creation of the *Volk,* a nation or people made up of the most superior of the human races, excluding all others to maintain purity, demanded a one-party state where Hitler was accorded unquestioning obedience from his citizens, who handed over their freedoms in exchange for their part in a smoothly functioning machine. *"Ein Volk, ein Reich, ein Führer:"* One people, one empire, one leader. The *Volksgemeinschaft* was the racist ideology forming the basis for the Nazis' largely successful attempts at mass extermination of the Jewish people.

A letter was sent to Günter on September 27, 1939, from Mengede, Germany, where Rose, Else and Fanni were visiting other members of the family.

From Rose:

> My dear Gunther,
>
> ... We also had letters from Gerta today and yesterday from August 21st and 30th with good news, thank God, about everyone's health and practice. We hadn't heard anything from there for weeks either and were twice as happy. Now all that's missing is news from Helmut. I think mail traffic is stalling too over there. ...

Today aunt Henny (*Henrietta Oppenheim Vorreuter, Albert's sister*) left us again, who surprised us the day before yesterday to speak to Uncle Eduard (*Eduard Oppenheim, Albert's brother*), who was also here and also left today. ... Walter *(Aunt Henny's son)* is still looking. ... I can't tell you how sorry I am for loved ones, dear Günter. If only the children were gone! But it is the purest doom with it. ...

I saw Amanda W., née Bachmann...and heard that she is alone because Erich and his family have recently moved to E (*Erez, Jewish Palestine, abbreviated because of censorship of mail*) I also met Max's *(Max Dahl's)* uncle, Mr. Neugarten *(Paul Neugarten, married to Sara Dahl's sister)*. He would really like to go to his family *(his son, Herbert Neugarten had emigrated to Jewish Palestine and later became a world-famous Israeli music composer)* ..., but it doesn't work out yet. Please tell Aunt Minna that I was ... at the cemetery ...and found the graves of dear uncle (*Albert Baum, Minna Oppenheim's late husband*) In perfect order. How happy are all who sleep there in peace. I am really longing for our dear father's grave in Aachen. God grant that we can go there again soon....We all fasted very well on Yomkippur.

From Fanni:

Best regards to you, Günter, for you and for dear Aunt Minna from your old grandmother who loves you.

From Else:

Dear Günter,

Your vacation is long behind you... It's just a shame that all the young people have no prospect of getting out. ...Thank you, dear Günter, for your good new year wishes. God help us and grant that we are allowed to spend the high holidays together again. You can imagine how wistfully we all thought of your good father, who was not with us for the first time. But we want to grant him his rest and fulfill our duties as if he were with us... from your Aunt Else who loves you

On November 8, 1939, a letter was sent to Günter from the family in Aachen, written in Mengede and forwarded on to him by a cousin, Toni de Lange, in Amsterdam. Mail was not flowing freely between Germany and the United States after the beginning of World War II.

From Rose:

My dear Günter,

... First of all, I want to tell you that, thank God, we are doing well, which I hope is the case with you also and it's always the main thing. Actually we wanted to go back to Aachen yesterday, we had already ordered the car, but upon Uncle Paul's request postponed the trip for 14 days... Do you know that Uncle Ed[*uard*]. in H. has employment? .... Unfortunately, there is no direct message from our Helmut...We are all so fond of Erich, he is so affectionate, very different from Margot, who almost never lets herself be heard, even though Grandma has so much fun when she writes... How do you like evening school, dear Günter? Hopefully you will learn well and be able to make progress. ... I just wrote to Gerda and Max, whose birthday is on the 6th of December.

write to your loving mother again soon.

Many warm greetings to you, dear Toni *(Toni de Lange, in Amsterdam, who forwarded this letter to Günter)*, as well as to dear Mark and Ernst, also from grandma and Else...

From Else:

For you, dear Günter, the warmest greetings. I got the package back because it contained cigarettes. I was very sorry for it. Sincerely, Grandma and Else too.

From Aunt Toni:

Dear Günther, I received this letter this morning, November 28th. 1939 and am forwarding the same immediately. I forwarded yours and Margot's letters.

Best regards   Your aunt Toni

Toni de Lange, the daughter of Aaron Hahn and Emma Vorreuter, was born on March 11, 1883, in Schlüsselburg/Minden/Westphalia. She emigrated to the Netherlands and was deported to Auschwitz concentration and extermination camp where she was murdered on February 1, 1943.

Another letter was sent, written in Aachen, sent from Amsterdam via Toni de Lange in Amsterdam to Günter on December 8, 1939.

From Rose:

My dear Toni and dear Gunther,

... Everything was fine in the apartment. We miss the piano... very much. Because of our grief for our dear, blessed Father, we hardly played because we don't feel like listening to music... Our life here goes by very quietly. We do our work, run errands, and read or study in the evening. God grant we can stay here until we find a new home with you! If only you earned better first! ... I also wrote to you that thank God we finally heard from Helmut. We also expect mail from Gerda and Max. Hopefully everyone is healthy there..... Much is being done and yet it is still too little for all the unfortunate people. ...

Helmut bought a used truck (just overhauled) and is happy with it. Hopefully he'll get a lot of work. He wants to move to Ramataim because it is more convenient for him. .... Stay healthy and soon delight with good reports, God willing, your ever-loving mother.

From Toni de Lange, written in Dutch upside down at the top of the page:

.   Hartelijke groeten *(hearty greetings)*   Aunt T.

From Else:

My dear Tony and Günter,

.... Max Goldschmidt is trying very hard to get his papers for Chile. Fritz in Bombay has returned from a long trip and his Lotte is happy about it... G lives at 3118 North 15th St. Philadelphia Pa, you know that dear Toni?... Grandma sends her regards.

The letter below mentions Hilde Vorreuter, both Albert's niece (his sister Henrietta's daughter) and Fanni's great niece (her brother "Solly" Vorreuter's granddaughter). Hilde was able to emigrate to Holland in her twenties and worked as a maid in various rooming houses and hotels. She looked after the young children of an English couple whenever they came to the Netherlands on business or for holidays. In 1939, they arranged for Hilde to obtain a visa to come to England as a nursemaid for their children. However, she had fallen in love and married Joseph Abraham in Holland, and he had no visa available. Hilde and her husband remained in Holland, where, after the Nazis conquered Holland in 1940, Hilde and her husband were deported to Westerbork, a Dutch concentration camp, and then sent on to Auschwitz.

December 27th, 1939

From Else:

Dear Günther,

.... We enjoyed a letter from Gerta on December 4th and from you on November 26th via Aunt Toni... What do you hear from Helmut? You can imagine how we always wait for that, because we only had mail from him only once since August. ... Today my cousin Leopold Liepmann... now in Amsterdam... *(who with his wife and daughter)* have been in Holland since July, where they have relatives and are waiting there for the USA, asked for Aunt Paula's address, since his son Werner is in New Orleans as an assistant at the hospital. ... Hilde Vorreuter had added greetings for us after your letter, she was probably just with Aunt Toni. The Christmas days were very lonely for us; on the 1st we went to the cemetery and visited the grave of your beloved father, who has now been resting for 3/4 years and has no more worries!

Mother and I are studying English hard. A course starts next week that we want to participate in 2 times a week. If only one could remember better and not always forget everything! ...

... Greetings from grandma and your aunt Else, who loves you.

From Rose:

My dear boy,

Aunt Else is just taking Grandma upstairs because she wants to go to sleep. Climbing stairs is so difficult for her on her own, that's why she helps her because our stairs are a little steep and not straight.

... How did you spend Christmas? With us the Christmas days were very lonely! On such days you feel twice as alone and feel even more what you have lost and what you have to do without. May the day come for all of us, too, when we can embrace each other in good health and never have to part from each other again! That is my constant wish and that hope keeps me going.

Dear Gunther, before I forget, would a new ink ribbon on your typewriter be very expensive? The red writing is getting so dull! But only if it doesn't cost that much! Are you still thinking about saving, dear boy? ... Or do you just use your savings without adding new ones? I hope not! I would be <u>very</u> happy if you could put something aside every week. I think about the future and how necessary we may all have it again...!

... The penultimate letter from Gerda is also missing. ... Everything is terribly difficult in Shanghai.

I wrote a birthday letter to Stanley... He should only answer in English, since I am currently learning

.

Your very loving mother

From Rose on the following day, December 28, 1939 (in the same envelope):

My dear boy,

… this morning your letter of November 17th arrived, so it was on the road for a long time and we were very happy. I'm glad you heard from Helmut and I hope you answered him quickly and always let me hear when he writes to you. If only he had success with the car and earned a living from it!

With you, dear Günter, I wish and hope that everything will develop to your satisfaction in the business and that your salary will increase and that you will get a better position also in other ways... I think about it so often! ... with 1000 greetings,

I am your mother with love.

Chapter 14: 1940

The progressively more devastating Nazi policies of 1933 through 1939 targeting the Jews in Germany continued into 1940. They were subjected to increasing economic boycott, loss of civil rights, jobs, and citizenship together with seizure of property and financial assets, both directed and random violence, mass deportations, and incarceration in prisons and concentration camps.

Although some Jews found temporary reprieve from this ongoing assault by expanding their own institutions and social organizations, such as the *Reichsvertretung der Deutschen Juden* (Central Organization of German Jews), founded in 1933 to represent the German Jewish interests through a unified response, most chose to leave Germany by any means possible. The initial desire of the German government to encourage Jewish emigration by placing few restrictions on such action had, by 1940, been replaced by recent actions to deprive Jews fleeing Germany of their property by levying an increasingly heavy emigration tax and by restricting the amount of money that could be transferred abroad.

Following *Kristallnacht*, the German government confiscated most of the remaining Jewish-owned property and entirely excluded Jews from the German economy. The desire for emigration increased dramatically as most Jews decided that there was no longer a future for them in Germany. Individuals and entire families became refugees, which ultimately was proven to be a fortunate situation only if they were given the opportunity to leave Europe.

In 1933, close to 600,000 Jews were living in Germany and 185,000 were in Austria. By 1940, half of these had fled to other countries. More than 100,000 German-Jewish émigrés traveled to western European countries, especially France, Belgium, and the Netherlands. Approximately 8,000 entered Switzerland and 48,000 went to Great Britain and various other European nations.

About 90,000 German-Jewish refugees were able to immigrate to the United States and 60,000 to Palestine, which was then under the British Mandate. An additional 84,000 German-Jewish refugees immigrated to Central and South America, and because the Japanese-controlled city of Shanghai in China did not require visas or certificates of good conduct from Jewish immigrants, 15,000 to 18,000 Jews found refuge there. These included Rose's daughter, my mother Gerda, her husband Max, and Gerda's parents-in-law, her sister-in-law, Ilse Dahl Radt and her husband.

As the number of people fleeing Nazi persecution increased, more and more countries refused to accept refugees, and by 1939 the number of havens available to Jewish refugees dwindled. Switzerland feared that massive numbers of German Jews would cross their border, and the British government continued to restrict Jewish immigration to Palestine. Unfortunately, by 1940, emigration from Nazi Germany became virtually impossible, and, in October 1941 it was officially forbidden by the German government.

Between 1933 and 1939, more than 300,000 Germans, 90 percent of them Jews, had applied for immigration visas to the United States. These included Rose, Albert, Else, Fanni and Uncle Paul Liepmann, his wife Agnes and daughter Ruth and many other members of my extended family. Despite the sincere intent of some American activists to assist refugees fleeing Nazism, strict immigration quotas, public opposition to immigration during a time of economic depression, and antisemitism in the general public and among some key government officials were serious obstacles to any relaxation of U.S. immigration quotas.

A strict quota system limited the annual immigration to the United States. Established by the immigration laws of 1921 and 1924, these were discriminatory and aimed at reducing emigration from "undesirable" areas of Europe, especially eastern Europe and the Balkans. American policy makers wanted to prevent thousands of penniless Jews from southern and eastern Europe from entering the U.S. While antisemitism was certainly a factor in formulating this aim, concern regarding communism and a general fear of poor people in a time of depression were equally influential.

The Immigration Act of 1924, which reduced the annual quota for immigrants to the United States from 358,000 to less than one half that number, intensified an already severe anti-immigration law that had been passed in 1921. The Act reduced the immigration limit from 3 percent to 2 percent of each foreign-born group "living in the United States," using census figures from 1890 rather than those of 1920. Thus the large influx of southern and eastern Europeans arriving between those thirty years was ignored in the calculation. Finally, the Act provided for a future reduction of the total quota to 154,000. In 1929, the new quota went into effect. Of the 154,000 people allowed into the United States annually, almost 84,000 were British and Irish, people who did not need to flee from the Nazis. While the new law reduced the quota for northern and western European countries by 29 percent, it slashed the numbers for southern and eastern Europe by 87 percent.

The annual German quota to the United States in 1936 was 25,957 people, meaning immigration officials could potentially fill this number from the applicant pool. As a matter of fact, the number of visas granted to people of German origin to come to the United States each year was considerably less, not because of a lack of applicants for a visa but rather due to antisemitic United States immigration policies. For the period beginning when Hitler came to power in 1933 through the end of 1937, less than twenty percent of the available German quota was granted a visa by US Immigration officials. The main obstacle was a 1930 U.S. State Department Regulation instructing consular officials abroad to adopt a new interpretation of regulations barring prospective immigrants that were likely to become "public charges." Instead of judging an individual's capacity to do useful work in the United States, the regulation was interpreted in such a way as to limit immigration because of the existing labor conditions in the United States. Anyone who needed to work to support himself or herself (i.e., anyone who was not independently wealthy) was considered likely to become a public charge and had their visa application rejected. Each Consul had wide-ranging discretion in determining eligibility of those applying to enter the U.S., using the restrictions stipulated in the LPC ("Likely to become a Public Charge") clause of the 1917 immigration act. Under LPC, a refugee could simply be denied entry if the Consul capriciously decided the candidate might become reliant on the US government for sustenance.

The Nazis had prohibited German Jews from taking substantial assets out of the country, which meant they could indeed be potential public charges unless they had close relatives in the U.S. with ample resources. As a result, American consuls rejected the applications of tens of thousands of German Jews who would have made fine hard-working American citizens, thus trapping them in the escalating Nazi persecution.

During the time prior to the end of World War II, the United States did not distinguish between immigrants and refugees nor was there any such thing as political asylum.

President Roosevelt in his first term of office considered changing the public charge clause to allow for the entry of more refugees from Germany. However, Jewish immigration was a sensitive issue with both Congress and the public. Critics of the Roosevelt "New Deal" referred to it as the "Jew Deal." Numerous State Department officials believed that American Jews alleging Nazi persecution in Germany were exaggerating, part of a Jewish scheme to reduce American barriers to increased immigration.

In 1936, American consular officials in Germany were told to soften their stance and change their criteria from whether candidates for immigration were "likely" to become a public charge to whether it was "probable" that they would. This was due to the quality of immigrants from Germany, the willingness of family in the United States to support immigrants, and the changed political atmosphere after the 1936 presidential elections. Immigration more than doubled between 1936 and 1937, but it was still less than half the permissible quota for applicants from Germany.

After Germany annexed Austria in March 1938 (*Anschluss*), President Roosevelt suggested liberalizing immigration procedures and combining the German and Austrian quotas to make it more likely for Jews in Austria to obtain visas to the United States. That led to the only two years where more than 90 percent of the full quota was used, occurring in 1938 and 1939. After the World War began in 1939, however, State Department officials instructed consuls-general not to admit anyone to the United States if there was any doubt about their political reliability. Fear of Axis spies entering the United States led to a significant reduction in the number of visas issued in 1940. In June 1941, Congress passed the Bloom-Van Nuys bill authorizing consuls to withhold any type of visa if they had reason to believe that the applicant might endanger public safety in the United States.

It would have been a simple matter for the Democrat-controlled Congress and FDR to increase the immigration quota at that critical time in the lives of my family and similarly terrorized Jewish refugees of Europe. Neither the White House nor Congress was willing to increase the quota. With the exception of adding the Austrian quota to the German one, quotas for immigration from Germany remained unchanged during the entire period of the Holocaust refugee crisis, preventing my family from qualifying for visas to bring them to the United States. While Roosevelt made it slightly easier to fill the quotas in 1938 and 1939, in 1940 the State Department made it more difficult again. Although most of the German quota was used in 1940, the majority of the visas were given to those German Jews who had already escaped from Germany. Some even had already emigrated to other nations in the Western Hemisphere, where they were safe.

As the Nazi regime's attacks intensified in the late 1930s, hundreds of thousands of Jews in Germany tried to immigrate to the United States. To enter the United States, each person needed an immigration visa stamped into his or her passport.

The bureaucratic hurdles facing German Jews attempting to emigrate in the late 1930s were overwhelming, requiring extensive documentation that was often virtually impossible to obtain.

My grandmother Rose, Albert, Else and Fanni were among the hundreds of thousands who applied to immigrate to the United State from Nazi territory and were unsuccessful. In 1937 they had first registered with the American consulate in Stuttgart and were given their quota numbers and placed on the waiting list. The paperwork that they presented for each of them included five copies of the visa application and two copies of their birth certificates. After Albert's death in 1939, his quota number, 46807, was removed from the waiting list.

The visa application required that each applicant supply two sponsors who would be responsible for each member of my family not becoming a public charge or burden on society. These sponsors were required to be United States citizens or have permanent United States resident status. Close relatives of the prospective immigrant were preferred as sponsors. The frequent mention of "guarantees" in the many letters from Rose and the family in Germany refer to this necessity for American personal sponsorship. Günter could not become a United States citizen until he had been in the country for five years, which would not occur until 1942, and, therefore, could not be one of the sponsors for his mother, grandmother, great aunt Else or for his uncle Paul and his family. Günter tried to circumvent this by making many unsuccessful attempts to have himself declared a permanent United States resident so that he could become a sponsor using that route.

Any potential sponsor in the USA was required to submit a plethora of certified personal financial information, plus bank and employer affidavits. It was no wonder that many US citizens, when begged by friends or relatives to become a sponsor or guarantor, would decline due to the effort required to surmount this bureaucracy. Remarkably, Günter was able to get a number of his friends and colleagues at work to submit sponsor applications for our family members of our family. However, despite frequently asking, he was never able to persuade Stanley Snellenburg, who possessed vast financial resources, to do so. I suppose Stanley felt that by providing a guarantee to Günter to obtain his visa and subsequently employing him at Snellenburgs and doing the same for Walter Vorreuter and Egon Baum, he had more than fulfilled all obligations to his family in Germany.

The only correspondence in my possession from the early part of 1940 consists of three postcards sent to Günter.

January 4, 1940

From: Rose

My dear Gunther,

.... This morning we were very pleased with your letter of 12/5, dear boy. Aunt Tony enclosed greetings, *(that letter and likely others were sent to Amsterdam and then sent forward to Aachen)*, and the picture sent along gave us a good idea of the size and the crowd at the soccer game. ... It was nice that you earned something from it and that the money was put to good use (*Apparently Günter, always industrious, was able to earn some additional income at a soccer game by selling some items at a sports stadium, either for Snellenburg's or privately*). I recently asked you if you would also bring something to the savings bank as you did in the past, so that it would get more interest there. That would make me <u>very</u> happy! ... To our delight, Aunt Henny wrote us that Stanley renewed the surety for Walter (*Vorreuter*). Hopefully his turn will come soon. It is said to go much faster in Stuttgart because many are gone. So Dinchen Sternberg heard on her request that it would be the end of this year or the beginning of next year. Her number is about 30,000 *(her waiting number for a US visa; Rose, Else's and Fanni's numbers were between 46 and 47 thousand)*. In a moment, I will go to the English course for the first time, where I hope to learn to speak proficiently. Aunt Else and I are studying diligently.

Dear Günter, I wonder how our Helmut is doing? Where does he live now? Please write to him and tell him to write a detailed letter to you for us! We don't hear anything from him... Hopefully you are alive and well like us, also Aunt Minna and all loved ones... Best regards from Grandma and Aunt Else.

As is the case with all communications, all available space is occupied by written words.

postcard from Rose to Günter, front and back, Jan 18, 1940,

January 18, 1940

From: Rose

My dear boy,

... You won't need Aunt Tony in the future, I think it'll just take longer. I don't know anyone in Italy. *(Rose is referring to Toni in Amsterdam forwarding letters both to and from the United States—apparently Günter had suggested in a letter that mail could more rapidly go through Italy.)* The postcards sent there on December 13th with an Italian ship have not yet arrived! Today we were surprised by Uncle Paul visiting us. He was worried about grandma. Thank God she is doing a little better. As I told you by letter, she has been in bed for 1 1/2 weeks, has had the flu and an inflammation in her right eye, so that she can hardly see anything with it. The doctor puts drops in it every day. God grant it helps. But Grandma is very lively and tells us a lot about the past. ... We are also so excited, dear Günter, what Christmas has brought you. May your hopes and wishes come true for your good.

... We had good news from Gerda. At the beginning of February an elderly couple will emigrate from here to Shanghai, as they have a married daughter there. They were always very rich people. Now the son-in-law has to pay the trip for her in foreign currency. You can only take with you underwear and clothes! *(Rose is referring to the Nazi edicts that prevented Jews leaving Germany from taking any possessions with them) ...*

With constant love your mother

On February 1, 1940, a postcard was sent to Günter from distant relatives ("J," Edith, and their children Ernst and Ursel) in Amsterdam regarding transmission of funds to secure a guarantor for Paul Liepmann, his wife Agnes and daughter Ruth.

Dear Günther!

Today I commissioned the Dutch bank Unie to send you the equivalent of 1200 Guilders in dollars for Uncle Paul. Uncle Paul wrote me today that the amount is for his guarantee... Please confirm reception of the amount upon receipt. There is no need to ask how you are, because you are so infinitely better off in happy America than we are in war-threatened Europe. I wish my children were there too!

Goodbye, dear Günther   Kind regards, Your Uncle J

My dear Günther!

Also take my warm regards. I hope that you continue to do well there. It is a comforting feeling for your loved ones that you have settled in so well there. For you surely the language will pose no more difficulties. Aunt Paula with husband and Erich are now united again with Margot. It must have been a great joy to see them again. Ilse and Ruth *(Sternberg, Agnes' sister)* write very sadly, the loss of our dear Erich *(husband of Ruth Sternberg)* is just too painful.

All the best, love Günter, and stay healthy. Again warm greetings from Ernst and Ursel.

Your Edith

Dear Günther, probably late, but thank you very much for the stamps you sent me. Please don't blame me for writing so late, but I wanted to wait for my parents.

For this time the warmest greetings and thank you again, Ernst

There is no preserved correspondence to Shanghai, Palestine, or Philadelphia between the above postcard from Amsterdam on February 3, 1940, and the letter below of October 7, 1940. Undoubtedly, countless letters were written and mailed and may or may not have been received. German censors were extremely active in burying letters which contained anything construed as anti-German and World War II was slowing international postal service.

Rose wrote almost weekly to the American consulate in Stuttgart, where her, Else's, and Fanni's application for a visa had been filed. She went there in person almost monthly during 1940, usually accompanied by Else for her support and well-organized mind. Each time, after a considerable wait in the large lobby with hordes of people requesting answers regarding seeking refuge in the United States, she would be seen by a clerk who would shuffle through some papers and announce that she would have to be patient. It clearly became apparent to Rose that the entire system of regulations and obstacles was practically insurmountable, but Rose continued to make the round trip to the consular office by train, hoping that this time it would be different. Perhaps she would even be allowed to speak to an undersecretary, rather than merely a newly employed clerk, who never knew anything or offered anything substantial.

On June 26, 1940, Assistant Secretary of State Breckinridge Long, whose duties included immigration and visa policy, and State Department Advisor on Political Relations, James Dunn, formulated a policy for the State Department to "delay and effectively stop for a temporary period of indefinite length" the entry of Jewish immigrants to the US. This could be accomplished, Long said, by "simply advising our Consul to put every obstacle in the way and to resort to various administrative devices which would postpone the granting of visas." Long wrote in his personal diary, not meant for publication, that he frequently briefed President Roosevelt on the tactics that he and his colleagues were using to restrict immigration. Long made a diary entry in October 1940 that, in a discussion at the White House on ways to curtail immigration, he "found that (FDR) was 100% in accord with my ideas," and "expressed himself as in entire accord" and was "wholeheartedly in support" of what Long and other State Department officials were doing.

Both Long and Dunn, members of Roosevelt's inner circle, played key roles in both preventing news about the mass murder of Jews in concentration camps from reaching Jewish officials in the United States and also obstructing efforts to rescue them. Dunn additionally was involved in ordering U.S. diplomats in Switzerland, in early 1943, to stop sending Washington reports about the slaughter of Europe's Jews. That order was later uncovered by Treasury Department officials and ignited a major controversy over the rescue issue. Dunn, furious that Treasury Secretary Henry Morgenthau, Jr., and his aides were taking an interest in rescue, remarked, "This Jew Morgenthau and his Jewish assistant (Josiah E.) DuBois are trying to run the State Department." Ironically, DuBois who was not Jewish, was a Treasury Department official who was instrumental in exposing the State Department's concealment of news about the Holocaust and barring opportunities for rescue.

The family in Aachen wrote to Günter on October 7, 1940.

From: Fanni

... Belatedly, dear Walter (*Walter Vorreuter, who had recently arrived in the United States was Fanni's grandnephew and, through a second relationship, Albert's nephew*), my deepest condolences on the passing of your dear father. After the suffering of the dear deceased, unfortunately so long, death is only a redemption for the dear departed. Your dear mother (*Henrietta Oppenheim, Albert's sister*) writes that she will visit us for the last holidays... Unfortunately, I can walk so badly. Regrettably, seeing and hearing are also getting harder and harder for me. At my age, 85, you can't expect much more from life..... We were also happy to hear that you, dear Walter, have already found employment through Stanley. If you have learned the language in a not too long time, God willing, it will not be so difficult for you to settle in. ... Please us, God willing, soon with good reports of your well-being and greetings from your loving aunt and grandma Fanny Liepmann.

We are still eagerly awaiting letters from the loved ones in Shanghai, as well as from dear Helmut. In Horn, where dear Ruth is at home for the festive season, she (*Ruth Liepmann was Fanni's youngest granddaughter and much more favored than Margot, in New Orleans, who never wrote*) already wrote a nice letter from Paderborn, again greetings, Your Oma

From: Rose

My dear Günter,

... We had a lot of fun with the nice photos of you, dear boy. I think you got a little leaner, or am I wrong? ...If you ever take pictures of yourself again, dear Günter, then put on something bright, because that will be the most beautiful, I think. You are sure to live on the memory of your wonderful vacation for a long time to come... The events themselves pass far too quickly, but the memory lingers forever. ...

Aunt Minna stayed longer and we are all looking forward to seeing her. *(Minna Oppenheim Baum, already a United States citizen, had returned to Germany despite the war to dispose of her household belongings which she had left in Mengede when she went to the USA in 1935. She returned to the USA via Lisbon and Cuba a few weeks after this letter was written. As a US citizen possessing a US passport, no visa was required).* She will meet Uncle Eduard these days in Mengede. Aunt Minna's household is to be dissolved... I think it's all supposed to be sold. Nebbich! *(Nebbich is a Yiddish term meaning "poor thing." Rose was referring to the fact that Aunt Minna would get only pfennig for her prized furniture.)* But <u>don't</u> tell Aunt Minna! As I found out, Max Baum's mother-in-law has taken over the dining room furniture because of interest arrears! It's good that Uncle Albert didn't live to see that! Uncle Eduard wrote to us that he hadn't heard from Heinz *(Eduard Oppenheim's son in the United States)* since the beginning of August, the letter was dated July 1st. ... The people of Halle are very worried about Heinz. They haven't heard from Herbert *(Eduard's other son, in England)* for a long time! ... We got a lot of mail for New Years, only nothing from Gerda and Max so far... Aunt Paula wrote to us that she ...is the only one who earns something and is very stressed. She sews on a borrowed electrical machine and has a lot of work. Robert *(Paula's second husband)* can't find a job!

It is surely a good thing that you go to night school again, dear Günter, even if it costs a lot of money. Make sure you study well there. ... Do you also think about saving something every month, dear boy! By the way, how did it go with the shirts? Do you still have a lot lying around, or did you sell most of them well? ... From Hilde *(Vorreuter, Walter's sister)* in Amsterdam I also got a letter in response to my condolence *(Hilde's father, Adolf Vorreuter, Henrietta Oppenheim's husband, had died recently).* She works in a boarding house all by herself, has a lot of work for 11 people, but everyone is so nice to her. Has my airmail letter from 9 September for Aunt Minna arrived? I wrote to you by airmail, dear Günter, on September 5th, on September 17th, on September 28th, and hope that everything reaches you in the best of health. Aunt Else is, thank God, mobile again and had a very bad cold. I had 4 teeth pulled but thank God I have things in order now. ... Best regards from your loving mother and all loved ones. Please write again soon and in detail!

With constant love your mother

"Walter" (Walter Vorreuter), referred to in many of the above and following letters, was then thirty years old. He was directly related to both Albert and Rose, being the son of Albert's sister Henrietta and also Fanni's great-nephew. He had been waiting for years to obtain a U.S. visa, finally receiving one from the Stuttgart Embassy on May 23, 1940. With German U-Boats patrolling the western Atlantic during this second year of WW II, there was no direct means to get to the United States. Germany did not invade Russia until June of 1941 and the routes from Germany to the east were still accessible. Walter made his way from the Third Reich via Russia and Siberia to Harbin, China, and then to the Japanese port city of Yokohama, leaving there on August 6, 1940, on the Steamship *Rakuyo Maru*, stopping in Hawaii on August 18, 1940, and arriving in San Francisco on August 28, 1940. He is listed by the US Department of Labor Immigration service as Walter Israel Vorreuter (although his middle name was not Israel), on the "List or Manifest of Alien Passengers for the United States." There were six other "aliens" on that ship. Four of those were classified, as Walter was, as being of the "Hebrew Race." The other two were a young married "German" couple, described as an "assistant Scientific Professor and his wife." Walter was one of approximately 500 Jewish European refugees who travelled to San Francisco from Shanghai and Yokohama in 1939 and 1940, according to ship passenger lists and Border Security and Immigration registries. Arriving passengers were further screened at Angel's Island off the coast of San Francisco, the west coast equivalent of Ellis Island in New York.

The SS *Rakuyo Maru* was a Japanese passenger and cargo ship built in 1921. Later, after Pearl Harbor, the Japanese Navy requisitioned the ship as a merchant vessel as part of their war effort. It eventually became a transporter of prisoners of war captured in the Pacific arena and being relocated to internment in the Japanese home islands. It was known by the Allied prisoners of war as a "hell ship," with the holds being floating dungeons, where inmates were denied air, space, light, bathroom facilities, and adequate food and water. Many POWs, primarily Americans, died on the *Rakuyo Maru* as they were being brought west after having been captured in the Battles of Midway, Coral Sea, Java Sea, and Guadalcanal.

During the Philippine campaign, the troopship was part of a convoy transporting prisoners of war (POWs) captured at the battles of Saipan and Leyte Gulf. Early in the morning of September 12, 1944, The *Rakuyo Maru* was carrying 1,317 Australian and British prisoners in its hold from Singapore to Formosa. While in the Luzon Strait, the ship was attacked by three American submarines, Growler, Pampanito and Sealion, using "wolfpack" convergence maneuvers, complex tactics initially perfected by the Germans and named *"Rudeltaktik"* or *"Wolfsrudel."* Not realizing the contents of the ship, the US submarine Sealion torpedoed the *Rakuyo Maru,* and it sank towards the evening. 1,159 POWs died, including 350 who had escaped in lifeboats but were bombarded by a Japanese navy vessel the next day. On September 15th, the three American submarines returned to the area and rescued some surviving POWs who were on rafts. Four more of them died before they could be landed at Saipan, in the Mariana Islands.

Walter took the train from San Francisco to Philadelphia, where he moved into the same rooming house at 3118 North 15th Street, where his first cousin, Günter, 11 years his junior, had been living. Walter, as Günter had been, was trained as a textile merchant in Germany, and was able to quickly obtain a job at the *Armon Company*, a five-story department store founded in 1927 at 35 South Second Street, selling textiles, home furnishings and home equipment, both wholesale and retail. On October 16, 1940, Walter registered for the United States Draft in Philadelphia.

Contained within the many letters to Günter from Rose, Else and Fanni during the time that my family was living in Aachen, there are many references to "Miss Nydick" and the "Nydick" family in Philadelphia. Günter's immediate boss at *Snellenburg's* was one of two spinster sisters, likely in their fifties or sixties, with maiden names of Nydick. Apparently, she had taken a motherly interest in Günter when he arrived from Germany, wet behind the ears. "Miss Nydick" had an unmarried niece, Sara Nydick, who was 21 years older than Günter. In 1944, Sara Nydick married Walter.

Walter Vorreuter with me, 1949, shortly after I arrived in the USA from Shanghai.

Walter and Sara Nydick, soon after they married.

The next letter received by Günter was written on October 16, 1940

From: Rose

My dear Günter,

... You don't believe, dear boy, how happy all three of us are when good news comes from you! I wrote you a long time ago that we were very happy with the beautiful photos of you. ...

Last week we had two letters from Gerda with good news, thank God. They wrote that they had recovered very well in Unzen *(a resort in Japan),* and that Max was very busy in the practice.

...The sheath must be very beautiful; Gerda wrote it too. How about the shirts, dear Günther? Did you sell well? Did you also go to service on the first day of New Year's? Ilse in Shanghai unfortunately lost her job at the newspaper because it went bankrupt. Nebbich! She got such a splendid letter of reference from the head of the newspaper. Hopefully she will find employment again <u>soon</u>. Old Frau Radt *(Ilse Dahl Radt's mother-in law)* is sick too. If only the inflation in Shanghai were over! The private apartment now costs 320 Dollars a month.

......did Walter receive his belongings? It would be terrible for him if the trunk didn't arrive. Did he have Helmut's things in it too? Lucky that he found work. How much does he pay for room and board? But you have not yet written to us that Walter pleased you so much, dear Gunther. What did he bring you?

Is Stanley back from his trip and does he take care of Walter a lot? I can imagine that it is not so easy to learn a new language at that age, but a lot can be achieved with diligence. I hope that you will also learn a lot through the courses at university, dear Gunther! I can imagine how difficult it may be to read and understand the English poets, especially in the old language. Is there no course where modern poets are read? ...

Dear Günther, if I'm not mistaken, you had a dark blue suit with gray stripes, didn't you? Our dear father got the same, but only wore it a few times. I now had a jacket dress made out of it, which turned out very pretty. If I were with you now, I would accompany you to the shop and choose a nice matching blouse there.

Before I forget, thank you very much for the many colorful stamps, so an old friend who collects them will be very happy! By the way, what does Ms. L. *(a young unmarried woman by the name of Levin, originally from Ludenscheid, where my father had a medical practice. Ms. L emigrated to Shanghai and then left there to go to the United States)* know about Max and Gerda's pecuniary circumstances? ... Please write to Helmut, dear Günter! How is he doing? I think about him so much, have dreamed of him so often at night! Our grandmother talks about Helmut so often, she can't understand why he doesn't let anyone hear from him.

... Now stay well, my dear boy, and soon write again to your mother who always loves you.

From Else:

Many warm greetings to you, dear Günther, from all loved ones... Grandma and Aunt Else

Typical letter with onion skin paper, every square mm. used by Rose and Else in their correspondence

The following letter received by Günter was written on October 27, 1940.

From: Rose

My dear Gunther,

I have just finished a letter to Shanghai and at the same time congratulated Max on his birthday *(he would be 40 on December 6, 1940)*, now I want to chat with you, dear boy... Thank God we are healthy too...... Aunt Henny has been here for a few days...and hope she stays a few weeks, but she has little peace of mind...

It's quiet here and you live like in the countryside. This is often better than the hustle and bustle... I hope you enjoy the course at the university and learn well, dear Gunther. What kind of things did Gerda send you? ... Gerda delighted me with a very pretty silver ring with an amethyst. There must have been a huge flood in Shanghai! Ilse's husband got a job as a teacher at a school, not earning much yet, but it will get better with time. ... Have you heard from Helmut in the meantime? If only he wrote you good things! How long, unfortunately, have we not heard from him? ... How is the business doing now? Hopefully you are busy and satisfied. ...

It's already really cold here ..., but our heating works well. Aunt Else takes care of it. ... Heinz's parents are very worried about him because he has not written since July. Hopefully he's healthy. Now please delight us again soon with a detailed report, dear Gunther, and warm greetings to you and to all loved ones from your loving mother

From: Aunt Henny (Oppenheim, Walter's mother, who was visiting in Aachen)

... dear Günther. The day before yesterday I also sent a letter to dear Walter, which I hope will come into his possession. You are together a lot, aren't you? Is Walter settling in well and is he getting on a little with the language? I like it very much here with your loved ones, it's so very cozy and you can relax well. Farewell, dear Günther, greet Walter, ... greetings from your loving Aunt Henny

From Else:

Dear Gunther,

How pleased we were with your lines! Hopefully you are all healthy and Walter is settling in well. ... Earlier we congratulated Uncle Hermann on his 70th birthday, which he wanted to spend in Horn; and Max in Shanghai for the 40th. We are very happy with Aunt Henny. It's getting late and it's time to go to bed.

Best regards from your aunt Else, who loves you

From Fanni:

Best regards, dear Günther, from your old grandmother who loves you.

On October 27, 1940, Rose sent a letter to Anton Bamfaste, the postmaster of Velmede, bringing him up to date regarding the Oppenheim family. She enclosed a postage stamp so that Mr. Bamfaste could reply to her request for information.

Dear Bamfaste family!

How many times have my thoughts lately been with you! If you had received the letter intended for you every time, it would have been a whole pile. First of all, I would like to thank you very much for your detailed report, Mr. Bamfaste, which pleased and interested me, because one always likes to hear from good friends from the old home. Hopefully you and your loved ones are in good health and otherwise. Is Alfons still in Minden and can Meinolf continue his studies? I want to wish it to him very much. Tony will certainly still be employed by the H. company. Should she ever have something to do in the local area, she is cordially invited. Nobody knows her here, and we live in a very quiet area, but close to the city.

How are your wife and you, dear Mr. Bamfaste? Hopefully you are both healthy and happy in business too. We currently have my sister-in-law visiting us (Henrietta Oppenheim Vorreuter) who recently lost her husband (Adolf). A few days before his father's death, their only son (Walter) started the long journey via Russia, Siberia, and Japan to the USA, which lasted 8 weeks. He is in Philadelphia, lives near Günter and is studying English hard. He found work straight away. Thank God Günter writes very satisfied, recently sent nice photos from Florida, where he had a nice vacation.

Our Gerda and her husband were in Japan for a rest and could not tell enough about the beauty of this country. I am very happy that our children are outside, and I only have the ardent wish that the 3 of us will live together with them again in the not-too-distant future, namely in the USA with Günter.

Minna, my sister-in-law with her son, lives there too. We haven't heard from Helmut for a long time, because no mail arrives from there. But he sent a good picture to Gerda, who sent it to me. I was very interested in all the news that you communicated, dear Mr. Bamfaste. I very much regret the death of Mr. Bültmann, who had such a tragic accident. Does Ms. Bäcker Burmann still live there? Has anyone from Velmede or Bestwig died in this war? How's it going at Huberts? Is Mr. Müller still a soldier and the hairdresser Anton Hengsbach and Anton Nieder junior?

Now I have a request, dear Mr. Bamfaste. Can you tell me the name and the exact address of the <u>district</u> (not local) farmer leader responsible for Heringhausen *(Bestwig)*. I need the same for a legal matter and would be very grateful to you. *(Rose was pursuing other avenues beyond her suits in an attempt to recover money owed to her and Albert from the sale of M. Oppenheim and their home, together with accounts still receivable from clients of M. Oppenheim, as described in the August 20, 1939, letter to Helmut).*

With best regards to all of you from my mother, sister, and me yours

Mrs. Albert Oppenheim

P.S.: Many greetings for Meier's mother and old Mr. Nieder.

On November 4, 1940, Rose and Else wrote to Günter.

From: Rose

My dear Gunther,

... Thank God we are fine, let's pray to God to keep us healthy and keep suffering and sorrow away from all of us! .... Heinz changed jobs, is now in northern U.S.A. and is making more. Herbert got engaged to his cousin Marianne Danziger ... Heinz wrote to his parents. But maybe you already know that, don't you? ... In the meantime we also had a detailed report from Gerda. I may have already written to you that she made me very happy with a pretty ring. How are the items that she got you, dear Gunther? Will you sell them too? Have you sold all the shirts? Be careful and above all economical and put something aside every month. Have you heard from Helmut in the meantime? If only he would write to you or Gerda in detail! A terrible storm has been raging here since yesterday and it's often pouring with rain... One wouldn't want to chase a dog out the door. I have a flower arrangement here for our dear father's grave but could not go there in the terrible weather. How happy are all those who sleep in peace, dear boy! How much worry they were spared! May God help us all! ...

I am very interested in ..., dear Gunther, about the speeches you have to give. You speak fluently, don't you? Or are you still missing expressions and words? ... What you wrote about Sylva, dear boy, amazes me greatly! You used to be so enthusiastic about her, and now all of a sudden this change! Aunt Henny and I both advise Walter and you not to get involved in things that do not concern you. If Sylva is not nice to Aunt Minna, Egon should correct her and set a good example for her and be especially nice to his mother. *(Egon, Aunt Minna's son was married to Sylva)*; Aunt Minna herself has her mouth in the right place and doesn't need an excuse. Walter and you only make yourself unpopular if you get in the way...

I hope you haven't seen or heard from Ms. Levin again. Please don't worry about her or her family! Gerda wrote that Ms. L. was absolutely no good, and that she was a lying so-and-so, that it was rather pathological with her. Gerda is very happy that she no longer has anything to do with her and you, dear Gunther, judged her correctly. It is best to avoid such people! You wrote that you gained twelve pounds, dear boy, but one can't see that in the photos you sent. How much do you weigh? .... Please let us hear from you again very soon, you always make your mother, who loves you, very happy.

From: Else

> Dear Günter, I also send the warmest greetings from Grandma and myself. ... We were sorry that Aunt Henny left again! – God grant that she will come to us again soon. We loved having her here. Mother asked Gerda to send 3 permits these days! If only we could be with you! God help us all and keep us from suffering and hardship. Say hello to everyone

> from your Aunt Else

In this letter, Else mentions in passing that Rose had requested Gerda in Shanghai "to send three permits." There is no detail given and this is unrevealed in Rose's correspondence of that date, likely due to the probability of German censors destroying the letter or worse, including sending the *SS* to their home in Aachen. Rose realized that their chances of getting to the United States was dwindling by the day. She knew from various sources that more than 300,000 Germans, 99% of them Jewish, were on the waiting list for U.S. visas. Rose had recently mailed affidavits of good conduct from two disinterested parties to the American consulate in Stuttgart, a new requirement as of September 1940.

The concept of going to China was now becoming a glimmer of hope. It had been rejected earlier because Rose realized that the trip would be too arduous for her mother to endure and she did not want to be a burden on Gerda and Max, who already were caring for his parents and, to some extent, his sister's family. Rose knew that she and the rest of my family would arrive in Shanghai destitute since her home in Aachen, her principal asset, would be worthless if she left Germany. The removal of all civil rights from German Jews by stripping them of German citizenship, called "denaturalization," had begun in 1933 but loss of all property rights initially was applied only to outspoken critics of Nazi policies who had fled abroad. On September 24, 1940, Reinhard Heydrich, chief of the Reich Security Main Office (RSHA), the successor to the Gestapo Central Office, warned that many Jewish emigrants had so far avoided denaturalization. Much property had escaped the Reich, especially in cases where Jews had succeeded in obtaining citizenship elsewhere. In response the Gestapo initiated negotiations with the government ministries to introduce legislation making all Jewish emigrants with German citizenship immediately subject to denaturalization. Rose was unable to sell the house while in Germany and were she to leave still owning the house, she would be "denaturalized," and the property taken by the government. Denaturalization allowed for the confiscation of Jewish property, whether or not the rightful owner resided in Germany. Rose's daughter Gerda and her husband Max had been fortunate that they were able to take their assets with them when they went to Shanghai in 1933. Hitler was determined not to let that happen again.

No visa was necessary to go to Shanghai, but one would have to book passage, and getting to China from Germany was becoming very competitive with Europe at war and the recent onset of the North African campaign. With the Middle East in turmoil, the Suez Canal was no longer a dependable route to the Far East.

As of September 1939, a US visa applicant had the additional requirement of having to provide proof of permission to leave Germany together with evidence that the prospective immigrant had booked passage to the Western hemisphere. Physical examinations at a US consulate were also required. These were all hurdles that my family still had to conquer, and they waited impatiently for their numbers to be called, with that process totally out of their control. Collecting these documents and keeping them in order was a task Rose and Else shared. Unfortunately, identity paperwork, police certificates, exit and transit permissions, and financial affidavits had expiration dates as did the prized visa itself. Everything needed to come together at the same time.

Potential immigrants also needed to have a valid ship ticket before receiving a visa. With the onset of war and the fear that German submarines would target passenger vessels, shipping across the Atlantic became extremely risky. Many passenger lines stopped entirely or at least reduced the number of vessels crossing the ocean, making it more difficult and expensive for refugees to find berths.

After World War II began in Europe in September 1939, and especially after the German invasion of Western European nations in the spring of 1940, many Americans believed that Germany and the Soviet Union were taking advantage of the masses of Jewish refugees to send spies abroad. The Department of State was the U.S. government agency most directly responsible for dealing with the refugees seeking to escape Nazi persecution. It had the power to grant visas, formulate refugee policy, and deal with foreign governments and international agencies. Between 1933 and 1941, as increasing numbers of Jews sought refuge outside of Nazi Germany, American consuls added severe restrictions to the already stringent U.S. visa regulations. With these restrictions, and in its opposition to increasing the number of refugees allowed into the United States under the quota system, the State Department reflected the prevalent public opinion on immigration restrictions. The American people rejected increasing immigration and felt that further immigrants, with their poverty, their European quarrels, and their pro-labor or even pro-communist ideas, would only destabilize American society. Even before the Great Depression, Americans overwhelmingly supported restrictive immigration quotas.

In 1938, with US unemployment again on the rise, four separate polls indicated that between 71 and 85 percent of all Americans opposed increasing quotas to help refugees. Sixty-seven percent of Americans favored a halt to all immigration. During the 1930s, for the first time in U.S. history, those leaving the United States outnumbered those entering. Specifically, the American people rejected increasing Jewish immigration. Immediately after *Kristallnacht* in November 1938, 94 percent of a sample poll by the National Opinion Research Center in Chicago disapproved of Nazi treatment of Jews, but 72 percent were opposed to admitting a large number of German Jews into the United States. Jewish leaders in America were deeply concerned about the dangers faced by German and Austrian Jews, but American Jewry, composed of disunited political factions, was unable to alter United States immigration policy. There were also some well-placed Jewish leaders who felt that they had worked hard to fully assimilate into American society and did not want a horde of Eastern European Jewish immigrants to upset their standing.

The State Department cautioned consular officials to exercise particular care in screening applicants. Rose heard many stories about German Jews who had American sponsors, which she had yet to acquire, having been told by US consular officials that all immigration quotas were filled and that they could expect to wait three or four years to come to the United States.

Hitler's vision of saving Germany involved expanding the country's borders to provide *lebensraum* for the German Aryan race while resisting and destroying Germany's enemies, directed by International Jewry. who were encircling the country. By mid-1940, he was well along on his goal to "secure predominance in Europe and the world." He believed that the Jews dominated and controlled the United States. Given the antisemitic actions of the Roosevelt administration, any critical thinker would have to disagree.

The highest-ranking Jew under Roosevelt in 1940 was Secretary of the Treasury Henry Morgenthau. Max Nussbaum, a German-educated rabbi and Zionist leader, arrived in the United States in August 1940, and met with Morgenthau about the existential threat to the Jewish people. Nussbaum recalled that the "burning question" for Morgenthau was whether Jews were spies for Germany. "I had the feeling that the great political questions of the Jewish people all over the world interested Mr. Morgenthau only marginally, and that Jewry – outside of the American sector – represented to him a world in which he does not identify and of which he prefers to speak in the third person." The first question Morgenthau asked Nussbaum was how many Jews he knew who were working for the Gestapo.

In keeping with the decision to achieve greater control over the immigration process, Roosevelt transferred Immigration and Natural Services from the Labor Department to the Justice Department in June 1940. Attorney General Robert Jackson, whom Roosevelt had appointed earlier that year, avowed that the move would accomplish "a more strict control of the privilege of entering this country." Jackson would not have issued such a declaration without the President's tacit approval.

On June 28, 1940, Roosevelt signed a bill requiring aliens to complete registration forms. At that point, there were approximately five million individuals residing in the U.S. who were not American citizens, including Günter. The Department of Justice maintained a card index system of all Germans in the country. In October 1941, he was required to register as an alien and report his income to the Department of Justice. In the meantime, Rose, Else and Fanni were continuously waiting for an order to appear at the United States Consulate in Stuttgart to begin the process of obtaining a visa.

On November 10, 1940, Rose, Else and Fanni sent a letter from Aachen to Günter and Walter Vorreuter, Fanni's great nephew, who had recently arrived in the USA and was living at the same Philadelphia rooming house as his first cousin Günter.

From: Fanni

My dear two boys,   Aachen, November 10th, 1940

... I will, dear Walter, also forward your letter to your dear mother these days. We would have loved to have had the good lady here for a longer time, but she had no peace to stay any longer now. Will God grant us for her to come back soon and then hopefully stay longer. We were happy when mother told us that thank God she had no more sugar at all. Looked well rested even, knock on wood. .... The loved ones from Shanghai wrote last week, thank God, very satisfied. Unfortunately there is no news from Helmut. The last letter from him was from April! Even in Horn our loved ones hear nothing from Hilde and Oskar *(also in Jewish Palestine)*. Ruth *(Liepmann)* from Paderborn writes happily. This week it is her grandmother's birthday in Horn. Unfortunately, Uncle Paul still doesn't know what to do!... My condition leaves a lot to be desired. Walking, seeing, and hearing, everything leaves a lot to be desired. At my age you can't expect much from life. Unfortunately, we hear so seldom from New Orleans *(her granddaughter, Margot)* now. But I am so happy when you, dear Walter and dear Günther, thank God, write with satisfaction...Write me please again soon with, God willing, satisfactory reports,

your loving old grandma and aunt Fanny

From: Rose

My dear boys

... We were so sorry to see *(Walter's mother)* ... leave again so quickly, but her restlessness was so great! But she promised God willing to come back soon. Incidentally, a few days ago we also received a card from *(Walter in)* Honolulu dated August 19th, that was the anniversary of your dear father's death. How well is he and who knows what sorrow and pain he has been spared. We want to grant him the rest! Hopefully you dear boys will be safe and sound as we are, thank God, when these lines arrive. ... I have just thanked Gerda and Max for their letter of October 13th (here on November 11th) and for a tin of very nice coffee, to which we have treated ourselves. Gerda's salary was raised to $ 100 a month by the medical company. She writes that that is not a lot, but she only works a few hours a week with it. If only it doesn't come to a war between the USA and Japan! ... How are your winter suits, dear boy? Is it still the ones you took with you? Make sure that the ones from dear father won't get the moth! Helmut will probably have a good use for it. He must be ragged in clothes. Have you heard anything from him? ... Do you already know that Margot from New Orleans went to Chicago, where she was accompanying a family to look after two small children, and never came back? She stayed there against her parents' wishes. Such a stupid girl! But now she should learn a trade. You can imagine how Aunt Paula *(Margot's mother)* grieves about it and Grandma grieves terribly too. Margot is by no means affectionate, and never writes a line to her old grandmother...

What can Margot do now alone in Chicago? Hopefully she stays good and well-mannered?... Well goodbye, write to your loving mother and aunt again very soon

Special greetings for Aunt Minna!

From: Else

Dear Günter and dear Walter, we were very happy with your lines, I hope you are safe and sound. It's good that the suitcase arrived. We want to hope that the other one will reach you too. Aunt Else.

The above letter is the among the last containing a section handwritten by *Oma*, grandmother, Fanni. As described in numerous letters primarily by Else, she had slowly been losing her sight and hearing and was sleeping in bed or in a chair most of the day.

The next letter was written on November 20, 1940, to Günter from Aachen.

From: Rose

My dear Gunther,

In my last letter to you on November 12th, Grandma and I thanked you for your and Walter's joint letter of October 24th. which pleased us very much on November 10th. I immediately sent Walter's lines to his mother, who is very astonished that Walter did not receive her various letters. Aunt Henny received a message from the forwarding agent that the suitcase that had been left in Berlin could be forwarded. It is back in Cologne and should be put on the road as quickly as possible. Were there a lot of Walter's things missing? ...

... Hopefully you are healthy and have nothing to complain about. ... How is the school going, dear Gunther? Are you making good progress in speaking? We have lessons twice a week, but unfortunately my memory is no longer as good as it used to be. I forget everything too easily, only what I have learnt, I have learnt. Aunt Else feels the same way, but in the end we learn something.

Oh, dear boy, if only we would soon be reunited with you! Local acquaintances, whose acquaintance Walter still made with us, received a notarized certificate from their brother, who has been living in New York for two to three years (he is a doctor there), that he would provide for a living in the USA. They hope that they may come to the country as visitors before their number is called.

Dear Günter, we would really like to have such a certificate from you or Stanley and would be very grateful to you. Perhaps such a letter can be of some use to us. Please talk to Stanley about it and send us the certified statement as soon as possible! God grant we can stay until our number is called! I also recently asked Gerda for three permits, but I hardly believe that there are any at the moment, as Japan does not issue any. The old permits that Gerda sent earlier have expired.

... My legal representative recently wrote to me that I had won the lawsuit against Padberg and Müller and that they would also have to pay the costs. I'm happy about that, of course, especially because they didn't get away with their bad behavior towards me.

How are you doing business-wise and has it gotten better in your department? Have you had a message from Helmut in the meantime? How is he doing? How dearly I loved to hear from him? ...

Your letters, dear boy, are the only joy we have! If only the Almighty would answer my prayer and bring us all together again in the not-too-distant future! How grateful and satisfied we would be, no matter how modest we lived. Now it is time to sleep, but one often lies awake and ponders everything! Stay healthy, my dear Gunther, please very soon with good reports, God willing,

your very loving mother.

From: Else

Dear Günter, we have been waiting eagerly for news from you for a few days. Hopefully we will soon hear good things from you all. Make sure that you can send us the relevant certificate. Stanley has helped a lot and hopefully won't let us down. It would be a small reassurance if we had something in our hands. If only we could be together again! Aunt Minna is lucky! Warm regards also from Aunt Else

Beginning December 1, 1940, the contents of the correspondence from my Aachen family to Gunther in the USA was becoming even more censored by Nazi authorities. Each page of every letter had the addition of two identical multidigit numbers, unique to each letter, separated by a hyphen or a backslash, each series written by a different hand in pencil, placed in the top left corner, signifying that the contents had been read. The first number was usually four-digits in length, while the second contained either three or four digits. For example, the letter below had the number "2658-1855" added to each page by censors. It is likely that one number designated the sender and the other the geographic area from which the correspondence derived, or possibly one of the numbers was related to the official performing the censoring.

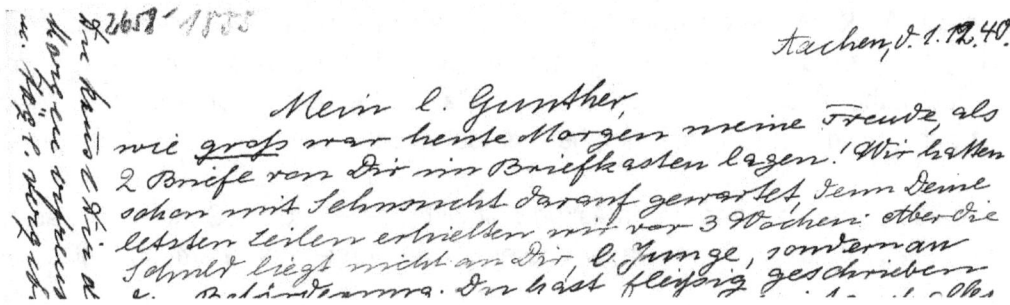

I have difficulty even imagining the anxiety that Rose endured each time she penned ink to paper, realizing that her words would be carefully read by a stranger who held her fate in his hands. Else's contribution to these later letters is mostly confined to expressions of emotions and everyday chit-chat and Fanni's greetings and utterances of grandmotherly love are usually transmitted briefly by Else. Else's writing is typically additive, confined to vertical space at the margins of each busy page, and made easier by the luxury of having already perused her older sister's comments and tone, adjusting her own written thoughts to repeat Rose's with different phraseology, only slightly embellishing the story, but rarely going down a new path of material.

For Rose the composition of each letter involved a careful combination of information and emotional outpouring, with words prudently chosen so that the epistle designated for "der Kleine" would not be assigned to the pile chosen for incineration.

The majority of her communications, both from Velmede and Aachen, refer to the specific dating of letters just received by her. I am certain that she kept a careful physical or mental record of the dates that she wrote each letter and that the communications that she received from her children abroad likewise contained references to the dating of their mother's letters. In this way, she would know whether specific letters never made their way to their designated addressee.

It is remarkable that her letters do not address the actions of World War II, which now was about to enter its second year and whose progress was well documented, albeit not truthfully, in the German newspapers she read daily. In addition, her letters do not include direct comments about the deteriorating situation all around her. In all of the letters written by my family from Germany to the children, the word "Hitler" is never used. References to politics are noticeably absent. This is a demonstration of Rose's grit and restraint, generated both by her desire to have her letters reach their destination and not wanting to be designated either *Volksfremden* (alien) or *Volksfeinden* (hostile). Undoubtedly, Rose personally knew many instances where friends or neighbors had received a knock on the door, followed quickly by one or more human disappearances at the hands of the Nazis.

Aachen to Günter, December 1, 1940

From: Rose

My dear Gunther,

How great was my joy this morning when 2 letters from you were in the mailbox! ... Hopefully when these lines arrive you will be as well as we are today, thank God. It has become ... really cold, but today ... the sun was shining so beautifully that Aunt Else and I went ... to visit a nice family (mother and daughter). We know the girl from the English class, she was recently seriously ill... but has recovered. They live here as long as we do, their father died at the same time as ours and is buried next to our dear father. Her only brother (formerly a lawyer) is now a gardener in Hollywood, and she hopes to go there with her mother when her number is called.

I read your description of the costume and masked ball with interest, dear Gunther. It was good that you chose the cheap costume. In any case, you enjoyed yourself just as much in it as in an expensive one. ...

... Did I already write to you, dear boy, that Aunt Marie got the papers for entry from Werner to be able to go. She can bring her clothes and household items. The lucky one! It is a lot that Werner, who has been out of work for so long, has already managed that. He still doesn't earn much and is struggling hard. The higher it is to be taken into account! The mother of Martha ..., now in the old people's home in Hannover, also received the papers for emigration from her son Iwan, who has a business in a small town in the USA. If only the consulates worked faster...

A few days ago we had a letter from Gerda and her mother-in-law dated October 25th with good news. ... The mother *(Sara Dahl)* had a letter from her sister Else in Australia, who is fine. The Salms have also been with their sons in the USA since August. It's strange that Helmut doesn't write to you or Gerda! If there is no mail getting out from there? They don't hear anything from Hilde and Oskar in Horn either! I would really like to know how Helmut is doing. It's nice that Gerda's belongings met with approval, dear Gunther. Be economical and think about later! Did you actually get rid of all the shirts? Or did you keep some? ...

Margot is purportedly in a mail order business in Chicago. She doesn't write a line to her old grandmother, which I find very unfair. She always speaks of her and wants to write to her, but we have not yet been able to find out the address...   Your mother who loves you always with good news

From: Else

You can imagine, dear Günther, how much we enjoyed your two letters this morning, after we hadn't heard from you for almost three weeks and were waiting for post every day in vain. It was a real Sunday joy. Yesterday, Uncle Paul gave us advance notice of a fruit package, which we are already looking forward to as our magnificent apples are running low! ... Greetings ... from Grandma and your Aunt Else

December 9, 1940, Aachen to Günter:

From: Rose

My dear Gunther,

We have just finished our supper and now comes the hour of chat with you that I have been looking forward to all day. May God grant it to us to have it cozy in our own home with you my dear boy again as in the past. Aunt Else and I had lessons today in the community center with six other nice people. We have a good teacher who speaks fluently. I wish I could speak as well as she does. I understand much better than I talk...

I ... hope you will get my lines... in which I asked you for a notarized certificate for emergencies only.

How are you, dear Gunther, health and otherwise? I hope and wish you are satisfied in every way. If you are often so tired, I would go to sleep earlier in the evening. In any case, you lack sleep. So take my advice and get a good night's sleep! Are you more satisfied with business now? ... How satisfied dear father and I were always when everything went so well and we had a hearty workload. Unfortunately that is all over now!

... By the way, as you intended, did you write to Helmut by airmail? How terribly happy we would be if we heard from him again. I can't understand why he's not writing to you and Gerda. Uncle Paul recently wrote to us that they had news from Oskar and Hilde indirectly, namely Oskar's mother wrote via USA... Oskar has five employees in his snack bar and is satisfied.

... Incidentally, did Gerda send you a parcel for sale for the second time and did you get the things early enough before Christmas? Max wrote thank God that the practice was to his satisfaction, which made me particularly happy...

Dear Gunther, please see to it that the moths don't get to father's suits. I am very happy that you want to give me a blouse. It is so nice of you! ... Now I ... therefore close with heartfelt greetings for you and all loved ones there. Stay healthy and please us again very soon with a detailed letter.

In constant love, your mother

From Else:

Dear Gunther, to you, Walter and Aunt Minna, the warmest greetings from Oma and me. Yesterday, Sunday, we were very pleased with your letter. We are always so happy when good news comes from you and Gerda.

Love   Aunt Else.

Aachen to Günter December 19, 1940

From Rose:

My dear Gunther,

... Hopefully you, dear boy, are in good health and otherwise, so that you have no reason to complain. Was the Christmas business satisfactory? During this time I think of earlier times so often; when we were still in Velmede and had so much to do from early in the morning until late in the evening that we hardly had time to eat. I see our dear father cutting off the wares that had been sold in the shop late in the evening and carrying them into the room at the front of the street. When it came to packing, the table in the living room was pulled out very long and an infinite number of large and small packages were packed and labelled with names. It happened like lightning! Nobody could pack as well and as quickly as our dear father. This is all over now and will never come back, unfortunately! Before I forget, please make a note of the fact that on March 30th, 1941, we have Yahrzeit from our good, blessed Father and that you have to light the … *(memorial candle)* on March 29th. Don't forget about it, dear Günter, and please tell Helmut, to whom you have hopefully written a long time ago, as you intended to do. Why is he not writing to you at all? Gerda hasn't heard from him for a long time either. If only he is healthy and in good spirits! Thank God we are fine, only grandma's sight leaves a lot to be desired. Walking and hearing are also very difficult for her. Unfortunately, she is always confined to her room, but what can you do, old age is a nasty disease. Grandma is also so worried about Margot, whose address we cannot find out, even though we asked Aunt Paula about it so much. Isn't that strange? ...

Dear Günter, do you have acquaintances in Chicago or other connections there? Aunt Paula recently wrote that it would not be right if we wrote to Margot, it would make her even more "stubborn!" Isn't that nonsense! Grandma is now very angry and grieved about it. I can't understand why Margot doesn't even write to her old grandmother. She didn't even congratulate her on New Years! Aunt Paula is very annoyed with Margot, who has cut off her future through her arbitrary actions..... Well, my dear boy, farewell and, with Walter, I warmly greet you. In constant love your mother.

From: Else

Dear Günter, I hope we will get mail from you very soon. Greetings and kisses from Grandma and Aunt Else

Aachen to Günter December 28, 1940

From Rose:

My dear Gunther,

I've just written to Gerda, and now it's your turn. Our old grandfather clock in the hallway is striking 10 o'clock and Grandma, who is sitting in the armchair, wants to go to sleep. Unfortunately, she can no longer do handicrafts or read in the evening, and this makes her evenings very long, while they always pass too quickly for me. ... Aunt Else and I visited our dear father's grave and found it in good order...

... God grant that you, dear boy, are safe and sound and that only the postal service is to blame for your silence. Did my letters arrive there? They were dated November 20th, December 1st, December 9th, and December 19th, all by air-mail. We wait eagerly for the postman every day, but we are always disappointed. We have also been without a sign of life from Gerda for three weeks, we are not used to that from her. Your letters are our only joy, dear boy! How are you? Was the Christmas business good and were you really busy? Did you also notice something about Channukah and do they light the candles there like in the past here? I think sadly of the happy years when your good father lit them and we all sang the beautiful old melodies together. Your homemade candlestick, which you made out of lots of rolls and then covered so beautifully with bronze, always reminds me of the past... Do you … notice that the courses at Temple University are helpful to you?

... Have you heard anything from Helmut in the meantime? I don't understand why he's not writing to you or Gerda... Dear Günter, I wrote you that Margot stayed in Chicago against her parents' wishes. She has not yet written a line to us from there. Grandma is very angry and grieved about this. ... Now we asked Aunt Paula for Margot's address, but to no avail. She gives the reason that Margot might be even more stubborn if we wrote to her. That's nonsense. I wouldn't write to her at all because she's so little affectionate, but Grandma is killing herself and talks about Margot all day. Aunt Paula wrote that she was in a wholesaling mail order office and was earning her living. The Comité continues to look after her there. ...Dear Günter, did you pack your father's suits away well so that no moths get to them? Do you ever use the glass that Walter gave you? You know it was a present from Gerda for the silver wedding anniversary! ... Now I wish you, dear boy, a happy and blessed new year! Stay healthy and ambitious and ensure that you move forward, you know how we all hope for you! ... I close in the hope that I will soon hear good things from you again. Be warmly greeted and hugged by your loving mother

From: Else

Dear Günter, this time the holidays were not so nice, because there was no mail from you! Hopefully you are healthy and we will soon hear good things from you and also from Shanghai! I wish You and Aunt Minna and Walter have a healthy, happy new year and greet you all very warmly, your Aunt Else

Despite the major political changes in Europe in 1940 and the increasing stranglehold of the Third Reich on the lives of German Jews, my grandmother Rose's letters continue to have the same themes, all centered about her devotion to her children and concern regarding their welfare. She is thankful for each letter she receives from them, carefully reading each word numerous times. News regarding Helmut in Palestine is sparse, and Rose often chooses to blame the mail service, since friends who also have relatives in the Middle East are also receiving letters infrequently. Rose has become a broker for clothing that Gerda purchases inexpensively in China and sends to Günter in Philadelphia to sell to supplement his meager income. Rose frequently counsels her youngest child to work hard and save some money for a rainy day. For Rose, the rainy days were already here, and the contents of each letter made reference to the existential question of how she, her sister Else and her mother Fanni will be able to escape from Germany and be reunited with her children scattered throughout a troubled world.

Chapter 15: 1941

Hitler's noose was tightening in Germany, Austria, and all of occupied Europe. By mid-1941, prior to the United States' entry into the War, the Nazis and their allies had taken control of an area nine times the size of today's Germany. Bulgaria, Hungary, Romania, Finland, and Italy had aligned themselves with Germany. Aside from Great Britain and France, officially at war with Germany, the only European countries not under Axis control were the formally neutral states of Ireland, Portugal, Spain, Sweden, Switzerland, and Turkey. By the end of 1940, despite the Molotov-Ribbentrop Treaty, Hitler had issued Führer Directive 21, a secret order for Germany's planned invasion of the Soviet Union to gain new territory on their Eastern Front to provide more *Lebensraum* for German citizens.

As the Nazi regime's attacks intensified in the late 1930s, my family, together with hundreds of thousands of other Jews in Germany, continued to attempt to get a visa stamped onto their passport allowing immigration to the United States.

The process of procuring that visa involved surmounting almost impossible odds, yet Rose spent many hours every day either thinking about procedures to overcome the obstacles, writing to friends and relatives to get advice, or visiting various offices to attempt to expedite acquiring that magical small piece of paper. She patiently had gathered all necessary documents since registering for the waiting list in 1938, paying multiple fees in Cologne and Stuttgart to obtain these documents, many of which had expiration dates which required renewing them more than once. Errors could set you back months and be extremely expensive. Rose continued to search for an American financial sponsor. Any communication with a prospective sponsor could only be by sending letters, which could take weeks to arrive at their destination. After September 1940, the United States government required two sponsors. Concurrently with this, Rose was attempting to buy ship tickets since she would have to prove, if indeed they were finally called from the visa waiting list, that they had booked passage out of Europe. These tickets were rare and extremely expensive, since transatlantic travel from Europe had become exceedingly challenging after World War II began in September 1939. Ports had closed and German submarines were attacking ships in the Atlantic Ocean.

By 1941, there were no longer any ships going from Germany to the United States and Rose was, at this time, also attempting to collect transit visas, those stamps on one's passport from all the countries which one needed to travel through to get to a yet unknown ship's unknown port of departure. These costly stamps required amassing in a specific order. One mistake could send you back to the same government office many times. Even if all the above were fulfilled, an American consular interview was required if one was called from the lengthy waiting list. At that interview, the State Department official would carefully read all of your paperwork to make sure you were financially stable, healthy, and would not be a threat to US national security. These officials often rejected applicants for economic or national security reasons or told them to return later with more documents. In the unlikely event that all was in order, the official would stamp a visa onto a page in your passport, and you would fill one of the quota slots available to potential immigrants that year. Rose knew the intricacies of the long, complicated, and expensive process of immigrating to the United States, but continued to hope that all hurdles would be overcome. Hundreds of thousands of people, mostly Jewish refugees, applied at American consulates in Europe but were unable to emigrate. My family, like so many others, became trapped in Nazi-occupied territory and were murdered in the Holocaust.

The letters from Rose to her children continued to be sent regularly. She felt that frequent communication with one's offspring was not only the duty required of any good mother, but also allowed her to express her concern about their well-being in all respects. Writing replaced feeding, making sure they were physically well, mentally fulfilled and planning for the future. She could no longer tuck them safely into their beds or wipe away a tear from their eyes. As Thornton Wilder wrote in *The Bridge of San Luis Rey,* "Henceforth letter-writing had to take the place of all the affection that could not be lived."

Each missive was often prompted by correspondence received from Shanghai, Palestine (rarely) or Philadelphia, but undoubtedly, Günter received the most mail from Aachen. After all, he was the baby, not even 21 years old, living in a foreign land, by himself, caring for himself. Gerda was ten years older and had the stability of a home and a husband who provided for her. As for Helmut, communication from him had always been sparse, initially causing a great deal of stress, but Rose had gradually become accustomed to seldom hearing from him. As the year 1941 went forward, the tone of the correspondence emanating from my grandmother Rose gradually changes. What had been hope and acceptance becomes resignation and then, slowly, there is the definite undertone of desperation.

No parent ever wishes to be a burden upon a child. Grief can be expressed but suffering is not a millstone that one plans to place upon a child's back, no matter how broad that may appear to others. Although every letter continues to speak about the ordinary, the conversation always returns to comments and questions about "guarantees" and "visas" and "passages." Without wishing to make the children responsible for her future, the anguish felt by both the writer and recipients becomes greater with each passing month.

In mid-1941 the Nazis decided to establish a Ministry for the Occupied Eastern Territories (*Ostland*), the German occupied Baltic states, Poland, and White Russia (Belarus), newly conquered from the Soviet Union. Hitler appointed Alfred Rosenberg as *Reichskommissariat Ostland* and directed him to both administer the territories and draft measures proposed "to implement the desired final solution of the Jewish Question." The Germans attempted to disguise their intentions, referring to deportations as "resettlement to the east." The victims were told they were to be taken to labor camps, but in reality, from 1942 onward, deportation for most Jews meant transit to killing centers.

In the latter part of 1941, officials of the RSHA (*Reichssicherheitshauptamt*), the organization which combined the intelligence service (*SS*), the Security Service (*SD*) the criminal police (*Kripo*) and the Secret State Police *(Gestapo)*, under the leadership of Heydrich began the policy of sending trainloads of German, Austrian, and Czechoslovakian Jews to the *Ostland.* The Nazi main political objectives for this area were the complete annihilation of the Jewish population, the expulsion of the native population, and the settlement of ethnic Germans in this new portion of German territory.

Within two months of the Polish takeover by the German *Wehrmacht,* the population of the Warsaw Ghetto in Poland, the area where all Jews in that large Polish city were imprisoned by the occupying Nazis, had swelled to 400,000. Food was rationed, those within the Ghetto being limited to under 200 calories per day. All sources of fuel were also withheld, and hundreds of Jews were dying daily of starvation or freezing to death. This situation was rarely reported to areas distant from Poland and I do not know whether my grandmother Rose was aware of current events in Warsaw and the rest of the *Ostland*. The absence of any comments in her many letters are not necessarily indicative of lack of knowledge since Rose was mindful that German censors reading her words in each letter would not look kindly on any information critical of Nazi policy.

As a matter of fact, the international press was remarkably silent in 1941 about the ongoing dreadful deeds of the Nazis. Although shortly after Hitler came to power in March of 1933, he resolved to eliminate Germany's "hereditarily unfit," the *New York Times* in October of 1933 merely reported that a German Ministry of Justice memorandum proposed that it shall be made possible for German physicians "to end the tortures of incurable patients, upon request, in the interests of true humanity." It was not until eight years later, in May 1941, that the *New Republic* published the first American report of Nazi atrocities. In that document, former U.S. Department of State official Michael Straight revealed that in the autumn of 1940, "85,000 blind, incurably ill, or aged Germans were put to death as casually as the SPCA chloroforms old and helpless dogs. They were not killed for mercy. They were killed because … the German hospitals were needed for wounded soldiers" and "because their death was the ultimate logic of the national socialist doctrine of the racial superiority and survival of the physically fit." An editorial in the Washington Post on May 5, 1941, echoed Straight's revelation and six weeks later, William Shirer's book, *Berlin Diary: The Journal of a Foreign Correspondent, 1934-1941,* was published in the United States. Regarding this *Gnadenstoß* (coup de grace), Shirer wrote that "It's an evil tale...The Germans advanced three reasons for the killings: That they are being carried out to save food, that they are done for the purpose of experimenting with new poison gases and death rays, and that they are simply the result of the extreme Nazis deciding to carry out their eugenic and sociological ideas....I am also informed that the relatives of the unfortunate victims…receive a stern warning from the secret police not to demand explanations and not to spread false rumors."

It was not until a year later, in May 1942, that the Polish-Jewish underground smuggled out a report which estimated that 700,000 Polish Jews had already been killed by the Germans.

In June 1941, the United States Department of State issued a "relatives' rule," forbidding the granting of a visa to anyone who had close family still in Nazi territory. This, for all practical purposes, closed the door for my family, who were all within "Nazi territory" at the time. Yet Günter remained undeterred in his attempts to bring his family to the United States in spite of repeatedly being told that it had become virtually impossible to get a visa for entry to the United States.

Despite public antipathy to revising American immigration laws, some refugee aid organizations tried to assist the hundreds of thousands attempting to flee Europe. Jewish and Christian organizations provided money for food and clothing, transit fare, employment, and financial assistance, and offered help in finding affidavits for endangered prospective Jewish immigrants. The most prominent of these groups was the American Jewish Joint Distribution Committee (JDC or "Joint"), originally formed in 1914 by the merger of two newly established relief committees, the largely Reformed American Jewish Relief Committee and the Orthodox Central Relief Committee, joined by a third committee one year later, the People's Relief Committee, composed of labor and socialist groups. The initial purpose of the Joint was to raise and distribute funds to help support the Jewish populations of eastern Europe and the Near East during World War I. Günter spent many weekends in 1940 and 1941 travelling to New York and Washington, D.C., to seek aid and advice from the JDC, all to no avail.

On July 1, 1941, the State Department centralized all alien visa control in Washington, DC, forcing every visa applicant to be approved by a review committee in Washington, and each was required to submit additional paperwork, including a second financial affidavit. At the same time, Nazi Germany ordered the

United States to shut down its consular offices in all German-occupied territories. After July 1941, emigration from Nazi-occupied territory was virtually impossible. Obtaining visas to some Latin American nations was the only legal way out of Germany. Only German refugees who had already escaped Nazi territory could obtain US immigration visas. At this point, the State Department canceled the visa waiting list, for which my family had registered more than three years earlier. The United States would not be at war with Germany for five more months, that event occurring after Pearl Harbor in December 1941.

Throughout this period Hitler and the Nazis continued their racial policies and confiscation of Jewish property by all possible means. In November 1941, the "Eleventh Decree" legalized the automatic confiscation of all property of German Jews "deported" to the East.

I am certain that Rose, tenderly penning letters to her beloved children located on three other continents, chose each word carefully. A major portion of each week was undoubtedly spent carefully composing her thoughts before putting her pen to the onionskin-like paper. In some of the missives she expresses the pleasure she receives from the mere anticipation of a written connection. There is rarely a letter where Rose does not articulate the pure joy she experienced upon reading the communications from her three children. Conversely, she is easily distracted and concerned if an anticipated correspondence is delayed, or she hears nothing from Helmut for months on end. For Rose, I believe that writing these letters to her children was undoubtedly the high point of each day. Many of these letters, but certainly not all, have survived. For me to touch them and read them allows me to experience the love with which they were composed and written. The letters Rose received from her children have, of course, not endured, but their contents can often be deciphered by Rose's reference to them in her subsequent writings.

On January 8, 1941, the family in Aachen wrote to Günter in Philadelphia:

From Rose:

My dear Günter,

In my last airmail letter to you …dated December 18, 1940, … I wrote you that I was waiting so much for mail from you because your last three letters of July 3rd and November 14th arrived here at the beginning of December and unfortunately we haven't heard from you (since)... You can imagine how eagerly we are waiting for a letter from you, dear Günter! Hopefully you are healthy and in good spirits, also all loved ones there and your silence is only due to a failure of the post office...

On New Year's and the day after we received two letters from Gerda and Max with, thank God, good content... We ... were really happy to finally hear good things. They also had a letter from you, in which you ordered some shirts. ... Unfortunately, Gerda didn't hear anything from Helmut. Did you get a letter from him, dear boy? I don't understand why he's not writing to you! If only he's alive and well! ... We can only wish that the new year will take away our great worries and we would walk towards a good future!

... Haven't you heard about a raise again, dear Günter? You mentioned it earlier.

On November 20th I asked you for a notarized certificate in case of emergency. Did you get the letter? I don't know if it's useful. Friends here had it sent from over there! I just heard from Aunt Henny that acquaintances in Stuttgart did not get the visa. Out of 25 people, only 3 received it that

217

day who have children over there. We also have very high numbers and have to wait a long time. May God just keep us healthy! Aunt Marie is probably going to Werner in Rio on the 22nd of the month. The journey is via Lisbon. You really have to be amazed that Werner can send for his mother so quickly; he hasn't had work long and doesn't earn much. Hilde's husband from Bücken recently went to Argentina alone (*without his wife*), where he has 1 brother... How is it in the school? I'm sure you're already speaking fluently, dear boy. Now please, please us soon with a long letter. Then the sun will shine for us too! Stay healthy and be with us always in spirit.

Love hugs you your faithful mother

From Else:

Dear Günter,

I hope you are healthy, and we will get mail from you soon. Best regards from Grandma and your aunt Else, who loves you

Back of envelope of January 8, 1941, letter from Rose to Günter. The middle name of "Sara" is used in this and all future letters as required by the Nazi mandate as of January 1, 1939.

On the same day, January 8, 1941, Rose's son Helmut from Palestine writes his brother Günter in the USA. The lengthy letter primarily concerns Helmut's experience with an extended bout of typhoid fever. There is no apparent major apprehension regarding the terrible situation in Europe and the tenuous existence of the family in Aachen. It is as if he has put on blinders because he cannot deal with the situation, having neither the means nor the temperament to do so. As he wrote: "but you know, I am an optimist and do not tend to always assume the worst. So I live in the belief that our loved ones in Aachen are doing well."

Magdiel, January 8, 1941

Dear Günter!

Your card from Miami, here at the beginning of November, your letter of September 23, here on November 25, have been waiting for quite a long time for a reply, and it came about this way: for I have afforded myself the luxury of being ill, and not too little. I spent more than five weeks in the hospital with typhoid fever. In itself, there would be nothing more to write about than the fact that today I am almost in full possession of my powers again, but since I assume that you are interested, I will be a little more detailed.

On Thursday, November 8, I was still working pretty hard in the Pardess *(Hebrew word for "orchard"),* so I was still healthy. When on Friday evening Löwes, with whom I always eat on this day, asked me to go for a walk after supper, I felt chilly, an otherwise unknown phenomenon to me, and went home early. You know I don't run to the doctor right away, although I have it free from the insurance, and dragged myself around like that for a few days, thinking it was flu. Headache towards evening mainly and fever, those were the symptoms. When I did go to the doctor and had aspirin given, he didn't think it was serious either. The aspirin caused a terrible sweating at night, also eliminated the headache, but the fever that I took three times a day at the behest of the doctor, persisted. On Tuesday I stayed in bed...and I did not lack warm food, just as I wished. The doctor came several times, expressed concern, and finally diagnosed typhoid fever with a fair degree of certainty based on a water test.

Thursday morning I sent the doctor's certificate to the "Department of health" in Jaffa. You must know that here in the country all infectious people are taken over and healed by the government, which maintains special hospitals for that. It is mandatory, there are no private institutions for such a thing, and it costs, by the way, nothing. By the way, already in the afternoon an extremely nice Arabic doctor with guards came in an ambulance, examined me again and took me away immediately, after I had packed the essential things together in a hurry... I was taken to a government hospital not far from Tel Aviv, which has only Jewish staff and only Jewish patients. Before I even knew what was happening to me, the guard had already shaved half my head. All the protest didn't help. The rules. Boy, was it bad there! The only things that deserve praise are the doctors, one of them a German, and the nurses. Everything else was below par! Every day the same food and so little that you were hungry forever. In addition, you don't get a hot bite, everything is almost cold, which is not supposed to be that way, but is due to deficiencies in organization, for which a "Miss" was responsible as the directrice, not the nurses. The beds were bad, most of the time you had ice cold feet, the furnishings were miserable, for example, if you needed a nurse at night, you kept the whole hospital awake, there were eight of us. ... getting up was forbidden, you were too weak to do so anyway. So I lay there for 28 days with a fever... I was in a good mood and didn't feel bad, but I dreamed of roast chicken and potatoes with gravy. Then another ten days of observation with somewhat better rations, one was given some bread for the last five days and had the possibility of having butter procured on the spot by one of the nurses, at least a relief. You could also buy sweets and chocolate or have them brought to you by relatives, without seeing them yourself. By the way, chocolate was dangerous, because you ate it all at once from hunger and had stomach ache afterwards. You also had to learn to walk again, you staggered like a drunk.

So, after 38 days, on December 22nd, happy as a king, I was able to make my return to Magdiel. Everyone said I looked terribly bad and I was still weak. But in the 2 1/2 weeks since then I have eaten my way out of it magnificently and the rest did the rest. But I don't save either, I can tell you that I have private meals cooked for me and only in butter, whatever I have an appetite for. Today I am actually quite all right again, except for my feet, which still get tired when I walk for a long time. Also look better again, almost like before and in the course of the next 8 days the first hair parting will be possible again. So I am fully restored and in great spirits, still have the same friends and still associate with the same mostly German families.

I still occupy the same room at Liffschütz's place... He behaved very indelicately toward me. Back then, when the bombs fell in Tel Aviv and Haifa... he would have liked to throw me out on the street so that he could rent to the city dwellers at fantasy prices. However, he picked the wrong person with me. Besides, the man so disgusted me also by other things that I do not like to see him around me anymore, particularly since there are now free rooms at reasonable prices. By the way, I am still "sick" in the sense of the health insurance since I receive sick pay, 8 piastres a day, which is not enough to live on, but is nevertheless nice to have. I have been granted 20 days.

After my complete recovery, I will certainly not earn 8 piastres a day here in Magdiel, because for the whole winter, not even one day of work can be expected. The situation in the orange economy is bleak, and there is nothing else here. The trees bend under the load of golden fruits, goods that have value only if they can be exported. And will they be able to do that!? Hardly! ... Harvest work will not happen at all and that was otherwise high season, from which not only the worker, but all branches of the economy benefited

I will not sit idle here for the winter, rather I will try to find some work somewhere in the country. I am thinking primarily of Haifa, where the country's industry is concentrated, and I will probably stay there for a longer period of time if necessary, and on that occasion I will also see Oskar and his family, and probably also have my meals there. I also want to go to Jerusalem, if only to be remembered by the American consulate. Since my written registration in March of last year, I received confirmation at that time, I heard nothing more on the matter.

... To return to me: If I don't find anything, I'll have to stay in good old Magdiel, where I like it quite a bit and where life costs me the least. Besides, I'll have work here, I would like to say as the first, the moment one works at all. Until my illness I was employed under the most pleasant conditions in a large Pardess, and the position has remained with me.

I almost forgot: My car was sold for a reasonably good price, for cash of course, so that I got off with a black eye. I still lost on the car itself, on the work with the car last winter, on money I didn't get and then some more in the course of the 5 years I'm here now almost. What I have received from home I know, namely 705 pounds, 300 pounds being shares at face value. What I still have I will add up in the next few days and let you know. Not considered are the occasional 10 Marks gifted.

Otherwise we've lived and still live quietly here in the country, even if one cannot know what the near future will bring. As far as food is concerned, everything is available in sufficient quantities, although prices are often not insignificantly higher than in peacetime. Hardware and household items have increased in price many times over, fabrics have also become expensive, and I had to buy some pajamas to my chagrin. Otherwise, I'm still outfitted pretty well, which means it's enough for here. You wear your clothes completely and mend them as long as you can. Suits that can be called "good" by European standards I have two, namely my black one and the gray one made in Mengede at the time. Everything else is patched up and mended, but still does its job perfectly. I guess I can say I am here very well dressed by Magdiel standards. In the summer you don't really need anything except shirts and a pair of khakis.

I still had a pair of Nazi boots, bought at the time for 12.50 Reichsmark at Stratmann, lying untouched in my suitcase, I sold them for 1,750 pounds, because I did not think they were practical because of the gaiter that opens at the side and also otherwise I am not a friend of such things. Instead, I had a pair of rough work shoes made for 1 pound, which I wear every day through the winter...

A few days ago in Tel Aviv I visited Neugartens ... Herbert has been divorced for a few weeks from his wife, who was and still is a dancer. *(Herbert Neugarten, a nephew of Sara Goldberg Dahl, my other grandmother, was born in Buer near Gelsenkirchen, Germany in 1912. He studied violin, viola, and double bass and came to Israel in 1937. He changed his name to Zvi Nagan and received his M.A. degree in philosophy from Tel Aviv University and after the War, worked toward a Ph.D. in musicology from Utrecht University in the Netherlands. Nagan is a well-known Israeli composer whose works include vocal choir music, pedagogic pieces for melodic instruments based mainly on Israeli folk tunes, and chamber pieces for various instrumental combinations. He died in Tel Aviv in 1986.)* It is better that way, in the long run living together was not possible, although one cannot say anything bad about Bella. Herbert's mother, a certainly very difficult, albeit good person, also did not help to make living together easier. ... The two of them live very happily together, even if they scold each other quite often and extensively, which I, as a connoisseur of the subject, in this case consider to be merely the outflow of excessive tenderness. Herbert has had work for months, and in all probability steady work, a rarity here in the country, namely as a private chauffeur for very rich people. He earns about eight pounds a month and food with his employer. This is certainly not a princely salary, but how one cannot get by on it, as the aunt claims, is incomprehensible to me. Complaining has become a habit for some people.

... But now to your card or letter: Dear Günter! If you notice that my last letter to you, - it contained two photos, - is dated August 31, then I must confirm the correctness with shame. Nevertheless, it was always letter after letter, only now there was a break due to my illness. Post and censorship are responsible for the fact that we hear so rarely from each other. By the way, two letters from Gerta are still waiting to be answered. Tomorrow I will take care of that, but you can be sure that the letter will be shorter. Once she wrote from Japan, the second time after her return to Shanghai, so I am pretty well oriented about home and the relatives, even if many things may have changed in the meantime, but you know, I am an optimist and do not tend to always assume the worst. So I live in the belief that our loved ones in Aachen are doing well. When I read that they are busy canning, including 50 pounds of peaches that they harvested themselves, I feel like peace time.

I take this opportunity to congratulate Walter (*Vorreuter*) on the final fulfillment of his wishes. I am convinced that he will quickly settle in and feel more comfortable. English is also a thing that is learned when one is forced to learn and speak. I envy him for the interesting trip, just a pity that Gerta found out too late about his stay in Kobe. What a wonderful country this is, where everyone can find work who is willing to work, for me today almost something unimaginable. The sad news of Uncle Adolf's (*Walter's father, married to Albert's sister, Henrietta Oppenheim*) passing has also shocked me. I can still see him during his frequent visits to Velmede, he never came without chocolate. I ask you to express my condolences to Walter... So the fate reaches today in this, tomorrow in that circle! I see a certain tragedy in the fact that he, who lived his life in Natzungen, was laid to rest in Siegburg, just as I would rather see our dear father rest in Meschede. *(The cemetery in Meschede was where Albert's parents, my great-grandparents, Moses Oppenheim and Lina Amant, are buried together with many other members of Albert's (and my) family. Had Rose and Albert not been forced to leave Velmede, he would undoubtedly have been buried there, rather than in the unfamiliar Jewish cemetery in Aachen.)*

You have really seen all sorts of things in your vacation, dear Günter. Here at the skat table a heated discussion arose about whether you had crossed the Mississippi or not, whereby fantastic views about the course of the Mississippi were expressed, until I could clarify the matter perfectly with the help of "Meyers Taschenatlas" (3 Marks) *(a pocket atlas).* For America it is still correct, for

Europe it gradually gets historical value. But the evening crowns the day. For God's sake, be content with your climate, even if your nose is a bit cold at the moment, and don't wish for the ever-shining sun of the south. What do you think, how gladly I would have a decent 15-degree cold north wind on the Kahler Asten *(this is a 3,000-foot-high mountain in Hochsauerland, a popular destination for tourists)* blow around my nose. The sentence before last is also valid in this respect. Do you often get together with Egon and Aunt Minna? What position does Egon hold in the business, and I must confess that I know very little about what you actually do. I am also interested in what you earn and roughly what you spend, as well as Walter's earnings and his current occupation... Are our cousins nice girls *(Lenore and Janet Oppenheim, the daughters of Max Oppenheim in New York, now in their late twenties)*? Say hello to everyone mentioned here, as far as you can.

If I wanted to write about politics, I would have to take two more sheets and "paper has become a very expensive article here." I just want to tell you that Roosevelt's speech a few days ago made a colossal impression on us. The press called it the most important speech since Wilson's on the declaration of war in 1917... Write home about me quite a lot and good things and do not forget to send my regards.

Sincerely, Helmut.

"Roosevelt's speech," referred to by Helmut in the last paragraph of the above letter, is the famous "Four Freedoms Speech" delivered by President Franklin Roosevelt on January 6, 1941. It has a short closing portion describing the President's vision in which the American ideals of individual liberties including freedom of speech, freedom of worship, freedom from want, and freedom from fear would be extended throughout the world.

Rose and Else wrote a letter to Günter on January 19, 1941:

From Rose:

My dear Günter,

I cannot tell you how great my joy was when your letter of November 21 arrived with Helmut's lines and his so well-taken photo on the 17th of this month, the day before yesterday. ...! The mail from there didn't seem to work. I am curious whether you received al all my letters dated ..... So thank you very much for your lines together, my dear two boys. I hope and wish that when these lines arrive, you will be safe and sound like me and us, thank God. We all want to trust in God and hope that it will be possible for us to see each other again in joy and to live together in a not too long time. The thought shines like a light in the dark!

Yesterday, when I came home from the service, I was very happy to find a registered letter from Stanley with something very important to us! He wrote very fondly and also praised you, dear Günter, which made me particularly happy because I had not yet received an answer from him to my question in this regard... He's really helpful and it's lucky that he takes care of us, I also mean mother and aunt Else. If our dear father had known that, how great would his joy have been! ... I think Helmut's picture is excellent! Good thing he went back to Magdiel. Apparently he feels most at home there. If only he were with you, dear Günter! The years there in the country are lost for him!

You have certainly heard that in this country this year, the numbers up to 30,000 are to be summoned to Stuttgart. You know well that we have a high number and that it will be a long time before it's our turn. If only we stay healthy in our cozy little house! Then this time will also pass quickly, God willing.

Today we were very pleased with a detailed letter from Gerda from December 16. ... Did you get rid of the second shipment of jewelry well? As a by-product of your order, Aunt Else got a very pretty ring that was enclosed with today's registered letter. It has a large jade plate and looks very good! ... Is Aunt Minna complaining about her daughter-in-law? It's best if you don't mix in and get on well with everyone.

We have a lot of cold ... but it's nice and warm (inside). We got coal a week ago and are now taken care of again. Aunt Else and I go to English lessons twice a week, which we enjoy. I wish I could speak as well as our teacher. For tomorrow I have to prepare my résumé in writing. I'll write English to Stanley so he can read it... Friends here in town...are among those now called up to Stuttgart, want to go to their son in Hollywood. ...Stay healthy and write to your very loving mother again soon.....

From Else:

Dear Günter,

How delighted we were with yesterday's letter, which this time was enroute for so long. Hopefully you are healthy just like us and we will soon hear from you more regularly. How are Aunt Minna and Walter? Greet them both warmly. Stanley's letter is a great comfort to us. Greetings from Grandma and let's hear from you soon! With love, your aunt Else.

The four members of my family had been assigned consecutive numbers far down on the visa waiting list, 46807 through 46810. In the above letter, Rose states that numbers up to 30,000 "are to be summoned" for interviews with the U.S. Consulate in Stuttgart. Rose assumes that Günter knew this state of affairs regarding the visas. It is uncertain what "something of importance" contained in the registered letter from Stanley Snellenburg represents. Rose was not going to give the Nazi censors reading the letter any excuse for interfering with the visa application process which was constantly lodged within her mind.

By the beginning of 1941, Günter had designated himself as the lead person in the battle to bring his family out of danger to a safer place. After all, the United States was a civilized country with a way of life that resembled the Germany that his parents had once known. China truly was a foreign land, with an alien language and strange customs, while Palestine was a primitive third-world area with a very uncertain future. Günter, immediately after his arrival in 1937, registered to become a United States citizen, which would occur after five continued years of residence. Until August 1942, he was still considered an alien. After that time, Günter, as a U.S. citizen, under U.S. Immigration law of the time, could petition the government to move his immediate family towards the top of the waiting list, something aliens with family abroad were unable to do. Günter had as his example the experience of his first cousin, Egon Baum, seven years his senior and also employed at *Snellenburg's,* who had arrived in the U.S. in 1933, and was able to bring his mother Minna to the U.S. when he became a citizen in early 1939.

During the winter of 1940 to 1941 and into the spring of 1941, Günter made frequent train trips to Washington D.C. to file inquiries both with the State Department and initially the Department of Labor and later the Department of Justice to inquire about progress with the visa application of his family. He had filed numerous affidavits of support and saw no progress regarding his efforts. He had also enlisted the assistance of the Philadelphia branch of the Hebrew Sheltering and Immigration Society (HIAS), walking to their location on South Ninth street frequently on his lunch break from work. That organization was founded in 1909 and in the 1930s was funded primarily by the American Jewish Joint Distribution Committee. HIAS at that time was attempting to assist refugees who, under US immigration law, had no special provision for escape from persecution. Their primary role was to counsel refugees on the process of acquiring immigration visas.

On January 20, 1941, Günter received a mailed postcard (form 576) acknowledging the Immigration and Naturalization Service's (INS) receipt of a previously filed form 575, a multipage affidavit of support for Rose Oppenheim, Fanny Liepmann and Else Liepmann. Similar boilerplate replies were received in respect to his documents submitted on behalf of Rose's younger brother Paul Liepmann and his wife Agnes and 12-year-old daughter Ruth. Günter had filled these out with utmost care, often tediously with the help of a German-English dictionary or one of his American friends living at his Philadelphia rooming house. The postcard is evidence of the chaos existing at the INS at that time. The printed "U.S. Department of Labor" has the word "Labor" over-stamped with the word "Justice," and words are crossed out and replacements written in their place in pencil.

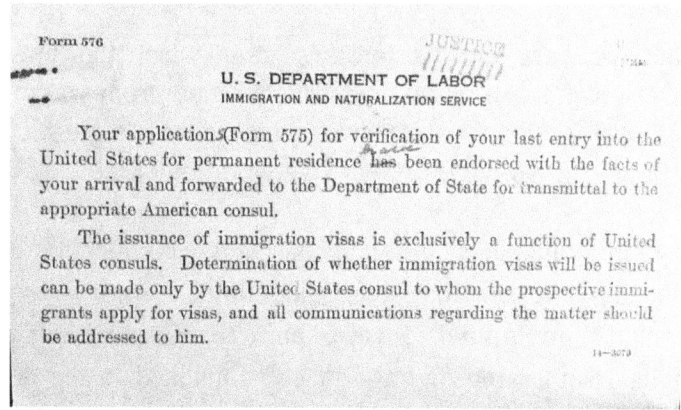

The text of the postcard is an exercise in pure doubletalk: "Your applications" (penciled addition of "s") (Form 575) for verification of your last entry into the United States for permanent residence have ("has" crossed out and "have" handwritten) been endorsed with the facts of your arrival and forwarded to the Department of State for transmittal to the appropriate American consul. The issuance of immigration visas is exclusively a function of United States consuls. Determination of whether immigration visas will be issued can be made only by the United States consul to whom the prospective immigrants apply for visas, and all communications regarding the matter should be addressed to him."

The only meaning that one can derive from this euphemistic gibberish is that multiple 575s had been received by an inflexible governmental department and sent on to another division for filing.

It is the nature of civil servants to fear they will be blamed—by the public, the media, agency leadership, or their immediate superiors—if favorable exercises of discretion later lead to negative publicity or outcomes. Restricting discretion or choosing to exercise it negatively avoids that risk of blame. Bureaucratic decisions denying benefits or relief are "safer" than granting relief, especially in the immigration context where the needy dependents of government action are invisible and powerless and—unlike powerful regulated industries—rarely able to impose any consequences or costs on an agency that takes negative action. Thus, the immigration process was agonizingly slow and open to interminable delay and potential manipulation by those who opposed change. In 1941, there was limited time remaining for action.

Beginning in 1940, Günter frequently sent notarized affidavits of support directly to the United States Consular offices both in Stuttgart and Cologne. Through his research, he had learned to include well-chosen words assuring the potential reader that his (and my) family would "never become public charges" and "will be properly received and cared for after their arrival in the United States." In addition, Günter wrote that "I shall see to it that they become acquainted with their new environments and that they eventually become useful American citizens."

On January 26, 1941, my family in Aachen wrote to Günter:

From Rose:

> My dear boy,
>
> I deem our last letter of January 19th is in your possession and hope that these lines will reach you safe and sound, as they, thank God, have left us. In the meantime I thanked Stanley in an English letter on the 21st for the affidavits sent to us *(Finally, but two years too late)*. Hopefully it has arrived already. A few days later, dear Günter, your registered letter arrived and we were <u>very</u> pleased. We thank you all 3 very much for this, dear boy. Hopefully you didn't have too much of an expense with it. I should be sorry for that! Even if our waiting numbers are very high, it is a comfort for us that we have the affidavits here. God grant that we can wait for our numbers to be called up in good health!
>
> Mr and Mrs B. also have their turn now, since they have 29,000..... I thought the company had given you some salary raise...
>
> The cold of the other day has given way to very mild weather. You can see that right away from the consumption of coal. .... Hopefully Uncle Paul will visit us soon. He hasn't been here since Uncle Adolf's death.
>
> Did you receive the things sent by Gerda and did they meet with approval? *(Gerda was buying inexpensive silk items and other relatively low-priced Chinese goods and sending them to Günter in Philadelphia for private resale—essentially a small Oppenheim import-export business.)* Don't you hear from Aunt Paula? We have not yet heard from New Orleans again, cannot get a hold of Margot's address in Chicago. ... We await your message.
>
> Thanks, dear boy, and many warm greetings to your loving mother

From Else:

> Dear Günter, I thank you from the bottom of my heart for the guarantee, please read Grandma's lines to Stanley; it is so difficult for her to write. But she really wanted to thank him. With love, Aunt Else.

From Fanni:

Dear Günter,

We were very pleased with your guarantee and thank you dear boy for it. God willing, these lines will also reach you in good health. We were also so happy to receive a letter from you from dear Helmut, from whom we have unfortunately not received a line for so long. Also our loved ones in Horn were so happy when we informed them of your offer. If only our Paul would know already where he can go with his loved ones! - Now, dear Günter, are you so good as to convey the enclosed letter to dear Stanley.

"Dear Mr. Schnellenberg.

I deem the letter from dear Rose from last week in your possession. I hope that these lines will find you in good health too. First of all I have to thank you very much for your big and loving offer. How can we ever make amends for you? - How vividly I remember now, while writing, your dear, blessed parents whom we last saw with us at Rose's wedding in Hannover *(Nathan Snellenburg and Minna Amant, who travelled to Germany from the USA in 1909)*. What sad things one has had to experience since then! So again, thank you very much. You must excuse my bad handwriting. I warmly greet you dear Mr. Schnellenberg. *(The name used by the German family, officially changed when they went to America)*.

Yours   Mrs. Fanny Liepmann."

From Else, who wrote this in English for Stanley Snellenburg:

Dear Sir.

We are happy when *("wenn")* that you will help us, if it is our turn. *(This is a typical grammatical English language error of German native speakers or writers: "If" and "when" in German are both "wenn." Here the intended meaning is "when" but Else translated it as "if")* Many thanks for your great kindness. I hope the best of you and all our dear ones.

With kind regards, yours very sincerely,   Else Liepmann

A letter was sent from Aachen to Günter on February 26, 1941. It includes a page written by Paul Liepmann, Rose's younger brother, who was visiting his family at that time.

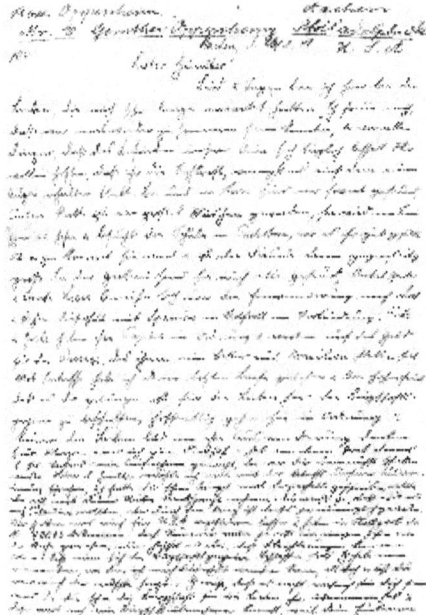

Page 1 of February 26, 1941, letter written by Paul Liepmann and Rose, together with the envelope that was "Opened (by the) Wehrmacht High Command. Note that the senders are "Rose Sara Oppenheim" and" Paul Israel Liepmann" with the added middle names mandated for all Jews by the 1939 edict.

From Paul:

Dear Günther!

For two days I've been here with the loved ones who have been waiting for me for a long time. …We in Horn are healthy so far; our Ruth has become a big girl, she will be twelve years old in June and goes to school in Paderborn, where she likes it a lot. Every now and then she comes home and the joy is mutual. In the nursery / tannery *(code for England where Edward, a son of Paul's maternal first cousin, and his family had escaped to in 1939)*, they are all still healthy. Uncle Gustav and Aunt Liese *(Gustav Spanier and Elise Sternberg, Paul's sister-in-law and her husband, who lived near Paul and his family in Horn)* are preparing to emigrate there and are therefore in contact with the Spaniers in Herford. Fritz and Grete *(Fritz Frank and Grete Sternberg, both born in 1898 and also Paul's sister-in-law and husband)* have their papers in order and are waiting for the money for the passage, which a cousin from Brazil is supposed to provide for them. I read your last letters with interest, and I am delighted that you have succeeded in obtaining the surety papers for the loved ones here. Hopefully they will be okay and the loved ones will soon be able to think about their emigration.

This morning I went to the cemetery and took a picture of your dear blessed father's grave, which we will send to you shortly.

Now, dear Günter, I would like to write to you about our emigration; ... You know that we wanted to go to Palestine first, but the war made this impossible. We had also registered for the USA and were given the number 48093 in Stuttgart. This number would only have been called up in a few years, but now it says that relief should come and that one should get guarantee papers. I now have no one to whom I can turn for this but you and you are also the closest in this to me. I know that it will not be easy for you because you have already taken on the guarantee for the loved ones here and therefore cannot take on another guarantee because your income is not sufficient. But I hope that you will succeed in finding someone among your circle of acquaintances who will provide the guarantee for me. I expressly state that we will not be a burden to them in any way, as Uncle J., Aunt Edith's *(Edith Snellenburg in Philadelphia)* husband, will help us in the first time. I don't know whether you can turn to Stanley for our guarantee, you know better yourself, maybe he would help us too if he knew our plight. I know you dear Günter will do your best and not let us down. Aunt Agnes was born on June 12, 1896; Ruth was born on June 7th, 1929, and I on January 5th, 1893...

    With love, your uncle Paul

In this letter, where Paul Liepmann begs his nephew Günter to do everything possible to save his family, Paul's desperation is clearly evident as he searches for any means to preserve the lives of his wife Agnes and his daughter Ruth. It is sardonically poignant that "Uncle Gustav and Aunt Liese" were "preparing to immigrate" to England. They both perished in the concentration camps of Poland in 1944. Likewise, "Fritz and Grete" who had "their papers in order and are waiting for the money for the passage" to Brazil, were both exterminated in a Polish concentration camp in 1943.

The letter continues:

From Rose:

    My dear Günter,

    ... Hopefully you, dear boy, are safe and sound and have no reason to complain in any way.

    ... We are all very happy with Uncle Paul, who surprised us by coming here. Grandma's eye has improved, thank God, so that the doctor was happy with it. Now may God grant that she may keep her eyesight in one eye. It is now said that all waiting numbers, regardless of their height, that have good guarantees and passage options, will soon have their turn. That would be very nice! However, I don't believe it yet. Will Stanley, who was so good to us, help us now again? Please write about it soon!

    Dear Günter, you can imagine how much we care about Uncle Paul's fate and that of his family. Please do what you can to help them! Unfortunately, they have no one else there. Will Stanley guarantee for him too? It may not be out of the question if they won't cost him anything. Or maybe Miss N *(Nydick)* or Harald's parents or other people you know can help you. Several of them can also provide a guarantee. You can for now disburse the costs! In any case, advice is needed. What do you think of Aunt Pauline in this relationship? Is there any point in reaching out to her? I'm thinking hard how to help Uncle Paul! He's always been so good to me and did what he can for me. So again, my dear boy, think about it and see that Uncle Paul is helped. How to take this great worry away from us. We don't have any other idea.

    How is business in your department doing and overall? ... Are you busy going to university? Now please, please us very soon with good news, God willing, and receive warm greetings from grandma and your mother who loves you.

From: Else

Dear Günter,

The warmest greetings from grandma and me to you and all loved ones. If only you could help Uncle Paul! With love, Aunt Else.

In March 1941, Adolf Eichmann, head of the Gestapo section for Jewish affairs, formulated definite plans to restrict Jewish emigration from Europe. Heinrich Himmler, leader of the *SS*, began plans for the expansion of the Auschwitz complex.

The next letter to Günter from Aachen was written 10 days later. The penciled censor number "1836-2v 3468" appears on each page:

March 6, 1941

From: Rose

My dear Günter,

Just a week ago today, a joint letter from Uncle Paul and me was sent to you by registered mail... How happy we would all be if you could help, you can imagine how depressed we are all that Uncle Paul has no one to issue affidavits to him. I know that you, dear boy, do everything in your power. Please write about it soon! On the way home, Uncle Paul visited Hermann in Essen, who is reasonably fine. He also wanted to go to Arnold L. *(Arnold Liepmann, a paternal first cousin of Rose's who still lived in Bücken)* and give him something, as he is unfortunately miserable financially. I have often sent him something too...

Well, dear boy, first of all I ...Thank you very much, dear Günther, for all three *(letters)*. .... I think that in it you tell a little more about the visit to the mother of the young girl that you met in Florida. Are they nice people? I surely grant you joy and pleasure, dear boy, but please don't forget to save. Traveling always costs a lot of money, and you mustn't forget how much we will need it soon. Are you carrying out your resolution and putting something aside every week? I would be <u>very</u> happy to hear from you that you bring something to the savings bank every month. You have to think about the future and moving forward!...

We received your registered letter with the affidavits you issued and we immediately acknowledged it with our thanks. I hear you can pay for the trip from here to Lisbon, but the rest of the money has to be paid for in foreign currency and we don't have that. As I learned, the consulate in Stuttgart only requests you to come there when the guarantees are good and sufficient and the passage has been paid for and documented. The height of the numbers should no longer matter! By the way, we have waiting numbers 46,808-10.

To my delight, Stanley praised you, dear Günter. Now make sure you continue to make an effort, then you will probably get a raise in salary soon. Hopefully Stanley will continue to help us too! It's sad that one can't even pay the travel expenses! One must not think about it!

Thank God we had good news from Gerda and Max on February 3rd here on March 2nd. They didn't hear from you and Helmut for a long time. ...

By the way, do you know that Gerd Neukam has already got engaged? ... Don't take this as an example, dear Günter! I wrote the English letter myself without outside help. Aunt Else and I study hard and also read English books. ...

Please do not forget to say Kaddish for our dear, blessed Father! I already wrote to you that it is Yahrzeit on March 30th. Hopefully these lines find you and all loved ones in the best of health. We too are healthy, thank God. Grandma is better again, God grant that it stays that way. ...

With best regards from the three of us, with constant love, your mother

From: Else

Dear Günther, we were very pleased with your three letters. Hopefully you are well with all loved ones.

Warm greetings also for Aunt Minna and Walter from Grandma and your aunt Else, who loves you.

The "official" document below was sent to Rose by the American consulate in Stuttgart, Germany, on March 11, 1941. It is a form letter in German originating with the "Foreign Service of the United States of America" and is regarding the holders of the U.S. registration numbers "46808/09/10," the waiting list "numbers" assigned to Rose, Else and Fanni for their desired emigration to the United States. It had been almost exactly two years since Rose had written to her daughter Gerda in Shanghai that, "You are quite right, dear child, that will definitely take more than five years." (For those numbers to be reached.)

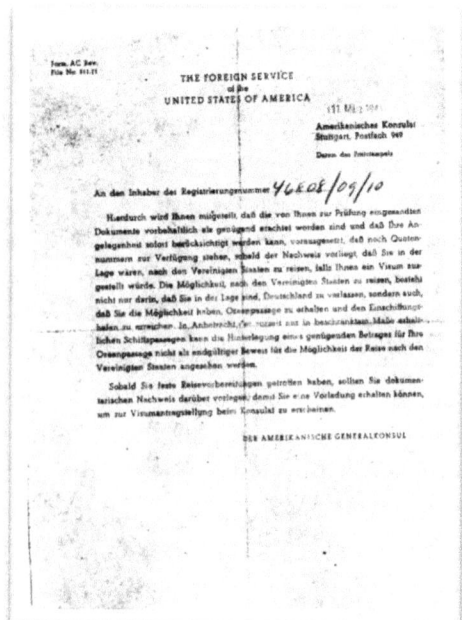

March 11, 1941, sent by the US Foreign Service to my family in Aachen.

The English translation of the above consulate letter above is as follows:

"This is to inform you that the documents you have submitted for examination have been considered sufficient subjectively and that your matter can be considered immediately provided that quotas are still available, once you have proof that you would be able to travel to the United

States if you were issued a visa. The possibility of traveling to the United States is not only that you are able to leave Germany, but also that you have the opportunity to receive ocean passage and reach the port of departure. Given that ship passes are currently available in limited quantities, a deposit of a sufficient amount for your ocean journey cannot be seen as a final proof of the possibility of travel to the United States.

Once you have firmly made travel arrangements, submit documentary proof of it so that you can receive a subpoena to appear at the consulate for visa application."

This "official" document conveys an unconscionable number of internal contradictory phrases. Rose and others were trying to hit a shifting target of obtaining immigration papers (a visa) to the United States, where not only were the goal posts always moving but also the rules could change even after the object had been theoretically attained. It essentially said that the documents you have submitted most likely are adequate to be on a waiting list for a visa and that once you have made (and paid for) travel arrangements to the USA, which will be very difficult to obtain, you may be asked to come to the US consulate where you can apply for a visa, which it is unlikely that you will get. Obtaining a visa could occur after the date of your intended travel has already passed. The visa, if obtained, would only be granted for a certain time period. As Rose wrote on March 6, 1941, "As I learned, the consulate in Stuttgart only requests you to come there when the guarantees are good and sufficient, and the passage has been paid for and documented."

An American refugee aid worker wrote at the time to her superior: "We cannot continue to let these tragic people (German Jews) go on hoping that if they comply with every requirement, if they get all the special documents required...if they nerve themselves for the final interview at the Consulate, they may just possibly be the lucky ones to get visas when we know that practically no one is granted visas in Germany today."

In the period 1940-1941, Rose had already sent the American consulate in Stuttgart, per the current document requirements, five copies of the visa application for each applicant, two copies of each applicant's birth certificate, together with the quota numbers she and her family had received establishing their place on the waiting list. In addition, she had submitted the necessary Certificate of Good Conduct from the German Police Authority, time consuming to obtain, but not yet impossible since Germany still was eager to both export the Jews and obtain any of their few remaining assets through taxes which would be levied prior to leaving the country. After September of 1940, two affidavits of good conduct from Germans, "disinterested parties," who were felt to be "responsible" by the authorities, were also required. She, Else and Fanni would also be required to have a physical examination at the US Consulate.

A large hurdle established by the United States to obtain a visa to emigrate there, one which Rose and Günter were trying to overcome, reflected frequently in their letters, was the support of the application by at least two sponsors in the United States. Close relatives of the prospective immigrant(s) were favored, and sponsors were required to be US citizens or have permanent resident status. In addition to providing six completed and notarized copies of an Affidavit of Support and Sponsorship, all sponsors were obliged to submit a certified copy of his or hers most recent federal tax return, and an additional declaration of facts from a bank regarding the sponsor's financial situation.

This form letter from the American consulate in Stuttgart was a precipitating cause prompting Rose to transmit a telegram early in the morning of March 19, 1941, to her son in Philadelphia. My uncle Günter was still two months short of reaching his 21st birthday. Sending a telegram in 1941 from Germany to the United States was extremely expensive and was, therefore, not a decision to be taken lightly. A telegram was usually reserved for only life and death matters. Learning that there was a telegram from Aachen waiting at the RCA office undoubtedly made Günter fear the worst—that someone had died, most likely his grandmother Fanni. This telegram did not convey a death, but Rose now considered the situation indeed to be a life and death matter.

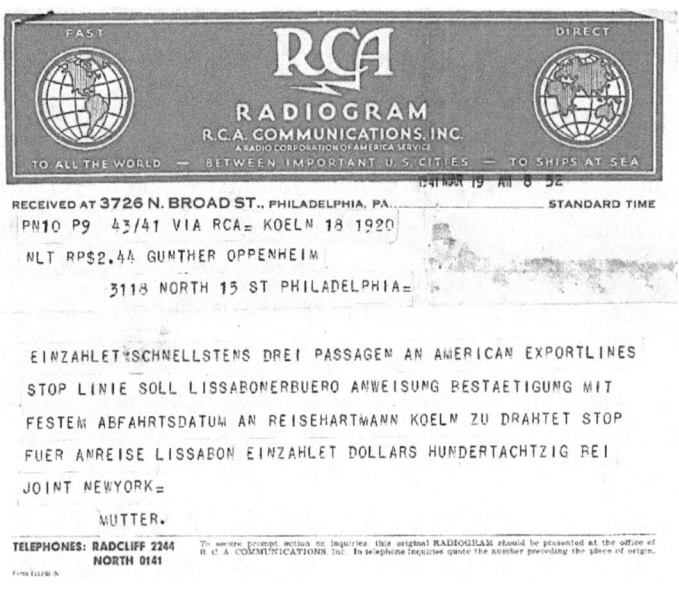

The telegram is translated:

"BOOK THREE PASSAGES AS SOON AS POSSIBLE ON AMERICAN EXPORT LINE FROM LISBON. SEND CONFIRMATION WITH A DEFINITE DATE OF DEPARTURE TO THE HARTMANN TRAVEL AGENCY IN COLOGNE WITH A TELEGRAM FOR PASSAGE FROM LISBON. PAY ONE HUNDRED EIGHTY DOLLARS TO THE NEW YORK OFFICE.

MOTHER."

Rose undoubtedly was referring to the American Export Lines passenger liner "Excalibur" which made seven round trip trans-Atlantic crossings in March, April and May of 1941 from Lisbon, Portugal, to New York. In October 1938, the Portuguese government had ruled that Jews were forbidden from settling in Portugal but were not prevented from passing through in order to reach a different destination. Every Jew seeking to enter Portugal had to prove to the Portuguese authorities that he was in possession of a visa to another country. These Lisbon-New York voyages were filled with Jewish refugees escaping Nazi persecution, extremely fortunate to not only have secured tickets for the ships' passage, but, of equal importance, had obtained permission from the United States to emigrate there. These lucky few had successfully navigated the US quota system which severely restricted the number of Germans who could enter America each year. They also had secured sponsorship by someone in the US who had previously signed an affidavit agreeing to be financially responsible for the immigrants. This was not a mere formality since transfer of any money out of Germany was illegal. They had also been forced to wait in seemingly endless lines to pass a thorough medical examination at an American consulate, an examination that eliminated many older people, often for frivolous reasons.

The Export Steamship Corporation had been organized in 1919 and began operating cargo services to the Mediterranean from New York. The word "American" was added in the 1920s to emphasize its ties to the U.S. In 1931, the American Export Lines placed four cargo-passenger liners, Excalibur, Excambion, Exeter, and Exochorda, known as the "Four Aces," into transatlantic service. These ships were expropriated by the U.S. Navy to become troop ships early in World War II. The Excalibur was renamed the *USS Joseph Hewes*, in memory of one of three North Carolinians to sign the Declaration of Independence. On November 8, 1942, the Joseph Hewes left Morocco after landing American troops there and a few hours later was torpedoed by the German submarine U-173 and quickly sank with the captain and 100 U.S. sailors going down with the ship.

Upon receiving the telegram, Günter immediately travelled by train to the New York office of the Hartmann Travel Agency and made a deposit of 180 dollars for three future American Export Line passages from Lisbon to New York. He was, however, told that visas for United States entry would be required prior to issuance of the tickets.

There was another imminent event that triggered the decision to have Günter purchase ship tickets from Lisbon. Beginning in October 1939, in Poland, the NSDAP established more than a thousand ghettos in the occupied areas of eastern Europe, enclosed spaces, where local Jews were forced to live. Tens of thousands of western European Jews were deported to these areas, the largest being in the cities of Warsaw, Lodz, Krakow, Bialystok, Lvov, Lublin, Vilna, Kovno, Czestochowa, and Minsk. The Germans saw the ghettos as a provisional measure to control and segregate Jews while the Nazi leadership in Berlin deliberated upon various permanent options for the removal of the Jewish population.

Crowded rooms and inadequate sanitary conditions within these ghettos made living conditions wretched for the inhabitants. Water borne infectious disease was rampant. The Germans ordered Jews in the ghettos to wear identifying badges or armbands and often to perform forced labor. Ghetto residents frequently smuggled food, medicine, weapons, or intelligence across the ghetto walls. Nazi-appointed *Judenraete* (Jewish Councils) were chosen to administer daily life in the ghettos. A ghetto police force enforced the orders of the German authorities and the ordinances of the Jewish Councils.

Smuggling and other such marginal, yet necessary, activities often took place without the approval of the Jewish councils. On the other hand, some Jewish councils and some individual council members encouraged the smuggling because the goods were necessary to keep ghetto residents alive. In August 1944, German SS and police had completed the destruction of the last major ghetto, located in Lodz. By then, more than 95% of former ghetto residents had been put to death through shooting, burning or the administration of poison gas.

The Nazis, unwilling to have native Germans living adjacent to such squalor, had never created ghettos on native German soil. As an alternative, houses in which Jews were concentrated and isolated had been set up in Germany since 1939 by the Nazi authorities independent of the deportation process. Various municipalities passed ordinances, under the direction of the Reich, to force Jews to self-segregate from the remainder of the population. These strict residence regulations forced Jews to leave their homes and relocate to live in designated "Jewish houses," accommodating unrelated parties, located in specific areas of German cities.

Such was the situation in Aachen in the late winter of 1941. A *Judenhaus* (Jewish House) was instituted at 28 *Försterstraße* for married couples who were in a so-called "mixed marriage" between a Jew and a Christian. On April 1, 1941, the City Council of Aachen implemented the instructions of the Nazi leadership to ghettoize the entire Jewish population of the city. Other "Jewish houses" were established at 95 *Alexanderstraße*, 249 *Eupener Straße*, 28 *Försterstraße*, 21 *Promenadenstraße*, 22 *Königstraße* and 285 *TriererStraße.* An additional Jewish "collective camp" was located in the *Gruenen Weg* (Green Way).

Judenhaus at 22 Königstraße, Aachen

Judenhaus at 228 Försterstraße, Aachen

Rose and her family were informed by the local authorities that all Jewish homes would have to remain unlocked at all times, so that the Gestapo and other police could freely enter without notice to search for anti-German or other "nefarious" activity. In addition, a black "Jewish Star" was placed on the front door, drawn large enough so that it could easily have been seen from the street. This marker and the inability to lock the door made the Oppenheim home in Aachen, as all other Jewish homes, excellent candidates for robbery, vandalism, violence or worse, essentially producing a situation in which remaining at 39 *NormannenStraße* was untenable. Aachen Jews scrambled to find a place to live at one of the above so-called *Judenhäuser* (Jewish houses), where there was communal living and a level of security could be organized.

Rose and Else had the resourcefulness and presence of mind to quickly arrange for a room at the *Judisches Altenheim* (Jewish old-age home), operated by the "Israelite Asylum Association." Their living with and caring for their mother, Fanni, who was 84 and in poor health, likely allowed them this opportunity. The *Altenheim* was a large house with approximately thirty rooms, originally occupied by one or two persons in each room, which also housed common cooking and dining facilities. There was a Jewish nurse in charge of its operation by the name of Greta Berger, who had considerable medical and administrative experience caring for the various health and other needs of the residents.

On March 24, 1941, Rose, Else and Fanni took their clothing, personal items and a few small pieces of furniture and moved to the *Altenheim* at 87 *Horst Wessel Straße*, where the three were to share a room for the next year. The family home and its remaining contents were expropriated by the local Nazi government.

The "Housekeeping Book" of the Israelite (Jewish) Asylum Association registration of residents of 1941, cover page. This book kept records of the names, birthdays and birthplaces of the residents and when they moved into the Altenheim. When they were deported, their name was crossed off. The address of 87 Kalverbende was correct prior to the street being renamed as a memorial for Horst Wessel.

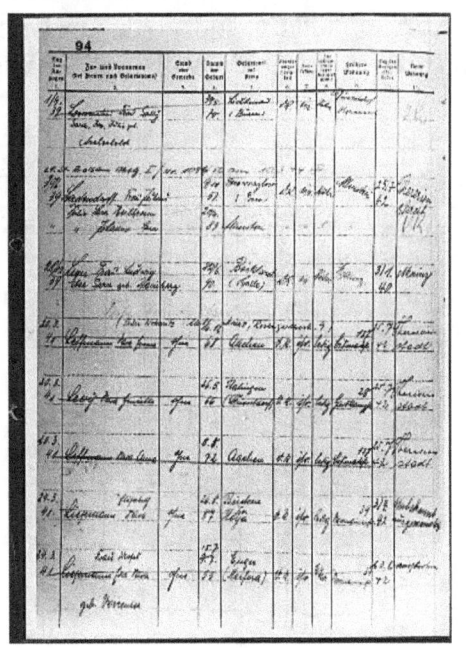

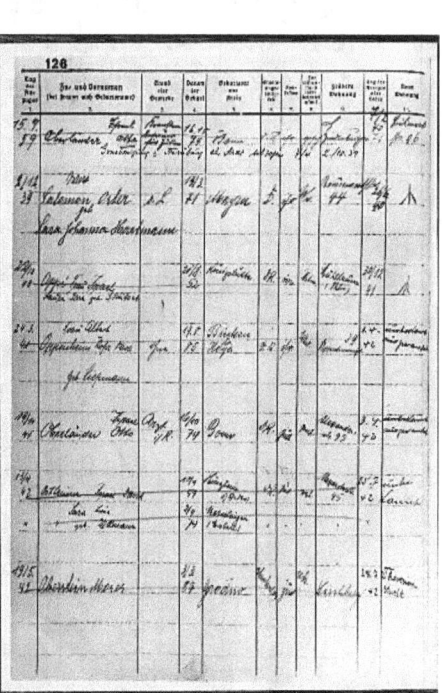

Pages 94 and 128 of the "housekeeping" book of the Judisches Altenheim showing the names of Else and Fanni Liepmann and Rose Oppenheim.

In the following letter of March 27, 1941, to Günter in Philadelphia (the correspondence referred to of March 16, 1941, has been lost or never received), Rose describes the conditions in the single room for the three of them at *Horst Wessel Strasse 87*.

From Rose:

In my last letter from March 16, I wrote you that unfortunately we had to leave our dear little house, which we loved so much, and moved to the local old people's home. The move to here is now behind us, thank God. We had difficult days, you can imagine that! Now we are happy that we are here and that we are in good hands. Many envy us for it! If only we had more space! All three of us live and sleep in one room that is of course very full of our various pieces of furniture, but we want to hope that we won't have to stay here for too long and that we will soon be able to emigrate. We received your cable answer on March 21st, dear Günter. If only you could manage to get a boat passage! The demand is certainly very high and not many ships are sailing. We are already preparing everything further. God grant that we will soon be with you!

But, dear boy, you are still so young and you still cannot maintain us! Surely Max and Gerda will help and Stanley will not let us down! Write about it, dear Günter! I am not allowed to think, otherwise I will get too much!

Our Gerda wrote a few days ago that in response to her dispatch she had a letter from Helmut, who unfortunately was seriously ill. The poor boy! I've thought about him so much and dreamed of him so often. If only I could help him so that he would soon be united with us and you! Helmut also didn't have work, he wanted to look for it in two larger cities. Did you also have a letter from Helmut? 2 letters he wrote to Gerda did not arrive. How are you, dear boy and all loved ones there?

Now our dear father has been resting for 2 years. Did you also think of the Jahrzeit, on March 30th you had to say Kaddish and light a candle on the 29th! How good it is that our dear father no longer lived through all of this. He would have been grieved to death! Here in the old people's home we are over 100 people, many acquaintances from the city moved in with us. We keep our room tidy and have meals brought to us. The home is a bit outside the city, beautifully surrounded by a garden. The forest is also close by, so God willing, we're going to get out there with grandma in the wheelchair.

Yesterday we were very pleased with your letter of February 19th, dear Günter. ... Yesterday, Aunt Tony delighted us for the second time with a wonderful food package. That's really nice of her! Uncle Eduard wrote today that Heinz was planning to spend his spring break in New York, Philadelphia, and Washington. Is he going to write to you? How is your business doing? What else is new? Are you actually in sales or what kind of work do you have to do?

It's getting late and I'm very tired, so that's it.

Farewell, dear boy, be embraced by your ever-loving mother

From Else:

Dear Günther,

It's good that we have the move behind us already. Those were days! Tell me how it is? When we come there it is surely not advisable to bring furniture of any kind? I mean because of the high transport costs that we probably can't pay from here. I wish we were all reunited already! But then we want to be happy and content with one another. We intend to bring linen and clothes.

Write in detail soon.

Greetings from grandma and your aunt Else, who loves you.

The above letter and all subsequent letters from Aachen were sent from the *Israelitisches Altenheim* (Jewish old age home). The building had been originally constructed as a large home at 87 *Kalverbenden*

Straße and later converted to a retirement home/nursing home. In 1933, with the Nazis in complete control of urban planning, the street was renamed, and the building's address became 87 *Horst Wessel Straße.*

Horst Wessel Platz, 1942

Horst Ludwig Georg Erich Wessel was as zealous a Nazi as one could imagine. Both Hitler and Goebbels knew that and turned him into a beloved martyr for the Nazi cause.

Wessel was born in 1907 and at a very young age founded an extreme right-wing youth group, entitled the *Knappschaft*, and at age 16 became an enthusiastic member of a paramilitary group, *Wiking Liga* (Viking League), which had as its purpose, the "establishment of a national dictatorship." After these two groups were banned in 1926, Wessel joined the Nazi party's brown shirted stormtroopers. He was happiest brawling in the streets with members of the *SPD* (Social Democratic Party) and the *KPD* (Communist Party). Goebbels was impressed by the fanatic young Nazi and designated Wessel a leader of a section of the *SA*. In January of 1930, at age 22, he was assassinated by two members of the *KPD*. His funeral was orchestrated by Goebbels, who delivered the eulogy, followed by a mass procession that was filmed for propaganda purposes.

Wessel had also been the writer of the lyrics of a song sung by Nazis as they demonstrated in the streets, which he called "Raise the Flag." That song became the Nazi co-national anthem, and a fictional film portrayal of his life, *Hans Westmar,* glorified his participation in the Nazi *Kampfzeit* – the history of their period of political opposition, struggling to gain power.

A letter from Rose "Sara," opened and censored by the Nazis, sent from the Judisches Altenheim on Horst Wessel Strasse 87 to Shanghai.

It is the harshest irony that Rose had to handwrite "*Horst Wessel Str 87*" on the back of each envelope that she used to enclose letters to her children.

Although my grandmother Rose wrote in the above letter that "we are over 100 people...here in the old people's home," other sources state that as many as 200 Jews were residents there. The Jews of Aachen residing in the various *Judenhäuser* were all subsequently "deported to the East."

Aachen to Günter April 2, 1941

From Rose:

My dear Günter,

Hopefully you have received my last letter of March 27, in which I told you about our move to the old people's home and at the same time asked for a deposit for the 3 passages. The consulate in Stuttgart sent us the so-called A.L. papers several weeks ago and informed us that the affidavits were sufficient. As soon as we could notify them of fixed ocean passages and provide documentary evidence of this, they would send us a summons to appear at the consulate to apply for a visa. Hopefully you, dear boy, will be able to secure places for us on some line, otherwise we cannot leave. Yesterday I wired again for this reason and await your answer.

Hopefully you and all your loved ones are doing well there and have no reason to complain. We have already settled in a bit here and are happy to have found accommodation here. Many envy us for it! God grant that we can stay here until we emigrate! This is our daily prayer! You can imagine that it was difficult for us to leave our dear little house. Now I have to ask you Günter to inform the consulate in Stuttgart underline immediately: The people listed under waiting numbers 46809 and 46810 are Miss Elsbeth Liepmann and Ms. Eva Liepmann (i.e., not Else and Fanni, but Elsbeth and Eva).

When obtaining the birth certificate for Grandma, it turned out that she is registered as Eva at the registry office, which we did not know beforehand either. Otherwise we could face great difficulties and Grandma and Aunt Else will not get the visa if you do not correct the matter immediately. On Grandma's birth certificate, July 15, 1855, is given as the date of her birth (not July 9, as we always believed). But the day probably doesn't matter, I mean just in case you were asked about it.

Yesterday we enjoyed your and Aunt Minna's joint letter very much. ...I was very happy about Bernice's engagement and will write her and also to Carla Bachmann. Is Franklin Josef a decent person? *("Bernice" Oppenheim, born in New York City in 1914 was the only child of Luis Oppenheim, Albert's brother.)*

Keep the building plan of the house there with you. We don't need it anymore. The house is rented out through a trustee who also sets the rent. If you, dear boy, want to write us an English letter, just do it. Hopefully we understand everything correctly. However, when it is important, it is better to write in German so that there is no mistake. How may our Helmut be doing? I think about him so much. The poor boy was sick with typhus in the hospital for 6 weeks and then alone in a foreign country! He wrote it to Gerda, from whom we found out. Helmut also didn't have work and wanted to look in some town for a job. Nebbig *(A Yiddish term for "how unfortunate.")* If only Helmut could be over there soon! How glad I would be if the prospect existed that we could live together again!

238

The blouse for me, dear Günter, was already in Shanghai, but it was supposed to cost so much customs that Gerda had it sent back. Don't be sad about it, dear boy. I take your goodwill for action. See that the shop takes it back and if it doesn't, put it aside for me. ...

I wish you had to pay a lot of income tax, then you would earn a lot too, dear Günter. Hopefully Aunt Minna lives by the rules so that the diabetes disappears. How proud she will be as a grandmother. I wish Sylva all the best...

We have <u>one</u> room here, it is quite spacious, but there is so much furniture in it that it seems cramped. But it's cozy. There were 80 people here in the home and 40 have now been added. Everything is very crowded. The home is a bit outside of the city, surrounded by a garden, many friends are here and there is no boredom.

Thank God we heard good things from Gerda... Finally it occurs to me that your birthday is approaching. I congratulate you, my dear boy, with all my heart and wish you all the best, a happy and blessed new year of life. Stay healthy and good and may it be granted to us to celebrate your next birthday with you. Very special greetings for Stanley!

Your mother hugs you in constant love.

From: Else

Dear Günter,

Grandma and I also congratulate you on your birthday and wish you the best of the best. Stay our sunshine as you always have been and see that you clear up the mistake in Stuttgart. Fanny and Else were only nicknames and the registry office counts!

With love, greetings and kisses your aunt Elsbeth

In April 1941, Germany invaded Yugoslavia and Greece, and both nations quickly capitulated to the German forces.

Aachen, April 14th, 1941, to Günter, Philadelphia, PA

Horst Wesselstrasse 87

From: Rose:

My dear Günter,

I have just congratulated the father in Shanghai on his birthday on May 1ˢᵗ *(my grandfather, Nathan Dahl)* ... Who would have thought that we would no longer spend the Easter days in our lovely little house! It's just a good thing we hadn't already dug up and sown the garden! But it was still too cold and wintry for that. Aunt Else and I had recently sprinkled artificial fertilizer and raked it in! But we want to be satisfied that we live here and that we are not accommodated like many good friends. *(The word "accommodated" is used to describe friends who had already been deported to forced labor camps or concentration camps "in the East." As always, Rose is aware that all her letters pass through the hands of censors.)* If you, dear Günter, only manage to get passages for us! You will certainly make enough effort! A well-known to us family from here got passage for 3 people for October. He has a brother who is a doctor in New York and a sister in Philadelphia. The joy is great! One even hears that berths have already been booked for January 1942. You, dear Günter, have certainly received my dispatch of April 2nd, in which I asked for payment for the tickets. The answer to this is still missing, at least you had not yet managed to get a boat place. In any case, you can find out <u>there</u> how others do it. I heard the money had to be paid for the Joint beforehand. *(The Joint Distribution Committee, known as "the Joint" with offices in Lisbon and The USA was attempting to assist European Jewry with matters related to immigration)* Please inquire <u>exactly</u> how it is correct. Hopefully cousin Stanley will help you with that. I have no other advice!

Hopefully you received our registered letter of April 3rd and <u>immediately</u> gave the consulate the requested correction, namely that grandma's first name is <u>Eva</u> and aunt's name is Elsbeth (not Else). Otherwise there is error and anger. Grandma was born on July 16, 1855 (this is what her birth certificate says, we always celebrated July 9). Aunt Elsbeth was born on August 26, 1887.

But first, dear boy, how are you? Hopefully you are safe and sound and satisfied in every respect. We have already settled in here; we can say we are lucky to be in this home! We have our meals at regular times and our order. It's just crowded with three in one room in which we sleep, eat and sojourn during the day, but you get used to it if you have to. Here are many old people and we are among the youngest. In the mornings we volunteer to help out in the kitchen, as there is still a lack of staff. The home is in a garden outside the city and not far from the forest. Hopefully it will be warm and summery soon so Grandma can spend time in the garden. Most of all she will miss the terrace, where she loved to sit. Thank goodness our room has running water, it used to be the doctor's room.

Your letter of March 16 arrived yesterday, dear Günter, and we were very pleased. It is very nice of Miss Nydick to give you some of the bonus. I think it is a sign of her satisfaction with you! Hopefully you took the money to the savings bank. Didn't you get another raise?...

... Gerda wrote to us a few days ago from March 11th that they had heard from you in detail on January 29th and that you again ordered all sorts of things. Have you already received the things and were you able to sell them well? Gerda also wrote that you could write such good English letters and that you made few mistakes. Please write to us in English, dear boy!

Haven't you heard from Helmut again? How does he feel after the serious illness? If only he already was with you ! He will find work because he is hardworking. We recently had a letter from New Orleans, all three of them wrote. Only Margot didn't write anything, the lazy one! She should be ashamed of not sending a line to her old grandma. Aunt Marie is still waiting for her visa!

Well goodbye, dear Günter. It's late, Grandma and Aunt Else are already asleep. Please send my best regards to all loved ones, especially Aunt Minna, Stanley, Walter. Be hugged by your mother who loves you...

From: Else

Dear Günter,

As always, we were delighted with your letter. Now the first days of Easter are already over. What did you do? …

How about passages, dear Günter? I wish we were there already! Greetings to you and everyone from grandma and your aunt Else, who loves you.

Rapid transmission of written messages had its birth in 1844, using Morse Code transmitted through wires connecting the transmitter and receiver. The first transatlantic cable was laid in 1866, allowing telegraphic messages in code to be sent between the USA and Great Britain at the rate of 8 words per minute.

In 1921, the Radio Corporation of America (RCA) built a center in Long Island to transmit telegraphic messages using low-frequency radio waves, rather than wire cables capable of traveling thousands of miles. Sending an RCA Radiogram was extremely expensive, priced at about twenty cents per word in 1941. Punctuation marks were each charged as if they were a word. Out of necessity to keep the cost down, users would send terse messages, omitting many verbs and all punctuation marks.

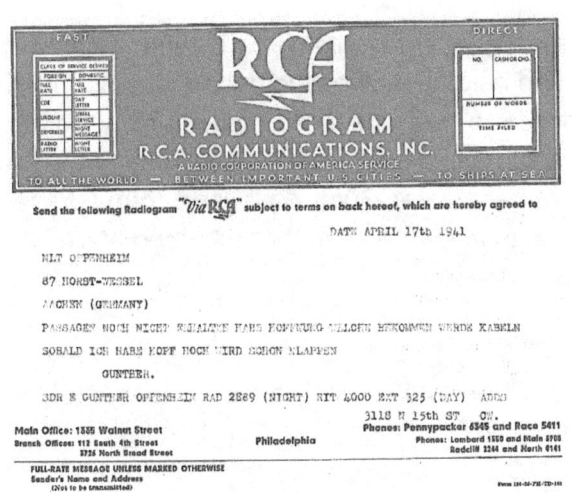

On April 17, 1941, Günter sent an RCA Radiogram (telegram) to my family in Aachen. It is translated:

"(SHIP) PASSAGES HAVE NOT YET BEEN RECEIVED(.) (I) HOPE TO GET (SOME.) (I) (WILL) CABLE (AS SOON AS) I HAVE (THEM.) (KEEP YOUR) HEAD(S) UP(.) (YOU) SOON (WILL BE) FINE(.)"

GUNTHER

A few days later, April 21, 1941, my family in Aachen wrote to Günter.

From: Rose

My dear Günter,

… The day before yesterday on April 19th your dear letter of March 22nd arrived here …and we saw from this that, unfortunately, you had not yet managed to secure us a ship. I can imagine how huge the demand is, but we still don't want to lose hope and we think that you, dear boy, will manage to secure passage for us at a not-too-distant point in time. I am convinced that you are doing your best and I know that Stanley will help you as much as he can. If only you were successful! Only the hope, God willing, to live united with you again, dear boy, keeps one going!

I …hope that everything reached you in the best of health and that you are safe and sound... We are also mobile (except for colds and coughs) and have now been in the new apartment for four weeks. Time flies by! One mustn't think back. You can imagine that it is not easy to make a trade like us, to leave such a lovely house where everything was so comfortably and nicely arranged.

Walter and Aunt Minna knew everything and must have told you many times how magnificent the terrace with the garden was. But tempi passati - just don't make any comparisons! We want to pray to God that he will keep us healthy and that we can stay here until we emigrate.

Dear Günter, please inform yourself <u>exactly</u> how it is with the payment of the passages. Friends of ours (Walter knows them) received a cable from their brother, the doctor in New York, that they have reserved places for them on a certain ship for October 26th. One hears here that the money would have to be deposited with the shipping company <u>beforehand</u>, but once again inform yourself very carefully from people who know it and are <u>honest</u>, so that you cannot be cheated out of the money!... If only the USA would have mercy and issue visas then many could be helped out of need!

We received the A.L. papers from Stuttgart many weeks ago with the notification that we would be summoned there to get the visas, as soon as we have a ship. Gerda and Max will certainly contribute; of that I am sure. I'm sorry enough, but I have no other advice! It is not easy! You can believe that, dear Günter.

I wrote to Uncle Paul and forwarded your letter. How happy we would all be if you managed to get the necessary papers for the three. Maybe you will find helpful people who understand our need! As far as I know and understand, the 180 Dollars that are to be transferred by Joint New York to *Reisehartmann (a travel agent)* in Cologne are intended for the journey from Irun to Lisbon. The trip from here to Irun can be paid for in German money from here. Dear Günter, please inform yourself again, I assume these 180 Dollars would have to be paid in advance. Isn't there a friend there who is in the same position as you, whose relatives want to come too? ...

We had news from Gerda yesterday of February 20th. She wanted to send you the things you ordered. Max *(my father)* recently had sciatica all of a sudden, was taking radiation and thank God, it improved quickly. Haven't you heard from Helmut again? ... Hopefully he's healthy. ... Well goodbye, dear Günter, stay healthy and please your mother who loves you very soon with good news, God willing.

From Else:

Dear Günther,

We were very pleased with your last lines! Hopefully you will be able to help us and also provide advice for Uncle Paul. I know it is not easy, but that you will try hardest. It is all fraught with such great difficulty. But we still don't want to lose our courage and hope for the best. God help us all and on Him we want to set our hopes that the sun will shine again for us, too.

... Let us hear from you soon. Greetings from grandma and your aunt Else, who loves you.

In the above letter, Rose references "Irun," a Spanish Atlantic coastal city immediately south of the French border. It is apparent from the correspondence available to me that Rose had concluded that the best way to reach the United States was to leave the European continent from Lisbon in Portugal. In April 1941, even though France had surrendered to Germany in June 1940, it was still theoretically possible to leave Aachen, Germany, by rail transportation, travelling first to Bruxelles and then turning south to go through the occupied portion of France, rather than the Vichy-controlled eastern portion of France, which collaborated with the Nazis in the hunting down of Jews. Rose, Else and Fanni would arrive at the southernmost French coastal town of Hendaye, just southwest of Biarritz and then cross the Spanish border to Irun where a change of trains would be necessary because of the difference in train track gauge, established under the terms of a diplomatic agreement between France and Spain in 1864.

Rose and the other members of my family then planned to travel by train southwest from San Sebastian, through the heart of Spain through Salamanca and then cross the border into Portugal at *Fuentes de Oñoro/Vilar Formoso* and continue to the Port of Lisbon.

Spain and Portugal were both officially "neutral" nations in World War II. However, Francisco Franco, the dictator of Spain, did write to Hitler offering to join the war on Germany's side in exchange for assistance in rebuilding Spain's colonial empire. Antonio Salazar, Portugal's leader, maintained an open trade policy with both Allied and Axis nations, but sold its vital natural resource, wolfram, a source of the important mineral tungsten, preferentially to Germany.

Neither the Spanish nor the Portuguese governments wanted emigrating European Jews to stay in their nations for more than a few days. When successful in applying for entry into either of these countries through application for a transit visa to their consulates in Germany, Jews were granted permission to remain in those nations for very short periods of time.

It would only be six months later that the Nazis would decree that all voluntarily emigration of Jews from Germany would immediately cease, with the exception of deportations of German Jews to the *Ostland.*

In the letter below to Günter, Paul is again urgently requesting Günter to assist him with obtaining "guarantees" to facilitate his bringing his family to the United States. In addition, Paul mentions "Uncle Eduard" getting a guarantee "from his son, who is already earning a lot as an aviator." Eduard Oppenheim, Albert's younger (by four years) brother, had a previously successful retail business in Halle, the largest city in the German state of Saxony-Anhalt, where Eduard had moved after completing his schooling in Velmede. Eduard had three children with his wife Meta Brandenstein, Herbert, Heinz, and Hannelore, who died as a teenager. Meta passed away in her early forties and Eduard remarried Erna Baum. Both sons emigrated initially to Palestine in 1934 and then later to England. Eduard and his wife were able to obtain visas for the United States through the US Consulate in Leipzig in 1935. They departed from Bremen on November 19, 1935, on the *SS Europa* of the Hamburg-American line bound for New York, stopping in Southampton. They left their younger son Heinz, who was visiting them in Halle, in Southampton to live with his brother Herbert in England. Uncle Eduard and his wife Erna continued on to New York. They spent time in the United States visiting with Eduard's brothers, Max and Luis, and their families. They returned to Germany to dispose of their business and their visas expired shortly thereafter.

By 1940, Germany was at war, visas to the United States were scarce and "guarantees" by "an aviator earning a lot" were meaningless in terms of obtaining those precious life-saving visas. I am certain that Heinz, having moved from England to the United States, did his best to accelerate the process of bringing his father and stepmother to the United States. However, the quota system was rigid, and one could only move ahead of others in the process of visa allocation if a child was a US citizen, which Heinz (now having changed his name to Henry) was not, since he had not been in the United States the required five years prior to achieving citizenship. Their other son, Herbert, residing in England, also did his best to have his parents come to him but Great Britain was already at war with Germany.

On June 1, 1942, Uncle Eduard and Aunt Erna were rounded up by the SS, together with hundreds of other Jews in Halle, and transported to the *Vernichtungslager* (death camp) at Sobibor, Poland, where they both were murdered in gas chambers on June 3, 1942.

Einsatz Reinhard (Operation Reinhard) was the code name for the German plan to annihilate all the Jews residing in Poland and the eastern part of Germany. It was named after SS General Reinhard Heydrich, the chief of the *Reichssicherheitshauptam* (Reich Security Main Office),who had been tasked by Adolf Hitler and Hermann Göring to personally find a permanent solution of the "Jewish question." Heydrich died in June 1942 from injuries sustained during an assassination attempt by Czech partisans.

Operation Reinhard was initiated in the autumn of 1941. In order to implement the plan, The German *SS* and police constructed three killing centers (*Tötungszentren*) in the winter and spring of 1942 near the small Polish towns of Treblinka, Sobibor and Belzec. Before the end of 1943, almost 2 million Jews were murdered in those "concentration camps" per Operation Reinhard's instructions.

Uncle Paul Liepmann in Horn, Germany, wrote to Günter on April 24, 1941:

Dear Günther! (*Some people spelled his name with an additional "h"*)

Your detailed letter from March 22nd reached your loved ones on April 19th and was forwarded by them to me here. We had been waiting with longing for it and we are happy that you are healthy, which thank God I can say about us, too. Your dear mother, grandma, and aunt Else are also in good health and have already made themselves comfortable in the old people's home, where they have a nice room. In the meantime you will have heard from them repeatedly and they are waiting with longing to come to you soon. We have read your letter, dear Günther, with great interest and we find it touching of Stanley how much he supports you and your loved ones. I can also fully understand if you don't want to approach him about us; and you have to know this best yourself. It is nice of you that you want to give the guarantee for us, but since you have already taken on one for the loved ones in Aachen, certain additional guarantees will be required. Hopefully you have managed to get one in the meantime, I am convinced that you, dear Günther, will do everything possible to help us, because you know how urgently it is needed. If the consul should ask for a deposit for us at a local bank when the guarantees are here, which we don't hope, you would have to use the amount that Uncle S. made available to you for the passage. I would then try to get the passages from here; however, none is said to be available here before October. But this only comes second, the main thing is that we have guarantees that are in order. One had also heard here that the Export Line was trying to rent the "Manhattan" or "Washington" there, which would certainly be a great relief regarding passages, if only it came true.

You always hear all the news from the family from the loved ones from Aachen; We expect Uncle Hermann from Essen here shortly when the weather improves. Aunt Liese and Uncle Gustav are doing well; they are expecting guarantees from Spaniers in Hadfort; Fritz and Grete are waiting for the passages, otherwise they have everything in order. Aunt Hermine is with Irma in Berleburg, where Käthe from Berlin is currently as well. Why doesn't Uncle Eduard actually get the guarantee from his son, who is already earning a lot as an aviator? Ruth *(Paul's daughter, age 12)* spent her Easter holidays with us and is already looking forward to the summer holidays! Now, dear Günther, I want to close because Aunt Agnes wants to add a few more greetings. Stay healthy and write again soon.

Your loving uncle Paul

From: Aunt Agnes Liepmann, Paul's wife

Dear Günther,

Even if we don't always hear from each other directly, we are always up to date thanks to the loved ones in Aachen - we are happy that you are doing so well. We would be so grateful if you could get the guarantees for us, we know that everything is not that easy, but we also know that you will help when it is possible. - God willing, we can make it up to you later.

All the best, heartfelt greetings and kisses from your Aunt Agnes.

Rose and Else wrote to Günter on April 28, 1941:

From Rose:

My dear Günter,

... I hope you are safe and sound and have no reason to complain. .... I am happy with you about your raise in salary. Just keep on being hardworking and ambitious and don't spend a penny unnecessarily. I recently shared the contents of Walter's lines with Aunt Henny and am awaiting her answer. I am also curious to see whether she had to move out and where to. ... Did you dispose of Gerda's silver things well? I am sorry, dear boy, that the blouse came back to you and that you only had to pay for it. But don't be angry about it. If you haven't given it to Aunt Minna yet, you can put it away for me.

Today we received a long letter from Shanghai with good news, thank God: Yes, dear Günter, God willing, you will soon become an uncle if everything stays healthy in September. *(This is the first mention of my expectant birth).* We were all completely flabbergasted about this news, and of course we were very happy about it. We thought Max's hint to you, which you mentioned in the last letter, was nonsense. Gerda wrote that, thank God, she was feeling very well and wanted to go back to Japan in June to escape the heat. Max also joined in the letter, is very happy. Now let's hope that everyone stays healthy. At last at the end of March they had received a very detailed letter from our Helmut from the beginning of January; he wrote about his illness, had been in the hospital for four weeks with a fever, had good doctors and nurses, but very little food. I think with typhus one is almost only allowed to eat potatoes and sauce.

... Kurt Radt, Ilse's husband *(in Shanghai)* also received a salary allowance so that they now earn their living (with very modest demands). They are happy about it. Dear Günther Uncle Paul wrote to you himself but forgot to give his registration number. Here it is: 48093. If only you could manage to get the papers for him too! How about passage for us, dear boy? A friend here in the home was given space for October 31st. She also got a message from Lisbon through the American

Export Line. It is still a long time until October and a lot can happen. But I just wish we had seats *(tickets).* Well I know that you are doing what you can and Stanley will certainly help you too.

.... How is Aunt Minna? Please greet her warmly. Hopefully she'll be a happy grandmother soon *(Her son Egon had recently been married in Philadelphia and he and his wife Sylva were expecting a child.)* Our grandma sits in the armchair and sleeps. She slumbers a lot even during the day, unfortunately she can no longer do handicrafts nor read and write. Otherwise she would love to write to you herself. Now goodbye, my dear boy, stay healthy and be embraced by your mother who loves you

Write again <u>soon</u>! Extra greetings for Walter.

From Else:

Dear Günter,

How happy we are with you about the salary increase for you and Walter. What do you think of the upcoming family event in Shanghai? Many things have already happened to you, but not yet that! Now let us hear good things from you again very soon. We were happy thanks to Gerda to hear from Helmut: It's good that he sold the car; he just had trouble with it.

Greetings to everyone from grandma and your aunt Else, who loves you.

The next letter is dated May 5, 1941

From: Rose:

My dear Günter,

It's almost midnight and it's time to go to bed, but I've just written Gerda and Max and now I want to continue with you. ... Has the stork been with Sylva and Egon? My last letter of April 28th has certainly reached you and in any case you are happy with me that Gerda and Max are also expecting a baby. God keep everything healthy! A marriage without children is not nice either, and I think Gerda often wished for a child. She wants to go to Japan in June to avoid the heat and hopes to come back in August. Yes, dear Günther, it would be nice if you could visit Shanghai! How much do you think I would like to take you there!

Before I forget, you wrote that you wanted to ask Gerda to send me a blouse! Please don't do that, I don't need it so much and I would like to ask you to send our Gerda six beautiful, mercerized baby jackets. Don't use the smallest number, but size 2. As Gerda writes, there are only woolen baby jackets there, which are not so easy to wash. I would love to send it to her, but it won't work. You can send the jackets individually or in pairs as a "sample of no value!"

Aunt Paula also sent 1 affidavit for Aunt Marie so that she could use it if getting to Werner won't work out. Mr. and Mrs. Bachmann thanked us for our congratulations on Carla's wedding and wrote that their children had given them ship passages for September 12th from Lisbon on that day. How happy they must be! Hilde, Anneliese, and their children are probably still not in the USA. In the meantime, your letter of March 30th arrived here on the 4th, yesterday *(It was apparently taking more than five weeks for mail from Günter to reach his mother).* Thank you for that dear boy... How did you spend your birthday yesterday? How terribly I would have loved to be with you, dear Günter.

You have taken a load off our mind! Many thanks for your kindness! Now I wish you could manage to get 3 berths for us. I can imagine how great the demand is and I know that you will spare no effort and leave no stone unturned to help us. Aunt Irma from Berleburg wrote to us that Ruth paid $ 420 for the passage for her, but she doesn't have a permanent ticket yet... The Hallers *(the family from Halle, Eduard and Erna)* wrote that Stanley's papers had been renewed. They probably also asked him for the passage *(money)* now, I think. Do you know anything about it? Everyone turns to Stanley! Are the other brothers doing nothing for their relatives? Lucky Stanley isn't like them! Did you ask Gerda for help for us? It is really difficult for me to take away their savings right now. But what to do!

... Why does Helmut write to you so seldom? Hopefully he will be completely restored after the serious illness. I wrote him 25 words through the Red Cross and am very curious to see whether I will get an answer. He sold his car for cash and almost without damage, wrote Gerda...   Dear boy, stay healthy and write again very soon. Many warm greetings to ... especially for you, from your very loving mother

From Else:

Dear Günter,

We have often thought of you these days and our thoughts were with you on May 4th. How did you spend your birthday? Hopefully you and all our loved ones are doing well. ... Kind regards to Aunt Minna and Walter; but especially for you.

from grandma and aunt Else

The phrases in the letters of 1941 reflect the sense of desperation felt by my grandmother Rose, tempered by her awareness of censorship and her desire to not upset her younger son, who had just turned 21 on May 4. The subjects of financial sponsors, ship tickets and visas are echoed, with stories of those friends or family who have achieved one of these necessary steps for immigration to the United States providing hope to both the writer and reader of the letters.

This type of correspondence would have been repeated in tens of thousands of Jewish families in Germany with relatives in the United States. Unfortunately for my family and so many others in remarkably similar situations, the unsurmountable hurdle was the U.S. State Department's restrictive immigration regulations and visa requirements. Officials in the State Department raised the barrier to come to the USA from Europe at precisely the time that the refugees were desperately seeking a safe haven.

In 1941, Breckinridge Long was the U.S. Assistant Secretary of State in charge of political affairs. overseeing immigration and refugee policy for countries impacted by the war, including the issuing of visas. Long was an extreme nativist with a pathological suspicion of Eastern Europeans. He frequently complained to his staff that he was continuously being attacked by "the communists, extreme radicals, Jewish professional agitators, and refugee enthusiasts." It was Long's policy to make the visa application process for applicants such as Rose, Else and Fanni linger in the files of consular offices forever. Long's views, shared by many in the

Roosevelt administration and not suppressed by FDR himself, were that immigrants, particularly those non-Christian newcomers from central and eastern Europe, were socially offensive and potentially subversive. Anti-Jewish attitudes in Long's State Department were deeply ingrained and often reflexive. Long could have saved many Jews and chose to do nothing to alter the course of history. One Treasury Department official would later call Long and his staff an American "underground movement...to let the Jews be killed."

Even without Long's successful attempts to prevent migration to the United States, Rose, Else and Fanni were already dealing with a system that had stacked the deck against them. Long pointedly put additional insurmountable roadblocks in their path to reach the United States and find freedom and life. An official interdepartmental memo sent by telegram from Long to his staff in June 1940 reads, "We can delay and effectively stop for a temporary period of indefinite length the number of immigrants into the United States. We could do this by simply advising our consuls to put every obstacle in the way and to require additional evidence and to resort to various administrative devices which would postpone and postpone and postpone the granting of the visas."

Using the excuse that Nazi spies were hiding among the refugees seeking admission to the United States, Long designed a secret policy to further tighten the immigration requirements, effectively slashing admissions by half. A year later, Long's department cut refugee immigration once more, this time reducing admission to about a quarter of the relevant quotas. A regulation known as the "relatives' rule" required any applicant with relatives in German, Russian, or Italian territory to pass an extremely arduous security test. At the same time, all would-be immigrants were required to undergo a very thorough security review by inter-departmental committees. If any of the committees gave an applicant an unfavorable review, a visa was refused.

In 1943, Long obstructed other initiatives to save Europe's Jews. In a closed Congressional hearing, Long greatly exaggerated the number of refugees to have reached the U.S. since Hitler came to power and claimed that everything that could be done to save the Jews was being done. Ultimately, the effect of the immigration policies set by Long's department was that, during American involvement in the war, 90 percent of the already restricted quota places available to immigrants from countries under German and Italian control were never filled. Had they been granted admission, according to PBS, "an additional 190,000 people could have escaped the atrocities being committed by the Nazis."

Günter received the following letter, written by my Aachen family on May 14, 1941:

From Rose:

> My dear Günter,
>
> ... since I have just finished dusting and cleaning our room, I want to chat with you until lunch. Aunt Else is helping a little in the kitchen this morning, where we are always welcome. There is a lot of work to be done in an operation like this and there is a lack of staff. There are 120 people at the table, 40 arrived with us here at the same time. We live 1 hour away from our previous dwelling, which was rented out after it was renovated. But I had nothing to do with the craftsmen, the trustee took care of that. The rent goes to an escrow account.
>
> It's good that there is a garden here too, if only because of Grandma. Although it is not as comfortable as it used to be, when she went straight out of the living room onto the terrace and sat

there all day. Yesterday Aunt Else and I took her to the nearby forest, which is very beautiful. We have a nice wheelchair available here. It is terribly difficult for her to walk. This afternoon we have English lessons again after a long time. We take the electric tram there and come back on foot. You, dear boy, can write to me in English. This is good exercise for you and for us too.

.... I wish our Gerda would have made it through the time happily too! A few days ago she wrote in great detail about her birthday and the upcoming Seder evening. She was very pleased with your letter and its contents, dear Günter! ... Gerda sent us tea, but we're here with full provisions and I wrote her that she didn't need to send any more. If only the terrible rise in prices over there stopped. It is all incredibly expensive! (*China was experiencing hyperinflation: Using the wholesale price index of Shanghai with May 1937 equaling 1, by the end of 1941 the Shanghai wholesale price index stood at 15.98. By the end of World War II, it had reached more than 175,000.*) Did you, dear Günther, get mail from Helmut for your birthday? We hope that his letter contains good things.

But first of all, thank you very much, my dear boy, for your letter ... and, as always, pleased us very much. If you only managed to get us a ship's passage! I am convinced that you, dear Günter, will do everything to help us and it gives me great comfort that Stanley is financially willing to help out in any way possible. Acquaintances of ours got tickets for January 1942, others again like, for example, Mr. and Mrs. Bachmann for September of this year. We have to be patient and wait! God grant that we can stay here in the home, where we are in good hands, until we emigrate!

You are right, dear boy, there are so many cheaters! Be careful that you and we do not fare like the Natzungers with Cuba. Walter will have told you! Irma from Berleburg doesn't have a place on a ship either, but Ruth paid $ 420 for her there, as she wrote to us. Before I don't have any places, I don't want to apply for a declaration of no objection, because then the Reich's flight tax is due immediately. Your proposal with Portugal is not feasible.

... Dear Günter, just don't eat too much! This is more of a habit than anything else and is definitely not wholesome and pretty! If you feast on less (for example 16 Matzoh dumplings) you are also full. The loved ones in Horn are very happy about your willingness to help. Hopefully the guarantees will suffice. They also stand by us here in every way, not just with good advice, and are very concerned for us.

We had letters from Aunt Paula, Erich, and Robert. They also gave an affidavit for Aunt Marie. Now she has the choice. It's just very difficult to get away. Erich has to go to school for another 1/2 year. He doesn't yet know what to become... Did you get rid of all of Gerda's things? ... Well dear boy, stay healthy and please write <u>soon</u> to your mother, who loves you

From Else:

Dear Günther,   I hope you and all loved ones are fine. These days we went to the cemetery. The pansies on Father's grave are blooming so beautifully. Best regards from Grandma and Aunt Else.

After France capitulated to the Germans in May 1940, an armistice agreement was signed, dividing France into occupied and unoccupied zones. The German *Wehrmacht* (the armed forces of the Nazi Third Reich) would occupy northern and western France, including the entire Atlantic coast. The remaining southern two-fifths of the country would become the "French state," *(L'État Français),* in contrast to the prewar "French

Republic" *(République Française.)* The new Nazi-controlled government, with its capital at Vichy, granted extraordinary powers to its chief of state, Marshall Philippe Pétain.

On May 16, 1941, Pétain, in a radio broadcast, approved collaboration with Hitler and the Nazis. In the next two years, the Vichy government passed and enforced antisemitic legislation, "Aryanized" Jewish property, arrested "undesirables," primarily Jews. and periodically rounded up thousands of foreign and French Jews to transport first to transit camps and later usually to Auschwitz, where most of them were murdered.

On that same day, all German consulates were notified by The Central Office of Emigration in Berlin that Reich Marshal Herman Göring, Hitler's second-in-command. had banned emigration of Jews from France and all other occupied territories. That directive quotes Göring's mention of the "doubtless imminent final solution," the first official Nazi reference to the plan for mass extermination of all Jews in Europe.

In May of 1941, Günter was busy preparing affidavits not only for his mother, aunt, and grandmother, but also for Paul, Agnes and Ruth Liepmann. In order to give credence to Günter's claim that he would provide financial support for any relatives allowed to emigrate to the United States, he submitted a notarized letter, dated May 15, 1941, from his place of work, *N. Snellenburg*, signed by his first cousin Stanley, attesting that Günter "has been employed since September 7, 1937," and "has held the position of Assistant Buyer in the Housedress Department since January 15, 1940, at a salary of $25.00 per week."

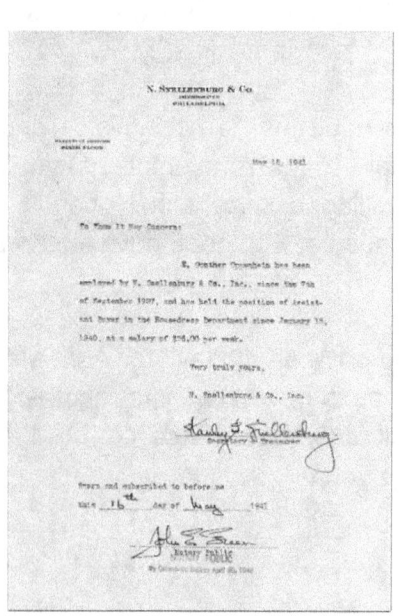

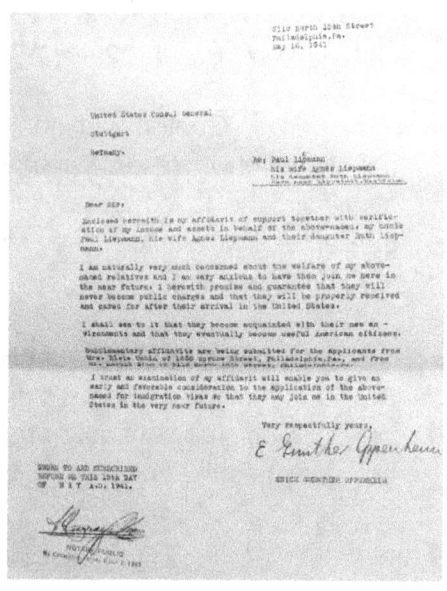

Left: attestation of Günter being gainfully employed

Right: Günter's Affidavit of financial support for Uncle Paul, Aunt Agnes and Cousin Ruth.

Günter had developed some close friendships at the boarding house at 3118 North 15th Street, where, by early 1941, he had lived for almost four years, initially sharing a small room with a stranger who quickly became a buddy, and later, after his salary had been increased to twenty dollars a week, was able to afford a private room. Today in Philadelphia, it is difficult to find a legal rooming house or boarding house, defined by city officials as rent-by-the-room establishments where more than three people unrelated by blood or marriage live and share a bathroom and sometimes kitchen facilities. Although accommodations at such facilities are currently in high demand because of affordability and accessibility, there are now less than eighty such legal dwellings as a consequence of strict licensing requirements, zoning regulations, fire laws and the fact that establishments of this type are generally unwelcome in most neighborhoods.

It was not always this way. In the 1930s, a Philadelphia Tribune report stated that 50,000 such facilities then existed in the city. For young immigrants like Günter, a rooming house provided an inexpensive place to live, where there were communal meals, English was spoken, and which was usually convenient to the workplace. The experience delivered continuing exposure to the American idiom and rapid immersion into American life, a place where one experienced first-hand the slang, customs, and attitudes of a new nation.

It was in this setting that Günter befriended Harold Blum, three years his senior. The two often ate together and talked into the night about their aspirations. Harold was an American and introduced Günter to some of his friends. For many years Philadelphia was one of the leading manufacturers of cigars ruth the United States and Harold worked as a foreman at the Philadelphia factory of Bayuk Cigars, the largest air-conditioned factory in the world to make cigars by machine. The company had its origins in 1896 when Sam, Max and Meyer Bayuk pooled $325 and opened their first factory in a rented Philadelphia attic. By 1941, Bayuk Cigars, Inc., was a successful enterprise, building on its early success in 1910 when the company introduced the "Philadelphia Hand Made Perfecto," which the smoking public quickly adopted, shortening the name to "Phillies." In 1933-1934, 365,000,000 of these were sold in just two years at 5 cents per cigar, propelling the brand to #1 in the United States (and probably the world) in cigar production in 1935.

Günter was able to persuade Harold to provide affidavits of guarantees for not only Rose, Else and Fanni, but also for Paul Liepmann and his family, all of whom Harold characterized as "friends," although obviously he had never met them. Harold also attached his personal financial information and a notarized affidavit from the plant manager at Bayuk Cigars, M.L. Wurman, attesting to his permanent employment as a foreman at Bayuk since March 1939, and that Harold Blum was an "honest, steady and reliable worker of excellent character."

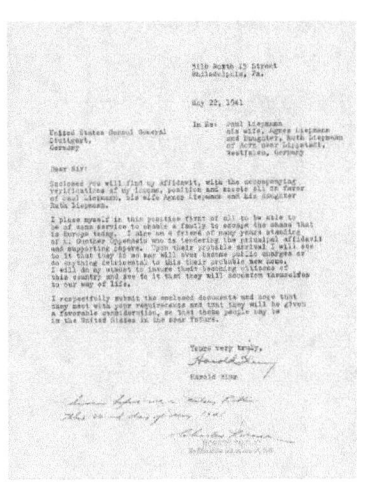 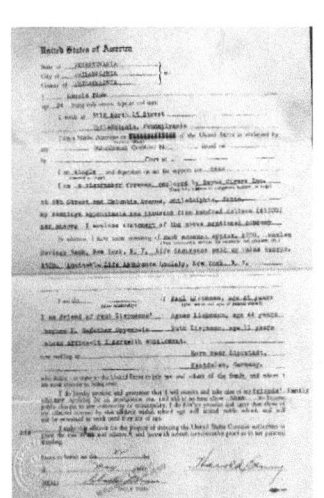 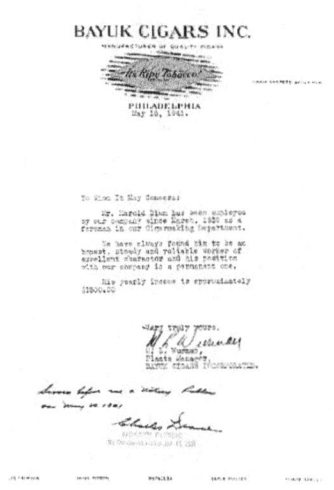

L: Harold Blum's notarized affidavit of financial support for Uncle Paul, Aunt Agnes and Cousin Ruth.

Center: accompanying list of salary and financial assets of Harold Blum

R: Notarized verification of Harold Blum's employment by his foreman at Bayuk Cigars

During the course of his work as a wholesale purchaser buyer of dresses to be sold at *Snellenburg's*, Günter befriended an older woman, Mrs. Elsie Uchin, who was the owner of a dress factory in Philadelphia. Günter also persuaded her to sign an affidavit in June of 1941, promising and guaranteeing to "receive and take care of my friend's family." As part of this guarantee, Mrs. Uchin submitted copies of cancelled checks made out to the U.S. Internal Revenue Service, signifying that she was an American taxpayer. These checks, written through accounts at the Central-Penn National Bank and the Corn Exchange National Bank and Trust Company, were for quarterly payments of personal federal income tax for the tax year 1940, totaling approximately 104 dollars.

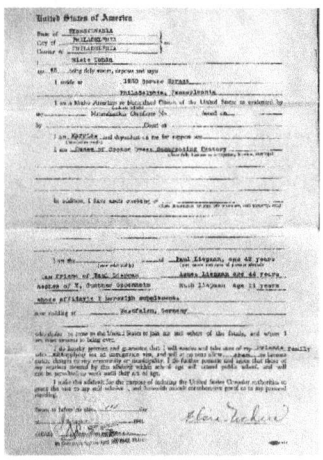

The next letter to Günter from Aachen was written on May 22, 1941. On page 2 of the letter, there is written in different handwriting, in pencl, "917 – 3291," representing the Nazi censor's identification number.

:

5/22/1941 envelope opened and stamped on back, pasted label "geöffnet (opened), stamp: "Geprüft (inspected) Oberkommando der Wehrmacht,"

From: Rose

My dear Günter,

I want to use this morning to chat with you, I've just finished dusting our room and I'm not going to help in the kitchen today, as I usually do. Aunt Else went to town, where she runs errands. ... First of all, I would like to thank you very much for your telegram on Mother's Day, dear Günter! You made us very happy, it arrived perfectly on time, and the whole Sunday was bright and beautiful! Aunt Henny got one from Walter too. She still lives in her apartment and is very happy about it. ... Thank you very much for the detailed report that we read with great interest. We were very happy with your photo, dear boy. I think you've got a little thinner in the face. So now cousin Joe *(Joseph Snellenburg, born in Philadelphia in 1872, the son of Albert's aunt, Minna Amant. who had been rescued from Albuquerque by the Snellenburg family)* died after all! I read the attached newspaper piece about his life with interest. Surely there was a huge following at the funeral. .... Is Aunt Minna happily back from Habana and got everything done? *(Minna Oppenheim Baum, Albert's sister and a widow, had emigrated from Germany to Philadelphia in 1937. In May 1941, she flew from Miami to Cuba, staying at the Hotel Sevilla in Havana, and attempted to transact some business related to her real estate holdings in Germany.)* Walter must have found a suitable boarding house a long time ago. Many warm greetings for Aunt Minna, Walter, and all loved ones!

Helmut's letter was on the road for a long time, I hope he's healthy and in good spirits. I immediately wrote to B. and asked for the certificates. I should be surprised if they send them! Let's hope the best! Did you hear from Helmut on your birthday and is he still in M. *(Magdiel, Jewish Palestine)*? Yesterday Aunt Else and I wrote an English letter of condolence to Stanley. He will certainly show you! ... You, dear Günter, really made an effort for us because of the passages. It's not your fault that you haven't had any success so far. Hopefully you will still be able to get some in a not too long time. We want to *(the following sentence in the original English):* "keep up our spirits and let us hope for the best!" Dear Günter, it's nice that you are satisfied with your business. Just see to it that your salary goes up and ask, if you are not informed automatically. Be thrifty dear boy, you know how necessary it is! Yesterday a letter from Gerda dated April 22 arrived here. They spent the Seder evening so beautifully, the two Goldschmidt boys were with them too *(Max Ludwig and his brother Fritz Goldschmidt, first cousins of Rose via the Liepmann side)*. Max can do it so splendidly. *(He certainly could!)* Unfortunately, both Max and Gerda were very depressed, but didn't let anyone notice. Just think about it, their good friend Dr. Meyerbach from Aachen, who has been in Shanghai for as long as they have and has a good practice as an ophthalmologist, poisoned himself with veronal. Max was called to him that day. Nobody knows the reason! Dr. M. slept for two days without waking up again. He wasn't married and has his old mother, a really nice lady, with him. She is most to be regretted, but she thinks her son has had encephalitis. When Gerda came to visit in 1935, Ms. M. visited us in Halle when we were there by car. That's why I know her. Nebbig! *(German-Jewish or Yiddish term meaning "what a pity" or "poor thing.")* It was such a good relationship between the son and the mother! Thank God, Gerda was doing well in health terms. She felt very comfortable! Hopefully it will stay that way. Has Egon become a happy dad? Dear Günter, it is entirely in my interest that you are very careful with paying the fare for the boat trips so that you are not cheated. Did you hear anything about the cargo steamers? Farewell, my dear boy, warm greetings, from your mother who loves you.

From: Else

I hope you are healthy and Aunt Minna and all loved ones alike. Just ask Walter if he knows Lotte Rosenthal from Recklinghausen? She sends her best regards. She takes care of the household here *(at the Altenheim)* and is very nice. *(This is likely Lieselotte Abraham, née Rosenthal, who the Nazis deported from Düsseldorf on July 25, 1942, to the Theresienstadt Ghetto and from there to Auschwitz in 1944. She is one of the few fortunate enough to have survived Auschwitz).*

The following letter to Günter was written on May 27, 1941, with the censor's number in pencil "3091-999/2" on page 2.

From Rose:

My dear boy,

This morning we were very pleased with your letter of May 7th with Walter's address... I'll send the greetings to Aunt Henny (*Henrietta Oppenheim Vorreuter, Walter's mother*) in a moment. She still lives in S. (*Siegburg*) in her apartment. Hopefully this letter reaches you in the best of health, thank God we are also well. It is now so wonderful outside in nature, as the fruit trees are in full bloom and the forest is emblazoned in all colors... May has been very cool so far. When we don't have an *(English)* class in the afternoon, we take Grandma to the nearby forest. She likes to be there, and we sit down on some quiet bench and test each other on phrases and vocabulary... Do you come home from work so late on Wednesdays, dear Günter, that you start writing shortly before midnight? Better go to bed, otherwise you won't be fresh for work the next day. I've already asked you to be <u>extremely careful</u> when buying the ship tickets, dear boy, so that you don't get cheated and the money is gone. That would be terrible! So first ask for advice from people who understand something about it.

Skip the Portuguese line if you don't trust it! I thanked you in my last letter for your telegram on Mother's Day, dear Günter, which delighted us immensely and punctually. That the birthday went so well and that you received so many presents is nice and pleases me... Just don't lose the beautiful pocket knife from Stanley! Yesterday Aunt Marie sent us 2 letters from Aunt Paula, one from May 7, 1941, and the other from May 20. Where have they been for so long? They are all healthy and make a living.... They also sent 1 affidavit for Aunt Marie, because it doesn't work out with her going to Werner. Paula and Robert's neighbors joined in the guarantee. Dear Günther, have you got the papers for Uncle Paul in order and sent off? Otherwise take care of it! The Horners (*the relatives in Horn, Germany—Paul, Agnes, and Ruth*), actually received the request from Stuttgart to send in their papers. Ruth spent a few days in the hospital in Paderborn, where the growths were removed. Hopefully she will be all right again. My cousin Max Sp. (*Spanier*) in Enger also received the A.L. papers from Stuttgart and his two sons in the USA arranged places for their parents with the Joint there. *(Max Spanier and his wife Adele née Seligman were deported to the Theresienstadt camp in Czechoslovakia, where they died. Their two sons, Edward and Arnold, were indeed in the USA. They had been fortunate to get there through England in 1939.)* Hopefully Sylva and baby are doing quite well! I suppose she has become a happy mother by now. How does Egon feel as a "dad" and Aunt Minna is surely a proud grandmother! I wish our Gerda had everything happily behind her too! ... Is your business doing well? Here there's a very nice, large garden with lots of flowering trees and bushes. A gardener works in it all the time. Well goodbye, dear boy, stay healthy and soon please us with good news, God willing, your ever-loving mother.

Special greetings for Walter and Aunt Minna!

From Else:

Dear Günther, also grandmas and my best regards. I hope you are fine. As always, your letter pleased us very much. ... All the best to you and Walter! Greetings and kisses to you again, Aunt Else

Aachen to Günter, May 30, 1941, with censor 3084/139 in pencil:

From Rose:

My dear Günter,

I am sending you 2 birth certificates and 2 police clearance certificates, which have just arrived. Hopefully they will reach you quickly and in good health and, above all, have the desired success! I wrote to you in detail, dear boy, three days ago, confirming your and Walter's letter of May 7th. I also asked you to be extremely careful when paying for the passages, so that you don't get cheated like the Natzungers *(This refers to a member of the Vorreuter family living in Natzungen, a village in Westphalia, who had paid for ship tickets to the United States and did not receive them)* back then! A letter just arrived from Gerda and Max, they now know our new address, and of course they were very shocked about it. They had mail from you on March 22nd and from Helmut on March 23rd. Gerda sent me what she wrote to Stanley (she enclosed it with your letter). I agree. Stanley has promised us his help for years, even back when father died. It certainly doesn't make him poorer, he's single, very rich and doesn't have a family to take care of. He helps strangers and what does the small sum mean to him? Gerda and Max, on the other hand, sacrifice almost all of their assets if they send the sum now, given the bad state of the Chinese dollar. Our dear blessed father would certainly have preferred to accept the money from dear Stanley rather than from Max and Gerda. You don't have to think about it and worry about it. Maybe we can make it up to Stanley after all! Now I only wish that Helmut would soon be reunited with you, dear boy! He doesn't shy away from work, you know that. May God let us see the day that we live together with you again in health and contentment! The day after tomorrow is Pentecost already! It is with sadness that I remember the wonderful time past, when you children were still at home with us and we all drove into God's beautiful world in our car very early in the morning on Pentecost. Do you still remember the Harz Mountains and the wonderful Rhine, dear boy? You never forget something like that! .... Please write again very soon, dear Günter! ... So who is vouching for the affidavit for Helmut now? Stay healthy and be hugged by your always loving mother.

From Else:

Dear Günther, ..., I send you, Aunt Minna, and Walter my warmest regards; and hope you are all healthy. Let us hear good things from you soon. With love, Grandma and Aunt Else

Uncle Paul from Horn again wrote to Günter on that same date, May 30, 1941. In addition to the addressee, the writing on the front of the envelope is translated "Airmail letter; By Airmail to North America; With Clipper via Lisbon – Portugal." The Boeing 314 Clipper was an American long-range flying boat (a type of fixed-wing seaplane with a hull, allowing it to land on water, if necessary) produced by Boeing from 1938 to 1941. One of the largest aircraft of its time, it had the range to cross the Atlantic or Pacific oceans. Twelve Clippers were built, nine of which served with Pan American Airways. The latter flew the aircraft from Lisbon to New York and back, carrying first class passengers and mail through mid-1941. The plane cruised at 150 miles per hour, making a one-way journey in 27 hours, including a stop at Horta in the Azores. Paul (and Rose) often wrote the above on the front of envelopes to ensure that the mail to America would indeed arrive.

May 30, 1941, letter to Günter from Paul Liepmann

From Paul:

Dear Günter! *(The name spellings are somewhat inconsistent; here Paul clearly writes "Günter" (no h) and "Gerta," and "Helmut.")*

I hope you received our letter of April 24th on time and that these lines find you as well as they leave us. I wanted to tell you today that we have received a request from the consulate in Stuttgart to hand in our papers and I would like to hear when you sent them off. You can probably imagine how much we are waiting for them. Did they go directly to the consulate, or did you send them to Horn? We heard from the loved ones in Aachen that Sel. *(shortened German word "selig," meaning deceased or departed)* Schnellenberg *(Paul is using the German form of "Snellenburg," which was used by that family before they came to the United States in 1857)* has died in the meantime, he was the main doer with you and I'm curious as to who will be his successor. Surely it was a big funeral, were you there too? How did Walter Vorreuter settle in? And what is his job? Is Aunt Minna back from Cuba? ... At the moment our Ruth has been with us for 3 days and will stay until after Pentecost; her polyps *(nasal)* were taken out and she was given a rest for a few days. We're expecting Uncle Hermann from Essen for a while next week, he's doing quite well again. Gustav Spanier, Grete, and I now go to Soest once a week for English lessons, taught by a Fraulein Rosenbaum from Essen. I wish I could already speak it as well as you!

(Penciled censor number 3636 is on page two) Have you heard from your Helmuth? We had various messages from the Red Cross from Oskar and Hilde that they now have a garden restaurant in Haifa, which is supposed to be going very well. In January, Oskar's father suddenly died of a heart attack, he had been ill for a long time... Thank God there is also good news from Shanghai, Gerta will probably have started her planned trip to Japan by now! Well, dear Günter, stay healthy and write again soon! Warm greetings with love Your Uncle Paul

From Ruth, in juvenile handwriting:

Dear Günter!

I gladly take the opportunity to add my warmest regards. Hopefully we can get there soon, and you manage to send us the guarantees. I'm happy to be home for a few days again, but time always goes by too quickly.

Greetings and kisses, Ruth

256

From Agnes:

Dear Günther,

The dear Aacheners sent us a picture of you for our information, you look healthy, but have become slimmer. We always hear from your loved ones about your letters and are happy that you are doing so well -

Warm greetings and kisses from yours

Aunt Agnes.

Trude and Werner say hello. (*Relatives of Agnes Sternberg, all of whom perished in the death camps of Czechoslovakia or Poland*).

On June 1, 1941, mob violence directed against Iraqi Jews broke out in Baghdad, instigated by Nazi sympathizers. Jews had lived in Iraq (the historical region known as Mesopotamia situated within the Tigris–Euphrates River system) since the sixth century BCE, one thousand years before the establishment of Islam, and had been an accepted group through most of that period of time. In 1941, 135,000 Jews lived in Iraq, 3% of the population at the time of this anti-Jewish uprising, known as the *Farhud* (an Arabic term translated as "pogrom" or "violent dispossession"). It was a turning point in the history of the Jews in Iraq. According to a recent article in the *Times of Israel*, there are now less than five Jews remaining living in Iraq.

Although Rose likely knew nothing about the *Farhud*, she certainly was aware that many Muslim leaders in the Middle East were eagerly working together with Germany in its quest for annihilation of world Jewry. The former Grand Mufti of Jerusalem, Hajj Amin al-Husayni, pursued by the British Army for his anti-British activity, had fled to Iraq in 1939. Hitler met with al-Husayni in Germany in November 1941. Since this event was well publicized in the German press, Rose undoubtedly was cognizant of this. Al-Husayni remained in Europe until 1945, living in splendor in Berlin and collaborating with Nazi Germany and Fascist Italy by broadcasting anti-Jewish propaganda by radio and inspiring and indoctrinating Muslim men to serve in Axis military and auxiliary units. He would compare Jewishness to infectious disease and Jews to microbes or bacilli and, in at least one speech attributed to him, he advocated killing Jews "wherever Arabs found them." Following the end of the War, Britain and France, eager to exert post-War influence in the oil-rich Middle East, allowed him to leave Germany. He lived in Egypt and Lebanon until his death in 1974, continuing to devote his life producing and disseminating anti-Zionist, anti-Jewish, and anti-Israel propaganda.

The next letter to Günter from Aachen was written on June 4, 1941, with censor mark "3675-2 (checkmark) 337/2:"

From Rose:

My dear Günter,

Your last letter of May 7th was answered on the 27th, the day it arrived. Then the desired birth certificates and certificates of good conduct were sent to you by registered mail on May 30th! I hope you received everything and that by the time these lines arrive you will be safe and sound, like us, thank God. ... Grandma is sitting in the garden under the chestnut trees in bloom. The air smells wonderfully of lilacs! ... As far as my letter today is concerned, dear boy, there is a special reason. The gentleman who is helping me with the emigration told me that at the beginning and end of August there are likely to be ships leaving from Spanish ports on which places might be available. The matter goes through the North German Lloyd, with whom I made enquiries myself yesterday. I was advised there to cable you <u>immediately</u>, which I did yesterday. But the telegram first went to Cologne and, God willing, has long since reached you. It read "pay dollars... for three passages to North German Lloyd, to Joint $126 for departure, since there may be an opportunity to leave the country at the end of August. <u>If you agree</u>, send wire and pay in." Hopefully you will have <u>done your research</u> before you paid in, dear Günter, so that the money is not lost. *(Two months earlier, Günter had already travelled to the New York office of the Hartmann Travel Agency and made a deposit of 180 dollars for three future American Export Line passages from Lisbon to New York.)* We women here don't know what to do! What attracted me to the matter was that *Norddeutscher Lloyd* was in charge. I don't like that it's Spanish or another foreign ship.

Of course, I would prefer if you could book for us there with the American Export Line. This would also be safe in the event of war! Well, dear Günter, my head is heavy with all the brooding! You must do what <u>you</u> think is right. In any case, it is probably a risky thing, because in the event of war everything would be lost. God grant that it doesn't come to that! I'm excited to see what you're wiring back and when! Uncle Paul just sent us a package that made us very happy. We might want to take economy class on the Spanish ship. But our acquaintance didn't exactly know the price for this, so he didn't fill out the price here, this was done in Cologne. Have you heard anything else positive from your many efforts regarding the passage, dear Günter? ... I'm closing in the hope of hearing good things from you soon. With best regards to Aunt Minna and Stanley, especially for you, your mother who always loves you

From Else:

Dear Günther,

I wonder how you did it in the end? Hopefully right, because one soon no longer knows what is right and what is wrong! We've been brooding for days, what to do? How are you and all your loved ones? Is Aunt Minna back and everything alright? Has Walter found a good boardinghouse? How about the affidavits for Uncle Paul? He asked about them today. If only you, dear Günther, could send them to him very soon. You have so many acquaintances and good friends. Uncle Paul is so worried about the papers, so see and do what you can. I know you're already doing it.

All the best and warm greetings from Grandma and your loving Aunt Else

I am certain that the "choice" between taking a ship operated by the American Export Line or North German Lloyd to reach the United States was discussed at great length by Rose and Else. As Else writes in the above letter, "we've been brooding for days, what to do?" Given the ultimate outcome, I hope that those conversations were engaged in optimistically by both, rather than a charade played by the two sisters, each one trying to hide the truth from one another. Additionally, the stress placed on Günter in Philadelphia must have been overwhelming with his wanting to make the correct decisions on our family's behalf. Else comments on Günter's choice, "Hopefully right; because one soon no longer knows what is right and what is wrong!" Letters took almost a month to cross the Atlantic and one never was certain whether or not communication was being received on the other end.

Günter read the next letter, written from the *Altenheim* in Aachen on June 13, 1941:

From Rose: All letters now have the censors' penciled numbers.

My dear Günter,

.... I hope you are healthy and happy when you receive these lines and satisfied in every respect, also all loved ones there. How is little Anthony Albert doing? *(Anthony Baum, Egon Baum's newborn son, the grandson of Minna Oppenheim Baum. His middle name is after his grandfather, Albert Oppenheim, as is mine.)* Is Sylva okay? Has the relationship with Aunt Minna improved? Your last letter from May 21st delighted us on June 7th. It's very gratifying that you're so busy. Hope you get an allowance soon! Do the others in your department also have to work in the shop that late in the evenings? ... Yesterday we had a letter from Halle. Uncle E. was ill (dizzy spells) but is better again. If possible, they want to go to *Friedrichroda (a spa resort in Thuringia, Germany)* for rest and relaxation. They recently received a letter from Heinz, who had also heard from Herbert, that they were fine.

The day before yesterday we received a letter from Gerda dated May 12th. They are, thank God, healthy and Gerta felt very well. Max complains about the practice, he feels it very much that many foreigners have left. Gerda will probably not travel to Japan because everything costs a lot and they still have to buy all sorts of things. Maybe she'll go to Tsingtao, which is also much easier to get to. I am curious when you will reply to my last telegram, for which I paid 50 Marks, and what your answer will be: From there you can best judge which shipping line to choose. I'd prefer to go with one from there! Inquire carefully beforehand, dear Günter, so that the money is <u>not</u> lost. Did Edgar answer you? Yesterday Aunt Frieda wrote to us that on July 28th she is leaving from Lisbon for New York on the steamer Nyassa. Her children sent her a cable that they had rebooked and that Frieda should go directly to New York instead of Cuba. However, she has not yet been to Hamburg to receive the visa. Hilde Selig is leaving Bilbao for Buenos Aires at the end of this month, where her husband is already *(Hilde Liepmann Selig was a cousin of Rose and Else, also born in Bücken, but a generation younger. She did indeed leave on a ship from Spain to South America on June 6, 1941, one of the last successful exits from the German Reich)...* An old woman in the home was over there in Scranton Pa when she was 16 years old. It's not far from Philadelphia. She was there often and I often converse with her in English, she speaks it fluently. Now, dear boy, I am absolutely to give you the address of her relatives in Scranton. She says they could help you if you asked them. Her cousin's address is E.J. Goodman, 730 Monroe Ave, Scranton, Pennsylvania. He is in a "building association" *(words written in English)* and doing very well. He lives with his sister, who is a "teacher at the high school" *(5 words also written in English)*. The two gave the affidavits for the daughter of this old woman and family and paid the money for 3 passages. Now they are waiting for ship slots. I had to read a very kind letter from the cousin from Scranton to his cousin here, Mrs. Jaffé... Greetings and regards also to Aunt Minna and Stanley. Please write again soon! Where are you going on your vacation? Be frugal, dear Günter! With love, mother

From Else: (written vertically in the left margin).

Warmest greetings to you, dear Günther, as well as Aunt Minna and Walter, in the hope that you are doing well. With love, your grandmother and aunt Else

The next letter to Günter was written one week later, on June 20, 1941:

From Rose:

My dear Günter,

... Thank you, my dear boy, for the two detailed letters. You've actually been very busy lately and I can empathize with how tired you are so late in the evening. But it's also a lot of fun when business is going well and success is not lacking. Well, I hope and wish that you personally will notice something of this and that your salary will be increased a bit! First of all on behalf of Grandma, who can no longer write well because of her eyes (which she regrets immensely, you know how much and how often she wrote), many thanks to you and Walter for your birthday wishes, which make her very happy. May they come true and may we all see each other again in good health over there in the not-too-distant future! Nothing came out of the berths on the *Nyassa,* because otherwise we would have received news anyway. I hope the deposit that Stanley made available to you is not lost, dear boy! That would be terrible! I will thank him myself these days for everything he does good for us. Did Walter receive the affidavits from friends in Natzung? Now all travel plans will probably be postponed.

It's been nice summer weather here for a few days, we sit a lot outside in the large garden under the shady trees. The forest is also very close and beautiful. Today I immediately sent the letter from Oskar and Hilde to Horn, where they are sure to be very happy. You didn't even mention what Helmuth wrote in his letter, dear Günter! Have Uncle Paul's affidavits been dispatched by now? The fact that you can already determine the prices in your department yourself is quite something. The heat there must be huge and not everyone can stand it. Is Aunt Minna still dressed as elegantly as she used to be here? How are Sylva and child? ... a silver plate was a practical, beautiful present.

A letter dated May 21 arrived today from Gerda and Max with good news, thank God. They shop for children's supplies. Gerda writes that thank God she feels very well and would probably not travel to Japan. It's all very expensive because of the inflation, and they're right about saving. In the practice, Max notices that many well-paying foreigners have left the city... I've been taking baths here for a while and hope they will banish my often-recurring lumbago! Aachen is famous for its hot springs, which are said to be good for rheumatism and gout. In any case, Edgar's parents will now have to postpone their trip to the children! That's how it is for infinitely many! However, one must not lose hope! Where are Heinz Ferber's parents? By the way, you didn't write us anything about your visit to Gisela Lenneberg, dear boy. Here Dinchen Sternberg read us their letter, which said that you tried so hard to get places for us. Now I hope that these lines will find you in the best of health, as they are leaving us, thank God. ... May you be embraced by your ever-loving mother

From Else:

Dear Günther, Grandma's birthday. Be careful with flashlights *(this is a code for something).* It probably didn't work out with the passage, otherwise we would have heard from you by now. With love and in haste, Aunt Else.

Also from Grandma and me the warmest greetings and thanks for the good wishes for Grandma.

Five days earlier, Reinhard Heydrich, head of the Gestapo (security police) had briefed the *Einzatzgruppen* (operational groups) commanders on the implementation of the "Final Solution." As early as 1938 Heydrich had already stated that simply restricting the Jews, whom he called "the eternal subhumans," was insufficient, one had to completely get rid of them.

On June 22, 1941. under the code name Operation "Barbarossa," Nazi Germany launched the largest German military operation of World War II, a surprise invasion against the Soviet Union, its ally in the war against Poland. Despite the signed strategic and political pacts between the two nations, the German High Command placed into action Nazi Germany's ideological goal of conquering the western Soviet Union to create more *Lebensraum* (living space) for long-term German settlement, repopulate it with Germans, use some of the conquered people as forced labor for the Axis war effort while acquiring the oil reserves of the Caucasus as well as the agricultural resources of various Soviet territories, including Ukraine and Byelorussia. Their ultimate goal was the eventual extermination of the indigenous Slavic peoples by mass deportation. By the end of the year, The *Wehrmacht* had advanced eastward hundreds of miles to the outskirts of Moscow and was well on its way to permanently eliminate the perceived Communist threat to Germany.

The Nazi "*Endlösung der Judenfrage*" (Final Solution to the Jewish Question) was a Nazi euphemism for the deliberate and systematic mass murder of all European Jews.

Soon after the invasion of Soviet Russia, special elements of the *Sicherheitsdienst-SD* (Security Police and the Security Service), were trained as mobile killing units to conduct the murder of Soviet Jews. These *Einzatzgruppen* were deployed immediately behind the rapidly advancing front lines of the German military and would immediately conduct mass shootings of Jews, of which there were three million in the Soviet Union. They were often assisted by local Russian antisemites recruited to help.

In 1941, after the *Schutztaffel* (*SS*, officers totally under Hitler's control), established extermination camps in Poland, located at Chelmno, Belzec, Sobibor, Treblinka, Auschwitz-Birkenau, and Majdanek, Heydrich took the job of coordinating the deportation of European Jews to these camps.

Although there is no mention of the German invasion in any of my grandmother's correspondence for obvious reasons, there is no question in my mind that Rose was reading the newspapers which extolled the successful German *Blitzkrieg* (lightning strike) against the Russians and was realizing that the Nazi war machine was making headway in its goals.

The family in Aachen wrote to Günter on July 1, 1941:

From Rose:

> My dear Günter,
>
> Your last two letters from May 28 and June 5 which arrived here on the 19th and 20th of June, I already answered on June 20 and expected a sign of life from you every day, but in vain. That's why I want to let you hear from me again today, so that there isn't too much of a pause in our

correspondence. I hope you're doing well, dear boy, in terms of health and otherwise, and you're not suffering too much from the heat. There were some very hot days here last week, which we mostly spent in the garden, where we also ate our meals because grandma finds it so difficult to walk. Everyone else eats in the dining room. But after a thunderstorm it cooled down considerably, even too much! Everything is blooming so beautifully outside. The large garden is kept in order by a gardener. Dear Günter, it didn't work out with the ship passages you advised! Hope you don't lose the money! That would be terrible! How much had Stanley given you for it? Did you actually get my telegram of June 8th? I don't know exactly when it went off. I paid 50 marks for it with a reply and sometimes I think it didn't go off at all! Gerda and Max last wrote on May 29th. The letter arrived here on June 27th. Gerda felt very well, thank God, and is busy with the baby equipment. Unfortunately, Max had a number of kidney stone attacks with severe pain all of a sudden during the night. A doctor gave him morphine injections, which helped. God grant that he is fully restored. He wrote that he had no time to be ill, nor could he afford the luxury! Everything costs a lot of money, especially now. Aunt Henny recently wrote that they have to move. She stays with Erna and Leo, doesn't yet know where they are going. Uncle Eduard was ill, but he's getting better.... Did Helmuth's birth certificate and certificate of good conduct sent by registered mail arrive and have you ever had a letter from him? How is he? Why doesn't Aunt Minna write? We haven't seen <u>one line</u> from her for a very long time! Does Walter still have the same job and still live in your room? How is your business and where are you going for vacation? Uncle Hermann is visiting in Horn at the moment. 32 years ago today was our wedding anniversary! Ah, dear Günter, what has one experienced since then! The dead have been spared a lot, they rest in peace. ... One can't do anything with it now anyway. One must not lose courage and hope and, above all, trust in God. Well, my dear boy, stay healthy and soon please with good reports, God willing, your ever-loving mother

Special greetings for Walter, Stanley, and Aunt Minna!

From Fanni:

Many thanks, dear Günter, for your kind words and good wishes. Unfortunately, writing is getting harder for me every day. At my age you can't expect much from life. One must be satisfied! Warm greetings from your old loving grandmother also for dear Walter and Aunt Minna

From Else:

Dear Günter, I hope you and all loved ones are healthy there and we'll hear good things from you very soon. You're probably looking forward to your holiday. Spend it pleasantly and recover well. Sincerely,

Aunt Else

The next letter was written on July 17, 1941:

From Rose:

My dear Günter,

A week ago today I confirmed your telegram for Grandma's birthday in a letter that was also intended for Gerda as well... I have already answered your letter of June 10 (here on July 9). How are you, dear boy? Do you still have so much to do and what are you all doing? Thank God we are still healthy and are glad about it every morning! – May God continue to protect us so that we will meet again in joy in a not-too-distant future! Dear Günther, yesterday the travel agency *Hartmann* from Cologne informed me that according to the new entry regulations, a <u>new visa application </u>has to be submitted to the government in Washington. *Hartmann* thinks it advisable that I inform my guarantor <u>as soon as possible</u> so that the application can be made and we can be registered <u>in good time</u>. I hope you, dear Günther, have<u> already arranged all this</u>, because according to your telegram you have known about it longer than we have. That's why I wouldn't send you a cable. I know you are doing what you can to help us. Write to me about this very soon. I've spent so much money on cables and it's all been for nothing! After all, there are no ships sailing for us! But we don't want to lose courage and trust in God! Have you heard from Helmuth and Gerda again? ... Just during Uncle Paul's being here we had a lot of excitement. But thank God the horror passed *(I am uncertain of what my grandmother is alluding to; perhaps the Nazis came to the Altenheim searching for people and/or possessions)*. Where are you going to spend the holidays this year, dear Günter? By the way, I wanted to tell you that this summer I'm wearing the light silk dress that you gave me for my birthday a lot and I like it a lot. I like it so much and it's so light. I really enjoy it, dear boy! Now I shall write warm greetings also for Walter, Aunt Minna and especially for you from Aunt Else and your mother who always loves you.

The next letter was written six days later:

From Rose:

My dear Günter,

Your dear letter of June 30th, which you had already begun on the 23rd, finally arrived yesterday. We expected mail from you every day and were happy to receive a sign of life from you. .... I think my last letter of July 17th, enclosing a few English lines for Stanley (it was sent by registered mail) has reached you. I also shared with you a message from the travel agency *Hartmann* in Cologne. Attached is a photocopy of the A.L. papers with our registration numbers. I don't know if it will be of any use. Our acquaintances here sent them all to their guarantors there. We want to leave nothing undone! It is very unfortunate that all your and our efforts have now been in vain, dear boy! But we still don't want to give up hope and trust in God. May he help us! I don't understand what you wrote about applicants who still leave relatives here and that they don't get any visa. What is that supposed to mean? For example, do we belong in this category too? I am very glad that the travel money deposited by Stanley was not lost. I would have been <u>very</u> upset about that! So, dear Günter, see what you can do to help us. You know that better there than we do here. In any case, I thank you very much for all your work and effort, even if it was in vain. It's not your fault! ... Did you ask for a salary raise and with what result? We haven't heard from Gerda and Max for a <u>very long</u> time! How may they be doing? Did you also have news from Helmut? Can't you make sure that he at least comes over there, dear Günther? We don't have many hot days here this summer, we sit in the garden a lot, it's very nice that grandma can be outside. Then she is happy. Just think, dear Günther, Hans D. died in Hannover from mental depression and poor memory in the hospital! It's very hard for his elderly mother and family! I'm floored that Dinchen would do nothing.

Aunt Paula and family congratulated grandma on time. Margot didn't write <u>one line</u>! Well my dear boy, stay healthy and warm greetings and hugs from your loving mother, grandma and aunt Else

On July 31, 1941, Hermann Göring instructed SS Reich Security Service chief Reinhard Heydrich by letter to evacuate and eliminate all European Jews presently in German-held territory. The letter mentions a "a complete solution of the Jewish question in the German sphere of influence in Europe."

In early September 1941, a gas chamber with poison gas Zyklon-B was first used in Auschwitz to murder six hundred Soviet prisoners of war and 300 Jews. On the Russian front, the *SS* and police, supported by locally recruited auxiliaries, continued to indiscriminately shoot the residents of Jewish communities in the captured territory.

The next letter was written to Günter on September 1, 1941:

From: Rose

My dear Günter,

I want to use the quiet that reigns throughout the home after dinner to chat with you, so that I can bring the letter straight to the post office when I go bathing. I have often felt a kind of lumbago and hope to eliminate the evil with thermal baths. The springs here are said to be very good, they are very close by, so the walk is short. The water comes out of the ground very hot and has to be cooled down before you can bathe. I will probably never have it more comfortable again. So let's hope it helps! I assume my last letters of August 15, 18 and 24 are in your possession and I hope you will let Gerda and Helmut read them! You can imagine how I particularly miss the news from my loved ones from Shanghai! Have you perhaps had a letter from them in the meantime, as well as from Helmut? Hope everyone is safe and sound like us, thank God. How are you, dear boy? ... I hope you have recovered very well and are going to your work with new strength and fresh courage. I hope you'll tell us a lot about your stay in beautiful Florida. You get to see a lot of the world. I also always had so much joy when I used to go on beautiful trips with dear father every summer. For me, traveling is the best thing there is! It's all over now! Only the memory remains!

Meanwhile, on August 30th, we were delighted by your dear letter of August 13th. How much was your ticket to Miami, dear Günter? The train must be magnificent! How I would have liked to sit with you! Miss Nydick is actually very nice to you and Walter! I will write to her in English myself tomorrow. Has she recovered well and is her niece fully restored? I was also very interested in the contents of the cards you were sent. I wish I could write such a lively letter style too! Recently Uncle Paul delighted us with magnificent plums from their garden. We're really hungry for fruit. There is little and you can hardly find any. If only we had a little of last year's excess! Aunt Henny and Erna also sent us pears and plums. They seem to be able to buy some there! ... Aunt Frieda wrote us a card before she left Spain. Now she must have landed in Cuba. Hilde from Bücken has also arrived happily with her husband in Argentina. Aunt Marie, on the other hand, cannot get away; she's very anxious. If you have nice photos of yourself from the holidays, dear boy, send them to me! If you hear from Gerda, please write to me immediately! Now stay healthy and please send our regards to Walter and Stanley. With love and hugs from your loving mother.

From Else:

Dear Günther,

(In English) Many thanks for your last letter. Did you enjoy the holidays and are you busy as before. Oma and I send you and all dear ones the best wishes. Yours truly   Aunt Else.

September 10, 1941, letter to Günter with Else writing in English, which she was studiously learning in preparation to go to the USA, within the left margin.

In September 1941, as the German Army began its 900-day siege of Leningrad in the Soviet Union, Hitler proclaimed, "Leningrad will be starved into submission." That month, the deportation of the Jewish population of Germany, 338,000 men, women, and children, commenced. Initially, they were sent to overcrowded ghettos in Eastern Europe, where space was made for the German Jews by annihilating the local Jewish residents. In Minsk, the regional *SD*, German Army, and local collaborators gathered approximately 25,000 of the Jewish ghetto inhabitants, drove them to a local ravine, and killed them. Similar murders took place in Riga.

The following two-page letter was written on September 15, 1941.

From: Rose:

My dear Günter,

Now it's time for me to write to you, because I just saw that my last letter to you was sent on September 1st. It also contained New Year's wishes for Aunt Minna, which you sure have passed on. A letter also went off the next day for Miss Nydick. I hope she received it and was happy with it. Did you read it? I just want to know if it contained any errors and if the style was reasonable *(It was written in English as Miss Nydick was not proficient in German)*. Meanwhile, on the 12th, we were very delighted by your detailed letter from Miami dated 8/26. It must be very beautiful there and I hope you have recovered very well and have regained strength and went back to work refreshed. Thank goodness we are healthy too. It must have certainly been a mutual joy when you saw Aunt Paula and family again. Nebbig, now they have to start all over again. They also wrote from New York to Aunt Marie, who mailed the letter to us. The old woman has experienced many disappointments lately in not being able to get away. She seems very down with her nerves! Now she suddenly had to move with her boarding house, lives with many others in Limmer in a suburb of Hannover. - How sorry I am for Aunt Marie! *(Apparently Aunt Marie had been forced out of her home in Hannover into a "Jewish house," just as my family in Aachen)*. May God help us!

Aunt Else and I went to Aunt Henny's very early yesterday for a few hours, where we spent a few cozy hours and had a lot to talk about. The loved ones have it comfortable, although they live close together. They share the kitchen with another family. Erna and Leo have a bedroom and Aunt Henny shares hers with Leo's mother. Leo works hard. *(Leo Levy, then 31 years old, had married*

Henrietta (née Oppenheim) Vorreuter 's youngest child, Erna (Eva), Walter's sister. Leo was likely working "hard" in a slave-labor camp. Erna and Leo were deported to a concentration camp and were murdered in 1942. In that same year Henrietta was deported to Auschwitz where she suffered a similar fate. Just as Rose expressed happiness in knowing that he husband Albert would not have to suffer through this horrifying experience, Henrietta, whose husband Adolf died of natural causes in 1940, must have felt the same way). Well, we probably won't be seeing each other again any time soon! *(Beginning on September 15, 1941, all Jews over the age of six in Germany had to wear a yellow Star of David displayed on their clothing in public at all times. This essentially made it impossible for my family to travel on public transportation).* ... Didn't your salary increase? You wanted to ask for it! How is business going with you? Did you hear anything from Gerda and Helmut? In those days they awaited her last month of waiting for their child. You can imagine, dear boy, how much I'm waiting for a sign of life. God keep everyone healthy! I don't understand why Gerda doesn't write to you! *(During all of 1941, there was extremely limited postal service between Germany at war and Shanghai, China, which was occupied by the pro-Nazi Japanese. Civilians had to use very specific formats for the transmission of messages sent and received, usually through the International Red Cross or by telegram. In Palestine, after Great Britain declared war on Germany on September 3, 1939, British-controlled Palestine suspended all postal services with Germany and intricate postal systems were implemented via the Red Cross and Lisbon post office boxes. Any communication that Rose would have with her two older children would have to go through Günter in the United States).*

What did Aunt Paula tell you about Margot? You wrote: She deals in love. *(The German phrase Rose uses is "Sie macht in Liebe." The term "machen in" is usually utilized for businesses describing what they are making or dealing in).* That sounds awful. I crossed it out in bold blue so Grandma wouldn't see it. Please enclose a separate note and give me true information about it. Margot must have caused her parents a lot of grief already! Has Robert had so much to do with ulcers and what does Erich want to be. ... How are Aunt Minna, Stanley and Egon with family doing? Uncle Paul and Aunt Agnes just wrote. They fear that Ruth will not come home often in the future either *(because of having to wear a Jewish Star).* By the way, they were very disappointed that you didn't send them the promised affidavits. If you had sent them at the time, as you wanted, they probably would have received the A.L. papers on it. Maybe that would have been of use to them. I don't understand either, dear Günter, why you didn't do that! The Horners are so good and do whatever they can for us. May God help us all and stand by us! His ways are often dark, but he does not forsake his own! Aunt Frieda must have landed in Cuba in the meantime. How long will she stay there? Did you find out anything new about the emigration affair, dear Günter? – If only one could get a visa! A lot of new people have recently moved here with us *(at the Jewish Altenheim on Horst Wessel Straße)*, so that we will soon be 150 people. That means a lot of work!

Kind regards to Walter and Aunt Minna as well as to Stanley.

From: Else

Dear Günther,

You must have liked it in Miami! It must be wonderful there and I know that you saw Erich again. Too bad you didn't see Margot personally as you were intending to. She wrote that she had a friend from Mannheim and that she visited his parents on Sundays. I hope and wish she doesn't throw herself away!   With love, Aunt Else and Grandma

The above letter has a non-stated reference to the requirement that Jews had to be clearly identified by a yellow star of David on their clothing when they were in public spaces. Decrees that ordered Jews to wear special badges for purposes of identification were not exclusive to the Nazi era. Over the course of more than ten centuries, medieval bishops and Muslim caliphs used an identifying badge to mark Jews. A 12th century letter from Baghdad describes decrees regulating Jewish clothes: "two yellow badges, one on the headgear and one on the neck. Furthermore, each Jew must hang round his neck a piece of lead with the word *dhimmi* on it. He also has to wear a belt round his waist. The women have to wear one red and one black shoe and have a small bell on their necks or shoes." These proclamations ordering identifying badges were rarely isolated acts. They were often part of a series of anti-Jewish measures designed to segregate Jews from the rest of the population and reinforce their inferior status.

In late September 1941, Hitler authorized the Reich Railroads to transport German, Austrian, and Czech Jews to locations in German-occupied Poland and the German-occupied Soviet Union, where German authorities would kill the overwhelming majority of them.

In that same month, Gunter excitedly opened a letter he received from the Visa division of the United States Department of State:

> Dear Mr. Oppenheim: September 28, 1941
>
> I have your letter of October 8, 1941, transmitting documents prepared on behalf of Rose Oppenheim, Else Liepmann, Paul Liepmann, Agnes Liepmann and Ruth Liepmann, residents of Germany, who desire to obtain immigration visas.
>
> Since there are no American consular visa services available in the territory in which Mrs. Oppenheim and the Liepmanns are now residing, it has not been possible for the Department to give consideration to their cases.
>
> In the event these aliens are able to proceed to some territory in which they may appear in person at an American consulate for the purpose of making application for visas, the Department, upon being furnished with some definite information in this respect, will give further consideration to their cases.
>
> Sincerely yours,   A. M. Warren   Chief, Visa Division, Washington, D.C.

The author of this letter, Avra Milvin Warren, was the Chief of the Visa Division of the United States State Department in 1941. During that time Warren enforced stringent immigration controls and delayed acceptance of refugees from Nazi persecution in situations where he could not actually legally deny them. Max Nussbaum, a former Berlin Rabbi, writes in his testimony to Yad Vashem in 1958 that "During those days after the outbreak of war, the American Vice-Consul Warren was the greatest misfortune for the Jews in Berlin. Inherently, emigration at that time was still possible since the USA had not yet entered the war and the Germans still approved applications. However, Warren sabotaged the whole emigration procedure, and he is responsible for the death of hundreds of Jews."

The next letter from my family was written on September 26, 1941:

From Rose:

My dear Günter,

... It's about time you heard from us again, so you know we're healthy, thank God. In it I confirmed your letter from Miami, where it must be wonderful, and at the same time I wrote to you about our cozy stay at Aunt Henny's in S., which unfortunately only lasted a few hours because we didn't want to get home late in the evening. Meanwhile New Year's Day passed and very quickly, as we had many visits from good friends and acquaintances. Our room still looks like a flower garden today. Your telegram with congratulations arrived on time, dear Günter! ... A detailed letter would have given me even more pleasure and would have been cheaper. But I think you probably thought of writing too late because of the holidays, didn't you? ... In the meantime, your letter from the "Champion" has also arrived with the enclosed prospectus. I read it with great interest and we can learn a lot from the description. It must be a magnificent train. I wish I could take it just once in my lifetime! Dear Günter, people are still getting away, via Cuba. Can't you help us to get there? As I have now heard, if you have the A.L. papers like we do, you don't need $3,000 per person, but $1,000 for Cuba. However, this money is not lost, it is only intended for living expenses in Cuba. If this doesn't last long and you can immigrate to the USA soon, you get the rest back. Please, dear Günter, inquire about it! You know that our cousin Frieda recently took this route. Ask her kids about it in New York.

Then I want to confide something in you alone! I don't think we can take Grandma with us, who is very frail and can hardly walk. I don't think the old woman is up to the rigors of the journey. She could stay here in the home, and we know an older, very nice girl here who our mother is very fond of. She would be looking after mother and caring for her with joy, has often offered this to us. But Else stays with me, I don't want to part with her! Dear Günter, discuss it with Stanley, he might lend you the money at interest. But don't put it off, maybe the path will soon be impossible! Please write your answer on a separate piece of paper because Grandma shouldn't know anything about it for the time being. I'm sitting here in the garden under a wonderful old chestnut tree and I'm writing. It's just after dinner, almost everyone is asleep. You know how I always liked to go for a walk in the forest and in God's beautiful nature. In the last few days that has all changed. I prefer to be here in the garden, there you have peace, and nobody takes notice of me! *(Rose is referring to the recently enacted Reinhard Heydrich decree that all Jews in the Reich wear two yellow stars on their clothing, one on the front left side and one on their back, so that anybody in front of or behind them could easily identify them as Jewish. The word Jude (Jew) on the badges imitated the appearance of the Hebraic type. This was the latest infamy that the Nazi's used to alienate Jews as "the other)."* How are you, dear boy, and all loved ones? Hopefully as you wish. Did I write to you that Helmut wrote to me through the Red Cross at the beginning of July. I received it recently. He is healthy and lives quietly, is all too alone and wants to go to the USA as soon as possible. Isn't there a way for him to come to Cuba, dear boy? Surely he has the means to do so! Help him if you can! I'm really looking forward to the announced pictures! We had a lot of mail from far and near for the holidays, unfortunately mostly only sad news. Henny L from H wrote particularly anxious and sad, as did Aunt Marie. Both have moved! *(code for forced into Judenhausen)*, Ruth couldn't spend the holidays at home this time, which everyone deeply regretted. Otherwise she was always there! If only mail from Gerda and Max arrived here with good news. We haven't heard from them for three months. ... How is business there? ... Well, my dear boy, stay healthy. Please us very soon with a long detailed letter. Please say hello to Minna, Walter, and Stanley! Be hugged by your loving mother.

From Else:

> Grandma sends her regards. The decision will not be easy for us, but there is probably no other solution. May the good Lord turn everything for the better.
>
> With love your Aunt Else.

Throughout this period of dark times, the letters from my grandmother Rose display constant optimism and hopefulness. She conveys to her children the expectation that her family will be reunited. Each piece of correspondence returns to the matters of guarantees, ship tickets and visas with the anticipation of success. Despite the evidence of growing darkness pervading her environment, she is still able to glimpse light at the end of the tunnel.

Rose's communication never suggests that her hope emanates from belief in a higher being. Although many letters use the term *"Gott sei dank,"* I believe she is using a colloquialism meaning "thank goodness" rather thanking God, which is the literal translation. I am certain that she frequently verbalized the phrase as a figure of speech throughout her life's conversations without signifying that she was praying to God or thanking God for his actions. She was expressing that she was pleased that something had (or had not) happened. She might as well have said "thank heavens" which, in German, is the phrase *"Dem Himmel sei Dank,"* and is almost never used in spoken or written German.

For Rose and my family in the late summer of 1941, the belief that tomorrow could be better provided the possibility of enduring the hardships of the present. Hope in the future made the current situation seem less insurmountable and gave them solace.

The painful decision communicated to Günter in the above letter required a great deal of courage but allowed Rose and Else to still maintain hope. I am certain that Rose and Else had many conversations over an extended period of time prior to reaching the conclusion that Fanni's health would not allow her to travel, even under the best of circumstances. My great-grandmother could no longer walk, slept most of the day and had serious impairment of her abilities to both see and hear. As Else put is so well, "the decision will not be easy for us, but there is probably no other solution." Once that judgment had been made, they were moving forward by finding a surrogate at the *Altenheim* who would lovingly care for her, just as they would have.

Else had lived with her older sister for all of her 54 years. They were the best of friends and there was never a question that Rose would write "But Else stays with me, I don't want to part with her!"

On September 27, 1941, the day after that painful revelation, I was born, Rose's first (and only) grandchild. My physician father delivered me at Shanghai's 125-bed Country Hospital, built in 1926. The Hospital was primarily staffed by European physicians and was easily accessible to the inhabitants of the French Concession, whose residents included a variety of nationalities. Today the Country Hospital is the "Number 1" Building of Huadong Hospital, a teaching hospital affiliated with Fudan University.

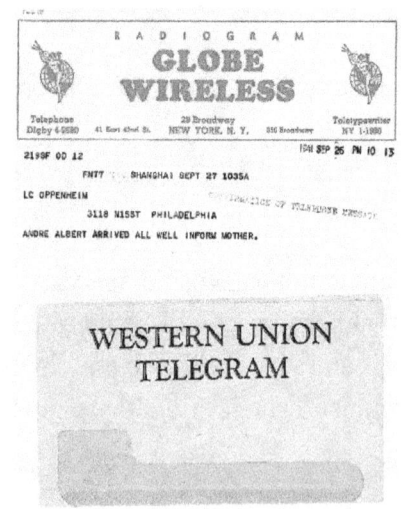

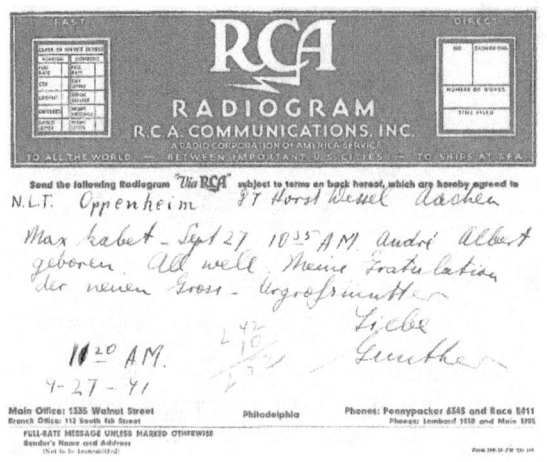

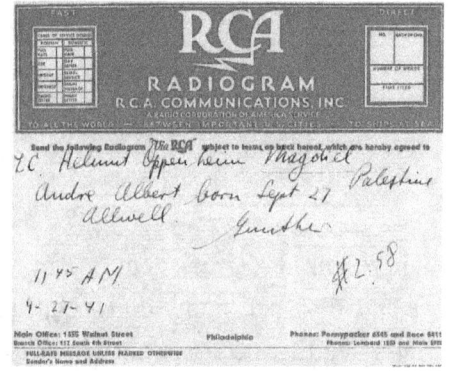

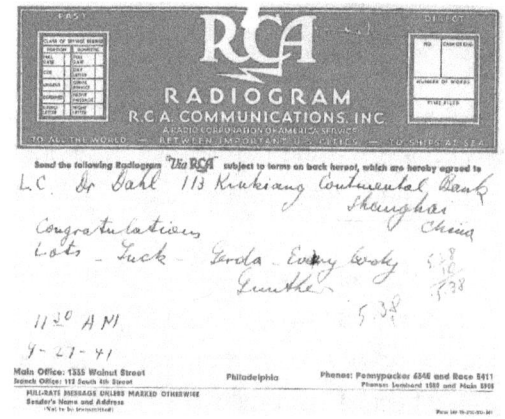

Globe Wireless Telegram sent from my father in Shanghai to Günter in Philadelphia: "André Albert arrived All Well Inform Mother."

RCA Telegram sent from Günter in Philadelphia to my family at 87 Horst Wessel, Aachen , Germany: " Max cabled Sept 27 10:35 AM André Albert was born All well My congratulation to the new great grandmother and grandmother. Love, Günther."

RCA Telegram sent from Günter in Philadelphia to Helmut in Magdiel, Palestine: " André Albert born Sept 27 All well   Günther."

RCA Telegram sent from Günter in Philadelphia to my father "Dr. Dahl" at his office on Kiukiang Road, Shanghai: Congratulations. Lots Luck. Gerda-everybody. Günther."

:

I am certain that there was a great deal of joy and tears that day in that tiny room occupied by Fanni, Rose and Else at the vastly overcrowded "*Israelitisches Altenheim*" on *Horst Wessel Strasse*, as they spoke of my arrival 6,000 miles away. After all, it was Fanni's first great-grandchild and Rose's first grandchild.

On the next day, September 28, 1941, Rose sent Günter the next letter:

From Rose:

My dear Günter,

Just the day before yesterday I wrote you a detailed letter and asked you to help us to emigrate via Cuba if possible. Many go, as one hears, this way. Wouldn't Stanley lend you the money? Please give us an answer about this very soon. In the last few days we had beautiful autumn weather and spent a lot of time in the garden. Lucky that it is so shady and big. I don't enjoy going for a walk anymore. – I prefer the lonely paths the most! The forest is so close and I always loved going for walks.

It was such a great joy this Sunday morning, dear Günter, when your cable brought us the good news of the little boy's birth in Shanghai! How happy we are all about that! Thank you very much for the telegram and your congratulations on the birth of my first grandson and I warmly return them on your new dignity as uncle. I immediately wrote to Gerda and Max today, I would have loved to wire, but it's not possible. One can only send a dispatch in cases of emigration. Hopefully our letter, which I airmailed to San Francisco, will also arrive. I've been thinking about Gerda so much lately and I ask God every day that they may all stay healthy. As soon as you have a letter from Gerda and Max, let us know. We haven't heard a word from them for three months. How nice that they named the little one after our dear blessed father. I hope he'll be as good (*the German adjective used here is "brav," which is a word with many connotations—honest, good, well-behaved, upright, worthy*) as he is.

Have you had mail from Helmut? Can't he also come to you via Cuba? That would be my greatest joy! I wrote him 25 words again through the Red Cross, also that Gerda has a little boy. Have you heard from Aunt Paula and family? How are they doing? The news from Aunt Marie and everyone I know from Hannover is very sad. Marie lives with many others in Limmer *(likely in a Judenhaus)*! They changed residences. How are you, dear boy? I hope you are healthy and had a good rest in Miami.

The letter is concluded on the following day:

It's good that I'm not finishing the letter until today, so I can also confirm your letter of September 9th with the lines from Gerda and Max, which made me <u>very happy</u> this morning because they reported good news and we hadn't heard anything in forever. Hopefully the postal service will work better again in the future. Have you, as you wrote, made the trip to New York for the holidays (*the Jewish High Holidays, Rosh Hashanah, the Jewish New Year, and Yom Kippur, the Day of Atonement*) and where did you sleep at night? ... Aunt Else and I sometimes help in the kitchen in the morning. So I almost always make dumplings on Friday for the soup on Friday evening. They taste just like matzah balls, made from dry white bread. I then make 270 pieces because everyone gets 2 dumplings. (*This may be a means of communicating the number of people in the "Jewish house"*) Please ask Walter if he still remembers Lotte Rosenthal. She worked together with him in Recklinghausen and often danced with him. She is the wife of our caretaker and cooks together with his mother (*Rose is writing about Lotte's mother, Ida Abraham, a contemporary of hers who, with her husband Siegfried, who had died in 1939, formerly owned a hotel in Bebra, Germany. Her son, Leo had married Lieselotte née Rosenthal and the three of them lived at the Jewish house on Horst Wessel. On July 25, 1942, Leo, his wife Lieselotte and his mother-in-law were all deported by the Nazis on Transport VII/2, from Aachen/Düsseldorf to Theresienstadt, Czechoslovakia. On September 29, 1944, Leo was transported to Bergen-Belsen concentration camp, where he was murdered in October 1944. Lotte was sent to Auschwitz-Birkenau concentration camp on October 1, 1942, where Ida was also taken two weeks later. Ida was killed there. Lieselotte survived until Auschwitz was liberated by the Russian Army in 1945, lived in Munich after she recovered her health, and then emigrated to Bolivia via Paris and Brazil to join her brother. She later moved to New York where she remarried. A number of sources have listed her as dying in Auschwitz. It is a shame that there are not more of these stories.*) You should see the giant pots here!

The young Abrahams are very nice people, as is the man's mother, whom everyone calls Grandma, although she isn't one yet. Now I want to take this and Gerda's letter to the post office immediately and also 25 words to Helmut through the Red Cross. God grant that all three find you, dear children, in good health. Please write again very soon, dear Günter! Warm greetings to all loved ones there from your always loving mother. I will convey your New Year's greetings.

From Else:

"Dear Uncle Günther,"

I congratulate you warmly on your first nephew. You must be very proud! We were very happy with your and Gerda's lines. Have you gotten used to work again? How are Aunt Minna, Walter, and Egon and the Fintz family? Did Miss Nydick get Mother's letter? Has the niece recovered? Well let's hear from you very soon. Say hello to all loved ones, also from grandma, who is always in the garden when the weather is good. I've been busy in it all morning and everyone is happy how clean it is now!

With love your Aunt Else.

On that same date, September 28, 1941, a letter was sent to my father's office in Shanghai.

From Rose:

My dear children,

Will these lines reach you? I hope so, tried so many times without hearing from you for 3 months. I last wrote to you at this address on September 10th and at the same time congratulated you and your dear parents *(my other grandparents, Nathan and Sara Dahl)* on the turn of the year. Maybe Günther let you know about us. I would like to believe so. Well, dear children, I am so glad and happy that this Sunday morning I was informed by Günther via cable of your telegram. So, dear children, I am so happy with you about the birth of your dear little André Albert, who, to your delight and that of all of us, may grow up and become a good, capable person. It is a particular pleasure for me that he bears the name Albert like our good, unforgettable father. If only he could have lived to see that! My congratulations to you, dear Sara and Nathan, are just as heartfelt. How I would love to be with you and see my first grandchild and take it in my arms! How are you, dear Gerda? Can you nurse the little one and is he growing profusely? How proud you will be, dear Max, of your boy! If only I would get a <u>very</u> <u>detailed</u> letter from you very soon! I'm so curious to hear from you again.

Various acquaintances here at the home have received mail from Shanghai dated July 2nd in the last few days. I was really jealous. I hope to hear from you soon too. Surely you were in hospital for the delivery, dear Gerda? Please write me in detail. My thoughts are always with you. Thank God we are healthy and are taking advantage of the beautiful sunny weather of the last few days to stay in the large, beautiful garden. For example, I write under a magnificent old chestnut tree, with Aunt Else sitting next to me and reading. Grandma takes her afternoon nap in the room. Do you know that Aunt Else and I recently visited the loved ones in Siegburg *(Henrietta Oppenheim Vorreuter and her remaining family)*. We spent a few leisurely hours. They live in very limited quarters but are in good health and she is not bothered by the sugar that much anymore *(reference is to diabetes)*. They hear good things from Walter, who is doing well in business. Our little one *(Günter)* spent wonderful holidays there in Miami. He last wrote to us from the train on the return journey. I have now asked him to discuss with Stanley whether we can go to the USA via Cuba, as many do. It's a question of money. Frieda G has succeeded. *(Frieda Liepmann Goldschmidt was indeed able to reach the United States).* How is her son Max Ludwig *(Max Goldschmidt had been fortunate to emigrate to Shanghai and there was unable to find steady work and lived in the ghetto. He was at my parents' apartment for dinner at least once a week during the entire War)*? At New Year's we had a lot of visitors, our room was full of flowers. We got a lot of mail, unfortunately mostly sad news, especially from Hannover. Aunt Marie no longer lives in her boarding house there, all the other friends have also moved. *("Aunt Marie" Hornthal, mother of Paula Hornthal, the widow of Max Liepmann, Rose's brother. Rose's prior correspondence always was so optimistic regarding Marie obtaining guarantees from multiple people to assist her in getting to the US: "Aunt Marie got the papers for entry from Werner to be able to go. She can bring her clothes and household items. The lucky one!" She and the friends that "have moved" is a euphemism for being forced from their homes to move into a "Jewish house." Marie was deported to Theresienstadt on July 23, 1942, and was murdered in Treblinka three months later).* Martha L. *(Martha née Vorreuter, a niece of grandma Fanni's)* wrote to us today in desperation, wired her Hilde to request her as soon as possible…I got mail from Helmut through the Red Cross the day before New Year in reply to my April letter. It was dated July 11th. He was healthy, just felt too alone and wanted to see Gunther as soon as possible. Yes, if only he and we were there!

Dear children, as soon as possible send a picture of your dear boy! What does he look like and who does he resemble? Is he well behaved? Now please us soon with good news please, God willing, and stay healthy. Has your kidney problem been completely resolved, dear Max? I've asked about it so many times! I would have loved to send you a cable, but unfortunately I can't. Are you satisfied with the practice, dear Max? Many heartfelt greetings also for the parents and Radts. With constant love, your faithful mother and grandmother

From Else:

If only we finally had news from you again. How much we miss your detailed reports, dearest Gerta. How nice that you called the little one Albert! May he follow suit with his Opa.

My dears, we were delighted at the arrival of your son and heir. Congratulations to the dear parents and grandparents! To you, dear Gerda, speedy recovery. Many greetings to all loved ones and prosperity to the dear child.

your dear Aunt Else.

From Fanni:

My beloveds,

I am delighted to congratulate you, dear Gerda, Max, as well as your dear parents and siblings on the birth of your dear new citizen of the world. May God let him grow up and thrive to the joy of all of you. How pleased I am that you, dear Gerda, endured this time well, God willing. God protect you and your beloved child. Heartfelt greetings to you all,

with true love from your old grandmother Fanny Liepmann

From Rose as postscript:

Today, on Sept. 29th, we were finally <u>tremendously</u> pleased to receive your letter of July 29th.

Another letter was sent to Shanghai on October 8, 1941.

From Rose:

My dear children,

In our last joint letter of September 29th, which contained our congratulations on the birth of dear little André Albert, I briefly acknowledged the arrival of your detailed lines of July 29th, which therefore took exactly two months. How happy we were with that, dear children! They were the first sign of life from you again since the end of June! I would have loved to send congratulations via cable, but unfortunately that wasn't possible! How long will it be before you get the letter!

First of all, I would like to tell you that, thank God, all three of us are healthy. Hopefully that's the case for you too. How are you, above all, dear Gerda and the dear boy? I always think of you! You can imagine how terribly I would like to see you! Can you nurse the little one yourself? Please write me everything in detail. Who does the dear child resemble? How long were you in the hospital? God grant that you are restored again and that the dear little one is healthy and strong. How proud you are of your boy, dear Max! I can only imagine you, dear Sara and Nathan, as grandparents. If only my dear Albert had lived to see that too!

Dear Gerda, did you actually receive the four baby jackets sent by registered mail? Now the first days of Tabernacles are over. They were accompanied by the most beautiful sunshine. Yesterday all three of us had coffee at Dinchen's *(Dinchen and Anneliese Sternberg were relatives of Paul Liepmann's wife Agnes. They were deported from Aachen in 1942 and were killed in an unknown concentration camp)*. We took Grandma there in the wheelchair. The way is through the forest about half an hour and was quite leisurely. The lonely paths are our favorite, especially lately. You have to get used to the new situation *(having to wear the Jewish star on clothing)*. – If only we could get to Günther via Cuba. People are still getting there. It's all a question of money. As I hear it is supposed to cost 1400 dollars per person via Cuba for travel etc.

I recently asked Gunther to ask Stanley for advice. Maybe he'll lend him the money for Aunt Else and me. It's probably impossible to make the trip with Grandma. She can hardly walk anymore, unfortunately! We'd have to leave her here, and a very nice older girl, whom Grandma thinks <u>highly</u> of, would be more than happy to take care of her. But I haven't talked to anyone about it *(except Günther in the last letter)*. What do you say about it? Write your opinion separately on a piece of paper. Grandma shouldn't know before the time comes and I don't think we'll get anywhere after all. Yesterday, Aunt Henny sent us a letter from Günther, which was for her for New Year's, with good news, thank God. Walter is happier than he's ever been, G. wrote. He got another raise, now earns $23 a week. After much effort, Günther has now gotten Walter to the point where he has forgotten everything that happened before and no longer speaks of the past. The little one pretends to be the older one! It's funny!

How are the Radts and Brauers and Max Ludwig doing? His mother has landed in Cuba. The lucky woman! Incidentally, his brother Fritz is also expecting an addition to the family. Aunt Marie is very unhappy about her move. She wasn't lucky, neither was Henny L. in Hannover, who lost all her undergarments. I sent her some underwear and towels and handkerchiefs. A blind lady here, Mrs. Hemmel, asked me to give Mrs. Meyerbach her best wishes. How is the old lady? Does she want to stay there?

Aunt Marie just sent us a letter sent by Paula from Rochester *(NY)*. She and Robert immediately found work/men's clothing store and large factory. Erich wants to train as an optician. Rochester must be a beautiful garden city. Aunt Paula writes about it with great delight.

How did you come up with the name André (is it spelled correctly?) dear children? How are you getting on at home now? A child turns the whole household upside down. Is the little one well-behaved? Settle him in right away *(meaning do not spoil him)* and don't carry him around too much. Will he also be taken for walks outside? There are so many things I would like to ask, hopefully a letter with good news will arrive from you soon.

Now everyone stay healthy and be warmly greeted and kissed by your loving mother and grandmother.

From Else:

My dears,

I hope you are healthy like us and the little one is thriving. How curious are we to hear how he's doing. You, dear Gerda, are completely restored, God willing. Many warm greetings from Grandma and your dear Aunt Else.

In the above letter, Rose says, for the first time, regarding the future, "I don't think we'll get anywhere after all." Although she tells my mother that the ship passage would be expensive, the true obstacle is not finding the money. It is primarily getting visas and, secondarily, simultaneously finding available space on a steamship to cross the Atlantic.

A postcard was sent from my grandmother to Günter on October 12, 1941, to be routed to America via Lisbon. As always, the Nazi-designated Jewish middle name of "Sara" is apparent as addressee.

My dear Gunther,

Hopefully these lines will find you healthy and cheerful and we will soon be hearing from you in detail. In any case, you have received our registered letter of October 10th with the urgent request to speak to Stanley and help us to Cuba, also those with the same content from September 26th and 30th. There is no time to waste! The sons of my cousin Max Spanier from Enger cabled their father a few days ago that they had paid the amount for Cuba for him and their mother. Now the two will probably get out soon. The boys haven't been over there long either! They probably borrowed the money. *(Max Spanier and his wife Adele, née Seligmann, were deported to Theresienstadt in the summer of 1942. He died there in 1944 due to malnutrition, but his wife survived and immigrated to the United States after the war. The two sons, Edward and Arnold had been arrested on Kristallnacht, taken to Buchenwald and, a month later, were released from the camp after signing a document stating they would leave Germany within four weeks. In April 1939, Edward and Arnold Spanier immigrated to the United States by way of the Netherlands).*

Please think it over with Stanley and ask him to do it! Hopefully he won't leave us! The whole thing is just a question of money, and as I already wrote to you, the amount paid in will be paid back. Please get in touch with my cousin Frieda's children right away, how they managed it. They live at 1815 Riverside Drive New York. Via Cuba is the only way so far! – Uncle Paul thinks you should do it for us too. This is for Aunt Else and me.

As I already wrote you, Grandma is not up to the hardships of such a journey and will stay here.

We last heard from you through Aunt Henny, who sent us your letter of September 16th. In the meantime, we had reports from Aunt Paula and Erich through Aunt Marie, who wrote terribly sad. They like it very much in R(ochester), where they immediately found work. How happy they were to see you! Erich also has an apprenticeship as an optician. Well my dear boy, stay healthy and help us! With many warm regards also for Stanley, Walter, and Aunt Minna,   always your loving mother

Another postcard with both sides full, was written from Aachen to Günter on October 19, 1941.

From Rose:

My dear Gunther,

We haven't heard from you since the letter you sent to Aunt Henny on September 16th and we hope that your silence doesn't mean anything bad and that you and all loved ones are well. Thank God we are healthy too. Have you received my two letters of September 26th and the registered letter of October 10th and the postcard of October 12th? In all three I made an <u>urgent</u> request to speak to Stanley and help us to Cuba. Today I am repeating this urgent request once again! Please help us while it is still possible! You, dear boy, know me, and you know that I would not so easily ask cousin Stanley. God grant that he will help us when we need his help so much! Autumn has come here with storm and rain. It's best (to stay) in the room. I don't enjoy going for walks anymore. Have you heard from Gerda and Helmut recently? We have not for a long time. How may things be going with the little one and Gerda? Hopefully all are alive and well.

Are you doing well in business? Aunt Henny and Erna wrote today and I was very happy that they are all healthy in S. We also heard from Uncle Paul. If only everyone didn't have so many worries! Now please write very soon and in detail to your mother, who sends her best regards to you and all loved ones.

From Else:

Dear Günther,

I too send you and all loved ones my warmest regards and I urgently ask you to help us if at all possible. Let us hear from you soon.   With love your Aunt Else

The following letter was sent to Günter on October 23, 1941.

From Rose:

My dear Gunther,

…That was a great joy …when two letters arrived at the same time (by registered mail), one from September 25th and the other from Gerda for you and us. Thank you so much for everything, especially for the beautiful photos! I've looked at them so many times, with and without a magnifying glass. The landscapes are magnificent! I do believe you that M*(iami)* is wonderfully beautiful! You too, dear boy, are very fetching and look so healthy and happy, as do your friends and Walter. How come you're shirtless in Mrs. Peters' yard while the others are in full dress? You mustn't laugh, but Grandma <u>only</u> likes the pictures in which you are fully clothed. She constantly talks about how it looks like you have <u>nothing</u> left to wear. Now she has found a topic! But like I said, that's grandma's point of view. You can occasionally send her a picture of you in your best suit to give her peace of mind. Yes, dear boy, old people are often whimsical and have funny views.

Incidentally, yesterday we again received 1 letter from Gerda that was sent via the USA and was dated August 11, while the one that arrived the day before was from the beginning of September. So you can see that it goes much faster through you. I was glad that both Gerda and Max wrote with satisfaction. They only complained about the heat and the high prices! It's pure inflation there. Hopefully Gerda and the child are quite well. If only I'd hear about it from her! We are healthy here, thank God, and it is our daily prayer that we can stay <u>here</u> until we emigrate to there. If only you could take these <u>big worries </u>away from us and cousin Stanley helps us to leave for Cuba soon! My letters of September 26th and October 10th and card of October 20th had the same urgent request. I'm waiting so much for an answer from you, dear Gunther! It's just a question of money. My cousin Max in Enger received 1 cable from his two sons in New York that they had paid the amount for the parents for Cuba. Now they are waiting for the decision of the Cuban consul in Berlin. That is the next step. His mother-in-law will be with him. How did he do it? The sons live in New York at 1815 Riverside Drive.

I hope you asked Stanley for his help. You have no idea how worried we are about the future! - This won't let us sleep at night! A good friend of mine just got a message from the Lloyd travel agency that emigration to Cuba is still possible at the moment if the necessary entry permit is obtained by the family living in the USA. People still leave from here to Cuba via Spain. But speed is of the essence before it's too late. Today Mrs. Bachmann, to whom I had written about the birth of little

André, wrote me back very kindly. I asked if they still live in K. Thank God that is the case, but unfortunately her husband has been in the asylum *(the Jewish Hospital)* there for three weeks (heart disease). Edgar and Liesel are also expecting a baby in winter. The children are doing well so far. Trude's mother, whom I asked about, had to go on a long journey. – Will she ever see Trude again? *(This is most likely code for "was deported," especially followed by remarks that relatives may never see those who had to "go on a long journey.")* The old Sterns from O. are still there, Julius works in K. *(Rose often uses only the first letter of German locations, so that censors would not be able to identify those that she wrote about).*

Dear Gunther, I would like to know if you still think about saving and have a certain amount left over every month. I mean, you didn't have to go back to New York for New Year's, as you just got back from vacation. It all costs money! So please, dear boy, think about saving! Did you deliver the English letter attached to your letter for Stanley the other day? It was July 17th when it was mailed. Aunt Else is in town to take some gray linen that I still had, for a rucksack *(Probably meaning that Rose and Else were preparing for a "long journey" themselves. Why else would they need backpacks?)* – I prefer to stay at home lately. I don't enjoy going for walks anymore. – Did the giant advertisement for the thousands of dresses have the desired success? ... I heard that Elfriede Friedemann née Matthias has left for a long journey. *(Again, a reference to deportation.)* Her husband is in southern France. Will she ever see him again!

What a coincidence that you met Leo Salm *(my other grandmother Sara Dahl's brother-in-law, who lived in New York)* on the street, dear boy. I recently met his brother and his wife here. He visited good friends, lived in Düsseldorf, but is now on a long journey *(and yet another deportation)*. – How are Aunt Minna, Walter, Stanley and Louise Buchdal and husband? Greet them all warmly. Hope you write again very soon! It's our only joy! Could we see you again soon, dear boy! Pray for us and may God help us and protect us from the hardest! What do you hear from Helmut?

With love, your mother

From Else:

Dear Günther,

... We were very pleased with your and Gerda's lines and the beautiful photos! It's a pity that you don't ever visit the Heilbrunns or Ilse and Ruth in New York. What Mister Joe Moes told you is nice. But it would be even nicer if he kept his word and you got a higher salary to be able to save more!

With love your Aunt Else

In October 1941, the orders for deportation of <u>all</u> German Jews from Germany to the east were given. Trains deporting Jews from the German Reich to the ghettos of Lodz, Riga and Minsk accelerated in number and size.

On October 23, 1941, an order was sent from Berlin by the *Schutzstaffel (SS,* the paramilitary organization under Adolf Hitler and the Nazi Party (NSDAP) in Nazi Germany) forbidding emigration of Jews from the Reich. The top-secret document read in part:

"The Reichsführer SS and Chief of the German Police has decreed that the emigration of Jews is to be prevented, taking effect immediately.

I request that the internal German Authorities concerned in the area of service there may be informed of this order.

Permission for the emigration of individual Jews can only be approved in single very special cases; for instance, in the event of a genuine interest on the part of the Reich, and then only after a prior decision has been obtained from the Reich Security Main Office."

Thus, no more Jews were allowed to emigrate; it would be preferable to kill them. Any chance, however miniscule, that my family had to escape from Germany prior to this had now disappeared.

On October 28, 1941, Paul Liepmann, Rose's younger brother, sent a letter to Günter from Horn, Germany.

From Paul:

Dear Günter!

The loved ones from Aachen sent us your lines of October 7th, from which we happily learned of your well-being. We were very glad about the birth of the little heir with Gerta and Max and congratulate you on your new uncle honor. Would you please forward the enclosed letter to Gerta. Your loved ones have always kept you informed about our health, we are healthy enough if only we weren't so worried that we don't make progress with our emigration. I know very well that you, dear Günter, first have to take care of the Aacheners and that you try to do so; I wish you could also manage to get them to Cuba with the help of Stanley. As an intermediate country, this is currently the cheapest, there are other options, for example Ecuador and Bolivia. Check with the Joint there what it takes to do this, and then discuss it with Stanley; he who has always been helpful will not let you down. We are also always thinking about what we can do about our emigration. Unfortunately we don't have any children outside and Oskar and Helmut are too far away but they would certainly add to the expense if you wired them. Dear Günter, please get in touch with Paula and Robert Brunell and also with Walter Alexander, who recently visited you, he will also help you if he can. I beg you urgently leave no stone unturned to help us, we don't want to be a burden to anyone and will make up for everything later. The boys from Enger (from Uncle Max), who have only been there for a short time, cabled him that they had arranged everything for Cuba, you should be able to manage the same with your relationships. *(Max Spanier, a grandson of Abraham Liepmann and Rose's first cousin, never made it to Cuba despite all the efforts. It was too late already. He died in Theresienstadt on December 24, 1944).* So, dear Günter, write to us soon what you have done. ... For today, best regards and kisses, your Uncle Paul

From Agnes:

Dear Günther,

I too congratulate you warmly on your new uncle status. Hopefully there will soon be a letter from Shanghai with a detailed report; the loved ones in Aachen are eagerly waiting for it and then will impart us everything. So we are always informed about everything, including your activities, dear Günther, and we are very happy when good news arrives.

I want to join Uncle Paul's plea, take care of us too if you can. We thank you very much for that.

Paul included a letter to be forwarded by Günter to Gerda and Max in Shanghai. Mail could still be sent to China from the USA, but not from Germany.

My dears!

That was such a joy when the news of the birth of your heir arrived from Günther! Accept our congratulations on the happy event, which also extends to Grandma and Grandpa Dahl, may little André Albert grow up to the joy of the whole family. I hope you, dear Gerta, got through everything well and have now fully recovered; you dear Max are surely proud of your new fatherhood. So far, I can only tell you good things about our well-being; if only we didn't have to worry about our emigration; can't you dear ones help us? Please get in touch with Günter about this; hopefully he will be able to get the loved ones in Aachen to Cuba. We always read your reports to Aachen with interest and are happy that you are doing well and that you, dear Max, are busy. Hopefully you will be spared from the war there, I would like to wish you that from the bottom of my heart. Dear Agnes wants to join in writing, so I'll close, all the best for the future. With love your Paul

From Agnes:

My dears,

From Aachen we were always informed about your health dear Gerda and we thought about you a lot - we were very happy when we got the news of the birth of the little heir - I congratulate you wholeheartedly on the beautiful event. May the new citizen of the earth grow up to everyone's joy and may all your loved ones in the not-too-distant future be able to join in your happiness and enjoy the development of the little one. – You are probably always up to date about our well-being through your loved ones in Aachen, we are also worried because we are not making any progress with our emigration. – Our health is decent; - then one should be satisfied. Our Ruth is still in Paderborn, she has grown into a big girl, she always talks about that she wants to be a kindergarten teacher. She is also very eager to take care of children and has the patience for it. Because of the situation, she's a bit behind at school. – Well, dear ones, stay healthy, warm greetings and love from your Agnes.

A postcard was written to Günter on November 1, 1941. Rose's usual optimism is very subdued, although as a mother, she does not refrain from inquiring about her child's health. However, for the first time, she uses the phrases "Who knows what's in store for us!" and "You can be sure that I'm driven by fear and worry." The feeling that something must be done immediately is also conveyed by Else. Both Rose and Else realize very well what is going on all around them—friends and relatives are disappearing. They are grasping at straws and my uncle Günter cannot provide them with drink, no matter how much they ask and how hard he tries.

From Rose:

My dear Gunther,

Hopefully this card will reach you in the best of health, as all loved ones there. Have you received my latest letters of October 10th, 12th, 23rd and 26th? In all of them I asked you, dear boy, to speak to Stanley in order to ask for his help. I sent him an English letter myself, by registered post, on the 28th, which I hope he received. If it were possible, I would have cabled long ago! I'm so waiting for an answer, dear boy! Who knows what's in store for us! People always get away via Cuba, and there is also a route via Ecuador as an intermediate country. The latter is said to be cheaper than Cuba. Please ask the aid association there! The two sons of my cousin Max Sp*(anier)*, who have only been there a short time, wired the registration numbers for their parents here a few days ago. Now they got the visa from the Cuban Consul and can then leave. Lucky ones. I have no other advice, dear Günther! You can be sure that I'm driven by fear and worry, otherwise I wouldn't write. Did you have mail from Gerda and Helmut?

We had a visit from my cousin Arnold's wife, who is very good and sympathetic. *(Arnold Liepmann, Rose's first cousin, the son of Levy Liepmann, had been taken by the Nazis to a slave labor camp near Berlin, leaving his wife, Hulda Karoline Amalie née Strothenke, alone. She was known to the family as "Li.")* Her best friends and acquaintances are no longer in E(nger). (*These people had already been taken away by the Nazis*). So they feel very lonely. Winter came early here with cold and snow. Stay healthy, dear boy, write to your very loving mother again soon. 1000 greetings to all loved ones.

From Else:

Dear Günter,

We are waiting so much for your answer and how things are with Cuba! Let us know immediately. Warm greetings from grandma and your aunt Else.

Günter, in Philadelphia, had hardly disregarded the frequent references made regarding emigration to Cuba. That nation as a possible destination for my family had been on his mind since Rose first mentioned it in a February 1939 letter. It was not written about again until April 1941, but since then, almost every letter received by him from Rose contained references to the ray of hope offered by Cuba. Throughout 1941, Günter wrote to the Cuban embassy in Washington, D.C. on numerous occasions and visited their office in that city and their consulate in New York to make inquiries regarding entrance to Cuba for our family. He was at last able to procure the name of a Jewish attorney in Havana, Cuba, Miguel Gurvitz y Antonil, who was also a public prosecutor. Miguel was born in Riga, Latvia, and educated in Vilna, Lithuania, and emigrated to Cuba in 1924. His daughter, Nedda Anhal, writing about Cuba in 2011, in the most read Jewish periodical in the Spanish-speaking world, *Enlace Judío*, published in Mexico, regarding "the adventures and misadventures that the Hebrews have suffered on this Island," commented "For Jews seeking economic opportunities fleeing the Inquisition, as well as antisemitism, pogroms or later, Nazism, Cuba, in those difficult times, was, with few exceptions, a much-appreciated refuge." For her parents "it seemed the entrance to a true paradise." Nedda's mother, Helena Zuchowicz, who was from Warsaw, first met her future husband when visiting Cuba as a tourist. While there, she was inside a "Hebrew" store when "a Cuban priest entered and, coincidentally meeting a Jewish acquaintance, the two merged into a brotherly embrace. For my mother, witnessing that was like inhabiting an episode of magical realism. Such an encounter would never have happened in the antisemitic Warsaw in which she lived. It was precisely that image, engraved in her heart and in her mind, that provoked in her the decision that Cuba would be, from that moment on, her beloved homeland." As she had promised her mother, she returned home to Warsaw and, a year later, she traveled again to Cuba to marry Miguel.

Miguel Gurvitz y Antonil learned to speak Spanish without a foreign accent and wrote it perfectly. In 1933, he became the first Jew in Cuba to be appointed as a "Public Attorney." By 1941, when Günter first contacted him, Antonil was well established and had earned a reputation for facilitating the procurement of Cuban visas. He wrote Günter that he could help him, but it would take some time and the cost of each visa allowing for entry to Cuba would be 500 US dollars plus his fee. After some thought and receipt of additional letters from Aachen, Günter, who had been saving money and working overtime for such an opportunity, decided to proceed and paid $1,500 for three future entrance visas.

In early November 1941, Antonil sent a letter to Günter, informing him that entrance visas to Cuba had been obtained for Rose, Else and Fanni. Now, Günter "only" needed to find a ship to bring his family to Cuba. He immediately sent a telegram to Aachen on November 10th with the good news.

A letter was sent back to Günter from Aachen on November 11, 1941.

From: Rose

My dear Gunther,

...My last card was dated November 1st, before that letters were sent to you on September 26th – September 30th – October 10th (registered mail) – October 12th – October 23rd – October 26th. – Letter to Stanley on 10/28. I think they all reached you. They all contained the same urgent request, dear boy, which unfortunately cannot be fulfilled at the moment because there is no possibility of leaving the country. God grant that this regulation will be changed and we will soon be reunited with you. You can imagine how sad we are, dear Gunther, not to be able to travel despite your help. Yesterday morning your cable arrived, which I answered on the same day: "Currently no possibility of leaving the country. Will wire if possible to leave the country." Now we have to wait and see! May God keep us all healthy and hear our prayers. If only we can stay here! - We are in God's hands. May he help us.

My cousin Max *(Spanier)* and his wife wanted to leave on November 3rd. Since they didn't get packing permission so quickly, they only wanted to travel with hand luggage. But they were notified by phone that they would have to wait. I don't know when they can travel now. Please ask around there too, dear boy, I will do the same here and cable you as soon as there are travel opportunities for us again. Did Stanley provide you with the amount? Please write to me in detail about everything! You can imagine how depressed and sad we are! But despite everything, we don't want to lose courage and our faith in God! I wrote to you that Mr. Bachmann has been ill in the asylum in C for several weeks. He suffered a nervous breakdown; as Ms. B. writes to us, he is no better.

Uncle Eduard and Aunt Erna are healthy, recently wrote to us that Aunt Minna's cousin Betty and her husband no longer live in K. Trude's mother has also moved. (*This information is all encoded to avoid the known censors—these people have all been taken away by the Nazis*). Aunt Wanda and daughter Trude wrote very sadly because they loved being in D. but had to say goodbye (*Gertrude (Trude) Aronstein and her family were among the people who were deported to Minsk, Belarus, in late 1941, where they were killed*). Aunt Irma also got a cable from her children that they had deposited the money for Cuba for her. She also wanted to prepare everything for the journey. I don't know exactly whether Irma is already 60 years old, I have asked her!

How much did the cable cost, dear Gunther? Are you frugal and don't spend anything needlessly? How is business with you? We also recently had a letter from Aunt Henny. One is always very happy when everything is healthy and unchanged. Have you heard from Gerda after the little one was born? Hopefully she and the child are doing well, as are Max and the parents. Did you send Helmut the birth certificate etc.? Aunt Henny wrote that your friend had to go away for 2 1/2 years. (*This is likely an encoded allusion to one of Günter's friends being drafted into the US Army*) Is that true? Does it refer to Bill or Harald? I hope you have time with that, dear boy.

We often hear from Uncle Paul and Aunt Agnes and are always very happy when everything is the same in Horn. Aunt Johanna will be 70 tomorrow (*This is Albert's sister, Johanna Oppenheim, who was institutionalized at an early age*). Ruth can't easily often come home now. They miss that very much. (*Ruth was away from home at a private Jewish school and was fearful of travel because of the necessity of wearing a Jewish star*).

How is Egon's little one doing? Are you going to night school again, dear Gunther. ... To you, my dear boy, warm greetings and kisses from your faithful mother.

From: Else

Dear Günther,

We were very happy with your cable and thank you very much for it, if unfortunately it cannot be of any use to us at the moment, let us hope that the regulations will change soon and then, God willing, we will see each other again. Anyway, we are very glad that you managed to help us. Unfortunately, too late. We received your last letter of October 14th on November 1st and answered you about it. Warm greetings from Grandma and your loving Aunt Else.

The next letter was sent to both Günter and my mother Gerda one week later, November 18, 1941. Note that although the letter was sent by "registered" mail, it did not arrive in Philadelphia until January 6, 1942. The penciled "1-7-42" on the front of the envelope was written by Günter and is the day he actually received and read it.

This letter was opened twice by mail censors; once in Germany (Geoffnet by Oberkommando der Wehrmacht) on the bottom, and again by US censors on the left side. Both pasted their labels over the opening slits.

From: Rose

My dear Gunther, dear children,

On November 15th the post brought your letter of October 24th, dear Gunther, with your letter and the photo of Aunt Minna with her grandson and at the same time your letter of July 3rd, dear Gerda, which really was long enough on the way. Nevertheless, we were very happy with it! How nice that at least 2 jackets arrived (*this refers to baby clothing for me*)! The rest, including Helmuth and Gunther's lace hat, will probably never appear again. Thank you very much, dear children, for your lines, and also Aunt Minna for the well-taken picture, which made us particularly happy. I'll be writing to her myself shortly! Aunt Minna looks really happy and has reason to be. How I would laugh if I could have my picture taken with my little grandson in my arms! I just wish I had some good news from you, dearest Gerda, after the birth of the child. You can imagine how we are waiting for it.

I don't understand why Walter hasn't heard from his mother for so long, so I asked them straight away. Aunt Henny also wrote recently that she hadn't heard from him for three weeks. I hope everything is still the same there in S., otherwise we would have found out by now.

Our cable of November 10 with the answer to your telegram, which arrived here on the same day, dear Gunther, you must have received for a long time. Although there is currently <u>no</u> possibility of leaving the country, it might be useful later if we received visas for Cuba. Wouldn't the amount paid (*I assume deposited at a bank in Cuba*) be paid back if nothing came of the trip? Inform yourself about it carefully, dear boy. We are so thankful to Stanley that he wants to help us in our need! God grant that the regulations change and we can get to you. If it were possible, we would of course like to take Grandma with us. Our only fear is that she is no longer up to the rigors of such a journey. She still knows everything and is mentally up to scratch, but unfortunately, she can't walk and see very well.

Has Aunt Frieda arrived safely with her children? Our cousin Max Sp(*anier*) and wife are still at home. They were informed by telephone 1 day before their departure that the transport had been postponed. Now they are waiting in their empty apartment! Aunt Johanna in H. tripped and hasn't been able to use her foot since. She recently turned 70. (*Apparently the institution where Johanna was housed was in Horn, near Uncle Paul's home*). Aunt Agnes and Uncle Paul also have their toil with the old people. They are all so good. Today Uncle Paul delighted us with beautiful fruit from their garden. You wouldn't believe what a delicacy this is for us! Last year we harvested so much from our little garden and all wonderful varieties - but we don't want to think about it and not mourn the past!

We are very interested in what you write, dear Gunther, about Miss F. from Chicago. Don't you have a picture of her? How old is she and what is her father's job? From where in G(ermany) is her mother from? I agree with you, in 10 years you'll be there soon enough, dear boy! (*Over the years 1937-1949, Günter had his share of girlfriends including "Miss F. from Chicago." He was charming, handsome, and entertaining*).

Did you get our last letter of November 11 with Aunt Else's and my picture? A friend took it here in the garden. I sent you the same thing, dear Gerda, in a letter on November 4th and then wrote you a card on November 14th. I hope you are healthy and happy and the dear little one is developing splendidly! Did you hear anything from Helmut? Has Ilse found a job and how are the dear parents doing? Is your business doing better now, dear Gunther, and how satisfied are you with the practice, dear Max? Aunt Else and I recently went to the cemetery and brought beautiful fir tree branches to our dear father's grave and also visited Mrs. M's graves, which are in order. How many people have died lately! One no longer needs to mourn when someone has to depart this world. Herr Bachmann is apparently doing better. He's still in the hospital in K, had a nervous breakdown. Frau B wrote to us that Edgar and Liesel are expecting a child in the winter. Uncle Hermann in E. is seriously ill again due to excitement. His housekeeper Miss R., who looked after him for so long, had to go on a long trip (*again, cryptic for "deported or jailed"*). – Well, my dear children, stay healthy and please us again soon with good reports, God willing. Pray for us! With love forever

from your mother.

From Else:

My dears,

We were very happy with your lines, although your birthday congratulations arrived a bit late, dear Gerda. Does your acquaintance in Chicago know Margot? Hardly likely.

What about our emigration now? If only it were possible to get to Cuba. How happy we would be! The Cuba visa may be of great use to us; and valid for 1 year. 1000 warm greetings from Grandma and Aunt Else

On November 24, 1941, the Nazis established a ghetto in Theresienstadt (*Terezin*), a walled garrison town in Northwestern Czechoslovakia. Hundreds of young Jewish men from Prague had been brought in as slave laborers by Adolf Eichmann to complete the project. Theresienstadt was run by the *SS* and served as a transit camp for Jews enroute to extermination camps. Many older German Jews were sent here, including other members of my family.

The next letter was written to Günter six days after the prior one, November 24, 1941. It arrived in Philadelphia on January 28, 1942, more than two months later.

From Rose:

My dear Gunther,

My last registered letter for you and Gerda was dispatched on the 18th. I hope you received it, like today's, in the best of health. Thank God we are well, we just have a lot of worries that don't let us sleep at night. May God help and protect us! Your cable arrived the day before yesterday, dear Gunther! Many thanks to both you and Stanley for your help! Unfortunately, unfortunately there is currently no possibility of leaving the country as I had wired you. Don't know if it will stay that way! Cables don't work either, otherwise I would have done it immediately. As soon as we can, we will do everything necessary, unfortunately nothing can be done at the moment, dear Gunther! Did Stanley deposit a lot and is some of the money lost if we don't get away? All the thinking and brooding will get your head completely confused!

I sent your cable to Aunt Henny. Leo *(Henrietta Oppenheim Vorreuter's son -in-law)* should take it to the Hilfsverein *(Relief Organization of German Jews)* and ask himself. Of course I did the same here and was told that nothing can be done at the moment. Pray for us that we will soon be united with you, dear Günther! That would be too nice! If only we can stay here until then. – Your cable read: "Cable received Mother Else Henny Visa number 27123 Cuban legation Berlin Telegram number Hababa Berlin *(telegram number)* 10005 Passages available January Notify if extra booking needed Gunther."

Now I expect to receive news from Berlin shortly. Now we have to wait. Today we had a letter from Aunt Henny. She shares our concerns! Many of their old friends and acquaintances are no longer at home *(have been taken away by the Nazis)*. Unfortunately, we heard from Aunt Marie from H. that she fell and broke the neck of her femur. She is in the Ellernstrasse hospital *(the Jewish Hospital in Hannover)* and wrote in desperation. That's the last thing she needed. We sent her a package, luckily we still had a can of tinned food *(These were indeed dire times when a can of food was sent as a present for a person in the hospital)*.

How are Walter, Stanley, and all loved ones there? Is business good with you? Did Stanley get my English letter? Did you have mail from Gerda and Max? How may they and the child be doing? I want to get the letter out today, so I have to be brief. With the warmest regards for you, dear boy, and all our loved ones there and in the hope of hearing from you again very soon. Greetings to all our relatives. Grandma and Aunt Else went for a walk, they also send greetings.

your very loving mother

On December 1, 1941, SS Colonel Karl Jäger, commander of an *Einsatzgruppe* (paramilitary death squads made up of *Schutzstaffel (SS)* that were responsible for mass murder, primarily by shooting), reported to Berlin that 85 percent of Lithuanian Jewry (136,442 Jews) had been killed since June 1941.

In early December 1941, the *Reichsministerium für die besetzten Ostgebiete* (Reich Ministry for the Occupied Eastern Territories) decreed that the Nazi occupiers and their local collaborators should continue to kill all Jews regardless of any economic consideration (i.e., that unpaid Jewish labor could be used for various menial tasks).

On December 6, 1941, the Soviet Union launched a major offensive against the center of the German 1,000-mile Eastern Front deep within Russia. The exhausted German Army, insufficiently supplied with food and medicine, was vulnerable to the Soviet counterattack. It would be more than six months before Germany could resume the offensive and finally reach the outskirts of Stalingrad.

On December 7, 1941, the Imperial Japanese Navy Air Service attacked the United States' naval base at Pearl Harbor, Honolulu. Until then, the U.S. was a neutral country in World War II. 2,403 Americans were killed, and more than 180 US aircraft were destroyed. On that same day, Japan also bombed airbases held by the British Empire in Malaya, Singapore, and Hong Kong. On December 8, the United States Congress declared war on Japan and four days later Hitler's Germany and Mussolini's Italy each declared war on the US, which responded with its own announcement of war against both countries.

The entrance of the United States into the War and the Alliance between Japan and Germany essentially ended any postal service between Rose, Else and Fanni in Aachen, and Gerda in Shanghai, Helmut in Palestine, and Günter in the United States. I am certain that lengthy letters continued to be written by Rose to her children, but the above communication of November 24, 1941, is the last postal service communication that reached any of Rose's children. Even prior to that date, I have no idea how many letters were undelivered, either disposed of by German censors or lost in transit.

I am also firmly convinced that my mother Gerda and my uncles Helmut and Günter sent hundreds of letters to their mother during the years that they were far away from her. Rose's letters make frequent reference to her pleasure in receiving these but, for obvious reasons, none of them have survived. There is no doubt that Rose's children continued to write to her beyond the time that civilian postal service officially ceased, hoping that at least some of these missives might get through.

The International Red Cross (IRC) began setting up a message service in 1936, with the purpose of allowing emigrants to stay in touch with relatives who had remained in Germany even if they could not use the regular postal service. Once Germany had prohibited corresponding by regular mail with any nation with which it was at war, the only means of communication was through the IRC, which was a difficult, inefficient, costly, and lengthy process.

Family members were allowed to write messages of up to twenty-five words on a standard form, but it often took several months for the messages to reach their recipients. These communications were heavily censored by the Nazis and the letter-writers, fearing reprisals, used harmless-sounding phrases to relate bad news. Rose and her children were already accustomed to this, having frequently described relatives' or friends' deportation as a "long trip" or "vacation" in many letters.

Although the IRC provided these essential services, that organization failed to protect the Jews persecuted and murdered by the Nazi regime. The Red Cross inadequately understood the uniqueness and inhumanity of the Holocaust. It lost its moral compass and never tried to live up to basic principles of humanity. The IRC responded to the outrageous with merely standard procedures. It drew inexcusably false conclusions from perfectly valid observations. More than 25 years ago, the IRC publicly finally recognized that the organization's failure to speak out was a defeat for decency.

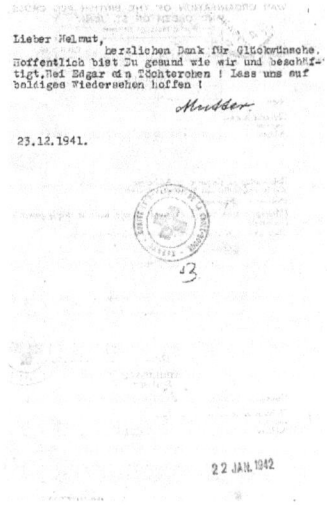

The above is a communication sent by Helmut to his family in Aachen through the Red Cross on October 29, 1941. It was received on December 18, 1941, and the reply that Rose penned was sent on December 23, 1941, and presumably accepted by Helmut on January 22, 1942. The round trip took almost three months.

Helmut writes on the form with his address as "Perlman's House, Magdiel, near Tel-Aviv" as the *sohn* (son) of the addressee. The instructions on the form are in English and German. This postal message form is meant to communicate from a *fragesteller* (enquirer or questioner or interrogator/ writer) to an *empfänger* (recipient receiver or addressee). From the office in Palestine the message is transmitted by the "War Organization of the British Red Cross and Order of St. John" via "Jerusalem (Palestine)" to the "Comité international de la Croix-Rouge" in Geneva, Switzerland and from there to Aachen, Germany.

The "enquirer" is instructed to send a "message not to exceed 25 words (of) family news of strictly personal character." Helmut writes:

> To You, dear Oma, Mother, Aunt Else Hearty congratulations on the baby André Albert Hope you well at your new home. Am healthy and satisfied. Herzlichst *(warmly or with kind regards)*, Helmut

The back of the form allowed a reply, also of 25 words or less. Rose responds on December 23, 1941:

> Dear Helmut Many thanks for good luck wishes. Hopefully you are healthy as we are and busy. Edgar had a daughter. Let us hope we see each other soon Mother

I am not surprised that Rose uses part of her word allotment to tell Helmut that "Edgar had a daughter." She wished to interject a sense of normality into a message that was undoubtedly written with fear and trepidation and received with doubt and despondency. Edgar Bachmann, after all, had been frequently mentioned in prior letters when the situation was not as dire. Edgar was the oldest child of the Bachmann family in Velmede, the Jewish owners of the other general store in the village. Edgar was born in 1910 and went to elementary school with his contemporaries, Gerda and Helmut. Recently Rose had written both Helmut and Günter that Edgar, able to emigrate to the United States and getting married there, was expecting a child.

On May 5, 1941, and again on May 14, 1941, Rose had written to Günter that Edgar's parents, Max and Klara (Wolf) Bachmann, had been given "ship passages" to the United States for September 12 from Lisbon by "their children," including Edgar in America. I am sure that Günter must have felt extreme guilt for his inability to do the same.

The elder Bachmanns had left Velmede to move to *Köln* (Cologne), the largest city in North-Rhine Westphalia, in 1937, shortly after they were also forced to sell their store in Velmede for a pittance to non-Jewish merchants. Shortly after Kristallnacht, Max Bachmann was arrested and, at age 63, was sent to the Sachsenhausen concentration camp near Berlin, the first new concentration camp to be established following the appointment of Heinrich Himmler as the Chief of the German Police in July 1936. There, Bachmann became a slave laborer, forced to work in workshops and factories owned by the SS in the camp's industrial yard as well as in various punishment details such as the "Klinkerwerk" (the world's largest brickworks factory) to supply building materials for the massive megastructures planned by the Nazi leadership in the Reich capital city. He was released from Sachsenhausen after a few months and returned to *Köln,* where he lived in an apartment with his wife until May 1941, when the Gestapo started to concentrate all Jews from Cologne in so-called Jewish or "ghetto" houses, similar to what occurred contemporaneously in Aachen.

As was the case with other Jewish families who had successfully struggled to obtain ship passage to the United States, Max and Karla Bachmann were unable to get the necessary visas for entry into the United States. Their ship left Lisbon, as planned, on September 12, 1941, but they were not on board.

In her letters, Rose documents that, in October, 1941, Max Bachmann was hospitalized at the *Israelitisches Asyl für Kranke und Altersschwäche* (literally translated, "the Israelite asylum for the sick and those decrepit from old age"). This Jewish Hospital, built on Cologne's *Ottostraße* in 1907, immediately developed an excellent reputation throughout the Rhineland and 80% of the patients seeking care there were non-Jewish. In 1936, the National Socialists (Nazis) banned the admission of non-Jewish patients, decreeing *"Zur ärztlichen Behandlung ausschliesslich von Juden berechtigt."* (Only Jews entitled to medical treatment.).

In that first letter, Rose writes that the hospitalization was for "heart disease." In a communication a month later, she informs Günter that Max Bachmann was still in the hospital and had "a nervous breakdown." It is not without cause that he was suffering from depression and anxiety: He had survived a slave labor camp, lost his home and possessions, undoubtedly had a drastically difficult financial situation and living condition, and the hope of salvation from this had been removed just prior to its fruition.

Deportation to the East began in Cologne in October 1941. In September 1942, Max and Klara Bachmann were taken to a detention facility in a large building at the Cologne Trade Fair complex. On September 26, 1942, they, together with many other Jews of the area, were taken to the lower level of the Cologne train station, where they were loaded onto Transport III/6, no. 2 and taken to Theresienstadt in Czechoslovakia. Max was murdered there on November 2, 1942; his wife Klara suffered the same fate on January 16, 1943. Günter's guilt had been generated by love for his mother but was unnecessary. Of the 50 Jews of Cologne on that train to Theresienstadt, only two survived the War.

For Rose, Else and Fanni, the year 1941 ended unimaginably worse than it had begun. In March, they had been forced to leave their spacious Aachen home and were now confined to a sparse single room for all three of them at the *Israelitisches Altenheim* at 87 *Horst-Wessel-Straße*. They were relatively fortunate with respect to the space they did have, since it is likely, given the size of the house and that there were almost 200 occupants, that some rooms must have housed at least eight people.

One can certainly imagine the nature of the conversations that occurred each and every day, both among the members of my family within their chamber and the exchanges that they had with others in the hallways and the communal dining and kitchen areas of the house. Although there may have been some elderly residents who had arrived at the old age home voluntarily prior to 1941, the vast majority were those who were forced to come to a "Jewish house" after their homes were taken by the Nazi government. Many had known each other through the Aachen Jewish community for years. They had much in common beyond their mutual despair.

There is a Swedish proverb that says "Shared joy is a double joy. Shared sorrow is half a sorrow." Undoubtedly, many tears were shed both in solace and in company but the sorrow was easier to tolerate knowing others were in identical situations. In that house. the air was constantly filled with expressions of concern, apprehension, anxiety, trepidation, dread and panic. Everyone had outside sources who wrote to them, providing them with information by mail, some true and others false, some exaggerated and others understated. Tales of what had happened to relatives and friends, was currently ocurring, and what the future held permeated every dialogue. Although Dante Alighieri has written, "There is no greater sorrow than to recall happiness in times of misery," I can only wish that there were brief moments where my family was able to share stories of happier times with each other and their new housemates. Perhaps thoughts of my birth and the pleasure that I was giving to her daughter allowed my grandmother Rose to sustain some hope for the future, if only briefly.

The oppressive nature of the close quarters, food scarcity, absence of medical care, the inability to walk in the neighborhood without fear and the sudden reduction in the number of letters received all added to their distress. Rose and Else, in 1941, were close witnesses to their mother's physical deterioration, to the point that they reached the conclusion that, if they left the home, either on their own volition or through force, Fanni would need to be left behind.

Chapter 16: 1942

In the closing days of 1941, with the world at war, United States President Roosevelt and Britain's Prime Minister Churchill met at the White House for the Arcadia Conference. There, Roosevelt created the term "United Nations" to describe the Allied countries fighting in World War II. Churchill acquiesced with that phrase and the text of the "Declaration by United Nations" was drafted on December 29, 1941. On New Year's Day 1942, Roosevelt, Churchill, Maxim Litvinov of the USSR, and T. V. Soong, of China, signed that document, and the next day the representatives of twenty-two other nations added their signatures. During the War, "the United Nations" became the official term for the Allies. To join, countries had to sign the Declaration and declare war on the Axis powers. The drafting of the Charter of the United Nations was completed over the following two months. It was signed on June 26, 1945, by representatives of 50 countries.

Although the UN officially only came into existence on October 24, 1945, those signing the Declaration of the United Nations four years earlier already knew enough about the horrors of Nazi brutality and mass murder of Jewish civilian men women and children to establish the United Nations War Crimes Commission in January 1942, to manage future prosecution of Nazi war criminals.

Documents declassified under the Nazi War Crimes Disclosure Act of 1998 is additional evidence that the American and British intelligence communities knew of Hitler's plans for the Jews even prior to America's entry into the War. On November 24, 1941, a Chilean diplomat sent a dispatch to the US Office of Coordinator of Information (COI), a predecessor of the Office of Strategic Services (OSS) discussing the Nazi intent to eradicate European Jewry. It states that "it has been decided to eradicate all the Jews... The German triumph [in the war] will leave Europe freed of Semites... Germany will expedite the destruction of Semitism, as she accuses international Judaism of all the calamities which have befallen the world."

Additionally, in the United States there was already sufficient proof of Nazi atrocities directed against those innocent of any crime except being Jewish. On New Year's Day 1942, the Counter-Intelligence Corps (CIC) was established to investigate and arrest suspected Nazi war criminals.

Yet there was no action taken to prevent what would only later be termed the Holocaust, the premeditated state-sponsored, systematic murder of six million European Jews by the Nazi German regime and its allies and collaborators. The fact that the U.S. State Department and the British Foreign Office had information of this type did not lead them to any degree of conviction that the unthinkable was indeed occurring.

Deborah Lipstadt, recently named US special envoy to monitor and combat antisemitism, a position in the Department of State with the rank of ambassador, has pointed out that Holocaust historians have described three groups of people within the Holocaust, "victims, perpetrators and bystanders." Lipstadt argues that "bystanders" should be defined as those who saw what was happening but lacked any real power to change things. She suggests an additional larger group, that of "enablers," who allowed, through their silence, for the Holocaust to take place. Ideologies such as antisemitism were enablers as were "governmental and non-governmental entities." The silence of the Vatican and others, as early as 1933, "was interpreted by the Germans as a clear signal that they could continue doing what they were doing without any consequences."

On January 13, 1942, the governments-in exile of Belgium, Czechoslovakia, France, Greece, Holland, Luxembourg, Norway, Poland, and Yugoslavia met at St. James' Palace in London for the Inter-Allied Conference and condemned German atrocities against their citizens without specifically mentioning Jews. The British Foreign Office approved the declaration, also failing to make any statement concerning Jews.

In 1941, the Nazi leadership had begun mass deportations of Jews from the German Reich to ghettos and extermination camps in the occupied areas of Eastern Europe. The first transport of approximately 1,000 Jews was from Düsseldorf, perhaps symbolically because it had been the home of the diplomat Ernst vom Rath, whose assassination had prompted *Kristallnacht*. It left there on October 27, 1941, with the destination being the Lodz ghetto. This was the first of seven transports in 1941 of the Jews of Düsseldorf. Prior to each of these transports, the Jews were rounded up and taken to the stockyard of the municipal slaughterhouse immediately adjacent to the freight train station. There they were registered, their remaining belongings were taken from them and on the following day, after a night of horrible uncertainty, were forced to board the trains travelling to the *Ostland*.

On January 20, 1942, Chief of the *SD*, *SS-Obergruppenführer* Reinhard Heydrich invited senior Nazi officials to a conference at a *SS*-owned Berlin villa on the shores of Lake Wannsee. There, he revealed to them his strategy for the "Final Solution *(die Endlösung der Judenfrage)*," a euphemism for the Nazi plan for the annihilation of the Jewish people. This included Europe being "combed through from west to east for Jews." The Wannsee Conference was the beginning of the bureaucratic coordination required for the massive efforts to be undertaken throughout Europe for the purpose of killing the 11,000,000 Jews of Europe.

A top-secret report of the meeting was prepared from Adolph Eichmann's meticulously kept minutes, later edited by Heydrich himself, and presented to Herman Göring, *Reichsmarschall* of the *Wehrmacht* (the German armed forces), a special title created for him by Hitler. The report enumerated what had already been accomplished, the expulsion of the Jews from every sphere of life and living space of the German people and the enforced speedy emigration of Jews from Germany, the latter financed totally by the Jews themselves through exorbitant taxes and seizure and sale of their possessions

The Wannsee report continues with an enumeration of the current location of the 11 million Jews of Europe. Estonia is listed as being "Judenfrei," (an area "cleansed" of all Jewish presence during the Holocaust). Germany had invaded and occupied Estonia in 1941 and the Nazi *Einzatsgruppe*, the *SS* paramilitary death squads responsible for mass murder, had already shot and killed more than 1,000 Estonian Jews. They were aided by Estonian collaborators, members of the Estonian Home Guard, who participated in unprecedented atrocities committed against the Jewish people. Any remaining Estonian Jews fled to the Soviet Union or were deported to locations to the East. Later in 1942, about 10,000 Jews were transported to Nazi concentration camps in Estonia from other parts of Europe. Very few survived.

The report resulting from the Wannsee conference also outlined the definition of a "Jew" to be exterminated, including persons of "mixed blood." That death sentence designation could also be applied to anyone with any connection to Judaism who "looked like" a Jew or behaved "as a Jew."

The "final solution" should be carried out "as quickly as possible, since…the Jew as an epidemic carrier represents an extreme danger and on the other hand he is causing permanent chaos in the economic structure…Jews will first be sent, group by group, to so-called transit ghettos, from which they will be transported to the East…During the course of the Final Solution…, able-bodied Jews will be brought to build

292

roads, whereby a large number will doubtlessly be lost through natural reduction....Any final remnant that survives will doubtless consist of the elements most capable of resistance. They must be dealt with appropriately, since, representing the fruit of natural selection, they are to be regarded as the core of a new Jewish revival." Heydrich did not mention the fate of Jews who were not fit to work, but according to his subordinate, Adolf Eichmann, who took the minutes, Heydrich's murderous intentions were obvious and understood.

Despite the use of euphemisms rather than terms like "murder" and "kill" in these transcripts, the goal of the Wannsee Conference, clearly understood by all the participants, was the physical annihilation of the European Jews. A few months later, more than twenty mobile gas chambers were hard at work in Poland.

On January 30, 1942, in a speech commemorating the ninth anniversary of his taking power, Hitler declared that the end result of the War will not be the destruction of the Aryans but will be the complete annihilation of the Jews. The speech was monitored in Washington, D.C. and London.

On January 31, 1942, 11 days after Wannsee, Adolf Eichmann, head of the *Reichssicherheitshauptamt* (*RSHA*, Reich Security Main Office), informed all Gestapo headquarters that "the recent evictions of Jews from several areas of the Reich to the east are but the beginning of the 'final solution' of the Jewish problem." Eichmann added that "the evacuation measures were initially restricted ...(and) new reception sites are presently being arranged with the aim of deporting additional contingents of Jews." On the basis of criteria that Eichmann set forth, the Gestapo in Düsseldorf, which also oversaw these operations in Aachen, was to present the *RSHA* with a list of Jews from the North Rhine-Westphalia region for deportation by February 9, 1942.

Eichmann's Department in Berlin on January 31 also issued "Guidelines for the Technical Implementation of the Evacuation of Jews to the General Government" which was sent to all offices of the Reich Security throughout Germany.

Rose, Else and Fanni, in the Jewish *Altenheim* in Aachen, together with the other residents in that extremely crowded facility, had no knowledge of the conference that was deciding their ultimate fate. What they certainly did know was that there was very little food to share and that, due to the scarcity of fuel to heat the large building, their bones always felt cold despite wearing many layers of the sweaters and winter coats that they had brought to 87 *Horst Wessel Straße* following the forced abandonment of their Aachen home. The Jews remaining in Aachen numbered approximately 500 all of whom would be deported in 1942. The residents of the other *Judenhäuser* (Jewish Houses) were even more unfortunate, since they had even less space and lacked the resourcefulness and experience of the Superior of the Jewish Home for the Elderly, Grete Berger née Löwenstein, who at 48 years of age had boundless energy and experience in managing a large communal home for adults.

The first *Sonderzüge* (special trains) filled with German Jews began departing from central Germany in October 1941, bound for ghettos in occupied Poland. These ghettos were liquidated beginning in 1942, with other trains taking that condemned population to the death camps at Bełżec, Chelmo, Sobibór, Majdanek, Treblinka, or Auschwitz-Birkenau.

In January 1942, at Belzec, near the Polish city of Lublin, Christian Wirth, a Nazi executions expert, hooked an armored-car diesel engine to a wooden building to murder the victims inside using carbon monoxide. This method was found to be too slow, unpredictable, and inefficient. In that same month, killings of Jews on a mammoth scale using Zyklon-B commenced at Auschwitz-Birkenau, the largest of the Nazi death camps. Auschwitz was established near the Polish city of *Oswiecim* (Polish for the German word "Auschwitz") near the prewar German-Polish border. This concentration camp could hold 150,000 inmates at any given time. On February 15, the first mass gassing of Jews at the Auschwitz death camp began. It is estimated that the number of people murdered at Auschwitz was in excess of three million, the vast majority being Jews. Most prisoners held at Auschwitz died in gas chambers, though many were murdered by shooting squads, forced labor, starvation and as a result of atrocious medical experiments.

Zyklon B had been used in Germany prior to the War as a common disinfectant and insecticide utilized in ships, buildings, and machinery. It was used at Auschwitz, first experimentally and then routinely, as an agent of mass human annihilation. The Zyklon used at concentration camps was produced by a division of *IG Farbenidustrie AG*, the principal chemical manufacturer in Germany. IG Farben's stock traded on German markets until 2012. Zyklon B consists of diatomite, a naturally occurring sedentary rock *(kieselguhr)*, in granules the size of fine peas, saturated with hydrogen cyanide (prussic acid). These pellets release a highly poisonous gas when exposed to air. In view of its volatility and the associated risk of accidental poisoning, it was transported to the camps and stored in hermetically sealed metal canisters.

Zyklon B proved to be a highly effective, very efficient, and very cheap way to kill large numbers of people. Jewish and other captives arrived at the camp by train and those who were felt to be unfit for work in forced labor areas were sent directly to the gas chambers. The Nazis kept this a secret and told the unsuspecting victims that they had to undress for a bath. The prisoners were led to a camouflaged airtight gas chamber, disguised by the Nazis to look like shower rooms, and there found themselves trapped inside when a large door was sealed behind them. Then, an orderly, wearing a gas mask, opened a vent on the roof of the chamber and poured Zyklon B pellets down the shaft, subsequently closing the vent to seal the gas chamber. The Zyklon B pellets turned immediately into a deadly gas, suffocating all inside within minutes. After it was determined that all had died, the poisonous air was pumped out. Once it was safe to go inside, the door was opened and a special unit of prisoners, known as the *Sonderkommando*, hosed down the gas chamber and used hooked poles to pry the dead bodies apart. Rings were removed from the fingers of clenched hands and gold plucked from teeth. The bodies were sent to the crematoria, where they were turned into ash.

The gold extracted from the teeth of the murdered together with the gold coins and jewelry of the Jews of Europe were processed under the direction of the Nazi German *Reichsbank* and deposited with the Bank for International Settlement (BIS), formed in 1930 in Basel, Switzerland, with the original intent of processing Germany's World War I reparation payments and providing liquidity to European governments struggling to survive the world-wide Depression. Countries assigned their gold reserves to BIS accounts, although the gold itself might be stored elsewhere, and payments between countries were processed by Swiss officials.

After Hitler rose to power, unleashed his war machine, and initiated the Holocaust, it was obvious that no reparations would be paid by Germany. Rather than going out of business, the BIS, under German direction, received the gold bullion of Austria after the March 1938 *Anschluss* and that of Czechoslovakia after the annexation of the *Sudetenland.* Likewise, following Germany's conquest of the remainder of

294

Czechoslovakia, the BIS credited Germany with the gold of that nation, releasing all this stolen gold to Germany to buy fuel and machinery, essentially financing the war effort.

The BIS achieved immunity from basically all banking regulations and international laws. Although it functioned as a central bank, it was virtually self-governing and, located in neutral Switzerland, gained another layer of protection by not being subject to even the notoriously secretive Swiss banking laws. For years it never bothered to even put a sign on its door.

Although the United States stored no gold with the BIS, an American, Harvard graduate Thomas McKittrick, was president of the Bank from 1940 to June 1943. McKittrick played a crucial role in abetting Hitler's war allowing the BIS to willingly accept looted Nazi gold, carrying out foreign exchange deals for the *Reichsbank*, and recognizing the Nazi invasion and annexation of conquered countries. McKittrick fundamentally legitimized the role of the national banks in the occupied countries in appropriating Jewish-owned assets while simultaneously assuring Swiss authorities that the bank would not "undertake political activities of any sort whatsoever on behalf of any governments or national organizations."

The *Reichsbank*'s Nazi vice-president Emil Puhl, who was later tried for war crimes, referred to the BIS as the *Reichsbank*'s only "foreign branch." In the closing months of the war, while other Americans were dying in France and Germany, McKittrick was arranging deals with Nazi industrialists to guarantee their profits after the Allied victory. When McKittrick died in New Jersey in 1970, the New York Times eulogized him as a world financier.

On February 5, 1942, Rose sent a communication via the International Red Cross to my father, Dr. Max Dahl, addressed to his office on 113 Kiukiang Road, in the Continental Bank Building in Shanghai:

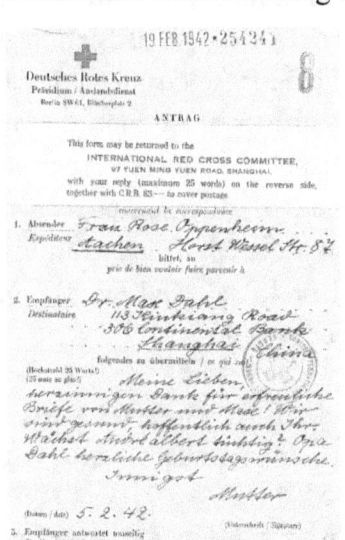

Communication from Rose to my parents in Shanghai.   February 5, 1942

My Dear Ones,

A hearty thank you for your joyful letter from "mother" and Max. We are healthy, hopefully you are the same. Is André Albert growing strong? Give Opa Dahl *(Nathan Dahl would be 72 on May 1, 1942)* our hearty birthday wishes.

Dearest "Mutter"

On the basis of criteria that Eichmann set forth, the Gestapo in Düsseldorf was to present the *RSHA* with a record of all Jews in the area for deportation by February 9, 1942. To prepare the list, the Jewish Affairs Department of Gestapo-Düsseldorf telephoned its branches on February 6 to immediately prepare files of all Jews living in their areas. On February 7, Georg Pütz, head of the Düsseldorf Department, drew up a list of Jews who could be deported from the area, including Aachen. According to this *Judenkartei* (catalog of Jews), 3,547 Jews remained in the area under the jurisdiction of Gestapo-Düsseldorf and 1,238 of them were eligible for transport to Izbica, a transit ghetto near Lublin, Poland.

On February 24, 1942, Hitler issued a proclamation celebrating the 22nd anniversary of the Nazi Party. He expressed his determination "to settle accounts with the conspiracy of…Jewish capitalism and Communism... As before, during, and after the First World War in our country, so today the Jews and again only the Jews have to be held responsible for tearing apart the nations... My prophecy will be fulfilled that this war will not destroy the Aryan, but, instead, it will exterminate the Jew. Whatever the struggle may bring, however long it may last, this will be its final result. And only then, after the elimination of these parasites, a long era of international understanding, and therefore of true peace, will come over the suffering world."

By February 1942, the residents of the Aachen "Jewish houses" at *Gruenen Weg, 95 Alexanderstraße, 20 Frankenbergerstraße, 39 Emmichstraße, 22 Königstraße, 249 Eupenerstraße, 28 Försterstraße,* and *21 Promenadenstraße*, together with my family and others residing at 87 *Horst Wessel Straße*, had certainly heard rumors regarding the fate of their families, friends and other Jews after they were deported to the East. Speculation, stories, and anecdotes were constantly shared, embellished, and denied, but there were no detailed reports of the truth. Had there been, it would have been too terrible for my family to comprehend the impending tragedy. In *The Origins of Totalitarianism,* Hannah Arendt writes, "It is inherent in our entire [Western] philosophical tradition that we cannot conceive of a 'radical evil'." In that book, she argues that the evil of the Nazis was absolute and inhuman, driven by an audacious, monstrous intention to abolish humanity itself. Psychologists tell us that it is part of the natural condition for a person to repress or exclude painful and disturbing visions of the future automatically or unconsciously from the human mind. The mind attempts to evade or dispel terror by relying on the sacrosanctity of the values of our culture. My hope is that my family, in those times of extreme anxiety and overwhelming fear, achieved some measure of inner peace by developing a much more appreciative attitude for those aspects of their life they had taken for granted before, grateful for their friends and family, grateful just to be alive, grateful to be able to perceive and experience the world around them.

On March 5, 1942, Rose sent a Red Cross transmitted "letter" to my parents, Gerda and Max Dahl, in Shanghai. It was delivered to my father's office on Kiukiang Road on April 10, 1942.

The translation (expanded by me to beyond the 25-word limit) reads:

My Dear Children,

Please write soon *(and let us know)* how you are doing. We are healthy *(and)* have heard nothing for a long time from you, Helmut and Gunther. How is André Albert?

Warmly, Mother

My mother Gerda replied on the back of the document.

My dear ones

We received with heartfelt pleasure your letter of March. I hope you are all well. We are all healthy. Andy gives us much joy *(crossed out, likely because of verbiage in excess of 25 words: he is crawling and trying to walk)* and is making wonderful progress *(in his development)*.

Greetings and kisses,   Gerda

My mother retained a copy of her reply. Since it was mailed on or after April 10, 1942, and returned to Aachen, it is doubtful that Rose ever received and read it, since she was deported from Aachen on March 22, 1942.

On March 6, 1942, Eichmann summoned Gestapo representatives from all over the Reich, including Düsseldorf, for a meeting to discuss the deportation of 55,000 Jews from the Reich. He instructed them to give the Jews no advance notice of their transport. Eichmann added that the date of the transport would be divulged to the local Gestapo offices only six days in advance. This precaution was evidently meant to forestall the spreading of rumors among the Jewish population about the impending deportation.

Transports of Jews from the Reich, including Austria, to localities in the Lublin district of the occupied *General Gouvernement* began in March. The destinations became transit camps for the implementation of the "Final Solution," although sometimes the deportees were taken directly to extermination camps.

The initial deportation of the Jews of Aachen was on Train # 17, known as part of Transport III, departing from *Koblenz* (also spelled Coblenz), about 160 kilometers southeast of Aachen, on March 22, 1942. "Zug" is German for the English word "train."   The term "*Zug Da 17*," includes the abbreviation "*Da*" which was a code for deportation trains. It stood for "*Da(vids) züge*," poignantly the trains occupied by people forced to wear the yellow six-pointed Jewish star of David on their clothing.

On March 4, 1942, the Gestapo office in Düsseldorf planned this transport. Six hundred twenty-six Jews were to be deported from Aachen, including 241 actual residents of the city, with the remainder from nearby Rhineland towns such as Düren, Eschweiler, Stolberg, Lendersdorf and Geilenkirchen. Those from Aachen included 27 persons from the "Jews' houses" at 87 *Horst Wessel Straße* and 25 from the 249 *Eupenersraße* home. They would travel to Koblenz where they would join 337 additional people from the area around Koblenz. For the vast majority of the Aachener Jews being deported, the Aachen *Hauptbahnhof* (main train station), from which the train to Koblenz departed, was the last location of their life that was familiar to them.

Aachen Hauptbahnhof

The *Da 17* train was originally planned to take its occupants to the Trawniki concentration camp about 40 kilometers southeast of Lublin, Poland. That facility originally housed Soviet prisoners of war during Operation Barbarossa, but at the time of deportation it had become both an *SS* training camp for Ukrainian collaborationist auxiliary police and a slave labor camp for Jews, the latter working on behalf of the Nazi war effort under appalling conditions and with little food. Towards the end of October 1943, the entire Trawniki slave-labor workforce in the area was ordered to begin the construction of "defensive air raid" trenches, which would soon become their mass graves. On November 3, 1943, all 12,000 Jews imprisoned at Trawniki were told to get into the pits and were promptly slaughtered by guns manned by the Ukrainian auxiliary units. This military operation, with the code name *Erntefest* (Operation Harvest Festival) occurred simultaneously at other concentration camps in the Lublin/Majdanek area and, with approximately 43,000 victims, was the largest single German massacre of Jews in one day during the entire war.

At the last minute, due to logistic problems involving a lack of "Russian trains," the final destination of train *Da 17* was changed to Izbica, a transit ghetto in the Lublin district of southeastern Poland. Some deportation trains, as they passed through Germany from west to east made stops to load on additional Jewish deportees. *Zug Da 17* did not do this, taking all of its prisoners from the collection point of Koblenz directly to Izbica.

Two of those passengers were my grandmother, Rose Liepmann Oppenheim, and her sister Else Liepmann. Not a single one of these approximately 1,000 deportees survived World War II. All were murdered by gas or bullets if they somehow had avoided dying of disease or starvation.

In my exploration, I discovered evidence placing Rose and Else instead on Train *Da 52* departing Düsseldorf on April 22, 1942, and arriving in Izbica three days later. That information was compiled by Traces of War, part of STIWOT, a Dutch foundation which continues to compile factual material regarding those murdered in World War II. In addition, the United States Archives lists the Aachen deportees in (*ia600305.us.archive.org/23/items/DeportationszuegeAusAachen/Deportationszuege.pdf*). There, "Rosa" Oppenheim and "Elisabeth" Liepmann are documented as being on Train *Da 52*. Other sources place them on Train *Da 17*. However, the most compelling evidence of my family being on Train *Da 17,* a month earlier, departing from Koblenz on March 22, 1942, is the fact that I have three postcards written by my family from Izbica, two of which were written and postmarked prior to Train *Da 52's* arrival in Izbica on April 25, 1942. The written content of these postcards also confirms their arrival in Izbica at the end of March, rather than the end of April.

Finding information regarding the Aachen deportees on that train brings the human dimension to the vast numbers such as one thousand on this train or the inconceivable mind-boggling six million Jews murdered by the Nazis. Each of these people, to a greater or lesser extent, had navigated life's passages and shared family milestones such as births, ritual circumcision and bar mitzvahs of males, weddings, religious and secular family celebrations and funerals. He or she had experienced satisfaction from accomplishments and disappointments as a result of failure or bad luck. Some had been fortunate to find true love; others had experienced heartbreak. Prior to the Nazis coming to power, Germany's Jews were well integrated into German society, although some faced discrimination on a social level. Despite this assimilation, Germany's Jews still maintained a sense of Jewish identity and celebrated their history and traditions. Some were more religiously observant than others, but all enjoyed the family Seder on Passover, the sharing of gifts at Chanukkah and the solemnity of Rosh Hashanah and Yom Kippur.

Hitler's plan for a "Final Solution" relied on careful mobilization and scheduling to efficiently shuttle millions of victims, including entire Jewish communities, across the European railway systems to the death camps, where victims were rapidly murdered. The complex logistics of this effort were solved through the involvement of the *Deutsche Reichsbahn* (German National Railway). There were more than 1,600 trains that were organized by the Reich Ministry of Transportation, most bound for the killing camps of Poland. Without the *Reichsbahn*, employing almost half a million civil servants and 900,000 additional workers made available by the Reich and knowingly participating in the killings, the industrial murder of millions of people would not have been possible. Although the prisoner trains took away valuable track space, they allowed for mass scale and shortened time over which the extermination needed to take place. The process involved carefully kept timetables, dependable contingents of drivers and precise coordination with the military that always had priority over the tracks. The fully enclosed nature of the locked and windowless "cattle wagons" greatly reduced the number and skill of troops required to transport the condemned Jews to their destinations. The use of railroads enabled the Nazis to lie about the "resettlement program" and, simultaneously, build and operate more efficient gassing facilities, requiring limited supervision. In researching for this book and translating German documents related to my family, I am repeatedly struck that, in these, as with so many other Nazi documents, there is an enormous chasm between the "civilized," orderly record-keeping and the barbarity of the act that is being recorded.

The trains were pulled by the *Deutsche Reichsbahn's* Class 52 German locomotive powered by coal. They were built in large numbers during the Second World War. Using fewer parts and less expensive materials to speed production, this steam engine was perfect for the economic circumstances of wartime

Germany, taking into account the shortage of materials, ease of maintenance under difficult conditions, resistance to extremes of weather, and the need for rapid, cheap mass production. German locomotive building firms employed primarily Polish nationals from concentration camps and other forced labor to construct the locomotives.

Class 52 Nazi steam locomotive

On Train *Da 17* and others going to the Lublin area, the number of deportees assigned to each train was to be 941 as a minimum and 1051 as a maximum. The Nazi death machine had decided that this was operationally the most efficient range of numbers. Most of the female deportees were middle class *hausfrauen* (housewives) who had spent their adult lives working hard to shop, cook, clean and take care of the children and to make a home that was comfortable for their husbands. Many men were employed by or owned small businesses in the towns and cities of Germany. Jews also worked as tailors, civil servants, doctors, lawyers, journalists, bank clerks, factory workers, professors, and teachers. A few were wealthy business owners. Most of these deportees considered themselves as belonging to a religious group. They were Germans who practiced Judaism. A minority saw themselves as an ethnic group. They were Jews who lived in Germany. For Hitler, it made no difference.

In their cramped room at 87 *Horst Wessel Straße*, Rose and Else felt blessed that their mother's hearing was sufficiently impaired to allow the two sisters to speak of the latest events without the distress that Fanni become agitated or alarmed. They discussed many things, often far into the night while their mother slept, sharing their fears, hope, and desperation, and during the days attempted to maintain a pleasant countenance and attitude when around her in the room. Rumors of all sorts abounded, a natural occurrence, given the nature and veracity of the verbal and written information provided to inhabitants confined to the "Jewish Houses" of Aachen.

All belongings left behind by deported Jews were considered property of the German Reich. Confiscations of property were directed by the Finance Ministry, which tried to prevent last minute disturbances of the contents of apartments by persons possessing some inkling of impending deportations. The Finance Office in Aachen sent a letter to both the local protective police and the *Geheime Staatspolizei* (Secret State Police), abbreviated *Gestapo*, instructing them that "To guard the (Jewish) property in the interest of the Reich, everything must be done to avoid the possibility that unauthorized third persons lay their hands on movable belongings of the Jews before we can take them over. We request, therefore, that all appropriate steps be taken to guard the property of the Jews until the moment they are removed. Among other

300

things it may be useful to have police officers watch the Jewish apartments several days in advance (of their deportation)." After enumerating the addresses of the various Aachen "Jewish Houses," the document continues, "The above-mentioned Jewish apartments are to be watched with special care by the patrol force."

Train #17 would carry approximately 1,000 Jewish deportees, abducted and transferred from throughout the heavily industrialized Ruhr Valley region and brought to Koblenz. The logistics of this was managed by the RSHA, *Reichssicherheitshauptamt* (Reich Security Main Office) headed by Reinhard Heydrich, Heinrich Himmler's deputy. The section of the RSHA organizing and operating this train was Office IV B 4, led by Adolf Eichmann. It was designated as the *Eichmannreferat* (Eichmann's Unit) or the *Judenreferat* (Jewish Unit), coordinating the deportation of Jews from Western, Central, and Southern Europe to ghettos, concentration camps, killing sites, where Jews were shot on a massive scale, and "killing centers," sometimes referred to as "extermination camps" or "death camps." Hundreds of concentration camps for the detention of civilians seen as real or perceived "enemies of the Reich" functioned primarily as detention and forced labor camps, but also were sites for the murder of smaller, targeted groups of individuals. In the forced-labor camps, the Nazi regime brutally exploited the labor of prisoners for economic gain and to meet labor shortages. Prisoners lacked proper equipment, clothing, nourishment, or rest.

Shortly after the Wannsee conference, Heinrich Himmler, Chief of the Security Police and the *SD* (*Sicherheitsdienst*, the Nazi Party intelligence service) determined that "of the approximately 2.5 million Jews in question (in the *Generalgouvernent,* consisting of the districts of Warsaw, Krakow, Lublin, Radom and Lvov), the majority are anyway unfit for work." The code name for the secret plan to eliminate these Jews was *Aktion Reinhard* (Operation Reinhard), named after Reinhard Heydrich, the leading planner of Hitler's Final Solution. Operation Reinhard began in March 1942, coinciding with opening of the death camp Belzec and the building of Sobibor and Treblinka, at the eastern border of the General Government. The geographical location of the killing sites was compatible with the pretext that the Jews were being deported to ghettos in the East, allowing their disappearance to be explained as merely transportation to labor camps in the huge areas in the Soviet Union occupied by the German armed forces. A special organization was set up in Lublin to prepare for the Jewish extermination, and continued its assigned task until November 1943, at which time the mission was complete.

The term extermination "camps" is rather inaccurate. These sites, which were used for the "factory" killing of people, were not places where prisoners would usually be kept overnight. Rather, the people arriving there by train were typically immediately murdered with gas. In these locations there were only small detachments of prisoners who had to support the "work" of the SS men and their helpers. These were the *kapos,* Jewish inmates who were forced by the Nazis to serve as "stand-in" guards. Being a *kapo* blurred the lines between perpetrator, collaborator, and victim. There was significant manpower and cost savings by recruiting and deploying an army of *Kapos,* since only a small number of *SS* men was required to oversee an ever-increasing camp population. Jewish *Kapos* played a pivotal role in the history of the Holocaust, driving a wedge between inmates, turning groups against groups and victims against victims. The strategy of "divide and rule" paid off. *Kapos* eventually were also victims of the Nazis; they were murdered after a shorter or longer time.

The "killing center" was a facility established totally for the assembly-line style mass murder of human beings immediately upon arrival to the site. Small numbers of prisoners were selected from each transport to support the main function of the death factories. Those survived, only temporarily, in a *Sonderkommando* (special detachment), working as *Arbeitsjuden* ("work Jews.") They removed bodies from the gas chambers and initially buried them in mass graves. Other prisoners selected for temporary survival facilitated detraining, disrobing, relinquishment of valuables, and movement of new arrivals into the gas chambers. They also sorted the possessions of the murdered victims to prepare those items for transport to Germany and were responsible for cleaning out freight cars for the next deportation. German *SS* and Trawniki-trained Ukrainian auxiliaries periodically murdered the members of these *Sonderkommando* Jewish laborers, replacing them with persons selected from newly arriving transports.

There were five killing centers for the murder primarily of Jews: The Chelmo killing center in German-occupied Poland was the first stationary facility where poison gas was used for the mass murder of Jews. The SS and police began killing operations at Chelmno on December 8, 1941, locking people in trucks in which the exhaust pipes had been reconfigured to pump carbon monoxide gas into a sealed space behind the cabs of the vehicles. Belzec and Sobibor were located in Poland's Lublin district, where Train 17 would be heading, and Treblinka was within the Warsaw District. Of the more than one million people sent to Belzec, Sobibor and Treblinka, only approximately three hundred prisoners survived.

The fifth and the largest killing center was Auschwitz-Birkenau, located in Upper Silesia, the area where my father was born when it was a part of Germany, becoming part of Poland after the Treaty of Versailles and reacquired by Nazi Germany during the 1939 conquest of Poland. Immediately after the Wannsee conference, Himmler established Auschwitz-Birkenau as the "final" destination for many European Jews, most killed within hours after arriving there.

Throughout this period of time Isaiah Bowman (1878-1950) strongly influenced President Franklin D. Roosevelt's view of the Jewish refugee problem. He was deeply antisemitic and, as President of Johns Hopkins University, Bowman discouraged the hiring of any Jewish faculty, saying "there are already too many Jews at Hopkins." After *Kristallnacht*, Roosevelt enlisted him to undertake a two-year examination of settlement possibilities for Jewish refugees. Bowman and his team found virtually every country they studied to be unsuitable for "a large foreign immigrant group." Bowman warned that there is "the danger (of) Jewish control…if too many are allowed into the country and particularly the cities." Bowman, positioned to wield great influence on the President, simply helped reinforce Roosevelt's preexisting bias regarding Jewish statehood (Zionism). Bowman strongly opposed the creation of a Jewish state in Palestine and, in a discussion with FDR, characterized Zionism as no different "from Hitler's *Lebensraum*." In 1942, FDR named Bowman to chair the Office of Post-War Planning. Bowman and his staff of more than 30 reported to Roosevelt that admission of significant numbers of foreigners would endanger America's racial well-being writing, "Our civilization will decline unless we improve our human breed. To support the genetically unfit and also allow them to breed is to degrade our society." Bowman also strongly defended America's right to take preventive action "if it decides that its character will be improved by excluding certain populations."

On March 5, 1942, the Düsseldorf Gestapo implemented a directive from the Berlin *RSHA* stating that when Jews were deported to the East, their destination should not be recorded. The Nazis were deflecting any inquiries regarding the place of arrival, continuing the dehumanization of the process. Within the non-Jewish German people, the fate of the deportees was hardly discussed. Very few spoke about the mass murder that was occurring, not because there was a lack of information or fear of reprisals, but due to the absence of interest regarding the fate of neighbors and acquaintances. The Gestapo did everything they could to dispel any rumors that were emerging regarding each train's terminus.

Rose, Else and Fanni would mark the first anniversary of their residence at the "Israelite Home for the Elderly" on March 24, 1942. At the time of their arrival in 1941, they still maintained some semblance of faith that some event would occur to deliver them from the confined existence that had been forced upon them and that, in one way or another, they would be reunited with their family. Hope is a crucial part of dealing with life's problems and retaining resilience in the face of obstacles. Even a glimmer of faith that our situation will turn around can keep us going and gives us something to live for. During that year, massive obstacles were presented, preventing my family from feeling in control of their lives. A few of their acquaintances in the various "Jewish Houses" had lost all hope and decided that suicide was the best solution. Albert and Rose were good friends and contemporaries of Professor Paul Maas and his wife Ida from Aachen. He had been a successful ear, nose, and throat medical specialist. The Maas couple were brought to the *Israelitisches Altenheim* in May of 1941 and saw Rose, Else, and Fanni daily, often sharing meals together. Paul and Ida Maas poisoned themselves two days prior to their planned deportation.

Rose's spirit enabled her to maintain hope by setting very simple and achievable goals. She and Else cared for their mother to the best of their ability, fed themselves within the constraints of inadequate supply and tried to keep warm, sharing meals and conversation. Reaching those minimal goals provided the self-validation that instills hope. When they lay down to sleep, they could say to each other and to themselves that they had gotten through another day. Most importantly, they had each other to share stories of the better times of the past.

A few of those to be deported from the *Altenheim* had been residents of the old age home for greater than a year because of disabilities or infirmities, but most had arrived there in 1941, forcibly displaced from their Aachen homes in a fashion similar to that of my family. There were the Fritzler sisters, Julie and Betty, originally from Arnsberg, who were about Albert's age and had known the Oppenheims socially for many years when they lived in Velmede. The others were mostly widows and widowers, with a few in their forties but most ranging in age from their late fifties to mid-seventies. My great-grandmother Fanni, at 87 years, was by far the oldest of those selected for expulsion.

My family and the others chosen were told that they would be "resettled" to a labor camp in the Lublin area of Poland, where they would receive more spacious accommodations, be adequately fed, and employed doing tasks suited to their age and skills. Since they would be living among fellow Jews, they would also be safe. The Nazi death machine depended on deception. The Jews needed to believe that they would be treated well upon their arrival at their destination. Otherwise, they would resist. The entire apparatus of death rested on the calm, orderly transfer of the Jews of Europe to the death camps. The Nazis disguised their "Final Solution" as the mass *Umsiedlung nach (dem) Osten* ("resettlement to the east.)"

Rose had become a good friend of Grete Berger, the head nurse and administrator in charge of the *Altenheim*. Margarethe Berger née Löwenstein was one of two twin sisters born in Lichtenau, Germany, near the French border, in 1893. Ms. Berger had been interacting and negotiating with the local Gestapo since 1939, either directly or through Jewish leadership intermediaries, on behalf of the welfare of her residents. After discussing the matter at length with Rose and Else, Grete went to the *Geheime Staatspolizei* (Gestapo) office at 14 *Theaterplatz* in Aachen and spoke there with an official whom she knew. She tried to convince him that my great-grandmother should not be deported on Train 17. She argued that Fanni was very elderly and unable to walk and that her inclusion in the transport would seriously impede the efficiency of the entire operation. A few days later, Rose learned that her mother had been removed from the list and would remain at 87 *Horst Wessel Straße* at least temporarily.

Gestapo headquarters, 14 Theaterplatz, Aachen, where Grete Berger arranged for my great grandmother to avoid deportation.

Shortly thereafter, Rose, Else, and the other future deportees were provided with detailed instructions regarding their personal preparation for the journey. The operational specifics of the arrangements had been laid out in a top-secret document which only came to light at the 1960 trial of Adolf Eichmann, charged with crimes against humanity, crimes against the Jewish people and membership in a criminal organization. *SS Obersturmbahnführer* Adolf Eichmann fled to Argentina at the end of World War II and was kidnapped by Israeli agents in 1960 and brought to Jerusalem to stand trial.

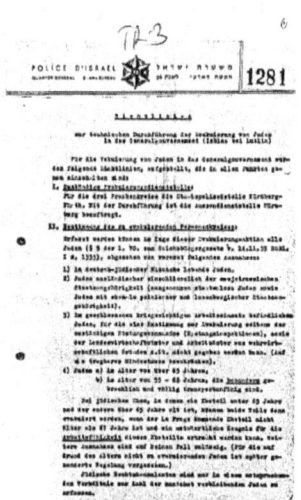

Page 1 of official document entitled "Guidelines on techniques for carrying out the evacuation of Jews to the general government (Izbica near Lublin)," as presented at the trial of Adolf Eichmann, 1960.

Rose and Else were told that they each could take only a small suitcase or backpack bearing their names. According to the directive, they were instructed to pack two weeks' worth of provisions consisting of "bread, cabbage, grapes and sweets," together with a plate or pot and a spoon. They should bring a "full set" of clothing and "ordinary" shoes. Only hand luggage was permitted, which should be light enough for the owner to carry comfortably when walking for long distances without assistance. It should bear a firmly affixed, clearly written tag with the owner's name, birthday and place, residence, and identification card number. They were prohibited from bringing any German or foreign currency, gold, silver, or platinum with the exception of a wedding ring. All of these items together with securities, other valuables, or ration cards were proscribed to be turned over to the Nazis prior to deportation. The carrying of any weapons, explosives, rocks, or poison was *"verboten"* (forbidden).

The rules for the handling of Jewish property belonging to those people on this transport were more complicated than for previous ones. The new "guidelines" stated that every item expropriated now had to be classified by the deportee's specific category of "dispossession." Therefore, a list of ninety-two "Jews who recently held former Polish citizenship or stateless Jews who also did not hold German citizenship before 1933" was prepared for this transport. The names of three Jews from Krefeld who had committed suicide shortly before the transport were also added to the list. Rose and Else were among the vast majority in the group who had been German citizens "before" 1933.

Each deportee had to pay a transportation charge of 60 *Reichsmarks* per person for their "resettlement to work in the East." This was collected before the trip by the Aachen Jewish community and then turned over to the Gestapo, which forwarded part of this money to the German Transport Authority to pay the German Railways for transport of the Jews. Children under 12 years of age paid half price, and those under four went free. The receipts taken in by the state-owned *Deutsche Reichsbahn* for mass deportations in the period between 1938 and 1945 reached a sum of more than 650 million US dollars.

On March 17, a specific train was designated to carry the deportees on "Da 17" from Koblenz to Poland five days later. That particular train would be in arriving in Koblenz after bringing in Russian slave laborers to various locations in Westphalia from Brest-Litovsk, a city in present-day Belarus, which had been the location of the March 1918 peace treaty between Russia and the Central Powers, thereby ending Russia's participation in World War I.

The entire operation of that train was under the direction of 32-year-old Hermann Waldbillig, a member of the Gestapo's *Judenreferat* (Jewish Department) of the Reich Security Main Office (RSHA) in Düsseldorf. It was his responsibility to transport the selected Jews from the area on the list to the train and then to ensure an orderly transit to Izbica, where he would complete their financial plundering.

According to the plan drawn up by Waldbillig for the transport of the Jews in preparation for departure to the *Ostland*, the deportees from Aachen and nearby towns were to be delivered to the city of Koblenz one day earlier, on March 21, 1942, in designated passenger cars coupled to a regular passenger train. Two Gestapo staff members were posted to each of these trains as guards.

On March 21, 1942, the Gestapo converted the deportees' money into *Reichskreditkassenscheine* (Reich treasury notes) at a branch of the *Reichsbank* (German central bank). The total sum of approximately 50,000 *Reichmarks*, having been collected from the approximately 1,000 men, women and children scheduled for Train 17, was presented to the commander of the transport, a member of the *Schutzpolizei* (security police), before departure. When the transport reached Izbica, the commander transferred the money to the officials in charge there. When Rose and Else obediently paid for their "tickets," they did not know that they were about to embark on a "transport to extinction."

As stated in a report which the Gestapo-Düsseldorf sent to the RSHA on March 29, 1942, four days after Train *Da 17* arrived in Izbica, the transport comprised 387 Jewish men and 554 Jewish women and includes data on each deportee's' place of birth, birthdate, sex, *familienstand* (marital/personal status), *konfession* (religious denomination) and *beruf* (occupation or profession). My grandmother Rose is listed as *verwitwet* (widowed) and my great-aunt Else is recorded as *ledig* (single). Their religion is documented as *Israelitische*, as was everyone else on the train. They have no occupation registered, identical with the vast majority of the women accompanying them on that train.

During the brief time that Rose and Else were informed of their deportation date until their leaving 87 *Horst Wessel Straße* on March 21, 1942, both of them had to cope with intense emotions. Thankfully they knew that they would remain together on their journey to the unknown and could commiserate with each other during the seemingly endless waiting period and beyond. The other residents of the *Altersheim* who were to accompany them on *Zug Da 17* had similar feelings of fear and frustration regarding their destination and many hours were spent in individual and group discussions considering what was in store for them. Many had heard stories or read reports and were all too willing to unburden themselves by relating these to others.

What distinguished Rose and Else's situation from the others was the imminence of leaving their beloved mother behind. That reality engendered reactive sadness, anger, frustration, grief, and guilt, usually comingled in moment-to-moment variations and intensity. Although they were sisters who had lived together all of their lives, they were unique individuals with different psychological patterns and emotional reserves. The above feelings affected each of them collectively, yet at different times of the day or night, depending on their mood pattern, the assortment of sensations experienced by Rose and Else was often quite distinctive.

I cannot be certain of what exactly Rose and Else explained to Fanni regarding what was about to occur. I am confident that they did not just disappear on the appointed day. Most likely, they gently and repeatedly told her that they were obligated to go on a trip and she, given her physical condition, would not be able to accompany them. They emphasized that Fanni would be far more comfortable remaining in familiar surroundings, well taken care of by both Grete Berger and the many friends they had made in their year at the Jewish house. Rose and Else promised that they would be back as soon as possible and would frequently write to their mother.

Although Rose and Else could not change Fanni's circumstances, speaking about it with her relieved some of their stress and allowed them to sense that they were at least somewhat in control and found it possible to accept their emotional lability as normal, given the state of affairs.

They had heard from residents of the *Judenhaus* at 249 *Eupenerstraße* that the Gestapo would come for the residents to be deported on the March train one day prior to its scheduled departure from Koblenz. Rose was not at all surprised when they were told on March 20th that they would be leaving very early in the morning on the following day, Saturday, March 21st.

After a sleepless last night at the *Altersheim*, Rose and Else got out of bed shortly before dawn to put food and water into their small suitcases, previously carefully packed with personal items, clothing and a few small pieces of jewelry placed into the clothing pockets. The March climate in Aachen is relatively cold with centigrade temperatures ranging from lows of 3 degrees to highs of 10 degrees, with occasional light snowfall. Although springtime was imminent, they had planned to wear their coats over multiple layers of clothing in order to be prepared for colder weather at their yet unknown destination. The suitcases needed to be manageable, and they did not wish to make them too heavy to carry. They had no appetite for breakfast.

Two motorized vans, each driven by a member of the RSHA's *Sicherheitspolizei* (*SiPo*, security police) arrived at 87 *Horst Wessel Straße* shortly before eight in the morning to transport the 22 chosen deportees to the Aachen *Hauptbahnhof*. Rose and Else had resolved to be able to contain their tears as they hugged and kissed their mother goodbye; there would be ample time to cry later in their journey. Wooden steps had been taken out of the trucks to allow them to climb into the back of the trucks, where they told to sit on two wooden benches, one on each side of the vehicle. They had never ridden in a windowless van before, but the presence of their friends made the experience more tolerable. It took them only twenty minutes to reach the train station familiar to all, twenty minutes where the passengers remained predominantly silent, each one wrapped in thought regarding their impending voyage and unknown fate. The vans stopped at a side entrance of the train station, the back door was opened, light streamed in again, and the steps, housed in the van with them, were placed by the drivers for them to walk onto the pavement, all carrying their suitcases. To any passerby, the scenario seemed rather ordinary, except perhaps that the group members each had only one suitcase, moved slowly and were wearing winter coats. There was no additional security—the *Sicherheitspolizei* knew that this was an elderly collection of people who knew each other, hardly a group whose members were likely to create a ruckus or try a getaway. In other locations, with larger groups containing younger people, the RSHA employed additional armed guards prepared to shoot anyone attempting to escape.

Rose and Else had been at the Aachen *Hauptbahnhof* many times during the previous five years, but never before entered through a side door that needed to be unlocked by a *SiPo* guard. Rose, in a whisper, asked her younger sister if she recalled a visit to the Aachen train station at its previous location outside the city walls. They had come with their parents and two brothers on a summer holiday to Belgium. Rose remembered that Paul was not with them on that trip—either he had not yet been born or they had left him as a baby with their grandparents Abraham and Rosette in Bücken. Likely Else was too young to recollect that trip. Fanni was then likely fifteen years younger than Rose and Else were now, still in her late thirties and vigorous. Their lives seemed to have flown by and for a brief moment Rose thought of happier times. She could not hear Else's reply because of the noise within the main hall.

The travelers were led to the last train platform, where there were already some people from the *Eupenerstraße* Jewish house, most of whom Rose and Else knew. They were told that the train was scheduled to depart at 2:46 p.m. with arrival in Koblenz at 5:17 p.m. During the five-hour wait, Rose and Else took turns walking briskly up and down the platform while the other watched their belongings. Shortly after 2 p.m., a rather ordinary third-class passenger train pulled slowly into the station adjacent to their ramp. The uniformed police told my grandmother's contingent to get into the empty last car of three, sit down and wait. Rose and Else entered and took a seat next to one another with their suitcases at their feet. The doors were closed by the two guards and after some discussion, one official sat in front and the other in the back of the car. After ten minutes the sisters felt too warm and both stood up, took off their coats and then sat with them on their laps. By this time, the group had, to some extent, regained their composure and were again eager to speak with each other. They noticed a few people on the platform unaccompanied by any police entering the two railroad coaches in front of them. There were businessmen carrying briefcases, workmen with tools in sacks or attached to their belts and women carrying groceries or holding a child's hand. The day had grown unseasonably warm and most of these people were not wearing their warmest coats. The chatter in Rose's car was hopeful, the seats were comfortable, there was heat on the train and this appeared to be an ordinary train also carrying everyday travelers to Koblenz. Not at all the horror stories that they had heard and worried about.

A few minutes later, Rose heard the rumble of the engine in front, a horn was sounded, and the train began to move slowly out of the station. The afternoon sun streamed through the windows into the carriage. Hearing the familiar "clickety-clack" sound as the train wheels rolled over the rail joints, her mind wandered to thoughts of trains that she had taken from the Bestwig station near Velmede with her husband or her children.

Following the train's departure from Aachen, the occupants were deleted from that city's population registry with the date indicated as March 25, 1942, which was the day they were to reach their final destination. The occupants of the train were registered as "Transport III" after their arrival in Izbica. In the "Housekeeping Book" of the Israelite (Jewish) Asylum Association, where they had lived for almost a year, Rose's name was deleted on April 1, 1942, and Else's was removed on April 3, 1942.

The train ride took almost three hours, stopping briefly in *Köln* (Cologne) to allow passengers in the first two cars to exit and to gather regular passengers and passing through Bonn without stopping. Rose knew they were going quite slowly for the 160 kilometers from Aachen to Koblenz, perhaps to save the fuel that was scarce in wartime. She had made this trip between the cities before, and it had never seemed as long.

Koblenz Hauptbahnof,
where Rose and Else's train
from Aachen arrived.

As the train pulled into the Koblenz *Hauptbahnof* (main train station,) the police guard in the front told everyone to stay seated until the other two train cars emptied their passengers. Approximately ten minutes later, the engine was turned off and the officer told everyone to gather their possessions, follow him outside, and be prepared for a long walk. Rose and Else combed their hair, put their coats on, grasped their suitcases, and exited the train.

The group left the station through its western doors onto *Karthäuserstraße*, a street named after the charterhouse (monastery) built there in the 14th century by the Roman Catholic Order of the Carthusians. The motto of the Carthusians is *Stat crux dum volvitur orbis* (the cross stands firm while the globe continues to turn). The Catholic Church indeed remained inflexible as millions of Jews were being murdered in the Holocaust. Pope Pius XII, its leader during World War II, placed the papacy's supremacy above the plight of Europe's Jews, and was called "Hitler's Pope" because of his refusal to publicly condemn the Nazis. The Vatican dismissed reports of mass killings, saying "we don't believe we have information that confirms this serious news in detail" and Jews "easily exaggerate."

They walked north parallel to the railroad tracks and Rose could see to her right in the distance, the hill topped by the *Festung Ehrenbreitstein* (Ehrenbreitstein Fortress), which was first described in a 12th century written document. It was getting dark.

Ehrenbreitstein Hill with its fortress as seen by Rose across the Rhine River on March 21ˢᵗ, 1942.

Within the first few hundred yards, the assemblage had rapidly changed from a bunched crowd to a long single-file column, with the older and frailer members falling quickly behind, despite encouragement from the officer at the rear. Rose and Else were at the front of the troop and were walking with Alfred Seelman who, at 46, was the youngest of the people from *Horst Wessel Straße*. Some could no longer carry their suitcases and had to drag them, slowing them down even more. Rose and Else were still physically relatively strong, having until recently been taking long walks together until the edict forcing them to wear a Jewish star on their clothing made this no longer viable. Now, of course, shopkeepers and passersby could discern that these were Jews being deported, not only from the yellow star that all displayed on their coats, but also from their suitcases and despondent expressions. This was a familiar scene to residents of this area of Koblenz. They knew that this miserable pack was walking towards *Blücherstraße*, where they would spend the night before being sent to the *Ostland*. They had already seen two larger, but similar, groups pass by earlier that day.

Rose was grateful that she and Else had each brought a smaller suitcase and that they had packed efficiently. As they watched their friends falling further behind, they were thankful that Fanni had been left in Aachen. There was no way their mother would have been able to navigate this walk, which already was approaching one kilometer in length. In the past few weeks, it had been an ordeal to merely help her get down the stairs to the dining room for meals and they often had brought her breakfast or midday meal up to the room.

They turned left, away from the Rhine River, onto *Bogenstraße* and then merging into *Hoevelstraße*, skirting Koblenz's *Altstadt* (old town). My grandfather had often travelled to Koblenz on business to purchase fabrics and Rose recalled visiting that part of Koblenz with Albert on one of these trips. She had been captivated by the area's picturesque winding narrow streets with their variety of charming squares, restaurants, and cafés. Everything now appeared tired and grey, and the half-timbered architecture was oppressive in its heaviness. They turned north on *Merlstraße* and entered the *Moselweiß* district, a part of Koblenz since 1340, and crossed *Schwerzstraße* ("heavy" street), which had intermittently housed Jews for centuries. Jews had been banned from Koblenz in medieval times until, in 1512, a doctrine allowed five Jewish families to return. The synagogue, built in 1702, was destroyed on *Kristallnacht* and the adjacent Jewish cemetery, consecrated in 1203, had been vandalized many times in the centuries since then.

The *SiPo* official in the rear had grown tired of answering *"bald"* (soon) in response to the recurrent questioning of when they would arrive at their destination. On her right, Rose caught glimpses of the Moselle

River near the promontory where it flows into the Rhine at the *Deutsches Eck* (German Corner). She raised her free arm and pointed her finger, telling Else that she had stood there, on at least one trip with Albert, at the base of the monumental equestrian statue depicting *Wilhelm I* (William), the first German Emperor, who had unified Germany in 1871.

A Nazi rally at the Koblenz statue of Emperor Wilhelm I

A few hundred yards later they crossed the intersection of *Steinstraße*. The guard just in front of her said "we are going there," pointing to a large building on the right. They turned right onto *Blücherstrasse* and soon were facing the back entrance of the *Freiherr-vom-Stein Grundschule* (primary school) in the *Rauental* district of Koblenz. They had walked more than two kilometers in about ninety minutes.

The school was named after a Prussian statesman, Heinrich Friedrich Karl Reichsfreiher vom und zum Stein, who had been exiled from Germany because of his anti-Napoleonic opinions, He then briefly was an advisor to the Russian Czar Alexander I before returning to Westphalia to centralize the teaching of medieval studies and hold various governmental administrative roles promoting aristocratic special interests.

Today the structure was being used as a collection point to intern approximately 1,000 Westphalian Jews for one to three nights prior to transporting them to Izbica. My grandmother and her sister stood there in the waning light of dusk while they waited for about 30 minutes until the last of the 22 exhausted residents of the *Israelitisches Altenheim* arrived at the school. The group then entered a small hallway and were ordered into a large open space which served as the gymnasium for the school. It was packed with hundreds of people, some milling about and others sitting on the stone floor, partially covered with straw. This was a major task – not only the planning and organization of the deportation, but also its practical implementation. Probably all the *SS* men of the Koblenz Gestapo plus local police and detectives were on duty. The stone schoolhouse also had to be cordoned off, and this large group of people there had to be guarded.

Rose and Else were led to a "registration" area where two Gestapo officials were sitting behind a long table. It was dark outside by the time they were registered, and their names were recorded by Hermann Waldbillig, representing the "Jewish Department" of the Gestapo-Düsseldorf. Rose and Else were interrogated, then filled out and signed various forms. Rose noted that although the space was full of deportees, everything done was performed in a very orderly manner.

They were then led to another area of the gymnasium where their luggage was examined and anything suspicious or disallowed was removed. The Gestapo had requested the judge responsible for the municipality to provide two bailiffs to be in control of seizure of the property of the Jews staying at the collection point. My family had a few pieces of jewelry remaining from those not previously sold to pay for food. They were required to hand over these valuables and the small amount of currency they had in their possession and were forced to sign a declaration detailing these various assets and legally authorizing the transfer of their property. This was the Nazi "settlement of property matters."

A few Gestapo personnel under Waldbillig's command searched the men. Body searches of the women were performed by two female members of the *Kripo* (criminal police) and a few female employees of the Gestapo. Although there was no privacy, Rose and Else were asked to undress completely for this procedure. Any further valuables found were confiscated. The belongings of the deportees were given to organizations such as the "National Socialist People's Welfare" or the "German Red Cross," which passed them on to bomb-damaged families and to soldiers at the front. Anything remaining was auctioned off publicly, with exact records kept of which items were acquired by whom and for how much money. Even amounts as low as ten *pfennigs* for a plate with a spoon were listed. Documents record an "extraordinarily high" demand from the German population for looted property, including property that had just been confiscated. The successful bidders were well aware of the origin of the auctioned goods and wanted to profit from the expulsion of the Jews. The auction proceeds were transferred to the government coffers.

By the time they got dressed again, they noticed their friends were no longer congregated with them. Rose's group had been among the last to arrive at the gymnasium and it was 10 p.m. by the time they were ready to find a spot to spend the night on the hard floor. They quickly ate some of the cold food they had taken with them and began to walk around the area. The 337 Jews of Koblenz had arrived one or two days earlier and had appropriated most of the straw for themselves to make sleeping more comfortable. Else was finally able to find some space for two more people and they put down their coats on which to lie down. It was good to have some respite from having to listen to ever-changing unverified information of uncertain origin. They had quickly tired of hearing the incessant chatter about where they were going next. It was good to be able to have a private conversation and quietly voice their common concern regarding their mother's situation and condition. Although they had seen her just this morning, it seemed that a significant amount of time had already transpired since leaving Fanni.

The gymnasium had three walls of windows and a handful of incandescent light bulbs hung from the high cement ceiling over wooden rafters, casting shadows throughout the large space. There were latrines in two corners of the area. Those sanitary facilities were primitive and became more unsanitary as the evening progressed. The stench coming from there, together with the smells of elderly people who had been unable to wash off their anxious sweat for at least one day, assaulted Rose's nostrils. It was an odor which would get more offensive during the night, one which was impossible to erase from one's consciousness.

For Rose and Else and many other deportees in the gymnasium, it was a long, largely sleepless night. Everyone had brought food with them although appetites were shrunk by apprehension, and, thankfully, there was access to water to drink, water that was presumed to be potable. During the hours of darkness outdoors, the bright lights remained on, illuminating the many scattered groups occupying the vast space. Although the chamber was remarkably quiet at times with most of the occupants too weary and disoriented to engage in conversation, there was the intermittent noise of crying children or shouting adults, made worse by the common enduring distress of its dwellers.

There is no contemporaneous information as to the environment in that hall during that specific night. Any written communications of significance from those imprisoned there would have failed to pass through the censors' hands without being altered, if not destroyed. The sender would also have been punished and likely shot. According to accounts of the grim conditions that typified similar transports, however, one may surmise that the situation was very bad, particularly given the large number of deportees. Later testimonies from survivors of this space recall the surroundings: "The hall is naked, damp dirty and contains an unbearable stench." A survivor of a different Koblenz transport testified at the Eichmann trial that there were many wet areas on the floor, and it was impossible to lie down and sleep during the night. I would hope that conditions on the night of March 21st were not as extreme.

Morning finally arrived. A new shift of Gestapo and *Kripo*, accompanied by leashed German shepherd dogs, arrived at 6 a.m. to relieve the officials who had spent the nights sitting in chairs watching the entire group while smoking, drinking, and chatting. Rose and Else were already awake, having been unable to find a comfortable position on the cold stone floor to sleep, when an announcement was made that they should gather their possessions and be prepared to leave the gymnasium at seven o'clock. Promptly at that time, the 963 men, women and children were told to form a procession and were escorted out of the building back onto *Blücherstrasse*.

During late 1941 and 1942, more than 100,000 Jewish men, women and children from Germany had to gather in comparable halls prior to boarding transports originating in various cities. They were similarly registered, searched, and robbed, forced to spend the night in similar primitive conditions, full of uncertainty about what was to come. The next morning, they were deported to ghettos in occupied Eastern Europe including Łódź, Minsk, Riga, Izbica and Theresienstadt. The ghettos were only waystations on the way to camps of mass murder. Rather than being "evacuated" and "resettled" for "work assignments," death awaited the vast majority of those deported to ghettos. Few survived the Shoah. In fact, after mid-1942, many trains went from Germany directly to Auschwitz or other death camps.

On Sunday, March 22nd, the entire entourage took their belongings and were marched under guard north across the Moselle River to the freight yard of the Koblenz-Lützel train station, much smaller than the city's *Hauptbahnof,* where they had disembarked the day before. This station was built in 1860 within the fortifications of the Kaiser Franz fortress, under the direction of William I when he was still King of Prussia prior to becoming Emperor. The station, located in the Koblenz suburb of *Lützel*, included a passenger station, a freight station, and a freight repair yard. The repair yard was an ideal spot to load deportees onto trains on a large scale well out of view of the public.

They crossed over the Moselle River on the *Balduinbrücke* (Baldwin Bridge), a stone arch structure built in the 14th century by Archbishop Baldwin of Luxembourg. Rose and Else exited the bridge and could now see their destination. Although they had walked less than a kilometer, the march seemed more arduous than that of the day before. Some of the older participants again fell behind and were repeatedly pushed ahead by the police guards. A few members partially emptied or even abandoned their suitcases in an effort to keep up with the group.

That morning, March 22, 1942, multiple identical cables were sent by the Jewish-Affairs Department of Gestapo-Düsseldorf. The recipients included the RSHA, the area commander of the *Sipo* (Sicherheitspolizei, Security Police), the SD (*Sicherheitsdienst*, Security Service) in Kraków, and the Police and SS leader in the Lublin District, which was the train's destination. The telegrams reported that the transport was being commanded by a longtime Sturmabteilung (SA) *Standartenführer* named Herbert Gehrke, and that the area commander of Sipo and the SD in Kraków, Poland, SS-*Oberführer* Karl Eberhard Schöngarth, was required to place someone in charge of receiving the Jews when they arrived at their destination in Poland. The telegrams also stated that three Jews had taken their lives during the night at the gymnasium and that five others had somehow managed to elude the transport and were classified as either "escapees" or "absentees." There is no way of knowing whether Rose and Else were aware of this.

An *Einsatzgruppe* led by Schöngarth had already murdered more than 5,000 Jews from the Brześć Ghetto in Poland in July 1941, and Schöngarth was also responsible for the killings of approximately 10,000 additional Polish Jews in the ensuing two months. He had attended the Wannsee Conference in January 1942. By his own admission, he ordered mass executions in the Netherlands. In 1944, an American pilot, Americo Galle, was captured alive after his plane crashed behind enemy lines in Holland. Schöngarth issued an order to kill Galle and for this after the war, he was tried by a British military court in *Nordrhein-Westphalia*. The prosecution never mentioned Schöngarth's colossal crimes in Poland and Holland. He was found guilty only of killing the airman and sentenced to death for that crime. He was hanged in 1946 by professional executioner Albert Pierrepoint, who was descended from a long line of similarly trained specialists.

Everyone was on the loading platform by 8:30 in the morning, three hours and five minutes before the train was scheduled to depart. They were randomly divided into clusters of about fifty people and Rose made certain that her sister was in her group just as others tried to avoid separation from their families. She correctly surmised that each group would occupy one car of the train. One male in each unit was seemingly randomly designated as a steward and given an armband to identify him as such. It would be his duty to ensure quiet and order during the journey. Rose commented to Else that their *Horst Wessel Strasse* housemates looked far more tired and disheveled than they had when they left the Aachen railroad station less than 24 hours earlier. Clothing had been slept on and folded into pillows. The SS and security police had confiscated all jewelry and watches. Standing, waiting for the train to arrive to transport them to Poland, the people around them were mostly strangers, since the band from the Aachen *Altersheim* had rapidly become dispersed among the large contingent. Even though they saw few familiar faces, the countenances of those around them were similar, expressing frustration, loss, and fear. What they had in common was their immediate fate and the Jewish star that had been sewn onto their outerwear.

Just before eleven in the morning, Rose heard the rumbling of a train engine and a few minutes later she saw the train slowly backing onto the tracks leading to the end of the loading platform of the freight yard. Although the events of the past day had been unique, she was not prepared for what she now saw—a large number of boxcars pulled by a locomotive. There was a single passenger car in the middle of the boxcars. Rose and Else spoke to each other simultaneously. Similar conversations could be heard emanating from the other parties of people. They would be travelling to Poland in these boxcars, not in passenger carriages.

The special train *Da 17* was now awaiting its passengers, at least 950 Jewish people to be placed in twenty boxcars leaving Koblenz for Izbica on March 22, 1942. 96 of those individuals had the identical address, 49 *Hindenburgstraße* in Bendorf-Sayn, a suburb of Koblenz. The *Israelitische Heil und Pflegeanstalt der Reichsvereinigung der Juden* (Jewish clinic and mental institution) was located there. This had originally been established as a Jewish Hospital in 1870, referred to as the *Jacoby'sche Anstalt* (Jacoby Institute). In 1940 the German Reich Ministry of Internal Affairs decided that "Jews and Germans" were no longer to be accommodated in the same place and ordered that all Jewish patients at "clinics and mental institutions" of the German Reich should be collected and put together at Bendorf-Sayn, which became a transit camp for mentally ill Jewish patients. Only Jewish doctors and nurses were hired to administer and care for their strictly Jewish patients. There were far too many patients at this "insane asylum" and conditions were terrible with lack of adequate food and medicine.

Windowless box car of the type used to transport Rose and Else from Koblenz, Germany, to Izbica, Poland, March 22-24, 1942.

Rose, Else, and the others were told that the boxcars were not very large, and their luggage would be placed in a separate car. They were instructed to remove their food and carry only that onto the train. Luggage was placed in the two rear cars, which were uncoupled before the rest of the train left the railyard. My family would not see their luggage again. Some of it remained in Koblenz and was stored both in the mortuary at the Jewish cemetery and in the Gestapo building at *1 Straße am Vogelsang*. Koblenz residents appropriated whatever they liked from the mortuary in the days that followed, and in the evenings items that had been taken were sold in the bars of the Old Town.

The transport was compiled of Jews of both sexes of various ages – from babies to 70-year-olds. In the middle of the convoy of cattle cars was a passenger car housing military police, Gestapo, and their dogs. These men were supplied with two blankets, cooking utensils and field stoves, warm clothing, furs, and warm boots, together with pistols and sufficient ammunition. They had orders to shoot anyone who tried to escape. Searchlights were available if any escape was attempted after dark. The Gestapo instructed the Reichsbahn to place the car for the guard detachment at the center of the train. This was essential for the supervision of the transport.

The train *Da 17* travelled eastwards through Cologne, Düsseldorf, and other cities throughout the Ruhr Valley without stopping. The three-day journey then continued, entering the province of Lower Saxony, moving through Northeim, Nordhausen in Thuringia, Halle (Saale) in Saxony-Anhalt, and to Cottbus, into the province of Brandenburg and Sagan, before crossing into Lissa, Poland, formerly a portion of Prussia ceded by the Germans to Poland by the Treaty of Versailles, and now, of course, part of the "General Gouvernment," the area occupied by the Germans since 1939. The train then passed through Ostrowo, Widzwe, Skarzysko, Kamienna, Rdom, Deblin and Lublin to finally reach Izbica in the Lublin district.

Zug Da 17
Koblenz To Izbica

Rose's train travelled a distance of 1300 kilometers. This would ordinarily take approximately 24 hours. However, much of this train route had only a single rail track and since these human transports, called *Sonderzüge* (special trains), were of low priority related to the actual German war effort, the voyage was often held up for long periods of time while the transport waited on an adjacent railroad spur for as long as it took for more important train traffic to pass.

The freight cars (*Güterwagen*) were designed to carry either livestock or covered goods, not human beings. At times these boxcars were each packed with up to 150 deportees, although 50 was the number proposed by the *SS* regulations. Rose and Else were fortunate that *Zug Da 17* had an average of "only" 45 occupants per *Güterwagen.* Later in 1942, during the mass deportation of Jews from the Warsaw Ghetto to the extermination camp in Treblinka, trains carried up to 7,000 victims each, distributed among less than 80 boxcars.

Each car measured about 10 meters in length, was unheated and lacked sanitary facilities, being outfitted with only a bucket latrine. A small, barred window provided irregular ventilation, which often resulted in multiple deaths from either suffocation or exposure to the elements. In 1944, a train carrying residents from Corfu left Athens and arrived in Auschwitz 18 days later. When the doors were opened, everyone was already dead. Between 1941 and December 1944, the official date of the closing of the Auschwitz-Birkenau complex, an average of 1.5 trains per day arrived at that destination. The number of freight cars of each transport averaged 50 with an occupancy of at least 50 innocent civilian prisoners per car. Week after week after week, more than 25,000 souls appeared there for the final day of their life.

Rose and Else entered the windowless unheated cattle wagon as directed and immediately felt the singular crippling dread that they would constantly experience within the next three days. The only belief that separated them from sheer terror was the trust in the Nazi promise that they would be treated well upon their arrival. They were given no nourishment since the armed guards were forbidden to supply any food to the Jews.

The train would periodically stop to allow them, under the watch of guards, to hurriedly fill their long-empty water bottles from a pump adjacent to the railroad. The latrine would be emptied along the side of the tracks. I have no direct knowledge from my grandmother regarding the circumstances on that three-day journey. I am certain that the environment was miserable, and the suffering was intense. An occupant of a similar boxcar wrote "The wagon shunted backwards and forwards for ages, adding to our sense of insecurity ... people screamed, and children and the sick cried constantly." Before this, the series of events impacting my family during these last years had been incrementally worsening, allowing the unbelievable to become

315

the believable and, ultimately, the normal. Yet what was now happening could never be considered ordinary or customary by the victims, although, for the perpetrators, it was habitual.

Many similar cattle cars were so packed with deportees that it was usually impossible to sit or kneel down. Comparable railway wagons had signs on the door stating that they were designed to transport "eighteen horses." Rose and Else were in a wagon that had less than fifty people, allowing them places to sit and even lie down in the inhumane conditions. It was also fortuitous that they were travelling in March and did not have to endure the intense heat of summer or subzero temperatures during the winter, both of which could prove lethal by dehydration, heat stroke or freezing. The necessity to relieve themselves inside the railcar without proper toilets was a nadir of humiliation. The absence of ventilation together with the stench of body fluids, vomitus and spoiled food added to the prisoners' mortification and suffering. The incessant loud noise generated by the boxcar's wheels encountering structurally necessary gaps in the tracks accompanied by whistling of the engine, grinding, squealing, and vibration of the cars themselves, combined with the cacophony of crying, loud talk, and screaming by the train's occupants, added to both the inability to rest and sleep and the degradation of mental health.

Jan Karski was a Catholic member of the Polish resistance and, beginning in 1940, he reported to the Polish government in exile and the United States and British authorities on the situation in Poland both regarding the destruction of the Warsaw Ghetto and the Nazi extermination of Polish Jews. At war's end, Karski remained in the United States and began graduate studies at Georgetown University, receiving his Ph.D. in 1952. In 1954, he became a naturalized citizen of the United States and taught Eastern European affairs, comparative government, and international affairs at Georgetown University for 40 years. In his book, *"Story of a Secret State,"* published in 1944, Karski vividly describes the process of filling of freight cars with human beings, with German policemen shouting and "the SS man bellowing like a madman, 'Ordnung, Ordnung!' ('Order, order!') ...while "the two policemen echoed him hoarsely."

Undoubtedly Rose and Else experienced the bellowing *"Ordnung, Ordnung!"* on numerous occasions both on this journey and at additional times at their destination. The Germans had been trained to treat the Jews as sheep, herding them into the trains by whatever means possible and then maintaining order during the transport however necessary, swinging and firing their rifles, either into the air or into the bodies of their prisoners. The word "order" immediately brings to mind a sense of peace and harmony. In this case, it was a threatening command uttered by a member of the dominant "master race," an expression of power which could not be disobeyed and, if doubted in any way, would be met with ruthless consequences. It was all part of a plan and design, to which all Nazis were fanatically committed, to annihilate all Jewish people. As stated in the opening remarks of the prosecutor at the Nuremberg trials, "These crimes were organized and promoted by the Party leadership, executed and protected by the Nazi officials, and outlined by written orders of the Secret State Police itself."

The Nazis considered every Jew a "mortal threat *(tödliche bedrohung)*" to the German "race." The residents of the "Jewish Houses" at 87 *Horst Wessel Straße* or 249 *Eupenerstraße* deported from Aachen/Koblenz on train #17 were friends or acquaintances of Rose and Else. None survived the Holocaust. These are some of those "mortal threats:"

Bernhard Arensberg, his wife Paula and their 17-year-old son Kurt were on that train to Izbica. Less than two months later, Bernhard, age 44, and his son were transported from Izbica to the nearby extermination camp, *Konzentrationslager Lublin*, nicknamed Majdanek ("little Majdan") by local residents, as it was adjacent to the Lublin Jewish ghetto of *Majdan Tatarski*. Bernhard was murdered there in one of the seven gas chambers on September 24, 1942, during the first month after they became operational. The gassing was performed in plain view of other inmates, without as much as a fence around the buildings. His son either met the same fate or succumbed to one of many mass shootings by the *Trawnikis*. the central and eastern European Nazi collaborators who took a major part in Operation Reinhard. Called *Trawnikimänner* because they were men who had been trained at a special camp at Trawniki outside of Lublin, they belonged to a category of *Hiwis*, the German abbreviation for *Hilfswilliger*, literally "those willing to help." German Order Police performed roundups or mass arrests inside the Jewish ghettos in German-occupied Poland, shooting everyone unable to move or attempting to flee, while the *Trawnikis* conducted large-scale civilian massacres in the same locations. Paula (Wolf) Arensberg apparently died in Izbica.

Josef and Julie (Mann) Herz were distant relatives of my family by marriage and were on *Da 17* with their 31-year-old daughter Betty. Although they survived for less than six months after their arrival in Poland, they were comforted by the "knowledge" that their two sons, Hans and Paul, had escaped a similar fate. Hans Jakob Herz fled to Belgium in 1937 at age 30. Paul Jakob Herz, three years older, had fled to the Netherlands at about the same time. What their parents did not know was that the Germans were making plans to deport the Jews of both Holland and Belgium. In July 1942, the Nazis converted the Dossin de St. Georges military barracks in Mechelen, Belgium, into a transit camp. Mechelen, with 60,000 residents, was considered an ideal location for this purpose. Located halfway between Antwerp and Brussels, which contained most of the Jewish population of Belgium, the city had good rail connections to the killing centers of the East. Between August 4, 1942, and July 31, 1944, a total of 28 trains carrying 25,257 Jews left Mechelen for Auschwitz-Birkenau. Hans, the Herz' younger son, was taken there and murdered in 1943. In early 1942, the Germans began preparations to deport Dutch Jews. Later that year, the Herz' older son, Paul, was removed to the Westerbork transit ghetto in the Netherlands, near the German-Dutch border. The Nazis interned all non-Dutch Jews in Westerbork, 20,000 of whom were refugees from Germany. Most Jews stayed in the camp for only a short period of time. Paul was deported to Gross-Rosen, a small Nazi concentration camp established in August 1940 near the German town of Striegau in Lower Silesia, and then to Auschwitz, where he somehow survived until early 1945. He was then transferred to Buchenwald where he was murdered on February 24, 1945, at age 42. Less than six weeks later, Buchenwald was liberated by US soldiers, including my uncle Günter, from the 6th Armored Division, part of the Third Army, who found more than 21,000 people still barely surviving in the camp, abandoned by the Germans only days earlier.

Willi Neckarsulmer and his wife Martha Hellwitz were also on *Da 17*. Willi's father, Bernhard, was born in 1844, and was the oldest resident in my grandmother's *Altersheim* in Aachen. He had been a successful merchant who, together with his brother Phillip, founded *Gebrüder Neckarsulmer* in Aachen, wholesalers of modern fabrics and leather. Bernhard married Pauline Wiesbaden in 1875 but had been a widower since 1912. On April 7, 1941, the Gestapo came to the Jewish *Altersheim* on *Horst Wessel Straße*, forcibly removed the 97-year-old gentleman and promptly murdered him. His son Willi, who resided at the Jewish house on *Eupenersraße*, had been a furniture manufacturer in Aachen and a prominent member of the Aachen synagogue community. His business was taken by the Nazis on December 31, 1938. Willi's brother Alfred had died unexpectedly at age 26 in 1902. His other brother, Dr. Karl Neckarsulmer, was killed in action on October 10, 1918, during the last days of World War I while serving as a senior reserve physician. Specific records from Izbica deportations to death camps are scanty. Willi and Martha apparently both perished in Izbica.

Leo Wolf, age 50, had lived at the Jewish House on *Eupenerstraße* with his 36-year-old wife Helena Brüll and their 14-year-old daughter Margot, ever since being required to leave their Aachen home. Leo was separated from his family and deported on *Zug Da 17* with my family. His wife and daughter were also taken to Izbica, one month later on *Zug Da 52* from Düsseldorf. All three died in the Shoah. (In Hebrew, "shoah" literally means catastrophe or calamity. It is a synonym for The Holocaust, derived from the Greek word *holocaustos* and the Latin word *holocaustum* meaning "something completely burnt up.") Yom HaShoah is the Hebrew name for International Holocaust Remembrance Day, or Holocaust Day, observed as Israel's day of commemoration for the approximately six million Jews murdered in the Holocaust by Nazi Germany.

Zug Da 17's destination was the transit ghetto of Izbica.

Izbica, pronounced "Izbitsa," is a small town in the Lublin District of eastern Poland in the Wieprz River valley. It is located 12 kilometers south of Krasnystaw and 50 kilometers south-east of the regional capital, the city of Lublin. In the middle of the 18th century, Jews were brought to Izbica after having been forbidden to live in the neighboring village of Tarnogóra, whose residents exercised that prerogative under the so-called *"privilegia de non tolerandis Judaeis,"* which was also adopted by many other towns in Poland. From that time on Izbica became a center of commerce and trade, a *shtetl* (a Jewish island within the surrounding non-Jewish populace bearing certain socio-economic and cultural connotations, pious communities following Orthodox Judaism, socially unchanging despite outside influence) inhabited almost entirely by Polish Jews. There was a grain mill, a sawmill, a bentwood furniture factory, tanneries, shoe repair and tailor's shops, a comb factory and, of course, a synagogue.

On the eve of World War I, the population of Izbica amounted to 4,451 inhabitants, almost all of them Orthodox Jews, whose pace of life was regulated by tradition. Rabbinic law superseded Polish law. Cultural life was highly vibrant. There were beerhouses, there were six libraries, there was a cinema, and there was an amateur theatre. Many of the residents of Izbica played musical instruments, often gathering together to provide concerts of both classical music and traditional Jewish melodies. Following the establishment of the Polish Republic after World War I, the town grew significantly. Streets were paved and the marketplace rebuilt. A train ran from Lublin directly into Izbica. Life was relatively good for the 6,000 Jews of Izbica. All of that would soon change.

In mid-September 1939, Izbica was seized by the *Wehrmacht* (unified armed forces of Nazi Germany) after a brief unsuccessful defense by the Polish Army. The Germans, immediately upon entering Izbica, seized goods from Jewish shops as a "tribute." The Polish Home Army (Resistance Movement) operated briefly in the area. The Germans blamed Jews for the resistance and hanged seven Izbica residents and placed 40 Jews on the German front lines, of which about one third were killed. Towards the end of September 1939, the Soviet Army entered the town for a brief period. Fearing further German reprisals, a group of Jews from the town left Izbica together with the withdrawing Red Army.

Shortly after the German occupation a local station of the German Security Police (*Sicherheitspolizei, SiPo)* for the County of Krasnystaw was established in Izbica, consisting of two sub-departments, the *Geheime Staatspolizei* (Gestapo or secret state police) and the *Kriminalpolizei* (Kripo or criminal police). *Hauptscharführer* (Head squad leader) Kurt Engels was appointed as its head and *Volksdeutscher* (an ethnic German) Ludwig Klemm as his deputy. The highest rank of the enlisted staff of the paramilitary *Schutzstaffel* (SS) was that of *Hauptscharführer,* typically functioning as the chief non-commissioned officer of a *SS-Sturm* (company) or assigned to a security agency such as the Gestapo or to serve in concentration camps. It was Engels and Klemm who first organized the arrest of leaders of the Izbica Jewish community from Izbica and Tarnogóra and subsequently launched the mass persecution of Jews. On Engels's order, Izbica's Jewish cemetery was razed, with the tombstones repurposed to build a jail and to pave the streets.

The area of Poland which included Lublin and Izbica had been designated as the "General Government" after the German invasion and occupation. The General Government area was also known colloquially as the *Restpolen* ("Remainder of Poland"). For logistical purposes, it was run by Germany as a separate administrative unit under the direction of Hans Frank, a dedicated Nazi who had been Hitler's personal legal adviser and the chief attorney for the Nazi Party. Governor-General Frank oversaw the segregation of the Jews into ghettos, including the huge Warsaw ghetto.

Jews were brutalized and robbed from the beginning of the occupation. Looting of Jewish homes by roving Nazi soldiers continued in waves. Almost immediately, the Germans established a Jewish ghetto in the poorest part of Izbica and within a few months, the entire town became a ghetto with the German authorities prohibiting the Jews from engaging in trade and also from leaving the town to barter with the surrounding population.

The requirement that Jews wear white armbands bearing the star of David did not apply to Jews under the age of 14. Jewish children were able to furtively leave the ghetto, often during the night, to exchange goods and personal possessions for food, helping to stave off starvation in the community. In this manner, trade between the Jews of Izbica and Christians of the surrounding areas continued *subrosa* illicitly.

From 1940, Jews began to be resettled to Izbica from the western regions of Poland previously incorporated into the German Reich after the Nazi invasion. Early that year, a Jewish Council (*Judenrat)* was formed in Izbica with Abraham Blatt appointed as its head. At first, the main task of the *Judenrat* was to formulate a list of able-bodied men and women to perform forced labor. The tasks included street cleaning in various towns and digging trenches on the German-Soviet border. After a few months, even the elderly and infirm were sent to do labor for a month at a time. Thomas (Tovi) Blatt, Abraham's nephew, was born in 1927 in Izbica. Tovi, one of only 14 Jews of Izbica to have survived World War II, later wrote that "if the council could not deliver the required number of workers, the Germans, they indiscriminately would go from house to house, beat and shoot the occupants ... The Ukrainians, who worked with the Nazis together ... simply caught people on the streets until they got" the required number. In 1941, about 1,000 Jews from Lublin were forcibly brought to Izbica to live. With two occupying armies in the region, food became even more scarce, homes were often ransacked and living conditions rapidly further deteriorated.

In the spring of 1941, in preparation for the attack on the Soviet lines in eastern Poland, German military storage facilities were set up in Izbica, and kept under heavy guard. Ransacking and pillaging of homes often accompanied by indiscriminate violence perpetrated on the local population became a daily occurrence.

In March 1941, Governor-General Hans Frank informed his subordinates that Hitler had made the decision to "turn this region into a purely German area within 15–20 years." He explained: "Where 12 million Poles now live, is to be populated by 4 to 5 million Germans. The General Government must become as German as the Rhineland."

At the end of 1941, the Germans confiscated furs from the Jews in Izbica, with their ultimate destination being the German army on the cold eastern front.

In late 1941, Heinrich Himmler, leader of the *SS,* and the second most powerful man in the Third Reich, informed his staff that a transit ghetto should be established in Izbica to temporarily house Jews transported from Germany. Space for these new arrivals would be made by murdering the Jewish inhabitants who currently lived there.

In mid-December 1941, Hans Frank, the "General Gouvernment's" chief, met with his senior officials and said, "Gentlemen, I must ask you to rid yourself of all feelings of pity. We must annihilate the Jews wherever we find them and whenever it is possible." Under his guidance mass murder became a deliberate policy. The General Government, consisting of the central territory of Poland, was the location of four of the six major extermination camps: Belzec, Treblinka, Majdanek and Sobibor. Auschwitz-Birkenau and Chelmno were located in the western part of Poland, which had been incorporated by the Germans into the Third Reich. The Eastern territory of Poland was incorporated by the Soviet Union.

By late 1941, the massive, forced resettlement of Jewish and non-Jewish Poles was well underway in the Lublin district, including Izbica. The operation was the culmination of the policies carried out since the 19th century when Poland was partitioned among foreign powers. In accordance with Nazi ideology, the Jews were considered to be less than subhuman, and the majority of the non-Jewish Slavic people were also deemed inferior or *Untermenschen* (undermen) destined for expulsion to Asia or slave labor or worse. The expression "under man" was first used by American Ku Klux member Lothrop Stoddard in his 1922 book, *The Revolt Against Civilization: The Menace of the Under-man*. Stoddard applied the term to those unable to function within a civilization, in general due to their race. The Nazis later adopted it from the 1925 translation of this book into German, *Der Kulturumsturz: Die Drohung des Untermensche*. It is possible that Stoddard constructed his "under man" as an opposite of the German 19th century philosopher Friedrich Nietzsche's superman (*Übermensch*) concept. The term *Übermensch* was used frequently by Hitler and the Nazi regime for their belief in a biologically superior Aryan master race, although Nietzsche himself was not a nationalist or fervent antisemite.

A few months earlier, my grandmother's train destination, Izbica, had been secretly designated a transit ghetto *(Durchgangslage),* an area to hold Rose, Else, and their fellow travelers from Germany prior to their ultimate fate. The choice of Izbica as a transit ghetto reflected its location on the main train line between Lublin and Belzec, the location where the Nazis started construction of the first death camp in November 1941, and which became operational in March 1942.

Typical loading of boxcar, 1942

I have no direct knowledge of Rose's specific car on *Zug Da 17* but hope that the emotional suffocation was not overwhelming during those three long days between Koblenz, Germany, and Izbica, Poland. From the three postcards they sent from Izbica, I know that my grandmother Rose and her sister survived the journey. Writing about his deportation, Nobel Prize winner Elie Wiesel has written "Life in the cattle cars was the death of my adolescence. How quickly I aged." There is no method of determining how many of those primarily elderly people on Train #17 perished during the journey due to their already depleted physical state together with the appalling conditions or how many souls attempted to leap from that train when the doors were opened at water stops. Those that did were quickly captured and either killed or beaten and returned to the train, often with their hands and legs bound together. If by some miracle they were able to flee from the train, they were soon reported to the local Gestapo by the area's German or Polish townspeople.

Some Jews tried in different ways to convey their situation and feelings to loved ones left behind, hastily writing them notes, often in code, on scraps of paper they found. The writers threw these "letters" out through the slits of light coming from the outside or under the doors of the train, having faint faith that someone would pick them up and send them on to their destination. The deportations cleared the deportees from humanity as they knew it and disconnected them from it conclusively. The world they understood was stolen from them forever.

For Rose and Else, the train journey was a compressed culmination of their disengagement from ordinary life and, to some extent, a preparation for life in the camp after their departure from the train. They recognized that their lives were itinerant, uncertain, and without a future, although they had been promised "resettlement." The conditions in the trains were profoundly offensive, violating, and traumatizing. They were not prepared for what an inescapable dark space did to smell, sound, and touch.

In preparation for the arrival of my family and other deportees from Germany, the existing population of Izbica had been removed by the Nazis. Officially, this was termed the "resettlement of native Jews to Russia and the settlement of Reich Jews." The first mass deportation of the Izbica existing ghetto Jewish inmates to the Belzec extermination camp took place in mid-March 1942. Several dozen Jews were also shot on the spot, mainly by the SS officers Engels and Klemm. The bodies of those who were shot were taken to the Jewish cemetery and buried there. This was conducted by the *Ordnungspolizei*, (paramilitary Order Police), under the leadership of the SS, together with Ukrainian Nazi collaborators, who also took an active role in the extermination of Jews at the nearby death camps of Belzec, Sobibor and Treblinka.

Tovi Blatt later wrote that in the morning of March 24, 1942, one day before the arrival of Rose and Else, "Our sleepy town was awakened by shots. Another round up! Frightened Jews quickly dressed, ran, and hid. On the hills encircling Izbica, silhouettes of armed soldiers began to appear. The whole area was surrounded. Bands of Ukrainian collaborators rushed into Jewish homes. They took every Jew they encountered – children, old men, and women, even cripples."

Every subsequent morning in Izbica during March 1942, the German Order Police performed roundups (*Aktions*) on a smaller scale inside the Ghetto of Izbica, shooting everyone unable to move or attempting to flee, while the Trawnikis murdered men, women, and children in the streets of the town. Those captured were forced to board a train and never returned. Seeking an answer, the *Judenrat* paid a Christian to follow one of the transport trains. Tovi writes "He came back and told them the Jews were not taken very far away, maybe only 50 kilometers to a small village, Belzec. His uncle worked at the Belzec train station and told him that he saw transports of thousands of Jews arriving every day from different parts of the country, even from Krakow and Lwow...The train would be directed to a side track where a gate would open, he said, and an area he couldn't see into, surrounded by a barbed wire fence, would swallow the whole trainload. Then the train would leave empty."

The diary of Joseph Goebbels, Hitler's propaganda minister, has an entry dated March 17, 1942, regarding the ongoing population exchange: "From the General Gouvernement, beginning at Lublin, the Jews are now being deported to the East... On the whole, one can probably conclude that 60 percent of them must be liquidated, while only 40 percent can still be put to work...A rather barbaric and indescribable procedure is being used here, and there is not much left of the Jews themselves...The ghettos that become vacant...will now be filled with Jews deported from the Reich, and here, after a certain time, the process will be renewed."

Between mid-March and mid-May 1942, 30 transports, with some 30,000 Jews aboard, reached the General Government from various parts of the Reich and from Austria and the Protectorate. The train carrying my grandmother was one of them. Neither she, Else, nor the almost 1,000 other occupants of *Zug Da 17* knew that, while they were travelling, Gestapo and SS men had made room for these "Reich Jews" in Izbica by deporting 2,200 local Jews to the newly built Belzec extermination camp, one hour to the south by train, and murdering them there in gas chambers.

Early in the afternoon of March 25, 1942, *Zug Da 17* came to a stop. Rose, Else and the others in their boxcar were told that they were halting in Lublin for a few hours to allow the German officers on the train to have a hot meal and stretch their legs prior to the last part of the journey to Izbica. Had any of the deportees ever heard of the small eastern Polish city of Lublin, it was likely from an obscure footnote in a geography book they had studied in school. They could not have known that nine days earlier, on March 16, 1942, from this very train station, 1,500 Jews of Lublin were deported to the death camp at Belzec, marking the beginning of Operation Reinhard. The Germans had expelled people from their homes in the Lublin ghetto, killing the sick and infirm on-site and marching the others to the Maharshal Synagogue, and then two kilometers to the railway siding known as Lublin's *Umschlagplatz* (collection point, a German word that technically denotes a place where all goods for rail transport are handled). The Nazis used the term as a dehumanized euphemism for the location where people would be deported to the death camps. The ambiguous language disguised the ultimate purpose of the *Umschlagplatz*. By mid-April 1942, around 28,000 Jews had been transported from Lublin to Belzec and immediately murdered in the newly created gas chambers.

Most first-person testimony of surviving victims of the Holocaust depicts the process of deportation but often omits the on-train happenings which Rose and Else experienced and certainly remembered until the end of their days. Primo Levi, an Italian Jew who survived Auschwitz, described his feeling of doom on the train in his 1946 book, *If This Is a Man (*published in 1947 in the US as *Survival in Auschwitz),* "Almost always, at the beginning of the memory sequence, stands the train which marked the departure towards the unknown not only for chronological reasons but also for the gratuitous cruelty with which those (otherwise innocuous) convoys of ordinary freight cars were employed for extraordinary purposes."

Levi, of course, had the superfluity of existence when he later recollected his train experience. My grandmother experienced the train and likely what followed did not allow her to mentally regurgitate the voyage with lengthy hindsight. I can only abstractly imagine the feeling of isolation within the overcrowding, the shame and suffering due to lack of privacy, the fear, and the terror of that grotesque journey. Most narratives of the mass dislocations do not deal with the victims but rather with the perpetrators, the Nazi bureaucracy and its timetables, procedures, traffic management and delivery of human cargo. Deportation is portrayed as a banal administrative practice, a compliant procedure without violence, impact, or suffering. We all have seen this passivity so often in the contemporary photographs of group togetherness, with people walking in columns or waiting in crowds. My family was there for the initial push into the freight car, the rush for sitting and standing space, the unconfirmed rumors of the train's destination, the compression of bodies, and the violation of social boundaries. Yet this was nothing compared to the overpowering sensory storm of misery, feces, urine, and vomit and the dearth of water and food, the magnitudes of violence and violating actions that become acceptable and endorsed when civilization breaks down.

After three seemingly endless days and two interminable nights, *Zug Da 17,* arrived in Izbica shortly after dark on March 25, 1942. The confinement was ending but the containment was hardly over. Although my grandmother must have experienced a certain relief when her swollen feet encountered solid pavement rather than the unstable clattering floor of the train, I cannot imagine the trauma of the sensory incursions she had experienced in the absence of light within the boxcar, the psychological ruin that the journey, although limited in time, had caused, the degree of long-lasting emotional pain having little relationship to the actual duration of the trauma.

The train station. Izbica, 1942: Rose and Else's first views.

Rose and Else's train was one of 15 deportation trains from the German Reich arriving in Lublin between March 1942 and the beginning of June 1942, carrying a total of approximately 17,500 Jews. One half of these were sent on to Izbica. After June 1, all trains with that "destination" never arrived, having been sent directly to the Sobibor death camp after stopping in Lublin.

Three postcards Rose and Else mailed from Izbica are the only first-person information that I have regarding my grandmother's experience there. All other material is based on testimony by the few survivors of Izbica, correspondence sent by other deportees, and my translation of Steffen Hänschen's comprehensive book, published in 2018, *Das Transitghetto Izbica im System des Holocaust (The Izbica Transit Ghetto in the System of the Holocaust.)*

On arrival of *Zug Da 17,* the Izbica train platform was illuminated by electric lights allowing the gathered police and Gestapo to see the deportees as they slowly made their way off the train. The sliding door of each of the 18 boxcars was unlocked and opened one at a time so that there could be no disorder caused by a mass exodus. The officials had gone through this routine before and were prepared for most eventualities. They knew that Rose and the others would have joints stiffened by three days of extremely limited movement. They would be dispirited, hungry, thirsty, and frightened. The Nazis desired them worried, even terrified, but did not want a situation of panic involving 1,000 people within a limited space. The key to achieving order was organization and instilling sufficient fear of reprisal if orders were disobeyed.

Rose, Else and the other occupants of their box car were greeted by *Hauptscharführer* Kurt Engels of the SS, commandant of Izbica. He told them that their train had carried "bread, flour and legumes" sufficient for the first two weeks of their residence in Izbica. After that, they would be on their own. They would receive their luggage "in the next few days." They were then introduced to a member of the *Judenrat* (the Jewish Council), which would be responsible for day-to-day life in the Izbica ghetto. Following the occupation, the Nazis had forced each ghettoized community of Jews in Poland to elect a *Judenrat*, which would then be in charge of the enforcement of Nazi orders.

Most Jewish Council members, ensnared between the often-violent ultimatums of Nazi officials and the tremendous needs of the Jews for whom they were responsible, grappled with daily moral decisions. They were given responsibility for organizing and maintaining everyday life in a community burdened by scarcity, violence, and uncertainty. Jewish Councils were authorized to distribute food rations and supplies, manage access to medical care, and organize housing. These groups were required to establish a Jewish police force to carry out Nazi directives within Izbica. *Judenrat* members often were responsible for choosing which residents of the ghetto would be selected for work, deported to concentration camps, or sent to death camps. Often representatives of the *Judenrat* and Jewish police force were granted certain "privileges" such as more food for their families. It is not surprising that other Izbica residents often accused Jewish Council members of collaborating with the Nazis to obtain special treatment.

A member of the *Judenrat* led my grandmother and her sister and their group, each carrying their pocketbooks and a few other paltry items, from the train platform onto a muddy street, where they walked past a row of decrepit wooden buildings. Every few minutes the Council member would point to a few members of the assemblage and signal that they were to enter a specific house. Rose and Else were directed to go into a dwelling, indistinguishable by any features from those they had already passed. This was to become their new home, to be shared with many others similar to them.

On the following day, a member of the *Judenrat* came to their room to present Rose and Else with a new Star of David armband which they had to wear day and night. The Jews shipped in from Germany and Austria were differentiated from Polish Jews by the color of the obligatory color of the Star, yellow for German Jews, and blue for the Polish, the remnants of whom were housed on the other side of the railroad tracks to keep them separate from the new arrivals.

The Jewish Religious Association of Württemberg, Germany, was commanded by the Nazis to prepare a document regarding the living situation in Izbica. This heavily censored official "report" was issued on May 13, 1942, while Rose and Else were there. The narrative stressed the presence of an "independent" Jewish self-government, a fact that would make the reader feel that life in Izbica was good. The document states that "Izbica is a small spot...," where the emigrants live in "houses...not in barracks, as could be erroneously assumed from the designation 'block'...(They) have received their luggage without exception... In Izbica, at first glance, the dirt and mud on the streets is particularly noticeable (in front of the houses 30 cm. deep!) This will, however, improve very soon with the warmer weather... Everything now depends on those who are able to work beginning immediately with clearing up and repair work. The emigrants are very much left to themselves in their new abode... There is undoubtedly ample opportunity for those able to work to find employment both in agriculture, which appears to be well cultivated, and in smaller industries. The land is fertile. Everything is to be had."

An uncensored and more accurate description of conditions in Izbica can be obtained from a letter written by Ernst Krombach, a young man from Essen who was deported on the same train from Koblenz as Rose and Else. A Christian friend of Krombach's, an auto mechanic employed by the *Werhmacht,* drove to Izbica to visit him. Krombach provided his friend with a letter to be delivered to a girlfriend in Essen, who had sent him some food. Krombach wrote "… You can imagine my feelings and my joy! Everything you sent us, which for a while has taken away our worries about our daily bread!... I shall tell you my story, so you can see it for yourself... It was a rainy evening when we arrived at Izbica. Once arrived, we were met by Jewish Police and the SS who then shoved us into the cave–like dwellings. An optimist might think of 'Carmen' if the reality hadn't been so hard, particularly for the elderly. Izbica is a village hidden in a valley. It used to be home to about 3,000 Polish Jews. Its geographical situation is superb. The 'houses' are mainly built of wood and clay and consist of one or two 'rooms'. Everything is filthy and infested. A few of the houses have the luxury of beds, tables, chairs, or cupboards... There are 12 of us living in the 2 x 4 meters hovel: ... At the front of the room, we have: 2 tables, 2 wooden benches we made ourselves, 4 chairs which we 'organized', one stove: at the back of our room, on the luxury of a wooden floor (elsewhere, clay) and sacks of straw the 'beds', side-by-side on the floor... Before the first transport arrived here, Izbica was cleansed of its Jewish residents. The SS drove them out with weapons and clubs... The transports came thick and fast... The legal code is simple to describe: the death penalty..... Everything is forbidden, the penalty as above. Leaving the ordained district before 7 a.m. or after 7 p.m., bartering, buying, or selling or speaking to Polish Aryans, baking bread. buying rationed groceries such as butter, eggs, bread, potatoes, etc., sending letters or any other form of correspondence, leaving the borders of the town, possession of gold or German money, or at all any money, jewelry, silver etc. Unfortunately, such offences…have cost many lives... In the meantime, many transports have left here. Of the approximately 14,000 Jews that arrived only 2-3,000 are still here. They go off in cattle trucks, subject to the most brutal treatment, with …only the clothes they are wearing. ... We have heard nothing more of these people... After the last transport, the men who were working outside the village returned to find neither wives, nor children, nor their possessions... Whenever I`ve had the opportunity to join the police I`ve always refused. Mainly because of the unpleasant work: Jews against Jews. But I was unable to avoid getting involved in the evacuation of Polish Jews. You have to suppress every human feeling and, under supervision of the SS, drive the people out with a whip, just as they are – barefoot, with infants in their arms. There are scenes which I cannot and will not describe just the thought of it... Food is a principal concern... Many go under through malnutrition. There's no one here to care for them. There is some 'welfare,' which provides hardly any help besides water and soup... Various private individuals give lunch to people. Those who have no money, no relatives, no acquaintances in Germany to send them things and nothing left to sell must either starve or steal... Yours! E."

Prior to 1939, 90% of the approximately 6,000 residents of Izbica were Jewish. Of these, only 14 survived the Holocaust. Of the 17,500 additional Jews deported to the Lublin District from Germany in 1942, less than twenty survived World War II.

Gerda in Shanghai, Helmut in Palestine and Günter in Philadelphia had no idea that my grandmother was no longer at the *Altersheim* in Aachen. They had heard nothing from her since the telegram of February 5, 1942. Ms. Berger may have attempted to contact Rose's children, but the lines of communication had been broken by the war. Had they been notified that their mother and great aunt were no longer at the Jewish home, they certainly would have made numerous "official" inquiries to determine her location, a fruitless task condemned to failure. Ernst Elsberg from Oberhausen in *Nordrhein-Westphalia* was 40 years old when he was deported from Düsseldorf to Izbica on train #52, one month after Rose and Else. According to the files of the Düsseldorf Gestapo, Ernst's mother, Mathilde, exercising her rights as a "citizen of the Reich" repeatedly inquired about her son's whereabouts, including writing to the German police authorities in Lublin. On May 11, 1943, more than a year later, the commander of the *Sipo* and *SD* in Lublin informed her that her son's whereabouts were unknown. The local police, certainly cognizant of his murder, wrote that "…It could only be established that in April 1942 a transport from the Reich was accommodated in Izbica, but that it had to be transported away again on October 1, 1942. It is possible that E. was on this transport [;] however, it cannot be determined where these persons were transported to, because no documents exist for this."

In my research, I came across a copy of a typewritten letter from the Izbica *Judenrat* dated March 29, 1942, four days after Rose and Else's arrival, mailed to the Jewish community office in Wuerzburg, Germany. The letter indicates that 2,000 additional Jews had arrived in Izbica from cities including Aachen and Koblenz. "German authorities have come to meet us and will involve those who are able to work in the labor process. We urgently need funds for the subsistence of the unemployed, mostly sick and elderly people and men, which is why we send you the polite and urgent request that you send the largest possible amount of money after you have received this letter. We also ask you to make preparations now, so that we are regularly sent money, possibly clothing, laundry, and permitted food. A committee formed from the newly arriving Jews from the Reich will take care of the fair distribution of these as long as possible. We ask you to comply with our requests immediately and thank you from the bottom of our hearts for everything you do for us." The letter is signed by Dr. A. Lob Pauner for the Izbica *Judenrat* and Ludwig Israel Weinhaber, Dr. Nathan Rosenthal and Hugo Kalb as representatives of the German Jews. Ludwig Weinhaber and Hugo Kalb had been deported from Nürnberg (Nuremberg), Bavaria, Germany and reached Izbica two days after my family's arrival.

Izbica, 1942

Rose and Else learned that Izbica commandant *Hauptscharführer* Kurt Engels had recently decided that the new deportees from the German Reich were permitted to purchase postcards and stamps and mail them to recipients in Germany. Obviously, no correspondence could be sent to enemies of The Reich such as the United States, Palestine, controlled by the British and Shanghai, ruled by Germany's ally, Japan. No letters in envelopes were allowed and the postcard's authors knew that the card's content would be carefully scrutinized by Izbica authorities, if not Engels himself.

Rose needed a close relative in Germany to whom she could send these postcards, hoped that they would arrive, with the remote chance that information about her whereabouts could, in some manner, be transmitted to my mother and my uncles.

My grandmother and her sister had grown up in Bücken together with the children of her paternal uncle, Levy (Louis) Liepmann. One of those first cousins was Arnold Liepmann, born in 1880. Rose and Else had been at many family gatherings in Bücken with Arnold, his parents and brothers and sisters prior to Arnold moving to Essen. After Rose married Albert and established their home in Velmede, Arnold and his wife, Hulde Karoline Amalie Strothenke, nicknamed "Lina," or, at times, "Li," who had no children, would often take the one-hour train ride to visit with the Oppenheim family and take great pleasure in observing Gerda, Helmut and Günter growing up.

Rose learned from Essen residents now in Izbica that Arnold and Li had not yet been deported, although someone had related to her that Arnold had been sent to a slave labor camp in Sachsenhausen, north of Berlin, leaving Li by herself. Rose and Else made the decision to write to them and hoped that the cards would pass through various censors and reach the Liepmanns in Essen.

The front and backs of the first of three postcards sent from Izbica, dated April 5, 1942, and postmarked April 7, 1942.

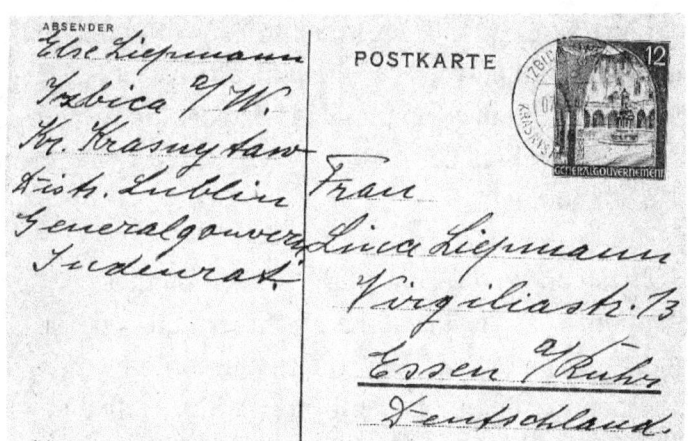

The first *postkarte* had a prepaid stamp and was written on April 5, 1942, ten days after their arrival in Izbica. The front has a postmark dated April 7 and says "Generalgouvernement Izbica (Wieprz) About Krasnystaw (Distr Lublin)." The postcard is addressed by Else to "*Frau* (Mrs.) Lina Liepmann, Virgiliastr. 13. Essen a / Ruhr, Germany." The sender is "Else Liepmann Izbica a / W. Krasnytaw Distr. Lublin, General gouvern[ment] Judenrat." The entire card is handwritten by Else. When I first saw this, I thought my grandmother Rose might not be alive anymore, having succumbed on the train ride or later, either from malnutrition, an infectious disease, being immediately sent to an extermination camp or shot upon arrival at the train station or later on the streets of Izbica by the *SS*.

Izbica, dated April 5, 1942.

Dear ones,

I hope you are healthy like we are. Have you spoken to Hermann? Give him our best regards and ask him to send us money soon. The hoods and the tote bag are very useful to us, we wear the former all the time. If you can, please send us something to eat. Is Paul still in H(orn). We think a lot of all of you, especially our poor mother! Stay healthy and give us notice immediately. With love, Your Rose and Else.

I was not initially certain of "Hermann's" identity." Given the information from this postcard, he seemed to be well off financially.

Hugo Goldscheider was born on December 4, 1902, in Rokycany, Czechoslovakia. He came to Izbica on March 13, 1942, with the first transport of Czech Jews from Theresienstadt, two weeks before the arrival of Rose and Else from Germany. He later wrote that, upon entering Izbica, he was jointly accommodated with the Stadler family, acquaintances from his hometown, together with 35 other people, in a 4 x 10-meter room in the only building in Izbica that had a floor and not just bare earth. There were no beds or bedding. It is clear that Rose and Else's "lodgings" were equally appalling, if not worse. In the fall of 1942, Goldscheider escaped from Izbica while working in the fields. He continues "In the beginning, the parcels still came twice a week. Later, it was still allowed to write letters, no more parcels came. As long as we still had parcels and something to sell, it was possible to live. For work one got nothing."

Passover, the Jewish Feast of Unleavened Bread, began on Wednesday, April 1, 1942. In those difficult times, Jews around the world gathered together in their homes, as they had for almost two thousand years, to celebrate a Seder, the initial and central ritual of this weeklong holiday originating shortly after the destruction of the second Temple, almost 2,000 years before, as a traditional family gathering to relive Moses' leading the Israelites' exodus from Egypt. My grandmother could not remember any year when she had not participated in a Seder, first with her parents and siblings in Bücken, then with Albert and her young family in Velmede, and later, after Gerda, Helmut and Günter had scattered to the ends of the earth, with Albert, Else, Fanni and often friends in Velmede and then Aachen. The Seder in 1941, at the *Israelitisches Altenheim* on *Horst Wessel Strasse*, had been very different, but at least they had *Haggadahs (*prayer books) together with the traditional Seder plate holding matzah, parsley, a boiled egg, salt water, a shank bone, horseradish and charoseth. Even though the door was opened at the appropriate time, there had been no children present to believe that Elijah might indeed come and partake of the goblet of wine set aside for him.

Rose and Else, one week after their arrival in Izbica, gathered with their roommates and with Jews from adjoining dwellings, to hold a Seder service. During the Crusades, the Black Death persecutions and the Inquisition, courageous Jews managed to find ways to celebrate Passover despite conditions that placed lives at risk. This time, any Hagaddah that someone had the presence of mind to bring with them had been lost with their luggage and there was no matzoh or wine. Although all present were able to ask the initial question

"Why is this night different from all other nights?" and end with "next year in Jerusalem," the familiar prayers or songs in between were overshadowed by their harrowing situation. Izbica was an eleventh plague, not brought by God to strike down their foes, but rather wrought by their enemies. It was impossible to understand that the Festival of Freedom was not a misnomer.

Yala Korwin, a young Jewish woman from Lvov who somehow survived the Holocaust, wrote a poem entitled "Passover Night 1942":

not a crumb of leavened

or unleavened bread
and no manna fell

no water sprang out
of the bunker's wall
the last potato was gone

we sat and we munched
chunks of potato-peels
more bitter than herbs

we didn't dare to sing
and open the door
for Elijah

we huddled and prayed
while pillars of clouds
massed above our heads

and pillars of fire
loomed like blazing traps

Two weeks later, another postcard was sent by my family from Izbica.

The front and backs of the second of three postcards sent from Izbica, dated April 16, 1942, and postmarked April 17, 1942.

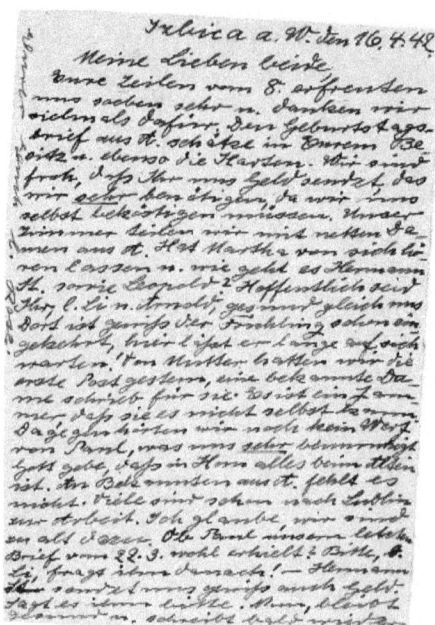

The second *postkarte* also had a prepaid stamp and was written on April 16, 1942, three weeks after their arrival in Izbica. The front has a postmark dated April 17 and the card is addressed to "Herrn Arnold Liepmann, Essen (Ruhr), Virigiliastr. 13." The sender is "Else Liepmann, Ixbica a. W. District Lublin, Kreis Krasnystaw, General Gouvernement. Block II/266 III. Transport."

It has long been customary for Germans, when providing the name of a town located on a river, to add the name of the river as part of the name. Else, writing this postcard, uses the term "Ixbica a. W." Ixbica was an alternative spelling and is located "a.W." on (or at) the Wieprz River, one of the largest rivers in eastern Poland.

Else and Rose's "address" in Izbica appears to have been "266 in Block II." "III. Transport" was the designation for the deportees who arrived in March 1942, the third month of the year. Izbica was located in the county "Krasnystaw."

Although the "sender" was Else, the majority of the contents of this card were written by my grandmother. Rose writes:

> Izbica a. W. April 16, 1942
>
> Dear ones both,
>
> Your lines of the 8th have just made us very happy and we thank you very much for them. Treasure in your possession the birthday letter from Aachen and also the cards. We are glad that you send us money that we need very much, because we have to feed ourselves. We share our room with nice ladies from Aachen. Have you heard from Martha and how are Hermann St. and Leopold? Hopefully you are, dear Li and. Arnold, healthy like us. Spring has certainly already arrived there; it is a long time coming here! We had the first mail from Mother yesterday, a friendly acquaintance lady wrote for her. It's a shame she can't do it herself. On the other hand, we haven't

heard a word from Paul, which worries us very much. God grant that everything remains unaffected in Horn. There is no lack of friends from Aachen here. Many have already gone to work in Lublin. I think we're too old for that. Has Paul received our last letter from March 22nd? Please, dear Li, ask him about it! - Hermann St. will certainly send us money too. Please tell him. Well, stay safe and write again soon.

Else adds the following, upside down on the front of the postcard under the sender information:

My warmest greetings to both of you. Let's hear from you again very soon. We always think of you. With love, Else.

It now apparent that "Hermann" is Herz "Hermann" Sternberg, born in 1870 in Horn, Germany, and an uncle of Agnes Sternberg, Paul Liepmann's wife. He was also living in Essen at the time, the destination of the three postcards Rose and Else sent from Izbica. His munificence, although greatly appreciated by my family, unfortunately did not save him from a similar fate. Hermann was deported from Düsseldorf to Theresienstadt Ghetto in Czechoslovakia on July 21, 1942, and died there on September 9, 1942.

The "Leopold" referred to in this postcard is Leopold Liepmann, Arnold's brother and another paternal first cousin of Rose and Else. He was also born in Bücken on March 31, 1876. He was arrested in Oldenburg, Germany, on *Kristallnacht* and on the following day, sentenced by the Nazi court to be sent to the Sachsenhausen Concentration Camp, north of Berlin. This camp primarily held political prisoners, including Herschel Grynszpan, whose actions initiated *Kristallnacht*. Leopold was released and returned to Oldenburg on November 22, 1938, to his wife, Erna Therese née Weinberg, who had grown up there, and their two children, Werner and Ingeborg (Ingrid). Leopold and his family escaped to Holland in July of 1939. Werner was then sent to Britain via the *Kindertransport*, "children's transport," the British-organized rescue effort that lasted nine months, brought 10,000 children to safety from Nazi Germany, and was ended by the outbreak of World War II. Leopold, Erna, and Ingeborg, hiding in Holland, were captured by the Nazis and sent to the Westerbork transit camp in the center of the Netherlands. Ironically, Westerbork was originally established by the Dutch as a refugee camp for the tidal wave of German Jewish refugees who fled Nazi persecution prior to the German occupation of the Netherlands in May 1940. In 1942, Westerbork became the Nazi waystation to death, the place where 100,000 Dutch Jews, including Anne Frank, were assembled in the remote countryside before being transported to death camps deep in Eastern Europe. Deportations from Westerbork occurred every Tuesday and Thursday. 1187 men, women, and children, including Leopold, Erna and Ingeborg Liepmann, left Westerbork on May 4, 1943, on transport # 10 by train to the Sobibor death camp in Poland, where they were all murdered 3 days later. Only 5,000 Jews who passed through Westerbork survived.

"Martha" is Martha Estella Weinberg, Leopold's wife's sister. Martha married Ludwig Tebrich, an engineer, in 1915. The Tebrichs had tried to emigrate, but their effort also failed. They were deported to Theresienstadt from Hamburg on July 15, 1942, and, six months later, were sent to Auschwitz, where they both were promptly murdered in the gas chambers.

There is nothing in this correspondence regarding the horrors that Rose and Else were experiencing at every moment. It was obvious to them that whatever they wrote would be read by a rabid Nazi in the *Durchgangslager* (transit ghetto), perhaps even *Hauptscharführer* Kurt Engels or his deputy, Ludwig

Klemm. There is not even a hint regarding the unfavorable living conditions of the ghetto, including lack of food, water, and living space, nothing about Jews dying daily in Izbica from starvation, disease, or Nazi violence. To any outside observer, this card appeared to be speaking of lack of money and asking about the health of their family, nothing that would warrant any reprimand or punishment. "Paul" is, of course, Rose's younger and favorite brother, and she takes this and every opportunity to inquire about him and his family in Horn. The remarks that "we share our room with nice ladies from Aachen" and "there is no lack of friends from Aachen here" are pieces of disinformation that Rose is using, deliberately intending to mislead the Nazis while, at the same time, attempting to give any family member that might read the card the impression that her situation is not that bad. When Rose writes "Many have already gone to work in Lublin," I pray that she indeed believed that and remained unaware that those "friends" had been sent to a death camp.

Hitler, in *Mein Kampf* ("My Struggle"), penned in prison while serving a sentence for a failed coup attempt in 1923, wrote "The function of propaganda is … not to weigh and ponder the rights of different people, but exclusively to emphasize the one right which it has set out to argue for. Its task is not to make an objective study of the truth, in so far as it favors the enemy, and then set it before the masses with academic fairness; its task is to serve our own right, always and unflinchingly."

The Nazis were masters of propaganda, cynically describing Theresienstadt as a "spa town" where elderly German Jews could "retire" in safety. That location was in reality a collection center for deportations to killing centers in Nazi-occupied eastern Europe.

Rose was an excellent student of Nazi propaganda. In her "Aachen" comments, she intentionally combined factually accurate content with false contextual information to manipulate the censors.

To me, the sentence "Treasure in your possession the birthday letter from Aachen and also the cards," has an appropriately sinister hidden meaning. In the fourth line Rose uses the word "*Schätze* ," which is derived from the German noun "*schatz*," meaning "treasure " or "darling" (sweetheart). Here, in this context, it is a verb grammatically expressing the imperative mood, one of 3 moods of the German language besides the indicative and the subjunctive. The imperative is used for expressing an order. As in most languages, there is no pronoun used in this sentence—the implication being that the writer is requiring "you" to perform a certain action.

Arnold and Li both celebrated their birthdays in April and apparently Rose had sent a birthday card from Aachen to them. Rose is asking her uncle and aunt to "treasure" that birthday card together with these postcards from Izbica, to preserve them and to share them with other members of the family as a remembrance of her existence. Indeed, this is exactly what occurred. Although the "birthday letter" was lost at some point in its history, the three postcards sent to Arnold and Li have come to me by a rather circuitous route, to be read and touched as a "treasure," a remembrance 82 years after their writing, an essential part of my finding my grandmother Rose.

Rose is thankful for money that apparently had been sent by Arnold and Li, "because we have to feed ourselves." A preoccupation with food was the rule among the prisoners in Izbica. For the Nazis, hunger was a weapon to be wielded against their enemies and victims. The prisoners suffered terribly from extremely low caloric intake. Insufficient nutrition would quickly begin to destroy the body, which gradually used up its stores of fat, muscle mass, and the tissues of the internal organs. This led to emaciation and famishment illness, the cause of a significant number of deaths in Izbica. Those doing forced hard labor needed to consume even more calories to avert starvation.

Rose and Else needed money to buy food; their requests for funds were hardly capricious. Prisoners who worked in the camp kitchens were at an advantage, with access to extra food to steal. Those who labored in facilities (*Effektenlager*) which stored the stolen belongings of prisoners could procure goods for themselves and other inmates. These warehouses were known as "Kanada," because the prisoners considered them the land of plenty. Those that worked there were known as *Aufräumungskommando* ("clearing-up commando") or *Kanada Kommando*. Neither Rose nor Else could meet the criteria necessary to attain such choice positions.

Prior to my family's arrival, the *Judenrat* established a ghetto soup kitchen to distribute food to the Izbica inmates. Before the United States entered World War II, this was funded primarily by the Joint Distribution Committee, headquartered in New York. By March 1942, the communal dining center was obtaining only minimal food from the Germans, supplemented that with contributions from Jewish community offices in Germany, some of which were still barely functioning. Those residents fortunate enough to receive mailed food packages from relatives would generally not share their treasure with others.

Three times a day, Rose and Else would put on their coat and hat and trudge through the muddy streets, usually accompanied by others in their dwelling, to obtain nourishment at the food supply building. As they drew nearer to that center, they always encountered other prisoners either approaching or leaving the facility. In the morning they would receive a half liter of "coffee," which consisted of boiled water with a grain-based substitute. There was neither sugar nor milk to accompany this to make it more palatable, but the warm liquid felt good. At times, a brew of herbal tea was substituted, and they often joked regarding what substances had been used to concoct this. As sisters and lifelong companions, they had shared much hilarity. Now, making jokes lessened anxiety and diminished fear, an alternative to the despair of their situation. To laugh was an act of courage, a means through which they could detach themselves from their circumstance and subconsciously rebel against their captors. At noon they were each given a liter of soup consisting of hot water, potatoes, cabbage, root vegetables and a small amount of flour and food extract. Initially they found this repugnant in taste, but as their hunger increased over the weeks, it became tolerable, if no more appetizing. Approximately a half pound of black bread made up the evening meal, sometimes accompanied by a small piece of sausage or cheese and, on a good day, some leftover soup from lunch if the *SS* guards had not stolen the remnants. That dinner bread was intended to be partially saved to be eaten the following morning. As Rose and Else spoke daily about their mother, they would sometimes jest about whether Fanni would ask whether the sausage was kosher and whether they could fool her, thinking only of her physical welfare, into believing that it contained no pork.

This daily menu obviously would not suffice to prevent weight loss and ultimately emaciation. It consisted of few calories, little fat or protein and few essential vitamins. Rose and Else could supplement this diet with the packages that they received through the efforts of Arnold and Li. Living in close quarters, my family did not notice that their roommates, or themselves, were becoming thinner on a daily basis. When they encountered fellow Aacheners on the street after not seeing them for several weeks, however, the accelerated aging, the haggard faces, the slumped shoulders, the change in image and attitude, all this was readily apparent.

A prisoner suffering from starvation sickness was referred to as a "*Muselmann*," a term used amongst prisoners of ghettos and concentration camps to refer to those suffering from a combination of hunger and exhaustion, as well as those who were resigned to their impending death. The *Muselmann* prisoners exhibited severe emaciation and physical weakness, an apathetic listlessness regarding their fate, and unresponsiveness to their surroundings owing to their barbaric treatment. The term possibly comes from the *Muselmann's* inability to stand for any time due to the loss of leg muscle, thus leading them to spend much of their time lying on their bed. In *Remnants of Auschwitz: The Witness and the Archive*, Giorgio Agamben defines the *Muselmann* as having a "bare, naked, unassigned and unwitnessable life…the body stripped of all personality, deprived of the power of life, sense and soul." In using the label *Muselmann* the Auschwitz prisoners were constructing a new category for people who were slipping into a state of being non-human. In Yiddish, *Muselmann* also literally means "a Muslim" and the prone position may have invoked the image of the Muslim practice of prostration during prayer. Nazis equated the prisoner's apathy to their circumstances, the result of weakness and acute hunger, to Islamic fatalism. Primo Levi has written in his autobiography that "this word '*Muselmann*', I do not know why, was used by the old ones of the camp to describe the weak, the inept, those doomed to selection...Their life is short, but their number is endless: they, the *Muselmänner*, the drowned form the backbone of the camp, an anonymous mass, continually renewed and always identical, of non-men who march and labour in silence, the divine spark dead within them, already too empty to really suffer. One hesitates to call them living; one hesitates to call their death death, in the face of which they have no fear, as they are too tired to understand."

Holocaust survivor and Nobel Laureate Elie Wiesel, speaking at the White House at the invitation of President Clinton in 1999, said, …the most tragic of all prisoners were the "*Muselmänner*," as they were called. Wrapped in their torn blankets, they would sit or lie on the ground, staring vacantly into space, unaware of who or where they were, strangers to their surroundings. They no longer felt pain, hunger, thirst. They feared nothing. They felt nothing. They were dead and did not know it."

In the transit ghettos of Poland as well as in the concentration and death camps, understandably the most repetitive topic discussed among the prisoners was food. There was a daily challenge in getting food, eating food and, in many cases, stealing food. The common goal shared by all people living in Rose and Else's room in Izbica was to avoid starvation. A survivor of another transit ghetto later said "Hunger and fear are the most fantastic weapons which Hitler was a master of. To be hungry slowly – not just to miss breakfast or to have the day of fast, but to be really hungry, to have less and less, day by day, month by month; so that at the end you only think about one thing: to get something to eat."

Some prisoners managed to survive by trading goods on the thriving black market in the camps. Anything and everything was traded, from food to buttons or clothing. People would trade half of their daily ration of bread for a needle and thread, for example. Those mobile enough to walk up and down the streets looking to trade food could sometimes sell a slice of bread for some soup and a few minutes later, exchange that soup for two slices of bread. Another survivor has written, "Really, it became the law of the jungle, you couldn't afford to be nice to others. I remember coming across three Jewish brothers and they used to pinch each other's bread ration. There were no standards; no right and wrong, you just looked after yourself if you could."

"The cooks would dole out the soup from barrels and as you got to the bottom of the barrel, the soup got thicker; people would play these strategic games to position themselves in the line in order to get the soup at the bottom of the barrel. You then came back with your soup: was it thick or was it thin? How many pieces of meat did you find?"

It is likely that Rose and Else romanticized food in their conversation. They would talk about ingredients of their favorite recipes and how they both made the mistake of eating less when they were girls trying to maintain trim figures. Discussing food as a fantasy, an ultimate wish for a better future, became so essential to their survival that the absence of that hope, that dream, was to become a *Muselmann*, the precursor of death.

For centuries, the source of Izbica's water had been from natural artesian wells, into which buckets were lowered by the residents to collect water. Any well water is subject to any of the standard contaminants of an untreated water source – bacteria, viruses, parasites, lead, chromium, arsenic, and pesticides. Water-borne illness has always been a problem in any community without properly managed water facilities. In 1942, with the arrival of thousands of prisoners and the absence of any sanitary facilities, the water in the muddy streets of Izbica now contained vast amounts of human waste which seeped into the underground water supply. Rose and Else, walking to obtain their food subsistence, would regularly see fellow prisoners relieving themselves on the sides of the streets. The drinking water promptly included pathogenic microorganisms causing serious illnesses such as cholera, typhoid fever, giardiasis, amebic dysentery, and hepatitis, all contracted by drinking the foul water. Worm infections and gastroenteritis were ubiquitous and *Durchfall* (diarrhea) was commonplace, exponentially adding to the water pollution. Many lost more fluids and calories than they were able to take in. Rose and Else knew that all water had to be boiled before drinking but this was almost impossible to adhere to, given the primitive setting, where the only source of heat was the burning of wood, which was scarce.

Tuberculosis was common among the prisoners and was easily spread via the respiratory system within these crowded conditions. *Hauptscharführer* Kurt Engels was especially fearful of contracting tuberculosis from a prisoner and issued an order that anyone with this diagnosis would be quickly transferred to the Belzec extermination camp.

The most common and deadliest infectious disease, however, was neither transmitted through drinking water nor breathing the air. This was epidemic typhus, caused by a type of bacteria called rickettsia and transmitted by lice between human hosts. A disastrous decline in personal hygiene, filthy clothes, interiors, and bedding promulgated the survival of lice. Those infected with *Fleckfieber*, the German name for the illness, experienced acute symptoms of high fever, headache, weakness, and a skin rash a week after having been bitten by a louse previously infected by feeding on a person with the disease. This was often followed by pneumonia, kidney failure, coma and cardiac failure with death occurring in approximately 30% of those infected, with older people more at risk for a fatal outcome. Antibiotics for the treatment of typhus only became available after World War II. In Izbica, under its congested and unsanitary conditions, typhus spread on a scale which would have been impossible normally.

Among the deportees in Izbica, there were a number of skilled German Jewish physicians who attempted to treat the sickest patients with very limited tools. They would make charcoal to decrease the diarrhea of gastroenteritis and beg the Nazis for more food for those suffering from starvation. Quarantine was necessary to limit the spread of infectious disease, but there was no facility to house those requiring isolation. Personal hygiene was impossible to maintain. There was no toilet paper. The doctors encouraged the boiling of water but had no control over the water used in Nazi food preparation. The food itself often contained pathogenic bacteria such as E. Coli. and prisoners had to share unwashed bowls and spoons. Swarms of flies and other insects infested the premises where the food was stored, cooked, and dispatched. The *Judenrat* tried to supply the doctors with used sheets, discarded by Nazi officers, to fashion bandages for the injuries that occurred daily. Most wood in the area was quickly utilized as fuel leaving the physicians only scraps to fashion splints for the treatment of fractures.

With contaminated water and no antiseptics, minor skin injuries became major problems for the prisoners, with many developing abscesses or even gangrene.

The *Judenrat* established a makeshift infirmary, where those prisoners who had been nurses in Germany did the best that they could for their patients. A survivor of another Polish ghetto has written "Purulent, unwashed patients lay two a bed in their day shirts that were grey with dirt and full of fleas. They were covered with one blanket, and accommodated in a stuffy, stinking room...... All the nurses could do was to distribute the food and sometimes to provide a bed pan. There were around six of those pans per block of 800 patients. I don't think they were ever washed and were covered with faeces."

There was always someone ill in the room shared by my family and they rapidly became accustomed to the endless outbreaks of epidemics and seeing those around them succumbing to their maladies. Many people fell sick within the first month of their arrival. Somehow, Rose and Else carried on, struggling to maintain their optimism and hope. To do otherwise would be a death sentence.

Most of those deported from Germany to Izbica owned only the clothing that they were wearing during their train transit. Rose and Else were fortunate that they had donned many layers for that trip, since all the other packed apparel never arrived at their destination. In general, everyone living in "266 in Block II" had only one set of clothing. They had been brought up with an almost sacred belief in cleanliness and Rose had tried to convey this principle to Gerda, Helmut, and Günter while they were children. Now she protected herself from the cold with the same outfit and tried to wash her undergarments as frequently as possible. Given the close quarters, it was difficult to keep her coat, which she generally left under her bed when inside, from becoming lice infested. She developed a daily routine of brushing her coat outside with evergreen branches to prevent that from occurring. A bed sheet and blanket were present on the bed when they arrived, and she was careful to frequently shake them outside to remove blood sucking skin parasites. Rose's shoes quickly became filthy and chronically wet from walking in the streets, but she tried to clean them to the best of her ability and guarded them from theft, since their loss would be devastating. A ghetto survivor later said that shoes were, "more important than bread, in high demand among inmates and constantly stolen during sleeping hours." The memoir of another survivor describes the efforts taken to protect shoes from being stolen during sleeping hours: "To protect my own, I bound them together with my belt, wrapped the belt around my neck, kept the end of the belt between my teeth all night and clutched the shoes under my arm."

In March 1942, Joseph Goebbels, Hitler's minister for propaganda, made an entry in his diary regarding the gassing of Jews in the Lublin district of Poland. He wrote "A judgment is being visited upon the Jews which, barbaric as it is, they have fully deserved. Führer's prophecy of the fate in store for them if they started another world war is beginning to come true in the most terrible manner. In these matters, one must not give way to sentimentality. If we did not fight them, the Jews would destroy us. It is a life-and-death struggle between the Aryan race and the Jewish bacillus."

336

In their speeches to the citizens of the Third Reich, Hitler and his assassins frequently used the German verb *"vernichten"* as a synonym for annihilation in regard to the Jewish people. There are other definitions of *vernichten* (or the noun *vernichtung*) besides the obvious one of murder. Devastation, ruination, elimination, exhaustion, wearing out, laying waste to, destroying, and exterminating all come to mind. For the prisoners in Izbica, the restriction of the clothing available and the lack of a decent pair of shoes was part of the continuing dehumanization process prior to their ultimate fate. In addition to providing protection from the elements, clothing allows the individual to assert some normalcy — however small and trivial it may have been—over their lives. Dressing was one of the few acts in which a semblance of control was still possible, even though prisoners generally had no choice about how they dressed. The inability to "look decent" only added to the loss of self-dignity, morality, or respectability. One survivor has said that after the process of becoming accustomed to her disheveled appearance, the discovery of lice in her clothing was the breaking point — "It was beyond endurance."

The third and last of the postcards from Izbica was sent four weeks after Passover, is dated April 28, 1942, and postmarked April 30, 1942, five weeks after Rose and Else's arrival at the *Durchgangslager*. As was the first card, this one is again addressed to *Frau* Lina Liepmann, Virigiliastr. 13., Essen a / Ruhr. It is postmarked Izbica (Wieprz) April 30 [19] 42-11, About Krasnystaw (Distr Lublin.) The sender once again is "Else Liepmann, Izbica a / W. Distr. Lublin, Krasnystaw General-gouvernment, Block II / 266.

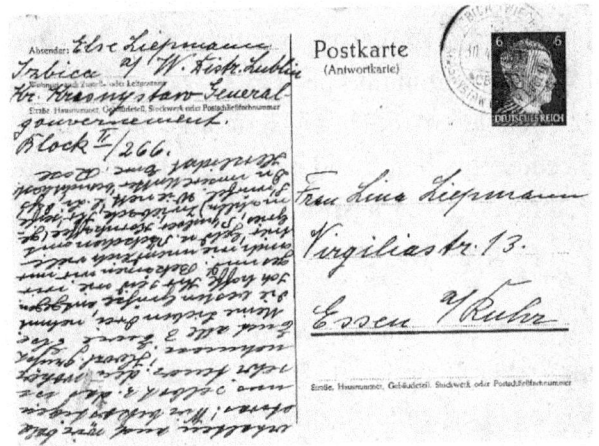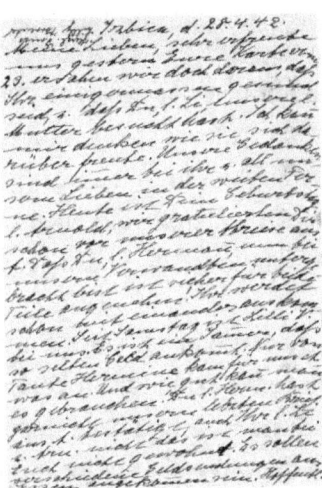

The front and back of the last of three
postcards sent from Izbica, dated April 28,
1942, and postmarked April 30, 1942.

Although the vast majority of the contents of the letters over the years to Rose's children had been penned by my grandmother, it is hardly surprising that this card is primarily written by Else, given that both were first cousins of Arnold Liepmann and his wife Lina.

Izbica April 28, 1942

My dear ones!,

Yesterday we were very happy with your card of the 29th, as we learned from it that you are reasonably healthy and that you, dear Li, have visited our dear mother. I can imagine how happy she was. Our thoughts are always with her and all our loved ones far away. Today is your birthday dear Arnold, we congratulated you already before we left Aachen. That you, dear Hermann, are now staying with our relatives, is certainly pleasant for both parties! You will get along well. Lilli V. has been with us since Saturday. It's a shame that money arrives so rarely. We only received something from Aunt Hermine. And how well it can be used! You dear Hermann didn't confirm our last letter from Aachen, neither did you dear Li and Arnold, which is so unlike you. Various mailings of money are said to have arrived from Essen. Hopefully we too will receive something soon! We feed ourselves and that is very expensive, because where to get it from!

Greetings to you all 3,   your Else

Rose Adds:

My dear three, take the best regards. I hope you are healthy like us. If only we would get, like an infinite number of people here, money and parcels with semolina, pudding powder, ground coffee, rusks, curd soap, soup cubes. How nice of you, dear Li, to visit our mother!

Kindest regards,   your Rose

The card referred to that had arrived in Izbica from Li on March 29, 1942, has, of course, been destroyed. Rose and Else must have been overjoyed at the news that my great-grandmother Fanni was visited at the Aachen Jewish *Altenheim.* At least she was alive and had not been deported. Herz "Hermann" Sternberg had moved in with his cousins Arnold and Li in Essen, likely because his home had been seized by the Nazis. These are "the dear three" that Rose references. Else again refers to Arnold's April birthday and reminds the Liepmanns that "congratulations" had been sent before they were deported from Aachen.

"Lilli V." who "has been with us since Saturday" is Lilli Vorreuter, another cousin previously living in Essen, who was transported to Izbica from Düsseldorf on train *"Da 52"* on April 22, 1942, the train on which I first had thought Rose and Else had been deported. Lilli V., together with 352 other Jews from Essen, was carried from the Essen central train station 60 kilometers northeast to Düsseldorf on April 21, 1942, on a special train consisting of five to seven passenger cars and two freight cars, provided by the *Reichsbahn* administration in Essen, solely for containing deportees.

Düsseldorf Hauptbahnof

The municipal slaughterhouse of Düsseldorf, where Lilli Vorreuter spent the night of April 21, 1942, together with almost one thousand of the other deportees on Train #52

The Grossviehmarkthalle of Düsseldorf's Alter Schlachthof, (the livestock market hall of the municipal slaughterhouse of Düsseldorf)

I am certain that Lilli told her cousins how their group, many of them elderly, had to walk, dragging their suitcases with all their worldly possessions, in single file from the Düsseldorf *Hauptbahnhof* for more than three hours to reach the *Schlachthof* (municipal slaughterhouse) adjacent to the Derendorf train station, where, one day later, they boarded the boxcars which would take them to Izbica.

Rose and Else compared their own experience while Lilli related how a thousand people spent the night sleeping on the cement floor of the *Grossviehmarkthalle* (livestock market hall) of Düsseldorf's *Alter Schlachthof*, which had been used as a collection point to intern Westphalian Jews for one to three nights on prior transports. During late 1941 and 1942, almost 6,000 Jewish men, women, and children from the entire administrative district of Düsseldorf had to gather in this hall for a total of seven transports. The *abattoir* was a functioning slaughterhouse where large cattle were initially brought for slaughter. The vast area was stark with a blood-stained floor made of hammered granite slabs. Before each deportation, the Gestapo had to coordinate and plan the exact procedure with the management of the municipal slaughterhouse so that normal business operations would not be interrupted.

Testimonies from deportees on the transport from Derendorf to Riga on December 10, 1941, recall the horrible conditions of the Düsseldorf slaughterhouse. "We were over one thousand people in the huge room and everything was deep in water. It was a terrible night." One survivor of this train to Riga testified at the Eichmann trial that the market hall "was flooded with water "up to the ankles," and that the crowded conditions made it impossible to lie down and sleep during the night.

These cards stress the necessity of obtaining funds to buy food for their sustenance. "Aunt Hermine" is Hermine "Eva" Vorreuter Aronstein, my great-grandmother Fanni's younger sister and an aunt to Else and Rose. Hermine was an 84-year-old widow at that time living in Berleburg, Westphalia. A few months after sending money to her nieces in Izbica, "Eva," despite her old age, was deported on July 30, 1942, on "Train *Da 72*" from Dortmund to Theresienstadt where she died on May 6, 1943. Her daughter Kathi was murdered in the Sobibor death camp in 1942, and her daughter Gertrud was deported to the Minsk ghetto where she succumbed in 1942. Her only child to survive to adulthood, Anna Aronstein, was fortunately able to escape to New Jersey.

Else is suggesting that perhaps letters with money from Hermann, Lina and Arnold did not get through to them, despite other mailings with money from Essen reaching other Izbica recipients. It is apparent that, given the close quarters and commonality of their situation, the deportees in Izbica had many conversations about their means for survival. Rose reiterates that "an infinite number of people," their fellow Jews in Izbica, were receiving money and food from friends and relatives. Her frustration, to say the least, is palpable.

Rose specifically mentions needing "semolina," a type of flour made from a species of wheat called "durum," rather than common wheat. Semolina is coarser than regular flour. The German word for semolina is *Weichweizengrieß*, but she uses the more common term *Grieß*. In Velmede, my family cooked semolina with milk and sugar and then topped it wth a little butter or cinnamon to make *Grießbrei*. Semolina could also be mixed with milk, sugar and whipped egg whites, dried fruit and nuts and then baked in the oven to make a cake called *Grießauflauf*. In Izbica, there was no milk or sugar or other ingredients available unless one could pay exorbitant sums of money for them. Rose and Else would have mixed semolina in boiling water to make a porridge with relatively high protein content.

The "pudding powder" was something Rose and Else had also grown up with as children in Bücken and used in their Velmede kitchen. It was a mixture of cornstarch, dry milk powder, sugar, and salt. At home, they would add egg yolks, whole milk, a touch of salt and vanilla beans in certain proportions to make *Vanillepudding*, a popular dessert at that time. Rose could have made the powder from scratch, as Fanni did for her family, but it became far easier to have Albert bring packets of Vanilla Instant Pudding Mix when he came from *M. Oppenheim*. That product was manufactured in Bielefield, Westphalia, by a company called "Dr Oetker," in 1891. The company today is one of the world's largest producers of frozen pizzas and convenience foods. In a new book, "*Dr Oetker and the National Socialists*," Munich history professor Andreas Wirsching points out that the company aligned itself with the Nazis after the extreme right seized power. The Oetker manager, a dedicated Nazi, often went to Berlin to meet with the chief of the German police, Heinrich Himmler. He was "able to seamlessly incorporate the anti-Jewish government policy into his view of the world," while the company's owner donated large sums of money to Himmler's cause and provided the German army with large amounts of free products from the company. In 1937, the Nazis rewarded Oetker's generosity by inviting him to a reception at the chancellor's residence, where he met Adolf Hitler. He later spoke of how the encounter thrilled him. Rudolf-August Oetker, son of the founder, joined the Nazi Party in 1940 and in July 1941, volunteered for the notorious *Waffen SS*, the elite separate army run directly by the Nazi Party. Wirsching writes, "his support for the NSDAP went well beyond 'simple opportunism'."

Had they received any "pudding powder" in Izbica, Rose and Else would have had only water to mix it with, but it could serve as a good source of carbohydrates due to its large starch content. It in no way resembled the *Vanillepudding* of their former lives.

My grandmother's request for "ground coffee" would have been difficult, if not impossible to fulfill. It was a sought-after commodity at that time, even in the United States where, in November 1942, coffee rationing was implemented, limiting households to 1 pound of coffee every five weeks, the equivalent of one cup per day. The Roosevelt administration prioritized its consumption for those in the military since the caffeine allowed them to function better on the battlefield. Thomas Czekanski, senior curator at The National WWII Museum, has said "You could argue that coffee is something that helped influence the victory of the democracies in World War II because we had it, and the Axis didn't."

The "rusks" that Rose asked for are the English translation for *zwieback,* which literally means "twice baked" from *zwie* (twice) plus *backen* to bake. It is a hard dry biscuit made from flour, eggs, and sugar, originating in East Prussia.

Because Germany lacked fats to make soap, the government made "curd soap," containing no trace of the scarce oil needed for the war effort. This is what Rose requests. A person at a Jewish old age home in Luxembourg was hastily deported because she used real soap rather than "war soap." The art of survival in Izbica included washing daily, something to look forward to, especially if there was soap and warm water.

Rose's appeal for "soup cubes" recognized that bouillon cubes can be mixed with water to stretch ingredients into a full, and filling, nutritious meal. Napoleon Bonaparte once said, "an army travels on its stomach. Soup makes the soldier." In her kitchen in Velmede, my grandmother likely always had a few packages of Knorr soup cubes, manufactured by the German food manufacturing Carl Heinrich Theodore Knorr, who began experimenting with dried soups in 1873 and finally introduced the soup cube in 1910.

On April 8, 1942, an additional trainload of Polish Jews was sent from Izbica to Belzec to make more room for the deportees from the west. On May 14 and 15, the Czech Jews in Izbica were rounded up and placed on two trains, one to Sobibor and the other to Belzec, the two nearby death camps.

April 28, 1942, is the last date of any contact with my grandmother. There is no mention of her children or me. Everything is about scarcity and need. The absence of such concerns makes the marked degree of emotional despair obvious. Less than one month later, according to a special order by the RSHA (*Reichssicherheitshauptamt*), the prisoners of the Izbica transit ghetto were no longer allowed to send any written communication to areas outside the Lublin district. Polish Holocaust Historian Robert Kuwałek (1966-2014), Lublin-based director of the Museum at the former Belzec death camp, dates the banning of postal traffic by the deportees in the *Generalgouvernement* to May 15, 1942.

Thousands of people continued to be deported to Izbica. From March to May 1942, between 12,000 and 14,000 Jews were transported to Izbica, including Rose and Else, German engineers, doctors, economists, professors, and Austrian army generals suspected of plotting treason against Hitler. One thousand Jews from Vienna arrived on April 9, 1942, and 1570 from Germany on April 22 to April 26. On April 27, 1942, an additional one thousand primarily German Jews came from Theresienstadt. In May 1942, thousands more arrived in Izbica from Vienna, Slovakia, and Germany, including another thousand individuals originating in Koblenz. The new arrivals had to wait for available places to stay, and the ghetto became more incredibly overcrowded. Most arrivals were elderly or women and children since young able-bodied men were commonly removed from the train at the stop in Lublin and sent to the Madjanek concentration camp, located on Lublin's outskirts, where they were used as forced laborers before being put to death. The final trains to Izbica arrived on June 13 and June 15, 1942, carrying a total of 3,000 German Jews. By this time there was a net outflow of Jews from Izbica to the nearby places known as Belzec and Sobibor.

During the Holocaust, the establishment of ghettos was an essential measure within the dedicated Nazi endeavor of heartlessly separating, persecuting, dehumanizing, and ultimately destroying Europe's Jews. Some ghettos were created by the mere whim of an SS-*Gruppenführer* and could exist for only a few weeks before its inmates were shipped elsewhere. The Nazis counted on a large percentage of ghetto residents quickly perishing from the cold, starvation, disease, or suicide, the latter often due to hopelessness caused by repeated "resettlement." For the Germans, the ghettos were a provisional measure to control and segregate Jews while the Nazi leadership in Berlin deliberated various options regarding the annihilation of the Jewish population. Once the "final solution" was devised and implemented, there was an exodus of Jews from the ghettos to the established "Operation Reinhard" killing centers.

In Izbica at that time, few, if any, of the residents were aware that these death camps existed. On July 10, 1942, Polish underground officials in occupied Poland sent a report to the Polish government-in-exile in London. This account details the killing process in the Belzec camp and other Operation Reinhard camps. The descriptions were soon shared with the British government, other Allied organizations in western Europe, and Jewish organizations. The report was met with incredibility and distrust as to its veracity. No action was taken to warn those Jews still in ghettos about the camps.

The movement of Jews out of Izbica to other areas was termed "relocation" for the purpose of population redistribution. With diabolical precision, *Hauptscharführer* Kurt Engels created ethnic divisions among the Izbica Jews to "decide" who would be sent to Belzec, the SS killing center devoted exclusively to the destruction of human beings, first by mass shootings, and after July 1942 within gas chambers. Belzec was located along a major rail line connecting Jewish population centers in Lvov, Krakow, and Lublin. By the end of July 1942, 350,000 Jews from these cities, plus transit ghettos such as Izbica, had been sent to Belzec or to the nearby Polish death camp of Sobibor to be murdered.

Engels had his own private Jewish police squad, recruited from German-speaking Czech Jews. He created a separate Czech Jewish faction within the *Judenrat* as well as a Czech Jewish Ghetto Police Force (*Ordnungsdienst*). Often German or Czech Jews who spoke German fluently were members of the *Judenrat* and Jewish police in the ghettos. These groups were told to remove "inferior Polish Jews" from Izbica. The Czech *Ordnungsdienst* were frequently loaded onto the last car of a particular transport, after having participated in their round-up of Polish Jews, where they were taken to Belzec and subsequently gassed together with the Poles.

Some of those Izbica prisoners were eager to be "relocated" from Izbica, since they had witnessed Engels walking the streets of Izbica early each morning, enjoying randomly shooting Jews before returning to Gestapo headquarters for his hearty breakfast. Engels chose Izbica as the place to practice murder. He drove around the town on a motorcycle looking for victims to shoot. He killed people, including young children, while they slept in their beds or were just walking in the streets. This was a witnessed reality—the stories about Belzec and Sobibor were just vague rumors.

The first mass Nazi Gestapo killing operation (known in German as an "*aktion*") after Rose and Else mailed the last postcard took place between May 12 and May 15, 1942. Several hundred Jewish men – both Polish and non-Polish – were taken from Izbica to the Majdanek concentration camp in Lublin, originally planned to be the largest source of inmates to perform free labor for the Third Reich. There the Jews would work in construction sites and factories to support the German war effort. They would literally work themselves to death in the absence of adequate food and presence of infectious diseases, and once deemed unproductive and, therefore, useless to the Nazis, would be sent to Belzec or Sobibor.

At the same time, a second group of approximately 400 people was deported directly to the death camp in Sobibor.

The few Polish Jews that remained in Izbica in May and June of 1942 would often try to escape by hiding in the village or the surrounding forests when an *aktion* was announced. Most of the non-Polish Jews at this time obediently assembled on the Izbica marketplace, then were led away in columns to the Izbica railway station. These Jews recognized more slowly the fate that awaited them.

On June 8, 1942, another deportation *Aktion* took place, now directed against the many Jews in Izbica who were deemed unfit for work. Approximately 2,000 Polish and non-Polish primarily older Jewish women were deported, probably to the Belzec death camp. One month later, the Germans rounded up Jews who had fled Izbica to avoid previous *Aktions* and had returned when they felt it was again safe. They were deported to the Sobibor death camp on July 8, 1942.

For the next three months, the situation in Izbica was relatively calm with no additional deportations being carried out. However, both within the town and also the surrounding fields and especially at the Jewish cemetery, Jews were arrested and immediately executed on the personal orders of Engels and his deputy, Ludwig Klemm. The executions were carried out on the grounds that Jews were trading illegally, having contact with Poles, storing weapons, or corresponding with other Jews by mail or by carrying messages.

On August 19, 1942, *SS* official and chemical engineer Kurt Gerstein was sent to Belzec to inspect the gas chambers. He was so horrified by what he saw that, upon his return to Germany, he leaked a report of the mass killing to the Vatican and other Catholic Church officials in Germany, Swiss and Swedish diplomats, and the Dutch government-in-exile. Again, these groups either doubted or were indifferent to the report and did nothing.

During this period, Polish Jews from neighboring ghettos were still being transported to Izbica. One of the events was recalled by survivor Tovi Blatt: "In September 1942 all Jews from the small neighbouring ghettos of Krasnystaw and Zamosc were resettled in Izbica. The resettlement was a bloody one. The people had been formed into columns and forced to walk the entire 21 kilometers; Engels guarded them with a machine gun manned from the roof of the truck. It was a caravan of horrors. He shot to kill those who lagged behind. Riding alongside in horse-drawn wagons were Ukrainian guards, who executed Jews at will and with pleasure."

Thousands of refugees for whom no accommodation could be found wandered about Izbica's streets or huddled in hallways. German and Ukrainian guards working in shifts surrounded the Jewish quarter and made sure that no one escaped.

On October 22, 1942, Engels called members of the *Judenrat* and *Ordnungsdienst* to his quarters. He announced a deportation order and made the two councils responsible for its successful operation. On this occasion, everyone in town including members of the *Judenrat* had to go directly to the train station and stand at attention until Engels arrived to personally select who would go and who would stay. What happened at the train station was horrible. Tovi Blatt remembers that day: "Since there were not enough boxcars, Engels decided to make a selection. Everyone was screaming and crying... There was chaos. Engels became furious. As he rested his machine gun on the shoulder of the *Judenrat* chairman Abram Blatt (Tovi's uncle), he mowed down a group of people and forced the others into the boxcars. They were packed so tightly that some suffocated to death before the train even left town. Those who could not fit in the boxcars, including my family, were told to go home."

A few days later, the Germans liquidated the orphanage in Izbica by shooting all the children there. Engels personally shot the chairman of the *Judenrat*, Abraham Blatt, and his deputy.

In early November 1942, the final mass liquidation of the Izbica Jews occurred. After this, about one thousand Jews remained in Izbica. They were concentrated in one street and employed in collecting and organizing the property left behind by the Jews who had been sent to the death camps. During this time, some young Jews who had managed to hide in nearby forests returned, erroneously believing they would be exploited for work, rather than being harmed. In January 1943, about 750 of the remaining Jews were sent to Sobibor, and the others, numbering about 300, were also sent there in April 1943. The Izbica Transit Ghetto had been totally liquidated.

Jan Karski, a non-Jewish member of the Polish resistance movement against the Nazis, entered the Warsaw Ghetto in August 1942, during the Nazi's mass deportation of the Jews of Warsaw to the Treblinka death camp. He met with Adolf Berman and Leon Feiner, two Jewish leaders of the secret organization, *Żegota*, the Polish Council for Jewish Aid, whose aim was to rescue Jews from the Holocaust. They persuaded Karski to visit Izbica on a fact-finding mission to further witness the brutal treatment of the Jews by the Germans and subsequently to both inform the Allies about the mass extermination of Polish Jewry and present them with plans to stop this.

Karski visited Izbica in September 1942 disguised as a Ukrainian policeman. He was guided by an actual Estonian guard. In his own words, this was his first impression of the Ghetto: "As we approached to within a few hundred yards of the camp, the shouts, cries and shots cut off further conversation. I noticed, or thought I noticed, an unpleasant stench that seem(ed) to have come from decomposing bodies mixed with horse manure. This may have been an illusion. The Estonian was, in any case, completely impervious to it. He even began to hum some sort of folk tune to himself... We passed through a small grove of decrepit -looking trees and emerged directly in front of the loud, sobbing, reeking, camp of death... The chaos, the squalor, the hideousness of it all, was simply indescribable. There was a suffocating stench of sweat, filth, decay, damp straw, and excrement."

The Estonian led Karski to the train station. "He proceeded eagerly to enlighten me. 'That's the train they'll load them on. You'll see it all." Karski continues, "(Engels)... turned to the crowd (of prisoners), planted himself with his feet wide apart and his hands on his hips and loosed a roar that must have actually hurt his ribs. It could be heard far above the hellish babble that came from the crowd. 'Quiet, Quiet! All Jews will board this train, to be taken to a place where work awaits them. Keep order. Do not push. Anyone who attempts to resist or create a panic will be shot.' He stopped speaking and looked challengingly at the helpless mob that hardly seemed to know what was happening. Suddenly accompanying the movement with a loud hearty laugh, he yanked out his gun and fired three random shots into the crowd. A single stricken groan answered him. He replaced the gun in his holster (and) smiled... For a moment the crowd was silent. Those nearest the *SS* man recoiled from the shots and tried to dodge, panic-stricken, toward the rear. But this was

344

resisted by the mob, as a volley of shots from the rear sent the whole mass surging forward madly, screaming in pain and fear. The shots continued without let-up from the rear and now from the sides too, narrowing the mob down and driving it in a savage scramble onto the passageway (to the train) ... It was twilight when the forty-six (I counted them) cars were packed."

After returning to Warsaw, the *Żegota* gave Karski a microfilm of hundreds of documents and he made his way by train to Berlin, onto Vichy France, crossed into Spain, and reached London via Gibraltar to share the evidence. Early in 1943, he appealed to British Foreign Secretary Anthony Eden, who told him that "Great Britain had already done enough by accepting 100,000 refugees."

In July 1943, he travelled to the United States and met with President Franklin Delano Roosevelt. Karski's message failed to convince him of the critical plight of the Jews. He also had a conference with Supreme Court Justice Felix Frankfurter, a close friend of the President's. Karski remembers Frankfurter's reaction: "'Mr. Karski,' he says emphatically, 'A man like me talking to a man like you must be totally frank. So I must say: I am unable to believe in what I have just heard, in all the things that you have just told me.'"

Although Karski's efforts were valiant, they largely fell on deaf ears, unwilling to listen and comprehend the enormity of human evil. Years later, Jan Karski was recognized as being one of more than 16,000 Christians included as "Righteous Among the Nations" at *Yad Vashem*, Jerusalem's World Holocaust Remembrance Center.

Had Karski been able to convince world leaders of the existential predicament of European Jewry and had there been subsequent major efforts to rapidly remedy the situation, it nonetheless would have been too late for my grandmother and her sister.

There is no means of determining exactly when, where, and how Rose and Else perished. On April 13, 1942, the Würzburg Gestapo, having intercepted some letters written from Izbica to Franconia, Bavaria, asked the Reich Security Main Office in Berlin to intervene and stop the mail traffic. Although Kuwałek, the historian, dated the institution of the ban to May 15, 1942, there are a large number of surviving postcards mailed from Izbica after that, some postmarked as late as August 1942. Outgoing mail from Izbica to recipients in Germany in fact came to a definite standstill at the beginning of September 1942. Given Rose and Else's proclivity to correspond frequently, I would have expected that they would have sent a fourth postcard no later than mid-May 1942, had they still been alive.

Detailed accounts of specific individuals killed during Operation Reinhard are almost nonexistent. This was a tightly secret process and, if any records were kept, they were deliberately burnt or otherwise destroyed by the Nazis before the end of the War for fear of future incrimination. In addition, a large percentage of murders have to be attributed to widespread shooting, since a "Holocaust by Bullets" took place in parallel with what occurred in the gas chambers. During the three months of August, September, and October 1942, it is estimated that a minimum of 1,320,000 victims were murdered by the Nazis in the area of the General Government, of which 292,000 were slaughtered by bullets.

While Auschwitz had a reasonable number of survivors to reconstruct the history of some individuals, very few survived the camps of Operation Reinhard to convey their experiences. Six hundred thousand Jews were exterminated at the Belzec death camp and there were only two survivors to provide first person accounts.

On August 15, 1942, the Fuhrer, chagrined with the pace of the extermination of the Jews in the "General Gouvernment" ordered "all action speeded up!" In his book, *The Holocaust: A History of the Jews of Europe During the Second World War,* British historian Sir Martin Gilbert devotes the chapter, "At a Faster Pace" to a similar directive by Hitler, which he dates to July 23, 1942.

These three months were unarguably one of the most destructive and murderous in the history of human civilization. Biostatistician Lewi Stone of Tel Aviv University has written that Operation Reinhard "was extreme in terms of three elementary indices of the severity of a genocide—kill rate, number, and proportion of population killed …which highlights the singularly violent character of this genocidal event."

Due to the Nazis' inhuman barbarism, there were relatively few living Jews remaining in the General Government by December 1942. Because of the difficulty of rounding up new victims, Himmler reported to Hitler that Operation Reinhard was now complete.

Undoubtedly Rose and Else had died, either by starvation, disease, or gunshot in Izbica or shooting in Belzec or asphyxiation in a gas chamber there. My grandmother would have been 57 years old in August 1942; my great-aunt would have her 55th birthday that same month. They had rarely been separated for almost 55 years. My hope is that they remained together until the very end, that neither sister had to witness the other's murder and that each of them had only a brief time to be alone after the other had left this earth.

Chapter 17: EPILOGUE

The last of the three postcards from Rose and Else in Izbica was mailed on April 29, 1942, and was likely received by their first cousin Arnold Liepmann and his wife Li in Essen, Germany, during the first week of May 1942. Because of the War, it was impossible for them to communicate Rose's location to Gerda in Shanghai, Helmut in Palestine, or Günter in the United States. The Nazi postal system, the *Deutsche Reichspost*, did not allow mail from Germany to be sent to countries which were at war with Germany, including Palestine, then under British rule, China, in the midst of the Second Sino-Japanese War, and, of course, the United States.

Rumors of mass deportations of German Jews to the *Ostland* were circulating in China, the Middle East, and the United States. My mother and her two brothers remained uncertain about their mother's specific situation, and they continued to hope that Rose, Else and Fanni were still surviving in Aachen. In 1942, Germany was winning the War and no end of the hostilities was in sight. Günter had continued his efforts to obtain entrance visas to Cuba for his mother, aunt, and grandmother. His attorney there responded to his repeated inquiries.

Letter from Cuban attorney, May 18, 1942

May 18, 1942

Dear Sir:

I beg to confirm receipt of your favor dated 10th inst., and took best notice of the contents of same. I can quite understand your standpoint and I think it is the right thing to recall the deposit now, as for the time being there is no possibility of bringing your folks into Cuba.

I regret, however, to inform you that I cannot help you at all in this respect, as the Landing Deposits of $500.- each have to be recalled by the intermediary of the Bank or institution, which has brought up same, so that you would have to address yourself to the Bank by which the money has been deposited in order to get it back.

Hoping that you will be able to settle this matter soon, I remain

Always at your services

Miguel Gurwitz y Antovil

Günter had lost the entire $1,500, which he had paid the Cuban government for three entrance visas plus the attorney's fees, representing five years of his savings. He was not about to give up the hope that Rose, her sister, and her mother were alive and well. He continued to write to and visit various United States agencies and was always told that, due to the war, there was no information available regarding his family's whereabouts.

On June 23, 1942, my great-grandmother Fanni Vorreuter Liepmann passed away of natural causes at the *Israelitische Altersheim* just short of her 87th birthday. She had survived her husband Moses by 45 years. She had outlived three sons, Gustav, Max, and Louis, who died as a child, and likely also had survived her two daughters, my grandmother Rose and her sister Else. Paul, her youngest child, was still alive and living in Horn, Germany with his wife Agnes and daughter Ruth. In 1943, that family was deported to the Theresienstadt camp in Czechoslovakia where Agnes died. In 1944, Paul and Ruth were sent to Auschwitz, where they were murdered. Paul was 48, Fanni's granddaughter Ruth, my first cousin once removed, was 15 years old. An entire generation had been wiped out. I was Fanni's only living great-grandchild at that time, to be thankfully joined later by Eric Liepmann Brunell's children, Susan and Peter, and Margot Liepmann Sonneman's children, Jane and Donald.

After the War, we learned that her nephew and niece, Arnold and Li Liepmann, came from Essen to Aachen for her funeral and that Fanni's end was peaceful. She was buried at the Aachen Jewish Cemetery. Her gravestone is inscribed on both sides, the first at the time of her death with her name etched as "Eva" and a wrong birthday "July 15, 1855." In April 1941, Rose had written to Günter to inform the U.S. Consulate "immediately" that Fanni was registered by the authorities with the wrong name and birthday. In 1949, Helmut had the back of the tombstone chiseled with her correct name (nickname of Fanni or more formal Fanny) and proper birthdate (July 9, 1855).

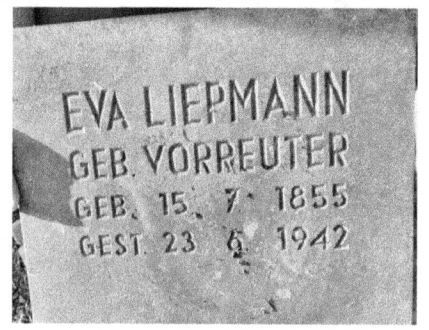 

Left: Original (1942) incorrect headstone inscription.

Right: Corrected (1949) headstone inscription added on reverse of original headstone.

On June 1, 1942, Transport *Zug Da 57* left the city of Kassel, passing through Halle to load more Jews, including my grandfather Albert's brother Eduard and his second wife Erna. The 1009 passengers were bound for the Sobibor death camp. They were told that they had arrived at a transit camp where they would be housed and fed, but instead all were immediately murdered upon exiting the train in Sobibor. Because of political constraints, my mother in Shanghai rarely communicated via Red Cross-delivered letters with Helmut in Palestine and Günter in America. They heard rumors that Rose had been deported to the concentration camp in Theresienstadt, Czechoslovakia. In 1941 the Nazis had established a ghetto in Theresienstadt (Terezin), a garrison town in Northwestern Czechoslovakia, run by the SS, as another transit camp for Jews en route to extermination camps.

Theresienstadt was founded at the end of the 18th century by Emperor Joseph II and named after his mother Empress Maria Theresa (1740-1780), whose anti-Jewish policy reached its climax when she ordered that all the Jews of Prague be expelled. Theresienstadt became an army garrison. Here there were homes, taverns, a post office, and a bank. The little town seemed by observers to have been forced onto the countryside, secluded in the blue hills, and green meadows, much as the concentration camp would be more than a hundred years later. There the Nazis interned, among many others, elderly German Jews and persons of "special merit" in the Reich. For Rose's children, this made sense, since Albert had served as an officer in World War I. In 1943 and 1944, Theresienstadt was presented as a "model Jewish settlement" for misinformation purposes. As part of Nazi propaganda, the Germans permitted an investigative commission of the International Red Cross to visit in June 1944. It was all an elaborate hoax. Prior to the inspection, the Germans intensified deportations to Auschwitz from the ghetto to reduce the overcrowding and the ghetto itself was "beautified." Gardens were planted, houses painted, and barracks renovated. Fake stores, a coffee house, bank, school, and kindergartens were opened throughout Theresienstadt. The commission held carefully orchestrated meetings with selected prisoners The Nazis staged social and cultural events for the visiting dignitaries. After the visit, the Nazis produced a propaganda film, widely distributed throughout the world, about the wonderful new life of the Jews under the auspices of the Third Reich. My mother and her brothers, having themselves seen the "excellent" conditions in Theresienstadt, came to the wishful conclusion that Rose was indeed there and continued to hold that belief until after the end of the War. Once the Red Cross visit was over, the Germans resumed deportations from Theresienstadt, which did not end until October 1944.

Unbeknown to them at the time, those interviewed in the film, together with all of the Jewish leadership (*Judenrat*) and most of the children in the ghetto, were sent to the gas chambers of Auschwitz-Birkenau. More than 155,000 Jews passed through Theresienstadt until it was liberated on May 8, 1945; 35,440 perished in the ghetto and 88,000 were deported to be murdered.

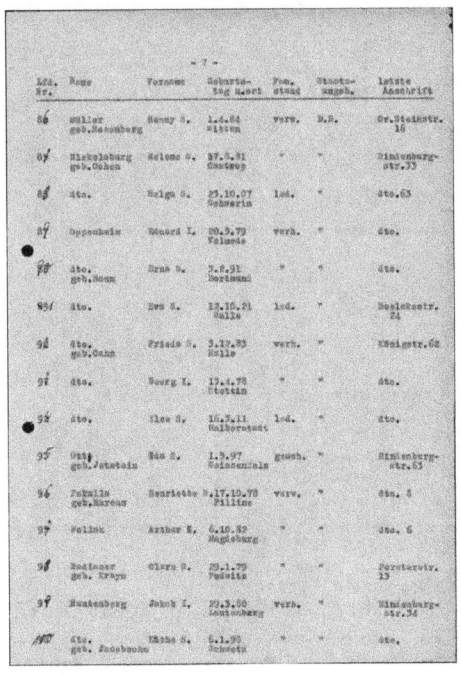

Portion of list of deportees on Transport train da 57 from Halle (Kassel) to extermination camp Sobibor, including Eduard and Erna Oppenheim, June 1, 1942.

By the end of 1942, the German Reich had deported more than two million Jews to death camps. Additionally, hundreds of thousands more Jews had been murdered by *Einzatsgruppen* and police battalions.

Helmut joined the British Army after the second battle of El Alamein in October 1942 and was stationed in Egypt at Abbassia on the outskirts of Cairo. With the outbreak of the Second World War, the British retook effective control of Egypt, which became an important military base in the Middle East, although Egypt remained nominally an independent country.

In July 1942, resigned to the fact that any path to the United States for his mother was closed, Günter volunteered for the United States Army to fight the Nazis himself. He was still considered a German alien and was accepted by the U.S. Army only after filing many forms and submitting letters of support, having a background check, and undergoing multiple interviews. He was then granted a "Notice of Alien's Acceptability for training and service in the armed forces" in late August 1942.

NOTICE OF ALIEN'S ACCEPTABILITY

Date of mailing ___August 26, 1942___

To ___Gunther E. Oppenheim___

Address ___3116 North 15th Street, Phila. Pa.___

Order No. ___S-3337 V___

Local Board No. 58
Philadelphia Pa.
AUG 26 1942
Hunting Park & Schuyler St.
Philadelphia, Pa.
(Local board stamp with date)

You are notified that, after considering your status as an alien, the * Army ~~Navy~~ ~~Marine Corps~~ has found that you * are, if otherwise qualified, ~~are not~~ acceptable for training and service in the armed forces of the United States.

Mabel E. Costello
Member or clerk of local board.

* Strike out portion not applicable.

NOTE

1. If you were found not acceptable to the armed forces, your classification will be changed to Class IV-C.

2. If you were found to be acceptable, your classification will remain unchanged.

D. S. S. Form 697

A few weeks later, having passed his physical examination he was ordered to report for induction into the United States Army.

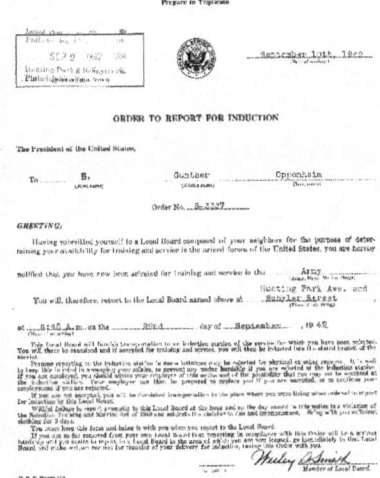

After undergoing basic training, Günter was assigned to the 80th Infantry Division. He proudly became a naturalized U.S. Citizen in December 1942. He had an Army desk job as a clerk until September 1943, when he was recruited to become a "Ritchie Boy."

MY PREVIOUS MILITARY EDUCATION HAS BEEN AS FOLLOWS (*State military training and experience in chronological order.* Use insufficient):

80th Rcn Sq 80 Inf. Div	basic	Oct–Nov 1942
E. Co. 319 Inf 80 Inf Div	"	Nov–Jan 1943
I&R Hq 319 Inf 80 Inf Div	int.	Jan–Mar 1943
G–2 Sec Hq 80 Inf Div	int. clerk	Mar–Sep 1943
MITC Camp Ritchie, Md.	IPW Course	Sep–June 1944
CC "B" Hq 6th Armd Div	Interrog.	June–Sep 1945
3rd Army Int. Center Screening	"	Sep–Oct 1945

List of Günter's U.S. Army assignments, 1942-1945

MITC= Military Intelligence Training Corp

IPW = Interrogation of Prisoners of War

Prior to Pearl Harbor and the entry of the United States into the Second World War, American military observers were sent to England to learn from British combat units. After their return, they recommended that the United States establish a centralized training center for intelligence staff. The Army did not have a program for training officers and noncommissioned officers to gather or analyze battlefield intelligence, particularly through interrogation of prisoners of war. In 1942, General George Marshall, the chief of staff of the US Army, presented a plan to the Secretary of War, Henry Stimson, to establish a top-secret Army facility at Camp Albert C. Ritchie, in Maryland, for specialized training in military intelligence including counterespionage and interrogation of German prisoners of war. Approximately 20,000 soldiers were chosen to undergo this intense training at Camp Ritchie during World War II. Ten percent of the soldiers who were taught at Camp Ritchie were German Jewish refugees, who had escaped Nazi persecution and violence and had immigrated to the United States. Their fluency in the German language and knowledge of German customs enhanced their intelligence work. These 2,000 soldiers, including Günter, were known as the "Ritchie Boys," and uncovered important information that saved the lives of thousands of other American soldiers during World War II. This extraordinary unit was responsible for more than half of all combat intelligence gathered on the Western Front and their efforts were pivotal to the Allies' victory.

Camp Ritchie, Maryland, 1943

At Camp Ritchie, Günter and the other Ritchie Boys took classes in "Terrain Intelligence," "Signal Intelligence," and Morse code. Günter learned close-combat fighting techniques from a 320-pound instructor named Frank Leavitt, who was previously known as Man Mountain Dean, a professional wrestler. This was just part of the "Intense Physical and Weapons Training" to prepare him for the front lines.

During that training, Günter perfected his already extensive knowledge of American slang, and became a chameleon, able to pass both as an American soldier or a German combatant. Because of his special skills, he was ordered to stay at Camp Ritchie for a longer period of time and received additional instruction in how to detect and identify potential enemy spies and saboteurs. He had to memorize up-to-date information about the various enemy commanders, unit structure, location, and weapons. He was also taught psychological warfare tactics, survival strategies when behind enemy lines, operation of mobile radio broadcasting equipment and how to write Allied propaganda aimed at enemy soldiers and civilians.

The culmination of Günter's training at Camp Ritchie was learning how to interrogate prisoners of war. The interrogators were told they could never physically assault a prisoner of war, but they could persuade the prisoners to talk in other ways. Camp Ritchie contained a fake German village which included a house with one of the walls removed so students could watch the staff demonstrate tactics for capturing and interrogating potential enemies.

A few of the exceptional students were asked to remain to teach new students. Günter was one of these, remaining as an instructor in Interrogation of Prisoners (IPW) until June 1944. My uncle was a natural for his role as an interrogator of German prisoners. He spoke both English and German without an accent. With his blond hair and blue eyes, he looked like an Aryan willing to give favors to German POWs. His fluency in German, knowledge of German customs and familiarity with the German mentality made his work notably easier. He was highly motivated to return to Europe to defeat Nazism, having left loved ones in Europe and hoping to reunite with them. He also wanted Nazis and other perpetrators to be brought to justice.

After completing training at Camp Ritchie, many German Jewish refugee soldiers "Americanized" their name, in part to prevent the Nazis from being able to identify them as Jewish if they were captured. Thus, at the courthouse in Hagerstown, Maryland, Erich Günther Oppenheim officially became Edwin G. (for Günter) Olden, known to his friends as "Guy."

In August 2021, the United States Senate passed a bipartisan resolution honoring the service of the Ritchie Boys. In 2022, the United States Holocaust Memorial Museum named the Ritchie Boys as the recipient of the Museum's highest honor, the Elie Wiesel Award, for "their remarkable actions and heroism in helping to end the war and the Holocaust."

Guy was transferred to England just before D-Day and assigned to an infantry battalion of the "Super Sixth" Armored Division

Oxford England, June 1942

Guy's Insignia of the "Super Sixth"

Six weeks after the D-Day invasion of western Europe, Guy and his 6th Armored Division landed on Utah Beach in Normandy. Guy would be involved in combat in Normandy, Brittany, Ardennes-Alsace, the Rhineland, and Central Europe.

Normandy July 18, 1944

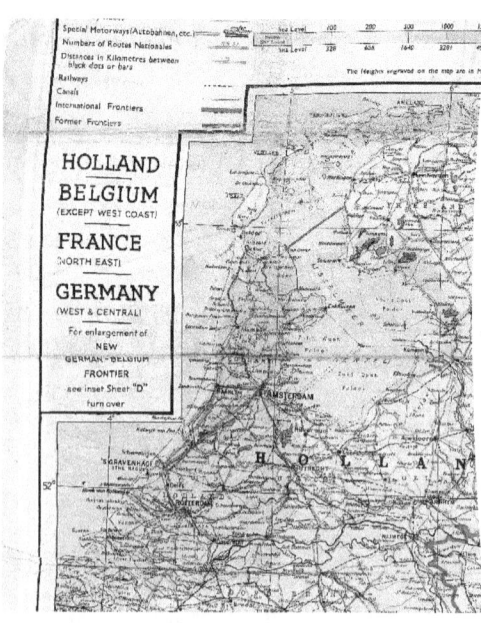

Map carried by Guy during the campaign in France, Belgium and Germany, 1944-1945.

Guy enjoying the fruits of victory in Normandy.

Guy moving west towards Brest, September 1944

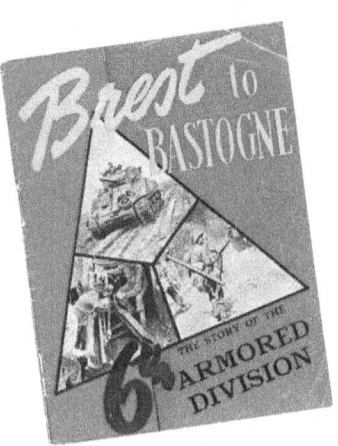

Guy and the "Super Sixth" were subsequently assigned to General George S. Patton's Third Army and fought in the Battle of The Bulge during the winter of 1944-1945.

Guy with his C.O. after the Battle of the Bulge, January 1945.

Guy, Nancy, France, early March 1945.

While in Bastogne, located less than 150 kilometers south of Aachen, Guy asked his commanding officer for permission to go to Aachen to search for any information regarding his mother Rose. His request was granted, but his brief visit to Aachen provided no other information about the whereabouts of our family.

On March 22nd, 1945, Guy's Sixth Armored Division traversed the Rhine River into Germany at the medieval town of "Oppenheim," the name that my ancestors had chosen in 1787, when Emperor Joseph II ruled that German Jews assume last names.

Guy crossing the Rhine, March 22, 1945.

Guy commissioned in the field as an officer (2nd Lieutenant).

As the "Super Sixth" advanced across the Southern Rhineland through Frankfurt, 100 miles south of Guy's birthplace, Allied forces captured 1,500,000 German prisoners. This created many opportunities for Guy and the other Ritchie Boys to practice their interrogation skills. General Patton was present while newly commissioned 2nd Lieutenant Guy Edwin Olden was grilling a German POW. Patton liked his looks, methodology, style, and sense of humor, befriended my uncle and asked Guy to become one of his jeep drivers.

Guy driving his jeep, March 1945

The Super Sixth crossed the *Main* River on March 28 and within a few days the *Fulda, Wehre and Werra* Rivers, placing the division in the heart of the province of *Thüringen* (Thuringia). Their entry into most towns was greeted by white flags of surrender. In Guy's home, many years later, I found an article from a German newspaper with a photograph of proud Nazis titled "Thuringian deputies of the last *Reichstag* and old fighters of our district." In the margin Guy had written "17- Siekmaier was arrested by me."

Gauleiter Heinrich Siekmeier, a member of the Nazi *Reichstag* and "State Councillor" of the Thuringian government, was a highly ranked Nazi leader and subordinate only to the position of *Reichsleiter* (Reich Leader) and to the *Führer* himself.

The Buchenwald death camp was constructed in 1937, ten kilometers northwest of Weimar. As US forces approached Buchenwald, the Germans began to evacuate tens of thousands of prisoners, many of them forced onto death marches. In the afternoon of April 11, 1945, Guy and the Super Sixth liberated the 21,000 remaining inmates at Buchenwald

Freed Prisoners at Buchenwald,,
April 12, 1945

Adolf Hitler committed suicide in Berlin on April 30, 1945, the Battle of Berlin ended on May 2, and Germany unconditionally surrendered to the Allied Forces on May 8, 1945. On May 12, 1945, Second Lieutenant Edwin G. Olden was awarded the Bronze Star for his valuable work as an interrogator of prisoners of war. In attendance at the ceremony was Supreme Allied Commander, General Dwight D. Eisenhower, who would be elected President of the United States in 1952.

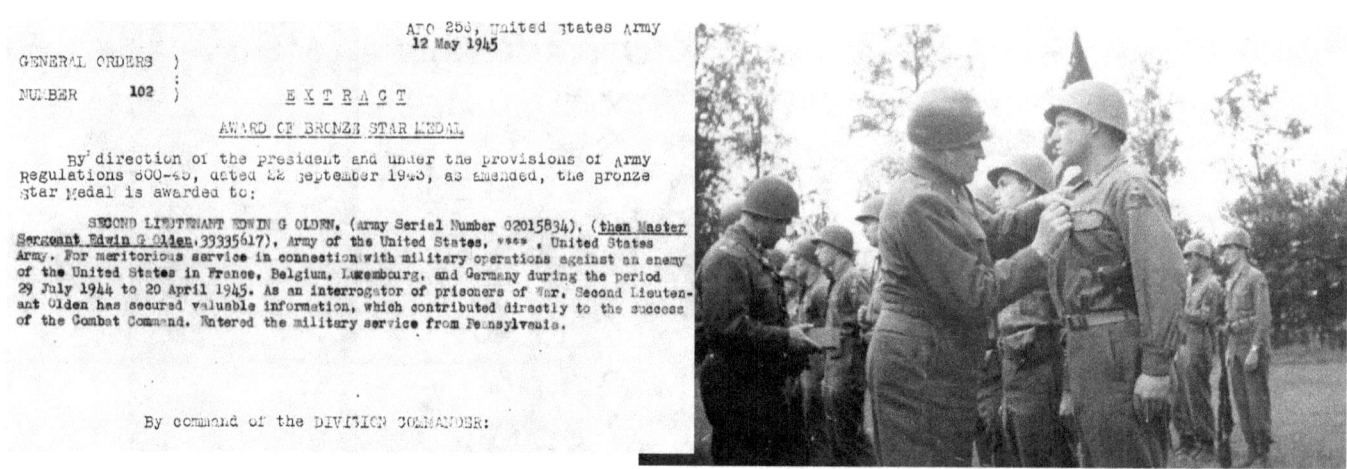

Guy, now stationed in Neumark near Buchenwald, waited for an opportunity to travel by any possible means to Theresienstadt to find his mother, since he and the rest of my family firmly believed that she had been deported there. In order to drive the 350 kilometers from Neumark to Theresienstadt, he would have to pass through the Russian-controlled area of Germany.

Post War zones of occupation, 1945.

B = Buchenwald

T= Theresienstadt

Guy was successful in navigating to Theresienstadt in his Jeep and after returning to Neumark, wrote the following lengthy letter to our family. Since fighting in the Middle East had terminated, he mailed the letter to Helmut in Palestine, rather than trying to reach his sister, my mother Gerda, in Shanghai, where the Japanese were still at war with the Allies and maintained control of the city.

2nd Lt. Edwin G Olden 0-20158J4

HQ   00 "B"   APO 256

25 May 1945   c/o Postmaster New York, N.Y. U. S. Army

Dear Helmut—

As you all know I am not in the habit of putting carbon paper to use in writing my letters but since this is going to be a rather lengthy report which interests 5 different persons you will all please excuse me for writing a rather stereotype letter. One copy of this letter each will go to my brother Helmut, my cousin Walter, my cousin Stanley, my cousin Heinz Oppenheim, and my aunt Paula Brunell. All the above-mentioned relations of mine will please pass this letter along to whoever may be interested in its contents. I am particularly thinking about my aunt, Minna Baum.

As you all may know, ever since I have been on the continent it has been my desire to have enough time off which would enable me to look around for my mother and finally on 23 May 1945 an opportunity presented itself to me. At present I am located in Neumark, Germany which is appr. 15 km North West of Weimar and the notorious Concentration Camp Buchenwald is in our immediate vicinity. On the morning of 23 May I reported at Buchenwald as assistant convoy commander for a 14-truck convoy which was to go from Buchenwald to Pilsen, Tschekoslovacia taking appr. 250 Tschecs and Slovaks who were formerly inmates at Buchenwald back home. Today Buchenwald looks of course so much better already in comparison to the first days shortly after we had overrun it, but still it is a very depressing feeling to stand out on the tremendous, big "Appel Platz" where newcomers to the camp got their first christening by the SS consisting usually of standing for 12 hours or more out in the open, rain, snow, or shine, under the supervision of some Obersturmbannfuehrer and his clique. This morning however the scene was an entirely different one. The American Army had come with 2 ½ ton trucks to bring Tschec Nationals back home and everyone, even though very weak yet in body, was in good spirits and milling busily about bringing little bundles along and boarding our trucks. Most of the people all men from 15 years of age up to 50 wore still the striped zebra Buchenwald clothing and today they wore it with a certain amount of pride. Talking to all these unfortunate characters one got the impression that almost all of them didn't even know what they were going back home for. Their families were split up and no one had had any news from home for 4 or more years. In spite of all that as soon as they boarded the trucks which were colorfully rigged up with streamers and painted signs, their national colors and what have you, the whole gang began to sing, and I realized then once again what they were singing about. All in all, it was a long ride of about 200 miles, and we reached Pilsen at 9:30 PM that night. Just in case someone wants to know what route we took here it is: Buchenwald, Weimar, (via the Autobahn Frankfurt Dresden to vic. Jena) at that time we turned South on the Autobahn Berlin Nuernberg to Hof (Bavaria) Asch Eger, Pilsen.

I remained in Pilsen for the night and the next morning I contacted a lot of people who might be able to-give me some information on how to go through Russian lines to Theresienstadt. Theresienstadt is the place where my mother was supposed to be. I couldn't get any satisfaction at any of our units in Pilsen about obtaining an official pass through the Russian lines. There simply isn't any liaison with the Russian forces and nobody seems to know where the Russian front lines run nor has anyone an idea whether one can go into their territory or not. Most of the Staff officers at corps I spoke to told me not to go into Russian lines since some of our boys had gotten themselves into heaps of trouble. Since I was determined to get to Theresien Stadt to find out about my mother I selected a route with my peep (*army jargon for "jeep"*) where Russian Forces were either non-existing or very thin. From Pilsen I went via Theusing-Petschau-Schlaggenwald-Elbogen- Karlsbad-Schlachenwert-Kloesterle-Komotau-Bruex-Dux-Teplitz-Schoenau   —   Lobositz-Theresienstadt. Halfway between Karlsbad and Komotau the Russian lines began, and all road markers turned suddenly into Russian script, which was very unfortunate for me.

It is peculiar about the Tschcs for although most of them speak a good German they hate to use it and rather stumble along with some French phrases, which they may or may not know. As a whole the Russian soldier looked to me as a very determined soldier and it was funny to note on the road between Pilsen and Karlsbad which must in my opinion constitute the American Russian border line, I found almost every fifty yards a GI guard and then again a Russian tommy-gunner. The Russian infantrist looks very rugged and he is naturally not half as well dressed as our boys. "Rusky" was extremely eager to salute us, and I was more than happy to return his salute. Were it not for him God only knows where we would be today. Tschecoslovacia was decorated all over with their national colors and just as many Russian flags were displayed. Miles and miles of road that is to both sides of the road is piled up with destroyed German motorized or should I say once motorized equipment. Most of that I suppose was caused by our air force. It once again looked like the escape routes which the Germans used out of the Ardennes where our air force had several field days. One very peculiar thing which is worthwhile noting was the female Russian MPs whom I found at ever so many road junctions and intersections directing traffic. The girls are rather smartly dressed handling one yellow and one red flag as traffic signals. The high black boots look good on them and their rifle belt around the waist plus a Sam-Brown belt cut with most Russian girls a figure which accentuates a wonderful bust line. The girls gave us riding by in a peep a big smile and a smart salute and naturally we did likewise. So much about that. At 6 PM 24 May I arrived at Theresienstadt. I had met a doctor shortly before whom I gave a lift into Theresienstadt and he helped me a great deal in obtaining information, securing sleeping quarters, etc.

My entry into the "Ghetto* that is really the only name for it is something which I will never forget. The first thing which struck my eye was a fenced off area and I was told by the doctor that four weeks ago typhus had broken out and all cases were kept in this segregated area. Shortly before the war's end the Nazis dumped an additional 15,000 persons out of concentration camps into Theresienstadt and since these poor people were overloaded with lice, typhus was the result. The Jews in Theresienstadt, an approximate 30,000, were terrified at this additional problem since the Ghetto so far had never quite experienced anything of that nature and there was nothing on hand to combat such an epidemic. Thousands died and only now that the Swiss Red Cross has taken over and brought in medical supplies has the situation become better. My first step in the Ghetto was to go to the information where all records of the inmates are kept, 'while a women looked for names which I had given her, I was patiently awaiting the results. Well --- no one was there anymore. I found out that the SS ordered all records to be burned before they pulled out and even all case histories had to be destroyed. That is the reason why there isn't any way one can trace a person unless one meets someone who actually knew when certain people were thrown into new transports to other concentration camp, Poland, or gas chambers at Auschwitz. Since mother nor aunt Else, nor your folks Walter or Heinz were present at Theresienstadt and therefore I resorted to certain folks at the ghetto who came from Aachen three years ago.

Quite by coincidence, I met a woman by the name of Grete Berger who was the head nurse at the home for the aged into which mother, grandmother and aunt Else moved at the end of 1941 and Miss Berger was a personal friend of mother's. Miss Berger, a charming woman, told me the following: Mother and aunt Else were shipped from Aachen on 22 March 1942 to Isbitza near Krasnodar on the Zieprs (Poland). Miss Berger had gotten postal cards as late as 1943 from mother and since she herself was shipped to Theresienstadt, there were no more communications. Mother and aunt Else left Aachen before grandmother died and grandmother's death was solely due to the fact that she had to remain behind all alone for she hung very much on her two daughters who did everything in their power for her. Miss Berger-told me that for Oma it sure was the best solution and for her funeral uncle Paul who at that time still lived in Horn, came to Aachen. She was buried at the same cemetery father was buried only there wasn't time enough left to give her a tombstone and that was the reason why I couldn't locate her grave while I was in Aachen not too long ago.

Miss Berger explained to me exactly what took place when mother and aunt Else were evacuated from Aachen and this constituted the first Jewish transport out of the Rheinland at that time. Although all people were allowed to take one suitcase of clothing along and food supplies for three days she doubts very much whether they were actually allowed to keep their personal belongings upon their arrival at their destination, which in mother's case was Isbitza. I was assured furthermore that mother as well as aunt were at the time in good physical condition and Miss Berger, who acted as head nurse in Theresienstadt and still does, felt pretty sure that she - mother and aunt - may have well been put to work in some sort of a textile mill in which case she may have lived through all this and still be around somewhere. Many people from Isbitza who were not capable of working and meant a burden to the Nazis were sent to gas chambers, but to tell you the truth I still have hope to find mother and many more of my relatives.

Miss Berger also personally knew Paul Liepmann who came to Theresienstadt sometimes in 1943 with his family. His wife Agnes and daughter Ruth were there with him. It is a fact that Agnes died in Theresienstadt shortly after her arrival. She was a weak person anyway and had been troubled in her youth by TB. It is not known as to what happened to her body. Paul Liepmann and Ruth went from Theresienstadt with a transport to Lublin Poland and since then no one at the ghetto has heard. On 24 May from 6 PM. to 11 PM., I interviewed quite a few people who may give me some clues on people I am looking for. In the course of conversation, I spoke to a certain Mrs. Falkenstein, also from Aachen who knew your father, Heinz Oppenheim. It appears that she had met him at Bad Wildungen and later on saw him in Aachen at my parents' I feel sure , since this lady is an old inmate of Theresienstadt that her statement never having seen your father there, Heinz, is correct, for she knew almost everyone there and certainly would know people whom she had met before. I am just reading over my notes which I had made while I was talking to various people, and I see there that Paul Liepmann with Ruth may have also gone to Birkenau or Auschwitz. All in all, you can see that for an almost 600-mile ride in a peep, which is only of secondary importance, I accomplished very little. However, I am grateful that I finally have some definite clues by which I can go now. At this moment I recall the moments shortly before I entered Theresienstadt, and these hours were the most hopeful ones of my life. Yet the results were — NIL —.

Now I will elaborate on some things which I spoke about in Theresienstadt although not pleasant but true and these things should always be remembered. When the ghetto was instituted by the SS the town had been cleared of all other people and all things which could have made lives a little pleasant for the masses of people who came there later were naturally removed. There was no light, there was not a stove, there were no medical supplies, in short there was nothing. Within a short period of time the place was overcrowded, and it remained that way. Food was so inadequate that all old and feeble people died away in short order. That apparently was the principal purpose of the whole thing.

All in all, some 100,000 Jews passed through this ghetto and from there were decentralized again to various places either for working purposes or extermination. The younger ones were selected for the first and the older ones for the latter. Clothing at Theresienstadt could be bought also. Yes, all the clothes which the people had brought into the ghetto originally were taken away from them, sorted out, and of course the good items went to the German Welfare and the rags were put up for sale again in the ghetto store. Yes, money the inmates had too. But the currency was a special one. It was a note valid only in Theresienstadt bearing a picture of Moses holding the Torah signed by "Der Aelteste, der Juden, Jacob Edelstein." Most people there drew from there otherwise frozen bank accounts a certain amount monthly and received for this German money, the Theresienstadt currency. It is very obvious why this system was instituted and needs no further explanation. All medical supplies which were being used at the ghetto were either smuggled in or received by bribing.

Today, the whole place looks actually like a model concentration camp and that is the reason why the Nazis used to bring in foreign reporters to prove to the world that it isn't as bad as everyone believed but not showing and telling certain things, which would have made all the difference in the world.

On May 24th another fellow and myself were the only two Americans in the ghetto which by the way is at present held under quarantine by the Russian forces. No one can imagine how these poor people fell all over us asking us to mail letters for them to all corners of the globe informing...

... Then we left and went back "home" via Chemnitz. Chemnitz is occupied today by Russian forces although American forces captured it. The town is in very bad shape and most likely will take years to be built up again. But Germany as such looks much too good yet for my money. I have no sympathy with them whatever and make every German responsible for the happenings during Hitler's regime regardless of what excuses they may ever make.

362

I would like everyone to do his utmost one way or other to initiate or at least further some sort of organization in the States which will concern itself with camps and ghettos of this nature. It would help - I believe - if you would put in a tracer, through the Red Cross for me from the States, giving mother's location as Izbitza. I will go there myself as soon as the possibility exists.

Helmut, this has turned out to be a very long report and I am very tired now. Only a few hours ago I came back from the above-described trip, and I am going to bed very shortly. Excuse the many mistakes but I haven't got the patience to read it over again. Write soon again and keep your chin up I am going to find mother yet. I am certain she is still living.

As ever

Edward

"Miss Grete Berger," who Guy refers to in the above was the Superior in the Jewish Home for the Elderly in Aachen when Rose, Else and Fanni were there. She was responsible for Fanni not being deported from Aachen with her daughters. Grete herself was deported on July 25, 1942, in the "Great Transport" from Aachen to Theresienstadt. 205 people were deported from the city of Aachen that day together with hundreds of others from throughout the Rhineland. 21 Aacheners remained on the train in Theresienstadt and were transported 500 kilometers east directly to Auschwitz-Birkenau. None of those survived. Of the remaining 184 Aachen residents forced to disembark in Theresienstadt, there were eight survivors, including "Miss Berger."

Grete Berger's name on the list of transportees of
Transport VII/2 Aachen – Düsseldorf – Theresienstadt.

Transport Card of Grete Berger

Sometime after Theresienstadt was liberated by the Soviet Army, two weeks after Guy's arrival, "Miss Berger" was relocated to the largest displaced person (DP) camp in Germany, located in Bergen-Belsen, Germany, near the death camp of the same name. It was controlled by the British, who refused to allow any of the inmates, known as the *"She'erit Ha-Petalah"* (the Surviving Remnant) and other survivors of the Nazi Genocide to find sanctuary in Palestine. On June 6, 1946, President Truman urged the British government to relieve the suffering of the Jews then confined to displaced persons camps in Europe by immediately accepting 100,000 Jewish immigrants into Palestine. Britain's foreign minister Ernest Bevin replied sarcastically that the United States wanted displaced Jews to immigrate to Palestine "because they did not want too many of them in New York."

In 1946, the British transferred administration of the camp to the United Nations Relief and Rehabilitation Agency (UNRRA). "Miss Berger," with the assistance of the American Joint Distribution Committee and HIAS (originally the Hebrew Immigrant Aid Society), traveled on a military carrier, the *SS Marine Marlin*, in January 1948 to the United States. She lived in New York City until her death in 1973.

While the United States, Canada and Cuba were turning away desperate German Jewish refugees, Shanghai continued to be a safe harbor, despite its occupation by Japan in 1938, with no visa requirement to gain entry. Twenty thousand Jews, primarily from Germany and Austria, hid from the holocaust in Shanghai. These included my parents, Gerda (Oppenheim) and Max Dahl and my paternal grandparents Sara (Goldberg) and Nathan Dahl and their daughter Ilse (Dahl) Radt and her husband Kurt Radt. Life there was often difficult, especially for those without financial means. The Japanese occupied and controlled the city and Japan, under pressure from Germany, forced most Jewish refugees who arrived in 1938 or later to live in a rather primitive one-square-mile district called *Hongkew*, known as the "Shanghai Ghetto," where conditions were crowded and unsanitary, often leading to infectious disease. My parents and I lived in the very cosmopolitan French Concession of Shanghai. My Dahl grandparents, Nathan and Sara, who arrived in Shanghai in 1939, initially were confined to *Hongkew*, but their son, my father Max, was able to bribe some officials to allow them to reside near us within the French Concession. Most Jewish residents of the French Concession were treated fairly while the Japanese issued regulations to make life for Allied nationals as unpleasant as possible.

My parents were stateless refugees, lacking any citizenship since Germany had revoked my father's in 1934 and my mother's in 1935. Except for curfews, unavailability of various supplies, food shortages and rationing, and severe restrictions to bank accounts, my parents did not directly feel harsh effects of the Japanese occupation. The curtains had to be closed at night to prevent Allied bombings and my father went out in the evening to enforce the curfew and lights-out policies in the neighborhood.

Generally Jewish refugees in Shanghai tried to recreate their previous lives in Europe to the best of their ability. Lawyers and doctors set up practices; Jewish schools and communities were established. Musicians formed orchestras and the *literati* established book clubs. Few, if any, of the refugees knew the unimaginable extent of the genocide from which they had escaped until after communications were re-established following the Japanese surrender on September 2, 1945. After World War II, most Shanghai Jews moved to Israel, the United States or back to Europe.

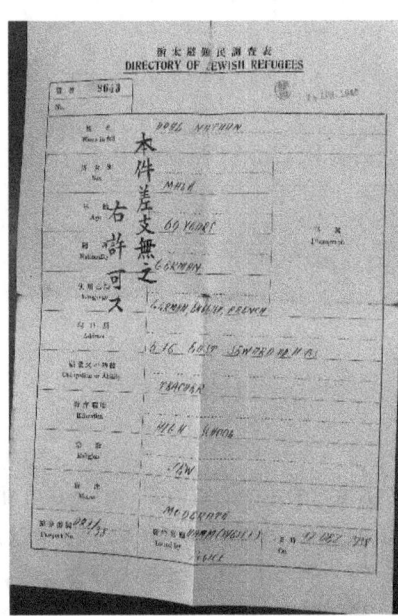

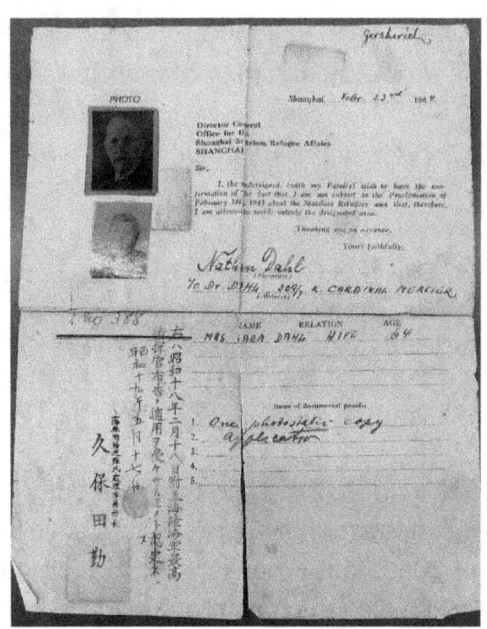

My grandfather Nathan Dahl is listed in the "Directory of Jewish Refugees" and was placed into the Ghetto after he and his wife Sara arrived in 1938.

My father was able to obtain this exemption of his parents from the stateless refugee class and allow them to live outside of the ghetto, near us in the French Concession.

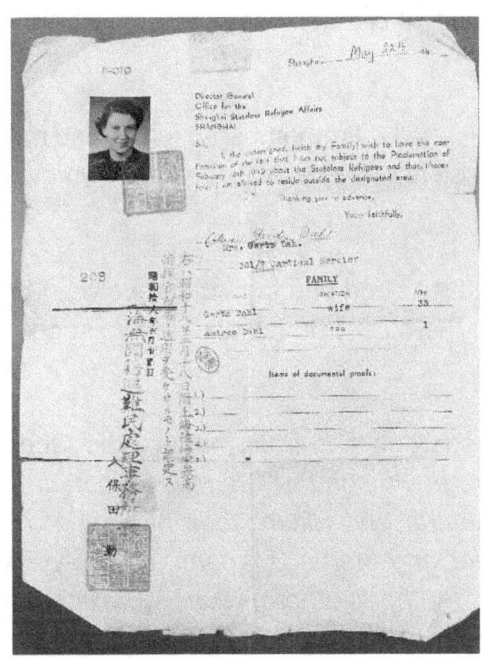

My parents, who arrived in 1933 prior to the Japanese occupation, always lived in the French Concession, but after 1938, had to annually provide evidence that they were "allowed to reside outside the designated area" for Jewish refugees in Hongkew.

In Palestine during World War II, Helmut served with the British Army in the North African campaign against the Germans. He was a member of the Palestine Regiment, an infantry regiment of the British Army that was formed in 1942, consisting of both Jews and Arabs, and deployed to Egypt and Libya.

On August 2, 1945, Guy, still in Germany, wrote to his brother Helmut in Cairo. I have excerpted portions of this letter:

2nd Lt. Edwin G Olden 0-2015854 HQ   HQ 00 "B"   APC 256

2 August 1945

Dear Helmut:-

My last letter to you dates back to June 17th and it is about time again that I'd have a little chat with you. In the meantime two letters of you reached me both airmail letters one of June 8th and the other of June 21st. Thanks a lot for both letters and I must say you have become a very diligent writer which pleases me no end... Eric Siebert, the brother of Herbert, who lives in New York, gave me the location of his mother. She lives at present in Absam which isn't far from Innsbruck, Austria. Since Herb and I had some sort of an agreement- that each one would take care of the others mother, depending who would get through this war o.k. So I took my jeep and another fellow and myself went down to see Mrs. Siebert taking plenty of canned food and money along for her. We went from here-via Aschaffenburg, Wurzburg, Ansbach, Ingolstadt, Muenchen, Mittenwald, Innsbruck. Mrs Siebert, a lady who is already 61 years old but looks much younger, is a splendid woman and it wasn't easy for me to tell her that her son Herbert had been killed in action especially so since she didn't even know that he had been in the armed forces. Eric in New York is anxious to have her join him in the states... I will see to it that Mrs. Siebert will be taken care of. The first thing I did was establish mail connections between Mrs Siebert and myself whereby I can also transmit letters from her son in New York to Innsbruck. This was accomplished by introducing Mrs. Siebert to a French captain there whom I can write to in her behalf. Innsbruck has become a French Occupational Zone, and I advised therefore for Mrs. Siebert to move into our zone. That way it is much easier for me to help her out in every respect.

From Innsbruck, I went up to Salzburg via Bad Reichenhall... I remembered father and mother who were there on their 25th wedding anniversary... Salzburg is a wonderfully located town overtowered by the old Salzburg.

The town itself is a bit destroyed by bombing, but it isn't bad and from there we went on to Bad-Ischl along very pretty mountain roads. Ischl is one of the cutest Badeplatze I have seen for a long time...

On my way-back I naturally went up to Berchtesgarden and from there to the Obersalzberg which once was the so proud Hitler's mountain retreat. *(It was on the Obersalzberg mountain 1200 feet above the alpine village of Berchtesgaden in Austria that Hitler made his home, along with Hermann Goering, Heinrich Himmler and Albert Speer and Martin Bormann. High level meetings were held here, and many important decisions affecting the lives of millions were made by Hitler sitting in his mountain retreat, which he called the "Berghof." Former U.K. Prime Minister David Lloyd George had a meeting with Hitler at the Berghof in 1936, and Prime Minister Neville Chamberlain had discussions with Hitler at the Berghof in 1938. Other important guests received there frequently included Benito Mussolini and the Duke and Duchess of Windsor. Lesser officials and diplomats visiting Hitler or his underlings usually stayed at the adjacent Hotel Zum Turken, which began as an inn in 1630. Hitler's walled-off underground bunker connected with an elaborate system of bunkers built under the Hotel),* Today the whole place is completely leveled, and our bombing was done so well and precise that Berchtesgaden itself only a mile or so away from Obersalzberg did not get a single bomb hit. Today even civilians can go up to the Obersalzberg which during the Third Reich was only allowed to a few privileged bastards of that certain clique. From there we passed through Muenchen which is very badly hit and we halted for a few-minutes at the Buerg Gerbraue where in 1923 Hitler staged his putsch. Today whatever is still standing of the place has been taken over by the American Red Cross to serve American coffee and doughnuts which is a national dish. Just in case you don't know what doughnuts are, here is the explanation: Berliner Pfannkuchen. So much about the 1000-mile trip I took...

... Just now I am trying myself to get a more or less permanent job with the CIC which is equivalent to the British FSS. You see all over the American Zone permanent CIC Detachments (*United States Army Counterintelligence Corps*) have been set up and one ...is located between Ulm and Augsburg and the boys ... on this team were taken out of the 6th Armored CIC. I know almost all of them and they still have a vacancy for two men. Therefore I would like to go on their team. It isn't so easy to get accepted into the CIC Corps but with a recommendation from the Commanding General of this division I hope I won't have any trouble. You see in CIC one works rather independent from regular Army units and one is more or less his own boss. It is about the closest to civilian life one can get while in the Army and ...the work as such is interesting too.

This letter to you will have a lot of enclosures... No. 3 are three letters of mother which were given to me by Anton Bamfaste while I was in Velmede. He had saved them all this time... In Philadelphia I have quite a few letters yet which were written by mother so you can keep these...

... What have you done so far to effect a transfer from there to the British Occupational Forces in Germany? It may not be a bad idea for you to write a letter to the FSS Detachment located in Arnsberg, Westphalia; maybe they can use you right there if you tell him that you know that sector well. Tell me if I can help you out any in this respect and I will do everything in my power, maybe even take a trip to Arnsberg myself. I really wish you could come over here... Write soon again and take care of yourself.

As ever,

Edwin

Guy (Edwin G) sent another letter to his brother three weeks later. Here are excerpts:

2nd Lt. Edwin G Olden 0-2015834

HQ   CC "B"   APO 256 US Army

23 August 1945

Dear Helmut:

It has been a hell of a long time since I have had my last chat with you. I believe my last letter to you left here on August 2nd. Since then, a lot of things have happened and the most important of all of course is the end of World War II. Who would have ever believed that the Japs would fold up so shortly after Germany's capitulation. I am certain that the atomic bomb had a lot to do with the sudden end of hostilities.!!!! At present I don't even know what's going to happen to me. I may get sent to Third Army Headquarters or headquarters Military Intelligence Service awaiting new assignment...

The other day I took a quick trip from here to Krumbach and on the way down on the road a transport halted filled with people who were being brought back from Theresienstadt to Koeln. I naturally was interested in who was in the transport so I spoke to several people hoping that they may be able to give me some news on mother. Well they didn't know about mother, but I was introduced to a certain Mrs. Irma Salomon. After talking with her for a while I found out that she came from Plettenberg. I naturally asked her whether she knew Paul and Otto Sternberg and what do you think she told me.? "Yes, of course, they are my uncles." In other words Irma Salomon -a girl of about 28 - turned out to be a distant cousin...relation of ours. Paul Sternberg...is now somewhere in New York and Herbert Sternberg, that is Irma's brother...is in England. How do you like such a coincidence of meeting Irma? I already have written to relations of hers in New York and I will be the middleman to transmit mail to her.

Then another thing. Walter Vorreuter sent me a cable not so long ago telling me that his sister Hilde has been located and gave me her address. She is married by now and her name is: Hilde Abraham-Vorreuter, Biesboschstr. 56/2. If you want to, Helmut, you can drop Hilde a line I am sure she will be happy to hear from you. *(This is incomplete information: Hilde had been married and survived Auschwitz, but her husband did not).*

So you are busy these days driving back and forth from Cairo to Palestine. Quite a trip each time but when I come to think of it, I have been taking a lot of trips lately too which were equally as far. How far have you gotten Helmut in regard to a possible transfer which you may get for the British Occupational Zone of Germany... Say Helmut, what is the British attitude toward the discharge plan of soldiers now that the war is over. Have they made any changes as yet and will you be able to become a civilian sooner than you had originally expected?

Enclosed you will find some pictures which I had taken some time ago while on the trip down to Innsbruck, Berchtesgaden, Salzburg, Bad Ischl and Gemuenden. I am sure you'll enjoy the pictures especially those of the Obersalzberg. That is just about all for today. Write soon again and take good care of yourself.

As

Edwin

Helmut's driver' license of the 1940s was issued by the "Government of Palestine." He, like the other Jews living in the biblical home of the Jewish people, were "Palestinians" prior to the founding of the modern State of Israel in 1948. He also had a "Palestinian" passport.

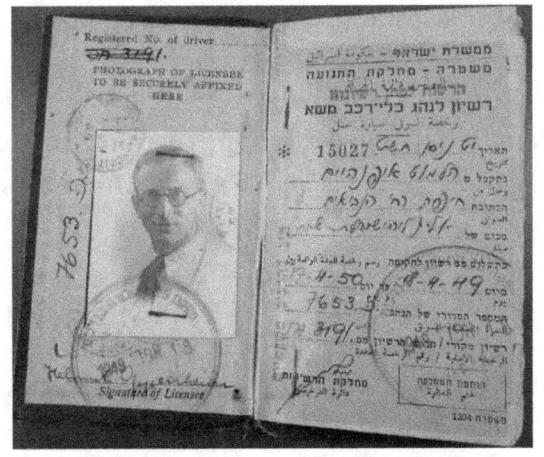
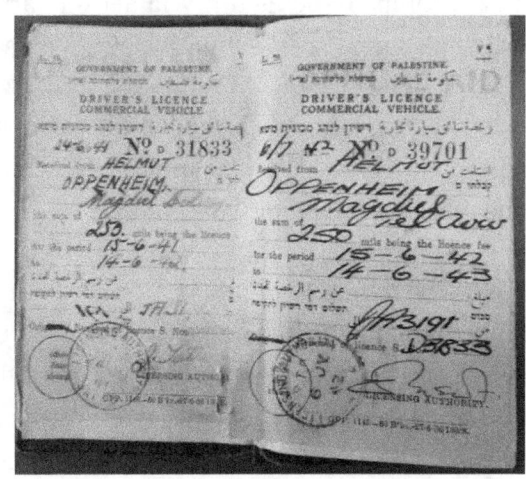

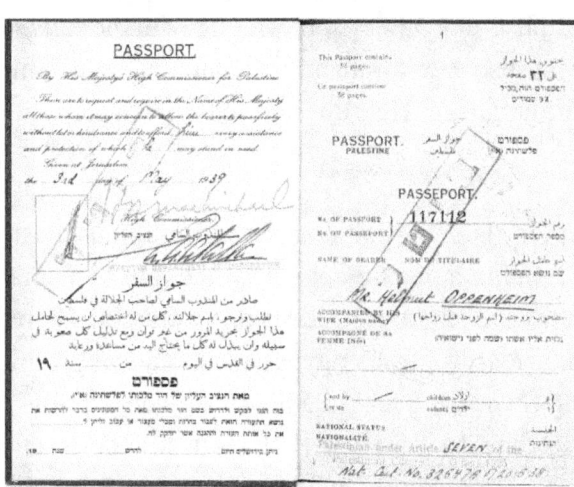

My uncle, Helmut Oppenheim, also fought with the Israeli Army during the War of Independence in 1948, as did many other Jews who had served in North Africa with the British Palestine Brigade. Following that, he remained in Israel and worked as a driver and chauffeur at various kibbutzim. He remained unmarried. He could never be persuaded to emigrate to the United States or even visit his brother or sister there.

In 1953, the German government decided to pay reparations to direct survivors of the Holocaust. This politically sensitive endeavor was named *Wiedergutmachung,* literally meaning "to make good again" or to compensate. Individuals who were persecuted for political, racial, religious, or ideological reasons by the wartime German regime became eligible for money from the German government under the terms of the Federal Compensation Law. The legal process in Germany was often extremely difficult, involving hiring attorneys specializing in restitution, and entangling oneself in bitter fighting which sometimes lasted for decades and over generations. The results of this effort was never certain.

As a result of this activity, Helmut was able to regain ownership of the Aachen house at 39 *Normannenstraße* and he moved there in the early 1960s. In the summer of 1964, I received a fellowship to do research work at Guy's Hospital in London and then traveled to continental Europe and went to see Helmut in Aachen for the first and only time. My mother Gerda refused to ever return to Germany but would often have Helmut accompany her and my father on various European trips to other countries. Guy and his wife Ruth ("Curly") also made contact with Helmut on a few of their trips abroad.

While in Aachen, Helmut worked in the casinos of eastern Belgium in the evenings exchanging German *marks* for Belgian *francs*. He died in an auto accident in 1977 while returning to Aachen from a Belgian casino in the middle of the night.

Zionism, the yearning to return to Zion, is the movement for the self-determination and statehood for the Jewish people in their ancestral homeland, the land of Israel. The vast majority of Jews around the world feel a connection or kinship with Israel, whether or not they explicitly identify as Zionists, and regardless of their opinions on the policies of the Israeli government. Its advocates believed that a modern Jewish state would provide Jews with a safe haven from the bigotry and endangerment they suffered perennially as a minority culture among non-Jewish majority cultures and ensure that Jews have the same right to nationhood and self-determination as any other people, along with the same protections that are typically afforded to other nations. Zionism was also a cultural and national renaissance movement which sought to enable the Jewish people to revive their language, Hebrew, and reestablish self-determination over their traditions, culture, religion, and education.

The current Israeli-Arab conflict is a religious clash between Jews and Muslims with the key element of the conflict being a dispute regarding the fate of a small piece of land that currently consists of the State of Israel and the area known as Judea and Samaria. There, three millennia ago, five hundred years after Moses brought the Hebrews from Egypt to the Biblical promised land, the first Kingdom of Israel was established under King Saul. King David united the twelve Tribes of Israel and King Solomon built the First Temple in Jerusalem in the 10th century BCE. After its destruction by the Babylonians in 586 BCE, the Jews of the Kingdom were forced into exile for 50 years where they lamented "By the rivers of Babylon, there we wept as we remembered Zion." A second Kingdom of Israel existed briefly in the second century BCE. That connection between Jews and the land, and the hope for repatriation, is deeply embedded in Jewish prayer, ritual, literature, and culture to the present day. A constant Jewish theme has been the desire to return to a rebuilt Jerusalem. Throughout the Jewish Diaspora, Jews have prayed *L'Shana Haba'ah B'Yerushalayim,* meaning "Next year in Jerusalem," both at the end of the *N'eila* service on *Yom Kippur* and at the conclusion of the Seder service on the holiday of Passover.

After the United Nations General Assembly adopted the resolution to partition Palestine into an Arab and Jewish state on November 29, 1947, Britain announced the termination of its Mandate over Palestine, to take effect on May 15, 1948. On May 14, 1948, the State of Israel was proclaimed. Five Arab armies (Egypt, Syria, Transjordan, Lebanon, and Iraq) immediately invaded Israel. Their intentions were declared by Azzam Pasha, Secretary-General of the Arab League: "It will be a war of annihilation. It will be a momentous massacre in history that will be talked about like the massacres of the Mongols or the Crusades."

In 1946, two letters were transmitted to my immediate family. Both had been written by Arnold Liepmann (Levy Liepmann's son, the first cousin of my grandmother Rose, my first cousin twice removed). Arnold was a survivor of the Sachsenhausen slave labor camp near Berlin. It was Arnold who, while still living in Essen in 1942 with his wife Li, received the three postcards mailed by Rose and Else from Izbica.

The letters are in German and have been translated by me.

The first letter is written from Minden, Germany *(Dankerser Straße* 18, then in British occupied territory) on January 18, 1946, to his older sister Frieda (Liepmann) Goldschmidt in New York, who had been widowed in 1920 and subsequently emigrated to the USA before the Holocaust. Parenthetically, Frieda's son Ludwig Goldschmidt, Arnold's nephew, escaped from Germany to arrive in Shanghai in about 1938 and lived in the *Hongkew* ghetto. He struggled to make ends meet and was invited to dinner at my parents' apartment every Sunday. My mother always said that he ate enough to last him the whole week. He was my mother's second cousin and born in the same year, 1910. These are excerpts of that letter *(with my comments italicized within parentheses)*:

"My dear Frieda and all of you,"

"I don't know where to begin my correspondence with you after such a long silence between us. I just heard today about the possibility of corresponding to America through UNRWA and I wanted to write to you right away. I hope that all of your loved ones are still alive, enjoy good health and blessings and are otherwise satisfied.

We are still healthy, …only both our hearts will no longer be the same after everything which we had to endure…In the middle of 1944 all Jews in Essen *(Germany)* were rounded up by the Gestapo and placed in an internment camp in Berlin…What that meant you already know from reading the newspapers…The reports have not been exaggerated…The worst of the experience was the hunger…I was down to under 100 pounds. Since then, I have regained some of the weight… In all of Germany, I was the only one that came out of that camp alive.

There were about 1000 Jews in this camp—it was near Reinickendorf *(a suburb of Berlin where there was a subcamp of the Sachsenhausen concentration camp established by Nazi Germany)* … On the 21st of April 1945, the Russians moved into our area…On April 24th we were supposed to be transported to another camp to be killed by gassing. The Russians were, in the truest sense of the word, our liberators. They also brought us potatoes and bread so we could eat our fill.

You can imagine the joy I felt when I unexpectedly again found my dear Li.

If I wanted to tell your loved ones everything that was sad (and only sad things we experienced), I would have to write volumes. On March 5, 1943, we lost everything in a bombing attack in Essen and only barely were able to save our lives; *(This was the first day of the Battle of the Ruhr, a strategic bombing campaign in Nazi Germany carried out by the British Royal Airforce (RAF). The target in Essen was the strategic Krupp armaments factory. On that day 442 British aircraft destroyed 53 buildings at the Krupps works and destroyed more than 3000 houses, killing, according to German records, about 460 people).* We were lucky that we made it to the cellar and we survived. We could not even find a small room in Essen after this because nobody wanted to deal with Jews. The Gestapo wouldn't let me out of Essen either. Li stayed with your sister, and I wound up camping out in a bathroom in a Jewish house that I made my makeshift home. Twice more that house was bombed on different occasions. And the little things that some compassionate people had given us was again lost. You have no idea and in your wildest imagination cannot understand the destruction in Germany.

We have to think of the fate of our dear siblings and other relatives with the grimmest hatred in our hearts for the Nazis. With a heavy heart we remember the fate of our brothers and sisters and other relatives... Our dear Leopold and Martha and Erna *(Leopold Liepmann, Arnold's brother, his wife Erna (Weinberg) Liepmann and Erna's sister, Martha (Weinberg) Tebrich)* had to suffer such a terrible fate....We have heard nothing about when Leopold, Martha and Erna were deported. I met a woman by the name of Israel from Hannover while I was in the refugee camp in Berlin who told me that Martha was deported to Riga and died there...

... Rose and Else *(my grandmother and great-aunt)* were sent to Isbitzka in Poland and shortly after their being deported they wrote us for money... We sent it but the envelope with the money came back as undeliverable... We have tried to find them on many occasions but always in vain...

We did have some success in contacting and sending a few packages to Paul Liepmann and Max Spanier who were in Theresienstadt...after a short period of time this also was not allowed and later they were sent to Poland--they must have come to a terrible ending there. Agnes, Paul's wife, and Johanna Sternberg *(Paul's wife's mother)* died natural deaths in Theresienstadt. Mathilde Neuhaus and Rosalie Lowenstein and Aunt Lina, Martha's mother. were in Hannover in the Jewish community and then most likely went to Theresienstadt and then most likely were sent from there... I had sent letters to Mathilde...with my return address and they all came back as undeliverable... Finally we did get a notification from Inge. We were overjoyed with this communication since we had already assumed that the worst had befallen her.

Elise Sternberg and Gustav Spanier went to Poland... I had a chance to say goodbye to them, but never heard from them again *(they were both deported to the Ostland on 7/27/1942)* ... I have not been successful in getting any information regarding Paula and Grete Alexander's fate. Also have not heard anything about Gertrude Levy. Gertrude had again gotten married to a Mr. Stein before she was deported."

Have you had any information on Guenter Oppenheim, Rose's youngest? In Philadelphia? The boy must be devastated about the fate of his mother and also eager to learn about his uncle Paul and Aunt Else... Let us hear from you soon, so that we can have the opportunity to learn more from you We long for signs of life from you. With best regards and in constant love,

"From your dear brother and uncle Arnold Liepmann

... I will close with a communication from Dear Li *(Hulda Karoline Amalie "Li" Strothenke, Arnold's wife)*."

The following is a portion of Li's letter which Arnold enclosed:

"I am especially sad at what Rose and Else had to do, to leave their old sick mother behind. I was in Aachen a number of times and stayed with them. In April 1942, they took them away, these good loving people—I thought my heart would break. Rose and Else wrote to us after that saying we should always pray for them. In June 1942, Aunt Fannie *(my great-grandmother)* died... She could not get over the separation from her children. When I last visited Aunt Fannie, she already could not understand anything, and then a few days later she just went to sleep and never woke up. All of us were greatly relieved that the poor elderly lady did not have to be deported with her children."

"Li"

The second letter is written by Arnold from the same address three months later on April 17, 1946, to Arnold Liepmann's "nephew" (really first cousin once removed) "Guenter" Oppenheim (my uncle), who was then almost 26 years old and again living in Philadelphia after having returned from serving with the U.S. Army.

"Dear Guenter,"

"Since April 1 we have again been allowed to mail letters out of the country so I am taking the opportunity to send you this…I find it difficult to write you these things…Your dear mother and Aunt Else asked me, shortly after you left for America, to notify you if anything happened to them. The fate of all Jews in Europe and especially in Germany is probably well now known by you now. It is so sad and terrible, dear Guenther, what I must tell you. But it was equally as difficult for me when I was told. Without a doubt, we cannot count on your dear loving good mother and Aunt Else coming home again. I have to tell you that they have unfortunately met the fate of so many other poor, good human beings.."

"On Feb 2, 1942, your dear ones together with most of the other Aachen Jews were rounded up by the Gestapo and together were taken to Izbica in Poland. (*This was the first correspondence confirming that Rose and Else were deported to Izbica. The date of deportation is incorrect*). We received three cards from them, dated April 5, 1942, April 16, 1942, and April 28, 1942, in which they asked us to send money and food as soon as possible. Of course, we did this immediately... The money came back to us from Berlin with the envelope stamped 'forbidden by exchange regulations.' After the card of April 28th we never heard anything from those dear people again, even though we frequently sent letters. Then we began to hear the terrible rumors which were circulating."

"Uncle Paul (*Liepmann, my great uncle, Rose's younger brother*), Aunt Agnes, Ruth and Johanna Sternberg from Horn were taken to Theresienstadt one month later together with Max Spanier and his wife from Horn. Aunt Agnes and Johanna Sternberg died a natural death in Theresienstadt. Until early 1945, we had some spotty correspondence with Uncle Paul and Max Spanier and we were occasionally able to send a package through to them. Then they were sent to Poland (*from Theresienstadt in Czechoslovakia*) and all communication ceased. There is no doubt today what the word 'Poland' means."

"Grandmother (*my great-grandmother Fanni Liepmann*) died in the old age home in Aachen shortly after your dear mother was deported (1942). She had a decent death. Aunt Li visited her a few days before she actually passed away, and death was a blessing for her. I would have gone to her burial but it was difficult for Jews to get travel permits. Also my brother Leopold with his wife, my sister-in-law Martha, were murdered by the Nazis, the scum of the earth (*Leopold's son, Werner, saved by the British Kindertransport eventually came to the United States and became a physician, practicing in New Orleans.*) Also, Lieschen (*Elise*) Sternberg and Gustav Spanier from Horn. Even though you, dear boy, did not know some of these people personally, you certainly have heard them spoken about... I could go on and on with more information, but sadly, sadly everything is gruesome and sorrowful."

"I hope that this letter finds you well and happy. You have already been there for quite a few years and must have gotten accustomed to America. I am sure you hear regularly from Max and Gerda and Helmuth. I hope all is well with them. When you write them give them our heartiest best wishes...We are doing pretty well, except that Aunt Li and I have problems with our hearts—what we went through was too much and in addition to everything else I was jailed by the Gestapo for a year and was in a KZ Lager in Berlin. The term KZ will also be familiar to you. (*The term KZ camps is used world-wide today to define all types of German slave labour and extermination camps. etc., sometimes including even the German-instituted and subsequently eradicated central ghettos for Jews in the cities of Eastern European countries. The term KZ-Lager was actually utilized very early by Adolf Hitler himself in a public speech but should not be confused with the technical term KL, which was the official German abbreviation of the main SS-concentration camps).* The forced labour I had to do there was bad, but nowhere as terrible as the hunger I felt, which was overwhelming. I weighed less than 100 pounds when the Russians freed me on April 21, 1945. They could not have come much later, because I was scheduled to be transported east to the gas chambers on April 24."

"Here in Germany, it looks terrible. Essen where we lived for so long is basically destroyed. All the Jews in the neighbourhood were searched for and we did not go outside, even to get food. On May 23, 1945, we were extensively bombed *(by the Allies)* for the first time and we lost everything within a few minutes. Later on we were bombed a second time. As a Jew I was not upset very much. "

"The sun is setting and I will stop for now. Dear Guenther, you surely must frequently go to New York and stop by and see the Heilbruns. *(Anna Goldschmidt Heilbrun, born 1908, Arnold's niece, granddaughter of Levy Liepmann and daughter of Frieda Liepmann Goldschmidt lived in New York.)* Give them my regards and good wishes, also from Aunt Li."

"Your uncle,

Arnold Liepmann"

The vast majority of my extended family died in the Holocaust. One poignant survivor was Hilde Vorreuter Abraham, my mother's maternal first cousin. She had met her future husband Joseph Abraham in the Netherlands after they both had left Germany in 1938. Two years after the German occupation of the Netherlands, they were both taken to the Westerbork Concentration camp in Holland in 1942 and from there were deported to Theresienstadt on Transport XXIV/7, no. 4 on September 6, 1944. On October 1, 1944, they were taken by train to Auschwitz to await "the final solution." The Czechoslovakian database of Holocaust victims *(https://www.holocaust.cz/en/database-of-victims/)* lists them both as having been murdered. Although Joseph was indeed killed in the gas chambers of Auschwitz, somehow Hilde survived. She came to the United States after World War II to be near her brother, Walter Vorreuter. She never remarried.

In Shanghai, my parents, Gerda and Max Dahl, had been attempting to emigrate to the United States since the occupation of Shanghai by the Japanese in 1937. As refugees without any citizenship (their German citizenship had been revoked by the Nazis), it was as difficult to get a U.S. visa in Shanghai as it was in trying to obtain one in Germany-controlled Europe. Their will to leave China for the U.S.A. intensified after the outbreak of World War II in 1939 when they realized that they would never want to return to Germany. It was, however, impossible to get visas from Japanese occupied territories. They would have to wait six more long war-years before even initiating the process.

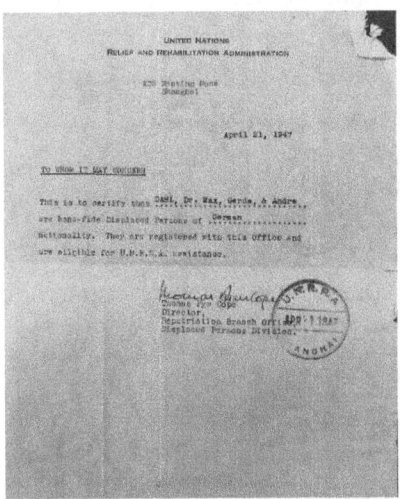

In April 1947, my parents were able to have the three of us certified as "bona-fide displaced persons of German nationality" by the Displaced Persons division of the United Nations Relief and Rehabilitation Administration.   The U.N., then and now, was a bureaucratic entity which moved at a snail's pace, especially when it dealt with Jews.

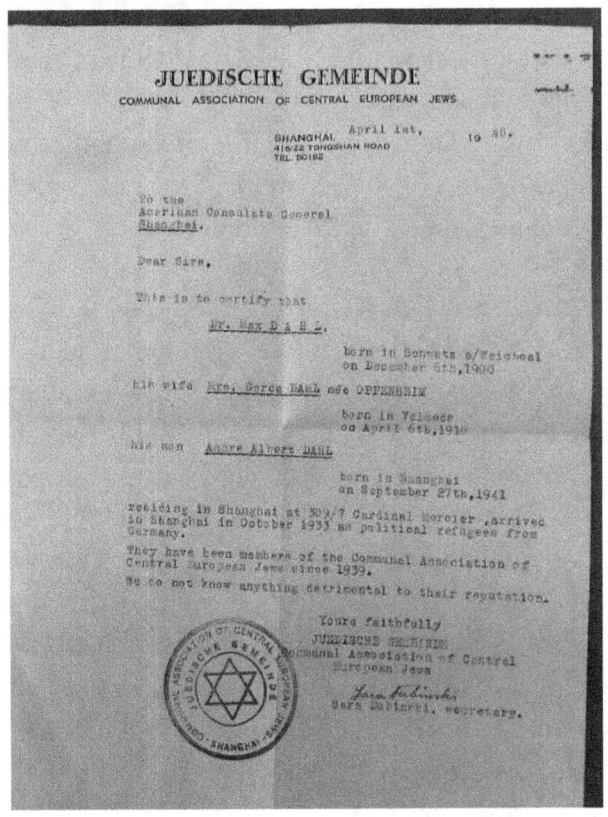

In April 1948. a document was transmitted to the American Consulate General in Shanghai from the Juedische Gemeinde (Communal Association of Central European Jews) certifying that my parents arrived in Shanghai in October 1933 as "political refugees from Germany," and that the three of us had nothing "detrimental to their reputations."

The two above documents, taking almost three years to acquire, moved us up in the line to obtain United States visas. A formal application, physical examinations and review were still needed to achieve that goal. We were set back six months by my first physical examination revealing the presence of an intestinal parasite, extremely common in China. Another half year was lost after my next physical examination included an abnormal chest x-ray, which supposedly revealed tuberculosis, which disqualified the necessary review. I was declared free of this disease after having another x-ray at a private hospital.

There was yet another major hurdle which my family had to deal with. Although my parents' German citizenship had been revoked by the Nazis, the United States did not certify them (and me) as "bona-fide displaced persons of German nationality," as the United Nations had done. The United States Immigration

Act of 1924, also called the National Origins Act, was reflective of the blatantly racist recommendations of a xenophobic congressional commission that classified countries according to the character of their people. A U.S. Foreign Service official had this to say regarding Polish Jews: "They are filthy, un-American and often dangerous in their habits, and lack any conception of patriotic or national spirit, and the majority…is mentally incapable of acquiring it." Africans were judged to be undesirable. Slavs were said to demonstrate carelessness as to the virtue of honesty. Scandinavians, meanwhile, were considered, quote, "the purest type." The number of visas to be granted to residents of each nation was proportional to the number of residents from that country already living in the US. 82 percent of all available visas went to Western and Northern European Countries, 14 percent went to Eastern and Southern European countries, and 4 percent went to the remaining Eastern Hemisphere (Asia and Africa) countries.

My mother Gerda was born in Westphalia, Germany, and was finally granted a visa in early 1949 under the German quota. As a minor I was able to accompany her to the United States. My father Max, born in a region of West Prussia that was ceded to Poland under the 1919 Treaty of Versailles, was considered to be of Polish nationality despite never having set foot in that country. He was denied a visa until mid-1950, forcing him to remain in Shanghai after the Communist takeover of China in 1949. My mother and I came to the United States on a Danish freighter, the *Marchen Maersk*, which transported goods between the Far East and the United States and also transported six passengers on the six-week voyage, stopping at ports in Japan, San Francisco and then passing through the Panama Canal to reach New York.

We briefly lived with Guy and his wife Ruth, nicknamed "Curly" because of her curly black hair, and then lived in a small space in a rooming house in Philadelphia, where communal meals cooked by "Mrs. Joseph" were shared with the other boarders, all of whom were young men just beginning their careers. My mother worked as a saleslady at Wanamaker's department store, the first full-time "job" she had taken since her marriage. My father joined us a year later and we moved to New York City. After passing the difficult examination to obtain a medical license in the State of New York on his first attempt, a very unique occurrence for a foreign-trained physician, we moved to Gowanda in Western New York State where my father was employed as a staff psychiatrist at a State mental institution. In 1954, we relocated to Poughkeepsie, N.Y., where my father became Assistant Director of the 6000-bed Hudson River State Hospital. I went to F.D. Roosevelt High School in Hyde Park, N.Y., before getting a B.A. from Wesleyan University and an M.D. from Cornell University Medical College, followed by a medical internship at the New York Hospital and an ophthalmology residency at Harvard. My father passed away in 1974, followed by my mother in 1990.

Guy and his wife never had children. They lived in Baltimore and opened a women's dress shop. After that area of the city developed urban blight, Guy became a landscape architect. His wife Ruth was a special education teacher.

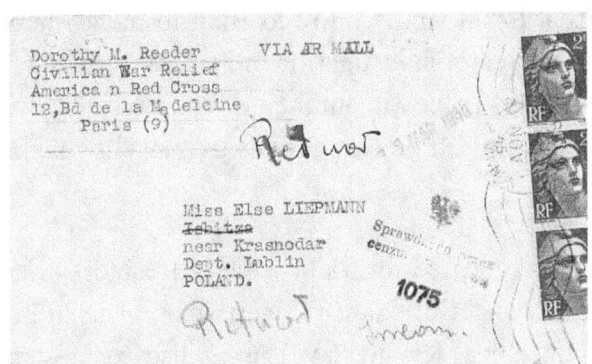

Ironically, in 1948, the above letter was sent from the Paris office of the American Red Cross addressed to "Miss Else Liepmann" in "Izbitza," Poland. It was returned to the sender. A family member (likely Gerda or Guy) had apparently asked the Red Cross for information regarding their aunt and the agency wrote to Else directly six years after her deportation there.

SS-Hauptsturmführer Kurt Engels, the commander of the Izbica Transit Camp, was only 26 years old when Train *Da 17* carrying Rose and Else arrived there on March 25, 1942. He had joined the Hitler Youth at age 14 and was utterly devoted to the Nazi cause, becoming a Storm Trooper *(SA)* in 1933 and joining the Protection Squadron *(SS)* in 1936. He became a member of the Secret State Police (*Gestapo*) in 1937, first assigned to Cologne and then was appointed to be district chief of the *Gestapo* in the Lublin district of Poland, assigned to Izbica.

Engels was known as "the devil of Izbitza." The last mass deportation of Jews from Izbica to the death camps of Belzec and Sobibor occurred on November 2, 1942, involving 4,000 prisoners. By nightfall, the trains stopped running back and forth and there were still more than two thousand Jews scheduled to be transported to their deaths. According to testimonies, Engels and the *Ordnungpolizei* crammed those remaining into a local fire brigade building designed to accommodate one tenth that number. He locked the doors, leaving those inside without food, water, and fresh air. Many perished over the next three days. The doors were opened and those Jews still alive were chased to the local Jewish cemetery. There, under Engels' direction, every prisoner was massacred in assembly-line-style by gunfire from SS guards and the *Sonderdienst* battalion of Ukrainian Trawnikis, trained killers who consumed large amounts of alcohol when they were not murdering Jews. The bodies were then dumped into hastily dug mass graves.

Thomas (Tovi) Blatt was almost fourteen years old when the train with Rose and Else arrived at his native town of Izbica. After most of his family was murdered, he was able to live hand to mouth until he was captured in the forest near Lublin in April, 1943. He was taken to the Sobibor death camp where he was selected to join the *Arbeitstjuden* (working Jews). His specific task was cutting off the hair of naked women prior to their gassing. On October 14, 1943, he, together with about 600 others, escaped from Sobibor during the prioner-led revolt, the most successful escape from a Nazi death camp during World War II, documented in the 1987 movie, *Escape from Sobibor*. At age 15, Tovi was one of the 47 people who survived the uprising in Sobibor.

Kurt Engels left his headquarters in Izbica in 1944 and vanished from view. After the end of the War, Tovi Blatt was determined to find him and bring him to justice. He learned that Engels had changed his name and married a chef in Hamburg, Germany, ultimately opening a restaurant there together with her in 1955 which he called "Café Engels" under his real name. This exercise in vanity allowed Blatt to track Engels down and report him to the Hamburg Police. After a multi-year secret investigation, an arrest warrant was issued against Engels on October 31, 1958 in Hamburg for an unknown number of murders. He was imprisoned but prior to his case coming to trial in court, he killed himself on New Year's Eve 1958 by taking poison tablets which he had sewn within the hem of his coat.

I have reviewed the 600 page dossier of German documents prepared for trial by the Prosecutors of the Hamburg Court. This collection, entitled "Engels, Kurt Hans Josef Christian, for participation in killing operations against Jews in the period from 1940 to 1943 in Izbica near Krasnystaw/Lublin district (Gestapo office Izbica, KdS Lublin) (Public Prosecutor's Office Hamburg 14a Js 2021/56, formerly 14a Js 208/56; 1 OAR 53/57)" was e-mailed to me at my request by the State Archives of the "Free and Hanseatic City of Hamburg."

These records detail many first-person accounts of Engels' sadistic atrocities. "He was by far the most fearful of the SS... I have very often seen with my own eyes how he walked the streets (of Izbica) with his adjutant named Ludwig (Klemm), gunning down the Jews fleeing from him - men, women and children." Another witness testified "Engels had a Jewish boy *Mojszełe*, who worked for him. He took care of the garden. Engels talked to him about growing flowers. He liked him. "You're a cool boy," Engels used to say to *Mojszełe*. "You will die the last one and I will shoot you personally so that you do not suffer." The witness confirmed that Engels had kept his word.

Ludwig Klemm, the other psychopathic murderer who served as Engels' assistant in their rule of terror, similarly went into hiding, taking the name Ludwig Jantz. He was arrested in Allendorf, Germany in early 1979 and, while awaiting trial for mass murder, also took his own life in May 1979, in the Limburg Prison.

The word "genocide" did not exist at the time of my grandmother Rose's murder in 1942. Although more than three million Jews were killed in 1942 alone, with two million from July to October, and nearly one and half million in just 100 days from late July to early November, it was not until 1944 that the term became part of our language.

Raphael Lemkin was born in 1900 into a Jewish farming family in Poland. He became an attorney and escaped to Western Europe when the German army invaded Poland, eventually coming to the United States, where he joined the War Department in 1942 as an analyst documenting Nazi atrocities. In his 1944 book, *Axis Rule in Occupied Europe,* he introduced the word "genocide."

In 1941, Winston Churchill had described the atrocities of the Nazis as "a crime without a name." Lemkin rectified this by combining the Greek word, *genos* (nation, race, or tribe), and *cide* from the Latin word for killing, to create a new term, "genocide," defined by him as "a coordinated plan of different actions aiming at the destruction of essential foundations of the life of national groups, with the aim of annihilating the groups themselves."

The Holocaust is considered to be the single largest genocide in history. Using Hitler's actions as an example, Lemkin classified the many deeds that constitute genocide. Politically, the Nazis occupied countries and established controllable puppet states. They manipulated populations by destroying social structures and eliminating clergy and intellectuals and disallowing any dissent. Any deviation from the Nazi standard of acceptable culture in literature, journalism, schools, and legal systems was severely punished. The Third

Reich reduced non-Germanic births through encouragement of non-Aryan abortions and starvation techniques, resulting in infant and child mortality. Hitler and his followers exterminated anyone they considered "sub-human," or who they felt was unable to contribute to a Teutonic society. The National Socialists allocated food and shelter on a racial basis and expropriated money and property to reduce standards of living. Genocide could be achieved both by overt killing or any other means affecting nourishment, health, and family life.

Lemkin identified 49 members of his family, including his parents, who perished during the Holocaust, some from starvation and disease, the others from extermination in the Treblinka death camp. I have discovered well over one hundred of mine.

In 1948, the United Nations General Assembly finally declared that genocide was a crime under international law. Under its *Convention on the Prevention and Punishment of the Crime of Genocide*, "genocide means any of the following acts committed with intent to destroy, in whole or in part, a national, ethnical, racial or religious group, as such: (a) Killing members of the group; (b) Causing serious bodily or mental harm to members of the group; (c) Deliberately inflicting on the group conditions of life calculated to bring about its physical destruction in whole or in part; (d) Imposing measures intended to prevent births within the group; (e) Forcibly transferring children of the group to another group."

It is indeed ironic that the United Nations, which laid the groundwork for the creation of the Jewish national homeland in 1947 under Resolution 181, is a continuing force delegitimizing the State of Israel. The General Assembly has been a vocal forum for isolating, chastising, and rebuking Israel, passing more anti-Israel resolutions over the years than all other nations combined. Since 2015, Israel has faced 140 condemnations at the General Assembly, while, Russia, a hotbed of human rights violation, received 23, and Syria encountered only 10.

The United Nations Educational, Scientific and Cultural Organization (UNESCO) has instituted financial sanctions against Israel. The UN Human Rights Council (HRC) has denied membership to Israel and unjustly targeted it as a violator of human rights, while ignoring the international human rights crises in other areas of the world. In 1975, UN resolution 339 declared that "Zionism equals racism," essentially stating that support for a National Jewish Homeland is a racist act. In 2001, at the United Nations' *Third World Conference Against Racism* in Durban, South Africa, the Israeli government and its policies were compared to *apartheid*, the system of racial segregation that existed in South Africa until 1994 and which was characterized by racial discrimination and white supremacy. Ever since the "Durban Hatefest," this analogy has been persistently used in discussions about Israel even though all Israeli citizens, regardless of their ethnic background, enjoy equal rights, access to all professions, and serve both in the legislature and the judicial system.

In 2008, the President of the General Assembly called Israeli policies a version of *apartheid* and vocally supported an international boycott of Israel. In 2009, the Goldstone Report accused Israel of committing war crimes in Gaza through the deliberate and premeditated targeting of civilians and Gaza's civilian infrastructure. Two years later, South-African Justice Richard Goldstone, in a Washington Post op-ed, after further review of the factual evidence, withdrew the charges against Israel he had made within the report.

On October 7, 2023, Palestinians belonging to Hamas, an internationally recognized terror organization, waged the deadliest attack on Jews since the Holocaust, crossing from Gaza into Israel and slaughtering babies, raping women, and burning whole families alive with grotesque brutality. The death toll reached almost 1200, primarily innocent civilians, and hundreds of additional civilians were taken hostage, many of whom were subsequently murdered. This event has spurred the use of Lemkin's "genocide" thousands of times, not in respect to the Hamas action, but paradoxically to describe Israel's self-defensive response in Gaza to the violent assault on its citizens. How an unprovoked slaughter initiated by leaders of a terrorist group and the defensive actions of a democracy can be seen as morally equivalent is beyond understanding. Extreme anti-Zionist rhetoric calling for the destruction of the Jewish State, which once would have been perceived as a fringe movement, has now been accepted as mainstream by many as has the alignment with terrorism.

Hamas originated in 1987 as an outgrowth of the Muslim Brotherhood, the same group that worked with the Nazis during World War II. Haj Amin al-Husseini, the Grand Mufti of Jerusalem, first met Hitler in 1941 when they discussed their cooperation towards the goal of exterminating European and Palestinian Jewry. For al-Husseini, the annihilation of the Jews was a necessary means of bringing salvation to the believers of Islam. Just as a Nazi cannot be a true Nazi without murdering Jews, so an Islamic Jihadist cannot be a true Muslim without murdering Jews. Both the Nazis and Hamas perpetrated acts of calculated systematically perpetrated evil to literally support similar Jewish-elimination programs. For fundamentalist Muslims, a dead Jew pleases Allah and provides the executioner entrance into Paradise.

Despite the fact that Hamas has adopted and tailored the Nazi's murderous agenda, faculty of many U.S. universities are charging Israel with genocide while, on their campuses, thousands of students are demonstrating against Israel and flagrantly and erroneously using that word. At class reunions, college alumni are calling for the destruction of Israel. Hamas' desire for the total obliteration of Israel is indeed a "genocidal" goal, accepted and abetted not only by other jihadist groups but also by "intersectional" western groups such as women's right's advocates, gays, and people of color. Nazi Propaganda Minister Joseph Goebbels would be pleased that his antisemitic rhetoric has been contemporized.

Regarding the current Israeli-Arab conflict, Israel Prime Minister Benjamin Netanyahu has said "If the Arabs put down their weapons today, there would be no more violence. If the Jews put down their weapons today, there would be no more Israel." The latter situation would indeed lead to a genocide.

"Never Forget" has been the mutual plea of survivors of the Holocaust. I have written this book in remembrance of my grandmother Rose, both an eyewitness and victim to the Nazi genocide of the Jews. In the first few years after the Holocaust, active antisemitism appeared to become less popular due to the world's guilt regarding the murders of six million Jews. However, the world's oldest continuous hatred, directed against Jews individually and collectively, has now again raised its metamorphosing head. Sinister forces that have been present for more than two thousand years do not wish to remember and are now forming a new wave of antisemitism. Today, antisemitism is based less on religious bigotry and paranoid fear of the unknown. It is part of the worldwide movement to vilify Western civilization and the intersectionality of perceived victimhood among many minorities who have little in common beyond Jew-hatred, plus the growth of fundamentalist Islam, whose genocidal wish for the Jews is well described in the Koran and was implemented by its prophet, Mohammed. There have recently been marked increases in incidents of antisemitism in the United States and the rest of the world, many of which demonize Israel and ascribe Israel's alleged transgressions to its Jewish character. The International Holocaust Remembrance Alliance formulated a definition of antisemitism in 2016 that has been adopted by the United States and 43 other countries. It states that "denying the Jewish people their right to self-determination, such as by claiming that the existence of a State of Israel is a racist endeavor," is an example of antisemitism. In addition, so is "applying double standards by requiring of Israel behavior not expected or demanded of any other democratic nation."

Since the October massacre, British Jews have felt unsafe going outside while displaying any evidence of their religion and nearly a half of them have considered leaving England due to Jew-hatred. In Germany, Chancellor Angela Merkel opened its borders to more than one million Muslims, with the majority not integrating into German society and harboring hatred for both Israel and Jews. The European Union calls Israel "apartheid, colonialist and genocidal," while the number of Muslims there grow at a far greater rate than other populations. They believe that Israel is unworthy of existing as is any Jew living in the Diaspora who is ideologically, religiously, or sentimentally or politically committed to it.

Just as the unification of Germany in 1871 produced a constitution that emancipated the Jews of Germany, the events of the 20th century in the United States brought a golden age for American Jews. This period of prosperity and safety is now in jeopardy due to anti-Jewish racism among a very broad and influential coalition of the Left together with fundamentalist Muslims who share a pathological form of poisonous Israelophobia, unwarranted hatred of the collective Jew. The BDS movement (Boycott, Divestment and Sanctions), directed solely against Israel, denies the Jewish state's right to exist. Israel, the first Jewish state to exist in two millennia, plays a key part in the narrative of the new antisemitism. This crusade has been promoted and joined by Muslims and their bedfellows, human rights advocates, feminists, other women's groups, Blacks, LGBTQ organizations, and college and university faculty and students. These groups were remarkably silent or delayed in their response regarding the violence of October 7, specifically because the victims were Jewish. The atrocities committed by Hamas were quickly overlooked and sympathy with the Gazan population who elected to be ruled by Hamas became the rallying cry of the activists. The reality that Hamas uses its Gazan civilian population as human shields is overlooked in this one-sided narrative, which has, at its center, the antisemitic trope of "the lying Jew." The quest for "social justice" directed against Israel is an acceptance of antisemitism disguised as political activism. The insidious support for Hamas ultimately seeks the eradication of Israel and its people for the purpose of perpetuation of the greater good, not unlike Hitler's desire to maintain the purity of the Aryan race.

In 1932, my grandmother could not envision the evolution of the Final Solution, a "machinery of destruction" which would include inexorable progression of antisemitism, identification and isolation of Jews through decrees and laws, substantive expropriation of Jewish property and business, assemblage of Jews in larger towns and ghettos, and ultimately annihilation by disease, starvation, killing squads, and gas chambers in death camps.

At every Passover Seder, we read from the Haggadah the historical fact that "In each and every generation they rise up against us to destroy us." No population on this earth holds a greater justification to fear for its continued survival than the Jewish people. Only time will tell whether the world in 2024 mirrors the Germany of 1932.